THE
HITLER
YEARS

THE HITLER YEARS

VOLUME 2
DISASTER
1940–1945

FRANK McDONOUGH

HEAD
of ZEUS

An Apollo Book

This book is dedicated to
my wonderful wife Ann,
the love of my life.

Picture research by Juliet Brightmore
Maps by Jeff Edwards
Designed by Isambard Thomas, Corvo
Printed and bound in Wales by Gomer Press

Head of Zeus Ltd
5–8 Hardwick Street
London ECIR 4RG
WWW.HEADOFZEUS.COM

The German Invasion of Western Europe 1940

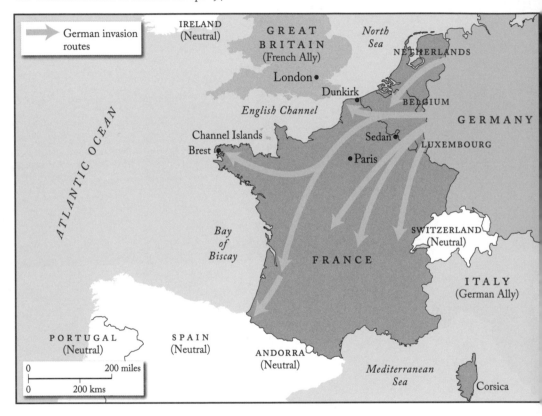

Operation Barbarossa: the Invasion of the Soviet Union 1941

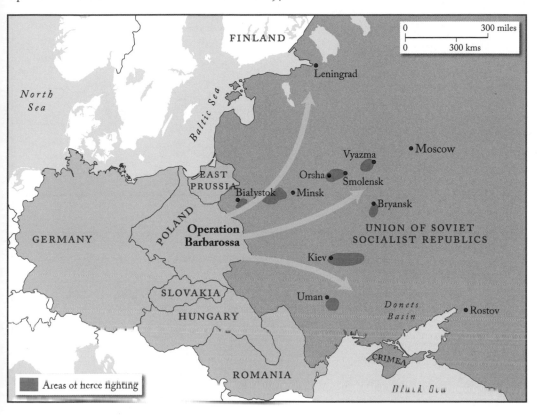

The Landing Sites of the D-Day Landings, 6 June 1944

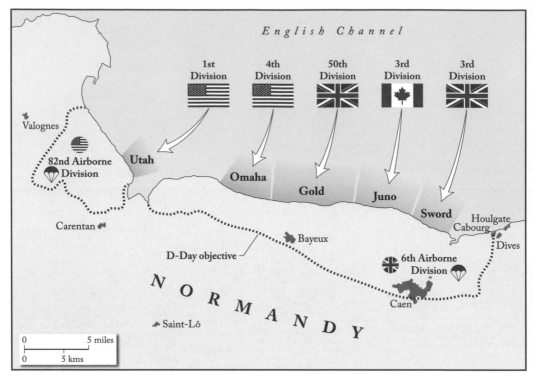

The Key Extermination Camps of the Holocaust

The Battle of Berlin, 1945

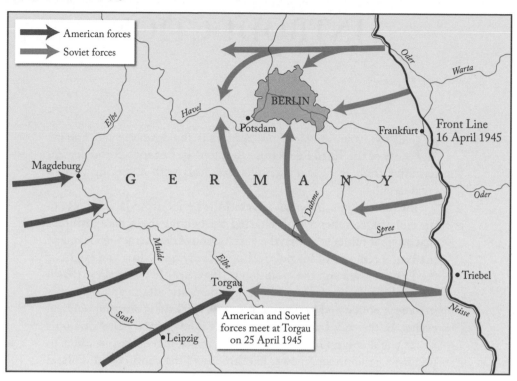

The division of Germany (left) and Berlin (right) after 1945

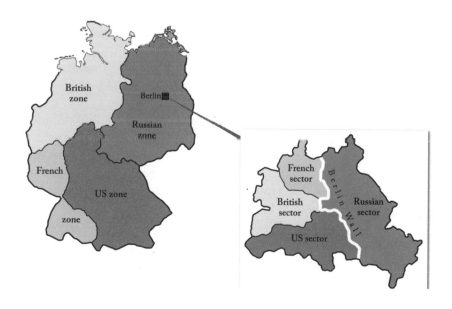

INTRODUCTION

Over two volumes *The Hitler Years* tells the dramatic and horrific story of the Third Reich from 1933 to 1945. I adopt a chronological narrative framework and each chapter deals with a specific year in vivid detail.

The first volume, *Triumph*, covered the period from January 1933 to the end of December 1939. It charted the behind-the-scenes intrigues that brought Hitler to power, the destruction of democracy in Germany, the brutal removal of his political opponents, including the Night of the Long Knives and the evolution of Nazi anti-Jewish policy. It also revealed the caution Hitler adopted in domestic affairs and especially in foreign policy, and his instinctive ability to exploit shifting political events. In the end, I argued that Hitler's fundamental belief that only a war could bring Germany the living space it required in order to become a genuine superpower led directly to the conflict with Poland, France and Britain that began in September 1939.

This second volume, *Disaster*, covers the years from 1940 to 1945, when Germany went from the zenith of its military power to comprehensive defeat. Accordingly, the central focus of this book is on Germany's role in the Second World War, particularly the military progress of the war and the key turning points for Germany, but it also shows how Hitler, as well as the Nazi elite, German officers, soldiers, and the German people, reacted to the conflict; in particular how the Germans coped with the ferocious Allied air attacks from 1942 onwards, and the gradual collapse of German society towards the end of the war.

Another dominant strand of this volume is the horrific mass murder of an estimated 6 million Jews, which the Nazis referred to as their 'Final Solution of the Jewish question'. It will be revealed how the Holocaust began with ghettoization in the German-occupied areas of Poland in 1939–40, then escalated to the mass shootings of Jews in the Soviet Union during the latter months of 1941, before leading to the creation of purpose-built extermination camps, eventually reaching its most murderous period in 1942, during Operation Reinhard.

Contrary to popular belief, historical knowledge of the Third Reich is by no means complete. New details on specialized areas emerge continuously and general histories need constantly updating. New general studies on this subject are therefore thoroughly warranted. Hitler biographies appear even more regularly, but they fail to explain the fact that there is no comprehensive collection of sources relating to how Hitler exercised his power as Führer, because near the end of the war he ordered the destruction of his most confidential private papers. Indeed, Hitler biographies are not really about Hitler at all, but record what other people thought about him. Some are general histories pretending to be biographies. It is really a distortion of history to see the Third Reich through the narrow prism of Hitler's mind. It must be understood that Hitler was one important ingredient in the historical events which unfolded, but he was ultimately powerless to control those events.

Adolf Hitler presented the conflict that began in September 1939 as a war of national defence forced upon Germany by 'Jewish wire-pullers' in Britain and France, who were determined to prevent Germany gaining living space. The same argument was used to justify the German attack on the Soviet Union in June 1941: again Hitler presented it as a 'preventive war' to stop the 'Jewish-inspired Bolsheviks' from attacking Germany. The decision to declare war on the United States in December 1941 was portrayed in a similar way. On that occasion 'Jewish wire-pullers' had apparently forced President Roosevelt to join the 'Jewish worldwide conspiracy'. A great majority of Germans accepted Hitler's totally false explanation of why Germany had been forced to go to war.

Two separate military conflicts are at the centre of events from 1940 to 1945 examined in this book. First, the epic German-Soviet War, which ran continuously from the beginning of Operation Barbarossa on 22 June 1941 to the end of the war on 9 May 1945. Four out of every five German soldiers who died in the Second World War were killed by the Red Army. Second, the separate war Germany fought against the British and French empires and the United States. The key events of this struggle were a protracted naval war; the war between Germany and the Anglo-French alliance in 1940, which lasted just six weeks; the German bombing war over Britain, particularly in 1940; the Anglo-American bombing war against Germany from 1942 to 1945; the key battles between Germany and Italy against the Anglo-American Allies in North Africa, in southern Italy, and in the period following the D-Day landings on 6 June 1944, ending in victory for the Allies in Western Europe in May 1945.

My aim here is to show that Germany's war against the Soviet Union was much more brutal and ideologically and economically driven, as well as more destructive and genocidal, than its conflict with the Western Allies, which was conducted mostly according to the Geneva Conventions on war. Germany's wartime conduct was undoubtedly influenced by Nazi racial ideology. Soviet prisoners of war were treated like animals and often starved to death, while Anglo-American POWs were treated well and given Red Cross parcels.

For all of Hitler's boasting, Germany at the start of 1940 remained a medium-sized economic and military power without easily defensible borders, surrounded by a range of potential enemies. As a result, Germany needed to limit the number of its opponents and any military campaign it undertook had to be rapid, because it lacked a sufficient industrial and financial base to sustain a longer conflict against huge economic powers.

Adolf Hitler outlined his key political and foreign policy objectives in *Mein Kampf* (*My Struggle*), which was published in two volumes, the first appearing in July 1925 and the second in December 1926. These ideas were supplemented by his Secret Book in 1928, although this was never published. Hitler's ideological ideas of space and race, as expressed in the 1920s, were founded upon the view that Germany had not lost the Great War of 1914–18, but instead was 'stabbed in the back' by Jewish-inspired socialists and democratic politicians on the home front. The remedy for this was to purge Germany of democracy, as well as socialist ideas and the 'Jewish menace'; only then could Hitler create a racially pure German 'National Community' and prepare it for another war. This second conflict would not only overturn the result of the Great War, but would also allow Germany to gain 'living space' (*Lebensraum*), primarily through a war of conquest against the Soviet Union, thereby paving the way for a German population explosion in these newly acquired areas. His eventual aim was to create a huge Greater German Reich of 250 million 'racially pure' Germans, completely self-sufficient in food and fuel resources: a land-based military and economic superpower to rival the United States.

War – 'the great purifier' – had always therefore been implicit in Hitler's foreign policy thinking. He avoided forming military alliances or signing multilateral treaties. Hence, it was inevitable that Germany would move forward unilaterally, step by step before the war. This modus operandi continued during the Second World War with Hitler never losing his faith in the element of surprise.

Hitler thought in the 1930s that the British government would not object to his foreign policy aims on the European continent, but he expected the French – 'the inexorable enemy of the German people' – to oppose him. By the time of the Hossbach Conference in November 1937, however, it became clear that the British government would not allow him to achieve his territorial aims without going to war. Hitler was therefore prepared to risk a war with Britain, although he hoped, even after the war began, that the British government would agree to a peace settlement on his terms. In this respect, Hitler totally underestimated the determination of the British people to prevent Germany from dominating the European continent.

The second dominant aspect of Nazi ideology was race. Hitler was not, as is routinely supposed, merely an extreme 'German nationalist'. He viewed human history not as a class struggle, but as a battle for existence between strong races and 'weak' and 'mixed' ones. The question of how the Germans would become the 'strongest race on earth' occupied a great deal of his attention in *Mein Kampf*. Hitler argued, mostly in private, that the pure Aryan or 'master' race extended to many other people in Europe, in particular, to the British and to Anglo-Saxons in the United States.

If the Aryan race possessed all the positive qualities Hitler admired, then the opposite was true of his two most hated enemies: Jews and Marxists. At the core of Hitler's ideology was a desire to exterminate Marxism. During his trial for treason in 1924, following the botched 1923 Munich Beer Hall Putsch, Hitler passionately told the court that he wanted to be the 'breaker of Marxism'. His first aim when he came to power remained the elimination of Marxism as a factor in German politics, and this he achieved within six months. From June 1941 he wanted to exterminate Marxism in the Soviet Union. Hitler's view of Russians as essentially 'Slavs' led him to believe that a German army could easily defeat these 'racial inferiors'.

Closely interlinked with Hitler's anti-Marxism was a virulent antisemitism. Whenever Hitler spoke of Marxists, he implied that they were either Jews or were controlled by Jews. It's important to understand that Hitler did not define the Jews as a race or a religious group, but as a nomadic 'non-race', which he thought was involved in a global conspiracy to undermine national unity. This Jewish plan for world domination was supposedly outlined in *The Protocols of the Elders of Zion*, a fabricated antisemitic text which was circulated widely in Germany before 1914.

Hitler believed that because Jews were a stateless people (the Jewish state of Israel was not established until 1948) they had sought to undermine the racial unity of every state they inhabited. Hitler ascribed every ill in the world to 'Jewish influence'. Antisemitism therefore had two functions in Nazi ideology: first, it provided a very simple explanation for all the divisions and problems in German society and the wider world; second, it suggested that a 'final solution' to those ills could be achieved only by eliminating Jews, first of all from German society.

It will also be shown in this volume, however, that many of the wartime initiatives that led to the genocide of the Holocaust grew out of the local circumstances faced by German SS bureaucrats in the General Government in occupied Poland, and also the activities of the SS *Einsatzgruppen* killing squads operating in the Soviet Union. It was the *Ostkrieg* – Hitler's war on the Eastern Front – that fundamentally radicalized SS policy towards the Jews.

The Holocaust was in fact a gradual process of 'cumulative radicalism', often the result of middle-ranking bureaucrats acting on their own initiative and seeking ever more radical solutions to the so-called 'Jewish question'. These vile acts were approved by Hitler, but were not directed or micromanaged by him in the same way as he controlled military decisions. The mass murder was devolved primarily to Heinrich Himmler and his SS empire. By the time of the Wannsee Conference on 20 January 1942, a meeting of SS leaders and Nazi officials, Himmler and Reinhard Heydrich had streamlined the killing process and sought to extend it to the rest of Europe.

It will also be shown here that the Holocaust was not financed by huge amounts of German government spending, but was expected by Himmler to be largely self-financing through the confiscation of Jewish goods and property, and by employing as few full-time SS officials as possible to carry out the exterminations. It was genocide on a limited budget. In sum, the Holocaust was not as coordinated or as predetermined as is often supposed.

Similarly, Hitler's ideas, as outlined in *Mein Kampf*, were never as fixed as is often assumed. He did not progress, step by step, along a predetermined path towards war with the Soviet Union and the horror of the Holocaust. A great many events between 1940 and 1945 had unintended causes and consequences. Even Germany's war against the Soviet Union was not purely ideological. Hitler's desire to destroy the supposedly 'racially inferior' Slavs was interwoven with his key economic aim of seizing sufficient territory and economic resources to establish the Greater German Reich.

For Hitler, too, the war with Britain was the 'wrong war'. He would have far preferred the British government to have continued with the policy of appeasement. The 'right war' for Hitler was the one against the Soviets. It fitted in perfectly with his long-term desire to turn Germany into a superpower by gaining *Lebensraum* and at the same time destroying 'Jewish-Bolshevism'. As we shall see, however, Hitler's war with the Soviet Union was by no means inevitable. He did explore other alternatives, but in the end he stuck to his original objective of attacking the Soviet Union. Maybe his gut instinct would always have led him in that direction, but it is not certain.

For their part, the Allied nations were not – as their propaganda insisted – fighting a morally 'good war' simply to destroy Hitler and National Socialism. They were defending their own powerful political interests in the world against the strategic threat of Germany's military aggression. This is one reason why the Allies devoted so little attention to stopping Hitler's genocidal activities, even though they had full knowledge of them. The Allies were more concerned with stopping Hitler's tanks, war planes and U-boats than with putting an end to his death camps.

At the centre of Hitler's activities during the wartime period – and examined in detail in this book – was his micromanagement on a daily basis of the *Wehrmacht*'s military strategy, in conjunction with leading German military figures. Hitler immersed himself so much in the military campaigns of the *Wehrmacht* from 1940 to 1945 that domestic policy was neglected. Hitler directed the German military offensive, while government on the home front was managed by a multiplicity of ministers, local leaders and numerous state and party organizations.

It's important to stress, however, that Hitler did not dictate everything that happened in the military sphere. The key German military commanders who had supported the general thrust of Hitler's foreign policy from the beginning went along with the attacks on Poland and in Western Europe. They also supported his attack on the Soviet Union, and his decision to declare war on the United States; and they were fully complicit in the Nazis' genocidal actions against Soviet civilians, prisoners of war, and Jews.

According to the memoirs and war-trial testimony of Hitler's generals, the German army was not defeated by superior military forces with better generals, better tactics and better equipment, but by Hitler's constant meddling. This was perhaps best summed up by the leading German commander Erich von Manstein in the title of his memoirs: *Lost Victories*.

The opening of new Soviet archives in the 1990s has led to a number of revealing and correcting military accounts of this period, which are incorporated here. They shatter the myth promoted by various German commanders that Hitler alone lost the war. They also provide a much-needed insight into the Soviet experience of the conflict, especially the gradual learning process of Soviet commanders, who in the end managed to break the German army.

The detailed archival work of the Military History Research Office of the German army has also shown the army's complicity in Nazi crimes in the east, and revealed that Germany never enjoyed a material or economic advantage over Britain and France in 1940, let alone when the massive combined resources of the Soviet Union and the United States were ranged against it after December 1941. Germany's early military victories were as much due to good fortune and the mistakes of its opponents as they were to greater German resources, superior equipment or better military leadership.

Hitler and his military commanders were much more united than his commanders were later ever willing to admit. The first plan to invade the Soviet Union, for instance, came not from Hitler but from an independent commission by the Army High Command (OKH). Anti-Bolshevik and anti-Slavic prejudices were commonplace among the German military's top brass. They all thought the Soviet Union was a colossus with feet of clay and they all expected a swift victory in 1941.

Hitler felt that he had to risk war in 1939 in order for Germany to achieve superpower status. He wanted to be in possession of sufficient territory before his enemies caught up with German rearmament. Hitler understood that Germany might win a short war, but not a long one. There was never any question of his consolidating the huge European-based empire that his military triumphs had created by the summer of 1940. Possibly, his mindset – essentially pro-British, but passionately anti-Soviet – meant that he was always going to risk everything to defeat the Soviet Union rather than concentrating all of his effort on the more sensible alternative of first defeating Britain and its empire, a course that might have turned Germany into a European superpower.

Overall, given the much more challenging role of being Germany's military commander from 1940 to 1945, Hitler lacked the flexibility he had demonstrated as a peacetime politician. In the end, the intense psychological pressure proved too much for him. His health deteriorated and gradually he was unable to cope with the repercussions of his own decisions. It was not only Germany that collapsed in 1945, but its Führer, who took his own life to escape the consequences of total defeat.

1940

·

BLITZKRIEG TRIUMPHANT

·

•

'We enter the most decisive year in German history,' Adolf Hitler declared in his New Year message on 1 January 1940. 'Eighty million people cannot be kept from participation in the world's wealth. All the measures we have already taken neither robbed nor harmed the rest of the world. They merely gave the German nation things that other nations had.' In 1939 Central Europe had been 'pacified' through a series of 'epoch-making events', including the destruction of 'the Poland of Versailles'.[1]

On 3 January 1940 the Italian Fascist dictator Benito Mussolini wrote a letter to Hitler, which was not delivered until 8 January. Most strikingly, Il Duce suggested that Hitler retain 'a modest, disarmed Poland', albeit 'liberated from the Jews'. This would deprive the Western democracies of any justification for continuing the war. At the same time Mussolini advised Hitler not to attack Western Europe. The solution to Germany's *Lebensraum* ('living space') problem lay in the Soviet Union. Mussolini further distanced himself from the general direction of Hitler's foreign policy by sneering at the Molotov–Ribbentrop Pact – the non-aggression treaty between the USSR and Germany – describing it as an abandonment of the anti-Bolshevik programme of the Nazi revolution. 'Until four months ago,' he wrote, 'the Soviet Union was world enemy Number One; it cannot have become, and is not, friend Number One.'[2]

Astonished by the strong anti-Soviet tone of Mussolini's letter, the Foreign Minister Joachim von Ribbentrop composed a stern memorandum for Hitler on its contents. Neither German nor Italian interests were threatened in any way by an easing of German-Soviet relations. As for Mussolini's suggestion that a reconstructed rump Polish state would pave the way towards peace with Britain and France, Ribbentrop pointed out that a peace settlement had already been offered to the Allies in October 1939 and roundly rejected by them.[3]

On 10 January 1940 Hitler set yet another date for the attack on France via Belgium and Holland: 17 January. On the same day an embarrassing incident occurred, which cast doubt on whether the original plan for the Western offensive, codenamed Case Yellow (*Fall Gelb*), could go ahead as planned. Major Helmut Reinberger, an officer in the German airborne division, was on board a reconnaissance plane from Loddenheide to Cologne when his pilot Major Erich Hoenmanns lost his way in freezing fog, before he mistakenly switched off his engine, leading to a crash landing near Mechelen-sur-Meuse in neutral Belgium.

Inside Reinberger's briefcase were secret plans for the German attack on Belgium, including detailed maps. After climbing from the burnt wreckage, Reinberger took the documents behind some bushes and set them alight, but Belgian soldiers had spotted the burning plane crash landing and were quickly on the scene.

Reinberger told Bernhard von Bülow, the German ambassador to Belgium, that he had only a few fragments of the documents he was carrying before his capture. After being taken to military quarters, he tried to burn the rest by throwing them into a stove.[4] What became known as the 'Mechelen Incident' led a furious Hitler to postpone Case Yellow and to reconsider his battle plan for the attack on Western Europe.

On 11 January Hitler hastily issued Fundamental Order No. 1, which related to the 'preservation of military secrets'. In future, no person who was not directly involved in the planning and decision-making of military operations would be allowed access to military secrets.

The Mechelen Incident created a huge international outcry and had enormous repercussions. The counsellor of the Belgian embassy in Berlin handed a diplomatic note to the German Foreign Ministry on 12 January, formally protesting about German aeroplanes flying over Belgium. Paul-Henri Spaak, the Belgian Foreign Minister, made it clear to Bülow that the documents they had retrieved clearly revealed a plan to attack Belgium. All that was missing was a time and a date.[5] The Belgians passed on details of these intercepted German plans to the British and French governments. The British thought the plans were genuine, but the French decided they were fake, a deliberate German attempt to deceive the Western Allies.[6]

On 24 January Hitler delivered a speech to 7,000 new army officer candidates in the Berlin Sport Palace (*Sportpalast*) on the anniversary of the birth of Frederick the Great (1712–86). Hitler often found such occasions difficult. The unconditional adulation he received in the Reichstag and at Nazi Party rallies was not always guaranteed when he spoke in front of a military audience.

[*overleaf*]
The German tanker Altmark.

Hitler argued that there was an imbalance between the size of the German population and its available living space. This had made war inevitable in 1939. Germany could only expand by dealing with the Western Allies by force and he promised that Germany would soon go on the offensive in Western Europe, concluding: 'We decide when these actions take place. Let no one entertain any doubt, however, that they will indeed take place. No struggle in world history was ever decided by inaction, by staying low or on the sidelines.'[7]

On 27 January Wilhelm Keitel, Chief of the Armed Forces High Command (OKW), issued a directive, ordered by Hitler, to armed forces chiefs, asking them to make preliminary preparations for the invasion of Norway and Denmark. German intelligence reports indicated that the Royal Navy was planning to mine Norwegian ports as a precursor to occupying Norway. Hitler stressed that he had not fully made up his mind about sanctioning the invasion of Norway, but because Swedish iron ore was vital to the German war machine, and it was imported during the winter months via Narvik in Norway, it was vital not to allow this port to fall into enemy hands. The capture of Norway was by no means a simple operation for the German navy, as the Royal Navy enjoyed naval superiority.[8]

On 30 January 1940 Hitler gave his annual speech commemorating his accession to power in 1933. For the first time it was not delivered in the Reichstag but at the Berlin Sport Palace, where Hitler delivered a blistering attack on the British government, especially Prime Minister Neville Chamberlain.

Chamberlain had recently issued the Allied war aims, which Hitler treated with derision, arguing the British had 'waged the greatest number of wars around the world', and Chamberlain was now hypocritically promising a post-war Europe based on the ideal of justice. Hitler reminded Chamberlain that Germany had been consistently denied justice by the Treaty of Versailles.

Hitler said he would take no moral lectures from a nation that had used extortion, tyrannical abuse and oppression to build its vast empire. Britain had waged wars for trade, opium, gold and diamonds. Now it wanted the complete destruction of Germany. Hitler claimed that Chamberlain's mask dropped when the 'supposed peacemaker' had declared war on Germany in September 1939. The British guarantee to Poland had proved worthless and Hitler's subsequent peace offering to the Western Allies had been flatly rejected.

Hitler warned the Western Allies that Germany had not been asleep since the end of the Polish campaign. On the contrary, its armaments programme had been greatly accelerated. The German people, he said, stood united behind National Socialism: 'Our enemies, they already cry out today: Germany shall fall! Yet Germany can give but one answer: Germany will live, and hence Germany will win!'[9]

On 2 February 1940 Hitler hosted a farewell party for the Italian ambassador, Count Massimo Magistrati, at the new Reich Chancellery. Afterwards, he spoke privately to Magistrati on the current military situation. He told him that he couldn't understand Britain's stubborn determination to crush Germany. The British seemed to be living in the Victorian era, he added, when all they needed to get their way in the world was to send out a few cruisers. The British needed to face a new world order. They were deluded if they still thought Britain was a major power. America was now a far more important power, even in the economic and financial fields. Japan no longer feared British power and neither did the Soviet Union. Hitler predicted that Britain and its allies would be completely dumbfounded when Germany began its upcoming military offensive in the West.[10]

The German tanker *Altmark*, carrying no armaments, crossed the Atlantic in early February, bound for Germany. On board were 299 British prisoners of war. They had been picked up from merchant ships sunk in the South Atlantic by the German pocket battleship the *Admiral Graf Spee* in December 1939.

As the *Altmark* sailed through Norwegian waters, the Royal Navy pursued it. At the insistence of the British government, the Norwegian Navy boarded the vessel on 15 February, but could find no British POWs on board. They were in fact locked in a hold, which the Norwegian boarding party had failed to inspect.

The *Altmark* next headed for Jøssingfjord, protected by two Norwegian naval vessels. At this point, two heavily armed British destroyers began to follow it. During the eventful evening of 16 February, one of these destroyers approached the *Altmark* and turned on its searchlights. British naval officers told the captain of one of the Norwegian torpedo vessels accompanying the *Altmark* that British sailors intended to board the German tanker and they expected the Norwegians to stand aside.

At 10.20 p.m. a Royal Navy boarding party from HMS *Cossack*, commanded by Captain Philip Vian, climbed on board the *Altmark*. After discovering the British POWs hidden in the hold, Vian's men killed seven German sailors defending them during the course of the rescue operation.[11]

The British government justified this daring action by insisting that Germany had violated Norwegian neutrality by transporting POWs through the waters of a neutral country. In its defence, the Norwegian government claimed that it was 'not obliged or able to resist a vastly superior naval force'.[12] The '*Altmark* Incident', as the press called it, convinced Hitler that the Norwegian government had been complicit with the British during the rescue.

In February Hitler decided that a rethink was required on the existing idea for Case Yellow prompted by the unexpected 'Mechelen Incident'. Hitler now wanted a less predictable plan. General Erich von Manstein, the chief of staff of General Gerd von Rundstedt, who was to be the Chief of Staff of Army Group A for the German attack in the West, was also unsatisfied with Case Yellow, which he thought resembled the Schlieffen Plan of 1914, suggesting an initial thrust through Belgium and the Netherlands.[13]

In seven memoranda Manstein argued that the main part of the Panzer attack in Western Europe should be led by Army Group A in a surprise thrust through the seemingly impenetrable Ardennes Forest, which was regarded as impassable by tanks; then they would bridge the River Meuse and break through at Sedan, before sweeping towards the English Channel, with the Panzers at the spearhead, thereby creating a corridor trapping the Allied armies on two sides.[14] A second assault, led by Army Group B, would attack through the Netherlands and Belgium, but this would be a diversionary assault designed to lure the Allied armies northwards and into the ingenious German trap.

This bold plan was supported by Rundstedt, but Walther von Brauchitsch, the Supreme Commander of the German Army High Command (OKH), felt the plan was far too risky. He feared the Panzer units needed to bridge the River Meuse would end up in a traffic jam and become a sitting target for Allied bombers.

Franz Halder, the Chief of General Staff at OKH, had effectively sidelined Manstein in the previous months by moving him to an insignificant post in Szczecin (Stettin in German) in Poland. None of Manstein's memoranda for Case Yellow had yet reached Hitler.

On 7 February 1940 Rudolf Schmundt, Hitler's chief military aide, listened to a talk by Manstein during a 'war game' conference in Koblenz and was deeply impressed by his ideas. Schmundt decided to invite Manstein to a military conference about Case Yellow with key army commanders at the new Reich Chancellery on the morning of 17 February. This gave Manstein the opportunity to present his plan

German officer Erich von Manstein.

to Hitler face to face. The Führer was transfixed as Manstein cleverly outlined how his plan would work. By the end, Hitler declared himself 'enthusiastic', especially about the deployment of Panzer units to spearhead the assault.

From this point on, Manstein's 'Sickle Cut' thrust through the Ardennes suddenly became the plan that Hitler had apparently favoured all along. Hitler felt that the unexpected nature of the attack would startle the Western Allied forces, thereby handing the *Wehrmacht* an important psychological and military advantage at the beginning of the campaign. It would also avoid the stalemate that had occurred on the Western Front at the outset of the First World War in 1914.[15]

Within a week a firm military proposal – codenamed *Sichelschnitt* ('Sickle Stroke') – was produced by the OKH. It drew together Manstein's ideas plus some minor amendments from Hitler.[16] However, this audacious plan went against the instincts of the traditionally cautious and conservative Army High Command, who were still wedded to the Schlieffen Plan. If Operation *Sichelschnitt* succeeded it would therefore increase Hitler's authority over the German military's top brass. It was not part of any preconceived *Blitzkrieg* strategy, but grew out of an unplanned and unexpected set of circumstances. It was another idea adopted on the spur of the moment, because it appealed to Hitler's own gambler's instinct.[17]

Hitler spoke at the Hofbräuhaus in Munich on the twentieth anniversary of the foundation of the National Socialist German Workers' Party (NSDAP) on 24 February 1920. One of his greatest achievements as Führer, he said, was the spread of equality of opportunity. The key difference in the new Germany that he was now building could be seen in the increase of people from lower down the social scale to positions of responsibility. When a ship was launched, there was no longer a 'sea of top hats', but 'real people' present.

It was the same among the leadership. People in top positions were no longer there by birth but due to ability. The result was a nation that had 'regained its self-confidence to an unprecedented degree'. In conclusion, Hitler said that he was determined to wage war to eliminate the 'despicable clique of world plutocrats' who ruled Britain and France.[18]

Meanwhile, Hitler continued to underestimate the military and economic implications should the United States enter the war in support of the Western Allies. He knew the American domestic economy was very strong, but he did not fully appreciate just how quickly it could be adapted into a war economy.

From late February to early March 1940 US President Franklin D. Roosevelt sent Sumner Welles, his Under-Secretary of State, on a peace mission to Europe. During his trip, Welles stopped off in Rome, Berlin, Paris and London.[19]

On 29 February Hitler circulated a directive to key German diplomatic officials on how the talks with Welles should be handled. He advised them to let Welles 'do most of the talking'. Political questions such as the future of the Polish state and the German protectorate of Bohemia and Moravia should be avoided. Hitler wanted his diplomats to emphasize to Welles that France and Britain had declared war upon Germany and not the other way around. He had offered generous peace terms to end the war, but these had been spurned by the Western Allies. Above all, German diplomats were to utter no statement that suggested Germany was interested in making peace to end the war. On the contrary, Hitler wanted to stress to Welles the 'unshakable determination' of Germany to fight and to win.[20]

Hitler's war plans in Western Europe continued uninterrupted. On 1 March 1940 he signed the first draft of Case Weser Exercise (*Fall Weserübung*), instructing the German armed forces to plan for the invasion of Denmark and Norway.[21] The plan was to prevent British encroachment into Scandinavia, which would threaten Germany's supply of iron ore from Sweden.

General Nikolaus von Falkenhorst, who had combat experience in Finland during the First World War, was put in charge of the German operation. The forces required were to be 'kept as small as possible'. All three military services would participate. The crossing of the Danish border and the landings in Norway would occur simultaneously.

Case Weser Exercise would precede the attack on France and it would be presented to the world as a 'peaceful occupation' designed to protect Norway's neutrality. The low level of manpower assigned to the operation would be compensated for by 'daring actions and surprise execution'. Hitler urged that both attacks had to be ready 'as quickly as possible', in case the enemy seized the initiative, especially in Norway.[22]

On the same day Hitler was planning an unprovoked war against Norway and Denmark, Sumner Welles met the Foreign Minister Joachim von Ribbentrop, seemingly to discuss peace. Following the line recommended in Hitler's briefing notes, Ribbentrop reminded Welles that Britain had declared war on Germany. The German people were united to carry on the war to a victorious conclusion. Germany had the biggest and best-equipped army and air force. The British blockade would not work this time – as it had done between 1914 and 1918 – because Germany now had free access to raw materials as well as food from the Soviet Union.[23] In a further meeting with Ernst von Weizsäcker, State Secretary at the German Foreign Ministry, Welles bitterly observed that if Ribbentrop really believed Germany's objectives could be achieved only by war then his peace mission to Europe had been utterly pointless.[24]

On the following day Welles met Hitler in the new Reich Chancellery. The Führer subjected the now jaded American diplomat to a long and predictable monologue. Britain and France, he said, were hell-bent on self-destruction. Germany wanted to secure through war the economic and territorial foundations for its long-term existence. All military preparations had been made to break the will of its enemies. Welles assured Hitler that he would convey his statements to Roosevelt, but in private Welles admitted to finding Hitler's bellicose rhetoric deeply intimidating and he saw little hope of peace.[25]

On 8 March 1940 Hitler finally got around to replying to Mussolini's letter of 3 January. First, he praised the Italian leader for his frankness. Then, regarding Poland, Hitler emphasized that there was no question of restoring the Polish state: the German General Government would rule Poland until the end of the war at the very least. Any other solution would bring chaos. On the Soviet Union, Hitler pointed out that since the departure of Maxim Litvinov, the Soviet Foreign Minister, in 1939 there had been a sea change in the Soviet Union's attitude towards Germany. Stalin had modified his Bolshevik internationalist principles in favour of a more nationalistic and patriotic stance.

Finally, Hitler expressed supreme confidence in the German armed forces winning the coming battle in Western Europe, and he predicted: 'I believe that sooner or later fate will force us after all to fight side by side, that is, that you will likewise not escape this clash of arms, no matter how the individual aspects of the situation may develop today, and that your place will then more than ever be at our side, just as mine will be at yours.'[26]

On 9 March Ribbentrop left Berlin on his special train to visit Rome for two days of talks with Mussolini. His first meeting with Il Duce took place on 10 March. Ribbentrop told him that there was no possibility of peace. Hitler was resolved to attack France and Britain as soon as possible. The French would be swiftly defeated and the British driven from the European continent. Ribbentrop then turned to the anti-Soviet tone of Mussolini's January letter. He mentioned that during his two visits to Moscow he had become convinced that Stalin had now renounced any idea of fomenting a world revolution. The question of whether Italy would enter the war was not discussed.[27]

Ribbentrop met the Fascist leader again on the following day. 'I am and always will be anti-communist,' Mussolini told him. Nevertheless, he accepted the fact that Hitler's pact with the Soviet Union was politically expedient, as it meant that Germany had to fight on only one front in the war. Mussolini stressed that there was no chance of Italy entering the war on the side of Britain or France. It was impossible therefore for Italy to stay out of the conflict for much longer. Italy would join the war on Germany's side at the 'proper time', but he added that Italy would only enter the war when it was militarily ready, so as not to be a burden on its German ally.[28] Ribbentrop swiftly conveyed to Hitler Mussolini's positive remarks about joining the war in the near future.

On 12 March Adolf Hitler met Colin Ross, a German of Scottish descent, who was an explorer and the author of several travelogues, as well as an informal adviser to Ribbentrop in Berlin.[29] Ross told Hitler that Germany had previously been viewed as a bulwark against communism in the Western democracies. Now, however, hatred of Germany was extremely strong, especially in the United States, which Ross had recently visited. The unjust treatment of Jews by Germany only added to this American anger.

Ross advised Hitler that if he wanted better relations with the American government he needed to adopt a 'positive solution to the Jewish question'. In reply, Hitler said that the solution to the so-called Jewish question was a matter of gaining *Lebensraum* or living space. He opposed the idea of a Jewish state but also admitted that there was not sufficient space in the General Government area of Poland to solve the so-called 'Jewish question'.[30]

On 18 March 1940 Hitler held a meeting with Mussolini at the Brenner Pass in the Alps, near the border between Italy and the German Reich. The two dictators arrived on adjacent platforms at the local railway station aboard their luxurious special trains. During a frank two-and-a-half-hour meeting, Hitler dominated the conversation.

Hitler explained that the purpose of their meeting was to apprise Il Duce of the current military situation. He stressed that if Germany was content to be a second-rate power it need do nothing, but if it wanted to be a first-class power, then Britain and France stood in its way. If

[overleaf]
Hitler shaking hands with Mussolini
at the Brenner Pass, in the Alps, on
18 March 1940.

Germany won the coming war, he told Mussolini, with Italy as an ally, then Italy would decide the future peace settlement in conjunction with Germany. Hitler admitted that he had originally favoured cooperation with Britain, but as Britain now wanted war, he had been forced to form an alliance with the Soviet Union. As for Stalin, Hitler thought him an 'out and out autocrat', but in the tradition of the Russian tsars.

Hitler was also keen to point out to Mussolini that his pact with the Soviet Union was one of political expediency for the time being and that in reality Italy was Germany's real ideological friend. In reply, Mussolini said it was impossible for Italy to remain neutral through-out the duration of the war. Italy's honour and its ideological interests demanded that it enter the war on Germany's side.[31] The two leaders parted on good terms, but Hitler told his interpreter Paul Schmidt not to submit a written copy of their conversation to the Italian govern-ment, because he thought it might be leaked to the Western Allies.[32]

The Italian Foreign Minister Count Galeazzo Ciano felt that the meeting had been 'cordial on both sides', although it was mostly a monologue by Hitler: 'Hitler talks all the time, but is less agitated than usual. He makes few gestures and talks in a quiet tone. He looks physically fit. Mussolini listens to him with interest and deference.'[33]

In France the public mood was one of increasing frustration at the protracted inactivity of the so-called 'Drôle de guerre' or 'Phoney War'. In the French parliament on 21 March a vote of no confidence was called against Édouard Daladier's increasingly unpopular government. The French government gained 239 votes, but 300 parliamentary deputies, a majority of those present, abstained. As a result of this humiliation, Daladier decided to resign, although he would stay in the cabinet as Defence Minister. The new French Prime Minister Paul Reynaud was determined to galvanize the French people into 'total warfare'.[34]

On 2 April 1940 Hitler issued a directive setting the date and time for Germany's attack on Denmark and Norway: 9 April at 5.15 a.m. It was only at this stage that Ribbentrop and the German Foreign Ministry were finally let in on the secret.[35] In a further military directive to Wilhelm Keitel, Chief of the OKW, Hitler stressed the importance of not allowing the kings of Denmark and Norway to escape during the joint invasions, so the royal palaces would need to be placed under armed guard quickly after German troops entered.[36]

On the day of the simultaneous attacks the German government would inform the Norwegian and Danish governments that informa-tion had come to its attention which indicated that Britain and France intended to occupy several important bases on the Scandinavian coast. To forestall this, German troops were occupying Norwegian and Danish bases to protect the neutrality of both countries.[37]

On 4 April 1940 the British Prime Minister Neville Chamberlain gave a speech in Central Hall, London, to the National Union of Conservative and Unionist Associations. 'German preparations in September 1939 were far ahead of our own,' he said, 'and it was natural to expect that the enemy would take advantage of its initial superiority to make an endeavour to overwhelm us and France before we had time to make good our deficiencies. Is it not a very extraordinary thing that no attempt was made? Whatever the reason – whether it was that Hitler thought he might get away with what he had got without fighting for it, whether it was after all the preparations were not sufficiently complete – however, one thing is certain: he missed the bus.'[38]

Hitler was not travelling by bus. On 7 April five German naval groups (*Marinegruppen*) put to sea, heading for six Norwegian cities. At three main ports – Narvik, Trondheim and Stavanger – German troops were hidden in the hold of merchant ships. Another five naval groups headed for Denmark. These forces were supported by thirty-one U-boats. The *Luftwaffe* deployed an entire air corps: 1,200 aircraft. Overall, 120,000 troops were involved in the daring operation.[39]

On 8 April the Royal Navy began Operation Wilfred. They laid mines off the coast of Norway, blocking the free flow of shipping, and in preparation for a pre-planned British occupation of Narvik. However, the Norwegian government protested against 'this breach of international law' and 'infringement of Norway's neutrality'.[40]

On the next morning at precisely 5.15 a.m. the joint German invasions of Denmark and Norway began. German warships entered Copenhagen harbour, while paratroopers captured the airport. The Danish navy and army offered no resistance to the German invaders. King Christian X of Denmark, though surprised by the German invasion, dutifully surrendered before lunch. It was one of the quickest conquests in military history.

The Danes, who were regarded as Aryans by Hitler, were rewarded with one of the mildest forms of German occupation. Denmark remained formally independent, the king stayed on the throne and the Danes could keep their own army and navy. The Danish parliament continued to function and democratic elections took place in 1943 at which time the Danish Nazi Party only registered 2 per cent of the vote.[41]

The German government appointed the former ambassador Cecil von Renthe-Fink as the first German plenipotentiary in occupied Denmark. His job was to supervise a small administrative staff, but he avoided interfering in domestic affairs. Meanwhile, the Gestapo deployed a mere twenty-five officers in the country. Denmark found a comfortable niche in Hitler's new order for Europe by supplying Germany with 15 per cent of its food requirements, including exports of bacon, butter, eggs and beef.[42]

If the Danes offered little resistance, the same could not be said of the Norwegians, who demonstrated a much more spirited defence of their nation from the beginning to the end of the invasion. The British and the French were taken completely by surprise as German troops landed from naval vessels and seized Narvik.

At 7.23 a.m. on 9 April a Norwegian coastal battery – based at the ancient fortress of Oskarsburg – fired a single shell and managed to hit and sink the German cruiser *Blücher*, killing 1,600 crew on board. However, this did not stop German troops from occupying Oslo after the Norwegian army surrendered.

Trondheim on the west coast of Norway also fell without a fight, but Bergen, the second-largest Norwegian port, put up stiff resistance. It was soon brought under German control, however, with the help of devastating *Luftwaffe* bombing raids. Sola airfield, the biggest in Norway, near the port of Stavanger, was swiftly captured by the Germans. The *Luftwaffe* now had a base from which to establish its overwhelming air superiority over Norway. Kristiansand and Egersund were also in German hands by the end of the first day.

Haakon VII of Norway, the only king in the twentieth century to be elected to the throne by voters, was awoken to be told that his country was being invaded. The German government asked him to capitulate, but he bravely refused, then left for the small village of Nybergsund.[43]

A Norwegian fascist leader, Vidkun Quisling, became the head of a new, pro-German collaborationist government in Norway. Soon his name would become synonymous with treachery. The king refused to accept the legitimacy of Quisling's puppet regime, as did – to Hitler's dismay – most Norwegians.[44]

Hitler wrote to Mussolini on 9 April to explain how the capture of Norway and Denmark was crucial for Germany's conduct of the war. They could not have been allowed to fall under Allied control and for this reason he had been forced to occupy the two countries.[45] Hitler always liked to play the role of reluctant invader. After reading Hitler's

Norwegian pro-Nazi collaborator
Vidkun Quisling.

letter, Mussolini commented: 'I approve of this decision down to the last detail. The Italian people will approve of it in exactly the same way, as it is aimed against England.'[46]

In Moscow the Soviet Foreign Minister Vyacheslav Molotov told Friedrich-Werner Graf von der Schulenburg, the German ambassador, that the Soviet government fully understood that the military measures which had been forced upon the German government were a consequence of the British government going too far by infringing the rights of neutral nations. Molotov concluded by saying: 'We wish Germany complete success in her defensive measures.'[47]

On 10 April a British naval task force arrived in Narvik harbour, headed by the battleship HMS *Warspite* and supported by a flotilla of heavily armed destroyers. Over the next three days the Royal Navy spectacularly outgunned the German navy in Norwegian waters. At Narvik, nine German destroyers were sunk, losses which made Hitler think that holding Narvik might not be possible.

Curt Bräuer, the German Minister in Norway, went to Elverum on 10 April to meet King Haakon VII, who was holed up in a school building. Bräuer explained that Germany's pre-emptive action had been prompted solely by the British desire to breach Norwegian neutrality. He assured the king that the Norwegian monarchy would be unaffected by the German occupation.

Bräuer implored the king to support the new Norwegian government formed by Quisling. The king said that he could not accept a government headed by Quisling and he promised that resistance to the German occupation would continue.[48] Bräuer sent a situation report to Berlin on 11 April, casting serious doubt on the survival of Quisling's government, given the opposition of the king.[49]

In Berlin on 13 April Hitler met Albert Viljam Hagelin, a key collaborator in Quisling's new puppet government. The Führer asked him what was the level of support for Quisling among the Norwegian people. Hagelin estimated that it was only about 15 per cent. Hitler advised him that Quisling needed to secure the active support of a much broader range of opinions in order to survive. Hagelin thought that only some kind of agreement between the Quisling government and the king would calm the population, but he doubted whether this would be possible.[50]

The following day Bräuer reported a severe deterioration of the political situation in Norway. Quisling was so unpopular that keeping him in power had become impossible. Bräuer suggested that the President of the Supreme Court could put together a coalition government that pledged loyalty to the German occupation authorities. Then Quisling could remain in the government, not as Prime Minister, but with duties connected to winding up military affairs.[51]

Ribbentrop told Bräuer in a telephone conversation that Hitler was prepared to accept Quisling being held in reserve, but he did not want him to be compromised. He advised that Quisling stepping down as Prime Minister needed to be accompanied by positive propaganda to stress Quisling's patriotism.[52]

On the next day Bräuer chaired a political meeting at the Hotel Continental with all of the key figures in the Quisling government. It was agreed it would be best if they all resigned and a new constitutional government was formed. Quisling pointed out that only the king could order the formation of such a government, and not the Supreme Court. Nevertheless, it was decided to establish a government appointed by the Supreme Court, because this would leave open the possibility of the return of the king as head of state. At the end of the meeting Quisling formally resigned and a Norwegian administrative council of seven people, headed by Ingolf Christensen, was then formed.[53]

Hitler was not pleased with this solution. He decided to appoint Josef Terboven, a staunch and ruthless Nazi – and formerly the regional leader (or *Gauleiter*) in Essen – as the new Reich Commissioner (*Reichskommissar*) for Norway. He was assigned the role of safeguarding non-military German interests. Terboven set up the so-called *Reichskommissariat* Norway on 24 April and it remained the civilian German occupation regime for the duration of the war.[54]

On 25 September 1940 Terboven took direct control of Norwegian internal affairs. He abolished the Norwegian monarchy, dissolved the political parties – except for Quisling's pro-Nazi National *Sammlung* (NS) – and formed a new State Commission to run the country, made up of German economic officials, mostly drawn from Hamburg.

Under German occupation the existing body of Norwegian law remained in force, but Terboven issued decrees as and when he wished. He appointed members of Quisling's NS as local mayors and he interfered with judicial appointments. All this was a serious rebuff to the Norwegian political elite, which is one reason why Nazi rule in Norway during the war remained deeply unpopular. Around 200 Gestapo personnel were deployed in Norway to track down opponents of the German occupation.[55]

On 20 April British and French troops landed at Namsos, a small port eighty miles down the coast from Trondheim. Another contingent of British troops was put ashore at Åndalsnes, a hundred miles south-west of Trondheim. Both groups aimed to attack the German-occupied port from the north and south. It was a poorly planned operation. The Allied troops were badly led and lacked maps, transport vehicles, radio communication, heavy artillery, machine guns, ammunition, skis and air support. A Norwegian army commander described the British troops as 'very young lads who appeared to come from the slums of London. They have taken a very close interest in the women of Romsdal and engaged in wholesale looting of stores and houses.'[56] The *Luftwaffe* bombarded the Allied troops night and day, preventing military reinforcements from landing. The situation for the Western Allies soon became hopeless.

Hitler informed Mussolini by letter on 26 April about the German capture of secret documents from the British and French consulates in Norway. They provided conclusive proof, he said, of Churchill's plans to occupy Norway on 8 April. Even if the Western Allies decided to defend Norway, Hitler predicted that 'they will never get the German divisions out of the country now'.[57]

On 29 April King Haakon VII and members of his government moved to Tromsø, where a provisional capital was set up. Allied troops in Norway were evacuated between 30 April and 2 May 1940, thus ending the first phase of Allied resistance in Norway. The southern half of Norway, including all of the main ports and cities except for Narvik, were now firmly under German control. Hitler gleefully told Mussolini that the British troops in Norway 'ran away faster than we could follow them'.[58]

In the Berlin Sport Palace on 3 May 1940 Hitler addressed 6,000 new officer candidates for the army, *Luftwaffe* and Waffen-SS. Hitler told them that the battle Germany was currently engaged in was a 'decisive struggle that will determine the future of our race, of our Reich'. The Western Allies were fighting to preserve a balance of power which had favoured them for centuries, whereas Germany was using its force to gain living space to secure its future as a great power: 'The earth is not there for cowardly peoples, not for weak ones, not for lazy ones. The earth is there for him who takes it and who industriously labours upon it and thereby fashions his life. That is the will of Providence.'[59]

The news of the humiliating evacuation of Norway by British and French troops was greeted with enormous anger in Britain. However, the major share of the blame was not heaped upon Winston Churchill, the First Lord of the Admiralty and the key instigator of the operation, but on the hapless and unpopular Prime Minister Neville Chamberlain.

During the tempestuous 'Norway debate' in the House of Commons from 7 to 8 May, the parliamentary opposition to Chamberlain was undeniable. In a speech defending his own actions regarding Norway, Chamberlain – who could not shake off his caricature as the 'apostle of appeasement' – sounded nervous, weak and deeply unconvincing.

The most scathing attack came in a devastating speech on 7 May by the Conservative MP Leo Amery, a former Chamberlain loyalist: 'This is what [Oliver] Cromwell said to the Long Parliament when he thought it was no longer fit to conduct the affairs of the nation: "You have sat too long here for any good you have been doing. Depart, I say, and let us have done with you. In the name of God, go!"'[60] In the vote of censure tabled by Clement Attlee, the leader of the opposition Labour Party, only forty Conservatives voted against Chamberlain's government, but sixty abstained.

The pressure was now mounting on Neville Chamberlain to resign. On 9 May he tried to form a new National Coalition government to include the Labour Party leader, but Attlee refused to serve if Chamberlain remained as Prime Minister. Two men seemed best placed to replace Chamberlain. Lord Halifax, the experienced Foreign Secretary, was favoured by Chamberlain himself, as well as by King George VI and most of the Conservative Party. Winston Churchill, aged 65, was still viewed as a maverick by many Conservatives, but as Hitler's biggest critic he was acceptable to the Labour Party. Halifax soon made it clear that he did not want the role.

And so, on 10 May 1940, Winston Churchill became Prime Minister. It was a key turning point in British history, because Halifax, had he been given the post, was still at heart a supporter of appeasement and he would most probably have come to some kind of peace terms with Germany and the course of the Second World War would have been very different.[61]

The political turmoil in Britain had no effect on Hitler's plan to attack the Western Allies on mainland Europe. 'When you receive this letter, I shall already have crossed the Rubicon,' Hitler informed Mussolini on 9 May, the eve of the German attack on France and the Low Countries. Hitler asked Mussolini to understand the circumstances which now compelled him to launch this invasion: 'It is a question of life and death for my people and the Reich for the next

500 or 1,000 years. I would be failing in my duty if I did not fulfil what my judgement of necessity demanded of me.' Hitler then promised to update Mussolini on events as they unfolded.[62]

In his reply Mussolini wrote: 'As in the campaign in Norway the press and the action of the [Fascist] Party will guide the mind of the Italian people toward understanding the necessity with which you were faced. I feel that time is pressing for Italy too, and I am deeply grateful for your promise to keep me informed of developments in the operations in order to put me in a position to make my decisions.'[63]

On 9 May 1940 Hitler issued a directive on the administration of the occupied territories of France, Luxembourg, Belgium and Holland in the event of a German victory. He proposed that the commander-in-chief of the army would initially set up a separate administration for each of the four countries. The provisions of the Hague Land Warfare Convention would be observed, which had not been the case in Poland. The people of Western Europe would not be treated as racial enemies, but any sabotage or passive resistance would be punished severely.[64] On the eve of the attack, Hitler told his generals: 'Gentlemen, you are about to witness the most famous victory in history.'[65]

On 9 May Hitler boarded his special train and at dawn the following day it arrived at a little railway station in the Eifel. From here, Hitler was driven to his new 'Führer Headquarters' near the spa town of Münstereifel which was about eighteen miles south-west of Bonn in the North-Rhine-Westphalia region.

The long-planned 'Case Yellow' (*Fall Gelb*) was finally being launched.[66] Its chief aims were not only to knock France out of the war, but to push the British out of the European mainland. Hitler had kept out of direct involvement in the military operations in Poland, but now he became deeply involved in the military decision-making during the Western European offensive. This was the beginning of Hitler's complete control of German military strategy that would continue for the rest of the war.

For the attack in Western Europe, the German army had a total nominal strength of 4.2 million men, supported by a million more attached to the *Luftwaffe*, plus 180,000 naval personnel and a Waffen-SS contingent of 100,000. In total 5.48 million men were available. Of these, 3 million were initially allocated to the attack. On paper the German army had 157 divisions, but only 135 of these were earmarked for Case Yellow and these included forty-two reserve divisions, most of which had only recently been formed and were inadequately trained.

British Prime Minister Winston Churchill.

In reality, the German army deployed ninety-three fully battle-ready divisions into Western Europe.[67]

They were divided into three army groups. Army Group A (*Heeresgruppe A*), at the centre of the assault, was commanded by Field Marshal Gerd von Rundstedt. It consisted of the forty-five divisions of the 4th, 12th and 17th armies. These forces were to advance through the Ardennes Forest, cross the River Meuse – with floating pontoon bridges – between Sedan and Dinant, then drive north-west along the line of the River Somme to Amiens, then Abbeville and finally to race to the Channel ports.

If Army Group A could make it across the Meuse it could move at a speedy forty miles a day. The seven Panzer Corps of Army Group A numbered 134,370 men, with 1,222 tanks, 41,140 motor vehicles and 545 other vehicles, all loaded up with ammunition, fuel and food. It was the first German deployment in battle of an autonomous tank force operating independently of the infantry. The supplies needed for the operation were calculated precisely beforehand. Amazingly, there was never any fuel supply crisis for Army Group A during the entire operation.

The second German attack force was Army Group B (*Heeresgruppe B*), commanded by Colonel General Fedor von Bock. It was composed of twenty-nine divisions split into two armies, the 6th and 18th. It would operate in the north, attacking into northern Belgium and the Netherlands. Its key aim was to draw the main bulk of the French army and the British Expeditionary Force (BEF) eastwards to meet it. Army Group B contained just three Panzer divisions. Bock was not pleased that his group was playing second fiddle to Army Group A and that his force was effectively acting as a diversion from the main thrust of the German attack by Army Group A.

The third German assault force was Army Group C (*Heeresgruppe C*), under the command of Field Marshal Wilhelm Ritter von Leeb. It had just nineteen divisions and two armies, the 1st and 7th. It contained no Panzer units at all. Army Group C would operate primarily in a defensive role in the south and, if required, it would engage with the defenders of the Maginot Line, the defensive fortifications along France's north-eastern frontier.

The German army was organized into three types of division: armoured (Panzer), motorized and infantry. Parachute divisions were also attached to the *Luftwaffe*. The authority structure came directly from Hitler, as the Supreme Commander, through the OKW, the

Supreme Command and the Army High Command OKH, then orders went from there to the commanders of the three army groups.[68]

The traditional historical view of the Fall of France is of German tanks racing unimpeded to the English Channel, as well as *Luftwaffe* dive bombers screeching overhead and the French army giving up without a fight. Yet the German army did not have the military superiority over the Western Allies, as is routinely imagined. The German army had 2,439 tanks, but the French had 3,254, supplemented by 310 British tanks. In addition, the Belgians had 270 and the Dutch 40. In total, 2,439 battle-ready German tanks faced an Allied tank battle-ready overall strength of 3,874. Furthermore, in terms of quality the Allied tanks had stronger armour and were more than a match for their German equivalents. It was how these tanks were organized and deployed that really made the difference during the battle.

The Allies lacked dedicated tank divisions, preferring to deploy tanks within traditional infantry divisions and thereby diluting their power. Furthermore, German tank divisions had better communications as a greater proportion of them were equipped with radios. Also, German tanks wisely avoided facing Allied tanks head-on during the invasion. One exception was at Hannut in Belgium on 14 May – the biggest tank battle of the war to that date – when the German tank losses exceeded the French by a ratio of three to two.[69]

In artillery the Western Allies were almost twice as strong as the Germans. The French had 10,700 artillery guns, the British, 1,280, the Belgians 1,338, and the Dutch army 656. A total of 13,974. Against this, the *Wehrmacht* had the lower total of 7,378.[70]

Perhaps the biggest *Blitzkrieg* myth of all is the alleged air superiority of the *Luftwaffe* during the Battle of France. The *Luftwaffe's* total strength of 5,446 aeroplanes was very impressive on paper, but only 2,589 German planes joined the attack on 10 May. Afterwards, the Allies deliberately exaggerated the strength of the *Luftwaffe* in order to diminish their own shortcomings.[71]

The French Air Force had 3,562 aeroplanes, but only 879 of these were ever deployed. A total of 1,528 fighters and 690 bombers remained on the ground. Within six weeks, the French had lost 892 aircraft. The Royal Air Force deployed 500 aircraft in north-east France from 10 May, but these figures do not tell us how many RAF planes participated in the battle: the RAF lost 1,029 aircraft and a total of 1,870 RAF planes took part in the conflict. To these figures can be added 377 Belgian and 124 Dutch aircraft.[72]

The *Luftwaffe* engaged about 75 per cent of its overall fighting strength during the invasion of Western Europe, while the French Air Force kept 75 per cent of its available aircraft on the ground. It was the RAF that really led the defence of France in the air. The two key advantages enjoyed by the *Luftwaffe* were (a) boldness: it threw every combat-ready aircraft into the Battle of France, and (b) modern radio communications to provide air support to the German army on the ground at vital moments during the battle.[73]

It remains a matter of conjecture whether *Luftwaffe* pilots performed better than Allied pilots during the conflict in Western Europe. The number of losses for both sides overall were 1,559 for the *Luftwaffe*, 892 for the French (only 306 of these during combat) and 1,029 for the RAF. The Western Allies shot down more German planes than they lost, yet the glaring error of the Allied effort in the air was the French decision to use so little of its available strength in the battle.

The French army in May 1940 was 5.5 million men strong, including soldiers of the French Empire. Of these, 2.24 million were deployed to meet the expected German assault. The French had 117 divisions available, with 104 manning the north-east front. To this total could be added the thirteen divisions of the British Expeditionary Force (BEF), twenty-two Belgian and ten Dutch divisions.

In total, the 93 German divisions faced 149 Allied divisions. The Western Allied Armies were organized into three army groups. The First Army Group played the major role in the battle. It consisted of the French 1st, 2nd, 7th and 9th armies, the BEF, the Belgian army and the Polish army in France. The Second Army Group consisted of three French armies: the 3rd, 4th and 5th. The Third Army Group was composed of the 8th French army and the Dutch army.

On paper, the Western Allies enjoyed an enormous numerical advantage over the Germans, but this obscured underlying weaknesses. The bulk of Allied soldiers were young and inadequately trained conscripts with little or no battle experience. The Allies had no radio communications either on the ground or with the supporting air forces. Another problem was morale. When Lieutenant-General Alan Brooke, a leading British general, had visited the Western Front in November 1939, he noted that the French recruits exhibited 'a complete lack of pride in themselves or their units. What shook me most, however, was the look in the men's eyes, disgruntled and insubordinate looks.'[74]

The Allied command structure depended upon the defence-minded 68-year-old General Maurice Gamelin, the French Supreme

French military commander
Maurice Gamelin.

Commander, who devolved his authority to General Aimé Doumenc, the Commander of Land Forces, as well as General Alphonse Georges, the commander-in-chief of the north-east front, who also controlled the three French army groups and the BEF, whose commander-in-chief was the British General Lord Gort.

Gamelin's headquarters were at the Château de Vincennes, a gloomy villa outside Paris, where the English king Henry V had died in 1422, and where the Dutch exotic dancer and spy Mata Hari had been executed in 1917. It was more like a monastery than the nerve centre of a modern military operation. It had no radio communications at all, which explains why communications between Gamelin and his Allied armies were often very slow.[75]

Gamelin favoured a defensive approach to Hitler's attack, for he wanted to avoid a repetition of the slaughter of 1914–18. As Captain André Beaufre, a member of the French General Staff, recalled: 'It was a period of decay, very deep decay, probably caused by the excess of effort during World War One. I think generally speaking we suffered from an illness, which is not peculiar to the French, that having been victorious we believed that we were right and very clever.'[76]

The German attack began at 5.35 a.m. on 10 May 1940 when a squad of German soldiers crossed the Sauer Bridge in Luxembourg, quickly overpowering the border guards. The German attack on Belgium and the Netherlands followed simultaneously.

The Dutch had assiduously maintained their neutrality throughout the First World War, but not this time. The bulk of the French army – backed up by the BEF – marched northwards into Belgium and the Netherlands on a defensive line running north–south from Breda in the Netherlands to Dinant in Belgium. But this was exactly what the *Wehrmacht* wanted the Allies to do.

In Belgium concrete defensive forts had been constructed along the three natural lines of canals, with the Albert Canal and Fort Eben Emael at their epicentre. It was at Eben Emael where the first daring German attack occurred. Light glider planes containing just 400 German troops landed on the roof of the fort and dropped hollow concrete piercing charges into its structure.[77]

By the end of the first day, the German army controlled the fort and two key bridges. Belgian forces retreated to the Dyle Line, the third and final line of defence, a series of bunkers and barricades stretching from Antwerp to Namur. Meanwhile, Dutch forces, numbering ten divisions, retreated to the waterlogged canal zone around Amsterdam and Rotterdam to try to hold up the German army.

On 13 May 1940 the first wave of German tanks crossed a newly created pontoon bridge over the Meuse River at the Pont Neuf, the northernmost bridge of Sedan, to begin the spectacular German attack. A bridgehead was quickly established. The following day a further 600 tanks had crossed the Gaulier Bridge. Indeed, the whole success of the German operation depended on this one pontoon bridge remaining in operation.

At the forefront of the German Panzer assault were two fearless tank commanders: Erwin Rommel and Heinz Guderian. Their tank forces punched a seventy-mile hole in the Maginot Line, capturing Sedan, the very same place where the self-declared Emperor Napoleon III had surrendered to the Prussian army in 1870.

Guderian and Rommel then ignored their orders to halt and wait for the infantry support to catch up with them, and instead raced boldly towards the Channel coast. Once again, the German troops driving the tanks made liberal use of Pervitin, a performance-enhancing amphetamine, which had kept them wide awake and feeling invincible during the invasion of Poland in 1939. An estimated 35 million tablets were taken by German soldiers during the Battle of France. The Germans were not just moving at speed through France, they were on speed.[78]

French defence forces in the Ardennes were relentlessly attacked by the *Luftwaffe*, which carpet-bombed their positions. In panic, the French infantry were forced to retreat. As one French soldier put it: 'Explosions came crashing all over the place. All you can feel is the nightmare noise of the bombs, whose whistling becomes louder and louder the closer they get. You have the feeling that they are zeroed in precisely on you.'[79]

The Allies soon realized that the Germans' pontoon bridges across the Meuse had to be destroyed or else a military catastrophe loomed. On 14 May 1940, 152 French and British bombers, supported by 250 fighter planes, mounted a huge Allied attack designed to destroy the German made bridges across the strategically important river.

The Allied air attack was a fiasco. Out of 109 RAF bombers, 47 were shot down and 5 French bombers were also destroyed. A further 50 Allied fighters were lost. In this single air engagement with the *Luftwaffe* the Allies had lost 102 planes and not a single German bridge had been put out of action.

The dire implications of the German breakthrough at Sedan were

[overleaf]
The German army motors through the
Ardennes Forest.

not lost on the French government and its military leadership. Defeat of a catastrophic nature now seemed certain for the Western Allies. On the morning of 15 May 1940 Paul Reynaud, the French Prime Minister, phoned his British counterpart Winston Churchill. Later, Churchill vividly recalled their conversation: 'He [Reynaud] spoke in English and evidently under stress. "We have been defeated." As I did not immediately respond, he said again, "We are beaten, we have lost the battle." I said, "Surely it can't have happened so soon?" But he replied, "The front is broken near Sedan: they are pounding through in great numbers with tanks and armoured cars."'[80]

On the same morning, Churchill held a crisis meeting with his War Cabinet. They immediately pledged to send more aircraft to assist the French. Churchill flew to Paris later in the day to try and lift Reynaud's spirits, but he encountered a French premier and a military leadership mired in despondency.[81]

At the French High Command headquarters defeatism spread like an uncontrollable virus. 'The atmosphere was that of a family in which there had been a death,' noted General André Beaufre. 'Georges [the leading French commander] was terribly pale. "Our front has broken at Sedan. There has been a collapse." He flung himself into a chair and burst into tears.'[82]

On 14 May the *Luftwaffe* bombed Rotterdam, flattening the city centre area and killing 814 civilians. On the following day, the Dutch army commander-in-chief General Henri Winkelman formally announced the surrender of the Dutch army. Queen Wilhelmina of the Netherlands and her government were evacuated to London aboard the British destroyer HMS *Hereward*. The Dutch Empire was unaffected by the surrender.

The people of the Netherlands had to endure German occupation until the end of the war. Hitler decided to adopt a traditional military occupation. The country was controlled by a Nazi governor, the slippery Austrian lawyer Arthur Seyss-Inquart. Hitler told him to encourage the local people to collaborate, but Seyss-Inquart ignored this order and imposed a strict policy of 'enforced conformity', eliminating all socialist parties and allowing only a minor Dutch Nazi party, the National Socialist Dutch Workers Party (DSB), to operate. Dutch civil servants carried on the business of civil administration, and Dutch law remained in force, except where it conflicted with Nazi racial policies.

Ruthless antisemitic policies were adopted by the Nazi occupiers in the Netherlands, especially by the SS and the Gestapo. The long-term goal of the occupation was to incorporate the Netherlands into the Greater German Reich, because the Dutch were considered valuable members of the Aryan race. The Netherlands would also become strategically important as a base for *Luftwaffe* bombing raids on Britain.[83]

In a military directive issued on 15 May 1940 Hitler observed that the Allies had already 'failed to realize the basic idea of our operation' because they continued to concentrate their defence in Belgium, neglecting the main thrust of the German attack by Army Group A. Everything was going to plan. The Meuse river crossings, Hitler added, had already provided the prerequisite of success.[84]

On 16 May the French premier Paul Reynaud made two appointments that would prove disastrous for France. First he invited the military hero of the First World War Philippe Pétain – who was serving at the French embassy in Madrid at the time – to become his Deputy Prime Minister. Next Reynaud approached another wartime hero, the 74-year-old General Maxime Weygand, who had been the Chief of the Army General Staff in 1918. Now that Maurice Gamelin had clearly failed, Reynaud asked the right-wing Weygand to replace the utterly discredited French supreme army commander.

Weygand's first action in his new role was to cancel a planned French counteroffensive. It was not until 22 May that he issued his 'Operations Order No. 1', known as the 'Weygand Plan'. This proposed a pincer attack to break the encirclement of the French 1st Army Group along the Channel coast. But Weygand cancelled this proposed assault twice, before finally shelving it completely.[85]

By 17 May, Army Group A's tank divisions had travelled forty miles inside French territory. Rundstedt, supported by Hitler, decided to halt them to allow the infantry divisions to catch up. This order undoubtedly slowed down the German advance towards the Channel ports. As Halder noted in his diary: 'An unpleasant day. The Führer is terribly nervous. Frightened by his own success, he is afraid to take any chances, and so would rather pull the reins on us. Puts forward the excuse that it is all because of his concern for the left flank.'[86]

On 18 May Hitler sent Mussolini an update on the progress of the German attack. Hitler reported that Belgium had already lost its entire canal system of defensive forts and that the Belgian army was 'largely smashed'. Meanwhile, the *Luftwaffe* enjoyed complete air superiority. Many British and French divisions no longer represented a serious fighting force. He added that all of this had been achieved with

minimal German losses. After eight days, Hitler felt that Germany was already in sight of victory.[87]

'I thank you for having found time during a pause in the tremendous victorious battle to send me a communication on the progress of the operations,' Mussolini wrote in reply. The battle was being followed with enthusiasm by the Italian people, he added, 'who are now convinced that the period of [Italian] non-belligerency cannot last much longer'.[88]

On 19 May the ambitious French general Charles de Gaulle launched a counter-attack against the advancing Panzer units of Army Group A, but it was short-lived and unsuccessful. Two days later, two divisions of the BEF, supported by two tank battalions, managed to attack Rommel's tank divisions at Arras, causing a brief period of German panic, but once again this failed to halt the seemingly unstoppable advance of Hitler's invasion force.

On 20 May the German Panzer divisions led by Heinz Guderian reached Abbeville at the mouth of the River Somme. They were now within fifty miles of the English Channel. Army Group A had created a corridor 130 miles in length and 86 miles in width. The BEF and the three French armies began to retreat to the coastal ports of Dunkirk and Ostend, hoping to be evacuated to Britain.

A German soldier wrote a letter home on the same day:

> The face of war is dreadful. Towns and villages shot to pieces, plundered shops everywhere, valuables are trodden on by jackboots ... We live like gods in France. If we need meat a cow is slaughtered, and only the best cuts are taken, and the rest discarded. Asparagus, oranges, lettuces, nuts, cocoa, coffee, butter, ham, chocolate, sparkling wine, wine, spirits, beer, tobacco, cigars and cigarettes, as well as complete sets of laundry are there in abundance.[89]

By 24 May 1940 the German army was just nine miles from Dunkirk and on the point of seizing it. In a few hours 1 million Allied troops would be trapped by the Germans. Then one of the strangest episodes of the Second World War occurred. At 12.45 a.m. the German army came to a shuddering halt, ordered by Hitler, under 'War Directive No. 13'. The order left Guderian 'speechless'.[90]

Hitler's decision to halt the German advance and give his enemies a chance to escape has been the subject of heated historical debate. Contrary to popular myth, Hitler was not exclusively responsible for the so-called halt order. The notion of stopping Army Group A was

The Allied evacuation from the port of Dunkirk.

first put forward by Field Marshal Gerd von Rundstedt, its commander on the previous day. The idea was then accepted and endorsed by Hitler. At the Nuremberg Trials, German generals tried to pin all the blame for the delay on Hitler, but the official war diary of Army Group A makes it clear that Rundstedt was chiefly culpable.[91]

Nevertheless, it is still suggested by some historians that Hitler issued the halt order because he wanted the British to escape in the hope they would accept a peace settlement. At the time, German tank crews couldn't understand why they were being ordered to halt. Ferdinand Krones, an Austrian-born German tank driver, with Army Group B, later recalled: 'I still cannot figure out why this decision was made by Army High Command, or whether it came straight from the top [Hitler]. My personal guess is that Hitler wanted to make a gesture to Britain, by making it possible for them to retreat without a fight. This was a gesture to the "blood relatives", our English cousins.'[92]

General Walter Warlimont, the deputy chief of Germany's Supreme Command, did not accept this explanation, commenting: 'I do not believe that he [Hitler] allowed the British Expeditionary Force to escape for political reasons and by this chivalrous attitude would obtain a chance of coming to terms with Britain. Such an assumption, apart from everything else, is in full contrast to Hitler's concentrating the whole power of the German Air Force on the coastline after the British retreat.'[93]

A far more plausible suggestion is that Hitler wanted the *Luftwaffe*, which was viewed as a Nazi creation, to gain the chief praise for defeating the French and British. Hermann Göring, the supreme commander of the *Luftwaffe*, did phone Hitler on 23 May to assure him that the *Luftwaffe*, acting alone, could carry out the operation. Göring also warned Hitler that if victory in Europe was perceived to be a victory by the generals, then 'they might win a prestige with the German people which would threaten your own position'.[94]

As it turned out the *Luftwaffe* proved incapable of preventing the evacuation from Dunkirk. The Royal Air Force played a major part in challenging German air superiority for the first time during the evacuation from Dunkirk. The newly introduced RAF fighter plane, the Spitfire, proved more than a match for the German Messerschmitt 109. The RAF lost 177 aircraft during the operation, but *Luftwaffe* losses were far higher.[95]

Between 26 May and 4 June, 388,682 Allied troops were evacuated in an extraordinary maritime and naval undertaking, codenamed

Operation Dynamo. At its heart was a brilliantly improvised Royal Navy-led armada of 900 vessels, including cruisers and destroyers, large passenger ferries and an assortment of 200 privately owned vessels, including fishing trawlers, yachts, motorboats and tugs. Contrary to popular belief, most were not manned by 'Sunday sailors', but by trained Royal Navy personnel. Of these, 272 were sunk, including 13 destroyers, with a further 15 severely damaged. About 200,000 troops of the British Expeditionary Force were rescued. Had they been captured by the Germans, Britain's ability to continue the war would have been seriously compromised.[96] As it was, the fleeing Allies were forced to abandon all of their equipment, including 63,000 motor vehicles, 20,000 motorcycles, 475 tanks, 2,400 artillery guns and huge numbers of handguns, rifles and ammunition.[97]

While the evacuation at Dunkirk was taking place, Hitler seemed totally unconcerned about exactly how many Allied troops were escaping. This is evident from a letter Hitler wrote to Mussolini on 25 May in which he admitted a willingness to risk the withdrawal of some Anglo-French troops in the Channel ports in order to have a 'lull in the advance', so as to allow the infantry divisions to catch up with the armoured and motorized divisions.

Hitler then offered Mussolini a brief overview of how the Allied forces had performed during the Battle of France. The Dutch had 'offered strong resistance' before surrendering. Belgian soldiers had fought bravely. The British were often brave, but had been 'miserably led by their officers'. The French had some excellent units, but overall they had performed abysmally, displaying very low morale.

As for the German armed forces, Hitler believed that they had demonstrated superiority on land and in the air, and they were emerging from the battle with minimal losses. He predicted that the remainder of the French army would be unable to resist the final German offensive.[98]

Mussolini noted in his reply that the information Hitler had provided was 'particularly interesting'. He then announced his decision: Italy would enter the war on 5 June, although he was prepared to delay 'a few days longer for the sake of better coordination with our plans'.[99]

Hitler informed Mussolini that he had been moved 'most profoundly' by Mussolini's decision to enter the war on Germany's side. It had strengthened his 'unshakable belief in the victorious outcome of the war'. Hitler then asked Mussolini to delay his entry into the war a few days to 8 June. Mussolini finally set the date for 10 June 1940.[100]

Behind the scenes, however, Franz Halder's diary reveals that Hitler did not care very much whether Italy entered the war or not, despite his polite response to Mussolini.[101]

Dunkirk was presented to the British public as a great victory – and the 'Dunkirk spirit' is still evoked today – but in reality it was a deeply humiliating defeat. The German media depicted the evacuation as cowardly and treacherous, the British were not only running away from the battle, but also shamelessly deserting their European allies. Churchill was also mocked in the German press for trying to dress up this scramble to escape as some kind of heroic triumph.

At a meeting of the War Cabinet on 26 May 1940 Lord Halifax, the Foreign Secretary, floated the idea that the British government might seek peace terms with Germany, using Mussolini as an intermediary. Halifax felt that with France heading for defeat and without firm American involvement, Britain and its imperial allies were not militarily strong enough to wage war against Germany alone and stand a chance of winning such a conflict. Churchill felt that much bigger moral issues were now at stake in the conflict with Hitler's Germany, such as liberty and British independence. He remained confident that the Royal Navy and the Royal Air Force could prevent a German invasion.[102]

The British Chiefs of Staff produced an optimistic analysis of Britain's wartime prospects, should France surrender to Germany, and this bolstered Churchill's determination to continue the war. Should the worst happen and the *Luftwaffe* gained air superiority over the British Isles, the Chiefs of Staff argued a German invasion would still be extremely difficult, due to the supremacy of the Royal Navy.[103]

Churchill was in no mood to sue for peace and he gained much-needed support from the Labour leader Clement Attlee and the Liberal leader Archibald Sinclair, as well as most of the War Cabinet. On 27 May the War Cabinet met three times. Halifax once again put a forceful case for seeking peace terms, even going as far as to offer his resignation if his views were dismissed. Halifax, at this stage, was much more popular with Conservative MPs than was Churchill. In a surprising intervention, however, Neville Chamberlain greatly assisted Churchill's case by observing that negotiations with the untrustworthy Mussolini would prove pointless. The man who had brought back 'peace in our time' from Munich had finally learned the hard way never to trust a fascist warmonger.

On 28 May the War Cabinet met once more. Halifax once more suggested that a wider peace settlement might be brokered by

Mussolini. A defiant Churchill insisted that another meeting of the War Cabinet should take place in the House of Commons. He then convened a further meeting with the members of the full cabinet.[104] Here, Churchill argued passionately that Britain should fight on, with the help of its imperial allies. Hitler's peace terms, he said, would reduce Britain to a 'slave state', run by a puppet, pro-Nazi government. When the War Cabinet reconvened, Churchill was then able to relay the fact that the majority of his cabinet endorsed his position. Lord Halifax had fought appeasement's last stand and lost.[105]

The novelist J. B. Priestley later claimed that he – and not Churchill – had been chiefly behind the rebranding of Dunkirk as a victory in his own famous BBC radio broadcasts:

> It was just after Dunkirk so I took the theme, the idea of victory coming from defeat, which is a very English thing, I believe. We're great improvisers, we English. I'm not sure about the British, but the English are, and that was important. Then, the feeling was very strong that now everything had happened we could really start, if you know what I mean, we're by ourselves now, and really we can get on with this war, which was very strong after Dunkirk.[106]

On 28 May the Belgian king, Leopold III, unconditionally surrendered to Germany. Churchill denounced Leopold for capitulating without consulting his own government or his allies, conveniently forgetting the fact that Britain had not consulted its allies before the mass evacuation at Dunkirk. An angry Paul Reynaud went further, branding Leopold a traitor. It was true that Leopold ignored his cabinet, but the Belgian army was in a desperate situation. Leopold was further criticized for remaining in Belgium under house arrest, as effectively a prisoner of war.[107]

A German military administration was established in Belgium under the control of General Alexander von Falkenhausen, a conservative aristocrat and career soldier. Thousands of captured Belgian soldiers became POWs and were used as forced labour for the German war machine.

King Leopold III mistakenly thought that Belgium would be treated as leniently as Denmark under German occupation, but Belgium was much more strategically important to Hitler, because it offered him a base from which to launch *Luftwaffe* air raids on Britain. To this end, the Eupen–Malmedy region in eastern Belgium was swiftly incorporated into the Greater German Reich. The German occupiers were assisted in running the country by the efficient and docile Belgian civil service and judiciary, which upheld existing laws and implemented the many new Nazi decrees. Belgian fascist parties also actively collaborated with the German occupiers. From 1942 onwards, however, the occupation of Belgium would become far more repressive, as Himmler's SS began their systematic persecution of the Jews.[108]

Britain was now in its most precarious position since the Norman Conquest of 1066. In a famous and inspirational speech, Churchill warned the House of Commons on 4 June 1940 that 'wars are not won by evacuation'. However, in a brave and defiant manner he promised:

> 'We shall go on to the end, we shall fight in France, we shall fight on the seas and oceans, we shall fight with growing confidence and growing strength in the air, we shall defend our island, whatever the cost may be, we shall fight on the beaches, we shall fight on the landing grounds, we shall fight in the fields and in the streets, we shall fight in the hills; we shall never surrender.'[109]

The aim of Case Yellow had been to encircle and defeat the Netherlands, Belgium, the main French armies and the BEF, and all of this had been accomplished in just twenty-five days. Now the second part of the German operation in mainland France began, codenamed Case Red (*Fall Rot*).

The French army was now in a hopeless position, with only sixty-six divisions remaining. The German army deployed fifty infantry and ten Panzer divisions for the final push to defeat France.[110] Hitler moved his military headquarters to the small village of Brüly-de-Pesche, near the Belgian-French border, from the cramped field bunker called the Felsennest ('Rocky Eyrie') near Bad Münstereifel. He now proudly gave instructions that his Felsennest should be preserved as a German national monument and museum.

On 5 June 1940 Hitler issued two personal statements to announce Germany's victory in the Battle of France. To the German people, he wrote:

> Our soldiers have emerged victorious from this greatest battle of all time. In a few weeks, we have taken over 1.2 million enemies as prisoners of war. Holland and Belgium have capitulated. The British Expeditionary Force has been largely destroyed, the remainder taken prisoner or driven from the Continent. Three French armies no longer exist. Your soldiers have fought bloodily

for this most glorious deed in history, at the risk of life and limb and with therefore the greatest of exertions. I order that flags fly from every roof throughout Germany for eight days. This is to do honour to our soldiers. I further order, for eight days, the ringing of bells.[111]

To Germany's soldiers, Hitler wrote:

The greatest battle in world history has ended. Soldiers! Mytrust in you was a boundless one. You have not disappointed me. The most daring plan in the history of war was realized, thanks to your unequal valour, your ability to endure the greatest pains, exertions and efforts. In a few weeks you have forced two states to capitulate in the most difficult battle, in many instances, an enemy of great valour. You have destroyed France's best divisions. You have defeated the British Expeditionary Force... Many soldiers have sealed their loyalty by giving their lives, others are wounded. The heart of our *Volk* is filled with profound gratitude.[112]

On 7 June 1940 the defiant King Haakon VII of Norway and his government were evacuated to London on HMS *Devonshire*. Allied forces numbering 25,000 troops had managed to drive the Germans out of Narvik in the previous week, but Allied difficulties in France meant that these troops had to pull out and be redeployed, thereby handing Germany total victory in Norway on 10 June, without any further fighting.[113]

The Germans lost 5,296 men in capturing Norway, compared to 4,500 British troop deaths. The French and Polish-exile army lost 530, and the Norwegian army around 1,800. The RAF lost 112 planes and the Germans 242. At sea the British lost three cruisers, seven destroyers, one aircraft carrier and four submarines. The German navy lost three cruisers, ten destroyers and six submarines. One important consequence of the Norway campaign was that Germany's naval losses in Norway made the idea of a German invasion of Britain totally unrealistic.[114]

Mussolini's Italy joined the war on Germany's side on 10 June by declaring war on Britain and France. The US President Franklin D. Roosevelt called Mussolini's action a 'stab in the back'. Without very much difficulty, four French army divisions held the twenty-eight Italian divisions which Mussolini had deployed. It was the first sign of Italy's military weakness. The Italian army lost nearly 5,000 soldiers in this one engagement alone.

Hitler wrote to Mussolini congratulating him on Italy's entry into the war: 'While we have always been very closely linked together ideologically by our two revolutions and politically by treaties, the increasing disregard shown by rulers in London and Paris for Italy's vital national rights has brought us together in the great struggle for freedom and future of our peoples.'[115] Privately, Hitler thought Mussolini was being extremely opportunistic: 'First they were too cowardly to take part, now they are in a hurry so they can share in the spoils.'[116]

On 13 June Hitler granted an interview to the German-born American journalist and war correspondent Karl Henry von Wiegand, who was opposed to the idea of America entering the war. Wiegand asked what Hitler thought of a supposedly neutral America quietly supplying aid to his enemies. 'An American intervention by mass deliveries of planes and war materials will not change the outcome of the war,' Hitler replied. He was convinced that Germany's enemies would lose because they were corrupt, unscrupulous politicians with no vision. Germany would win, he insisted, because 'we have the best army and the best equipment'.[117]

On that very same day Paris was declared an open city and Hitler issued 'Directive No. 15', reporting the 'collapse of the enemy' and the French government's flight from Paris to Bordeaux. The German army would now prevent the retreating French army from attempting to set up a new defensive front.[118]

In a final desperate attempt to prevent the French from capitulating, Churchill offered the French government a union with Britain, but it made no difference. On 16 June 1940 the French Prime Minister Paul Reynaud resigned. He was replaced by Marshal Philippe Pétain, who immediately requested an armistice from Germany. This move was supported by the French Army High Command and most of the French cabinet.

On 17 June 1940 Pétain spoke live on French national radio: 'I give myself to France to assuage her misfortune,' he said. 'It is with a heavy heart that I say we must end the fight. Last night I applied to our adversary [Hitler] to ask if he is prepared to seek with me, soldier to soldier, after the battle, honourably, the means whereby hostilities may cease.'[119]

On 18 June Winston Churchill told the House of Commons:

> What General Weygand has called the Battle of France is over
> ... The Battle of Britain is about to begin. Upon this battle
> depends the survival of Christian civilisation. Upon it depends
> our own British life, and the long continuity of our institutions

and our Empire. The whole fury and might of the enemy must very soon be turned on us. Hitler knows that he will have to break us in this island or lose the war. If we can stand up to him, all Europe may be freed and the life of the world may move forward into broad, sunlit uplands. But if we fail, then the whole world, including the United States, including all that we have known and cared for, will sink into the abyss of a new dark age made more sinister, and perhaps more protracted, by the lights of perverted science. Let us therefore brace ourselves to our duties, and so bear ourselves, that if the British Empire and its Commonwealth last for a thousand years, men will still say, 'This was their finest hour.'[120]

On the same day, General Charles de Gaulle – the self-appointed leader of the Free French, who had fled to London – gave a speech on BBC radio calling for the continuation of French resistance: 'The war has not been settled by the Battle of France,' he said. 'This war is a world war... whatever happens the flame of resistance must not and will not be extinguished.'[121]

In Munich, also on the same day, Hitler met Mussolini to discuss the French proposal of an armistice. Hitler, who dominated the conversation, felt it was important to negotiate with the newly formed French government, otherwise it might flee to London along with the French navy.

Hitler then outlined to Mussolini the terms he intended to offer. As a priority, the Germans would occupy all of the French Channel ports, while details concerning the occupation of the rest of France would be subject to further discussion. No French prisoner of war would be returned until a peace treaty had been concluded. If the new French government refused to accept his terms, Hitler promised to occupy a large part of France.[122]

In a final act of revenge, Hitler insisted that the signing of the Franco-German Armistice should take place in the very same railway carriage in which the Germans had signed the Armistice that had ended the Great War on 11 November 1918. Only now the roles of victor and vanquished had been reversed. The railway carriage was duly transported from a museum to Compiègne Forest.

At 3.15 p.m. on 21 June 1940 Hitler arrived at Compiègne by motorcade. Few of his generals had ever seen him in such a jubilant mood as on this day. At 3.30 p.m. General Charles Huntziger, heading the French delegation, sat down directly opposite the Führer. This macabre scene was filmed for the newsreels and photographed for the

[overleaf]
General de Gaulle, leader of the Free French, delivering his radio 'Appeal' for resistance on 18 June 1940.

newspapers. Wilhelm Keitel, Chief of the Armed Forces, was put in charge of the German delegation. He read out the German armistice terms and handed a French translation to Huntziger. Hitler, who never uttered a single word, then left the carriage as the final negotiations continued.

Keitel queried whether the French official had the authority to sign the Armistice. Huntziger told him that he was empowered to discuss terms, but could not sign the final agreement without the permission of the French government. Keitel told him the German terms were non-negotiable, but promised to answer any questions the French delegation put to him.

After carefully reading the terms, Huntziger put them down in front of him on the table in the cramped railway carriage and said that they were 'hard and merciless'. The terms were indeed much harsher than the Allies had imposed on Germany in 1918, but, given the extent of the French defeat, Hitler considered them fairly lenient.

France was to be split into an Occupied Zone, controlling Paris, the industrial north and the coastal areas of Atlantic France. A nominally autonomous region in Central France would be left to the French government of Marshal Pétain, who would be based in the small spa town of Vichy. France could retain its navy and its colonial possessions. The French army was reduced to 100,000, the exact figure the German army had been reduced to under the terms of the Versailles Treaty. Around 1.5 million French POWs would be deported to Germany to work in armaments factories. France was further forced to pay the entire cost of the German occupation.

Huntziger asked when the final peace treaty would be concluded. General Alfred Jodl, part of the German delegation, observed that a protracted discussion of the terms would lead nowhere. When Britain ceased hostilities, he said, a new situation would arise, and certain alterations to the terms would be considered and embodied in a final peace treaty.

Huntziger felt that although the terms were extremely harsh, the French people would have to resign themselves to a German occupation. Jodl explained that an Armistice Commission would be established at which the French government could discuss the finer details. The conference was adjourned until 11 a.m. the following day to allow the French delegation to discuss the terms of the Armistice with the French government.[123]

A telephone line was made available to the French delegation.

Huntziger used it to speak with French military commander Maxime Weygand. Huntziger told him that the Armistice treaty contained twenty-four articles which could not be altered. He thought them harsh, but felt that they did not offend French honour. Weygand said that the full text must be sent by air for the French government to read and make a final decision.[124]

The Armistice negotiations resumed at 11 a.m. on the following day. Huntziger explained that he had submitted the German terms to the French government, which had instructed him to put a few questions. Pétain had asked if the German advance on Bordeaux could be halted, while the negotiations continued. Keitel said that he was willing to consider this, but only after the Armistice agreement was signed.

Huntziger said that the French government accepted the terms, but he asked for military aircraft to be deleted from the list of war materials to be handed over. Keitel said that the final decision as to how French war materiel would be disposed of would be decided by the Armistice Commission. He then warned Huntziger not to haggle over such trivial matters any further.

Keitel gave the French an ultimatum to sign the agreement by 7.30 p.m. The French agreed, but only on condition that the following statement was issued:

> Under the stress of the fortunes of war, France has had to give up the struggle in which she was engaged along with her Allies. Very heavy demands are made of her under conditions which stress even more the severity of these demands. The French government is justified in expecting that in further negotiations Germany will be guided by a spirit which will make it possible for two great neighbouring peoples to live and work in peace.

Before finally signing the historic document, Huntziger, with tears in his eyes, said that he hoped the French delegation would not regret the gesture it was about to make. Keitel replied that it was honourable for the victor to honour the vanquished and he praised Huntziger for his courage during the negotiations.[125] The Armistice between France and Germany became effective at 1.35 a.m. on 25 June 1940.

It's difficult to fully establish the exact number of dead during the battles in Western Europe in the spring of 1940. The German death toll was officially reported as 26,500, but through further research it has now been more accurately determined at 49,000. The number of French killed has been estimated at 90,000. Belgium suffered 7,500

[overleaf]
Hitler entering Foch's famous railway carriage at Compiègne, France, prior to the signing of the Armistice of 22 June 1940.

fatalities, the Netherlands, 3,000 and 5,000 British army and air force personnel were killed. This pattern of relatively low death rates would continue for British land forces throughout the remainder of the war.[126]

Before returning to Germany Hitler wanted to visit Paris. On 23 June he undertook a three-hour, whistle-stop tour, accompanied by his favourite architects Albert Speer and Hermann Giesler, as well as the acclaimed sculptor Arno Breker. It was a cloudy day when Hitler arrived at Le Bourget Airport at dawn. The streets were completely deserted. Most Parisians had either fled the city or stayed indoors.

During his brief car journey Hitler visited the Paris Opera House, the Panthéon, the Eiffel Tower and Les Invalides. Hitler seemed visibly moved while viewing Napoleon's tomb. Napoleon was the last ruler who had attempted to conquer Europe but he had been stopped in the end by a more powerful international coalition. In 1940 it seemed doubtful that Hitler would meet the same fate.[127]

The triumph in Western Europe was undoubtedly Hitler's greatest military triumph. He already saw himself as a great politician, but now he considered himself to be something of a military genius. The generals who doubted him beforehand had been proved spectacularly wrong. Jodl later observed that after his military victories between 1939 and 1940 Hitler became convinced of the infallibility of his judgement.[128] Yet Germany's triumph was essentially a tactical victory made possible by Manstein's 'Sickle Stroke' thrust through the Ardennes.

It suited the Western Allies to attribute Hitler's victory solely to his *Blitzkrieg* style of tank warfare, conveniently overlooking the fact that only ten German divisions were fully mechanized. This 'myth of the *Blitzkrieg*' was used by Britain and France to conceal their own appalling lack of planning and military leadership during the German invasion of Western Europe. German equipment was not superior, but it was deployed much more efficiently and effectively.

It would be equally wrong to believe *Blitzkrieg* tactics were a direct result of National Socialist rule, as was suggested by Nazi propaganda. The German army, a superb fighting organization, had developed its offensive strategy during the period when the army had been reduced to 100,000. There still remained doubt amongst its best generals whether *Blitzkrieg* tactics would work in all circumstances.[129]

Hitler wanted the French people to collaborate with their German occupiers. This explains why he initially treated France as an independent state. Pétain's new Vichy government was given a mandate in the French National Assembly by 569 votes to 80 to revise

Adolf Hitler walking in front of the Eiffel Tower with Albert Speer (left) and Arno Breker (right) during his whistle stop tour of Paris on 23 June 1940.

the constitution. He abolished the Third Republic, adjourned meetings of the Assembly and appointed himself head of state with the right to issue decrees. He also appointed the pro-Nazi collaborationist Pierre Laval as his Deputy Prime Minister.[130]

To further please Hitler, the Vichy government put some of the leaders of the former French democratic governments on trial. Two former prime ministers, Léon Blum, who was Jewish, and Eduard Daladier, were placed in internment camps. A raft of anti-Jewish legislation was hastily introduced, restricting civil liberties and Jewish access to the civil service, medicine and law.[131]

The Germans imposed a Military Administration in Northern Occupied France, including Paris, and all the western coastal areas. This occupied zone consisted of 45 per cent of all French territory. It was more economically prosperous than the Vichy area. Around 100,000 German troops were stationed in the zone, but by early 1942 this fell to 60,000. A draconian exchange rate of twenty francs to one Reichsmark was imposed and it has been estimated that Germany took 50 per cent of French GDP. The French government claimed to have paid 20 million Reichsmarks per day during the Occupation.

Occupied France was run initially by Otto von Stülpnagel as a de facto dictatorship. The Gestapo established an HQ at 11 Rue des Saussaies in Paris, but the number of Gestapo deployed in the occupied zone never exceeded one hundred officers. From June 1940 to May 1941 German military courts sentenced ninety-three people to death, but of those only a third were executed. The German military occupying force cooperated with the Gestapo to deal with resistance activities and to implement anti-Jewish policy. A census of France's Jewish population was undertaken and all Jews were issued with identity cards. A large area of north-east France called the *zone interdite* ('Prohibited Zone') consisted of the areas of Nord and Pas-de-Calais. Here were the *Luftwaffe* air bases and camps for German troops stationed along the English Channel.[132]

The defeat of France, Norway, Denmark, Belgium, the Netherlands and Luxembourg – as well as the expulsion of the British Expeditionary Force from Europe – had shifted the balance of power dramatically in Europe. Germany was already in control of Poland, Austria and the territories of the former Czechoslovakia. Taken together, this was a formidable economic bloc and it gave Germany unrivalled industrial capacity as well as a large pool of labour.

Hitler had acquired a huge amount of territory in Western Europe.

If the European territories that Germany had invaded by 1940 had been formed into a single political and economic bloc, which it never was, it would have had a GDP greater than the United States and the British Empire combined. In 1940, with a population of 250 million people, German-controlled Western Europe accounted for 30 per cent of global GDP.

The profits from Germany's military conquests in Western Europe were huge. The reparations demanded of these defeated powers solved at a stroke Germany's pre-war shortage of foreign currency. The Reichsbank was soon sitting on a generous currency reserve of 10 billion Reichsmarks. The value of the Reichsmark against the currencies in the occupied territories was set so high that import prices to Germany were extremely cheap, while exports enjoyed a hugely favourable exchange rate.

The Reichsbank created a clearing system for all trade payments to and from the occupied German areas. This meant that the German government never had to settle bills for all the goods it purchased in the occupied territories, but simply added them to a huge government deficit. Surprisingly, the German government did not create a common currency and customs union in the occupied areas. This was a mistake as it would have allowed for even greater German economic exploitation.

As was the case in Germany after Hitler's rise to power, capitalist businesses in the occupied areas – provided they were not owned by Jews – had nothing to fear from the German occupation. Germany's civil and military administrators did not centrally control the economies of its occupied areas, but allowed capitalist companies the necessary freedom to continue functioning. In the Netherlands, for example, its major companies – notably, Philips, Unilever and Shell – remained in private hands and continued to generate large profits.

The German economy benefited greatly from the use of imported cheap labour, including prisoners of war captured in Western Europe. The German government even allowed big private companies in the occupied areas to purchase shares in German companies, often as a replacement for paying for imported goods.[133]

Stalin was shocked by the swiftness of the German victory in Western Europe. He had expected the conflict to last two years, thereby weakening Hitler's armed forces. To further increase the buffer zone between the Soviet and German borders, the Soviet Union swiftly occupied the Baltic states: Lithuania on 15 June and then Latvia and Estonia two days later. On 28 June Romania was forced to cede

Bessarabia and northern Bukovina to the Soviet Union. The German government offered no protests, but registered a concern – rather than a complaint – that it was important for Romania to retain its independence, not least because it exported some 1.2 million tonnes of oil per annum to Germany. The situation in Romania was further complicated by the long-standing territorial claims of Hungary and Bulgaria, which were now being pressed.[134]

Mussolini sent a letter to Hitler on 26 June 1940 suggesting the next task of the Axis powers was to conquer Britain, and he offered the 'direct participation of Italy in the assault of the island. I am ready to contribute ground forces and air forces and you know how much I desire to do so.'[135] Hitler, in reply, thanked Mussolini for his generous offer to make Italian army divisions available. However, he felt that they would not be necessary, although he would consider Italian air and naval support.[136]

On the crest of a wave, German forces occupied the poorly de-fended British Channel Islands – Jersey, Guernsey, Alderney, Sark and Herm – between 30 June and 4 July, during Operation *Grünpfeil* ('Green Arrow'). No military resistance was encountered. Churchill decided that the islands, with a population of 66,000 people, were of no strategic importance. Nevertheless, they were the only parts of the British Isles to be occupied by German armed forces during the war.

The Germans set up a military administration throughout each island, but they allowed local government to continue to function. Existing English laws remained in force. German rule of the Channel Islands was far less harsh than it was for the local populations of mainland Europe. There were love affairs between island women and German soldiers, many producing children. Active resistance was extraordinarily low.

Channel Islanders did not fight on the beaches or in the fields or in the streets. Instead they kept their heads down and accepted German rule. They did not revolt, even in 1945, when the Allies were marching to victory. There were four prison camps established by the German occupiers on the island of Alderney, but they operated primarily as work camps, with a population of 6,000. Many of the inmates were slave labourers shipped in from mainland Europe and they were very harshly treated. It's estimated that 700 of them perished. Only 570 Channel Islanders were sent to concentration camps on mainland Europe. Of these, thirty-one never returned.

Conditions worsened for the Channel Islanders after 1942, due to severe food shortages caused by the Allied naval blockade. The islands were not liberated until 9 March 1945. Some historians see the example of the Channel Islands as an indicator of how British people probably would have behaved if Germany had invaded Great Britain. Germany's unopposed occupation of the Channel Islands is hard to reconcile with the 'Dunkirk spirit' evoked by Churchill.[137]

After the defeat of France, Churchill quickly realized that the French navy could be of enormous advantage to any German plan to invade Britain. On 3 July the Royal Navy – in a bold and controversial move – opened fire on French navy ships anchored in the port of Mers el-Kebir, near Oran in French Algeria. The French battleship *Bretagne* was sunk and three other French vessels were severely damaged and 1,297 French sailors were killed. Codenamed Operation Catapult, this unexpected attack on the vessels and crew of old allies was clear evidence of Churchill's determination to fight on.[138]

The German Foreign Ministry saw the expansion of German rule in Western Europe as a new opportunity to find a solution to the so-called 'Jewish question'. To this end, discussions began between Heinrich Himmler, on behalf of the SS, the Department of the Interior and the Foreign Ministry. On 3 July 1940 Franz Rademacher, head of the Jewish Desk at the German Foreign Ministry, submitted a memorandum entitled 'The Jewish Question in the Peace Treaty'. 'The imminent victory [in the war] gives Germany the possibility, and in my opinion also the duty, of solving the Jewish question in Europe,' he wrote. 'The desirable solution is: All Jews out of Europe.'

Rademacher felt the Vichy government should make the French colony of Madagascar available for the solution of the so-called Jewish question. Madagascar would be transferred to Germany as a mandate under the terms of the final peace treaty with France. German naval and air bases would then be established and the island placed under the control of a German police governor, who would be under the overall authority of the SS. On Madagascar Jews would have self-government – their own mayors, police force, civil service, postal service and transport system. Jewish assets would then be transferred via a European bank, but Jews who lived there would not have German citizenship and Jews sent there from countries outside Germany would also have their existing citizenship rights withdrawn.

Rademacher's memorandum represents the first time Madagascar was mentioned by the Nazis as a solution to the so-called Jewish question in Germany. It was a recognition that emigration was no longer a practical solution. Hitler was initially attracted by the Madagascar plan, but it, too, was impractical, for it did not take into account the enormous difficulty of transporting Jews by sea in the face of British naval supremacy in the region.[139]

On 6 July 1940 Hitler made a triumphant return to Berlin. Cheering crowds lined the streets as he paraded in an open-topped limousine. Arriving at the new Reich Chancellery, Hitler acknowledged the cheers as a huge crowd, estimated at one million, congregated below his balcony window. Public opinion reports compiled by the exiled Social Democrats showed that there was genuine public exultation about Hitler's victory in Western Europe. Many Germans expected the British government to seek a peace settlement.[140]

Christabel Bielenberg, an Englishwoman married to a German lawyer, recalled the reaction:

> I think one could say that the actual defeat of France in six weeks
> came as a complete surprise to the generality of the German
> people. I found that there was a difference between my attitude
> to this defeat of France, and England being left alone. I didn't
> really ever feel England was going to lose the war, even in those
> days when it looked as if it was absolutely certain that a landing
> would take place and they would be defeated.[141]

The German Foreign Minister Joachim von Ribbentrop met Naotake Satō, the Japanese ambassador in Berlin, on 9 July 1940. Satō congratulated Germany on its stunning victory over France and he warmly welcomed Germany's new order in Europe. He also promised that Japan would seek good neighbourly relations with the Soviet Union. Satō said that Hitler's victory had prompted the Japanese government to seek much closer relations with Germany and Italy, too. In reply, Ribbentrop said that he favoured an invasion of Britain, which was now an encircled country. Germany was no longer interested in gold, he said, which was flowing to the United States. Germany was now economically independent and Britain's naval blockade was having a minimal impact.[142]

On 16 July 1940 Hitler signed 'Directive No. 16' on the 'Preparation of a Landing Operation against England'. It was codenamed Operation Sea Lion. It began: 'Since England despite her militarily hopeless situation still shows no sign of a willingness to come to terms, I have decided to prepare a landing operation against England, and if it is necessary to carry it out.'

The key aim of Operation Sea Lion was to eliminate the British homeland as a base for continuing the war. The German landing would be a surprise assault on a broad front from Ramsgate in Kent to the Isle of Wight. A total of 260,000 German troops were allocated to the operation. To make the landing possible, air superiority would first have to be established over the area, so the *Luftwaffe* would adopt the role of the artillery from the air. All preparations would need to be complete by mid-August 1940.[143]

There remains considerable doubt as to whether Operation Sea Lion was ever a serious plan, although at first the German Army High Command did seem enthusiastic about it. However, even assuming air superiority was achievable, the German navy doubted whether a large army could be transported across the Channel in the face of the overwhelming power of the Royal Navy.

The scepticism of the German navy seemed reasonable. After all, the German fleet had suffered huge losses during the Norwegian campaign. Admiral Erich Raeder, the commander of the German navy, had been assigned just three cruisers and four destroyers to oversee a huge German army landing force, the main part of which consisted of 2,000 unarmed, flat-bottomed barges that only stood any chance of making the crossing in very calm waters.

Meanwhile, in defence of the south coast of England, the Royal Navy had five battleships, eleven cruisers and thirty destroyers, with a reserve backup fleet based in Gibraltar. These figures show that Britain was never in any danger of invasion, even if the Germans had foolishly attempted it.[144] As the leading German Field Marshal Gerd von Rundstedt observed in 1945: 'The proposed invasion of England was nonsense, because adequate ships were not available. We looked on the whole thing as a sort of game, because it was obvious that no invasion was possible when our Navy was not in a position to cover a crossing of the Channel or carry reinforcements.'[145]

Even so, elaborate plans for the proposed invasion of Britain were compiled. The most detailed were created not by the armed forces but by Himmler's SS. Himmler envisaged six *Einsatzgruppen* units operating from headquarters in London, Manchester, Birmingham, Bristol, Liverpool and Edinburgh or Glasgow in the period following a German invasion. The SS would round up potential opponents, outlined in a list called 'The Black Book' or 'Special Search List GB' (*Sonderfahndungsliste*, GB). This list of 2,820 individuals who would be subject to immediate arrest after the invasion had been compiled by a young SD (the intelligence agency of the SS) officer called Walter Schellenberg, part of Himmler's Reich Security Main Office (*Reichs-sicherheitshauptamt* or RSHA).

It was a pretty idiosyncratic list, including the press baron Lord Beaverbrook and politicians such as Churchill, Chamberlain, Eden and Attlee. Others mentioned were the founder of the Boy Scout Movement Robert Baden-Powell, as well as writers such as H. G. Wells, Vera Brittain, Virginia Woolf, E. M. Forster, Aldous Huxley and J. B. Priestley. Academics Bertrand Russell, Beatrice Webb and Harold Laski were cited, as was the popular playwright, composer and wit Noël Coward, who ironically would go on to write a hugely popular hit called 'Don't Let's Be Beastly to the Germans' (1943). Austrian founder of psychoanalysis Sigmund Freud was on the list, too, even though he had died in 1939.

The list was an appendix to a detailed German invasion handbook. It was called Information Brochure *GB* (*Informationsheft GB*) and was a cobbled together travel guide offering details on British government institutions, political parties, the legal system, schools, universities, religion, the media and trade unions. It made some interesting if unreliable observations on British life, too, suggesting that British democracy was a sham and that the trade unions were not interested in politics. The universities and the Church of England seemingly formed 'the centre of an anti-German group'. The English aristocrat had 'no interest in philosophy, no knowledge of foreign cultures and views Germany as the embodiment of evil'. Other 'dangerous' elements included the public schools. This book was only discovered in the captured German archives after the war. It is not mentioned in the German military planning documents.[146]

In a speech on 19 July 1940 in the Reichstag, which was still sitting in the Kroll Opera House, Hitler blamed the outbreak of the war on Jews, Freemasons and Allied armaments manufacturers. The continuation of the conflict was due to the intransigence of the current British government, he said, and he poured scorn on Churchill's idea of fleeing to Canada to continue the war should Germany invade Britain.

Hitler then made what he called a 'final peace offer', appealing to the 'common sense' of the British people, and ended his speech by saying: 'I can see no reason why this war must go on.' Hitler was disappointed when Lord Halifax flatly rejected this so-called 'peace offer' in a live BBC radio broadcast three days later. There was no reason, Halifax explained, to expect Hitler to honour any pledges he either made in public or signed.[147]

After this rebuff, Hitler held a significant meeting at the Berghof with his military chiefs Brauchitsch, Halder, Jodl, Keitel, and the navy's representatives Raeder and Puttkamer, which began at 11.30 a.m. on 31 July 1940. Halder kept notes of the meeting. It was ostensibly called by the German Army High Command to discuss the existing plans for Operation Sea Lion. Significantly, the *Luftwaffe*, which had a key role in the operation, was not even represented at the meeting.

Hitler told his colleagues that he thought the war in Europe was already won, although he was dismayed by the continued intransigence of the British. He provisionally agreed that the planned invasion of Britain would begin on 15 September 1940. Due to the poor strength of the British forces he was convinced that if the German army could land – and it was a big if – they would easily defeat the enemy. The major difficulty was putting together a big enough landing force and getting it safely ashore. Hitler felt that thirty to thirty-five army divisions would be sufficient for the operation, but air superiority had to be established before a landing could even be contemplated. Hitler then reiterated the difficulties, primarily, the need for calm weather and the huge strength of the defending Royal Navy. Even so, he felt that the British army was now so weak that an attack was much more likely to succeed.

Admiral Raeder said that by 13 September 1940 he hoped all the naval preparations would be advanced enough for the landing to start, but that would depend on good weather. Between 20–28 September there was generally bad weather in the English Channel, he added, with better weather traditionally occurring at the beginning of October. Overall, Raeder expressed serious concerns about the operational difficulties of a seaborne invasion.

A discussion then ensued about whether the invasion should go ahead in the autumn of 1940 or perhaps be postponed. The navy favoured a postponement until the spring 1941, but the army was keen to act now, because a long delay would allow the British to build up supplies of men and equipment to resist a German invasion. It was finally agreed that 15 September 1940 was the best invasion date.

Hitler then turned to the Soviet Union. Britain still hoped that the Soviets might intervene on the Allied side, he said, but if the Soviet Union was smashed, then Britain's last hope would be extinguished and it would have to accept peace terms. This idea had been floated in a planning paper compiled by Franz Halder a few days before this meeting. Halder had argued that it made strategic sense to defeat the Soviet Union first, because defeating Britain might take at least two years and during this time the United States and the Soviet Union might intervene on Britain's side.[148]

Hitler, who had clearly been influenced by Halder's paper, then said that he was now personally resolved to attack the Soviet Union in the spring of 1941: 'The quicker we defeat Russia the better,' he added. 'Operation only makes sense if we destroy this state in one strike.'

Halder ordered German staff officers to draw up more detailed plans, before the issue of a formal directive to attack the Soviet Union.[149] Most historians view this meeting as the starting point for what would become Operation Barbarossa. They also suggest that Hitler was persuaded to foolishly rip up the Nazi-Soviet Pact because his ultimate objective of *Lebensraum*, as outlined in *Mein Kampf*, was to gain territory at the expense of the Soviet Union.

In fact, Hitler made no strong ideological case for an attack on the Soviet Union at this meeting. There was no mention of 'destroying Bolshevism' or of a 'war of annihilation'. Hitler made his decision, which was backed up by the German army, solely on the strategic view that knocking Britain out of the war quickly was unlikely to happen and therefore removing a potential British ally like the Soviet Union might induce the British government to give up the fight. What Hitler seems not to have seen at this stage was the danger of Germany fighting a war on two fronts at once, which was something he had warned against in *Mein Kampf*.

Operation Sea Lion depended on the *Luftwaffe's* ability to secure air superiority over Britain in just six weeks during what later became known as 'The Battle of Britain'.[150] As Johannes Steinhoff, a *Luftwaffe* fighter ace, later recalled: 'It was a battle in which very young men fought like medieval knights. Both sides not only recognized, but also adhered to rules of fair play.'[151]

On 1 August 1940 Hitler issued 'Directive No. 17 for the Conduct of Air and Naval Warfare against England'. It suggested the *Luftwaffe* needed to 'overcome the English air force' in the shortest possible time. Attacks would be directed against the planes and bases of the Royal Air Force and the factories that were building British planes. After gaining air superiority, harbours related to food supplies would be targeted, but attacks on the south coast – the proposed German invasion zone – would be kept to a minimum. The intensification of the air war was set to begin on or after 5 August 1940. The exact date and time would be decided by the *Luftwaffe*.[152]

Sir Hugh Dowding, the commander-in-chief of RAF Fighter Command, had to prevent the *Luftwaffe* from reaching its objective of air superiority. At the beginning of August, the *Luftwaffe* had 1,438 aircraft, with 949 fully ready for combat. In comparison, RAF Fighter Command possessed 1,112 aircraft, with 715 immediately ready for action. The personnel records of the RAF reveal that about 2,300 pilots served between July and November 1940. The *Luftwaffe* had 1,200 pilots, but at the outset only 900 were available for operations.

The RAF had a huge technological advantage in the upcoming British-German air war, most notably Radio Detection Finding (RDF), better known as RADAR (Radio Detection and Ranging). This secret invention could detect incoming aircraft at 1,000 feet or above so that fighter planes could be deployed to intercept them.[153]

Official RAF records designate 8 August 1940 as the beginning of the Battle of Britain. German documents show the German air offensive – codenamed 'Operation Eagle Attack' (*Unternehmen Adlerangriff*) – was supposed to start on 13 August 1940: Eagle Day (*Adlertag*). It actually began on the following day. The air struggle which began in August continued throughout the rest of the year. Neither side referred to it as the Battle of Britain, but that was how it was first described in a British pamphlet in 1941 and how it has been described ever since.

Between 13 August and 6 September 1940 there were fifty-three major German attacks on RAF airfields, but only thirty-two of these were on fighter stations. There were six main German raids against British radar stations, which killed eighty-five civilians. The largest was at Biggin Hill on 30 August. These attacks put enormous strain on the resources of RAF Fighter Command.

The battle in the air was fought by a comparatively small number of pilots. On 20 August 1940 Winston Churchill emphasized this point in his famous speech to the House of Commons:

> The gratitude of every home in our Island, in our Empire, and
> indeed throughout the world, except in the abodes of the
> guilty, goes out to the British airmen who, undaunted by odds,
> unwearied in their constant challenge and mortal danger, are
> turning the tide of the World War by their prowess and by their
> devotion. Never in the field of human conflict was so much owed
> by so many to so few.[154]

At the end of August, German Air Intelligence estimated that the RAF had lost 50 per cent of its fighters, against a loss of 12 per cent by the *Luftwaffe*. This estimate suggested that 791 RAF fighters had been shot down, against a total of 169 *Luftwaffe* planes. However, the real figures show that the RAF lost 444 aircraft between 6 August and 2 September 1940, with German records listing 443 *Luftwaffe* losses from 8 to 31 August 1940. In other words, despite the propaganda on both sides, the losses of aircraft on each side were broadly identical.

The next key phase of the Battle of Britain began on 7 September 1940 with the mass bombing of British cities. On that day 350 German bombers attacked London, causing enormous damage. The British, abbreviating the German word *Blitzkrieg*, began to refer to these air raids as 'the Blitz'. Between 7 September and 5 October 1940 there were thirty-five large-scale *Luftwaffe* raids over Britain, eighteen of them targeting London. This was when, for the first time, British civilians felt the cruel reality of the Second World War. In September 1940 6,968 British civilians were killed and a further 9,488 were seriously injured.

The decisive point in the Battle of Britain occurred between 7 and 15 September 1940. During those fateful days the RAF lost 120 aircraft, but the *Luftwaffe* lost 298. Ever since, 15 September 1940 has been celebrated as Battle of Britain Day. On that day 200 German bombers attacked London. The British press reported that 185 *Luftwaffe* planes had been brought down, but the actual figure was just 56, with 20 more severely damaged.[155]

Yet the *Luftwaffe* could not sustain losses of this magnitude. The failure to gain air superiority forced the *Wehrmacht* to reconsider its invasion plans. The Blitz would continue – to keep up the pressure on the British government and to weaken civilian morale – but for the rest of the war Britain was safe from invasion. As *Luftwaffe* pilot Johannes Steinhoff observed: 'I personally believe that the outcome of this air battle was a major turning point in the war. From that moment on, I knew we had lost control of the third dimension: the air space over Europe.'[156]

On 14 September 1940 Hitler held a crucial meeting of leading figures in the *Wehrmacht*, on the eve of what should have been the beginning of Operation Sea Lion. He conceded that the precondition of air superiority was 'not yet there', and reiterated the fact that any successful landing in Britain would require 'total command of the air'. Hitler therefore decided to postpone Operation Sea Lion 'indefinitely'.[157]

A successful invasion of Britain by sea in 1940 was not just difficult, it was impossible. Air superiority was only one aspect. To invade Britain required total naval superiority and the German navy was no match for the Royal Navy. A fully deployed Royal Navy would have outgunned any German invasion force before it had even landed, as had already been graphically illustrated in Norway.

One important key to RAF success in the Battle of Britain was superior British aircraft production. There were 4,283 British aircraft produced in 1940, a figure much higher than the German production figure of 1,870. Britain could also freely import planes from the United States, thus building up reserves to continue the air war. All the planes deployed by the RAF were new and state-of-the-art models. The Spitfire is often associated with victory in the Battle of Britain due to its greater maneuverability, but it was the less exalted Hurricane, which outnumbered Spitfires by a ratio of 65 to 35 per cent, that shot down 60 per cent of the German planes. The RAF planes were not without mechanical faults. The Spitfire relied on a carburettor rather than the more efficient fuel injection mechanism of the Messerschmitt 109 and could suddenly stall in flight with disastrous consequences, and the close proximity of the fuel tank to the cockpit in the Hurricane meant pilots were quickly engulfed in flames if the fuel tank was hit by enemy machine gun fire.

On 17 September 1940 Hitler sent Mussolini a letter updating him on the current military situation. The first task of the Axis powers, he argued, was the protection of the territory that had already been captured. Hitler noted that Norway and Denmark were securely under German control. The attack on Britain remained a central aim, but weather conditions had delayed it. For weeks, he added, 'we have been carrying on aggressive warfare of progressive intensity with our air force against the British Island'.[158]

On the German home front, Goebbels was using films not just as entertainment, but to popularize key aspects of Nazi ideology, in particular, a virulent hatred of the Jews. Before the war this had not featured heavily, especially in entertainment films, but in the latter part of 1940 three antisemitic films were shown in German cinemas.

The first was *The Rothschilds* (*Die Rothschilds*), released on 17 July 1940. It portrayed Nathan Rothschild as a ruthless, greedy, cut-throat capitalist, plotting to gain the advantage in London's financial markets. The film struck a decidedly anti-British tone. Lord Wellington, the hero

[overleaf]
Balham High Road, London, after a
German bomb attack on 14 October 1940.

of Waterloo, was presented as a shameless womanizer, with a reckless lifestyle, involved in shady financial dealings with Jews. Goebbels felt the film had dwelled too much on the corruption of English upper-class society and didn't show how the British were outwitted by the Jewish Rothschild family.[159]

To rectify this, he commissioned a second mass entertainment antisemitic film called *The Jew Süss* (*Jud Süss*), released on 24 September 1940. Directed by Viet Harlan, it had a big budget of 2 million Reichsmarks (the equivalent of 9 million euros today). Now considered one of the most antisemitic films of all time, it was a huge box office success at the time, viewed by 20 million Germans between 1940 and 1943. It took 12 million Reichsmarks at the box office (worth about 36 million euros today).

Set in Stuttgart in 1773, the film is based on the eighteenth-century Jewish moneylender Josef Süss Oppenheimer and loosely adapted from a 1925 novel by the exiled Jewish writer Lion Feuchtwanger. In Feuchtwanger's version it's a sympathetic story about the unfairness of anti-Jewish discrimination. His Süss is a man who acts as a Jewish financial stereotype, only to find out just days before his execution that he is really a Gentile.

In the Goebbels-commissioned German version, however, Süss is portrayed as an assimilated Jew who uses fake charm, bribery and guile to achieve unscrupulous ends. The film begins with the coronation of Prince Karl Alexander, the Duke of Württemberg, played by rotund Heinrich George, who swears a solemn oath of devotion to his 'beloved Swabians', promising them 'truth and honesty'. It soon becomes obvious that the duke is an extravagant rogue mired in financial trouble.

The local People's Council refuses to sanction the increased expenditure the duke requires, so he calls in the clever Jewish financier Joseph Süss Oppenheimer, played by the Austrian actor Ferdinand Marian, to help him. Süss, who is portrayed as a classic stereotype of a Jewish moneylender, advances the duke huge loans in return for the right to levy taxes on the local population for using roads and bridges. He also recruits a brutal mercenary army to keep the duke in power and persuades him to repeal a law that prevents Jews from living or trading in the city. An influx of Jews soon follows.

To add a further negative dimension to Süss's personality, he is shown to be sexually pursuing a blond, blue-eyed Aryan woman called Dorothea Sturm, played by the beautiful Swedish star Kristina Söderbaum. When Süss finds out that her father, who objects to his

Poster for the antisemitic propaganda documentary *Der ewige Jude* (*The Eternal Jew*).

hold over the duke, has allowed her to secretly marry her fiancé, he has her husband arrested and tortured on the grounds that he is the leader of a conspiracy against the duke.

In a disturbing scene, Süss entices Dorothea to his bedroom, making clear that if she succumbs to his sexual advances he will cease torturing her husband and release him. No actual rape scene is shown, but it is implied that she succumbs to his blackmail to save her husband from further torture. Dorothea is next seen leaving the residence of Süss in a distressed state. She drowns herself in a river and her husband, now released from prison, carries her lifeless body to the court to demand justice, blaming Süss for her death.

As many of the local population riot outside his palace, the duke is seen drinking champagne and he becomes very angry when told about the crowd outside. He then suddenly and theatrically dies of a heart attack.

Süss is arrested on several charges including abuse of office, blackmail, treason and having carnal knowledge of a Christian woman. (The sexual pursuit of Aryan women was a consistent theme of Nazi antisemitic propaganda.) During his brief trial Süss pleads for his life, arguing that he was nothing more than a faithful servant to the duke. Goebbels had the director edit this speech so that Süss is portrayed as a miserable coward desperately trying to save himself.

A sentence of death by hanging is announced, then Dorothea's father reads out a chilling message: 'All Jews must leave Stuttgart within three days. May our descendants forever hold fast to this law, so that they can be spared such harm and keep their property and their lives of their children and their children's children.' In a final chilling scene, Süss is seen hanging on a gibbet in an iron cage elevated high above the ground.

Jew Süss was hugely successful antisemitic propaganda. It focused exclusively on the flaws of the central Jewish character who sweet talks his way into a position of power, then exploits that position not for the good of the community, but for his own selfish needs and desires. The intensity of hatred towards Süss grows as he reveals some new disreputable trait in each successive scene.

Public opinion surveys by the SD revealed that German audiences were horrified by the suggestion of rape, but cheered when Süss was hanged at the end of the film. A rise in incidents of street violence against Jews was recorded in many cities after screenings of the film. Goebbels noted: 'A quite extraordinary success – a work of genius. The sort of antisemitic film that we could only wish for. I'm really pleased with it.'[160]

The third antisemitic film of the year was the harrowing documentary *The Eternal Jew* (*Der ewige Jude*), directed by Fritz Hippler, with a commentary written by Eberhard Taubert. It was released on 28 November 1940. Hitler hoped the film would strengthen support in Germany for more radical action on the so-called Jewish question. It aimed to attack the view that Jews were passive victims of relentless persecution.

By combining film shot in the Warsaw Ghetto with archive film, plus sombre music, historical and statistical facts and an authoritative-sounding narrator, *Der ewige Jude* gives the outward impression of being an accurate representation of the history of the Jews in Europe. The narration begins by saying that Jews shun physical work, especially in agriculture, and prefer buying and selling goods for profit. It's further claimed that Judaism makes lending money with interest acceptable. According to the commentary, the chief object of Jews is acquiring money and using it to exploit people. The so-called 'Wandering Jew' is depicted as moving from place to place, looting from the cultures of 'superior' races along the way.

Jews are described as 'parasites' and compared to rats carrying disease, as well as plague, dysentery, cholera and typhoid. The film chillingly connects the migration of Jews throughout Europe with the spread of rats, who are shown, in a harrowing scene, swarming near bags of corn. The cunning of rats is even compared to the cunning of the Jew.

Jews do not just spread disease, the film says, but they are also seemingly responsible for international crime. The commentary claims that whereas Jews represent just 1 per cent of the world's population, they account for 34 per cent of drug dealing, 47 per cent of robberies, 47 per cent of illegal gambling and 98 per cent of dealings in prostitution. It's then alleged that Jewish men in Western society shave off their beards and take off their skull caps and caftans in order to assimilate into society. It is this ability to change their true appearance that makes Jews so dangerous, the film warns.

Der ewige Jude also maintains that Jews, amounting to just 1 per cent of the German population, held a disproportionate share of influential jobs before Hitler came to power. It's then highlighted that in 1933 of every 100 state prosecutors, 15 were Jews; for every 100 judges, 23 were Jews; out of every 100 doctors, 52 were Jews, as were 60 out of every 100 merchants. While the average German annual salary was 810 Reichsmarks, the film claims that the average Jewish salary was 10,000 Reichsmarks.

The film then casts a critical eye on Jewish religious practices. Using footage from inside a synagogue, it is suggested that the Jewish religion is full of strange, ambiguous symbols, while rabbis speak an incomprehensible language. The kosher slaughter of animals is presented as cruel and barbaric.

The film concludes with an extract from Hitler's then famous Reichstag speech from 30 January 1939, when he promised: 'If Jews involved in international finance, inside and outside Europe, succeed in pushing people into another war, the result will not be a victory of Jewry, but the annihilation of the Jewish race in Europe.'

Der ewige Jude undoubtedly wanted to present the case for this annihilation. It attacked Jews for their appearance, their character and their business and religious practices. The highly emotive commentary and shocking juxtapositions of rats and Jews only served to reinforce the film's central message that Jews are dangerous aggressors that need to be exterminated. Killing a Jew is presented as a necessity, just like killing a rat.

The film was edited several times and Hitler's views were considered during the whole process. He approved of the extreme tone of the commentary, but when *Der ewige Jude* was shown in cinemas the German public found it off-putting. SD opinion reports noted that the film mainly attracted committed Nazis. When less committed members of the general public saw it, there were several instances of people leaving the movie theatre before the end. Hitler had made a film that appealed only to people like himself.

Der ewige Jude was a huge box-office flop, with only an estimated 1 million people ever seeing it. It was withdrawn from mainstream cinemas and ended up being shown in private screenings by the SS and the Hitler Youth. Goebbels, dismayed by the public's reaction, noted: 'We must film stuff that is true to life, portraying real people.'[161]

During the latter months of 1940 Hitler attempted to create an 'anti British' worldwide coalition and held a series of diplomatic meetings to test out this idea. Instead of employing bullying tactics, as he had done in his dealings with Austria and Czechoslovakia before 1939, his major weapons now were charm and persuasion. In no other period of the Second World War did Hitler ever engage in such proactive diplomatic activity as he did towards the end of 1940. These meetings in which he met a number of foreign leaders rather than expecting them to come to him show that Hitler was prepared to practise a little humility if it meant he might still attain his goal of eliminating Britain and its imperial allies.

Hitler's first diplomatic move was centred on the Balkans. He feared that Romania might collapse, but he couldn't let this happen as Germany depended on Romanian oil. Romania had already been forced to give up Bessarabia and northern Bukovina to the Soviet Union in June 1940. Hungary then demanded from Romania the transfer of large parts of Transylvania, while Bulgaria wanted the return of southern Dobrudja. Hitler persuaded the Romanian government to accede to the demands of Hungary and Bulgaria, but in return for this loss of territory he offered Romania a territorial guarantee and twelve German army divisions to bolster the strength of the army.

On 30 August 1940 the Second Vienna Award – dealing with the transfer of northern Transylvania to Hungary – was signed by Germany, Italy, Romania and Hungary. It generated anger among the Romanian people, leading to the enforced abdication of King Carol II on 6 September. This brought to power General Ion Antonescu, an admirer of Hitler, who set up a pro-Nazi dictatorship. Romania soon joined the Axis Tripartite Pact.[162] This meant that Hungary, Bulgaria and Romania were all now firmly in Germany's diplomatic orbit.

Hitler next tried to persuade the Spanish government to enter the war on the side of the Axis powers.[163] Ramón Serrano Suñer, the brother-in-law of General Franco and Spain's Interior Minister, arrived in Berlin on 17 September for talks. He met Hitler in the new Reich Chancellery. Franco thought that Spain could not stand aside in the fight for the new order in Europe, Suñer reported. Once the country's food and war materiel supplies were secure, Suñer promised that Spain would join the war on the side of the Axis powers. In reply, Hitler made no offer to help with Franco's supply problems, but he emphasized the common ideological bond that existed between Germany and Spain.[164]

Clearly pleased by the progress of the talks with Suñer, Hitler wrote a letter to General Franco the following day offering him his thoughts on the 'war that will decide the future of Europe'. Hitler stressed that Spain's entry into the war must begin with the expulsion of the British from Gibraltar. With Gibraltar secured, a key British naval base in the Mediterranean would be eliminated. If Spain decided to join in the war, Germany would stand by its side until victory was secured.[165]

In his reply, a seemingly enthusiastic Franco expressed the view that Germany and Spain seemed in complete agreement on the terms for Spain's entry into the war. He suggested a personal meeting with Hitler to discuss the matter in further detail, near the Spanish border.[166]

Meanwhile, Ribbentrop met with Mussolini in Rome on 19 and 20 September to offer him an update on the war against Britain. At the first meeting, Ribbentrop blamed bad weather for the delay to Germany's invasion of Britain. He even falsely claimed that Germany had achieved air superiority over the RAF and was bombing London night and day. If these attacks continued, 'London would in a short time be reduced to ashes and rubble'. British claims about German plane losses were pure propaganda, Ribbentrop insisted. The British government was being infantile if it could not see the hopelessness of its situation.[167]

At their second meeting, Ribbentrop discussed the possibility of Spain entering the war. He admitted that this might not be straightforward. The Spanish government had already opposed a German request to occupy one of the Canary Islands and he thought Franco wanted to capture Gibraltar without German help. Mussolini felt that the Spanish army was in favour of war, but he doubted whether Franco would live up to his promise to enter the war.[168]

A few days after Ribbentrop's meeting with Mussolini there was a further strengthening of the Axis. A ten-year Tripartite Pact between Germany, Italy and Japan was signed on 27 September 1940. The three powers agreed to cooperate with each other in the event of any one of them being attacked by an external power not currently involved in the European and Sino-Japanese conflicts: this clearly meant the United States.

The new agreement also promised that the efforts of Japan in Greater East Asia and of Germany and Italy in Europe aimed to establish and maintain a new order calculated to promote mutual prosperity. It was emphasized that the pact did not affect exiting political agreements between the three contracting parties and the Soviet Union.

Hitler was very pleased with the new Axis agreement as it fitted in with his embryonic plan of creating a broad anti-British coalition. The Japanese government felt the defeat of France and the weakening of Britain offered opportunities for Japanese military expansion in Southeast Asia. For Italy, the agreement offered the prospect of further Italian expansion in the Mediterranean and Africa, at the expense of the British Empire.[169]

On 4 October 1940 Hitler and Mussolini met at the Brenner Pass between Austria and Italy. Mussolini told Hitler that Chamberlain's recent resignation from the British cabinet was a sign of British domestic upheaval. Mussolini was obviously unaware Chamberlain had resigned on health grounds: he was suffering from terminal cancer and died on 9 November 1940.

Hitler was keen to update Mussolini on his recent negotiations with the Spanish government. He told Mussolini that it was Franco who had approached him in the first place about entering the war, advancing territorial claims on Gibraltar and Morocco. In return, Germany had demanded the use of one of the Canary Islands, but Franco had politely refused this request. Hitler said that Spain's assistance was necessary only for the conquest of Gibraltar.

Mussolini thought that an understanding with Spain was impossible, if Spain's claim to Morocco was openly advanced, because this would openly antagonize the French Vichy government. He felt that Spain was demanding a lot, while offering very little in return. Hitler promised to speak to Franco in plain language when he met him in person and tell him that his territorial claims were unreasonable.[170]

On 13 October Ribbentrop wrote a letter to Stalin, pointing out how advantageous the Nazi-Soviet Pact had proved to both countries. He was sure that the continuation of the policy of being good neighbours and the strengthening of political and economic collaboration would bring even greater benefits to the two countries moving forward. Ribbentrop reassured Stalin that the recently signed Tripartite Pact was not in any way aimed against the Soviet Union. To further clarify the current state of German-Soviet relations, Ribbentrop informed Stalin that he would welcome a visit to Berlin by the Soviet Foreign Minister Vyacheslav Molotov soon.[171]

On 19 October 1940 Mussolini wrote a letter to Hitler offering some further thoughts on their discussions at the Brenner Pass. He informed Hitler that Italian intelligence agents had discovered that the new French Vichy government hated the Axis powers 'more than ever before'. Given this, Mussolini advised Hitler not to pursue active collaboration with the Vichy regime.

Mussolini then turned to Spain, welcoming the appointment of Ramón Serrano Suñer as the new Spanish Foreign Minister, because he believed Suñer was favourably disposed towards the Axis powers. As Spain's economy was progressively weakening, Mussolini believed it was much more advantageous for Axis strategy if Spain continued

to remain neutral. Bringing Spain into the war was, according to Mussolini, a 'card we ought to play at the most opportune moment in accordance with the given circumstances, such as the prolongation of the war throughout 1941 or an overt intervention of the United States'.[172]

On 22 October 1940 Stalin replied positively to Ribbentrop's invitation for Molotov to hold diplomatic talks in Berlin. He thanked Ribbentrop for his 'constructive' comments and agreed to discussions for a further improvement in German-Soviet relations. He added that Molotov had already agreed to come to Berlin and suggested 10–12 November as the most convenient time for the meeting.[173]

To bolster his anti-British coalition, Hitler wanted to sound out the French Vichy government about closer French-German collaboration. First, he met the slippery Pierre Laval, the Deputy Prime Minister of Vichy France, in the Führer's private railway carriage at the Montoire-sur-le-Loir station on 22 October 1940. Laval wanted to speak with 'absolute frankness' about the prospects for closer German-French collaboration. He felt that the French declaration of war in September 1939 had been the 'greatest crime' in French history and now that Germany had been victorious he was convinced that French policy must now be based on firm Franco-German cooperation. Laval appreciated that no final peace settlement could be finalized while the war was continuing, but he also felt that Britain would soon be defeated. Laval frankly admitted that he wanted a British defeat because Britain had plunged France into war.

In reply, Hitler observed that against his own wishes the war was still going on. He was not waging war for the sake of it but in order to bring it to an end and to resume his ambitious domestic reforms. The outcome of the war was beyond doubt, Hitler added. Only bad weather had prevented the German invasion of Britain. As for France, as a defeated power it must expect to be held economically liable, but Germany was not motivated by vengeance.

Hitler promised that he was mobilizing all of his military resources to bring about the defeat of Britain and its imperial allies. The big question was: would the French Vichy government take a 'positive attitude' towards Germany in this struggle? After all, Hitler added, surely the best peace settlement for France would be at the expense of a totally defeated British Empire.[174]

The next day Hitler met General Franco at the Hendaye railway station on the border with Spain. Franco arrived late, much to the annoyance of Hitler and Ribbentrop, who waited on the platform for

Vichy French head of government Pierre Laval shaking hands with Hitler at their meeting in Montoire on 22 October 1940.

over an hour. When Franco finally arrived, Hitler was surprised by how small and overweight he was. Franco began their talks inside Hitler's special train by saying that he had always wanted to meet the Führer in person and to personally thank him for his support during the Spanish Civil War. Spain, he said, was always ideologically allied with the new Germany. In the current war, Spain would gladly fight on Germany's side, but this involvement required extensive economic, military and political preparations. At present, Franco admitted, Spain must wait and it would only enter the war at the right time.[175]

Hitler replied that he was not prepared to make Franco any promises of territorial gains if he joined the war. Germany's main priority was to swiftly defeat Britain, but this was proving difficult, because the operation to invade Britain had to be carried out across the sea, and Germany lacked naval superiority. Hitler next admitted that he was currently trying to make the French Vichy regime issue a public statement against the British, but this was proving difficult. There were two tendencies in France, he said: the pro-Nazi figures in the Vichy regime and those who wanted to carry on double-dealing with the British and the Americans in the hope that they would eventually triumph in a long war.[176]

By the time Hitler and Franco had concluded their lengthy conversation, the Spanish dictator had promised nothing more than deciding to inform Hitler when he thought Spain should join the war, and even this vague promise had been conditional on certain economic and territorial demands.

Hitler admitted that he found the meeting with Franco tiring and deeply frustrating, telling Mussolini that he would 'prefer to have three or four teeth taken out' than 'go through that again'.[177] Franco was equally exasperated, observing of Hitler and Ribbentrop: 'These people are intolerable. They want us to come into the war in exchange for nothing.'[178]

On 24 October 1940 Hitler met Marshal Pétain, the leader of the Vichy government, on his special train at Montoire-sur-le-Loir railway station. Hitler expressed regret at having to meet Pétain at such a distressing time for his country. For his part, Pétain said he was sorry that close Franco-German relations had not occurred before the war began. It was the British who had prevented that. Pétain added that he had personally opposed declaring war on Germany in 1939. In principle, he was supportive of close collaboration between France and Germany.

Hitler meets the Spanish dictator Fransisco Franco (right) at Hendaye railway station on 23 October 1940.

In reply, Hitler said that he was a man who had not wanted war, and now he wanted only to work out a clear road map for future cordial Franco-German relations. He was determined to carry out the 'annihilation of the British Isles', because it was the very centre of the British Empire. Weather conditions might compel Germany to put off the direct assault on Britain for a few weeks or months, he added, but he promised that in the end a defeated Britain would have to bear the major costs of the war.

Pétain concluded the talks by saying that he was personally in favour of cooperation along the lines Hitler had outlined, because this would ensure a better outcome for France. However, he was in no position to define the limits of French cooperation with Germany, because he needed to consult with the French Vichy government further before any decision could be taken about whether France should declare war on Britain.[179] Pétain had really promised nothing. Hitler's diplomatic talks with Franco and Pétain had left him no nearer to creating a broad anti-British coalition.[180]

Then came another unexpected disappointment for Hitler. Mussolini, without informing him, ordered the Italian invasion of Greece, beginning on 28 October 1940. The Greek terrain was difficult, with heavy autumn rain further hampering the poorly trained and ill-equipped Italian army. Italian soldiers had no maps, winter clothing or naval support. Within days the Greek army had held off the Italian advance. On 14 November the Greeks mounted a counteroffensive, supported by the Royal Air Force, which bombed Italian ports. The Italian army was soon pushed back into Albania, where the invasion attempt had begun.[181]

The poorly planned Italian attack on Greece was a humiliating disaster for Mussolini. The Italians lost 39,000 soldiers, with a further 50,000 wounded during the engagement. On 11 November 1940 the Royal Navy added to Mussolini's woes by rendering half of the Italian fleet inoperative after a bold aircraft-carrier raid on Taranto. Hitler began to view Italy as a military liability in need of constant German military assistance.[182]

Hitler met Mussolini and his Foreign Minister Count Galeazzo Ciano in the Palazzo Vecchio in Florence on the day that the Italians attacked Greece, but he did not mention his bitter anger at this decision. Instead, he promised Mussolini his full support, even offering parachute troops, if required, to occupy Crete.

Hitler also gave Mussolini a summary of his personal views on his

[previous pages]
Vichy French President Marshal Philippe
Pétain meets Hitler in Montoire on
24 October 1940.

recent meetings with Laval, Franco and Pétain. Laval, he said, was a 'typical democratic politician' who at heart did not believe a single word he said. Hitler knew that Laval was cooperating with Germany only because he had no choice. Hitler then spoke of his lengthy conversation with General Franco. Franco, he said, was not up to the challenge of leading Spain at this critical juncture. He thought the talks had been a complete waste of time, because Franco had given no concrete assurance of when – or even if – Spain would enter the war. Hitler had been more impressed by Marshal Pétain, who he felt was a true French patriot and not an opportunist politician. He thought Pétain had pointed out honestly the difficulties he personally would face if France decided to declare war on Britain.

Hitler then moved on to the subject of the Soviet Union. Italy and Germany were natural ideological allies, he told Mussolini, whereas his pact with Stalin was a matter of pure expediency. Hitler was as mistrustful of Stalin as Stalin was of him. Hitler also mentioned Molotov's forthcoming visit to Berlin and said he hoped that he could explain to the Soviet Foreign Minister why the Soviet Union needed to divert its attention away from areas of Europe that overlapped with German and Italian interests.[183]

At this time, the German Army High Command asked Hitler what his major goals now were for the coming period of the war. Attempting to clarify his position, Hitler issued 'Directive No. 18' on 12 November 1940. It listed a range of strategic options, without stressing any one key priority. Hitler claimed that German policy was to cooperate with the French Vichy government, but that for now France would remain a 'non-belligerent power' and it was unlikely to declare war on Britain. Hitler then moved on to the question of Spain entering the war. The key benefit of this would be to drive the British out of the Western Mediterranean by occupying Gibraltar, but Hitler noted that Franco had not yet agreed to enter the war. Hitler then gave the green light for German armed forces to support the Italian attack on Greece, and to hold in readiness an armoured division for deployment in North Africa. As for Operation Sea Lion, its feasibility would be considered again in the spring of 1941, but for the moment it remained impossible. Hitler made no mention of the future of German-Soviet relations.[184]

On the same day as Hitler's directive was issued the Soviet Foreign Minister Vyacheslav Molotov's special train arrived in Berlin at 11.05 a.m. The station was decorated with Soviet flags and swastikas. Ribbentrop, the chief instigator of the talks, greeted Molotov very warmly as newspaper photographers took pictures. Weizsäcker, the German State Secretary, thought the large Soviet entourage 'resembled extras in a gangster film'.[185] Hitler told Major Gerhard Engel that he viewed the talks as a means of testing whether Germany and the Soviet Union could remain closely associated in the future.[186]

The talks started shortly after Molotov's arrival, firstly, in Ribbentrop's study in Hindenburg's old Reich President's Palace. Ribbentrop explained that the purpose of these talks was to review the general situation. He told Molotov that the beginning of the end of the British Empire had now arrived. It was only a matter of time before the British government accepted this. In the meantime, the *Luftwaffe* was carrying out sustained bombing raids on British cities. He emphasized that Germany's key aim was to end the war as soon as possible.

As for the recently signed Tripartite Pact, this should not disturb relations with the Soviet Union at all. Ribbentrop suggested that the expansion of Germany, Italy, Japan and the Soviet Union should be directed southward to Africa and the Arabian Sea. He then asked Molotov to consider how the Soviet Union might collaborate with the signatories of the Tripartite Pact. Molotov, with his horn-rimmed spectacles perched delicately on the end of his nose, listened patiently and silently to Ribbentrop's long-winded summary.

In response, Molotov welcomed improved relations with Japan, but he pointedly reminded Ribbentrop that the Soviet Union remained a non-belligerent country in the current war. Molotov asked for further clarification of the concept of a 'Greater East Asian Sphere', which had been mentioned in the Tripartite Pact. Ribbentrop assured Molotov that the 'Greater East Asian Sphere' was a vague concept and he stressed that it had nothing to do with any of the signatories interfering with vital Russian spheres of influence.[187]

In the afternoon of 12 November 1940 Molotov met Hitler at the new Reich Chancellery. It was the first time the two men had ever met. Germany and Russia both had strong leaders at the helm, Hitler told Molotov. Men with the authority to shape policy in a definite direction. Neither country wanted to wage war just for the sake of it, but they both needed peace to carry out important domestic reforms.

Hitler stressed that the current situation was conditioned by the fact that Germany was at war and the Soviet Union was not. In the German-Soviet relationship, neither side could hope for 100 per cent agreement, but if they stood together there would be great advantages to both countries. If they worked against each other, however, the only beneficiaries would be other nations. When this sentence was translated, Molotov nodded firmly in agreement.

Due to the war, Hitler added, Germany had to extend its field of operations, particularly protecting its oil supplies from Romania. Some colonial expansion in Africa and Central Asia was also necessary, especially to bolster Italy. But under no circumstances would the vital concerns of the Soviet Union be affected. On the contrary, Hitler assured Molotov that Germany had no political interests in the Balkans at all, other than being determined to prevent Britain from gaining a foothold in Greece.

In reply, Molotov observed that Hitler's statements were of a general nature, and he could agree with much of what he had said, especially the importance of the Soviet Union and Germany collaborating, rather than fighting each other. Molotov then returned to the Tripartite Pact and raised several questions about its terms: what was the meaning of the new order in Europe and Asia? And what role would the Soviet Union be given in it? How far was Germany prepared to accept the USSR's interests in Bulgaria, Turkey and Romania? What was Germany's position regarding Finland?

In reply, Hitler avoided answering any of these questions directly, but he tried to reassure Molotov that the Soviet Union would not be faced with a German *fait accompli* in areas it regarded as its own spheres of influence. The Tripartite Pact, he added, only left open the possibility of further cooperation between Germany, Italy and Japan. Hitler would be more than happy if the Soviet Union agreed to join it.

Molotov said that Soviet participation in the Tripartite Pact seemed acceptable, provided the USSR cooperated as a partner with the other signatories. Due to an air-raid alarm the talks had to be broken off.[188] Hitler seemed visibly shaken by Molotov's forensic cross-examination. Hitler's interpreter Paul Schmidt couldn't recall any other foreign statesman speaking to Hitler in such a forthright manner before.[189]

On the following day Hitler and Molotov resumed their conversation. Hitler began by stating that Germany had honoured the Nazi-Soviet Pact from the beginning, while the Soviet occupation of the Baltic states in the summer of 1940 had occurred without any consultation with Germany. As for Finland, Germany had no political interests there and he accepted it lay within the Soviet sphere of influence. Nevertheless, Germany needed imports of nickel and

[overleaf]
Soviet Foreign Minister Vyacheslav Molotov (left) during talks with Hitler in Berlin on 12 November 1940 (in the middle is a German interpreter).

lumber from Finland and he certainly did not want another Russo-Finnish War.

This answer did not satisfy Molotov at all. He wanted to know why German troops were stationed there at all when the Baltic states and Finland had been assigned as Soviet spheres of influence. If Germany and the Soviet Union could agree on Finland, Molotov added, this would be a great help in easing tension. Molotov was clear: there must be no German troops in Finland and all anti-Soviet demonstrations there needed to stop.

Hitler replied that he had no influence over street demonstrations in Finland, but he promised that if a general German-Soviet agreement could be reached on Finland, then his troops would withdraw. Meanwhile, Hitler wanted to know if the Soviet Union wanted to resume war with Finland. Molotov was rather evasive on this matter, observing that it depended on whether the Finnish government ended its hostile attitude.

Hitler countered by saying that a war in the Baltic would place great strain on German-Soviet relations. Molotov did not see why there should be a war in the Baltic region. Hitler then asked if the Soviet Union would declare war on the United States if it became involved in the Baltic region. Molotov thought this was an unlikely scenario.

Molotov asked if Germany would object to a Soviet guarantee to Bulgaria. Hitler said this depended on whether the Bulgarian government wanted such a guarantee. He added that he needed to talk with Mussolini before he could give a definite answer on this matter. Molotov then expressed dissatisfaction with the German guarantee to Romania, without any consultation with the Soviet Union, but when he asked Hitler to revoke his guarantee to Romania, Hitler became 'markedly agitated' and reiterated that oil from Romania was vital for the German war effort.

Hitler then changed the subject to the opportunities presented by a German conquest of the British Empire. The Soviet Union would profit greatly from Britain's imperial territory being shared out. He admitted that in the long term he wanted to create a world coalition of Germany, the Soviet Union, Italy, Japan, Spain and France – all of which could profit from the end of the British Empire.

At this point, Hitler called Molotov's attention to the late hour and the possibility of a British air attack. By this stage, Hitler was so angry and perturbed after his grilling by Molotov that he sullenly withdrew from any further talks with him. He even failed to turn up to the farewell banquet for Molotov, held at the Soviet embassy on the following day.[190]

It was Ribbentrop who conducted the final conversation with Molotov, beginning at 9.45 p.m. in the underground bunker beneath the garden of the old Reich Chancellery. Ribbentrop said that he wanted to summarize the points of agreement to establish further collaboration between Germany and the Soviet Union. Molotov said that further talks were required to come up with a common formula between Germany, the Soviet Union, Italy and Japan.

Ribbentrop produced a draft of an agreement between the four powers – Germany, Italy, Japan and the USSR – designed to respect each country's natural spheres of interest. All four powers would agree not to join another combination of powers aimed against any one signatory, and also to assist each other on economic matters.

Molotov suggested that Germany was assuming the war with Britain was already won, and he joked that if this was so why were they meeting in an air-raid shelter, and who was dropping those booming bombs he could hear outside? As to the question of closer German-Soviet collaboration in the future, Molotov said that he approved of it, but there needed to be a full understanding on all issues before there could be any question of the Soviet Union joining the proposed four-power agreement. The meeting ended at midnight.[191]

Upon his return to Moscow, Molotov briefed Stalin on his talks in Berlin. On 25 November 1940, Stalin provisionally agreed to accept Ribbentrop's proposal of a four-power agreement, but only under certain strict conditions. These were: the immediate withdrawal of German troops from Finland; the signing of a Soviet-Bulgarian treaty; and the granting of a naval base on the Bosporus. The German government never even replied to Stalin's requests. Hitler described Stalin as a 'cold-blooded blackmailer' and wanted no further negotiations with the Soviet Union.[192]

The extremely tense meetings between Hitler and Molotov proved deeply significant for the future course of events. Hitler told Göring shortly afterwards that his encounter with the Soviet Foreign Minister had been crucial in making up his mind to attack the Soviet Union in 1941. Göring told him that Germany must first drive the British out of the Mediterranean, before turning on the Soviet Union, but Hitler would not listen.[193]

Ramón Serrano Suñer, the Spanish Foreign Minister, met Hitler at the Berghof on 18 November 1940. Hitler reiterated his demand for Spain to join the war and he saw no logical reason for delaying this decision. Suñer replied that Spain could not join the war until public opinion fully supported it and the country's economic position had greatly improved. He then outlined the current difficulties: if Spain entered the war, food imports from Canada would cease and a blockade of Spanish imports via the Atlantic would be closed off. This would be disastrous due to Spain's already serious food situation.

Hitler replied that as Spain was not a belligerent country, it could not be sent economic or military supplies before entering the war. Suñer said that Spain had come under pressure from the United States and Britain to publicly state that it would not join the war. Hitler then repeated his point that the war would be over more quickly if Spain entered now. The best time for an attack on Gibraltar would be January or February 1941. Suñer pointed out that war would hit Spain much harder economically than Germany or Italy. Hitler said the longer Spain waited on the sidelines, the more difficult it would be to conquer Gibraltar. Suñer was not convinced and once again made no firm promise of Spain entering the war.[194]

On 20 November 1940 Hitler wrote a surprisingly critical letter to Mussolini. He informed him that Germany wanted to postpone the attack on Greece until more favourable weather conditions prevailed, adding it had been a mistake for Italy not to have occupied Crete when it had the chance. The current situation now had grave psychological repercussions for the Axis. It was making his current diplomatic discussions about creating an anti-British coalition even more difficult. Bulgaria had considered joining the Tripartite Pact, but was now completely opposed to the idea, while Turkey had moved much closer towards Britain.

The military consequences were also very serious. Britain had acquired several air bases in Greece, which brought the RAF within striking range of the vital oilfields in Ploesti, Romania. In the face of this, Hitler realized that he had to continue to press Spain to enter the war. The main purpose was to seize Gibraltar and close the Strait to the Royal Navy.[195]

Mussolini replied to Hitler's letter two days later. His excuse for not giving Hitler prior knowledge of the Italian attack on Greece was to blame it on a postal delay. A letter Mussolini sent on 19 October 1940 had seemingly arrived after hostilities with Greece began. Mussolini then admitted that after a rapid early advance by Italian troops his invasion came to a standstill. The poorly equipped Albanian troops assisting the Italian army then deserted in large numbers. 'I am naturally aware of the unfavourable psychological repercussions which these events have caused,' Mussolini added, 'but I believe that these are passing phenomena. I am preparing a sufficient number of divisions (30) to annihilate Greece.'

Mussolini then turned to Spain and Yugoslavia. He felt that Spain should enter the war and he offered to meet Franco to put pressure on him to do so. Mussolini felt that Yugoslavian support was now even more important, and he was willing to offer a guarantee to Yugoslavia on the condition that it joined the Tripartite Pact.[196]

On 22 November 1940 Hitler met with the Romanian dictator General Ion Antonescu in Berlin. Antonescu said that he regarded the great work of the Führer with complete admiration and stressed that a great change had occurred in Romania on the question of joining the Axis, something he had personally supported ever since he came to power. Antonescu's key goal now was to contribute to the victory of the Axis powers and thereby to help bring the war to an end as soon as possible. Hitler was sure that Antonescu would achieve success in reorganizing the Romanian army and he was very pleased by Romania's promise to join the Tripartite Pact.[197]

Hitler next met Parvan Draganov, the Bulgarian Minister in Berlin, on the following day. Draganov informed Hitler that Bulgaria was now also willing to join the Tripartite Pact. This decision came after Molotov had asked Bulgaria if it would have any objection to a Soviet guarantee like the one given to Romania by Germany. Draganov said that Bulgaria would reject the Soviet offer. Draganov admitted that he was still fearful of a Soviet attack, but Hitler reassured him that Stalin was unwilling to clash with Germany. At the end of his conversation, Draganov asked Hitler what message he should convey to the King of Bulgaria. Hitler said to tell him that he was happy Bulgaria had rejected the Soviet offer of a guarantee and that he was pleased Bulgaria was taking defence precautions.[198]

On the night of 26 November 1940 members of the far right Iron Guard Party forced their way into a prison in Jilava near Bucharest, Romania, and killed a number of political prisoners. The next day, Nicolae Iorga, the former Romanian Prime Minister, was shot dead in the town of Strejnic. Hermann Neubacher, the German Minister in Bucharest, reported Antonescu's deep shock at these unexpected events. A humiliated Antonescu had even considered resigning, but he soon regained his composure. Neubacher felt that Antonescu's authority was now much stronger, due to the success of his visit to Hitler in Berlin. The actions of the Iron Guard showed their desperation, he added, because they had little widespread public support. The rumour that army generals were planning a coup against Antonescu were also untrue.[199]

Continuing his frenetic round of diplomatic meetings with Balkan ministers, Hitler met Yugoslav Foreign Minister Aleksandar Cincar-Marković at the Berghof on 28 November 1940. Hitler told him about his bold plan for a worldwide coalition to defeat the British Empire. The time had come, he said, for every European state to decide whether or not to join this grouping. Hitler wanted Yugoslavia to join his European coalition. Alternatively, he suggested Yugoslavia and Germany could conclude a non-aggression pact. Cincar-Marković listened patiently to Hitler's monologue, promised to convey Hitler's message to the Prince Regent of Yugoslovia, but he gave no indication of his own personal opinion.[200]

Hitler wrote to Mussolini on 5 December 1940 to update him on recent diplomatic developments. Antonescu had made a good impression on Hitler, who described him positively as a 'real nationalist fanatic'. He then gave details of his meeting with Cincar-Marković. Hitler had offered him the chance of developing friendly relations with the Axis powers, but he admitted to being unsure whether Yugoslavia could be won over.[201]

Admiral Canaris, the chief of the *Abwehr*, the German military intelligence service, held a meeting with General Franco in Madrid on 7 December 1940. Franco told him it was impossible for Spain to enter the war by 10 January 1941 as Germany had requested. The food situation in Spain was now perilous and military preparations were inadequate. For these reasons Franco ruled out Spain joining the war 'for the foreseeable future'. Months of frustrating discussions over the possibility of Spain entering the war had frustratingly gone nowhere.[202]

On 10 December Adolf Hitler signed 'Directive No. 19' for Operation Attila. It stated that in the event of breakaway movements developing in the French colonial empire, preparations should be made for the speedy occupation of the entire Unoccupied Zone (Vichy France), and at the same time to capture the French fleet. The invasion of Vichy France would use strong motorized groups, supported by the *Luftwaffe*. The time between the order and operations would be as short as possible. It was unlikely the French armed forces would offer any resistance. Hitler made it clear that the preparations for Operation Attila must be kept strictly secret.[203]

On 13 December 1940, Hitler signed 'Directive No. 20', codenamed Operation Marita. This was designed to provide military assistance to Italy in Greece. It stated that 'in the next few months' a force of German troops would be prepared in Romania. After favourable weather conditions had set in, 'probably March', this force would attack Greece via Bulgaria. The German contribution would consist of an armoured division, supported by seven infantry divisions. The *Luftwaffe* would support the operation.[204]

Marshal Pétain sent a letter to Hitler on the same day to report that Pierre Laval, a keen supporter of collaboration with Germany, had been forced to resign, because he 'no longer enjoys the sufficient confidence and authority in the country'. It was felt that Laval's openly pro-German attitude had made him 'suspect to Frenchmen for the undertakings to which he has addressed himself'. Hitler saw this as a huge rebuff to his desire for closer Franco-German cooperation.[205]

After all the feverish and frustrating diplomatic activity of the autumn of 1941, which had failed to create a broad anti-British coalition, Hitler now moved in a completely different military and diplomatic direction. On 18 December 1940 Hitler signed 'Directive No. 21', codenamed Operation Barbarossa: a plan to attack the Soviet Union. It began: 'The German *Wehrmacht* must be prepared to crush Soviet Russia in a quick campaign even before the conclusion of the war with England.' For this purpose, the *Wehrmacht* would 'have to employ all available units', but the occupied territories must be secured in case of any 'surprises'. The campaign would be supported by the *Luftwaffe*. The main effort of the German navy would continue to be directed against the Royal Navy. Preparations for the invasion of the Soviet Union were to be completed by 15 May 1941. The German General Staff had drafted and approved this directive, which Hitler duly signed. Significantly, there was no mention at this stage of any ideological motivation for destroying the Soviet Union.[206]

On that same fateful day Hitler addressed a group of officer candidates in the Berlin Sport Palace. He had dedicated everything to making Germany militarily strong, he declared, and in battle 'to stake everything on one throw'. If the national unity of the German people remained strong, 'then the future of Europe belongs to this *Volk*'. If not, 'then this *Volk* will perish, shall sink back and it will no longer be worthwhile to live in this *Volk*'.[207]

Oberkommando der Wehrm...
des Heere...

Geheime Kommandosache

Chef-Sache!
Nur durch Offizier!

Buch Nr.
Stü. Nr.

Jahrgang

ACCO
D.R.V.G.
Heffer
DB Trupp

von

bis

OKH - Gen StdH
Op Abt (I/N) Nr. 050/41 g.K.

30 Ausfertigungen
2. Ausfertigung

Aufmarschanweisung

„Barbarossa"

On Christmas Eve 1940, Hitler met Admiral François Darlan, the head of the French fleet, in his special train in the northern French city of Beauvais. Hitler was not in a very festive mood. Darlan told Hitler that a strong personal conflict had emerged between Pétain and Laval, which led Pétain to part with the Prime Minister and replace him with Pierre Flandin. Darlan then tried to assure Hitler that the policy of the Vichy government remained one of close cooperation with Germany. In response, Hitler angrily told Darlan that it was a matter of supreme indifference to him as to who ran the French government. If Laval was considered a disloyal member of the cabinet then it had been rather tactless of the French government to allow Laval to meet him in October. Hitler then warned Darlan that the French government needed to realize that any further attempt to undermine Franco-German collaboration would lead to France receiving a 'more terrible lesson' than the one that had already led to their complete military defeat earlier in 1940. In response, Darlan said that he could have sailed to America with the French fleet in June, which would have made the Armistice null and void. Personally, he had always supported German-French cooperation. The removal of Laval, he admitted, had been handled very badly, but due to Laval's unpopularity it was unavoidable. With that comment the very tense exchange ended.[208]

On New Year's Eve Hitler sent a letter to Mussolini to 'wish him good wishes for the coming year' and offered him an overview of the current military situation. He believed that the war in Western Europe had already been won. When weather conditions permitted, the final decisive attack on Britain would begin. In conclusion, Hitler wrote: 'I regard the future with calm assurance. Your people, *Duce*, will only emerge hardened from the first reverses.' In 1941, Hitler promised to do everything in his power 'to make this the year of final victory'.

What he did not tell his closest ally was that he had already decided to broaden the scope of the Second World War by attacking the Soviet Union, thereby breaking his previous injunction against starting a war on two fronts.[209]

War Directive 21, dated 18 December 1940, sanctioning Operation Barbarossa, the German attack on the Soviet Union.

1941

·

WAR OF ANNIHILATION

·

'A momentous year in German history has come to an end,' Hitler wrote in his traditional New Year's message. 'The enormous uniqueness of the events and their revolutionary significance for the future development of mankind will be fully acknowledged by later generations.' He promised that 1941 would see the combined might of the German army, navy and *Luftwaffe* enormously strengthened. 'The last of the war criminals will collapse under its blows,' he concluded, 'and thus the prerequisites for a true understanding among nations will be created.'[1]

On the following day, the German High Command presented Hitler with a gloomy report on the fighting capability of the Italian army. Even before the war began, the German General Staff had low expectations of the Italian army. Military setbacks in the Balkans and North Africa only confirmed this assessment. Operations in Greece and Albania showed that even when they were better equipped, Italian troops still performed badly. These Italian military failures were ascribed to poor leadership and the inferior quality of the troops. The report concluded that the Italians would always need substantial German assistance.[2]

In spite of the dire performance of the Italian troops, Hitler was still captivated by Mussolini's personal charisma: 'As I walked with him in the gardens of Villa Borghese,' he told a meeting of his generals, 'I could easily compare his profile with that of the old Roman busts and I realized he was one of the Caesars. There is no doubt that Mussolini is the heir of the great men of that period.'[3]

On 4 January 1941 Hitler met the Bulgarian Prime Minister Bogdan Filov at the Berghof. Hitler stressed to him the need for a common front against what he called the 'Bolshevik infection'. While Stalin was alive, he felt that it was 'absolutely impossible' for the Soviet Union to start a war with Germany. He advised Bulgaria to join the Tripartite Pact as a protection against the Soviet threat. In response, Filov said that the Bulgarian government feared Soviet intervention if it joined the Tripartite Pact.[4]

A planning conference for Operation Barbarossa was held by Hitler and his leading military and naval commanders on 8–9 January 1941. Hitler claimed that his planned destruction of the Soviet Union was based upon the premise of completing a very short campaign before the Russian winter set in. Victory over the Soviet Union would, he thought, cause Britain to seek peace, allow Japan to expand in the Pacific and would increase Germany's capability to wage a long war by exploiting captured Soviet economic resources.[5]

Hitler later recalled: 'I had no more difficult decision to take than the attack on Russia. I had always maintained that we ought at all costs to avoid waging war on two fronts, and you may rest assured that I pondered long and anxiously over Napoleon and his experiences in Russia.'[6]

Franz Halder, the Chief of General Staff at OKH, was not impressed by the current state of Hitler's plans for the attack on the Soviet Union, noting in his diary on 28 January: 'Barbarossa purpose not clear. We do not hurt the English. Our economic base is not significantly improved. Risk in the west should not be underestimated. It is possible Italy might collapse after the loss of its colonies, and we get a southern front in Spain, Italy and Greece. If we are tied up in Russia, a bad situation will be made worse.'[7]

The attack on the Soviet Union made no economic sense. Germany was still reliant on raw material imports from the Soviet Union. On 10 January, the German government signed a new economic agreement with the Soviet Union, specifying the delivery of huge amounts of commodities and raw materials, including 2.5 million tonnes of grain and 1 million tonnes of oil. Under a secret protocol, Germany had even renounced its claim to a part of Lithuania in return for 7.5 million in gold dollars. The deliveries from the Soviet Union continued on schedule, although German deliveries of war materials were slowing down.[8] During the first six months of 1941, Stalin did all he could to maintain the Nazi-Soviet Pact.

On 11 January 1941 Hitler issued 'War Directive No. 22', codenamed Operation Sunflower (*Sonnenblume*), on the cooperation of German and Italian forces in the Mediterranean. It emphasized that Tripoli must be held and that the collapse of Italian forces in Albania must be prevented. A German blocking unit for the defence of Tripoli was planned, supported by the *Luftwaffe*.[9]

In Moscow, on 13 January 1941, the leading Soviet commanders delivered a presentation to Stalin, summarizing the outcome of war games they had conducted into a possible German attack on the USSR during December 1940. One of the key contributors to the discussion was the talented Red Army General Georgy Zhukov, who assessed the impact of a potential German *Blitzkrieg* operation on the western frontier of the Soviet Union.

Zhukov gloomily predicted that German attackers, using heavily concentrated tank forces, but also with air support, would wipe out the defending forces, then drive deep into Soviet territory unimpeded. Stalin was deeply shocked by this assessment, but he quickly promoted Zhukov to the post of Army Chief of Staff on the basis that he championed the use of tank forces, which he argued could rectify the current deficiencies in Soviet defences.[10]

On 14 January Hitler met the Romanian Prime Minister Antonescu at the Berghof. The Romanian people were fully behind his pro-German stance, reported Antonescu. In reply, Hitler said that while he wanted Romanian support, he did not require a Romanian organization identical with the principles of National Socialism. The discussion soon moved on to foreign affairs. Antonescu thought that Romanian relations with Bulgaria were currently good, but there was distrust between Romania and Yugoslavia. Relations with the Soviet Union had deteriorated since Romania had joined the Tripartite Pact. Hungary remained on good terms. Romanian relations with Britain had been broken off and Antonescu now feared RAF attacks on the oilfields. Finally, Antonescu promised that Romania would offer military assistance to the Axis in the Balkans.[11]

Mussolini arrived at the Berghof on 19 January for a two-day visit. Goebbels noted in his diary that Mussolini 'had lost a great deal of prestige since his military disasters in Greece and North Africa'.[12] During their first meeting, Hitler told Mussolini that the situation in North Africa was becoming extremely difficult. During January 1941, British Allied forces had taken 130,000 Italians prisoner in Libya. Hitler argued that the Axis strategic position would greatly improve if Gibraltar were captured, but Franco was still refusing to join in the war. In response Mussolini said that he was willing to make another effort to persuade Franco to reconsider.[13]

On the next day, Hitler spoke for two hours to a small select group of leading German-Italian figures, including his Foreign Minister Ribbentrop, the German military commanders Keitel and Jodl, and the German naval intelligence officer Franz von Rintelen. Mussolini, the Italian Foreign Minister Ciano, and the leading Italian generals Alfred Guzzoni and Leonardo Marras were also present.

The key part of Hitler's talk was the German plan to invade Greece, which he said was by no means straightforward. A glance at the map showed that four Balkan countries lay between Germany and Greece: Hungary, Romania, Bulgaria and Yugoslavia. His latest diplomatic efforts had been aimed at binding these Balkan states to the foreign policy aims of Germany. The compliance of all four was essential before Germany could attack Greece. Each nation had already been offered territorial gains and economic incentives to come into Germany's orbit. Hitler then ran through the current state of progress of his talks. Romania was fully allied to Germany. Hungary was reluctant to become a German satellite, but would cooperate with German plans. Bulgaria was worried about upsetting the Soviet Union, but it had already agreed to the passage of German troops to attack Greece (and on 1 March 1941 Bulgaria would join the Tripartite Pact).

Hitler then stressed the geographical position of Yugoslavia made it vital for the attack on Greece. Yugoslavia had close economic ties with Germany, but its government was lukewarm about openly aligning itself with Hitler's foreign policy, preferring instead to preserve its independence and neutrality. For this reason, Yugoslavia had so far resisted joining the Tripartite Pact.

Hitler noted that the British and US governments had tried to influence the Yugoslavian government to resist German diplomatic and economic overtures. Prince Paul, the Yugoslav Regent, was pro-British, but the fall of France had convinced him of the might of the German armed forces and this had led Yugoslavia to consider joining the Tripartite Pact. But, Hitler added, there had been opposition to this move among the leading Serbian officers in the Yugoslav army.

Hitler then turned to German-Russian relations, but made no mention of Operation Barbarossa because the Italian government had still not been informed of this plan. Germany was bound to the Soviet Union by treaties, Hitler said. As a result, he was confident that the Soviet Union would not attack Germany, but Germany had to remain ready for such a possibility.

Hitler almost gave the game away about his proposed attack on the Soviet Union when he observed that German-Soviet relations were deteriorating rapidly. This was due, he argued, to the Soviets constantly offering a one-sided interpretation of the definition of the term 'spheres of influence' outlined in the Nazi-Soviet Pact. Hitler also expressed concern about the diplomatic pressure Stalin was bringing to bear on Bulgaria and Romania to resist German influence.

It was, therefore, necessary, Hitler concluded, to be cautious in all dealings with the Soviets, because they were constantly looking for loopholes in the existing treaties to expand their own territory.[14] Mussolini privately noted the 'anti-Russian' tone of Hitler's comments, but he had no inkling that his German ally was planning to attack the Soviet Union.[15]

On 21 January 1941 there was an unexpected revolt in Romania. The renegade Iron Guard, unhappy with Antonescu's increasingly pro-German stance, seized government buildings in Bucharest, but Antonescu's palace and the Foreign Ministry were left untouched. Antonescu called on the German government for military assistance. In a show of strength, German tanks rolled into Bucharest. The Iron Guard rebels soon surrendered and many were summarily executed. This incident bound Antonescu's regime even more closely to Hitler than ever before.[16]

Meanwhile, Eberhard von Stohrer, the German ambassador to Spain, held talks with General Franco. Stohrer reported Hitler's disappointment at the continued reluctance of Spain to enter the war. The German government refused to accept Spain's repeated economic or military excuses for non-participation. German economic aid would immediately follow a Spanish declaration of war. Stohrer also pointed out to Franco that his delay in deciding to enter the war had led Hitler to believe that Spain was not really convinced of a German victory.

In response, Franco expressed his 'astonishment' at Stohrer's pessimistic tone. The Spanish economic situation was dire, Franco pointed out, and he needed to be assured of food supplies to maintain the lives of his people. Without bread supplies it would be 'criminal' for Spain to enter the war. Franco ended by saying it was not a question of if Spain would enter the war, but only when.[17]

Stohrer met Franco again on 23 January 1941. He read him an uncompromising personal message from Ribbentrop, which began by pointing out that without Axis help Franco would not have won the Spanish Civil War. Hitler was now deeply disturbed by Spain's continued vacillation.[18] In a very angry tone, Franco told Stohrer that Ribbentrop's message was completely false. As a man of honour, Franco had never lost sight of the need to join the war, but Spain's entry would come only when the economic conditions were right.[19]

Stohrer held a third and equally frustrating meeting with Franco on 27 January. Franco once again gave him a lengthy explanation of the distressing food situation in Spain and he added that Spain was in no position to fight a long war. Stohrer reported back to Ribbentrop that Germany's constant diplomatic pressure on Franco had only served to injure the General's pride and make him even more intransigent.[20]

Ribbentrop replied to Stohrer on 28 January, criticizing him for the manner in which he had presented the German position to Franco during their recent conversations. Ribbentrop had simply wanted to make clear to Franco that only Spain's immediate entry into the war was of any value to the German government. Instead, Ribbentrop felt that Stohrer had allowed Franco to steer the conversation towards the economic reasons why Spain could not enter, with the result that Franco was now requesting that Germany send economic and military experts to assess Spanish needs. In this way, Ribbentrop felt that Franco could now claim a grievance if Germany failed to meet his economic requirements. Ribbentrop advised Stohrer to put an end to the pointless wrangling by telling Franco that, because he had rejected the idea of entering the war on the side of the Axis powers, that was now the end of the matter.[21]

On 29 January Stohrer met Franco one more time to ask him bluntly if Spain would enter the war or not. Franco, acting true to form, once again failed to give a straight answer. Instead, he once again listed the reasons why Spain could not join the war effort. Stohrer informed Ribbentrop after the meeting that in his view Franco never had any intention of entering the war and that he had spun out the diplomatic discussions in order to delay giving a clear answer.[22]

On 20 January 1941 the Grand Mufti of Jerusalem wrote a letter to Hitler, requesting German support for Arab independence in the British Mandate of Palestine. The Grand Mufti noted that in the case of the Palestine question all the Arab countries were united in their hatred of the British and the Jews. The Zionists, he added, were allied to the British in the hope of gaining a Jewish state in the event of a British victory in the war. If Germany aided the Arab independence movement these British plans could be prevented.[23]

A reply to this letter, composed by Ernst von Weizsäcker in the German Foreign Ministry, was not sent until 8 April. Weizsäcker informed the Grand Mufti that Hitler fully recognized the independence of existing Arab states and broadly supported the claims of Arab people for independence in areas where this did not currently exist. Hitler also agreed that the British and the Jews were common enemies. Germany was therefore willing to collaborate on a friendly basis wherever Arabs were fighting the British and to offer military and financial assistance. Further discussions would determine how this assistance could be given. Weizsäcker stressed to the Grand Mufti that the contents of this letter must be 'kept secret'.[24]

At the end of 1941 the Grand Mufti visited Berlin. He met Ribbentrop on 28 November, stressing the importance that Arabs attached to collaboration with Germany. Ribbentrop understood that the Mufti wanted a public declaration of Axis support for Arab independence, but he emphasized the fact that the German government had to proceed cautiously, even though Ribbentrop said that he personally supported the Mufti's point of view.[25]

On 28 November the Grand Mufti finally met Hitler in person. He first thanked Hitler for the sympathy he had always shown for the Palestinian cause. Arabs hated Jews, the British and communists, the Grand Mufti continued, and they were Germany's natural friends. He felt that a public declaration of support by Hitler would be extremely valuable to the cause of Arab independence.

In reply, Hitler said that Germany stood for 'uncompromising war against the Jews'. This naturally included firm opposition to a Jewish national homeland in Palestine. Hitler promised that Germany would furnish positive and practical aid to the Arab cause, but this would be material and only offered secretly. He stressed that if the German government issued a public declaration for Arab independence this might lead to the accusation that Germany was determined to break up the French colonial empire. At some moment in the future, Hitler promised, he would openly support Arab liberation, but that moment was not now.[26]

On 30 January 1941 Hitler delivered his traditional speech in the Berlin Sport Palace. Hitler made no mention of German relations with the Soviet Union, but he predicted that '1941 will be a crucial year of the great New Order in Europe.' He then launched into a lengthy attack on the British government, which he claimed was under the direction of a 'Jewish clique'. Britain had acquired a quarter of the territory of the world by robbery and force, and upheld a balance of power merely to prevent other powers from challenging its dominant position.

Hitler then ominously reiterated his prophecy from 1939 that if the world was plunged into a general war because of Jewish manipulation, then this would lead to Jewish annihilation. 'They [Britain and the United States] can still laugh about it,' he added, 'just like they used to laugh at my prophecies. The coming months and years will prove that here, too, I've seen things correctly.'[27]

Adolf Hitler meeting the Grand Mufti
(Haj Amin al-Husseini) in Berlin on 28
November 1941.

Hitler wrote to Mussolini on 5 February assuring him of his continued personal support. Hitler was still concerned about the continued reversals of Italian fortunes in North Africa. He promised to send Mussolini not only an army blocking unit, but a complete German armoured division.[28] In reply, Mussolini reported that Italians were extremely shocked and dismayed by the continuing military setbacks, but he assured Hitler that his own popularity remained strong. On Spain, Mussolini felt that Franco was in no position to enter the war, because the Spanish population was starving, its army lacked modern armaments and there remained a strong pro-British tendency among its nobility and middle classes.[29]

On 6 February Hitler appointed the brilliant tank commander Erwin Rommel – who had distinguished himself as commander of the 7th German Panzer Division during the Battle of France – as head of the Africa Corps, with the aim of reversing the Italian losses in North Africa. Rommel arrived in North Africa in mid-March and soon turned the tables on the British forces there. In just twelve days Rommel's Panzer units were able to regain all of the territory the Italians had lost in the previous autumn, driving the British back to the Egyptian frontier.[30]

On 6 February Hitler issued 'Directive No. 23' called 'Guiding Principles for the Conduct of the War against the English War Economy'. It noted that the economic war against Britain was reaching its greatest effort, with German U-boats inflicting heavy losses on British merchant ships. A further escalation of submarine attacks was to be expected during the year. The directive also observed that the effect of *Luftwaffe* attacks on British armament industries was difficult to estimate, but that a sharp decrease in British production could be expected. The effect of bombing on the British civilian population was equally difficult to assess. Due to the needs of Operation Barbarossa, the current scale of air attacks on Britain could not be maintained. After the attack on the Soviet Union, it would be better, therefore, to direct German air attacks on British economic targets, such as ports, rather than on the civilian population.[31]

During this period, Joseph Goebbels stepped up his anti-British propaganda campaign with the release of two films. The first was *My Life for Ireland* (*Mein Leben für Irland*), released on 17 February 1941. It tells the story of Michael O'Brien (the son of an executed Irish nationalist of the same name), who is sent, against his wishes, to St Edward's College, a boarding school in Dublin, staffed by English-born teachers who indoctrinate students with pro-British imperial ideas. School sports such as rugby and golf are mocked in the film as upper-class pastimes, while the English sense of fair play is twisted to mean it is acceptable to cheat if you can get away with it. Overall, the film depicted the British as cynical, unscrupulous and brutal, but suggests that they are no match for the passionately driven Irish nationalists. *My Life for Ireland* proved very popular with German cinema audiences.[32]

It was soon followed by *Uncle Krüger* (*Ohm Krüger*) which was released on 4 April. It was the most venomous anti-British film released during the Nazi era. It's based on the life of Paul Kruger, the leader of the Boers during the First and Second Boer Wars. In the film, the blind Krüger, who is exiled in Switzerland (and is played impressively by Emil Jannings), recounts his wartime experiences to a young nurse in a hotel in Geneva in several flashbacks.

The Boers are shown in the film as resolute and valiant, but ultimately the victims of ruthless British imperialism. The British figures in the film are crude caricatures: Queen Victoria is cynical and addicted to whisky; Joseph Chamberlain, the Colonial Secretary, is a conspiring diplomat who can't be trusted; Cecil Rhodes is portrayed as a ruthless businessman exploiting workers in his gold and diamond mines; and General Kitchener is presented as inhumane as he orders civilian farms and houses to be set alight.

Ohm Krüger also highlights the British use of concentration camps during the Boer Wars, emphasizing that women and children were denied food and medical attention. The British concentration camp commandant, who strongly resembles Winston Churchill, feeds his loyal bulldog steak, while shooting starving inmates if they complain of hunger. In the final scene, clearly derived from the famous Odessa Steps sequence in Eisenstein's *Battleship Potemkin* (1925), Boer women and children are massacred in the British concentration camp.

Most of the crimes the British were accused of committing in the film were currently going on in Nazi concentration camps and Jewish ghettos. *Ohm Krüger* was a blatant attempt to subliminally justify German actions by claiming that they were not acting any worse than the British did during the Boer Wars. It concludes with Krüger prophesying the destruction of the British Empire by a combination of world powers which he thinks will make the world a better place.[33]

On 6 February 1941 Hitler wrote a personal letter to Franco in a last-ditch effort to bring Spain into the war. It was stern in tone,

warning Franco that if Germany and Italy lost the war there would be no place for a national and independent Spain. He further reminded him of their meeting at Hendaye the previous autumn, when he was under the impression that Franco had promised to join the Tripartite Pact and enter the war.[34]

Mussolini met with Franco in Bordighera in Italy on 12 February. Franco told him that Spain wished to cooperate with the Axis powers, but it was not in a position either economically or militarily to enter the war. After the meeting, Mussolini advised Hitler to accept Franco's position and to keep Spain on the sidelines for the time being.[35]

On 14 February 1941 Hitler held talks with Dragiša Cvetković, the Yugoslavian Prime Minister, at the Berghof. Cvetković began by saying that he had always championed closer economic and political cooperation between Germany and Yugoslavia. In fact, since the war began, he continued, the Yugoslavian economy had been orientated towards Germany. In response, Hitler said that he regarded Yugoslavia as a natural and valuable trading partner. What currently concerned him was British intervention in Greece, which he regarded as intolerable. The Greek government had allowed itself to become a pawn of the British and this could no longer continue.

Hitler felt that a unique historic moment had arrived for Yugoslavia and he urged Cvetković's government to align itself with the Axis powers by joining the Tripartite Pact. Cvetković promised to convey Hitler's views to the Prince Regent, but he gave no commitment on the matter himself.[36]

The German drive to improve relations with Japan resumed. Ribbentrop invited the Japanese ambassador Hiroshi Ōshima to his estate in Fuschl, Austria, on 23 February 1941. Ribbentrop told Ōshima that Germany had already won the war. All that remained was to demonstrate to Britain that continuing to fight was futile. Regarding the Soviet Union and Germany, Ribbentrop said that Stalin was a shrewd politician who would not attack Germany. Ribbentrop then predicted that a war between Germany and the USSR would spell the end of the Soviet regime. As for the United States, he felt it was a bitter enemy of Germany and Japan, but even if America did enter the war it would not be able to do anything at the outset.

Hitler was determined to bring the war to a glorious conclusion in 1941, Ribbentrop informed Ōshima, and Japan's cooperation was important in achieving this goal. He suggested that a Japanese attack on Singapore would wipe out Britain's position in the Far East.

Emil Jannings in the 1941 film *Ohm Krüger*
(*Uncle Krüger*).

Ōshima agreed with Ribbentrop's overall analysis, and he assured him that preparations were already in motion for the seizure of Singapore.[37]

General Georg Thomas, head of the *Wehrmacht*'s War Economy and Armaments Office, met with Hermann Göring on 26 February 1941 to discuss his proposals to ruthlessly exploit the economic resources of the Soviet Union after its defeat, with grain from Ukraine and oil from the Caucasus viewed as the top economic prizes. Before this meeting, Thomas had been urged by Keitel to play down the huge economic benefits of invading the USSR. Yet in his presentation to Göring, Thomas did just the opposite. He argued that in the initial attack Germany could seize 70 per cent of Soviet industrial potential.[38]

Hitler sent a letter to Mussolini on 28 February making it clear that Spain did not want to enter the war and had never intended to. This was unfortunate, thought Hitler, because it eliminated the possibility, for the time being, of driving the British out of the Mediterranean.[39]

Hitler may have failed to persuade Franco, but his diplomatic charm offensive with the Balkan states was beginning to pay off. On 1 March 1941 Bulgaria joined the Tripartite Pact. This immediately led the Soviet Foreign Minister Vyacheslav Molotov to seek a meeting with Count von Schulenburg, the German ambassador in Moscow. Molotov objected that the Bulgarian move went completely against the spirit of the Nazi-Soviet Pact. In response, Schulenburg reassured Molotov that Germany had no territorial claims in Bulgaria, and he found the anxiety of the Soviet government 'incomprehensible'. Molotov countered by saying that the Soviet Union had special interests in Bulgaria. After the meeting, Schulenburg felt that – despite Molotov's protest – the Soviet Union would take no action.[40]

Hitler now turned his diplomatic attention towards neutral Turkey. He sent a letter to İsmet İnönü, the President of Turkey, on 1 March 1941, informing him that due to British attempts to gain a foothold on Greek territory, Germany had decided to take measures to prevent this. This action was in no way directed against the territorial and political integrity of Turkey. On the contrary, 'I should like to assure you that it is my deepest conviction that in the future, too, all of the conditions necessary for a really friendly cooperation between Germany and Turkey will exist.'[41] Replying, İnönü stated that his key aim in the war was to protect Turkish independence. His government wanted to keep out of the current war. There was no reason for any conflict with Germany, and Turkey would seek to maintain friendly relations.[42]

Meanwhile, the detailed planning for Operation Barbarossa

was stepped up. For the first time, the ideological implications of the German attack came to the fore. On 3 March 1941 Hitler gave instructions to Alfred Jodl, the Chief of the Operations Staff of the OKW, to work out 'Guidelines on Special Tasks' for Operation Barbarossa. These were to be based on the principle that 'it is not enough to defeat the enemy by force of arms; it is a conflict between two world views, no nationalist Russia must emerge after the defeat of Bolshevism; the Jewish-Bolshevist intelligentsia must be destroyed; the SS should take care of the immediate elimination of Bolshevist chiefs and commissars – without court martial.'[43]

On 13 March a new draft plan for Operation Barbarossa was agreed, now incorporating Hitler's ideological imperatives. The planned killing operation in the Soviet Union would be overseen by Himmler and carried out by paramilitary death squads (*Einsatzgruppen*), which would move behind the advancing German army and systematically execute Soviet ideological and racial enemies. The German army would be required to provide logistical support to these killing squads. It was emphasized that close cooperation would be achieved between the *Einsatzkommando* liaison officer and the intelligence officer assigned to each German army division. The military would also be kept informed of the orders issued by Reinhard Heydrich to the *Einsatzgruppen*.

Heydrich and Bruno Streckenbach, the head of personnel at the Reich Security Main Office (RSHA), selected the men to lead each *Einsatzgruppe*. They were drawn from the highest ranks of the SD and the Gestapo, as well as the criminal police or Kripo, the order police and the Waffen-SS. They were all committed Nazis, antisemitic ideologues and specialist bureaucrats, who fervently believed in the racial policy of the SS. All had higher educational qualifications, including doctorates – often in law – and experience in the police and security forces over many years.

Einsatzgruppe A, operating in the Baltic states, was led by SS Colonel Dr Walther Stahlecker; *Einsatzgruppe* B, venturing to White Russia, was commanded by SS General Arthur Nebe, *Einsatzgruppe* C, journeying to north and central Ukraine, was directed by SS Brigadier General Dr Otto Rasch; and *Einsatzgruppe* D, which operated in south Ukraine, the Crimea and the Caucasus, was controlled by SS Brigade Leader Dr Otto Ohlendorf. These four killing units were further subdivided into smaller units, referred to as *Einsatzkommandos* and *Sonderkommandos*.[44]

Each *Einsatzgruppe* task force was made up of 600 to 1,000

men, with some women in clerical and communications positions. The total *Einsatzgruppen* force deployed in the Soviet Union never exceeded 3,000 personnel. The units were fully motorized. Sometimes army support was required and used for the killing operations. The commanders were also instructed to encourage the local populations in conquered areas to assist in the murders: 'No steps will be taken to interfere with any purges that may be initiated by anti-communist or anti-Jewish elements. On the contrary, these are to be encouraged.'[45]

In a meeting on 26 March 1941 Göring told Heydrich that the army should be given a brief set of directions about the dangers posed by communist political commissars and Jews, so that they would know who to 'put up against the wall'. Göring assured Himmler that in the Soviet Union offensive the SS would have much greater independent authority than ever before to carry out mass murder, leaving the army little power to restrain the activities of the *Einsatzgruppen* even if it had wanted to. There was no mention in these very early discussions of Operation Barbarossa of any widespread plan to kill Jews.[46]

On 5 March Hitler signed 'Directive No. 24' regarding 'Cooperation with Japan'. It effectively condoned any Japanese aggression against Britain and the United States. Hitler felt that Operation Barbarossa would offer Japan opportunities for expansion in the Far East. His directive advocated the strengthening of Japanese military power by every means. Information on German battle experience would be shared with Japanese military chiefs. The following aims were outlined. First, the swift defeat of Britain, thereby keeping the United States out of the war. Second, the Japanese Navy should join the German attack on British merchant shipping. Third, Japan should seize areas that would gain raw materials to continue the war. Fourth, Singapore should be seized to damage Britain's position. Finally, 'no hint of the Barbarossa Operation' was to be given to the Japanese government prior to the attack.[47]

On 22 March Hitler issued a further directive on Operation Marita. It was decided to capture the entire Greek mainland during the operation and to occupy the islands of Thasos and Samothrace, off the Aegean coast. The commander-in-chief of the German army was authorized to build up attack forces in Bulgaria. German units would spearhead the attack on Greece, with Italian forces taking a secondary role.[48]

Germany now increased its pressure on Yugoslavia to join the Axis powers. Prince Paul, the Yugoslav regent, was known to be pro-

British. Educated at the University of Oxford, he once said that he 'felt like an Englishman'.[49] He was also anti-Italian and married to a Greek princess, so he had no desire to support a German invasion of Greece. Nevertheless, Prince Paul's resistance was gradually overcome by a combination of bullying and pragmatism. As Hungary, Romania and Bulgaria had all joined the Tripartite Pact, Yugoslavia was not in a strong enough position to resist Germany for very much longer and remain independent. In a meeting with Adolf Hitler on 4 March Prince Paul finally agreed to sign the Tripartite Pact on the condition that Yugoslavia would not provide any military assistance to Germany or allow its troops to cross its territory to invade Greece.

A lavish signing ceremony took place on 25 March 1941 in Vienna to celebrate Yugoslavia finally joining the Axis. When Hitler met with the Yugoslav Prime Minister Cvetković in the Hotel Imperial in Vienna shortly after the signing the atmosphere was very friendly. Hitler expressed satisfaction with the accession of Yugoslavia to the Tripartite Pact. By this act, Hitler told him, Yugoslavia had placed itself firmly on the side of Germany's new order for Europe. In response, Cvetković said that the Yugoslavians knew that the Führer had always been friendly to them and Yugoslavia was now ready to fully cooperate with Germany. Cvetković then spoke of the internal difficulties he had needed to overcome for Yugoslavia to join the Axis, but he was pleased to report these problems had been eliminated.[50]

This proved wishful thinking. The Serbian element in Yugoslavia had already decided to defy Hitler even before the signing ceremony occurred. On the night of 26 March 1941 a military coup began in Belgrade. It was led by a disgruntled group of army officers, most notably, air force general Borivoje Mirković and General Dušan Simović, the Serbian Chief of the General Staff of the Yugoslavian army. Denouncing the treaty with Germany, they overthrew the government of Prince Paul and his Prime Minister Cvetković, who both fled into exile.

Prince Paul's seventeen-year-old nephew Peter II was declared the new king. His government was led by Simović, now the Prime Minister. The Yugoslav *coup d'état* was a genuine popular uprising. Serbs – some of them carrying British and French flags – celebrated on the streets of Belgrade, thinking their ordeal was over.

It was, of course, never a good idea for a small country to defy the wishes of Adolf Hitler. When the Führer heard news of the uprising, his shock soon turned to outrage. On 27 March, Hitler summoned his leading generals to a meeting at noon in the new Reich Chancellery. The current Yugoslav situation was an uncertain factor in the forthcoming attack on Greece, he said, but he was now determined – without waiting for a possible declaration of loyalty from the new government – to smash Yugoslavia militarily and as a state. This knockout blow against Yugoslavia would be delivered with the utmost severity in a lightning quick operation. Operation Barbarossa would be postponed for four weeks as a result of the need to invade Greece and Yugoslavia simultaneously.[51] The Croats would be won over with a promise of independence.

Hitler ordered the attacks on Yugoslavia and Greece to begin simultaneously on 6 April 1941. 'I intend to make a clean sweep in the Balkans,' he told his generals. 'It is time people got to know me better.'[52] He swiftly issued 'Directive No. 25' after the meeting. It stated that the military coup in Yugoslavia had completely changed the political situation in the Balkans and that Hitler's intention was now 'to break Yugoslavia'.[53]

Ribbentrop decided not to allow the popular Croat leader Vlado Maček to take over as the leader of the proposed independent Croatian government, but instead turned to Ante Pavelić, the founder of Ustaše, the fascist, ultranationalist and terrorist organization, to form a government. This decision ultimately proved disastrous because it resulted in civil war and terrorism in Yugoslavia, which dragged on throughout the remainder of the war.

On 28 March Hitler met the Hungarian ambassador Döme Sztójay in Berlin, where the Führer vented his anger over recent developments in Yugoslavia. 'Whom the gods destroy they first strike blind,' he told Sztójay bitterly. Current developments in Yugoslavia were a remarkable misfortune for that country, he added. The young king Peter II 'was a puppet of divergent forces' and if it came to war, Yugoslavia 'would be liquidated quickly'.[54]

On 30 March Hitler delivered a frank speech to 200 top military officers in the new Reich Chancellery, beginning at 11 a.m. and lasting for just over two hours. The purpose was to brief them on the reasoning behind Operation Barbarossa. Halder recorded the contents of the speech in his diary. Hitler began by saying that as Britain's hopes were pinned on assistance from the United States and the Soviet Union, the Bolshevik foe had to be eliminated first. Hitler did not underestimate Soviet military strength on paper. In numerical terms, the USSR had the strongest armed forces in the world. It possessed huge numbers of tanks and aircraft. Even so, Hitler thought that the modern tanks and aircraft of the *Wehrmacht* would quickly overwhelm them.

Hitler then bluntly spelled out his racial and ideological aims for invading the Soviet Union. Bolshevism was 'social criminality'. The communist was not a comrade before the invasion, nor would he be one afterwards. Therefore, the invasion would need to be one of utter 'annihilation' and 'extermination', fought outside the existing international treaties on war established at Geneva. The German-Soviet War would not end with an armistice or a peace treaty. Captured Soviet territory would simply be 'colonized'.

The conflict against the Soviet Union would be very different from the war in Western Europe, he continued. It aimed to exterminate Bolshevist Commissars and the communist intelligentsia. Individual commanders needed to brief troops about the brutal methods that were to be deployed and of the ideological issues at stake.[55]

In order to legitimize genocide, Hitler told his generals that the Soviet Union had never been a party to the Hague or the Geneva conventions on warfare. In reality, the Soviet Union had indicated a desire on 20 August 1940 to accede to the Hague Convention, which regulated the rules for the treatment of prisoners of war, as well as non-combatants in war, and acknowledged that in time of war the USSR would be guided by the Geneva Convention. Yet in the spring of 1941 the Soviet Union was still not officially a party to the Hague Convention or the Geneva Convention. Germany, however, was a signatory to both agreements and it was expected to abide by them under international law. So the German government intended to flout international law during its invasion of the Soviet Union when it had no legal basis to do so.[56]

The instructions Hitler delivered to officers at this important meeting would be codified by the Army High Command into what became known as the 'Commissar Order', duly signed by Keitel on 6 June 1941. This drew on previous discussions and drafts, but it was a document prepared by the German army and not by the SS, thereby making the *Wehrmacht* complicit in the genocide that followed.

The 'Commissar Order' was narrowly focused on the destruction of the 'Jewish-Bolshevik' political intelligentsia and party functionaries. Captured individuals would be taken to an army officer, who, satisfied by their identification, would order their immediate execution. 'In the struggle against Bolshevism,' the order continued, 'we must not assume that the enemy's conduct will be based on principles of humanity or international law. In particular, hate-inspired, cruel and inhuman treatment of prisoners of war can be expected on the part of all grades of political commissars, who are the real leaders of resistance.'

This order complemented a previous directive, issued by the army on 6 May 1941, under which officers were expected to shoot all Soviet residents who took part in hostile acts or resisted the German armed forces. If necessary, it was envisaged, collective measures of German reprisal operations could take place against the villages from which oppositional acts occurred.[57]

This order was distributed to all German troops in a document called *Guidelines to Troops*, which was issued on 19 May 1941. It was very ideological in tone, describing Bolshevism as 'the deadly enemy of the National Socialist German people'. Accordingly, it continued the struggle with the Soviet Union 'demands ruthless and energetic measures against Bolshevist agitators, guerrillas [also known as partisans], saboteurs, Jews, and the complete elimination of any active or passive resistance'. It remained to be seen how German soldiers in the field would interpret this order, but it left open the possibility of Jews, even if they had nothing to do with Bolshevism, being arbitrarily murdered.[58]

The 'Decree on the Exercise of Military Jurisdiction' operative during the invasion of the Soviet Union did away with the former requirement for German officers to convene court martials or in any way to punish the murderous actions of their troops. The only stipulation was for officers at battalion and regimental level to sanction the execution of individuals caught in – or suspected of being involved in – 'anti German' activity.

Hitler's war against the Soviet Union, therefore, contained three interwoven elements. First, it was an old-fashioned imperial war of territorial and economic conquest. Second, it was an ideological conflict: the final showdown between Fascism and communism. Third, it was a racial war of annihilation involving plans for widespread genocide.

Meanwhile, the Hungarian Prime Minister Pál Teleki told his cabinet that he strongly objected to Hungary's involvement in the upcoming German invasion of Yugoslavia, arguing that Hungary had already signed a non-aggression pact with Yugoslavia on 12 December 1940. Teleki also made it clear that he wanted to maintain Hungary's non-aligned status in the war. He was soon outvoted by his own cabinet members, who agreed to allow German troops to march into Hungary in preparation for the attack on Yugoslavia. In utter despair,

Teleki composed a brief suicide letter in his office and killed himself just after midnight on 3 April 1941, with a single pistol shot.

Pál Teleki's death shocked the Hungarian public. Miklós Horthy, the Regent of Hungary, sent a letter to Hitler shortly after Teleki's body had been discovered. He described Teleki as highly educated and 'the symbol of exaggerated correctness, of purity, of devotion to duty'. In his suicide letter Teleki had protested the fact that his country had breached its Friendship Pact with Yugoslavia and that it continued to collaborate with Germany. His death, Horthy concluded, 'has deeply shaken me and with me the entire nation'.[59]

Otto von Erdmannsdorf, the German ambassador to Hungary, reported that 'senseless rumours' were now circulating about Teleki's suicide. It was being said that Teleki had asked Horthy to resign and this amounted to high treason. It was also being suggested in Allied newspapers that his death had been murder and not suicide. There were other reports saying that Teleki had family troubles and was exhausted by over-work.[60]

Yōsuke Matsuoka, the Japanese Foreign Minister, visited Germany, Italy and the Soviet Union for diplomatic talks during March and April 1941. Matsuoka had been a keen supporter of the Tripartite Pact in 1940 and the German government now wanted to encourage Japan to move against Britain in the Far East. Goebbels ensured that Matsuoka felt welcome when he arrived in Berlin: 'Hundreds of thousands of people on the streets,' he wrote. 'My instructions have been followed to the letter. Matsuoka, whom I help receive at the station, gives an impression of great intelligence.'[61]

Hungarian Prime Minister Pál Teleki.

Ribbentrop met Matsuoka four times between 27 March and 5 April 1941. At the first meeting, on 27 March, Ribbentrop told him that German-Soviet relations, although outwardly 'formal and correct', were not friendly at all and seemed to be worsening. The British government had been cultivating closer relations with the Soviet Union ever since Sir Stafford Cripps became British ambassador to Moscow. However, Ribbentrop thought that Stalin was unlikely to embark on a collision course with Germany.[62]

The two men held further talks on the following day. Ribbentrop told Matsuoka that Hitler desired much closer cooperation between Germany and Japan. Once again Ribbentrop brought up the current difficulties that Germany was encountering with the Soviet Union. It was possible that the Soviet Union would set off on the 'wrong road' in its foreign policy, he added. Matsuoka then asked whether Hitler had considered a Russian-Japanese-German alliance. Ribbentrop said that closer collaboration with the Soviet Union was an 'impossibility' since both nations were ideologically incompatible. Stalin had only agreed to the Nazi-Soviet Pact solely out of pragmatism. If the policies of Germany and the Soviet Union did not remain in harmony, then the USSR would be crushed, Ribbentrop added.

In response, Matsuoka pointed out that Japan's policy was not to provoke war with the Soviet Union. On the contrary, Japan was keen to build closer relations with the USSR and to conclude a long-term trade agreement. Matsuoka asked what the German attitude would be if Japan negotiated a non-aggression pact or a neutrality treaty with the Soviet Union. Ribbentrop made no comment, but during this exchange he had indiscreetly dropped big hints of a possible war between Germany and the Soviet Union.[63]

Talks with Matsuoka continued on 29 March. Ribbentrop was concerned about Matsuoka's visit to Moscow for talks on his way back to Japan. Ribbentrop advised him 'not to go into things too deeply with the Russians', because Ribbentrop 'did not know how the situation would develop'. Ribbentrop wanted to emphasize to Matsuoka that a military conflict between Germany and the USSR was 'always within the realm of possibility'. He then added, in confidence, his personal view that the Soviet Union wanted the war to drag on, because a long war would make the people of Europe ripe for a Bolshevik revolution. In a similar spirit of candour, Matsuoka then revealed that he had already proposed a non-aggression pact to the Soviets, but that Molotov had suggested a neutrality agreement instead.[64]

Ribbentrop met Matsuoka for a fourth time on 5 April 1941. Matsuoka was very impressed by the confidence of victory in the war that he had observed in Germany and Italy during his visits. Ribbentrop then summed up what he wanted Matsuoka to report back to Japan. First, to emphasize the fact that Germany had already won the war. Second, there were no conflicts of interest between Japan and Germany. Third, it was in the interests of Japan to enter the war, because the circumstances would never again be more favourable than now. He advised Japan to attack British possessions in the Far East, but warned against a war with the United States.[65]

Matsuoka also met Hitler twice during his visits to Germany. The first meeting was held in Berlin on 27 March 1941. Hitler told him that the war's outcome was already decided. The position of Britain was completely hopeless and Hitler felt that the United States was not militarily ready for war. This opened great possibilities for Japan to expand in East Asia, he said, especially at the expense of the British Empire.

Matsuoka agreed about the opportunities now available, but he stressed that unprovoked military aggression always carried certain risks. There were, he added, differences within the Japanese government between a pro-Axis stance and those who wanted to come to some sort of accommodation with the United States and Britain. Some of these people still occupied important positions in the government and the armed forces. Matsuoka personally favoured a pro-Axis policy, but it was by no means certain which group would gain the upper hand within Japan.

Hitler asked Matsuoka about his recent meetings with Molotov and Stalin in Moscow. Matsuoka said it was a courtesy call, but he assured Hitler that Stalin believed the Anglo-Saxon nations to be the greatest hindrance to the new order in Europe. Matsuoka had asked Stalin if the differences between Japan and the Soviet Union could be eliminated, and he showed a willingness to discuss this further. It was agreed that Matsuoka would meet Stalin again on his return to Japan via the Soviet Union.[66]

Hitler met Matsuoka for a second time on 4 April 1941 in the new Reich Chancellery in Berlin. Matsuoka promised Hitler that he would use all of his power and influence to convince the Japanese people of the sincere friendship and esteem in which Japan was held by the German people. Hitler told Matsuoka that a war with the United States was 'undesirable', but it had already been factored into his own calculations. He promised that if Japan became involved in a war with the United States, then Germany would take part. Matsuoka thought that war with the United States was 'unavoidable'.

Hitler felt that the position of Japan at this point reminded him of his own decision to reoccupy the Rhineland in March 1936. He had thought it was a risk worth taking and events proved him right. Japan now had a similar opportunity to strike against the British Empire.

Matsuoka then admitted that the views he was expressing to Hitler could not be discussed within leading political and military circles in Japan, nor could he discuss these matters with the Emperor. Nevertheless, Matsuoka felt that the Japanese government would soon come around to his position. Hitler told him that he could rely on German discretion regarding all the discussions he had held in Berlin.[67] Unlike Ribbentrop, Hitler dropped no hints about the upcoming attack on the Soviet Union.

On his return journey to Japan, Matsuoka stopped off in Moscow to meet with Molotov and Stalin. He proposed a non-aggression pact between Japan and the Soviet Union, but finally agreed to sign a neutrality pact, which was concluded on 13 April 1941. It was based on three principles: friendship, respect for each other's territory, and neutrality in the case of war. It was emphasized that this agreement did not affect the terms of the Nazi-Soviet Pact or the Tripartite Pact.

For Japan, this agreement made sense, because if Germany intended to attack the Soviet Union – and Ribbentrop had clearly but unwisely hinted to Matsuoka that this was the case – then Japan would not be involved. It also helped further Japan's military aims in the Far East against Britain and the United States, without needing to worry about the Soviet Union.[68]

Stalin and Molotov both attended Matsuoka's departure by train on the famous Trans-Siberian Railway, surrounded by the diplomatic corps and a large retinue of press and radio reporters. Stalin commented to Matsuoka: 'The European problem can be solved in a natural way if Japan and the Soviets cooperate.' Friedrich-Werner Graf von der Schulenburg, the German ambassador, was also present on the platform during Matsuoka's departure ceremony. When Stalin suddenly caught sight of him, he walked up to him, placed his arm affectionately on his shoulders, and said: 'We must remain friends and you must do everything to that end.' He also turned to Colonel Hans Krebs, the German Acting Military Attaché, who was also present: 'We will remain friends with you whatever happens.'[69]

On 5 April 1941 Hitler wrote to Mussolini, expressing his deep frustration with Yugoslavia, which he had hoped would enter into friendly relations with the Axis. Instead, the Yugoslavians had shown their true colours and they would have been unpredictable neighbours. 'I am entering this fight', he concluded, 'with fanatic determination, for, come what may, victory will be on our side in the end.'[70] Mussolini wrote in reply: 'Yugoslavia is the most authentic creation of Versailles and deserves its fate. That the Serbian soldier is brave and tough, there is no doubt, but as a mass they are probably less strong, in view of the ethnic composition and the cultural differences. The struggle will be hard, but as to the victorious result, my certainty, like yours, is absolute.'[71]

Operation Marita opened at 5.15 a.m. on 6 April 1941 with simultaneous devastating attacks on Greece and Yugoslavia. The German High Command expected the operation to take two months, but this grossly overestimated the enemy's military strength. A friendship treaty between Yugoslavia and the Soviet Union had been hurriedly signed the previous day, but this was nullified when news came of the German invasion. Hitler presented the attack to the German people as a measured response to Yugoslavia being taken over by a 'Serbian clique'.

The war between Germany and Yugoslavia was a total military mismatch. The Yugoslavian army numbered 1 million men, divided into 28 infantry and 3 outdated cavalry divisions, supported by 100 ancient tanks. The Yugoslav Air Force, numbering 450 aircraft, was largely destroyed on the ground. The German army deployed 500,000 soldiers, spearheaded by its fearsome Panzer divisions. They were supported by less well-equipped Italian and Hungarian troops. The *Luftwaffe* mounted a devastating raid on Belgrade, the capital city, killing more than 17,000 civilians.

On 10 April Zagreb was easily captured. Croatia then declared itself an independent state, with Hitler's blessing. On 12 April the German army entered Belgrade, which by then was reduced to rubble. Hitler issued 'Directive No. 27' on the progress of the Balkan campaign on 13 April which noted the Yugoslavian army was 'crumbling'.[72]

The Yugoslavian army surrendered on 17 April. It had been a brilliantly organized operation by the *Wehrmacht*, given that Hitler had only decided to mount the attack on 27 March. Victory was achieved in eleven days for the loss of just 151 German troops. Around 344,000 Yugoslavian troops were taken prisoner. Once again, it was the organization and professionalism of the *Wehrmacht* that achieved victory, but Hitler took the credit. Another of his spur-of-the-moment gambles had paid off.

After victory in Yugoslavia, the German government was determined to crush Serb influence and annexed the northern part of Slovenia. Italy took over the Adriatic Coast and the administration of Montenegro, while Hungary occupied Bačka and the Bulgarians seized most of Macedonia. The pro-Nazi fascist leader Ante Pavelić took over the newly independent Croatia, which quickly absorbed the territory of Bosnia-Herzegovina within its borders. Pavelić also set in motion a massive programme of genocidal ethnic cleansing against Serbs, Gypsies and Jews. All non-Croats were excluded from citizenship. An estimated 300,000 Serbs were the victims of genocide in Croatia during the remainder of the war.

The German attack on Greece, which also began on 6 April, was designed to bolster the Italians and remove the British from the country. During this brief conflict, Hitler refused to allow the *Luftwaffe* to bomb Athens, which he regarded as the cradle of Western civilization. The Germans deployed 680,000 troops in Greece, supported by 565,000 Italians. In contrast, the Greeks had 430,000 men, supplemented by 62,612 troops of the British, Australian and New Zealand Expeditionary Force.

The swift thrusts into Greek territory by the two German Panzer Corps proved devastating. The Greek Prime Minister Alexandros Koryzis shot himself on 18 April as defeat loomed. The bulk of Greek forces surrendered on 23 April. On 27 April German troops marched into Athens and the swastika was raised over the Acropolis.

German losses in the Greek campaign numbered 1,099 dead and 385 missing. British Allied losses totalled 903 dead, with 13,598 captured by the Germans. Greek losses totalled 13,400 dead and 270,000 captured. In another 'Dunkirk-style' evacuation, 43,000 British Allied troops were rescued but once again left behind huge amounts of valuable equipment. It was yet another British humiliation on land against the vastly superior German army.[73]

The Greek people suffered terribly under German wartime occupation. A pro-Nazi puppet government was soon installed, but real power lay with the German army. Rationing of food was held below subsistence level. In the first eighteen months of the German occupation, an estimated 43,000 Greeks starved to death as the Germans requisitioned olive oil, oranges and lemons for their own

The swastika flies in Athens after the Axis victory over Greece.

use. The Greek population was reduced by 300,000 during the entire duration of the war. The German occupiers dealt with any sign of resistance with extreme brutality.

In 'Directive No. 28' entitled Operation Mercury, issued on 25 April 1941, Hitler decided to capitalize on his military victory in the Balkans by ordering a German landing on Crete. The plan was to drive the British out of the Eastern Mediterranean and to acquire air bases from which to bomb Egypt and Libya.[74]

Schulenburg sent a memorandum from Moscow to Ribbentrop on 28 April stating that there was absolutely no danger of the Soviet Union attacking Germany. Weizsäcker was then asked by Ribbentrop to write a memorandum on the consequences of a German-Soviet conflict. In response Weizsäcker wrote that while it might seem attractive to deliver a death blow to communism, the real issue was whether the Soviet Union's defeat would really bring about the defeat of Britain, as Hitler assumed. If Germany believed Britain was close to collapse, Weizsäcker continued, then why give it an ally in the USSR? He admitted that Germany's attack on the Soviet Union might well secure food supplies for Germany to assist a longer war of attrition against Britain but it was more likely that the attack on the Soviet Union might give Britain a moral boost to continue the war.[75]

On 2 May 1941 General Georg Thomas held a conference on the economic planning for Operation Barbarossa. State secretaries from all the leading ministerial agencies involved in planning the invasion were present. There was no ambiguity at this meeting concerning the fate that awaited ordinary Soviet citizens. Thomas then outlined ideas identical to what became known as the 'Hunger Plan'. This had been drafted during the winter of 1940–41 by Herbert Backe, the State Secretary for Food and Agriculture, and the head of the Food Division of Göring's Four-Year Plan Office. Backe suggested that as the German army advanced through the Soviet Union it should be fed from the 'breadbasket' of Ukraine. Consequently, the urban population of the western Soviet Union would be starved to death. Backe estimated that some 20 or 30 million 'Slavs' would perish during the German invasion.

These genocidal plans were openly discussed at the meeting. The minutes recorded three agreed conclusions: '1. The war can only be continued, if the entire *Wehrmacht* is fed from Russia in the third year of the war [1941]. 2. If we take what we need out of the country, there can be no doubt that many millions of people will die of starvation.

Stalin with Yōsuka Matsuoka, Japanese Foreign Minister, prior to the signing of the Soviet-Japanese Neutrality Pact on 13 April 1941.

3. The most important issues are the recovery and removal of oil seeds, oil cake and only then the removal of grain.'[76]

On 4 May 1941, Hitler delivered a speech to the Reichstag to celebrate his victories over Yugoslavia and Greece but used the occasion to deliver a blistering attack on Winston Churchill: 'As a soldier he is a bad politician and as politician he is a bad soldier,' he said. He derided Churchill's decision to intervene in the Balkan conflict in the first place, which meant the British had 'managed to lose two theatres of war in one single blow'. As for Yugoslavia, he said that the coup, organized by a group of 'bribed conspirators', had provoked him to attack, because he was not prepared for Germany to be treated in such a manner.[77]

On the following day, Stalin spoke at a banquet at the Kremlin for Soviet officers and graduates of military academies. There are differing accounts of what he said at this gathering, but most historians suggest that he warned of the imminent danger of a war between the Soviet Union and Germany. In response to this new situation, Stalin announced on 6 May that he would be taking Molotov's place as the head of government (the Chairman of the People's Commissars), although Molotov would stay on as the Deputy Chairman and Foreign Minister. This change at the top was reported in the international press as a clear sign that relations between the Soviet Union and Germany were sharply deteriorating.[78]

After his military success in the Balkans, Hitler returned to the Berghof for some much-needed rest and recuperation. It was here on 10 May 1941 that he received the unexpected news that the Deputy Führer, Rudolf Hess, had taken off at 6 p.m. from Augsburg aerodrome, self-piloting an unarmed Messerschmitt ME-110 fighter plane bound for Scotland. Hess wanted to meet Douglas Douglas-Hamilton, the Duke of Hamilton, whom he understood to be sympathetic to Germany and Britain working together. It was a poorly conceived personal 'peace mission' aimed at negotiating an end to hostilities before Operation Barbarossa began.

Hess bailed out of his plane, with a parachute, twelve miles from Hamilton's stately home. At around 10 p.m. he hit the ground so heavily that he broke his ankle. A local Scottish farmer spotted him, then summoned the Home Guard, who arrested him. In a bizarre meeting with Hamilton, Hess claimed that if Germany won the war, the consequences would be catastrophic for Britain, and it was therefore sensible to conclude a peace settlement.

The wreckage of Hess's Messerschmitt Bf 110.

Churchill, on hearing of Hess's mission, refused to have anything at all to do with him. The Deputy Führer was brought to London and then imprisoned in the Tower of London. Hess was questioned by Ivone Kirkpatrick, the former First Secretary at the British embassy in Berlin and a fluent German-speaker. Kirkpatrick concluded that Hess's offer of peace differed little from what Hitler had been saying publicly and repeatedly ever since the war began. Hess became agitated when he finally realized there was no possibility of him meeting any prominent British cabinet minister, let alone the Prime Minister. Throughout his interrogation, he never mentioned the upcoming attack on the Soviet Union. He even denied the suggestion put to him by Kirkpatrick that it was imminent.[79]

In the period leading up to his flight, Hess had come under the influence of Albrecht Haushofer, an opponent of Hitler, but whose father had inspired Hitler's *Lebensraum* expansionist strategies. The younger Haushofer knew the Duke of Hamilton and wrongly thought that he had some influence over the higher echelons of the British government.[80] In a letter to his wife, written after his capture, Hess admitted that prior to his flight he had become 'not quite normal'. His personal secretary Hildegard Fath noticed that Hess had seemed 'in a world of his own' when she spoke to him in the days before he left.[81]

Hitler's first reaction was to suggest that Hess had completely lost his mind: 'It's a different person. Something must have happened to him – some mental disturbance,' he commented.[82] Goebbels noted in his diary:

DAILY MIRROR, Tuesday, May 13, 1941.

Daily Mirror

MAY 13

No. 11,675

ONE PENNY

Registered at the G.P.O. as a Newspaper.

HESS, HITLER'S DEPUTY, LANDS IN BRITAIN

THIS IS HESS

HESS, the man who was Hitler's confidant, his adoring friend, companion of his unsuccessful days, is 44.

This may not be the first visit Hess has made to this country since crisis came to Europe. It is confidently believed by some that the mysterious visitor who landed at Croydon from a German plane a few days before war broke out was Hess.

Handsome, dark, strongly built, he is the idol of millions of German women. If he hadn't been a Nazi leader he might easily have been a film star.

Hitler's right-hand man since the days of the Munich beer cellar putsch, he still carries the scar of a beer jug thrown while he was Hitler's bodyguard in one of the early Nazi riots.

Thrown into prison with Hitler when the Munich putsch failed, he helped him write Mein Kampf.

He was the one man in Germany allowed to see the Fuehrer without appointment.

Whenever Hitler had one of his fits, it was said in Germany, he allowed none to come near him except Hess.

Hess, son of a wealthy Ger-

man merchant, was born in Egypt. He went to an English school in Alexandria and speaks perfect English.

He would have been prepared, it is thought, to negotiate rather than go to war.

He has left behind him in Germany his wife and little boy aged 4.

How highly he was regarded by Hitler was evident in the speech Hitler made to the Reichstag on the day he invaded Poland.

Hitler then named Hess as his successor in war, with Hess as the man to follow Goering.

The wreckage of the plane from which Hess landed.

U.S. PINS VICHY

AMERICA wants to know what Count de Brinon, French representative in Paris, meant by the threat that if the U.S. tried to occupy Dakar it would have to be by force.

To obtain an explanation, Admiral W. D. Leahy, United States Ambassador to Vichy, has asked for an interview with Marshal Petain, says the British United Press.

Marshal Petain arrived in Vichy yesterday from Antibes and was to consider reports made by Admiral Darlan, French Vice-Premier, on his conversations with the Germans.

Darlan left Paris on Friday night and was reported in Vichy to have negotiated with "high German personalities"

RUDOLF HESS

RUDOLF HESS, Hitler's deputy, the man who knows Germany's every secret, has landed in Scotland, having flown from Germany in defiance of Hitler's desperate efforts to stop him.

How He Arrived

This is the story of how Hess reached this country, as telephoned on Sunday by a "Daily Mirror" reporter who was near the spot at the time.

A GERMAN airman who says he stole his plane has landed in a lonely part of Scotland. He baled out just before the plane crashed and landed in the fields of a farm near Glasgow. It was moonlight.

Overhead we had seen the plane circling for some minutes. It came down low. We thought it was searching for a landing place. It crashed.

A ploughman heard the noise and ran from his cottage. He saw the wrecked plane. Not far away was the pilot.

He limped. It was obvious he had injured one of his legs.

Tea in a Cottage

The German offered no resistance. The ploughman told me that as he approached the pilot, "a man about fifty," smiled and appeared glad he had landed in Britain.

The plane carried no bombs. Those who spoke to him told me this mystery pilot speaks good English. His first inquiry was: "Where am I?"

Then, to a few Scottish cranfrumen, he told how he had stolen the plane and flown it to this country.

The ploughman took his captive to his home and offered him a cup of tea. All he would drink was a cup of water. He remained in the cottage until Army officers arrived and took him to a military camp.

ONE DAY AT WHIT FOR NON-VITAL WORKERS

There will be no official Whitsun holiday this year.

But workers in non-essential trades and arms workers who can be spared will get one day.

"We hope factory chiefs will be able to arrange a day's holiday for workers," said the Ministry of Aircraft Production yesterday. "But men and women on vital jobs cannot be spared."

PANIC AT WAR RUMOUR

Tokio (Japan) stock market dropped sharply as the result of a persistent rumour that America is ready to enter the war.

This announcement was made to the Pressmen of the world at the Ministry of Information a few minutes before midnight last night.

The following statement was issued from 10, Downing-street, 11.20 p.m. last night:

"Rudolf Hess, the deputy Fuehrer of Germany and Party Leader of the National Socialist Party, has landed in Scotland in the following circumstances.

"On the night of Saturday the 10th inst. a Messerschmitt 110 was reported by our patrols to have crossed the coast of Scotland and to be flying in the direction of Glasgow.

Guns Unloaded

"Since a Messerschmitt 110 would not have the fuel to return to Germany this report was at first disbelieved. However, later on a Messerschmitt 110 crashed near Glasgow with its guns unloaded.

"Shortly afterwards a German officer who had baled out was found with his parachute in the neighbourhood suffering from a broken ankle.

"He was taken to hospital in Glasgow where he first gave his name as Horn, but later on declared that he was Rudolf Hess.

"He brought with him various photographs of himself at different ages apparently in order to establish his identity.

"These photographs were deemed to be photographs of Hess by several people who knew him personally.

"Accordingly an officer of the Foreign Office who was closely acquainted with Hess before the war has been sent up by aeroplane to see him in hospital."

The first news of Hess's flight
Continued on Back Page

VOICE OF THE GERMANS

Nominally Hitler's deputy, Hess was much more. He wielded tremendous influence over the Fuehrer, wrote his speeches, worked out policy with him, and more thca Goering was the power behind the scenes.

In recent years he was the mouth and more the voice of the German people, and there was a large section of the Nazi Party as well as of the ordinary people who thought Hess should have been appointed to succeed Hitler instead of coming after Goering.

SUEZ RAIDED AGAIN

Enemy aircraft raided the Suez Canal zone for the third successive night,

The Scots ploughman who found Hess.

I read the letters that Hess left behind for the Führer: totally confused schoolboy amateurism, saying that he intended to go to England, make the hopelessness of their position clear to them, bring down Churchill's government with the aid of Lord Hamilton in Scotland, and then make a peace which would save London's face. Unfortunately, he failed to realize that Churchill would have him immediately arrested. It is all just too stupid. A fool like this was the Führer's deputy. It is scarcely conceivable.[83]

Stalin was convinced that Hess had gone to Britain with Hitler's blessing as part of a pre-arranged plan to negotiate a peace deal. Lord Beaverbrook told Ivan Maisky, the Soviet ambassador: 'Oh, Hess, of course, is Hitler's emissary.' Beaverbrook's theory was that Hitler was counting on 'British Quislings' to overthrow Churchill and conclude an Anglo-German peace deal.[84] There is no evidence, however, to support the idea of any collusion between Hitler and Hess prior to his flight.

Hitler decided to abolish the post of the Führer's deputy, renaming Hess's office the Party Chancellery and appointing the loyal Nazi Martin Bormann to lead it. Goebbels considered Hess's flight to be so embarrassing that it was impossible for him to put any propaganda spin on it. He decided the best policy was to 'systematically keep quiet' in the hope the furore surrounding it would subside.[85] As for Hess, Goebbels noted: 'He is finished so far as the Führer is concerned. The Führer is shattered. He has been spared nothing. He condemns Hess in the strongest terms, but grants him a degree of idealism.'[86]

Ribbentrop met Mussolini at the Palazzo Venezia in Rome on 13 May 1941. Not surprisingly, the Hess affair was the chief topic of conversation. Ribbentrop told Mussolini that when Hitler heard the news he was completely 'dumbfounded'. Apparently, Hess had been suffering pain from a gall bladder complaint for some time and had 'fallen under the spell of hypnotists and natural medicine cranks'. Ribbentrop thought that Hess had acted from loyal motives in the hope of negotiating a peace settlement and he had convinced himself he could work with 'British pro-fascists' to achieve this. He failed to realize that the Duke of Hamilton was not remotely pro German and his plan was doomed to failure. In reply, Mussolini thought that this embarrassing affair would gradually blow over.[87]

On 20 May 1941 Operation Mercury – the German airborne occupation of Crete – began. Involving 14,000 paratroopers and 15,000 mountain troops, it was the first airborne invasion in military history. The capture of Crete had not been mentioned in the original plan for

Daily Mirror reports the bizarre flight of Rudolf Hess to Scotland on 10 May 1941.

Operation Marita. Hitler was unsure beforehand about the wisdom of an airborne assault, but he was persuaded by the *Luftwaffe* that the British and their imperial allies could be easily defeated. The island was defended by around 40,000 British, Australian, New Zealand and Greek troops.

The Germans suffered many casualties during the first day of the invasion and the prospects were good for a successful defence of the island by the British-led forces. Once reinforcements had arrived by air and sea, however, the Germans started to gain the upper hand, capturing valuable airfields, then gradually pushing the British Allied defenders southwards.

For the first time since the war began, tanks did not play a major part in a German offensive. They were unsuited to the mountain terrain of Crete. At any rate the *Luftwaffe* soon established air superiority, because the British did not have enough fighter planes available. The *Luftwaffe* also inflicted huge losses on the Royal Navy during the brief conflict. The aircraft carrier HMS *Formidable* and two battleships were badly damaged, while six British destroyers and three cruisers were sunk. A total of 2,011 British navy personnel perished. These were the worst losses the Royal Navy would suffer in any single engagement during the entire Second World War.

By 26 May British Allied forces came to the conclusion that the position in Crete was hopeless. Once again there was a humiliating British evacuation, which took place between 28 May and 1 June, with 16,500 men embarked. During the conflict in Crete, the British Allies lost 3,489 men and a further 11,835 became POWs. The Germans suffered 3,352 dead, with 220 planes destroyed. Hitler had proved that a massive paratroop attack was possible, but accepted it was a high-risk strategy, saying: 'Crete proves that the days of the paratroopers are over.'[88] Hitler refused to sanction any similar airborne assaults, which helped to save British-controlled Cyprus and Malta from falling into German hands.

Crete was another British-led disaster. Churchill's decision for the British Empire to fight on in 1940 was starting to look like a mistake by the spring of 1941.[89]

If Hitler had not been so single-mindedly determined to destroy the Soviet Union in the summer of 1941 he could have dealt the British Empire a mortal blow in Africa and in the Middle East. Yet Hitler never even discussed capitalizing on his triumph in Crete. He continued to think that the British would come to their senses. 'I believe that the end of this war will mark the beginning of a durable friendship with England,' he told his military generals. 'But first we must give her the knockout – for only so can we live at peace with her; the Englishman can only respect someone who has first knocked him out.'[90]

On 21 May all of the cadets at the Security Police training school in Berlin-Charlottenburg were assigned to *Einsatzgruppen* units for Operation Barbarossa. By this time, training courses were being held regularly at the border police training school in Pretzsch, north-east of Leipzig, and in two other similar training facilities in Düben and Bad Schmiedeberg in Saxony. The instructions given to members of the *Einsatzgruppen* at these meetings seemingly went way beyond the original 'Commissar Order' and included a secret order for the widespread killing of Soviet Jews in the USSR.[91] As Dr Walter Blume, an *Einsatzgruppen* unit commander, admitted in testimony at the Nuremberg Trials, at a meeting of the *Einsatzgruppen* commanders held at Prince Charles Palace in Berlin on 17 June 1941, a 'Führer Order' to murder all Jews in the Soviet Union was relayed by Heydrich and discussed openly.

When they met at the Brenner Pass on 3 June 1941, Hitler told Mussolini that German relations with the Vichy government were 'rather difficult' at present. He could not be certain whether or not the Vichy government was secretly cooperating with the Free French leader Charles de Gaulle in London. Hitler added that Germany had allowed 700,000 of the original 1.9 million French POWs to return home, but henceforth no further French prisoners would be released. Among the current French government, Hitler felt that Admiral François Darlan was the most reliable, as he was thoroughly anti-British. On the whole, however, Hitler suspected that most of the Vichy politicians were anti-German and that they would resist closer collaboration with Germany.[92]

Hitler met the Romanian leader Ion Antonescu in the Führerbau in Munich on 11 June. Antonescu congratulated him on his spectacular victories in the Balkan campaign and Crete. In reply, Hitler confided to Antonescu the fact that during the winter of 1940–41 Germany had come to the realization that the Soviet Union was now an enemy of the Reich. Recent Soviet troop concentrations on the eastern border had only confirmed this impression.

Hitler then promised that in return for military assistance in the German attack on the Soviet Union he would restore Romania's former provinces of northern Bukovina and Bessarabia, which had been seized by Stalin in 1940. An enthusiastic Antonescu said that there should be no delay in beginning the German attack on the Soviet Union. He was very optimistic about the outcome and he advised Hitler not to be deterred by the precedent of Napoleon's ill-fated invasion of Russia in 1812.[93]

İsmet İnönü, the President of Turkey, wrote to Hitler on 12 June to thank him for making positive comments about Turkey in his Reichstag speech on 4 May. He agreed that there were no points of divergence between Germany and Turkey, and he wanted to open talks to maintain relations based on mutual friendship and trust.[94] This led to the signing in Ankara on 18 June 1941 of a German-Turkish Treaty of Friendship and Non-Aggression, which became effective on the same day. It was agreed that both nations would respect the integrity and inviolability of their territories and would not take measures of any sort aimed directly or indirectly against the other party. This German-Turkish agreement remained in force until 23 February 1945.[95]

On 14 June the German High Command informed Army Group commanders that the codeword 'Dortmund' would be used to signify the start of the attack on the Soviet Union. The codeword 'Altona' would indicate a postponement or cancellation of the attack. On the following day it was finally confirmed that Operation Barbarossa would begin on 22 June at 3 a.m. (German time).[96]

Hitler sent a letter to Antonescu on 18 June giving him details of the 'definite position' he had now taken towards the Soviet Union. His intention, he said, was to employ the *Wehrmacht* in the near future to deal with Russia 'once and for all'. He would personally provide the unified command of this 'tremendous offensive operation'. As to the deployment of the Romanian armed forces, Hitler promised: 'I will take the liberty of submitting further proposals when the time is ripe.'[97]

For months before the attack on the Soviet Union, Stalin had received numerous intelligence reports indicating that Germany intended to invade, and most probably in mid-June. On 20 March, for instance, Sumner Welles, the US Under-Secretary of State, had warned Konstantin Umansky, the Soviet ambassador, the German attack would begin in June 1941. In Tokyo, Richard Sorge – Stalin's reliable spy, who had built up an impressive list of contacts with the German embassy and well-placed sources in the Japanese diplomatic community – warned Stalin of a planned attack by Germany. Sorge even predicted the attack date was 20 June 1941, which was only two days out from the actual date of the invasion.

The Soviet military attaché in Berlin had sent several reports to Moscow in June, noting that 140 German divisions were massing along the Russian border. The British and American governments saw multiplying evidence of plans for a German attack, especially in the huge build-up of troops in German-occupied Poland. Churchill and Roosevelt both sent secret intelligence messages to Stalin, indicating that an attack was coming soon. A sceptical Stalin marked these reports in pen with words such as 'suspect', 'disinformation' or 'suspicious'.

Stalin's faith in the Nazi-Soviet Pact remained unshakable. It seemed inconceivable to him that Hitler would risk a war on two fronts. Stalin could imagine Hitler lying to Chamberlain, but not to him. A copy of the actual Operation Barbarossa plan even came into the hands of the Soviet government days before the attack, but it was dismissed as not being genuine. Stalin's failure to heed the warning signs was in part due to a long-standing mistrust of the motives of Western capitalist states.[98]

On the eve of the attack on the Soviet Union, Hitler dictated a letter to his chief ally Mussolini, finally informing him that Operation Barbarossa would begin the following day. The letter began with a reference to Hitler's 'months of nerve-wracking waiting'. He felt that he could wait no longer, as this would only lead to disaster next year. The aim was to end any hope of the British for support from Stalin. It was also important to end communist rule in Russia, as this represented a great danger to the future of Europe. The invasion would also secure a common food supply for Germany and Italy in Ukraine. Hitler concluded:

> Since I struggled through to this decision, I again feel spiritually free. The partnership with the Soviet Union, in spite of the complete sincerity of the efforts to bring about a final conciliation, was nevertheless often very irksome to me, for in some way or other it seemed to me to be a break with my whole [ideological] origin, my concepts and my former obligations. I am now happy to be rid of these mental agonies.[99]

Mussolini was awoken at 3 a.m. on 22 June 1941 to read the contents of Hitler's letter. 'At night, I don't even disturb my servants,' he commented, 'but the Germans make me jump out of bed without the slightest consideration.'[100]

The next day, Mussolini replied to Hitler in an exceptionally positive manner. He agreed that the so-called 'Russian question' needed

[overleaf]
German troops moving forward during the attack on the Soviet Union in summer of 1941.

a 'radical solution'. For Mussolini, there were many advantages in defeating the Soviet Union: it would deprive Britain of its last hope on the European continent, and it would bring the Axis back to its anticommunist political doctrine, which had been abandoned for purely tactical reasons by the Nazi-Soviet Pact. In sum, Mussolini gave 'enthusiastic approval' to Hitler's decision to attack the Soviet Union and he predicted that the campaign would result in a 'dazzling victory'. He made no mention of the fact that Hitler had kept him in the dark until the night before the attack began.[101]

At 4.30 a.m. (Russian time) silence on the battlefield was shattered by German artillery booming out over the Soviet border positions. Within minutes, massed squadrons of *Luftwaffe* aircraft were bombing undefended airfields, administering a devastating blow to the Soviet Air Force while its planes were still on the ground. An estimated 1,200 Soviet bombers and fighters were destroyed on the first day of Operation Barbarossa.[102] With air superiority, German tanks swept across the largely undefended Soviet frontier, followed by the infantry on foot, with its vast horse-drawn supplies, and, bringing up the rear, the murderous *Einsatzgruppen*.

Never in the history of warfare had such a colossal invading force ever been deployed. The German army that attacked the Soviet Union seemed invincible at the outset. The aim was to destroy the Red Army up to the defensive Dvina–Dnieper River line, around 186 miles from the western border of the Soviet Union.

The attack on the Soviet Union was undoubtedly the defining event of Hitler's attempt to dominate Europe by force. The Soviet Union was the largest country in the world, twice the geographical size of the United States or China, and five times the size of India. Its rivers, lakes, steppes and mountains were all vast. In 1941 Russia's borders were 2,000 miles wide and it was flat land all the way to Moscow. To the west was European Russia. To the east was Siberia, stretching all the way to the Bering Sea and the North Pacific Ocean. To reach Moscow, any invading army would need to be sure of sustaining long supply lines.[103]

The fighting strength of the German army had increased from 5.7 million men in 1940 to 7.3 million in 1941: amounting to 85 per cent of all German males aged between 20 and 30.[104] A further 2.12 million teenagers aged 16 to 19 were also undergoing military training. The remaining men in the German population were either unfit for military service or deemed indispensable to the economy.[105]

For the initial attack on the Soviet Union on 22 June 1941 the German army deployed 153 divisions, with 17 Panzer and 13 motorized infantry units: a staggering overall total of 3.2 million troops.[106] The Germans could draw on 3,350 tanks, 600,000 motor vehicles, 2,770 aircraft and 7,184 artillery guns. Accompanying them, too, were 600,000 horses, dragging wagons full of moving artillery, ammunition and food supplies.[107]

The German invading force was further supplemented by Romanian and Finnish divisions, and, after 24 June, by Hungarian, Slovakian and Italian armies. Even a small volunteer Spanish unit, known as the Blue Division, participated in Operation Barbarossa. These combined forces brought the total strength of the Axis invaders up to 3.8 million.

As with previous battles, Germany's military leaders expected victory to be achieved in a matter of weeks. Hitler was convinced that communist Russia was a house of cards that would collapse under the military weight of the *Wehrmacht*, and he uttered the now famous phrase: 'You only have to kick in the door and the whole rotten structure will come crashing down.'[108]

It was not just Hitler who was overconfident. His faith in a swift victory over the Soviet Union was shared by his military commanders. Leading tank commander Heinz Guderian recalled that at meetings of the German High Command in the run-up to Barbarossa there was 'an unshakable optimism' in the success of the operation.[109] Another tank commander, Erich Hoepner, commented: 'The war with Russia is a vital part of the German fight for existence. It is the old fight of the German against the Slav, the defence of European culture against the Muscovite-Asiatic flood and the repulse of Jewish blood.'[110] The immense distances of the Soviet Union, the cruel winters and the lack of modern roads were ignored.

The German led attack forces stretched along the vast western border of the Soviet Union, from Finland in the north to the Black Sea in the south. The German army was organized into three huge army groups. Army Group North, commanded by the veteran Field Marshal Wilhelm Ritter von Leeb, aimed to move to the north – spearheaded by its Panzer divisions – to capture the Baltic states, before then speeding to Leningrad and laying siege to the city. It was supported by sixteen divisions of the Finnish army, which mainly operated in the Baltic states.

Army Group Centre, with fifty divisions, led by Field Marshal Fedor von Bock, was the strongest of the three German army groups.

It aimed to capture the former Polish cities of Minsk in Belarus and Smolensk in Russia, and would eventually head to Moscow, following the exact route of Napoleon's ill-fated 1812 invasion.

Keen to avoid history repeating itself, Hitler refused to make the capture of Moscow the key objective of Operation Barbarossa at the outset. Instead, he wanted to prioritize the seizure of important industrial and agricultural resources. This task was assigned to Army Group South, with thirty-three divisions, under the experienced field marshal Gerd von Rundstedt, supported by an assortment of Romanian, Hungarian, Slovakian, Italian and Croatian forces. Its principal objectives were economic rather than ideological: to advance south to capture the bread-rich Ukraine and its capital Kiev, and then to seize the oilfields in the Caucasus and eventually Stalingrad, the great industrial centre situated on the Volga River.

The only natural barrier to the German attack was the impassable, 200-mile-wide freshwater Pripet Marshes, which separated the operating areas of Army Group Centre and Army Group South. The rail network serving the north, leading to Moscow and Leningrad, was divided from that in the south, which passes through Ukraine, by the impassable Pripet Marshes.

In defence against the German attack, the Red Army deployed 240 divisions, with 158 of these (comprising 2.6 million men) deployed near the poorly defended western border. These were primarily infantry 'rifle' divisions dependent upon horses for transport. The Soviet Union had 24,000 tanks and 10,000 aircraft, but nearly all of these were outdated.[111]

At 5.30 a.m. on 22 June 1941 Goebbels read out on German national radio Hitler's proclamation to the German people, announcing the attack on the Soviet Union. The German public had no inkling this attack would happen beforehand. Goebbels adopted a sombre tone during the broadcast. He had to justify Germany starting yet another major war and breaking the Nazi-Soviet Pact.

Hitler's feeble explanation – in the address read out by Goebbels – was to claim that the German invasion of the USSR was really a pre-emptive strike to stop British encirclement; and also, it was falsely alleged, because Stalin planned to invade Germany. But an ideological justification was added: 'Now that the Führer has unmasked the treachery of the Bolshevik rulers, National Socialists and hence the German people are reverting to the principles which impelled them from the beginning – the struggle against plutocracy and Bolshevism.'[112]

According to Goebbels, Stalin and his 'Jewish-Bolshevik' leaders in Moscow had been planning to impose Bolshevism on the German people; they were constantly undermining the Nazi-Soviet Pact and secretly plotting with Churchill and Roosevelt. It was all part of a supposed conspiracy of the Jewish and Anglo-Saxon warmongers with the Jewish ruling powers in Moscow. To counteract this imagined conspiracy, Germany's mission in the war was no longer the protection of individual countries, but rather, in Hitler's words, the salvation of Europe: 'Today I have therefore determined to lay the fate and the future of the German Reich and our *Volk* again into the hands of our soldiers. May the Lord Almighty help us especially in this battle!'[113]

The attack on the Soviet Union was a major turning point in German attitudes towards the war. From the very beginning, the public was divided on the wisdom of waging war against the USSR. A report by the SD on the initial public reaction to the invasion noted that it had taken most people completely by surprise. Few had expected it. Worries were expressed about the prolongation of the war and its expansion into a world war. Women were particularly worried about the fate of family members directly involved in the fighting. It was easy, however, for the Nazis to tap into widespread anti-Bolshevik feelings. Many swallowed Hitler's propaganda line that the 'treacherous conduct' of the Soviet Union had to be met by force.[114]

By July 1941, despite the rapid German advance in the east, the 'general mood' was viewed as being 'depressed, embittered and angered'. For the rest of the year, the public mood continued to deteriorate.[115] An SD report in Stuttgart recorded: 'Everywhere one finds the opinion that in this war the little people are the losers once more.'[116] By September, letters home from the soldiers were deeply pessimistic.[117]

In Britain, on the evening of 22 June, Prime Minister Churchill (who had recently remarked, 'If Hitler invaded Hell I would make at least a favourable reference to the Devil in the House of Commons') made a powerful speech to the British public on BBC radio, offering full support to the Soviet Union and pledging: 'We are resolved to destroy Hitler and every vestige of the Nazi regime. We will never parley, we will never negotiate with Hitler or any of his gang.' President Roosevelt also promised to 'give all the aid we can to Russia'.[118]

In private, Churchill – who had little faith in the Red Army – thought that the Soviet Union would be swiftly defeated, but he welcomed the extension of the conflict, because he thought it made it more likely that the United States would now enter the war, especially if the Germans proved victorious in the Soviet Union and Hitler's power was further increased. Churchill felt that only America's entry into the war would ensure the defeat of the Axis nations.

The entry of the Soviet Union into the war meant that Britain and its empire no longer stood alone. The opening-up of a new front in the war brought welcome respite for British civilians. In the first six months of 1941 there had been 20,374 British fatalities from German air raids. However, in the last six months of the year this fell dramatically to 1,467. The total British civilian bombing deaths in 1942 were 4,150, falling to 3,450 in 1943. More people died in car accidents in Britain from 1942 to 1945 than in German bombing raids.[119]

Stalin immediately asked the British to open up a Second Front against Germany on mainland Europe. Churchill rejected this idea as 'impossible' in the short term, but he promised military aid and pledged to increase bombing attacks on German cities. Dropping bombs on German cities in the west instead of putting boots on the ground in the east became Britain's chief means of assisting the Soviet Union for the remainder of the war.[120]

The Red Army was totally unprepared for the huge German attack. On the night of 21 June, Stalin went to bed before midnight at his dacha in Kuntsevo, near Moscow. At 4.45 a.m. the phone rang. It was answered by a duty officer. On the end of the line was the Chief of the Army Staff General Georgy Zhukov, who asked to speak to Stalin. 'Comrade Stalin is sleeping,' came the reply. 'Wake him up immediately, the Germans are bombing our cities!' There was a brief silence. Stalin then picked up the phone. Still unable to believe that Hitler knew anything about this attack, Stalin ordered the Red Army not to respond with artillery or bombing. Then he asked Zhukov to assemble the Politburo in the Kremlin immediately.

The German invasion was a personal disaster for Stalin. The Nazi-Soviet Pact had been largely his own creation. He had trusted Hitler implicitly and he now felt bitterly betrayed. 'Lenin left us a great inheritance,' he said, 'and we, his heirs, have fucked it up.'[121] At the hastily convened meeting of the Politburo, Stalin argued that it was still not certain this was war, as the German government had issued no formal declaration.

In fact, Ribbentrop had already met Vladimir Dekanozov, the Soviet ambassador, in Berlin at 4 a.m. (German time) to give him an explanation for the outbreak of war. He blamed it on the Soviet Union's 'hostile policy' towards Germany and falsely claimed that the

Soviets were massing troops on the German border. This explanation did not satisfy Dekanozov at all, who called the German invasion an 'act of insolent and unprovoked aggression'.[122]

In Moscow, Friedrich-Werner Graf von der Schulenburg, the German ambassador, was summoned to the Kremlin by Molotov at 9.30 a.m. Schulenburg informed Molotov that a state of war now existed between Germany and the Soviet Union, although he never presented an official declaration of war. In reply, Molotov said: 'What have we done to deserve this?' The German pretext for war was all nonsense, he added, as there hadn't been any Soviet troop movements that threatened Germany.[123]

When Molotov informed Stalin of the news that Germany had indeed invaded the Soviet Union, something he had not fully taken in, he sank back in his chair in a state of shock. He then assured his Politburo colleagues that 'the enemy will be beaten, all along the line'.[124] Deeply depressed, Stalin retreated to his dacha and did not return to Moscow until 1 July 1941. It was left to Molotov to inform the Russian people on national radio at twelve noon that the German-Soviet War had begun. 'Our cause is just,' Molotov said. 'The enemy will be smashed; victory will be ours.'[125]

On 23 June 1941, a Soviet supreme command headquarters was established. On 30 June a Committee of National Defence was also set up, known as *Stavka*, consisting of Stalin, Molotov, Stalin's party deputy Georgy Malenkov, the former Minister of Defence Kliment Voroshilov and Lavrenti Beria, head of the fearsome People's Commissariat for Internal Affairs (NKVD), the secret police. To this group four other army figures were added: Semyon Timoshenko, Georgy Zhukov, Boris Shaposhnikov and Semyon Budenny.

Martial law was declared in the western Soviet Union. A labour conscription law compelled all men aged eighteen to forty five and all women aged between eighteen and forty to work eight hours a day constructing defences. The working day was extended by three hours. All leave and public holidays were suspended. Some 50,000 factories in the west, mostly small-scale workshops, were dismantled, brick by brick, then shipped east and rebuilt. This was part of a vast Soviet programme of industrial evacuation and relocation that was truly extraordinary.

On 16 August 'Order 270' was issued by Stalin, condemning all those who surrendered to or were captured by the German invaders as 'traitors to the Motherland'. Soviet soldiers, nearly all of them conscripts,

[overleaf]
Hitler at his military headquarters in Rastenburg, known as the Wolf's Lair (*Wolfsschanze*).

were expected to fight to the death. Meanwhile, the NKVD rounded up suspected rumour-mongers and defeatists. An estimated 168,000 Red Army soldiers were sentenced to death for alleged cowardice and desertion during the war. It would be wrong, however, to suggest that most Red Army soldiers were coerced into resisting the Germans. On the contrary, a large majority were deeply patriotic and wanted to exact revenge against the extreme brutality of the *Wehrmacht*.[126]

On 3 July 1941 Stalin finally addressed the Soviet people, on national radio, addressing them as 'Comrades, citizens, brothers and sisters.' Germany had launched an unprovoked attack, he said, before gloomily listing the current territorial losses: Soviet Lithuania, Latvia, western Byelorussia and parts of western Ukraine. Stalin then defended supporting the Nazi-Soviet Pact in August 1939. 'No peace-loving state could have rejected such a pact with another country,' he said, 'even if rogues like Hitler and Ribbentrop were at its head.' He called on the Russian people to defend the Motherland in a 'patriotic war' and committed to a scorched-earth policy: 'The enemy must not be left a single engine, a single railway car, a single pound of grain or a gallon of fuel.'[127] He called for every citizen to join in the struggle against Hitler's Germany. This was no ordinary war, he concluded, it was a total war: 'a choice between Soviet freedom or German slavery'.[128] This speech was a clear demonstration to the Russian people and to the world that Stalin had regained his nerve.

On 10 July 1941 Stalin assumed the title of Supreme Commander of the Armed Forces. On the same day, three defence fronts were established, corresponding to the three attacking German army groups: the North-western, commanded by Voroshilov, the Western under Timoshenko, and the South-western under Budenny. This was the first sign that the Red Army was slowly beginning to recover from the initial shock of the German assault. On 19 July Stalin replaced Timoshenko as Commander for Defence and took over himself as Russia's supreme war leader.

Despite being Germany's ally, Japan was given no prior knowledge of the attack on the Soviet Union. On 25 June Yōsuke Matsuoka, the Japanese Foreign Minister, went to see the German ambassador in Tokyo to demand an explanation. The Tripartite Pact remained the basis of Japanese foreign policy, Matsuoka said, but there was very strong opposition in the cabinet to supporting Japan entering the war against the Soviet Union. In Matsuoka's view, it was unlikely that Japan would join in hostilities while the victor of Germany's war on the

USSR remained uncertain.[129] Disappointed by this lukewarm response from the Japanese government, Ribbentrop soon began a campaign to get Japan to enter the war against Russia. He emphasized the fact that a swift German victory would offer Japan a unique opportunity to begin to dominate East Asia at the expense of the British Empire.[130]

Hitler had departed by special train from Berlin on 23 June 1941 for his new military field headquarters, dubbed the *Wolfsschanze* ('Wolf's Lair'), in a forested area near Rastenburg in East Prussia. It was from this gloomy complex, surrounded by barbed-wire-topped fences and hidden away in the Masurian woods, that Hitler would command the German-Soviet War. He would remain at the Wolf's Lair for most of the next three and a half years. Here he was cut off, not just from the centre of government in Berlin, but far away from the horrors on the battlefield and, later, the bombing of German cities. Hitler felt that this detachment would help him to make more rational, rather than emotional, decisions.

In Germany, Hitler gradually retreated from the public gaze. The speeches that had brought him huge popularity up to now became much rarer. German government on the home front was shared between a multiplicity of different and often overlapping bodies with no one coordinating it from the centre. There were no cabinet meetings. Of the 445 legislative measures of the German government in 1941, 373 were issued by individual government ministries without any consultation.[131]

The Wolf's Lair had been constructed in the previous six months. It was built on boggy soil near smelly and stagnant lakes and ponds. The complex consisted of ten windowless bunkers, reinforced by two metres of concrete, with associated barrack-style buildings containing a dining hall, conference rooms and administrative offices. There were around 2,000 staff based there, primarily German officers and soldiers on guard, with a retinue of civil servants and clerical staff.

As the danger of air raids increased, the concrete was gradually reinforced in the bunkers. It was surrounded by perimeter fencing, topped off by barbed wire and protected by mines. In the summer months the Wolf's Lair's residents were plagued by mosquitos. During winter, there was a daily cold fog to accompany the snow and persistent frost. There was an air ventilation system in the bunkers, but it often recycled the existing air. Hitler's bunker was the only one with fresh air pumped in. Dampness and breeding mold was a feature of bunker life for most of the staff on the complex.

An insight into Hitler's mind in the Wolf's Lair during 1941 and 1942 is provided by the written records of his evening after-dinner monologues, known as the 'Table Talk'. A party official, appointed by Martin Bormann, was allowed to attend, unobtrusively, in order to record Hitler's opinions.[132] The Hitler recorded at the Wolf's Lair is unmistakably the author of *Mein Kampf*, his desire to crush communism and the Jews once again coming to the fore as the war progressed.

The main event daily at the Wolf's Lair was the 'Situation Report' meeting, usually at noon, which ran for two hours. This was followed by a lengthy lunch, beginning at 2 p.m. Hitler would have a coffee break with his secretaries for some chit-chat around 5 p.m. At 6 p.m. there was usually a shorter military briefing, with dinner beginning at 7.30 p.m. If there was a pressing military issue, another meeting might occur at midnight or beyond. Invited guests from the Nazi elite would often visit.[133]

Although he was supremely confident of victory, Hitler became quite ill during the early phase of Operation Barbarossa. He was suffering from severe stomach pains, accompanied by fever and diarrhoea. His personal physician Dr Morell, who accompanied him to the Wolf's Lair, diagnosed dysentery and prescribed a cocktail of injected drugs, hormones and vitamins.

Morell recorded the various treatments he administered to Hitler for 885 days, from June 1941 to April 1945. Medications are recorded 1,100 times, with 800 different injections being mentioned.[134] Hitler's bedside table was full of pill bottles and liquid medicines. Along with opioid painkillers and amphetamines, Hitler used all sorts of vitamin supplements, steroids and hormone preparations. The aim was usually to combat stress, anxiety pain and exhaustion. It's an exaggeration to call Hitler a drug addict, but he was undoubtedly seriously dependent on many prescription medications, and they clearly contributed to his mood swings. A cardiogram taken by Morell in 1941 revealed that Hitler had developed serious cardiovascular disease and later he most probably developed Parkinson's disease.[135]

In the first weeks of the invasion of the USSR, the German army advanced further into Soviet territory and the destruction of the communist state seemed inevitable. Huge Soviet armies were encircled and destroyed as the German Panzer units penetrated more deeply. Soviet towns and cities were reduced to flaming ruins. The truly barbaric nature of the invasion was evident from the very beginning.

As Karl Fuchs, a German tank gunner, put it: 'The war against these subhuman beings is almost over, we really let them have it! They are scoundrels, the scum of the earth and they are no match for the German soldier.'[136]

By 25 June 1941 Army Group North, having advanced rapidly into Byelorussia, was fighting three encirclement battles simultaneously, one around the border area of Brest-Litovsk, one near Bialystok and one at Volkovysk. In all three places, the Red Army defenders were surrounded and subsequently decimated. The Panzer Corps of Army Group North was advancing at a rate of fifty miles a day.

The tanks of Army Group Centre were also speeding ahead at breakneck pace, threatening the destruction of fifteen Red Army divisions around Minsk. Army Group South quickly moved into Ukraine, supported by two Romanian armies, but met with much stronger Soviet resistance, commanded by Colonel General Mikhail Kirponos, who launched a bold counteroffensive. At first, the Soviets gained the upper hand, but on 26 June General von Kleist's Panzer Corps repulsed this attack and advanced towards Rovno. On 27 June German forces reached the Byelorussian capital of Minsk, already 300 miles inside Soviet territory. They captured 400,000 Russian prisoners in the first great battle of encirclement of the campaign in the Soviet Union.[137]

These early battles were extremely ferocious and brutal. Soviet soldiers fought far more bitterly than the Poles or the Western Europeans had done. As one German soldier noted: 'The Russian soldier is a tough opponent. We take hardly any prisoners and shoot them all instead.'[138] There was brutality on both sides. Some German soldiers never forgot seeing their own comrades killed by Red Army forces. One noted: 'The sight of bestially mutilated corpses which wear the same uniform as you cut into the whole mental map of who you are. But also, the staring faces of the hanged. The pits full of the shot.'[139] Other German soldiers became atrocity tourists, taking photographs of the aftermath of the mass shootings of Russians.

At the start of the German invasion, German officers warned soldiers about engaging in sexual activities with 'racially inferior' Soviet women. These instructions went largely ignored, with widespread instances reported of rape, gang rape, sexual enslavement and sexual violence being committed by German soldiers. Rape could often end in the murder of the victim. Military judges either ignored or issued relatively light sentences to soldiers accused of sexual offences. It's

[overleaf]
Captured Soviet prisoners during the early stages of Operation Barbarossa.

been estimated that 50 per cent of all men serving in the German army in the Soviet Union had 'undesirable sexual intercourse with ethnically alien women'.[140]

The extreme brutality of the German army in the Soviet Union proved counterproductive. German soldier Hans von Bittenfeld recalled that when the German army first marched into some parts of Soviet territory they were greeted as liberators. Many people in the Baltic states and Ukraine expected the arrival of the Germans to spell the end of Stalinist repression and collective farming, but the Germans' inhuman treatment of the population slowly eroded the goodwill of the population.[141]

Soon a vast number of Soviet soldiers were captured by the German army. During the German-Soviet war, the *Wehrmacht* took 5.7 million Red Army prisoners. Of these 3.3 million died, mostly in the first year of the campaign through appalling neglect. In Western Europe the *Wehrmacht* had taken 2 million POWs, but had managed to contain them and feed them and respected the rules of the Geneva Convention. In the Soviet Union there was no provision for feeding or housing any Soviet prisoners. The vast majority simply starved to death.

Helmut Schmidt, who later became a post-war German chancellor, was a soldier involved in the attack on the Soviet Union. He once saw a freight train full of POWs: 'They were in a pitiful condition. It wasn't that they had been mistreated, it was more that they obviously hadn't been given anything to eat. They stretched their arms out and shouted something I could not understand. I assumed they were asking for food.'[142]

In August 1941, Joseph Goebbels visited a POW camp in Zeithain and noted in his diary: 'The camp looks awful. Some of the Bolsheviks must sleep on the bare earth. It was pouring with rain. Some of them have no roof over their heads and insofar as they have one, the sides of the huts are open. In short, it's not a pretty picture.'[143]

On 30 June Hitler wrote to Mussolini from the Wolf's Lair. The war with the Soviet Union had been inevitable, he explained, and had he delayed it until 1942 then the Axis powers would have certainly lost the war. In the previous eight days the German armed forces had attacked and beaten or annihilated the enemy forces.

Hitler admitted the battles in the Soviet Union had been 'among the most difficult' that his troops had faced since 1939, because the Russians fought 'with a stupid fanaticism'. Commissars told the Soviet troops that if they didn't fight to the death they would be 'tortured and killed anyway', while Russian infantry were thrown into battles 'regardless of the sacrifices involved'.[144]

By early July 1941 Hitler seemed on the verge of yet another amazing military triumph. On 3 July Halder noted in his diary that it was 'probably no overstatement to say that the Russian campaign has been won in the space of two weeks'.[145] So swift were the German tank advances that the infantry units were having difficulty catching up. Between 22 June and 28 July the 12th German Infantry Division had marched a staggering 300 miles, an average of 15 miles a day, all while troops were carrying 50 pounds of equipment and in the height of summer.

On 8 July the German High Command estimated that it had already completely destroyed 89 Soviet divisions. Army Group Centre had captured 300,000 prisoners and destroyed 2,500 tanks and 1,400 artillery guns. Army Group North was accelerating rapidly towards Leningrad. Army Group South had made slower progress, because the defending Red Army had more tank divisions, but with the support of the *Luftwaffe* it was still advancing inexorably towards Kiev, the capital of Ukraine.

Army Group Centre captured Minsk on 9 July, taking 287,704 prisoners, and was soon moving to encircle twenty-five Soviet divisions at Smolensk, Mogilev and Vitebsk. This pocket was near the strategically vital Dnieper-Dvina land bridge. Fedor von Bock, the commander of Army Group Centre, aimed to keep his armies moving forward in good weather. On 16 July Smolensk was captured.[146] This meant the last major city on the way to Moscow had fallen, and the German army was now just 248 miles west of the Soviet capital.[147]

At a military conference at the Wolf's Lair, on 16 July, Hitler defined the objectives of the German subjugation of the Soviet Union. Germany needed to present itself to the world as a liberator of the Russian people from Bolshevism, he said. Once Germany was victorious, only Germans would be permitted to carry arms in the occupied territory. In the Baltic territory, military administration would be imposed as a transition to incorporating this region into the German Reich, along with the Crimea. In Ukraine, the nationalism of the Ukrainians would be encouraged; however, the main priority was not self-government but making sure the food supply was secure, so that it could be exploited for the German war effort.[148]

On the following day a Führer decree was issued on the administration of the newly occupied eastern territories. It stated that when military operations ended, the administration of the eastern occupied territories would pass from military to civil administration. These areas would be placed under the control of Alfred Rosenberg, the head of the Reich Ministry for the Occupied Eastern Territories, and divided into Reich Commissariats, then into regions and districts.

A Reich Commissar would take charge of each Reich Commissariat, a General Commissar in control of each General Region, and a District Commissar controlling each district. Hitler would personally appoint all of the Reich Commissars and General Commissars. The loyal Nazi Gauleiters Erich Koch and Heinrich Lohse were made Reich Commissioners for Ukraine and Ostland (the Baltic provinces and Byelorussia) respectively.[149]

On 21 July 1941 Yōsuke Matsuoka, the pro-Axis Japanese Foreign Minister, was suddenly replaced by Admiral Teijirō Toyoda, an opponent of the Tripartite Pact, who was firmly opposed to Japan invading the Soviet Union. The new Japanese cabinet, led by the Prime Minister Fumimaro Konoye, was largely under the influence of big business and it favoured a reconciliation with the United States. This was a blow to Ribbentrop's diplomatic mission to bring Japan into the war on the side of the Axis nations.

Hitler wrote to Mussolini on 20 July expressing his puzzlement about the fresh cabinet upheaval in Japan. He felt it was impossible to fathom why the Japanese government did not grasp the unique opportunity offered by the current international situation: 'I do not believe that Japan will be in a position to proceed against the Soviet Union before the middle of August,' he added.[150] Mussolini felt that 'Japan will remain in our camp', but it would not attack the Soviet Union, preferring instead to expand in Indochina, which might bring the United States into the war.[151]

Hitler sent a letter to Ion Antonescu, the Romanian Prime Minister, on 27 July, reporting his satisfaction so far with the progress of the German invasion of the Soviet Union. In just five weeks, some infantry units had travelled over 300 miles, while several bloody battles had resulted in the destruction of numerous Red Army units. Hitler claimed that his objective was 'not at all the winning of space, but the annihilation of the enemy, not only with regard to men but above all to materials'. Replacing manpower might be easy for the Russians, but he thought that replacing arms and materiel on a huge scale would be impossible.[152] On 30 July Hitler issued 'Directive No. 34', which reported the sudden appearance of 'strong enemy forces' confronting

Army Group Centre. This prompted Hitler to order two armoured divisions to halt for ten days to refit and switch to the defensive.[153]

Behind the advancing brutal German army in the Soviet Union came the even more deadly *Einsatzgruppen*. From the very beginning of Operation Barbarossa it's clear that the order to kill only communist political functionaries and bureaucrats was being ignored or interpreted more broadly by Hitler's killing squads on the spot. They were instead primarily targeting male Jewish civilians. The first documented order to kill 'all Jewish males' aged seventeen to forty-five was issued on 11 July 1941. *Einsatzgruppen* reports sent to the Reich Security Main Office in Berlin provide us with a written record of this escalation of the murder of Jews. Between 23 June 1941 and 24 April 1942 a total of 195 'Activity and Situation' reports were submitted and circulated to a select group of Nazi figures, including Hitler.

On 6 July 1941 *Einsatzgruppe* B reported that in three towns – Garsden, Krottingham and Polangan – 'mainly Jews were liquidated'. On 11 July *Einsatzgruppe* A recorded that in the first nineteen days of the German invasion 7,800 Jews had been killed in pogroms organized by local Lithuanian collaborators. The number of Jews being murdered then escalated rapidly. The killing figures for *Einsatzkommando* 3, operating in Ukraine, demonstrated this very clearly. In July, 4,239 Jews were killed. In August this rose to 37,186. In September the Jewish death toll was 56,459, including 26,244 women and 15,112 children. It seems the initial order to kill only males was now being ignored. These extrajudicial killings were carried out when Germany appeared to be winning the war in the Soviet Union, so this 'war against the Jews' cannot be interpreted as an act of vengeance or compensation for the invasion going wrong. The driving force behind the mass killing of Jewish people was undoubtedly Himmler's SS units, but the German army did not just turn a blind eye, it openly collaborated in the slaughter.

It is not until mid-August 1941 that an *Einsatzgruppen* operation report uses the chilling phrase 'Final Solution of the Jewish Question', alongside the key policy aim of making the Soviet Union *Juden Frei* ('free of Jews'). Between June 1941 and January 1942 as many as 750,000 Jews were killed in the mass shootings by the *Einsatzgruppen* in the Soviet Union. Out of the 240,410 documented killings of *Einsatzgruppe* A, 229,052 of the victims were Jews.

One of the most horrific Jewish massacres by the *Einsatzgruppen* in the Soviet Union occurred at Babi Yar, just outside Kiev, between 29 and 30 September 1941, when a staggering 33,771 people were

An den

    Chef der Sicherheitspolizei und des SD
    #-Gruppenführer H e y d r i c h

        B e r l i n.

      Jn Ergänzung der Jhnen bereits mit Erlaß vom 24.I.39 übertragenen Aufgabe,die Judenfrage in Form der Auswanderung oder Evakuierung einer den Zeitverhält-nissen entsprechend möglichst günstigsten Lösung zuzu-führen, beauftrage ich Sie hiermit,alle erforderlichen Vorbereitungen in organisatorischer,sachlicher und materieller Hinsicht zu treffen für eine Gesamtlösung der Judenfrage im deutschen Einflußgebiet in Europa.

      Soferne hierbei die Zuständigkeiten anderer Zentralinstanzen berührt werden, sind diese zu betei-ligen.

      Jch beauftrage Sie weiter,mir in Bälde einen Gesamtentwurf über die organisatorischen,sachlichen und materiellen Vorausmaßnahmen zur Durchführung der angestrebten Endlösung der Judenfrage vorzulegen.

killed in mass shootings. The *Einsatzgruppen* report on this incident suggested that it had been carried out at the request of local Ukrainian nationalists, who wanted revenge for the preferential treatment given to Jews under Soviet rule.[154]

Within weeks of Operation Barbarossa beginning, a fully developed SS policy of the systematic murder of all Jews in the Soviet Union was clearly under way, but a much broader plan was also taking shape. A Europe-wide 'Final Solution', proposing not emigration but physical extermination, was now being seriously contemplated. On 31 July 1941 Hermann Göring asked Reinhard Heydrich to make 'all the necessary organizational and technical preparations' to devise 'an overall plan', including financial costings, for a 'Final Solution of the Jewish Question'.

There is little doubt that the 'war against the Jews' escalated in the latter half of 1941. At a meeting at the Wolf's Lair on 18 August 1941 Goebbels presented Hitler with new proposals for the persecution of Jews in Germany. Hitler reminded Goebbels of his 30 January 1939 speech, in which he had prophesied that all Jews in Europe would be eliminated. By the end of this meeting Hitler had agreed that all Jews aged six and over in the Old Reich would be required to wear an identifying badge. This was publicly announced in Germany on 1 September and became operative on 19 September. In October 1941 all Jewish emigration from Germany was prohibited.

The introduction of the 'yellow star' in Germany was accompanied by a vociferous wave of anti-Jewish propaganda. Jews were persecuted in every walk of life. In Dresden, the Jewish former professor Victor Klemperer noted in his diary: 'I personally feel shattered, cannot compose myself, now Eva [his non-Jewish wife] wants to take over all the errands for me. I only want to leave the house for a few minutes when it's dark.'[155] Klaus Scheurenberg, a sixteen-year-old Jewish youth living in Berlin, recalled: 'I was terribly embarrassed. All of a sudden everyone could tell what you were. They could spit on you, beat you to death – you were suddenly unprotected.'[156]

The Jewish deportations from Germany were mostly viewed as a good solution to the Jewish problem. An SD report on 9 October noted: 'The Star of David regulation was welcomed and received with satisfaction by a vast majority of the population, particularly since many had expected such an identification for some time. Only from a small group, mostly Catholic and bourgeois, did isolated expressions of compassion emanate.'[157]

Hermann Göring's letter of 31 July 1941
to Reinhard Heydrich authorizing the
Final Solution.

On 25 October 1941, during an evening table talk in the Wolf's Lair, Hitler commented: 'From the rostrum of the Reichstag I prophesied that in the event of the war proving inevitable, the Jew would disappear from Europe. That race of criminals has on its conscience the two million dead of the First World War and now hundreds of thousands more.'[158] During a similar conversation on 5 November 1941 Hitler predicted: 'The end of the war will see the ruin of the Jew. The Jew is the incarnation of egoism. And their egoism goes so far that they're not even capable of risking their lives for the defence of their most vital interests.'[159]

Writing in *Das Reich* on 5 November Goebbels described the introduction of the yellow Star of David as 'an extremely humane regulation', designed to prevent Jews from 'sneaking into our ranks unrecognized and sowing seeds of discord'. The isolation of Jews from the National Community was 'an elementary rule of social hygiene'.[160] By the end of 1941 the number of Jews in the Old Reich (*Altes Reich*) had declined to 131,823 from a figure of 525,000 in 1933 when Hitler came to power.[161]

During the course of July it became obvious that the optimistic predictions of a swift German victory had been deceptive. Fedor von Bock, the commander of Army Group Centre, noted in his diary: 'Here a new operation is to start from this position with the slowly falling combat value of the troops who are attacked again and again. I don't quite know how yet.' A few days later, he noted equally pessimistically: 'If the Russians do not collapse somewhere soon, then it will be very difficult before the winter to hit them so hard as to eliminate them.'[162]

Around the same time Franz Halder commented:

> In the general situation what stands out is that we have underestimated the Russian colossus, which has consciously prepared for war with all the effort that a totalitarian state can muster. At the start of the war, we counted on about 200 enemy divisions. We have counted 360. These divisions are not as well armed or equipped as ours, they are often poorly led, but they are there. And if we knock out a dozen of them, then the Russian puts up another dozen.[163]

It was now clear that the original three-pronged attack on the Soviet Union along a broad front required some revision. In 'Directive No. 33', issued on 19 July, Hitler outlined the next stage of the German offensive. Army Group Centre's two Panzer groups, which now stood just 200 miles from Moscow, would be diverted to cooperate with the

A member of the SS *Einsatzgruppen*
preparing to kill a Ukrainian Jew.

advance in the north towards Leningrad and onwards to Kiev, joining up with Army Group South. The two focal points of the German advance were now on Ukraine, capturing Kiev, and on the operation to encircle Leningrad.

In 'Directive No. 34', issued on 30 July 1941, Hitler had ordered Army Group Centre to halt its drive towards Moscow.[164] This decision provoked bitter disagreement within the German High Command. Army Group Centre commanders wanted all formations to concentrate on seizing Moscow in order to inflict a fatal political death blow to Stalin's regime, but Hitler wanted instead to push southwards to secure the rich agricultural resources of Ukraine and the vital oil supplies in the Caucasus, which were more important to him than the ideological prize of capturing Moscow. The two leading German army commanders Franz Halder and Alfred Jodl strongly favoured heading to Moscow before the winter set in. As Halder noted after a long meeting at the Wolf's Lair: 'Hours of gibberish, and the outcome is there's only one man [Hitler] who knows how to wage wars.'[165] Jodl observed: 'Hitler has an instinctive aversion to treading the same path as Napoleon. Moscow gives him a sinister feeling.'[166]

The famed tank commander Heinz Guderian visited Hitler at the Wolf's Lair to try and convince him of the need to prioritize Moscow in the next phase of the German operation. Brauchitsch warned him beforehand not 'to mention the question of Moscow' in front of Hitler, but when Hitler brought up the matter himself, Guderian made an impassioned plea to continue the drive towards Moscow. This prompted Hitler to launch an angry tirade about how little his military commanders knew about the economic aspects of war.[167]

Keitel produced a detailed memorandum on 27 August entitled 'The Strategic Situation in Late Summer 1941'. It noted there had been 'mighty successes' since the start of Operation Barbarossa. Soviet forces had suffered enormous losses in the number of men dead or wounded taken as POWs, as well as in equipment. However, Keitel admitted that 'the enemy's resistance is still not completely broken' and this situation would most likely continue into 1942. The danger of Britain and its allies invading Western Europe was regarded by Keitel as 'removed for the time being'. However, it was expected that Britain would be in a better position to increase its air attacks on German cities during 1942. It remained a key German aim to defeat Britain and to force its government to make peace, but it was admitted *Luftwaffe* attacks alone had not been able to achieve this.[168]

British Prime Minister Winston Churchill knew that Britain and its empire could not defeat Hitler's Germany in Western Europe without America entering the war on the Allied side. Churchill and President Roosevelt agreed to meet for fresh talks in August 1941 in Placenta Bay off Newfoundland, Canada. Roosevelt, though charmed by Churchill, would not agree to enter the war. Roosevelt did agree to the issue of the much-trumpeted Atlantic Charter, signed on 12 August, which was released to the press on 14 August 1941. This document laid out key Anglo-American principles for a post-war world after the 'destruction of Nazi tyranny'. Britain and the United States would seek no territorial gains and promised self-determination to all countries currently occupied by the Axis powers, as well as lower trade barriers and the freedom of the seas.

Churchill and Roosevelt understood the propaganda value of the Atlantic Charter. Roosevelt privately promised Churchill that he would now adopt a much more strident anti-Hitler public stance and stress the common purpose of the Allies to defeat the Axis nations. The Atlantic Charter offered Britain and America an idealistic vision of a post-war world based on democracy, peace, free trade, self-determination and international cooperation.[169]

Ribbentrop sent briefing notes to Hitler concerning the Roosevelt–Churchill meeting. Ribbentrop felt Churchill pressed for the issue of the Atlantic Charter because he believed that the Soviet Union faced imminent defeat. The release of the Atlantic Charter was really a way for Britain to keep the war going, even if the Soviet Union fell. Roosevelt knew that he could make such gestures, because the United States could not be attacked so easily. Finally, Ribbentrop predicted that when the Soviet Union was defeated the United States would still not get involved in the war.[170]

Mussolini met Hitler in the Wolf's Lair on 25 August 1941 to give him a detailed account of the current situation in the Soviet campaign. Hitler felt that German military intelligence had been very poor prior to the attack and confessed it was not easy to defeat the Red Army swiftly. The Red Army was well equipped, with soldiers 'imbued with a veritable fanaticism' who fought with 'blind fury'. Hitler added that he remained determined not to allow the German army be drawn into street fighting in Soviet cities. His plan for the attack on Leningrad was to encircle it, but not to capture it.[171]

On 29 August 1941 Hitler and Mussolini issued a joint communiqué, in a blaze of publicity, obviously designed to counteract the recently

[overleaf]
US President Franklin D. Roosevelt with British Prime Minister Winston Churchill during the Atlantic Conference in August 1941.

announced Atlantic Charter. It stressed the two Axis powers aimed to create a new European order, following the 'destruction of the Bolshevik danger and of plutocratic exploitation', thereby creating 'the possibility of a peaceful, harmonious and fruitful cooperation of all peoples of the European continent in the political as well as in the economic and cultural and economic spheres'.[172]

On 13 September Stalin sent Georgy Zhukov to organize the defence of Leningrad. Zhukov quickly brought in more artillery guns. The population was conscripted to build defensive fortifications, including tank ditches, mines and trenches, to protect the 3.5 million citizens trapped within the city. People were starving to death in Leningrad at a rate of 5,000 per day. The only access to the city was via Lake Lagoda and from late November trucks operating in hazardous conditions brought food supplies over its frozen surface. It became known as the 'Ice Road'.

Zhukov advised Stalin to evacuate Red Army forces from Kiev, which was also under siege by the German army during the early days of September. In yet another spell-binding German military encirclement, spearheaded by the German Panzer Corps, Kiev had been surrounded. On 17 September, Stalin finally issued the Kiev evacuation order. The German army had won another stunning victory over the Red Army, with a monumental 655,000 Soviet soldiers captured in Kiev: the largest number taken in a single German operation.[173] With the flank threat to Army Group Centre ended, the way was now open to capture Moscow.[174]

Hitler now briefly paused to intervene in a political crisis in the Protectorate of Bohemia and Moravia, formerly part of Czechoslavia. Hitler summoned the Reich Protector Konstantin von Neurath to the Wolf's Lair then accused him of being far too lenient towards those Czechs who were engaging in strikes, resistance and industrial sabotage. On 27 September Hitler installed the ruthless SS figure Reinhard Heydrich, head of the Reich Security Main Office, as Neurath's deputy, thereby reducing the Reich Governor to a powerless figurehead. Heydrich promptly declared a state of emergency, then ordered the arrest of Czech Prime Minister General Alois Eliáš, who had maintained contact with the Czech government-in-exile. Within five days of his arrival in Prague, Heydrich (who would become known as the 'Butcher of Prague') had ordered the execution of 142 people.

With this messy matter out of the way, Hitler turned his attention to Moscow and finally gave in to the pressure from his leading generals.

On 6 September he gave the go-ahead for Operation Typhoon, which aimed to destroy the Soviet armies defending Moscow, in the region of Vyazma and Bryansk. Operation Typhoon had a launch date of 30 September, but it did not get under way until 2 October. German forces initially converged on Vyazma, threatening yet another huge encirclement of the Red Army. Six huge German armies – with 1.9 million men, 1,000 tanks, 1,390 aircraft and 14,000 artillery guns – participated in the lightning-fast operation.[175] In Vyazma and Bryansk, the German army captured a record 673,000 prisoners. German troops then entered Orel, while the local commuter trams were still running. A jubilant Jodl noted: 'We have finally and without exaggeration won this war.'[176]

On 4 October Hitler arrived in Berlin, his confidence sky high. In the evening, he gave a speech at Berlin's Sport Palace, ostensibly to launch the annual Winter Relief charity campaign. The front rows of the auditorium were reserved for the wounded of the German-Soviet War. Hitler informed the packed audience that he had just come back from the 'greatest battle in the history of the world' and he could assure everyone present: 'The Soviet enemy was defeated and would never rise again.' Hitler then offered the evidence for his prediction: over 2 million Soviet prisoners had been captured, 18,000 tanks destroyed, and 14,500 aircraft shot down.[177]

On 10 October Otto Dietrich, Hitler's press chief, held a press conference in Berlin for foreign press journalists. With Hitler's blessing and speaking in front of a huge map of the battle in the Soviet Union, which was displayed on a large cinema screen, Dietrich explained that day by day the Red Army was being destroyed. On the following day, a headline in one German newspaper read: 'Campaign in the East Decided. The Great Hour Has Arrived.'[178]

On the same day Hitler reported in a military directive that 'the bulk of Soviet Russia's armed forces in the main theatre of operations had been smashed or destroyed'.[179] The German High Command reported on 7 October that Hitler had decided no surrender of Leningrad or Moscow was to be accepted. No German soldier was to enter either city.[180]

In Moscow the situation was so dire that orders were issued to begin evacuating the Soviet government to Kuibyshev, 500 miles east of the Soviet capital. There was an enormous evacuation of industry at the same time: factories in Moscow were dismantled, transported eastwards in trucks and freight trains, then hastily reassembled. A total

[overleaf]
Soviet citizens during the siege of
Leningrad which lasted for 872 days.

of 498 industrial installations were moved in this operation alone. Out of 75,000 metal-cutting lathes, 53,000 were shipped to the east and used in armaments production. The movement of Soviet factories east of Moscow was little short of an industrial revolution.[181]

These were very grim days for the Soviet Union. The world held its breath. On 16 October, a Soviet radio broadcast issued a blunt statement: 'During the night of 14–15 October the position of the Western Front became worse. The Germans with large quantities of tanks broke through our defences.'[182] On 18 October, Army Group Centre captured the cities of Kalinin, 90 miles north of Moscow, and Kaluga, 100 miles south-west of the capital.

Zhukov had already been recalled from Leningrad to lead the defence of Moscow. He had just 90,000 troops left for this task by mid-October, but he was energetically scouting for reserves. By early November he had assembled 240,000 men. In addition, 250,000 Muscovites, 75 per cent of them women, were conscripted to dig anti-tank ditches around Moscow.

On 17 October there was another government crisis in Japan. The Konoye cabinet, which had sought to improve relations with the United States, suddenly fell from power. The new Prime Minister Hideki Tojo, a committed nationalist, adopted a much more belligerent attitude towards America, viewing its government as a group of 'bullying white supremacists'. The German ambassador in Tokyo reported to Ribbentrop on 21 October 1941 that 'increased tension with the USA is to be expected'. The German ambassador predicted that the Tojo government would now adopt an 'unyielding position regarding America's demands'.[183]

On 26 October 1941 Hitler met Count Ciano, the Italian Foreign Minister, at the Wolf's Lair. Hitler told him that Russia's forces were on the verge of total defeat. The Soviet Union had lost so much war materiel it could not recover, he added. The Germans estimated that some branches of Soviet industry had lost 75 per cent of raw materials and its railway system was progressively collapsing. After the expected capture of Moscow, Hitler said, the next major German objective would be gaining the Caucasus, because it was the main centre of Soviet oil supplies.[184]

In a confident letter to Mussolini, dated 29 October 1941, Hitler wrote: 'I can justifiably claim that the campaign in the east is not only won but as such has in the main been brought to a successful conclusion'. He then predicted: 'Leningrad and Moscow will fall, possibly without our being forced to put even a single man in the cities themselves and thereby perhaps sacrificing them.' Bolshevism was finally 'falling victim to its treacherous designs'.[185] In his reply on 6 November, Mussolini agreed that Bolshevism was crushed but thought that would mean 'America will intervene in the war', and that the USA would initially operate in North Africa to defend British interests there, especially in Egypt.[186]

In November 1941 Stalin decided to go ahead with the annual celebrations of the 1917 Russian Revolution in Moscow, even though the German army now stood only fifty miles away. The Soviet rally on the eve of the anniversary on 6 November was held in the ornate hall of the Mayakovsky underground railway station at which Stalin gave a rallying speech to the assembled party delegates. He spoke of vast German losses and grossly exaggerated them. He then claimed that the German *Blitzkrieg* had already failed. The Soviet Union was not disintegrating, but with Ukraine, Byelorussia and the Balkan states already lost, it was now a bitter fight to save the Soviet Union: 'If they want a war of extermination they can have one,' he added. 'Our task now will be to destroy every German, to the very last man.' He ended his speech with the defiant rallying cry: 'Death to the German invaders!'[187]

Hitler briefly left the Wolf's Lair for Munich on 8 November to deliver his annual speech, commemorating the failed 1923 Munich Beer Hall Putsch. He used the occasion to bitterly attack Winston Churchill, who he described as 'that insane drunkard who has been controlling England for years'. He then warned Roosevelt that if any American ship fired at a German vessel 'it would do so at its own risk'. The war with the Soviet Union was a struggle not just for Germany, he added, 'but also for all of Europe'.

Hitler poured scorn on Allied press claims that the German army had been forced to go on the defensive in the Soviet Union, pointing out the vast amount of territory and the 3.6 million prisoners they had already captured. Aware that victory had not been swift, he rejected the use of the word '*Blitzkrieg*' to describe German military strategy. It was a 'stupid word', he said, and he had personally never used it. He added a note of caution, warning that the German people would have to be prepared for more sacrifices before a final victory was achieved.[188]

By now the initial overwhelming fire power of the German assault on Moscow was diminishing in ferocity. During October the weather had noticeably worsened. Heavy rain and sleet turned roads into

[overleaf]
The crack winter-trained Siberian divisions who participated in the Soviet counter-offensive outside Moscow in December 1941.

quagmires so that tanks and motor vehicles could not move for days. Machine guns and rifles frequently jammed. As one German soldier put it: 'I don't think anyone has seen such terrible mud. There's rain, snow, hailstones, a liquid, bottomless swamp.'[189] Temperatures at night started to plummet below zero. German soldiers still wearing thin denim uniforms and worn-out leather boots seemed ill-prepared.

The German military death toll was now rising alarmingly. Between 22 June and 31 July 1941 the Germans lost 46,000 dead. The bitter battles for Kiev, Leningrad and on the road to Moscow came at the cost of another 118,000 deaths. By the end of November 1941, around 23 per cent of the original German invading force of 3.2 million was dead, missing, wounded or invalided out. Hitler was totally indifferent to the rising toll of German losses, commenting on 1 December: 'The life of the individual must not be set at too high a price. If the individual were important in the eyes of nature, nature would take care to preserve him. Amongst the millions of eggs a fly lays, very few hatch – and yet the race of the fly thrives.'[190]

The final climactic stage of Operation Typhoon resumed on 16 November 1941. The battlefield was now deep in snow. This final assault got to within twenty-five miles of Moscow by 28 November. One legend suggests that the German forward units saw the golden domes of the Kremlin, illuminated by a burst of sunshine, but this has never been verified. There is now a monument on the outskirts of Moscow in Khimski, a satellite city, which marks what the Russians view as the farthest point of the German advance. In 1941, this point was 15 miles from Moscow.

At the end of November 1941 the German advance suddenly ground to a complete halt. Hitler, always overconfident of victory, had not ordered winter equipment or clothing for his troops. Nor had his equally overconfident generals. German troops were now in a very vulnerable position, with insecure supply lines. Tanks failed to start, guns and artillery could not fire as lubricants froze in their recoil mechanisms. The Germans began to think Red Army soldiers were superhuman winter fighters. As Heinz Guderian later recalled: 'Only he who saw the endless expanse of Russian snow during this winter of our misery and felt the icy wind that blew across it, can truly judge the events that now occurred.'[191]

In the south of the Soviet Union, German Panzer units entered Rostov on 21 November, in much better weather than persisted around Moscow, but just five days later the Red Army retook the city. It was the first major German army retreat since Operation Barbarossa began. 'Our misfortunes began with Rostov,' Guderian later admitted. 'That was the writing on the wall.' Field Marshal Gerd von Rundstedt was summarily dismissed by Hitler for ordering the retreat from Rostov.[192]

Fedor von Bock, the commander of Army Group Centre, who was now suffering from severe stomach pains, realized that his troops could not take Moscow. Discipline was breaking down in the German ranks. Bock wanted to withdraw his forces to a more defensible position and reported to Halder on 1 December:

> The idea that the enemy was on the point of collapse was, as the fighting of the last fortnight shows, a pipe dream. To remain outside the gates of Moscow, where the road and rail systems connect with almost the whole of Russia, means heavy defensive fighting. Further offensive action seems to be senseless and aimless, especially as the time is coming very near when the physical strength of the troops is becoming exhausted.[193]

What Bock didn't know was that Zhukov was planning a huge Soviet counteroffensive against Army Group Centre outside Moscow. Stalin had initially resisted Zhukov's idea, but he finally gave the go-ahead in late November. This Soviet build-up of troops had gone completely undetected by German military intelligence.

Zhukov aimed to push German troops twenty-five miles back from Moscow. In late November the Soviet military intelligence officer Richard Sorge had reported back to Moscow that Japan was no immediate threat to the USSR, because it was preparing to attack the United States and Britain in the Pacific. This gave Zhukov an opportunity to bring in fresh troops deployed much further east. He ordered the transfer to Moscow of half of all the eastern divisions, including specialist Siberian units, men who were skilled in winter warfare. Karl Rupp, a member of a German armoured division outside Moscow, later recalled: 'These troops were excellently equipped – fur coats, fur caps, fur-lined boots and gloves. Our troops were a pitiful sight in comparison – light coats, rags wrapped around feet or shoes. I managed to get some felt boots. I'd taken them off a dead Russian.'[194] These Siberian troops were supplemented by fifty-eight reserve divisions, held to the east of Moscow, with 1,000 tanks and 1,000 aircraft. With 800,000 troops now assembled for the counteroffensive, the Red Army now roughly equalled the number of troops available to Army Group Centre for the Battle of Moscow.

At 3 a.m. on 5 December 1941 – in waist-deep snow, with bitterly cold temperatures at -25°C – the Red Army launched a massive and bold counteroffensive. The Soviet attack began north of Moscow, against German Panzer forces in the small town of Klin. These concentrated 'shock groups', who were brave and tenacious, quickly broke through German defences.

Hitler reacted with total disbelief to the Soviet counteroffensive. He could not understand where the Red Army had found all these fresh troops. On 8 December, he issued 'Directive No. 39', which stated that because of the 'surprisingly early arrival of severe winter weather in the east and the supply difficulties' offensive operations would cease, and the German army would shift to the defensive. This tactical defensive stand-off had three objectives: to retain areas of great importance to German arms production; to allow for the recuperation of German forces; and to prepare for a resumption of major offensive operations in the spring of 1942.[195]

The German retreat from Moscow soon threatened to degenerate into a full-blown military collapse. By 12 December 1941 the entire front established by Army Group Centre in European Russia was threatened with total disintegration. Halder frankly admitted that the *Wehrmacht* now faced 'the most serious situation' of the entire war and he warned that the German army was now in real danger of collapse.[196] On 13 December, Soviet radio announced that the German attempt to capture Moscow was over.

German army commanders were begging Hitler to let them retreat much further, but on 16 December Hitler issued an order demanding 'fanatical resistance', and to 'Stand fast, not one step back' in their positions 'to the last man' (the so-called *Haltebefehl* order).

On 20 December 1941, Guderian flew to the Wolf's Lair to outline to Hitler the dire position of the Army Group Centre outside Moscow and to ask him for permission to retreat even further. Hitler showed absolutely no sympathy for this line of argument, angrily telling Guderian that German soldiers should dig in and fight where they stood. Hitler accused Guderian of being 'too deeply impressed by the suffering of the soldiers. You feel too much pity for them. You should stand back more. Believe me, things appear much clearer when viewed at a distance.'[197] Hitler had no desire to hear about the suffering that he was inflicting on German troops. Guderian later recalled that although Hitler constantly spoke about his time as a soldier in the

The *New York Times* reports the surprise Japanese attack on Pearl Harbor on 7 December 1941.

First World War, his character 'had little in common with the thoughts and emotions of soldiers'.[198]

While Hitler's *Blitzkrieg* was being halted by the Red Army in front of Moscow, a hugely important event for the future course of the war happened in the Pacific when the Japanese Air Force launched a surprise air attack on the US fleet at Pearl Harbor on 7 December 1941 (Washington time). A total of 2,335 American servicemen were killed during this Japanese attack; the American Navy lost two battleships and two destroyers, and three other huge battleships were seriously damaged. In addition, 188 US aircraft were destroyed on the ground.

The tension between Japan and the United States had been intensifying for months. In July 1941, when Japanese forces invaded the southern half of Indochina, Roosevelt reacted by imposing a trade and financial embargo. Japan was given the stark choice: capitulate to American demands or attack southwards to gain oil in order to expand in Southeast Asia and to continue its war with China.

In evidence at the Nuremberg Trial, Ribbentrop admitted that when he had first heard about the attack on Pearl Harbor he had thought it was an Allied hoax. Ribbentrop would have welcomed a Japanese attack on the Soviet Union or on British possessions in Southeast Asia, but he 'never considered a Japanese attack on the USA would be to our [Germany's] advantage'.[199]

The day after the attack on Pearl Harbor President Roosevelt declared war on Japan, but an American declaration of war against Germany and Italy was not immediately forthcoming, even though Roosevelt had repeatedly said that Hitler's Germany was the biggest threat to the existing world order.

Hitler had not been informed of the Japanese attack, nor had he foreseen it, but he rejoiced when he heard the news: 'We now have an ally that has never been conquered in 3,000 years.'[200] Hitler had not encouraged the Japanese government to attack the United States either. Instead, he wanted Japan to seize British territory in the Far East. Under the terms of the Tripartite Pact, Germany was not even obliged to declare war on the United States. The German army had not prepared for the possibility of a war with America and had no plans as to how it might defeat this huge economic superpower.[201]

With the entry of the United States, the Second World War became a truly global conflict. On 11 December 1941, Hitler announced to the Reichstag that Germany was declaring war on the United States. He stressed that the United States, egged on by its 'Jewish financial wire-pullers', was hell-bent on the destruction of Germany: 'That the Anglo-Saxon-Jewish-Capitalist World finds itself now on one and the same Front with Bolshevism does not surprise us National Socialists.' He further claimed to be tired of endless American provocations. 'We always strike first,' he said. 'Roosevelt was as mad as Woodrow Wilson. First, he incites war, then falsifies the causes, then odiously wraps himself in a cloak of Christian hypocrisy and slowly but surely leads mankind to war.'[202]

It's often argued that Hitler's unilateral decision to declare war against the United States was a huge blunder. It must be remembered, however, that Roosevelt would almost certainly have declared war on Germany in the following days anyway. The US government was already giving moral and diplomatic support, as well as sending military and food supplies, to the Soviet Union and the British Empire.

German economic planners did recognize the danger America's war potential posed. In December 1941 a German planning memorandum entitled 'The Requirements of Victory' painted a very gloomy picture indeed, concluding that Germany required a further $150 billion US dollars in arms manufacture in the next two years just to stay in the conflict with the new Allied combination of the USA, the British Empire and the Soviet Union. This sum exceeded what Germany spent during the entire period of the Second World War. The report gloomily concluded that Germany did not have the economic means to defeat the Allies in a long drawn-out struggle. It's not clear whether Hitler ever saw this report.[203]

The increase of American arms production from 1939 to 1945 was quite extraordinary. In 1939 the United States was devoting less on military expenditure than any of the other major world powers. By 1944, the USA was producing 40 per cent of all the world's armaments.[204] In 1942 the US produced 48,000 aircraft; in 1943 this rose to 86,000 and in 1944 was up to 114,000. Germany could not hope to match armaments production on this scale. For instance, in 1940 Germany built 10,000 new aircraft; in 1941 it was 11,000 and in 1942 it was only up to 15,000.[205]

The immediate consequence of the United States' entry into the war was to radicalize German anti-Jewish policy. In numerous speeches since 1939 Hitler had promised that a truly 'global war' would herald the extermination of the Jews. Mass extermination of Jews had already begun in the Soviet Union, as we have already seen, primarily undertaken by the lawless execution squads of the *Einsatzgruppen*, but alongside this a more secretive, planned and mechanized form of mass murder was evolving.

Experiments with other methods of killing were under way. On 3 September 1941 the gas Zyklon B, an industrial pesticide, was used in the Auschwitz concentration camp to kill a number of Soviet POWs in an experiment to test its effectiveness. Gas vans began to be utilized by the *Einsatzgruppen* in the Soviet Union, using carbon monoxide piped in from the engine. On 8 December 1941 a gas van was used to kill Jews in an improvised killing facility in Chełmno.

On 29 November 1941 Heydrich invited a number of senior civil servants and key figures in the Reich Security Main Office (SA) to a meeting to map out a 'comprehensive solution to the Jewish question'. The date set for this gathering was 9 December 1941 at a picturesque lakeside villa in Wannsee on the outskirts of Berlin. Due to the Japanese attack at Pearl Harbor, this meeting was postponed until 20 January 1942. Two leading figures in the General Government – Hans Frank and Friedrich-Wilhelm Krüger – were added to the list of invitees to this meeting.[206]

On 12 December 1941, Adolf Hitler gave a speech to regional Nazi leaders in which he said, according to Hans Frank, who was present: 'We must put an end to the Jews.' Goebbels also noted in his diary: 'Concerning the Jewish question, the Führer is determined to make

[overleaf]
Adolf Hitler at the end of the speech in the Reichstag declaring war on the USA on 11 December 1941.

a clean sweep. He prophesied [on 30 January 1939] to the Jews that if once again they were to cause a world war, the result would be their own destruction. That was no figure of speech. The world war is here [with the entry of the USA], the destruction of the Jews must be its inevitable consequence.'[207]

Pearl Harbor helpfully diverted German public attention from the total failure of the German army to capture Moscow. Operation Barbarossa had already been dealt an enormous psychological blow. Hitler pinned the blame for the Moscow catastrophe on the German High Command, who, he argued, had pushed him to try and take Moscow when he had never considered it to be a top priority. Many leading army officers were now discharged by Hitler. On 19 December the commander-in-chief of the army Walther von Brauchitsch, who had been reduced to the role of little more than Hitler's messenger boy, was summarily dismissed. His health was already failing, following a recent heart attack, but Hitler now considered him completely incompetent. The Führer decided to appoint himself as commander-in-chief.

Fedor von Bock, the commander of Army Group Centre, who had seemingly lost his nerve outside Moscow, was also removed. His replacement was Field Marshal Günther von Kluge, who was already a high-ranking officer in Army Group Centre. The outspoken Heinz Guderian was also sacked. Gerd von Rundstedt, the commander of Army Group South, was replaced by Field Marshal Walther von Reichenau, the commander of the legendary German 6th Army. Field Marshal Wilhelm Ritter von Leeb, the commander of Army Group North, decided to resign before Hitler sacked him. He was replaced by Field Marshal Georg von Küchler. About forty other German army officers were demoted or sidelined during the wholesale army purge that followed the Moscow debacle.[208] Hitler had suffered a severe setback in his plan to swiftly defeat the Soviet Union, but he was now the undisputed master of the German army. He micromanaged not just its military strategy, but its leading generals too.

Hitler's long-standing distrust of upper-class and aristocratic German army officers now came to the fore. He constantly blamed himself for failing to Nazify the Army High Command before the war. As a radical Nazi, Hitler felt that he was constantly being forced into compromises with the conservative old guard who ran the army. 'Anybody can handle operational leadership – that's easy,' he declared. 'The task of the commander-in-chief of the army is to give the army

National Socialist training. I don't know any army general who can do this as I want it done.'[209]

By the end of 1941, the German army had lost about 25 per cent of its original battle strength at the outset of Operation Barbarossa. These men could not be replaced by soldiers of equal training and experience. As well as these irreplaceable losses, most of the armaments produced by German industry in 1941 had been lost on the battlefield. This did not mean that Hitler was heading for inevitable defeat. After all, Germany had gained more territory during 1941 than in all the battles in Western Europe in 1940, and German losses were small when compared to those of the Soviet Union. From June to December 1941 the Red Army lost a staggering 2,663,000 killed, with 3,350,000 taken prisoner.[210] Germany had complete control of the rich grain area of Ukraine. Around 33 per cent of the Soviet rail network was now behind German lines. Production of Soviet coal, steel and iron had been reduced by 75 per cent by the end of 1941. Only 130 million people lived in the still unconquered Soviet territories. German Army Group Centre had been forced to retreat, but it soon took up strong defence positions just 70 miles forward of where Operation Typhoon had begun.

1942

·

WAR
AGAINST
THE JEWS

·

•

Adolf Hitler spent Christmas 1941 at his gloomy military headquarters in Rastenburg. His traditional New Year message on 1
January 1942 adopted an uncharacteristically apologetic tone. 'I regret
this war,' he began, 'not only because of the sacrifices that it demands
of my German *Volk*, but also because of the time it takes away from
those who intend to carry out great social and civilizing work and
who intend to complete it.' Hitler pinned the blame for the war on
an 'international Jewish-capitalist and Bolshevik conspiracy'. Then he
issued a chilling warning: 'The Jew will not exterminate the European
people; he will instead become the victim of his own plot.'[1]

Hitler met with Hiroshi Ōshima, the Japanese ambassador, at the
Wolf's Lair on 3 January to discuss future Axis cooperation. This meeting
followed an agreement signed by the Axis powers on 11 December 1941
on the joint conduct of the war. The signatories pledged to continue the
war against the Allies until a successful conclusion had been reached.
Hitler told Ōshima that a new German offensive in a southerly
direction in the Soviet Union would begin once weather conditions
were favourable. He remained confident of victory in the German-
Soviet War, further promising that the German U-boat campaign in
the Atlantic would be stepped up. If Axis military operations were
coordinated, he said, then victory over Britain was certain, but he was
not yet sure how the United States would be defeated.[2]

On 18 January a new military agreement between Germany, Japan
and Italy was signed. The Axis powers divided up the world into two
'zones of military operations': an eastern zone covered by Japan and a
western one dominated by Germany and Italy. In reality, Germany and
Italy in Europe and Japan in the Far East fought entirely different wars.
There was little effort to coordinate Axis activity in these very different
theatres of war.

In the first half of 1942, Japanese armed forces expanded rapidly in
Asia, largely at the expense of the British Empire. Thailand and Hong
Kong had already been captured in December 1941. Then Malaya
(now Malaysia) fell on 31 January 1942, Singapore on 15 February, the

Dutch East Indies (now Indonesia) on 9 March, the Philippines on 11 March, and Burma (now Myanmar) on 16 April. Neither British and Commonwealth forces – nor the great ships of the Royal Navy or their American allies – could do anything to stop this spectacular run of Japanese military victories in the early part of 1942.[3]

On 5 January, Stalin held a meeting of the State Defence Committee in the Kremlin. With the German army in retreat outside Moscow, Stalin proposed a fresh general offensive. The aims were extremely ambitious: to end the Leningrad siege, crush Army Group North, strike a further devastating blow against the retreating Army Group Centre, and attack Army Group South, with the aim of pushing the Germans back in the Crimea. As Stalin put it: 'The Germans are in disarray as a result of their defeat in Moscow, they are badly fitted-out for winter. This is the most favourable moment for the transition to a general offensive.'[4] Stalin ordered this risky general offensive in temperatures averaging $-20°C$. Hitler's December order to 'stand fast' had been communicated to the three German army groups and discipline within the German army was quickly re-established. However, defence strongpoints had been held at a huge cost in lives.

By the beginning of February Army Group Centre had consolidated its new defence positions around sixty miles west of Moscow. In the south, the Soviet offensive was halted due to the bitter winter conditions. Army Group North was also able to maintain its siege of Leningrad.

In early March 1942, the Red Army general offensive shuddered to a halt. It soon became clear that there would now be a lull in the fighting on the Eastern Front. The Soviet High Command recommended that the Red Army groups moved to a 'strategic defensive' position during the summer, with the aim of building up well-equipped reserves, supported by tanks and aircraft to mount a major offensive later in the year. It was felt that the main threat during the expected German summer offensive would be spearheaded by Army Group Centre and would once again be directed towards Moscow.[5]

The Stavka, or High Command of the Soviet armed forces, calculated that there remained 16 million men of military age in the USSR and that during 1942 the current strength of the Red Army would be increased to 9 million. This figure excluded the 3 million Russian POWs who had been captured by Axis forces in 1941 and also those who had been killed. There were still enough Soviet soldiers to staff 400 new army divisions in 1942.[6]

On 15 January the Third Pan-American Conference of foreign ministers opened in Rio de Janeiro. The US government had convened it for the purpose of emergency consultation with Latin American countries in response to the recent Japanese attack on Pearl Harbor. Prior to the meeting, the Dominican Republic, Haiti, Cuba, Panama, Nicaragua, Honduras and Guatemala had all declared war on the Axis powers, and the United States wanted every remaining Latin American republic to follow suit.

On 28 January all the participants agreed to sever diplomatic relations with the Axis powers, but Argentina and Chile refused to do so. A joint declaration was issued, pledging all countries to consult on defence matters, to respect international treaties, to uphold morality in foreign relations and to declare solidarity with the United States in its war with Axis powers. Later in the year, Mexico on 22 May and Brazil on 22 August declared war on the Axis nations.[7]

A much more sinister German conference took place on 20 January 1942 in a villa on the south-western outskirts of Berlin, overlooking the picturesque Lake Wannsee. At the time the villa at 56–58 Am Großen Wannsee was being used as a guest house by the Security Police (SD). The meeting to organize the 'Final Solution of the Jewish question' had originally been scheduled for 9 December 1941, but it was postponed by Reinhard Heydrich due to the Japanese attack on Pearl Harbor. In his invitations to the conference, Heydrich had emphasized that he alone had been commissioned by Hermann Göring on 31 July 1941

to make the necessary technical and organizational preparations for a comprehensive solution to the so-called Jewish question. He attached a copy of this order to each invitation.[8]

The original list of invitees was expanded to include the state secretaries of government ministries for the Occupied Eastern Territories (Dr Alfred Meyer, Dr Georg Leibbrandt), the Ministry of the Interior (Dr Wilhelm Stuckart), the Ministry of Justice (Dr Roland Freisler), the Foreign Ministry (Martin Luther), the Office of the Four-Year Plan (Erich Neumann) and the Reich Chancellery (Wilhelm Kitzinger), as well as key officials from the General Government in Poland (Dr Josef Bühler, Dr Eberhard Schöngarth), and administrators from the Party Chancellery (Dr Gerhard Klopfer), the Reich Security Main Office (Otto Hofmann, Adolf Eichmann), the Gestapo (Heinrich Müller) and the *Einsatzgruppen* (Dr Rudolf Lange).

In all, there were fifteen attendees at the Wannsee Conference, including Heydrich, who chaired the meeting. All had lengthy experience of Nazi Jewish policy. They were all highly educated, eight of them holding doctorates, mainly in law. Only one person was over fifty and nearly half of them were under forty. These men were not dutiful bureaucratic functionaries with an essentially conservative outlook, but true believers in Hitler's antisemitic ideology.

There were some notable absentees. There was no representative from the Propaganda Ministry and no Reich Commissar for the Strengthening of Germandom. No officials from the Transport or Finance Ministries were present either, which suggests that the original purpose of the meeting was probably a narrow policy to organize the deportation arrangements for Jews from Germany as well as the Protectorate of Bohemia and Moravia, to the *Reichskommissariat* Ostland, the civilian regime established in the former Baltic states.[9]

Because the 'Final Solution' was viewed as an ideological, SS matter, representatives of the armed forced were not invited. The fact that representatives from the General Government were omitted from the original list of invitees adds weight to the idea that a Europe-wide solution to the so-called Jewish question was not the original intention of the proposed but cancelled December 1941 Wannsee meeting.

From early December 1941 onwards Jews had begun to be gassed to death in large numbers with carbon monoxide in gas vans at a camp in Chełmno, about fifty miles from the city of Łódź in the Warthegau. Arthur Greiser, the local Gauleiter, decided to reduce the population

The villa at 56–58 Am Großen Wannsee.

of the overcrowded Łódź ghetto by murdering 20,000 Jews and 5,000 Gypsies. Greiser gave the order to carry out these killings under his own initiative, without asking for permission from the Reich Security Main Office.

Herbert Lange was selected as the camp commandant at Chełmno. Once victims arrived, their property was confiscated. They were told to undress for a shower for delousing purposes. The victims were then herded up a ramp into the waiting gas vans. Their corpses were removed by Polish forced labourers and buried nearby in shallow pits. There were few survivors of the Chełmno killing operation. One man who did escape from a work crew assisting the killings was Szalma Weiner, who gave a detailed statement about the genocide at Chełmno to the leaders of the Jewish community in Warsaw. His account was then sent to the Polish government-in-exile in London.

Between December 1941 and March 1943 approximately 145,000 Jews were killed at Chełmno. The killing at Chełmno involved around eighty to a hundred SS guards and a small number of Polish labourers. The whole operation was self-financing and profitable. Guards collected huge amounts of cash, gold, silver and jewellery from the victims.[10]

Heydrich claimed that the Wannsee meeting was designed 'to obtain clarity on questions of principle' and to allow 'joint consultation' to achieve harmony between 'relevant central agencies' for handling the 'Final Solution' of the so-called Jewish question. He apologized for postponing the previous meeting, but simply stated that this was due to 'events which suddenly intruded'.[11]

The typed minutes of the conference were discovered only in March 1947 by the German lawyer Robert Kempner, who served as assistant US chief counsel during the International Military Tribunal into war crimes at Nuremberg.[12] He found them among a number of files seized by the Allies from the German Foreign Ministry. There were thirty copies made of the minutes, but the copy found by Kempner was the only one to survive.[13]

Heydrich began the Wannsee Conference by reminding those present once again of the order sent to him on 31 July 1941 by Göring. He stressed that the ultimate authority over Jewish policy rested with Himmler. He then delivered a short overview of the anti-Jewish measures of the German government since 1933. These had aimed to segregate Jews from society, remove their citizenship rights, cut them off from the economy and to accelerate emigration.

In October 1941 emigration, which had only been a 'provisional

Reinhard Heydrich who chaired the Wannsee Conference.

solution', was prohibited, due to the danger it posed during wartime. In its place the Führer had now authorized a much more radical solution: the transportation of the Jews of Europe to the 'East'.[14] In total, 11 million Jews would be affected by this policy. Drawing on estimates provided by Adolf Eichmann, Heydrich listed the number of Jews living in each European country, including those residing in areas under German occupation or control (Part A) and Jews resident in countries which were Germany's allies, in neutral countries and even in enemy countries not under German control (Part B).

Heydrich made clear that the 'Final Solution' involved tracking down all Jews in Europe and transporting them to the 'East'. Able-bodied Jews would be assigned hard labour, mostly heavy construction work, and would be eliminated by what was described as 'extermination through labour'. Older Jews (meaning those over sixty-five) from Germany and some Western countries would be deported to an 'old-age ghetto' in Theresienstadt concentration camp, where they would die from limited food rations. The 'unmentioned' remainder faced 'special treatment', which had already become an SS euphemism for extermination. First the Greater German Reich and the Protectorate of Bohemia and Moravia would be cleared of Jews, then the whole of Europe would be 'combed from West to East' and all Jews transported eastwards and held in camps and ghettos.

Heydrich then explained how an extension of the 'Final Solution' to the occupied and satellite countries would follow negotiations between local and military governments. Slovakia, Croatia, Italy and Greece would present no problems in cooperating, he said, but Hungary and Romania might offer resistance. As for France, Heydrich thought that it might prove difficult getting hold of every Jew there, particularly in the Unoccupied Zone. This might also be the case in Belgium and the Netherlands.

Martin Luther, representing the Foreign Ministry, thought that the Vichy government would cooperate in rounding up Jews, but he felt that the Scandinavian states – notably, Denmark, Norway, Finland and Sweden – would oppose transporting their Jewish populations. But the number of Jews living in these countries was low anyway, so Heydrich thought that deferring action in these nations would not be a problem.

Heydrich next moved on to discuss the situation of 'half-Jews' (*Mischlinge*) and those Jews currently in mixed marriages in Germany. First-degree *Mischlinge* were defined as people who did not belong to the Jewish religion and were not married to a Jewish spouse, but who had two Jewish grandparents; second-degree *Mischlinge* were people with one Jewish grandparent. This controversial topic was discussed in some detail. Heydrich proposed a radical solution by suggesting that first-degree *Mischlinge* should be deported to the 'East' with the rest of Europe's Jews. In total, he estimated that there were 100,000 'half-Jews' still remaining in Germany. The situation of Jews married to 'Aryan' Germans would be decided on a case-by-case basis. The number involved in mixed marriages was thought to be less than 20,000. Hitler always felt that the *Mischlinge* should be treated as 'Aryans', and he was generally unwilling to endorse drastic solutions to Jews of mixed parentage, because he was worried about how it would affect German public opinion.

The final part of the meeting was devoted to brief comments from other participants. Wilhelm Stuckart, from the Ministry of the Interior, pointed out the bureaucratic difficulties encountered in deporting *Mischlinge*, especially those in mixed marriages. As an alternative to deportation he suggested forced sterilization and raised the possibility that mixed marriages could be annulled by a new law. Josef Bühler from the General Government argued that the 'Final Solution' should begin in German-occupied Poland, where there were no major transport problems. An estimated 2.28 million Jews resided there at present, he said, and they were not part of the workforce, but were a source of epidemics in the ghettos. Bühler stressed that the authorities in the General Government wanted the Jewish matter to be solved 'as quickly as possible'.

The true significance of the Wannsee Conference on the Holocaust has long been debated by historians. Under cross-examination at Nuremberg, Hans Heinrich Lammers, the Chief of the Reich Chancellery, claimed that the Wannsee minutes 'weren't records. They were one-sided minutes compiled by the RSHA [the Reich Security Main Office].'[15] Others present denied that any concrete programme of genocide was ever discussed and suggested that the chief purpose of the meeting was the provision of forced labour for huge road-building schemes. Wilhelm Stuckart, for instance, commented: 'There was no discussion of the Final Solution of the Jewish question, in the sense in which it is now understood.'[16]

Another doubt concerning the significance of the Wannsee Conference revolves around whether the exact means of killing Jews was ever spelled out clearly by Heydrich to the delegates. The judges at the Ministries Trial at Nuremberg concluded that the term 'evacuating

Jews to the east' really meant 'physical extermination'.[17] In 1961, under cross-examination at his trial in Israel for war crimes, Adolf Eichmann explained that there had been references in off-the-record discussions to the 'annihilation of the Jews'.[18]

There now seems little doubt that genocide was being contemplated at the Wannsee Conference. Heydrich had made it perfectly clear that 'able-bodied' Jews would be worked to death, and that those surviving would then be 'eliminated'. Josef Bühler's comments also showed that he fully understood that Jews who could not work would be murdered in the General Government, and that he was keen for this to start soon and to be concluded quickly. The 'Final Solution' envisaged at Wannsee undoubtedly involved a combination of slave labour and extermination.

The Wannsee Conference was therefore a pivotal moment in the emergence of the 'Final Solution', signalling a more radical genocidal phase within Hitler's government. Heydrich was not asking the participants to organize the genocide themselves, but to cooperate in its implementation. Himmler, Heydrich and the SD-RSHA terror apparatus would take the lead in the operation. The civilian ministries present were collaborators, but they were not the instigators of the mass killing.

Heydrich's radical solutions to the *Mischlinge* and Jews in mixed marriages were never actually implemented. The Ministry of Justice sank the proposal to annul mixed marriages by law and the Reich Chancellery refused to allow compulsory sterilization of *Mischlinge*. In October 1943, Himmler agreed not to deport *Mischlinge* from Germany proper for the duration of the war. In December 1943, however, it was decided that the Jewish widows of Aryan men could be deported. For the most part, German-born *Mischlinge* and German Jews in mixed marriages were spared. For non-German Jews no such mercy was shown.

Whether or not the Wannsee Conference was the key factor, 1942 stands out as the peak year for the mass murder of Jews under Nazi rule. Up until the end of January 1942, fewer than 10 per cent of Jewish victims of the Holocaust perished, mostly in mass shootings and primarily in the Soviet Union, but between March 1942 and March 1943, 50 per cent of all Jews killed in the Holocaust were murdered.

Within days of the Wannsee Conference, Eichmann informed the main Gestapo offices in Germany about the recent 'evacuation of Jews' to the east. This was already occurring in several areas of the Reich, which he suggested marked the beginning of the Final Solution of the so-called Jewish question in the Old Reich, in Austria and in the Protectorate of Bohemia and Moravia.[19] At the end of February 1942 all the relevant government departments had received copies of the Wannsee Conference minutes.

The idea of 'extermination through labour' was also pursued by SS officials in the weeks following the Wannsee Conference.[20] During February 1942 the role of the concentration camps was being redefined. Oswald Pohl, the chief of the new SS Main Economic and Administrative Office, gave a much higher priority than before to the economic exploitation of prisoners in the camps. The whole concentration camp system was now seen as a key source of labour for Germany's war industries. The idea that unproductive prisoners would be killed now became accepted among those who ran all the concentration camps.[21]

On 25 January 1942 Adolf Hitler had lunch with Himmler.[22] Hitler was concerned about whether the German people were ready for the life and death struggle for their existence that was currently going on in the Soviet Union. 'Faith moves mountains,' he told Himmler. 'In that respect, I see things with the coldest objectivity. If the German people lost its faith, if the German people were no longer inclined to give itself body and soul in order to survive – then the German people would have nothing to do but disappear.'[23] Hitler also spoke bluntly on the fate of the Jews: 'The Jew must be ousted from Europe. If not, we shall get no European cooperation.'[24]

Hermann Göring arrived for talks with Mussolini in Rome on 28 January 1942. Hitler sent him there to press Mussolini for greater Italian military involvement in North Africa. However, the talk soon moved to a growing dissatisfaction among the Italian public with Mussolini's Fascist Party. Mussolini reassured Göring that he still believed that he had the population under his control, and remained convinced the Axis nations would win the war.[25]

On 30 January 1942 at Berlin's Sport Palace Hitler delivered his traditional speech commemorating his coming to power in 1933. He confessed that he did not know whether the war could be won in 1942, but he asked the German public to keep faith: 'God give us the strength to maintain freedom for ourselves, for our people, our children and our children's children, and not only for our people, but for the other peoples of Europe.' He then reminded his audience of his famous speech of 30 January 1939 in which he had prophesied that a world war would result in the annihilation of all European Jews. Hitler now promised that his prophecy would come true:

This war will not end as the Jews imagine, namely, in the extermination of the European-Aryan people; instead, the result of this war will be the annihilation of Jewry. For the first time, not merely others will bleed to death; rather, for the first time the old Jewish law "an eye for an eye, a tooth for a tooth" will be applied to them. And the more the fighting expands, the more antisemitism will spread.[26]

Goebbels, who was present, commented:

The speech made a tremendous impression both upon those present and on the entire German nation. We may now rest assured that the main psychological difficulties have been overcome. We are now standing with both feet on the ground again. The enthusiasm of the audience exceeded anything the mind can imagine. The Führer has charged the entire nation as though it were a storage battery.[27]

On 1 February the pro-Nazi Vidkun Quisling was appointed as Norway's Prime Minister in a move designed to transfer power from the German military administration to a native if puppet 'national government'. On 12 March Norway effectively became a one-party state. Goebbels commented: 'Quisling is hated violently in the entire enemy world.' He then advised the German press not to call Quisling a 'Führer' when writing about Norwegian affairs.[28]

On 7 February Fritz Todt – the builder of the autobahn network and the 'West Wall' (or 'Siegfried Line') – visited Hitler at the Wolf's Lair.[29] Todt, who had been Minister of Armaments and Munitions ever since March 1940, delivered a report to the Führer on the current armaments situation and afterwards they dined privately together. Albert Speer, who was also present in Hitler's HQ at the same time, noticed that Todt seemed 'strained and fatigued' after his meeting with Hitler, although Todt gave him no details about what was discussed.[30] On the next morning Todt's twin-engine Heinkel III took off, bound for Berlin. As it ascended, it quickly burst into flames and crashed. Todt was killed instantly.

Hitler initially suspected foul play and ordered the Reich Air Ministry to investigate. The subsequent report ruled out sabotage and concluded that the plane's engine had exploded at around sixty-five feet, then the aircraft had fallen out of the sky. It later transpired that Todt had expressed a fear of being assassinated and had deposited a large sum of money in a safe, earmarked for his personal secretary in the event of his sudden death.[31]

Goebbels noted his own feelings on Todt's death:

I feel numb over this loss. I hardly have time to think! There are so many people in public life who are as superfluous as a goitre. Death does not dare touch them, but when there is someone among them who has the ability to make history, a senseless and cruel fate tears him from our ranks and he leaves a void that simply cannot be filled.[32]

Todt was replaced as Armaments Minister by Speer. Ironically, Speer had declined a seat on Todt's ill-fated plane. The appointment of Speer, who remained in post until 1945, was something of a surprise, even to Speer, who admitted that he knew nothing about armaments. 'I have confidence in you,' Hitler reassured him. 'I know you will manage it.'[33]

Göring was very unhappy about Speer's appointment. He felt it undermined his role as head of the Four-Year Plan Department. Hitler made it plain to sceptics that Speer had his full support in a decree issued on 21 March, stating: 'The requirements of the German economy as a whole must be subordinated to the necessities of armament production.'[34] Soon afterwards, Göring assured Speer that he had his full support.

Speer was a master of self-publicity and used armaments statistics selectively to suggest that his policies had produced a German 'armaments miracle'.[35] Speer soon established a Central Planning Committee (*Zentrale Planung*), which helped coordinate armament production more effectively. His close relationship with Hitler added to his standing among the com-

Fritz Todt, Reich Minister of Armaments and Munitions.

mittee members. They met sixty-two times from 27 April 1942 until the end of the war, although most of these meetings took place from April 1942 to the end of 1943. The Central Planning Committee proved a crucial forum for coordinating the German armaments drive. Speer's primary authority was over the equipment needs of the *Wehrmacht* and within six months he had overseen an increase in gun production of 27 per cent, increased tanks by 25 per cent and ammunition by 97 per cent.[36]

Speer also introduced an imaginative incentive scheme to boost armament production. At its heart was a new fixed-price system. This replaced the existing government procurement system, which allowed armaments manufacturers to inflate costs and deliver armaments way over budget. Speer asked producers to make goods to a pre-agreed set price and stick to it. Any profits the companies made by reducing costs below the original price could be retained. It was a capitalist profit incentive scheme encouraging industry to reduce costs, rationalize labour and increase productivity.

Speer undoubtedly improved relations with big business. German business leaders feared a Soviet victory in the war, because it would spell the end of German capitalism. This had intensified their mutually beneficial links with Hitler's government. Speer left the responsibility for meeting his armaments targets to private industry. He also recruited industrialists to serve on his Subcommittees on Rearmament, so that they had a genuine input into policy decisions.[37]

At Fritz Todt's state funeral service on 12 February, broadcast live on German national radio, Hitler delivered a deeply emotional eulogy, outlining Todt's achievements and highlighting his many personal qualities. Hitler seemed so moved during his speech that he halted, seemingly welling up with tears, then admitted that Todt's death had hit him hard, as he had been very close to him.[38]

On 14 February Hitler met Dr Mile Budak the antisemitic Croatian ambassador at the new Reich Chancellery in Berlin. Goebbels was present and overheard Hitler telling Budak of his intention to massacre the Jews:

> The Führer once more expressed his determination to clean up the Jews of Europe pitilessly. There must be no squeamish sentimentalism about it. The Jews have deserved the catastrophe that has overtaken them. Their destruction will go hand in hand with the destruction of our enemies. We must hasten this process with cold ruthlessness. We shall thereby render an inestimable

Adolf Hitler walking with Albert Speer at the Wolf's Lair.

service to a humanity tormented for thousands of years by the Jews.[39]

In a speech to 10,000 officer candidates in the Berlin Sport Palace on 15 February Hitler argued that the whole world had once been the sworn enemy of Frederick the Great and Bismarck: 'Today I have the honour to be this enemy, because I am attempting to create a world power out of the German Reich.'[40]

For the first time, Hitler could not deliver in Munich his traditional 24 February speech commemorating the Foundation of the Nazi Party Programme. Hitler claimed it was impossible for him to leave his military headquarters during the worst winter for a hundred years. At any rate, he was now preparing for the 'final confrontation' with Stalin's Red Army. Instead, the Munich Gauleiter Adolf Wagner read out Hitler's speech. Hitler stressed that the German army had advanced in the Soviet Union by 621 miles from June to November 1941, until 'Snow and frost temporarily halted the triumphant advance of the German *Wehrmacht* that was unique in history.'

Hitler then issued another warning to the Jews: 'My prophecy – that this war will not destroy the Aryan, but instead, it will exterminate the Jew – will be fulfilled. Whatever the struggle may bring with it, or however long it may last, this will be its final result. And only then, after the elimination of these parasites, will a long era of international understanding and therefore true peace come over the suffering world.'[41]

On 6 March 1942 Goebbels appears to have read a copy of the minutes of the Wannsee Conference for the first time. Afterwards, he noted in his diary that the 'Final

Odilo Globočnik, the leading SS official who was the chief organizer of Operation Reinhard.

Solution' was now being decided in a 'Europe-wide context'. The first part of this process was to 'concentrate Jews in the east'. Goebbels was of the opinion that there could be no lasting peace on the European continent until the Jews were permanently excluded.[42]

On 15 March 1942 Hitler spoke at the Heroes' Memorial Day commemoration in Berlin's Courtyard of Honour. He remained both a statesman and a soldier, he said. The current winter had been the 'sole hope of the power-holders in the Kremlin', but he promised that 'the Bolshevik hordes, which were unable to defeat the German soldiers and their allies this winter, will be beaten by us into annihilation this summer'.[43] Goebbels thought the speech was 'excellent, indeed a classical speech both in style and content'.[44]

After the speech, German national radio broadcast Hitler conducting an informal conversation with a group of wounded soldiers from the Eastern Front. It was very rare for Hitler to seek the company of those directly affected by his military decisions and it reflected his fear of losing support on the home front. He talked in a warm, conversational tone of his 'inner connection with each soldier'.[45]

On 17 March 1942 the Bełżec extermination camp began its mass killing operation. It was part of what subsequently became known as Operation Reinhard (*Aktion Reinhard*), a plan to exterminate all Jews 'unfit for work' located in the General Government area of occupied Poland.[46] Preparations for this phase of mass murder had begun in the autumn of 1941, when Himmler ordered the leading SS figure Odilo Globočnik (known as 'Globus') to organize the planning and deportations of Jews to three new camps. He was also told to commission the construction of extermination facilities where these killings would be carried out.[47] Each camp was built near a railway line to facilitate the smooth transportation of victims. They were constructed in isolated, rural areas, as far away as possible from heavily populated cities. All were close to the border of the Soviet Union in order to maintain the subterfuge that Jews were being 'transported to the East'.

According to a surviving letter from Globočnik, dated 27 October 1943, a total of 450 men were involved in Operation Reinhard. They consisted of 153 police and SS personnel and ninety-two staff from the Reich Chancellery, who had all previously been involved in the *Aktion T4* involuntary euthanasia programme. These T4 staff all brought with them the grim experience of running gassing operations.[48]

A special organization established in Lublin was headed by

the brutal SS Major Christian Wirth, who was given the task of coordinating the entire killing operation in the Reinhard camps. He had also been a high-ranking officer in the *Aktion T4* programme.[49] All the staff involved in Operation Reinhard signed a declaration of strict secrecy. There was even a prohibition on the use of cameras by staff at any of the extermination camps. There were between twenty and thirty-five SS men involved in the killing operations at each location. Each member of staff was paid a daily bonus of eighteen Reichsmarks.

An additional security force was required in the extermination camps to supplement these experts in killing. They primarily consisted of two groups. First, guards of Ukrainian, Byelorussian, Lithuanian and Latvian origin, who were often extremely antisemitic already and eagerly volunteered for the task. Second, a group of strong Jewish prisoners at each camp, consisting of up to one hundred men. They were selected as they disembarked from the incoming trains and had no choice in the matter. It was their duty to carry out the gruesome tasks associated with the killing, including, removing corpses from the gas chambers, transporting them on trolleys and throwing them into the large burial pits. They also collected the clothes, suitcases, jewellery and even the gold teeth of the victims.[50]

The first Reinhard camp to open was Bełżec, located in the southeast of the Lublin district on the Lublin–Lvov railway line. It began life as a forced labour camp for Jews in April 1940, but was closed in the autumn of that year. Construction to convert Bełżec into a full-blown extermination camp began on 1 November 1941, after Wirth identified it as a suitable location. Polish forced labour was used to build the camp. By the end of February 1942 it was ready for operation.[51]

Bełżec occupied a small and compact area of just 1,220 square yards, which was ringed by a barbed-wire fence, with towers manned by guards equipped with machine guns. It was divided into two sections and surrounded by newly planted trees. The first section, Camp 1, had an administrative office and a barracks for the Jewish 'work teams' and the SS personnel. When victims arrived at the railway station, everything appeared eerily normal. None had any reason to believe Bełżec was not just an ordinary 'transit camp'. An SS officer gave a short speech – usually modified, depending on where the rail transport came from – stating that they were all going to work on farms. They were then told to form single-sex lines and to give up their suitcases and other belongings. Cash, gold and jewellery was handed over at a 'cash desk'. After this, they were told to proceed to an undressing area for 'hygienic reasons'. Women's heads were shaved for 'de-lousing purposes'. All the victims were ordered to undress while in the Camp 1 area.

Victims then went through a narrow passageway (called 'The Tube'), which led into Camp 2. This housed all of the extermination facilities and burial pits. This area was fenced off from the rest of the camp. The whole process from arrival to death moved at a very brisk speed.

Rudolf Reder, who escaped from a Jewish work team at Bełżec, vividly described what happened to women. He saw 'work-prisoners' appearing with stools and hair-cutting equipment to supervise the shaving of the women's hair. At this point, Reder recalled, the women usually began to fear the worst: 'There were cries and shrieking. Some women went mad. Others went to their death calmly, young girls in particular.' The women, naked and with their heads shaved, were then herded into the gas chamber, with guards bellowing, 'Faster, Faster.' 'Eventually,' Reder added, 'all the women were forced into the chambers. I heard the doors being shut. I heard the shrieks and the cries. I heard desperate calls for help in Polish and Yiddish. I heard blood-curdling wails of women and squeals of children.'[52]

There were initially three gas chambers at Bełżec. Each was four by eight metres and two metres high. They were soon to be replaced by six new airtight, rubber-sealed gas chambers housed in a much larger concrete building. The method of killing used was to pipe in carbon monoxide gas, connected to a large diesel engine. The killing at Bełżec began on 17 March 1942 and ended in December of the same year. The Polish Commission for the Investigation of German Crimes in Poland, which began in 1945, gave a figure of 600,000 people murdered in the Bełżec camp.[53] Most of the Jewish victims came from the districts of Lublin, Lviv, Galicia and Krakow. Jews from France, Slovakia, Germany, Greece and the Netherlands were also killed there.

Sobibór, the Nazis' second purpose-built extermination camp, was located near a small village near the Chełm-Włodawa railway line east of Lublin. Built between March and May 1942, it was operational from 16 May 1942 to 14 October 1943.[54] The area around the camp was swampy, wooded and thinly populated. Sobibór was rectangular in shape, measuring just 600 by 400 metres. It was surrounded by trees with an inner ring of barbed-wire fences, plus five elevated watchtowers manned by guards with machine guns.

Franz Stangl, a young but experienced SS official who had previously been involved in the *Aktion T4* programme, was drafted in by

[overleaf]
Jews being deported by train to the extermination camps.

Globočnik to run the Sobibór killing facility. Stangl had a reputation for taking orders without questioning them. Handsome and neatly dressed in a smart white jacket, black trousers and jackboots, he always carried a riding crop with him on inspections of the camp, though he never used it.[55]

Sobibór was divided into three areas: (a) the administrative section (Camp I) included the entrance gate, railway ramp and living quarters for the SS and the other guards; (b) the reception area (Camp II) had an undressing barracks, where the women had their hair shaved. Victims were then processed through a narrow passageway (also nicknamed 'The Tube'). This connected to (c) the extermination section (Camp III), which contained the gas chambers, crematoria and burial ground.

After the war SS officer Erich Bauer testified on the extermination process at Sobibór: 'Usually the undressing went smoothly. Subsequently, the Jews were taken through the 'Tube' to Camp III – the real extermination camp. The transfer through the tube proceeded as follows: one SS man was in the lead and five or six Ukrainian auxiliaries were at the back hastening the [Jews] along.'[56]

At the start of the killing operation at Sobibór, there were three gas chambers that used carbon monoxide fumes and were housed in a concrete building. They could kill 600 people at a time. Stangl ordered this to be replaced by a new and much larger building, operational from October 1942, which housed six new gas chambers, each capable of killing 1,300 victims at a time.

From May 1942 to October 1943 an estimated 167,000 to 250,000 Jews were killed in Sobibór. The Höfle telegram

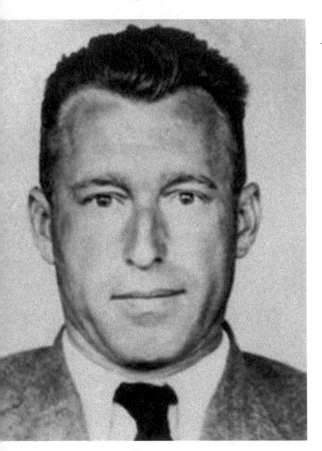

Franz Stangl, the commandant of the Treblinka and Sobibór extermination camps.

– a top-secret telegram from the SS officer Hermann Höfle to Adolf Eichmann, dated 11 January 1943, and intercepted by British intelligence – gives a figure of 167,000 people killed at Sobibór up to that date alone.[57] The victims were primarily Jews from the General Government area. In October 1943, there was a major uprising of inmates at the camp. It was then swiftly closed on a direct order from Himmler and all the gas chambers there were destroyed.

Treblinka was the third Operation Reinhard extermination camp. It was in a remote north-eastern section of the General Government, about seventy-five miles from Warsaw. A single-track railway line led to the camp, which branched off from the Malikinia–Siedlce railway line. Treblinka was built from April to July 1942 and was in operation between 22 July 1942 and October 1943. The camp was roughly the same size (400 by 600 metres) as Sobibór and it was similarly rectangular in shape. It, too, was surrounded by barbed wire, with heavily guarded watchtowers and camouflaged by tall trees.[58]

The camp was divided into three zones of roughly equal size: (a) the living area, containing barracks for the SS and the other guards; (b) the reception area, near the train platform, with storage for confiscated goods, and also the undressing area; (c) the extermination area, which initially contained three hermetically sealed gas chambers, each four by four metres in size and three metres in height, housed in a brick building. This area was completely isolated from the rest of the camp. The gas chambers were made to look even more like showers than in the other camps, with white tiles and mock shower-heads. A room attached to the extermination building contained a large diesel engine, which introduced carbon monoxide fumes through pipes. Nearby were the huge burial pits for the corpses of the victims.

A sign on the railway platform had an inscription which read:

You are in a transit camp [*Durchgangslager*] from which you will be sent to a labour camp [*Arbeitslager*]. In order to avoid epidemics, you must present your clothing and belongings for immediate disinfection. Gold, money, foreign currency and jewellery should be deposited with the cashiers in return for a receipt. This will be returned to you later when you present the receipt. Bodily cleanliness requires that everyone bathe before continuing the journey.[59]

The mass murder at Treblinka began on 23 July 1942 under the command of Dr Irmfried Eberl, an SS officer and another former *Aktion T4* operative. He proved extremely inefficient and corrupt. His staff confiscated the gold and currency of the victims and kept them for themselves. The gas chambers did not work properly and there was no plan of how to dispose of the dead. Rotting corpses were simply left in huge piles out in the open and the horrible smell soon made its way to the local village.

Reports soon spread of the chaos at Treblinka. Christian Wirth accompanied by Odilo Globočnik paid a surprise visit to see what was happening for themselves. Even these hardened SS men were horrified at the state of the camp. Eberl was promptly sacked on the spot. The reliable Franz Stangl was then drafted in from Sobibór, in early September, as the new camp commandant.

Stangl transformed Treblinka into an efficient factory of death. He built a fake railway station, complete with timetables, a ticket office and a painted clock whose hands never moved. A new brick building was completed in October 1942. It had ten gas chambers, each four by eight metres, which all branched off from a central long corridor. Each gas chamber could kill 2,300 people at a time. The ceilings were deliberately kept at a low level to reduce the time required for the carbon monoxide to have its deadly effect. A small glass window was fitted to each gas chamber for the guards to check that all the victims were dead before opening the door. At his later war crimes trial, Stangl estimated that between 12,000 and 15,000 people were murdered each day at Treblinka. The gas chambers operated from early morning to the late evening.

Stangl later revealed, with astonishing detachment, his personal feelings towards the plight of the victims, during a harrowing interview with the historian Gitta Sereny:

> To tell the truth one did become used to it... they were cargo...
> I think it started the day I first saw the *Totenlager* [extermination area] in Treblinka. I remember Wirth standing there, next to the pits full of blue-black corpses. It had nothing to do with humanity – it couldn't have; it was a mass – a mass of rotting flesh. Wirth said, 'What shall we do with this garbage?' I think unconsciously that started me thinking of them as cargo...
> I rarely saw them as individuals. It was always a huge mass. I sometimes stood on the wall and saw them [the victims] in the 'tube'. But – how can I explain it – they were naked, packed together, running, being driven with whips.

Treblinka was viewed by Himmler as the model extermination camp. Estimates of the killing at Treblinka range from 700,000 to

900,000 people. Most of the victims were Jews from the Warsaw Ghetto and the Radom and Lublin districts. The Höfle telegram recorded that 813,000 Jews were killed at Treblinka in 1942 alone.[60] In November 1943, a group of Jewish slave labourers were ordered by the SS to dismantle the camp.

Operation Reinhard was not financed by huge amounts of German government spending. These extermination camps were planned on the hoof, underfunded and created at breakneck speed. Everything was done on the cheap using basic building materials and conscripted slave labour. Each camp had only around twenty paid SS personnel. The Jewish 'work-teams' who were recruited from the prisoners were paid with small amounts of food and eventually all were killed. The guards were also cheap volunteer labour, similarly paid in food. Using carbon monoxide from diesel engines to murder people cost very little, too. As the victims were killed not long after their arrival, there was no expense on food.

Operation Reinhard was a self-financed and profitable operation. The confiscated goods and valuables of the dead played a huge part in funding the whole enterprise. Globočnik frequently submitted progress reports to the SS Main Office for Economic Administration in Berlin, giving a detailed breakdown of 'valuables' confiscated from the victims. The booty included banknotes from forty-eight different countries, gold coins from thirty-four countries, large amounts of gold and silver bars, diamonds, wedding rings, earrings, necklaces, watches and various spun fabrics and clothing. The total profit for Operation Reinhard, after deducting the cost of running the camps, was 178.7 million Reichsmarks, with 100 million of that sum transferred to the Reichsbank as profit. The value of the goods stolen from victims by the SS and the camp guards never appeared in Globočnik's official reports and can only be guessed at but must have run into millions.[61]

In March 1942 Reinhard Heydrich met with Paul Blobel, a commander in the *Einsatzgruppe* in Warsaw, and gave him the task of organizing the erasure of all traces of German mass murder. Blobel commissioned experiments on burning large numbers of corpses. The first experiment took place at Chełmno. All the victims killed there had been buried in mass pits, covered by a very shallow layer of soil. These rotting corpses were dug up, using a mechanical excavator, and then burned on wood fires.[62]

The fanatical antisemite Globočnik raised objections about covering up the traces of the 'Final Solution'. Germans should be proud of carrying out their historic mission to exterminate the Jews, he said. Despite this, the digging-up and burning of corpses soon extended to every Operation Reinhard camp. The process began at Sobibór. A special large 'roaster' was created by placing railway lines over wood-filled pits. The decomposed corpses were then placed on top like meat on a barbecue and set alight.

Stangl later described how the mass outdoor cremations at Treblinka were carried out: 'It must have been at the beginning of 1943. That's when excavators were brought in. Using these, the corpses were removed from the huge ditches which had been used until then [for burial]. The old corpses were burned on the roasters, along with the new bodies [of recent victims]. Around 2,000 bodies could be burned on each roaster at a time.'[63]

The number of Jews killed in Bełżec, Sobibór and Treblinka is notoriously difficult to calculate, but it came to an enormous total. No detailed reports on the number of victims was ever submitted. The entire operation was designated a 'Reich Secret Matter' and documents related to it were routinely destroyed by the SS towards the end of the war.

Estimates of the number of deaths have been calculated from various deportation documents, survivors' witness accounts, evidence submitted at war trials, as well as detailed population and census research carried out by various government agencies, committees and historical researchers. Putting all of this surviving evidence together, it has been estimated that 1.7 million Jews were murdered at the three Operation Reinhard camps. With 1.65 million of those killed in the short period from March 1942 to the end of February 1943.[64] In other words, nearly a third of all the Jewish murders in the Holocaust occurred during Operation Reinhard.

No trace of any of these extermination camps now exists. The buildings were bulldozed and the extermination facilities were dismantled. Local people knew what had happened there, of course. In the summer of 1944 a rumour spread in nearby villages and towns that hundreds of thousands of Jews were buried at these sites, with their gold teeth and jewellery. For months, locals were seen digging in the fields, ghoulishly looking for the valuables of the dead.[65]

The major killing centre for Jews during the Holocaust was, of course, at the more well-known Auschwitz-Birkenau, located near the town of Oświęcim, which was annexed and incorporated into the Province of Upper Silesia (*Provinz Oberschlesien*) within an administrative area called *Regierungsbezirk Kattowitz*.

The Auschwitz camp did not emerge as a central part of the 'Final Solution' until July 1942. Unlike the Operation Reinhard extermination camps, Auschwitz was a dual-purpose, forced-labour/death camp. The original camp, Auschwitz (Camp I), was formerly a Polish army barracks before its conversion into a concentration camp in May 1940. The first inmates were Polish political prisoners, housed in twenty brick-built barracks. Entry to the camp was via a wrought-iron gate, displaying the now infamous sign *'Arbeit macht frei'* ('Work sets you free').

On 4 May 1940 the leading SS officer Rudolf Höss, who had previously worked at Dachau and Sachsenhausen concentration camps, was appointed as the new camp commandant of the Auschwitz concentration camp. In September 1940 Oswald Pohl visited the camp, quickly seeing its potential for industrial development. To fund this gigantic project, Himmler brokered what is now called a government-private finance deal between the SS and the German industrial company IG Farben, which established a huge chemical plant on the site at Monowitz (Camp III), which was designed to make synthetic rubber (called *Buna*).

Himmler paid IG Farben camp workers three Reichsmarks per day. Auschwitz was the first German-run concentration camp to be fully financed and built by private industry. German civilian managers, scientists, administrators and clerical workers were housed in a residential area near to the factory.[66] Eventually, the Auschwitz complex covered eighteen square miles and included up to fifty different satellite camps. This vast expansion was facilitated by a huge influx of primarily unskilled Jewish slave labour, which was central to the construction of the local factories and the infrastructure surrounding the camp.[67]

In October 1941, Birkenau (Camp II) was constructed. This became the chief killing centre within the Auschwitz-Birkenau complex.[68] Birkenau predominately housed deported Jews, who were used firstly as forced labourers, before their extermination. It included a women's camp, a Gypsy family camp and a 'family camp' for Jews who had been transferred from the Theresienstadt camp.[69] The inmates of these family camps were eventually exterminated. At the Nuremberg Trial, Höss claimed to have been given an order by Himmler in the late autumn of 1941 to construct extermination facilities to carry out the 'Final Solution'.[70]

Auschwitz-Birkenau gradually evolved into a leading centre of mass murder from 1940 to 1943. Construction of Crematorium 1 in

[overleaf]
The entrance to the notorious Auschwitz concentration camp.

Auschwitz Camp I began in July 1940. It had six ovens with the capacity to burn 340 corpses per day and was designed in the first place for prisoners who were executed or died of natural causes. The mortuary inside the crematorium was then converted into a gas chamber.

The first experiment with gassing in the Auschwitz I camp occurred on 3 September 1941, when a group of Soviet POWs were killed. A can of Zyklon B crystals was thrown into the basement cell of Block 11, which was packed with prisoners. When the crystals vaporized inside the room they quickly turned into a deadly gas, killing everyone within twenty minutes.

Höss later admitted that he personally witnessed many of the subsequent gassings:

> I had to look through the peephole of the gas chambers and watch the process of death itself, because the doctors wanted me to see it. I had to go through this because I was the one to whom everyone looked, because I had to show them all that I did not merely issue the orders and make the regulations, but was also prepared myself to be present at whatever task I had assigned to my subordinates.[71]

The first gas chamber in Birkenau (Camp II) was a converted farmer's cottage called Bunker 1 (known as 'The Little Red House'). It became operational on 20 March 1942. This was followed by Bunker 2 ('The Little White House'), which was modified into a gas chamber in June 1942. The use of these two killing bunkers ended in July 1943 when four new crematoria became operational. These new gassing facilities were designated as Crematoriums I, II, III and IV. Another two large crematoria (V and VI) were planned, but were never built. These four gas chambers could kill 4,616 people per day, but this figure was rarely reached due to problems with the crematorium ovens, which often broke down. The main method of killing used at Auschwitz-Birkenau was not carbon monoxide gas but Zyklon B, licensed by the huge chemical company IG Farben.[72]

Unlike at Operation Reinhard camps, where arrivals were prepared for death immediately upon arrival, the selection process at the Auschwitz-Birkenau complex was much more discriminatory. It was possible to survive the arrival process. After the victims arrived on packed trains, SS doctors gave each of them a cursory medical examination. Children under sixteen, mothers in charge of children, the obviously very sick, old and the disabled were asked to form a single line. They were then told to climb aboard waiting lorries and were driven straight to the gas chamber building where they were murdered. Able-bodied men and women were placed in a different line and then taken into the concentration camp by the head of labour allocation. They were tattooed with a serial number on their left arm and officially registered for work.

In a further distinguishing process inside the camp, prisoners were grouped into different work categories and each wore a distinctive coloured identification symbol on their striped uniforms. Jews wore yellow stars. Other prisoners wore coloured triangles: green for common criminals, pink for homosexuals, black for lesbians and other 'asocials', brown for Gypsies, red for political prisoners, and purple for Jehovah's Witnesses.

Another category of prisoner was selected upon arrival: those deemed suitable for medical and anthropological experiments in the camp complex. Dr Josef Mengele, known as the 'Angel of Death', was often present when the trains arrived, eager to find suitable 'guinea pigs' for his experiments. He was particularly interested in twins, but also people with physical abnormalities, who were often killed and used in post-mortem experiments.[73]

One of the most controversial aspects of the killing process at Auschwitz-Birkenau was the use of Special Squads (*Sonderkommandos*) to dispose of the remains of the victims.[74] Most of the *Sonderkommandos* were the strongest, fittest Jews, selected by the SS upon arrival. They had to pick up the bodies piled in the gas chambers, remove any gold teeth, put the corpses on trolleys and push them into coal-fired ovens. These men lived at the very bottom of hell. One member of the *Sonderkommando* later explained how the will to survive made him carry out these grim tasks: 'You think that those working in the *Sonderkommando* are monsters? I'm telling you, they're like the rest [of the inmates], just more unhappy.'[75]

A non-Jewish inmate of Auschwitz-Birkenau had some hope of survival. A Jew was utterly defenceless and on the lowest rung of the camp hierarchy. As Holocaust survivor Yisrael Gutman put it:

> The Jews were the pariahs in the concentration camps and were regarded as such by the other internees. Antisemitism was perceptible in the camps and assumed its most violent forms. Attacks on Jews were encouraged by the Nazis. Even those who were not anti-Jewish and were able to oppose the tide of hatred which flooded the camp acceded to the accepted norms and

regarded the Jews as abandoned, miserable creatures who were best avoided.[76]

The number of Jews killed at Auschwitz-Birkenau remains a subject of enormous controversy. Unfortunately, the differing estimates produced since 1945 have only served to encourage Holocaust-deniers and antisemitic conspiracy theorists. The Polish government estimated, shortly after the war ended, that 4.1 million people had been killed, mostly by systematic gassing. In his Nuremberg testimony, Höss claimed that 2.5 million Jews were murdered there, but under strong cross-examination by Allied prosecution lawyers he conceded that he did not know the exact figure, because he had not kept systematic records.

Ever since, the death toll at Auschwitz-Birkenau has been revised downwards. In 1961, the Jewish-American historian Raul Hilberg put the minimum Jewish murder total at Auschwitz-Birkenau at 1.1 million, with a maximum of 1.6 million. In 1991 another authoritative study by the Israeli historian Yehuda Bauer estimated the total number of deaths at 1.35 million.[77] The current estimate, based on the most recent research, is that 1.1 million people were killed at Auschwitz-Birkenau, and 90 per cent of them were Jews from places as diverse as Austria, Belarus, Belgium, Croatia, Czechoslovakia (the Protectorate of Bohemia and Moravia), France, Germany, Greece, Italy, the Netherlands, Norway, Poland and Slovakia. In 1944 alone a total of 394,000 Hungarian Jews were transported to the camp and gassed there.[78]

A much less well-known camp involved in the 'Final Solution' was Majdanek. It was not located in a remote area, like all the others, but was near to the major city of Lublin in the General Government. Primarily a forced-labour camp, Majdanek originally contained a combination of Soviet POWs and ethnic Poles. It was run on a shoestring budget, with no branch railway line or sewage system or even a proper piped water supply.

The transformation of Majdanek into a death camp came in late 1942. In September 1942, construction began on three gas chambers, which mainly used carbon monoxide. Victims arrived in trucks from the main railway station in Lublin. When deportations to Bełżec ended in mid-December 1942, thousands of Polish Jews were diverted to the Majdanek camp and murdered in its gas chambers soon after arrival.

Further extermination transports to Majdanek followed in the spring of 1943 as the SS stepped up its liquidation of the remaining inhabitants of the Jewish ghettos. Entire families from Warsaw ended up being killed at Majdanek. The camp finally ceased operation on 23 July 1944. Majdanek was not strictly speaking an Operation Reinhard extermination camp, but it was connected to that project and it appears in several SS documents as being a part of it, but only as an afterthought, once the killing in the other camps had been scaled down or had ceased.[79]

The Soviets originally estimated that 1.7 million people had been murdered in Majdanek. This figure was reduced to 1.5 million at the time of the Nuremberg Trials. Both figures turned out to be wild miscalculations. The Soviets thought that so many had died there because they discovered 800,000 pairs of shoes in the camp storage warehouse. It was later proved that Majdanek had acted as a processing centre for the goods confiscated from the Operation Reinhard camps. In 2008 Thomas Kranz, the chief researcher at the Majdanek State Museum, estimated that 78,000 people were killed there and that 59,000 of them were Jews. This figure has now been generally accepted.[80]

On 20 March 1942, Goebbels visited Hitler at the Wolf's Lair. He found the atmosphere at the gloomy military headquarters even more depressing than usual. Hitler now seemed to have no time for relaxation and appeared lonely and isolated. Goebbels thought that the Führer was showing signs of the strain of the winter months. He was complaining of dizzy spells and admitted to having some difficult days. He was troubled by the thought that in December 1942 he might face the same fate as Napoleon.

Hitler blamed the misfortunes of the German army on his General Staff, who had proved unable to cope with the pressure. It was their fixation with capturing Moscow that had caused all of the difficulties. Stalin's 'brutal hand' had saved Moscow and Hitler thought that the German army would need to be just as brutal in order to come out on top in the coming struggle.

Hitler then told Goebbels that he had developed a clear plan for the next stage of the offensive in the Soviet Union, with key aims in the Caucasus, Leningrad and Moscow. This new offensive would begin probably at the beginning of June 1942, but he would not attack along the whole front as had happened in June 1941.

Finally, they talked about the so-called Jewish question and Goebbels noted: 'Here the Führer was as uncompromising as ever. The Jews must be got out of Europe, if necessary, by applying the most brutal methods.'[81]

On the next day Hitler appointed the committed National Socialist Fritz Sauckel to the new post of General Plenipotentiary for Labour Mobilization (GBA). Sauckel was from a lowly background: he was the son of a post-office clerk and a seamstress. He had previously served as the brutal Nazi Gauleiter of Thuringia. Now he was given the much larger task of mobilizing 30 million Germans, plus millions of foreign workers from the German-occupied territories, to work in German factories and agriculture. This huge forced migration created enormous logistical challenges. Most of the foreign labourers were widely dispersed among prisoner-of-war camps, barrack-style camps, hostels and concentration camps.

At the end of 1941, 1.2 million POWs, mainly Frenchmen, and 2.3 million civilian Poles were employed in Germany. From January 1942 to June 1943 Sauckel's GBA brought in another 2.8 million. By the summer of 1943 the total of foreign workers stood at 6.5 million. In September 1944 there were 7.3 million, amounting to 20 per cent of the total workforce. Inside Hitler's Germany – the country that he had promised would become 'racially pure' – the workforce was as ethnically diverse as anywhere in Europe.

The death rate of foreign workers under German rule amounted to a 'hidden genocide'. Of the 1.65 million concentration camp inmates held in Germany during the war, most were used as forced labour, and only 475,000 of them were still alive in 1945. Less than 50 per cent of the 1.95 million Soviet POWs held in Germany survived the war. About 170,000 Soviet civilians – also conscripted to work in Germany – perished in concentration camps. Around 130,000 Polish workers in Germany also died, mainly of starvation.

Many German industries meted out 'corporal punishment' to any foreign worker deemed to be 'underperforming'. These beatings were carried out by local factory foremen. A macabre system of 'performance feeding' was introduced in factories. It rewarded 'better performing' workers with more food and punished those deemed 'poorly performing' with reduced rations. Those who could not work hard enough ate less and died of starvation. These deaths were recorded under the bureaucratic term 'annihilation through labour', the term used by Heydrich at the Wannsee Conference.

The concentration camp system in wartime became a pool of cheap forced labour. Most camps were now attached to industrial projects and companies paid 'fees' to the SS for providing the forced labour, while the workers themselves received no payment at all. Those conscripted from

Fritz Sauckel, General Plenipotentiary for Labour Deployment.

the camps were mostly used in back-breaking construction projects and in industrial factories. The productivity level of these poorly fed workers was about 40 per cent lower than the average German waged labourer who received full wages. It proved more profitable to employ concentration camp labour in the construction sectors rather than in the factories where higher skills were required to produce finished goods.

The outlook for the foreign civilian workers who were brought to Germany was somewhat different. Such workers were housed and fed in more conventional labour camps mostly paid for by their employers. These workers were not confined to these camps. Companies who employed foreign labour paid a special tax on each worker to the government. In general, German industry employed foreign workers as a last resort, but as the war progressed they became the only labour available.[82]

Meanwhile, Hitler's anger concerning the lack of ideological zeal among his generals soon spread to the conservative-dominated judiciary inside Germany. Hitler believed these judges were still impeding the National Socialist revolution and that his own failure to fully Nazify Germany's institutions and social elites had severely impeded his radical approach to the war. He was most concerned about the lenient sentences being given to criminals, black-marketeers and opponents during wartime.

In the spring of 1942 he was particularly troubled by two recent court cases. The first concerned his sacking of General Erich Hoepner, an officer in Army Group Centre, for failing to carry out Hitler's 'halt order' in the Soviet Union during December 1941. Outraged by the removal of his occupational pension, which Hitler had personally ordered, Hoepner instigated a civil law case to regain his pension rights and he won. This incensed Hitler who was now determined to make sure that no such thing ever happened again.[83]

The second case was the highly publicized trial of Ewald Schlitt, which began in Oldenburg on 19 March 1942. Schlitt, from Wilhelmshaven in north-west Germany, had reportedly beaten up his wife because he felt she had lost her nerve during an RAF air raid. She was hospitalized with severe injuries, but died a few days later. Forensic tests did not determine whether her death resulted from being brutally beaten by Schlitt or from a pre-existing intestinal infection. At the end of the trial, the judge sentenced Schlitt to five years in prison. Hitler, who read about the case in a Berlin newspaper, felt the sentence was far too light for a man who he felt had 'beaten his wife to death'. He immediately ordered the sentence to be revised to a death penalty. As a result of the Führer's intervention, Schlitt was tried again on 31 March at the Extraordinary Criminal Division of the Court of Appeal and sentenced to death. On 2 April, he was executed.[84]

On 21 March 1942 Hitler issued a decree ordering that proceedings in criminal and civil cases should be simplified and speeded up. The role of defence lawyers would be greatly reduced and increased powers granted to judges to issue summary punishments. The role of the assessor of judicial decisions would be greatly reduced – thus undermining the existing appeal system. This new decree was a major interference by Hitler in the existing criminal justice system. He announced at the same time that he would now assume the role of Supreme Law Lord, effectively putting himself above the judiciary.[85]

At this time it is clear that Goebbels knew about Operation Reinhard. On 26 March in a detailed diary entry he noted:

> The Jews are now being deported to the east from the General Government, beginning with Lublin. A barbaric procedure, not to be described in detail, is being used here [Bełżec], and not much is left of the Jews themselves. In general, it can probably be established that 60 per cent of them will have to be eliminated, while only 40 per cent can be put to work.

In a further deeply significant passage in the same entry Goebbels commented: 'A judgement is being carried out on the Jews that is barbaric but thoroughly deserved. The prophecy that the Führer gave them [a reference to Hitler's 30 January 1939 speech] for bringing about a new world war is coming true in the most terrible fashion. There must be no sentimentality about these matters.'[86]

A special military conference was held at the Wolf's Lair on 28 March 1942. Only a limited number of the highest-level commanders from the German army and the *Luftwaffe* were invited. The main topic under discussion was the German summer campaign on the Eastern Front. Hitler explained that it was no longer possible to attack across the whole front. The focus of this renewed assault would be to seize the oilfields in the Caucasus in the south of the Soviet Union. The Army High Command and the *Luftwaffe* raised no objection to Hitler's plan.[87]

On 14 February 1942, the British War Cabinet issued an 'Area Bombing Directive' to the Royal Air Force, authorizing the bombing of civilian areas in order to undermine 'the morale of the enemy civil population'.[88] The new head of Bomber Command was Arthur 'Bomber' Harris, who believed that an independent air war could be fought over Germany.

The first major RAF target he selected was the German city of Lübeck. This medieval city had no armaments factories, but many vulnerable, half-timbered buildings, which would burn easily. On the night of 28–29 March 1942, 234 RAF aircraft dropped 400 tonnes of mainly incendiary bombs on the old part of the city, causing 325 deaths, destroying 1,104 homes and leaving 25,000 local inhabitants homeless. Even the historic Lübeck Cathedral, dating from 1173, could not be saved. For the first time, the German population had experienced the effects of a truly devastating air raid.[89]

The German leadership was deeply alarmed at the severity of the RAF raid on Lübeck, with Goebbels noting: 'Thank God, it is the north German population, which is generally more resilient than that of the south and south-east.'[90] Hitler immediately ordered a series of reprisal *Luftwaffe* bomb attacks on British towns and cities of 'architectural value', beginning with Exeter (23–24 April), followed by Bath (25–26 April), Norwich (27–28 April), York (27 April) and Canterbury (30–31 May). After this, German bombing raids on Britain gradually petered out.[91]

In contrast, British raids on Germany escalated. On 23 April, the RAF bombed Rostock in a raid involving 100 bombers over a four-day period which saw 6,000 buildings destroyed and 200 civilians killed. The first '1,000-bomber raid' was carried out by the RAF on the evening of 30–31 May 1942 on the major German Rhineland city of Cologne. Around 1,455 tonnes of incendiary bombs were dropped, killing 480 people, destroying 3,300 buildings, damaging 9,500 others, and leaving 45,000 people homeless. RAF bomber crews reported that Cologne looked as if a volcano had erupted within it. Churchill stressed in the House of Commons that the 'gloves were off' in the fight against Hitler's Germany, and he promised that other German cities, ports and war-production centres could expect similar air raids.[92]

Goebbels instructed the German press to highlight the cowardly nature of British bombing attacks, which were primarily aimed at killing defenceless civilians. Hitler was indifferent to the huge civilian casualties being inflicted by British bombers on Germany. He even suggested to Goebbels that Cologne had needed flattening anyway, in order to make way for his grand architectural plans for the city after the war. In that sense, he thought 'the enemy has done this work for us'.[93]

In the continuing naval war, Germany stepped up its U-boat attacks against the Allies during 1942. The primary aim was to sink British merchant ships because Britain still needed to import 66 per cent of its food. If the German navy could have seriously disrupted this trade, the British population would surely have faced starvation rations. It was German U-boats that posed the greatest threat to Allied merchant ships. In the course of the war, 70 per cent of all Allied shipping losses were inflicted by German U-boats, 13.4 per cent by air attacks, 6.5 per cent by mines and only 6.1 per cent by surface ships.[94]

The German naval commander Admiral Karl Dönitz reckoned that with a fully operational fleet of 300 U-boats Germany might have strangled the British merchant trade altogether, but in 1942 he had an average of only 100 available at any one time. As Churchill later recalled: 'The U-boat attack was our worst evil. It would have been wise of the Germans to stake all on it.'[95]

During the summer of 1942 German U-boats targeted the Allied Arctic convoys taking war supplies to the Soviet ports of Archangel and Murmansk. On 4 July 1942 the Allied naval Convoy PQ-17 consisting of thirty-five merchant ships, protected by six destroyers and fifteen other heavily armed vessels, came under sustained attack by German U-boats supported by deadly *Luftwaffe* torpedo-bombers. A total of 24 ships on the Allied convoy were sunk and 153 seamen killed. The loss of war materiel during these German U-boat attacks included 210 aircraft, 430 tanks and 3,000 motor vehicles.

The PQ-17 disaster was primarily caused by the decision of the British Admiral Sir Dudley Pound, who, thinking that the convoy faced attack from four powerful German warships – *Tirpitz*, *Admiral Hipper*, *Admiral Scheer* and *Lützow* – gave the order for the merchant ships to scatter, leaving them totally undefended and thereby exposing them to devastating German U-boat and air attacks.

In September 1942, when thirteen out of the forty ships in Convoy PQ-18 were sunk by German U-boats, the British Admiralty decided to suspend altogether the convoys to the Soviet Union. This action was endorsed by the British War Cabinet on 14 September. The success of German U-boats against the Allied Arctic convoys left Churchill deeply worried that if such losses continued the Allied naval effort might be totally compromised. In the end, there was no need for concern. Between 1939 and 1945, only 8 per cent of slow and 4 per cent of fast convoys ever suffered German U-boat attacks.

The losses from the PQ convoys in 1942 were not really that large, totalling 78 merchant ships, 829 merchant seamen and 1,944 naval personnel. In those engagements the German navy lost thirty-two U-boats, one battleship and three destroyers.[96] Whereas Allied losses could be replaced by new building, German losses could not. The US navy decided to supply the Soviet Union by other less hazardous routes, in particular from Persia (now Iran).

One of the main reasons why the Royal Navy had been so vulnerable to German U-boat attacks in 1942 was because the Germans introduced a new naval intelligence code, which the British decoding experts at Bletchley Park could not immediately crack. The results of this intelligence blackout were remarkable. In 1942 German U-boats sank 1,859 Allied ships, totalling 8.3 million tonnes. All this was achieved by just 100 operational German U-boats.

On 30 October 1942 some respite for the Allies arrived when the German U-boat 559 was hit by four British destroyers using depth charges. The captain and crew were captured, along with the German U-boat codebooks and other important secret operational documents. On 13 December 1942, Bletchley Park achieved another massive breakthrough by breaking the new German naval code. [97]

From this point, the Battle of the Atlantic began to shift inexorably in favour of the Allies. This was achieved by attacking German U-boats in groups, with greater bomber support and using new technological equipment that could track their location – most notably, centimetric radar-guided equipment and greatly improved radio communications. In 1943 Germany sank 812 Allied ships, totalling 3.6 million tonnes, but lost 242 U-boats in the process. On 24 May 1943 Dönitz decided to withdraw all German U-boats from the North Atlantic, effectively handing victory in the Battle of the Atlantic to the Allies.

The naval battle in the Mediterranean was a much fiercer and a more protracted struggle. Malta, the only offshore British naval outpost in the central Mediterranean, came under constant siege from the German and Italian navies, and especially from the *Luftwaffe*. This helps to explain why between 1940 and 1943 the Mediterranean was largely unusable as a supply route for the Allied armies. The Royal Navy sustained very heavy losses of military supply ships in this period. It was only from mid-1942 onwards that the Royal Navy began to improve its own supply lines and to seriously impede Axis naval supply vessels to North Africa.[98]

In the spring of 1942, Hitler remained convinced that the Soviet Union would soon be defeated. On 5 April he signed 'Directive No. 41', codenamed Operation Blue (*Fall Blau*). It stated that once the good weather returned, the German armed forces must 'seize the initiative again'. The key aim was to wipe out the defence potential of the Red Army and to cut it off from important centres of war industry.

The main focus of Operation Blue would be in the southern sector of the Eastern Front, led by Army Group South, and divided into four phases: (a) an attack eastwards, with the aim of capturing Soviet forces near Voronezh; (b) a thrust south to destroy the enemy defending the River Don; (c) an encircling operation intended to trap Soviet forces south-west of the city of Stalingrad; and (d) an advance along the Black Sea coast towards the oil-rich Caucasus, capturing Sebastopol and the Kerch Peninsula on the way. Elsewhere along the front, Army Group Centre was ordered to hold its current defensive position and Army Group North would attempt to end the siege of Leningrad, then join up with the Finnish army.

Hitler decided the exposed flanks of this huge Axis offensive would be protected by the weaker armies of Romania, Hungary, Italy and Bulgaria. Preparations for this new operation were conducted in complete secrecy. The key objectives of Operation Blue were not ideological but economic: to capture the USSR's oil supplies in the Caucasus region.[99]

Yet the German army was not as strong as it had been when Operation Barbarossa was launched a year before. Since the autumn of 1941, 900,000 German soldiers had been lost and only 50 per cent of those had been replaced. Around 90 per cent of motor vehicles lost in the previous nine months of battle had not been replaced either. These shortages in personnel and equipment meant that in 1942 the German army in the Soviet Union was far more reliant than ever before on its much weaker Axis allies.

The search to find additional boots on the ground to fight for Germany spread wider. Special 'collection camps' were established for captured Red Army soldiers who expressed a willingness to collaborate with their German captors. These Soviet 'volunteers' known as *Hiwis* were offered improved food rations as inducements to fight for the German cause. Army Group Centre even created full combat units of Soviet POWs, commanded by German officers. Volunteer units were also created in the Baltic states where pro-Nazi sympathies and animosity towards Bolshevism remained strong.[100]

Muslims in the Caucasus, Georgia and Armenia – who were also antagonistic towards Stalin's regime – also proved easy for the German army to recruit. In Muslim areas, the German-occupying authorities rebuilt mosques and prayer-houses. A Muslim cleric, speaking at a conference of the Tartar Committee in Simferopol in early 1942, declared that Muslims must take part in 'this Holy battle alongside Germans against Bolshevism'. The Germans ensured that Muslim soldiers who fought in German units were given the right to religious observance.[101] There were simultaneous efforts by Stalin's government to rally Muslims to fight against the Germans and to declare a jihad against Hitler, and these efforts were also often very successful.[102]

On 6 April 1942 new rations for meat, fat and bread were introduced in Germany. Nazi Party speakers were advised to stress the fact that the new rations were required because the *Wehrmacht* had an increased need for food, and the economy needed imported foreign labour for the armaments industry and they also needed feeding.[103] SD reports on German public opinion mentioned the 'crushing' effect that the April announcement of new rations had on 'a large section of the population'. The morale of workers in industrial areas was reported to be at 'an all-time low'. A report from Leipzig noted: 'Since the stomach is the determining factor, not only for the overall health of the individual, but also for the well-being of the population as a whole, a general depression is discernible.'[104]

On 26 April 1942 the final session of the Reichstag took place. Hitler had decided to dispense with these meetings, fearing they might be used to depose him in the future should he start to lose the war. This special session of the Reichstag was convened to pass a 'super Enabling Act', granting Hitler unlimited and arbitrary powers. Opening the proceedings, Göring explained that due to wartime conditions Hitler could no longer be bound by the pre-existing regulations. He now needed to be able to compel any German – whether a judge, a party functionary, a soldier, a worker or an employee – to follow his orders, and also to be able to dismiss anyone without recourse to due legal process. The term 'Supreme War Lord' was now invoked. It had last been used in July 1934 to justify Hitler's actions during the Night of the Long Knives. A compliant Reichstag overwhelmingly approved this new law.

Hitler then delivered his final Reichstag speech. It followed a familiar pattern: a long-winded explanation of events leading up to the war, then a bitter attack on Churchill and Roosevelt. He highlighted the brave struggle of German soldiers during the previous winter but gave no promise the war would be over by the end of 1942. Hitler then explained why he needed new dictatorial powers. Using the Schlitt case as an example, he bitterly attacked the judiciary for not dealing with such criminals much more harshly. From now on, Hitler promised to personally intervene in judicial and civil cases, overturning verdicts if he so wished, dismissing judges he thought were not fulfilling their role and punishing any German who misused public office or failed to carry out their duties.[105] On 20 August 1942 Hitler appointed Otto Thierack as the new Minister of Justice with a political brief to 'fully Nazify' the German justice system. Paperwork associated with legal cases was reduced to a minimum, sentences were increased and the right to appeal was restricted. Outside Germany, it was feared that by ending the independence of lawyers, judges and civil servants Hitler was now creating a genuine totalitarian dictatorship.

As part of what Hitler called his 'drive against corruption', he issued a special decree concerning the 'lifestyle of leading personalities'. This was in response to sustained Allied propaganda highlighting German corruption, especially among Nazi Party officials. SD public opinion reports showed that this was a constant gripe of the average German, most of whom were no doubt listening to foreign radio broadcasts. Initially, there was a crackdown on extravagant expenses claims by Nazi officials for 'pleasure trips'.[106]

On 28 April 1942 Hitler met Mussolini at Schloss Klessheim, an imposing Baroque castle near Salzburg. It came as a welcome break for Hitler from the gloomy atmosphere at the Wolf's Lair. The key aim of the meeting was to give the impression of a coordinated military strategy among the Axis powers, when in reality nothing of the sort existed. Mussolini, who was in very poor health with severe stomach problems, had initially refused to visit Hitler in Germany. This time there were no public displays of enthusiasm for Il Duce on his arrival.

At the meeting Hitler did most of the talking. He admitted that the German campaign in the Soviet Union almost ended in catastrophe near Moscow in December 1941, but he blamed this not on the prowess of the Red Army, but on the freezing cold weather conditions and the poor decision making of his own generals. Hitler did not discuss the details of Operation Blue with Mussolini at all, but he seemed optimistic about the prospects of eventual victory over the Soviet Union. He then dismissed Churchill's hope that America would make a huge difference in the war as a 'colossal bluff'. In North

Africa, he thought that the French colonies would support the Allies if there were an invasion. The Axis powers, in such circumstances, had to be ready to seize unoccupied areas of Vichy France.

Mussolini said very little during the meeting, except to point out the deep economic crisis that Italy was now facing as food shortages deeply affected the morale of the population. The meeting was filmed for the German and Italian cinema newsreels. Filmgoers thought Mussolini looked pale and thin. In London *The Times* suggested that Mussolini, whose popularity was now declining with the Italians, had met Hitler only to quell growing rumours that Italy was about to abandon the war.[107]

On 12 May 1942 the Red Army launched a poorly planned offensive to retake the major Ukrainian city of Kharkov (now Kharkiv). Within sixteen days, the 1st Panzer Army, commanded by Ewald von Kleist, had smashed through the Soviet defences; then the 6th Army encircled the three Soviet armies and largely destroyed them. A total of 170,000 Red Army soldiers were killed, captured or went missing during the engagement, and 650 tanks and 5,000 artillery pieces were lost.[108] The Soviet commander Semyon Timoshenko held Stalin responsible for this catastrophe, but Zhukov blamed the leadership of the Soviet South-western Front, which he believed had misinformed Stalin beforehand of the likely prospects of military success.[109]

The victorious 6th German Army was commanded by Friedrich Paulus. He had only taken command on 20 January 1942, following the sudden and unexpected death of Walther von Reichenau on 17 January, who had suffered a massive stroke while out jogging three days earlier. It was a huge promotion for Paulus, who had never commanded an army division or even an army corps before. Many books on the history of the Third Reich give his family name the prefix 'von', but Paulus did not come from an aristocratic family at all. He had a solid middle-class background. Paulus had very good manners and carried out orders without question, a trait which greatly impressed Hitler, who awarded him the Knight's Cross for his leadership role during the recent Second Battle of Kharkov.[110]

On 18 May 1942 a communist underground group based in Berlin led by the Jewish electrician Herbert Baum broke into an anti-Soviet exhibition which had been commissioned by Goebbels called The Soviet Paradise (*Das Sowjet-Paradies*). They wandered around setting off some small explosive devices that damaged several exhibits. Within days Baum and the other members of the group had been arrested by the Gestapo. He was severely beaten and tortured during his lengthy interrogation. He died on 11 June in Moabit Prison. The Gestapo recorded his death as 'suicide', although it was obviously due to their maltreatment of him while he was in custody.

Responding to these events, Goebbels, the Gauleiter of Berlin, ordered the immediate and arbitrary arrest of 500 Berlin Jews. Of these, 250 were shot dead by SS guards in the Sachsenhausen concentration camp. The rest were held as 'human hostages' to be killed in the event of 'further acts of sabotage' by the Jewish population. Baum's wife Marianne was also executed on 18 August 1942. Twenty members of the group suffered the same fate.[111]

On 23 May Richard Walther Darré was dismissed as the Reich Minister of Food and Agriculture. The official reason given was that he was taking 'extended leave of absence due to ill health', but in reality Hitler felt Darré had failed to maintain adequate food supplies in Germany.[112] He was replaced by the Nazi ideologue Herbert Backe, who was attached to the agricultural section of Göring's Four-Year Plan Office. It will be recalled that Backe was the author of the notorious 'Hunger Plan', which had mentioned the deliberate starvation of 30 million Soviet citizens during Operation Barbarossa.[113] Backe was brought into the cabinet by Hitler to exploit labour in the eastern occupied territories in a more ruthless manner and in conjunction with this to improve the current food situation in Germany.[114]

With the German government now envisaging a lengthy war, the food supply situation became crucial. Backe was determined to impose a hierarchy in the use of food supplies: Germans would receive the best rations, followed by 'civilian' foreign workers. Much lower down the food chain came concentration camp inmates, POWs captured in Western Europe and, at the bottom, Soviet POWs. Backe also decided that food deliveries from Germany to the German army on the Eastern Front would now cease. This meant the army was expected to feed itself by confiscating food in the occupied areas at the expense of the local population. Jews were excluded from the food rationing system in German-occupied Poland and in the other eastern occupied territories altogether.

The result was a starvation epidemic amongst the Jewish population in the ghettos. By the spring of 1942 only Jews classed as workers received any food rations at all. Murdering Jews in the extermination camps was ideologically motivated, but it also served an economic purpose by taking Jews out of a food supply chain upon which there

[overleaf]
German tank commander Erwin Rommel celebrating the capture of Tobruk in North Africa on 21 June 1942.

were growing demands. A total of 500,000 tonnes of grain was confiscated from the General Government in 1942 and sent to Germany, thereby intensifying the starvation of local citizens. The fate of all individuals under German rule now depended to a great extent on where they were in the food supply chain. Between 1942 and 1943 German-occupied Europe supplied Germany with 20 per cent of its grain, 25 per cent of its fats and 30 per cent of its meat.[115]

On 26 May 1942 Erwin Rommel's Afrika Corps – consisting of three Panzer divisions and supported by Italian infantry and the *Luftwaffe* – began Operation Theseus. In total, the Axis forces for this operation numbered 90,000 troops, with 560 tanks and 542 aircraft. The Allied Forces – spearheaded by the British and Commonwealth 8th Army – numbered 110,000 men, 843 tanks and 604 aircraft, including troops from India, South Africa, the Free French and a smaller number of Americans.

Rommel's key aim was to capture Tobruk, a central British supply port. On 31 May 1942 his tank forces began a major assault on British positions in the Battle of Gazala. Operation Aberdeen, a poorly coordinated counter-attack by the 8th Army, failed miserably. Axis forces next captured Bir Hakeim from the Free French on 10 June 1942, then spectacularly broke through the strategically important Gazala line on 14 June, forcing the British into yet another humiliating retreat. On 17 June Rommel began his attack on Tobruk, soon encircling it. On 20 June there was a huge *Luftwaffe* raid on the port. The next day Allied troops there surrendered and 35,000 of them became prisoners. Hitler promoted Rommel to the rank of Field Marshal, the youngest German officer ever to achieve such an honour. Mussolini did the same with General Ugo Cavallero, the Italian commander.

The loss of Tobruk was deeply humiliating for the British war effort. At the time the news came through, Churchill was chatting with President Roosevelt in the White House in Washington, D.C., during an official visit. 'This was one of the heaviest blows I can recall during the war,' he later wrote. 'Not only were its military effects grievous, but it had affected the reputation of the British armies.'[116] A deeply shocked Roosevelt promised to despatch 300 ultra-modern Sherman tanks to support the Allies in North Africa.

Neil Ritchie, the commander of the British 8th Army, was summarily dismissed by Churchill, even though most of the blame for the defeat was due to General Claude Auchinleck, who now assumed command of the 8th Army. He immediately withdrew the British and

Commonwealth forces to El Alamein to try and establish a new defensive line. Realizing that the British were in disarray, Rommel decided to step up the Axis offensive in North Africa. The British self-deprecating joke of the day was that Rommel had already booked a hotel room in Cairo. This turned out to be an overly pessimistic assessment. In the first Battle of El Alamein from 1–27 July 1942, British and Commonwealth forces halted Rommel's advance towards Egypt with a series of counter-attacks. Both sides now dug in and remained on the defensive.

By this time Rommel only had fifty functioning tanks left and even they were desperately short of fuel. He sensed that the German position in North Africa was much less secure than German propaganda suggested. General Walter Warlimont visited Rommel at the end of July and found him in a deeply pessimistic mood. Rommel pointed out that the German-Italian army now faced an enemy that was superior on land, sea and in the air, and it would only get stronger in the coming months as fresh American manpower and supplies began to make a real difference.[117]

Auchinleck had halted the seemingly superhuman Rommel, but Churchill refused to elevate the British general to the status of a hero. Instead, he replaced him as commander-in-chief with General Harold Alexander. He also appointed Lieutenant-General William Gott as the new commander of the 8th Army, but Gott was killed when his plane was shot down by the *Luftwaffe* on 7 August.

This opened up a huge opportunity for another British officer. On 13 August Lieutenant-General Bernard Montgomery (nicknamed 'Monty') took charge of the British 8th Army. 'Monty' had a huge flair for self-publicity, as well as a boundless self-confidence which he transferred to his troops. He knew that the Allies – now with growing American military support – stood an excellent chance of reversing the situation in North Africa. He immediately set about re-equipping the 8th Army for an autumn offensive. When Axis forces tried to break through the Alamein defence line in late August they were easily repulsed by Allied forces at the Battle of Alam Halfa.[118]

In reality, Hitler viewed the North African theatre of war as a sideshow to the main German-Soviet War, but he played up Rommel's success for propaganda purposes. There was a limit to the resources that Hitler was prepared to supply to Rommel. The situation in North Africa was of greater consequence to Italy than to Germany, because an Allied victory there could lead to an assault on the Italian mainland itself and threaten Mussolini's regime.

While the military situation for the Axis powers in North Africa was gradually deteriorating, Hitler was coming to terms with the recent untimely death of one of the key members of the Nazi elite. On 27 May 1942 Reinhard Heydrich, the Deputy Reich Protector of Bohemia and Moravia, was seriously wounded during a bomb attack in Prague. This daring attempt to assassinate Heydrich (codenamed Operation Anthropoid) was carried out by Czech exiles who had been trained in Glasgow and Dorking by the British Special Operations Executive (SOE). The operation was sanctioned by the Czech government-in-exile and eagerly supported by Churchill.

Two Czechoslovakian agents, Josef Gabčík and Jan Kubiš, had spent five months living in safe houses in German-occupied Czechoslovakia, carefully planning the attack. They observed that on most mornings Heydrich would drive from his headquarters at Panenské Břežany in a chauffeur-driven, open-topped Mercedes 320 Cabriolet B to Prague, without any bodyguards or armed motorcycle outriders accompanying him. He was a soft target for a would-be assassin.

It was about 10.30 a.m. on 27 May when Heydrich's car reached a hairpin bend in the road. As the driver naturally slowed down to turn the corner, Heydrich's car was suddenly ambushed. Gabčík stepped out from the pavement with a Sten gun, but it jammed. His companion Kubiš simultaneously ran forwards throwing an anti-tank grenade

under the car. When it immediately exploded, a seat spring punctured Heydrich's spleen. Not realising how badly injured he was, Heydrich jumped out of the car and fired at his fleeing assailants before suddenly collapsing on the pavement. He was rushed to Prague's Bukova hospital by a motorist driving a delivery van who had been stopped shortly after the attack by an off-duty policeman. At first, the hospital doctors thought that Heydrich's injuries were not life-threatening. The two assassins escaped arrest and hid for three weeks but they were soon betrayed by a Czech SOE double agent. On 18 June they were tracked down to the crypt of a church in central Prague. A bitter gun battle ensued, with 700 Waffen-SS troops surrounding the church. Rather than surrender, the two exceptionally brave men committed suicide by shooting themselves.[119]

Hitler signed 'War Directive No. 42' on 29 May 1942. It contained instructions to occupy Vichy France. The plan was originally called Operation Atilla, then changed to Operation Isabella and finally Operation Anton. The plan would become operative whenever there was a threat to German and Italian security in France or North Africa. Designed as a joint German-Italian operation, its key aims were to break the Resistance in unoccupied France and to take control of this zone using mechanized and mobile forces. German forces would then occupy the French areas currently controlled by the Vichy government. Italian units would occupy Corsica and blockade French naval bases, particularly in Toulon. The Italians were also instructed to prepare to occupy Tunisia. The High Command of the German army would make all necessary preparations for the entire operation if and when it became operative.[120]

On 30 May 1942 Hitler gave a speech at the Berlin Sport Palace to 10,000 young German officers. He told them that the summer campaign in the Soviet Union was critical. If the Red Army triumphed on the Eastern Front, he warned: 'Asiatic barbarity would plant itself in Europe.' German women would be 'fair game for these beasts', and the European intelligentsia and the German people would be exterminated.[121]

At this time, Hitler remained concerned that most of the high-ranking German officers surrounding him were not sufficiently committed Nazis. Wilhelm Keitel, the Chief of the Armed Forces High Command, formulated Hitler's thinking on this issue into a regulation on 'the responsibility of the German officer'. Issued on 31 May 1942, it stated: 'The officer must be capable of educating his

Reinhard Heydrich's car after the bomb attack on 27 May 1942.

[overleaf]
Hitler salutes Heydrich's flag-draped coffin prior to his state funeral on 9 June 1942.

soldiers to become convinced representatives of this *Weltanschauung* [philosophy or world view].'[122]

On 4 June Hitler made a flying visit to Finland to attend the seventy-fifth birthday celebrations of the famous Finnish Field Marshal Carl Gustaf Mannerheim. It was a rarity for Hitler to visit any area outside German control. His aim on this occasion was to stiffen the Finns' resolve to remain in the war. The meeting took place aboard Mannerheim's special train, near Immola Airfield, because the Finnish government did not want to give the impression it was an official state visit by Hitler. The Finns secretly recorded eleven minutes of Hitler's conversation with Mannerheim aboard the train.

Hitler, speaking off the record, in the conversational low tone that he reserved for close friends, admitted that there was a growing danger from the military forces of the Soviet Union. The German attack in 1941, he explained, had been a 'preventive' strike designed to head off an inevitable Soviet assault. He made no mention of his future military plans or of the forthcoming summer offensive. He was satisfied with the meeting, even though the Finnish government had promised him nothing.[123]

On the same day that Hitler was in Finland, news came through of Reinhard Heydrich's death. The wounds he had sustained in the bomb attack had turned septic while he was in hospital, leading to a severe fever. He slipped into a coma and never regained consciousness. Hitler felt that Heydrich had been extremely careless about his personal security: 'Since it is opportunity which makes not only the thief but also the assassin, such heroic gestures as driving in an open, unarmoured vehicle or walking about the streets unguarded are just damned stupidity, which serves the Fatherland not one whit. That a man as irreplaceable as Heydrich should expose himself to unnecessary danger, I can only condemn as stupid and idiotic.'[124]

The German occupying authorities in the Protectorate of Bohemia and Moravia were extraordinarily ruthless in their response to Heydrich's assassination. On 10 June 1942, in a vicious act of reprisal, the SD and the Order Police murdered every man over the age of fifteen in the small village of Lidice, numbering 173 victims. All of the 184 women in the village were deported to Ravensbrück concentration camp. Most of the eighty-eight children who also lived there were gassed at Chełmno, except for a few who were considered 'racially suitable' for adoption by SS families. The village was then set on fire and its buildings blown up with explosives. A further eleven men who

[previous pages]
Hitler walking with Carl Mannerheim,
Finnish Field Marshal, during their
meeting on 4 June 1942.

were not in the village at the time of the massacre were soon tracked down and killed.[125] German national radio justified these brutal actions on the grounds that Lidice had harboured Czechoslovakian partisans, who were supposed to have assisted the two assassins. This was, of course, false. There was no evidence that Lidice's inhabitants had been involved in the plot to kill Heydrich at all.

A crackdown followed against Czechoslovakian and communist resistance groups, and 1,357 people were subsequently sentenced to death. On 24 October 1942, 257 people were arrested on suspicion of helping Heydrich's assassins. They were shot during a day-long series of executions at Mauthausen concentration camp.[126] The Allies considered the extra-judicial killing of Heydrich to be wholly justified, and given his role in the Nazi genocide this is a thoroughly defensible position, but it remains a matter of debate among historians whether the deaths of so many innocent victims during the Nazi reprisals were a price worth paying as Heydrich's death increased Nazi terror rather than reduced it.

On 6 June 1942 the German Army High Command (OKW) produced a secret memorandum entitled: 'War Potential 1942'. Setting out the gaps and shortages in German manpower and equipment, it concluded that the combat potential of the *Wehrmacht* in 1942 was much lower than in 1941. In the upcoming summer offensive of 1942, therefore, it would be essential to inflict overwhelming losses on the Red Army. It's doubtful whether Hitler ever saw this document, but it highlights the gloomy outlook of the German High Command on the eve of Operation Blue.[127]

On 19 June 1942, Major Joachim Reichel, the operations officer of the 23rd Panzer Division, was on board a plane that suddenly veered off course and crash-landed behind enemy lines in the Soviet Union. The pilot was killed instantly and Reichel was shot dead trying to escape capture. Reichel had plainly ignored Hitler's order never to fly over enemy territory with secret plans because inside his captured briefcase was a copy of a detailed memorandum outlining the plans for Operation Blue, including detailed maps of the location of the assault. It gave the provisional start date for the operation as 22 June 1942. The captured documents were sent to Stalin's military headquarters in Moscow. They had made clear that Germany intended to strike southwards towards the oil-rich Caucasus. However, Stalin was convinced that the main thrust of the German summer offensive would be aimed in the direction of Moscow, so he dismissed the Reichel plane crash as part of

[overleaf]
Dead bodies lined up after the Lidice
Massacre on 10 June 1942.

an elaborate German deception which, of course, was untrue.[128]

German plans for a summer offensive in the Soviet Union were now an open secret. Newspapers in Britain and the United States even printed full details, including accurate quotations from the Führer's directive for Operation Blue. As Keitel later recalled: 'There could be no doubt but that there was treachery somewhere along the line.'[129] The intelligence leaks to the Allied press only served to fuel Hitler's already strong suspicion that he was surrounded by treacherous German army officers.

In fact, the most important sources for these German leaks (primarily to Soviet intelligence in 1942) came from the air force officer Harro Schulze-Boysen, who was based in the Reich Air Transport Ministry, and Arvid Harnack, a high-ranking civil servant attached to the Economics Ministry. Both men had access to copies of all the war directives and many other key German documents. They were part of an anti-Nazi resistance group known by the Gestapo as the Red Orchestra (*Rote Kapelle*). Its members were sympathetic to socialist ideas, but they were not linked to any German communist resistance group. As well as passing on intelligence to the Soviet Union and the United States, the Red Orchestra produced several anti-Nazi leaflets, calling for a popular uprising against Hitler's government. They also helped Jews to escape, and documented Nazi war crimes. It's thought that there were at least 400 members connected to the Red Orchestra. In July 1942 the Gestapo decoded the group's messages and after a wave of arrests, brutal interrogations and show trials followed with fifty members of the group executed, including Schulze-Boysen and Harnack, on 22 December 1942.[130]

Operation Blue – now renamed Operation Brunswick (*Braunsch-weig*) – began on 28 June 1942 in southern Russia, between Kursk and Taganrog. Hitler had not altered the original plan. A key initial aim of the German offensive was to seize the city of Voronezh, an important transport hub, halfway between the Donetsk region and Moscow. This operation was designed to give the impression that the main thrust of the German assault was still aimed at Moscow.

German tank units broke through Soviet lines with ease and after a bitter siege the German 11th Army captured Sevastopol on 4 July 1942. After a ceaseless bombardment of the city by the *Luftwaffe*, just eleven major buildings were left standing. During this engagement, the German army deployed a new artillery gun nicknamed 'Dora', an 800-millimetre giant, with a 30-metre gun barrel. The commander of

German operations in Sevastopol was Erich von Manstein, who had been promoted by Hitler to the rank of Field Marshal. The Germans took 95,000 prisoners and killed at least 18,000 Red Army soldiers during the capture of Sevastopol, but German losses were also high, with 25,000 dead and 50,000 wounded.[131]

On the same day Sevastopol fell, German forces reached the River Don, opposite Voronezh, but Franz Halder was concerned by the odd lack of Soviet resistance there, noting: 'There are two possibilities: either we have overestimated the enemy's strength and the offensive has smashed him or the enemy is conducting a planned disengagement to forestall being irretrievably beaten in 1942.'[132]

On 24 July 1942 the Germans, after a dogged struggle, did capture Voronezh, using flamethrowers to clear out the final remnants of Red Army opposition, street by street. There were 290,000 Soviet troops killed in this bloody battle, and a further 80,000 were taken prisoner. The Germans suffered 94,500 casualties, including 19,000 dead or missing. Many Red Army troops had escaped, thereby avoiding encirclement.[133] Red Army commanders had changed their tactics between 1941 and 1942. Instead of standing their ground, which had led to them being encircled and captured in 1941, Soviet soldiers in 1942 were now allowed to retreat from hopeless situations. This meant that the Germans captured fewer prisoners.

Despite these impressive series of German victories, Hitler thought the progress of the summer offensive was too slow. On 15 July he summarily dismissed Fedor von Bock, the commander of Army Group South, and replaced him with General Maximilian von Weichs.[134] Bock's diary entries reveal he was deeply sceptical about the likely success of Operation Blue from the very beginning. He doubted Army Group South had sufficient military strength to seize the Caucasian oilfields, and feared a huge Soviet counteroffensive at some point, which Hitler had refused to contemplate.[135]

On 16 July Hitler decamped from the Wolf's Lair in Rastenburg to another gloomy, forested area north-east of Vinnytsia in Ukraine. Codenamed 'Werewolf' ('*Werwolf*'), this austere complex consisted of twenty wooden cottages. There was a newly built 'Führer House' with a private courtyard, a sauna, a private cinema, an underground bunker and a swimming pool. Hitler's retinue of secretaries and other members of his personal staff all came with him; including his personal chef, who established a vegetable garden on the site. All the food Hitler ate was chemically tested and a taster sampled it before it

ever reached Hitler's plate. A clear example of Hitler's fear of being poisoned. During Hitler's stay, the temperature at Vinnytsia was a stifling 40 °C and the complex was plagued by swarms of mosquitos. It was built by forced labour, mainly Soviet POWs, many of whom were executed immediately afterwards to maintain the secrecy of the site.[136]

Hitler was once again isolated in the middle of nowhere. Ever since the attack on the Soviet Union began, he had spent much less time in the company of his young partner Eva Braun, who never visited him at either the Wolf's Lair or Werewolf. Among Hitler's inner circle and in the foreign press Eva was now openly described as Hitler's 'mistress' or 'girlfriend'.[137] At the Berghof, she had her own bedroom, next to the Führer's, and she often stayed there with him when he was in residence. She sometimes stayed at Hitler's Berlin apartment in the old Reich Chancellery at 77 Wilhelmstraße. Hitler telephoned her frequently, usually after 10 p.m.

At the Berghof, Eva was now the undisputed mistress of the household. While there, she often filmed home movies and took photographs of Hitler and his cronies. During the war, Hitler came to increasingly value his time with her. He seemed calmer and more humane in her company. He even talked of retiring to Linz and marrying her once the war was over.

Christa Schroeder, one of Hitler's secretaries, felt that Eva became 'more self-confident' during the wartime period. At the Berghof, Eva even dared to interrupt Hitler's long monologues, as they stretched way beyond midnight, and often urged him to go to bed. Hitler increasingly viewed the optimistic and cheery Eva as the ideal antidote to his increasingly strained relationship with his generals. Unlike them, she made clear her unconditional love and loyalty to the Führer. Goebbels described her as 'extraordinarily well-read, extraordinarily clear and mature in her judgement of aesthetic questions'.[138]

The German summer campaign in the Soviet Union was the first military operation that Hitler had fully directed. He now felt superior to his 'expert' military commanders, but they saw things differently. In their memoirs, Hitler's leading generals gave the impression that every military success was down to them and every failure due to Hitler. General Walter Warlimont is a typical example. He later recalled:

> Directions were given which were not based on military
> requirements but designed in at least equal degree to satisfy
> political, prestige and economic purposes; the conquest and
> occupation of territory was therefore placed first in importance.

German military commander
Fedor von Bock.

The resources necessary to reach the objectives were frequently
not available. Pursuit of these objectives was stubbornly
continued to the last man and the last round even when the
troops had long since been overtaxed.[139]

On 23 July 1942 German tanks moved into the heart of Rostov-on-
Don, which the Russians called the 'Gate to the Caucasus'. A total of
83,000 Soviet prisoners were captured during this single engagement.
The loss of Rostov was viewed as a disaster by the Soviet High
Command because it put in great danger the oilfields in the Caucasus.

By now Germany's officers and soldiers had fully regained their
confidence. As Count Clemens-Heinrich Graf von Kageneck, a
lieutenant in the 3rd Panzer Army, commented: 'We were charging
ahead exultantly.'[140] But the triumph at Rostov also heralded a return
of Hitler's own overconfidence, prompting Halder to note in his diary:
'The chronic tendency [of Hitler] to underrate enemy capabilities is
assuming grotesque proportions and develops into a positive danger.'[141]

On the same day Rostov fell, Hitler had issued 'War Directive No.
45', outlining what amounted to a completely new plan for the summer
offensive in the Soviet Union. Hitler argued that the main goals of
the German thrust south had already been fully achieved, which was
not true. Nevertheless, Hitler now decided to run three simultaneous
offensives, all going in different directions. To achieve this, he split
Army Group South into two groups: a northern sector called Army
Group A and a southern sector called Army Group B.

Army Group A was composed of the 17th Army and the 1st and
4th Panzer armies, and was commanded by Field Marshal Wilhelm
List. This would now advance along the River Don, occupy the eastern
coastline of the Black Sea, capture key oilfields in the Caucasus – most
notably Maikop and Grozny – then move to oil-rich Baku (a plan
known as Operation *Edelweiss)*.

The key objective of Army Group B – which consisted of the 6th
Army and the 2nd Hungarian, 8th Italian and 4th Romanian armies,
and was commanded by Maximilian von Weichs – was to capture
Stalingrad (Operation *Fischreiher*), an objective which had increased
in importance, and then to move on and capture Astrakhan on the
Caspian Sea.

Army Group North – in a separate military operation called
Operation Northern Light (*Nordlicht*) – was instructed to capture
Leningrad. Erich von Manstein's 11th Army would take charge of this

assault, even though his originally assigned role was to help Army Groups A and B should they get into unforeseen difficulties.[142]

The task of protecting the flanks of Army Groups A and B was now completely dependent on much weaker Axis forces from Romania, Hungary and Italy. When Wilhelm List first saw this revised military plan, he assumed that Hitler must have obtained secret intelligence information confirming the collapse of the Red Army in the south.[143]

On 23 July 1942 Hitler asked his loyal ally Martin Bormann to communicate to Alfred Rosenberg his ideas on the 'Treatment of Non-German Populations in the Eastern Territories'. Hitler now favoured using abortion and birth control to suppress the non-German population in these areas. The local population would also be deliberately denied healthcare and immunization injections, as well as housing and entry into higher education. As few regulations as possible would be enforced in German-occupied areas in the east in order to save spending on civil administration.[144]

On 28 July 1942 Stalin issued the famous Order 227 to Red Army troops, familiarly known as the 'Not a Step Back Order' (*Ni shagu nazad*). It was designed to boost morale and restore discipline in the battle against the German armed forces. Soviet commanders were ordered to 'eliminate retreat moods in the troops' and to 'stubbornly defend to the last drop of blood every position, every metre of Soviet territory, cling to every patch of Soviet earth and hold it to the limit of possibility'. Furthermore, 'defeatists and cowards must be liquidated on the spot'. Order 227 was read out to all officers and soldiers, and as one soldier recalled: 'The spirit and content of the order made possible the moral, psychological and spiritual breakthrough in the hearts and minds of those to whom it was read.'[145]

The order did not rule out tactical military retreats, but it stressed that they should not be undertaken without the approval of a high-ranking officer. The power of the 'officer' was now being enhanced by Stalin and the role of the communist political 'commissar' downgraded in each army division. The use of medals as incentives was now increased too. By 1945 the Red Army had issued 11 million medals to its troops, a great deal more than the 1.4 million the Allies awarded to theirs.[146]

There was by now a rising tide of anger among the Soviet population and a desire for vengeance against the brutal German invaders. As the Soviet writer Ilya Ehrenburg, returning from exile in Paris, wrote in an article in *Red Star* on 13 August: 'The Germans are not human. Now the word "German" has become the most terrible swear word. Let us not speak. Let us not be indignant. Let us kill. If you do not kill the German, he will kill you.'[147]

To take the pressure off the Soviet Union, Stalin was pressing the Western Allies to open a Second Front in Western Europe. At the end of May 1942 Molotov, the Soviet Foreign Minister, had travelled to Washington, D.C., and then London to discuss this key Soviet demand. He first met Roosevelt who told him that he was prepared to support eight to ten army divisions landing in northern Europe, and he also agreed to the issuing of a joint US-Soviet communiqué indicating that a Second Front would be created in 1942. Then Molotov went to London to discuss the issue with the British Foreign Secretary Anthony Eden but he expressed deep reservations about the feasibility of such an operation in 1942. On 29 July Roosevelt advised Churchill to handle the matter of a Second Front with great care during his upcoming meeting with Stalin, commenting: 'We have got always to keep in mind the personality of our ally and the very difficult situation that confronts him.'[148]

Between 12 and 15 August 1942 Churchill held talks on the military situation with Stalin in Moscow. It was the first face-to-face meeting of the two Allied leaders. At their first meeting on 12 August, Churchill came straight to the point, telling Stalin that a massive, cross-Channel invasion of France was currently 'impossible' because not enough landing craft were available. He then gave an exaggerated description of the devastation being caused by the British strategic bombing of Germany. Stalin suggested some alternatives: the recapture of the Channel Islands, the seizure of Cherbourg, or a landing of six divisions on the continent.

Churchill would only promise an offensive in North Africa (known as Operation Torch) and a small-scale, amphibious reconnaissance mission on the French port of Dieppe to test out the feasibility of a future major Allied attack on the Channel coast. This attack (known as Operation Jubilee) took place on 19 August 1942, with 5,000 Canadian troops, 1,000 British commandos and fifty American Rangers involved. The operation was supported by 237 ships and supplemented by 74 squadrons of aircraft.

The Dieppe Raid was utterly catastrophic. In a matter of six hours 907 Canadians were killed, 586 wounded and 1,946 captured by the Germans. British losses were equally dire with 550 dead or wounded. About 100 Allied aircraft were shot down and one destroyer and 33 landing craft were sunk. The Germans lost just 311 men and 280 were wounded during the military engagement.[149]

The final meeting between Stalin and Churchill began at 7 p.m. on 15 August 1942 and ended at 3 a.m. on the following morning. The atmosphere was enhanced by a huge buffet and several drinks. Stalin turned on the charm. At one point a huge, steaming roasted suckling pig was brought in for the leaders to eat. Stalin told Churchill that he was fully confident the Red Army would hold out in the Caucasus and at Stalingrad. By the end of the meeting, Churchill felt that Stalin had finally accepted there could be no Second Front in Europe in 1942. As Churchill observed: 'I feel I have established a personal relationship which will be helpful.'[150]

In early August, German Army Group A had advanced 350 miles, occupying the city of Elista, and seizing the key railway junction at Krasnodar. On 9 August the oil-rich city of Maikop on the Belaya River was captured, although its nearby oil installations were set on fire as Soviet soldiers retreated. Once again, the Red Army had avoided a huge encirclement. Halder noted: 'This enemy is running for dear life and will be in the northern hills of the Caucasus well ahead of our [tank] armour.'[151]

The German army was now at the foothills of the 600-mile-long Caucasus mountain range. On 21 August Bavarian mountain troops planted a swastika flag on top of Mount Elbus, the highest peak in the Caucasus and in Europe at 5,642 metres. When Hitler was told about this, he became extremely agitated, saying that he wanted tank advances in the Caucasus not mountaineering victories.[152] On 30 August, the Operations Staff Diary noted: 'The Führer is dissatisfied with the situation of Army Group A.'[153]

There were other worrying signs for the German summer offensive in the late summer of 1942. On 24 August a Soviet counter-attack at Rzhev threatened the 9th Army advance in the area. At a highly charged military conference, Halder asked Hitler for permission for German forces to retreat from Rzhev to a more defensible position, prompting Hitler to shout at him: 'You always come here with the same proposal, that of withdrawal and at the same time make a series of disparaging remarks. I expect commanders to be as tough as the fighting troops.' In response, Halder said defiantly: 'I am tough enough, my Führer. But out there, brave men and young officers are falling in thousands simply because their commanders are not allowed to make the only reasonable decision [to retreat] and have their hands tied behind their backs.'

[overleaf]
British and Canadian troops captured by
the Germans during the catastrophic
Dieppe Raid in August 1942.

Hitler was shocked by this riposte from Halder, replying angrily: 'How dare you use language like that to me! Do you think you can teach me what the man at the front is thinking? What do you know what goes on at the front? Where were you in the First World War? And you try to pretend that I don't understand what it's like at the front. I won't stand for that! It's outrageous.'[154] On 30 August Halder noted gloomily in his diary: 'Today's conferences with the Führer were again the occasion of abusive reproaches against the military leadership of the highest commands. He charges them with intellectual conceit, mental non-adaptability, and utter failure to grasp essentials.'[155]

In early September 1942 the offensive of Army Group A ground to a shuddering halt in front of the heavily defended city of Grozny, a key oil supply hub. A lack of fuel held up its Panzer divisions for days beforehand. The big objective for this operation was to capture Baku, the capital of Azerbaijan, which produced 80 per cent of Russia's oil supplies, but the Germans were still a long way from capturing it. The seizure of Russia's precious oilfields – the original key aim for the summer offensive – now seemed impossible.

Franz Halder, Chief of the German Army High Command (1938–1942).

Alfred Jodl was sent by Hitler to visit Army Group A's headquarters in the Caucasus. Its commander Wilhelm List told Jodl there was no hope of his troops advancing any further through the mountain paths in the Caucasus because Red Army defences were now blocking their way. List then blamed this developing catastrophe on Hitler's over-ambitious objectives for Army Group A in the Caucasus in the first place, which he thought had overstretched his forces. On his return to Hitler's military headquarters, Jodl told Hitler that List could not be held responsible for the current dire situation, because he was only following the orders of the Führer. Hitler was at first speechless and then outraged by Jodl's blunt assessment. 'That's a lie!' he shouted. On 9 September List was dismissed from his post and Hitler appointed himself as the new commander of Army Group A.

These bitter exchanges show how much Hitler's relationship with his key commanders was deteriorating. He was convinced that they were all conspiring against him. Returning to Hitler's military HQ after a few weeks on leave, General Warlimont observed: 'I entered the log cabin. Hitler fixed me with a long malevolent stare and suddenly I thought: "The man's confidence has gone"; he has realized that his deadly game is moving to its appointed end and that Russia is not going to be overthrown.'[156]

Hitler now brought in his own stenographers from Berlin to take verbatim records of all his daily military conferences. He took to eating alone, rather than in the staff dining room as was his custom previously. The map room, the fulcrum of military discussions, remained empty. The twice-daily military briefings became much more formal and tense. Keitel later recalled that Hitler did not even shake hands with him or Jodl from September 1942 to the end of January 1943.[157]

The biggest clash of personalities among the German High Command was between Hitler and Halder. Keitel felt that the personalities of the two men were totally 'unsuited'. Halder had grown progressively tired of Hitler's repetitive and long-winded arguments, while Hitler viewed Halder's interventions as a criticism of his own competency in commanding the German war machine.[158]

Halder told a Nuremberg Trial interviewer how his relationship with Hitler gradually deteriorated, before his eventual dismissal on 24 September 1942: 'The point upon which we had our final disagreement was the decision of an offensive on the Caucasus and Stalingrad – a mistake, and Hitler didn't want to see it. I told him the Russians would put in another million men in 1942 and get another [million] in 1943. Hitler told me I was an idiot.'[159] Hitler felt that if Halder had shared his own fanatical belief in National Socialism then harmony would have prevailed in their relationship.[160]

Halder's replacement as the Chief of the Army High Command (OKH) was Major-General Kurt Zeitzler. A committed National Socialist, Zeitzler was generally regarded as an energetic and efficient staff officer, skilled in managing large tank formations and known for being loyal to his superiors. Göring had already put in a good word for him, commenting to Hitler: 'I have had sleepless nights over your eternal difficulties with this fellow Halder. You must get rid of him, and I know a successor who will cause you no worry at all: Zeitzler, he is the right man for you.'[161] Hitler told Speer that he now had a reliable adviser who 'doesn't go off and brood on my orders, but energetically sees to carrying them out'.[162]

With the German army now bogged down in the Caucasus, the city of Stalingrad (modern-day Volgograd) began to assume much greater importance in the southern sector of the German offensive, spearheaded by Army Group B. Stalingrad was previously called Tsaritsyn and it was only named after Stalin on 10 April 1925 in recognition of his role in helping to save the city from the counter-revolutionary White armies during the Russian Civil War.

Stalingrad was located along the western bank of the River Volga: twenty-five miles long, but rarely more than four miles wide at any single point. In the south was its old town containing the dock area, the main railway station, key government buildings and apartment blocks, as well as shops, bars and theatres. The focal point in the city centre was the Square of Fallen Heroes. A huge concrete grain-storage factory known as The Grain Elevator was also located nearby. The Tsaritsa River ran through the middle of the city.

The south of the city was dominated by the 300-foot high Mamayev Kurgan, the ancient burial site of Mamai, the military commander of the Golden Horde. On top of a very high hill overlooking the whole city, it would become a focal point during the Battle of Stalingrad. Possession of the hill gave artillery guns a huge advantage and it changed hands repeatedly during the fierce fighting.

In the north there were four huge industrial factory complexes, all devoted to armaments production: the Barrikady (Barricades) arms factory; the Lazur chemical plant; the Dzerzhinsky tractor factory, which had recently been modified to make tank chassis; the Krasny Oktyabr (Red October) metal factory, which recycled metal; and finally the Schnellhefter factory block. Each of these buildings running along the river was half a mile long. This concrete factory district would play a huge role in the military fighting in Stalingrad. The Central Rail Station and the Southern Train Station were also fought over relentlessly, and these stations changed hands at least fifteen times during the bitter struggle. There was also heavy fighting in the city railway loop (known as the 'Tennis Racket').[163]

The entire population of Stalingrad was mobilized to defend the city. A Stalingrad Defence Committee was formed with 200,000 citizens organized into workers columns. Women played a key defensive role. They dug anti-tank ditches, planted barbed wire and laid anti-tank mines. They acted as doctors, nurses, medical orderlies, telephonists, sailors on the Volga ferries, anti-aircraft gunners and as pilots.[164]

In August 1942 the prospects of the Red Army holding Stalingrad looked bleak. Army Group B (now consisting of the German 6th Army and 4th Panzer Army) initially deployed 270,000 troops, 500 tanks and 600 aircraft. The Germans were supported outside the city by the 3rd and 4th Romanian armies, the 2nd Hungarian and 8th Italian armies. The Red Army defenders numbered 187,000 troops, including the 62nd Army defending the north of the city with the 64th Army in the south. The Soviets had 400 tanks and 300 aircraft to defend the city.

The Soviet 62nd Army, which fought battles street by street inside the city at close quarters, became one of the most legendary Red Army units of the entire Second World War. Its commander General Vasily Chuikov was given the thankless task of replacing General Anton Lopatin as its commander on 12 September 1942. Chuikov joined the Red Army in 1918, aged eighteen. He had returned to the Soviet Union only in July 1942 after acting as a military adviser to Chiang Kai-shek's Chinese army during its continuing bitter struggle with Japan.

Chuikov was not only fearless but a master of improvisation. He moulded his soldiers into a courageous band of brothers. He summed up the mission succinctly: 'We will defend the city or die in the attempt.'[165] He dubbed his soldiers 'the Stalingrad Academy of Street Fighters'. He was ruthless, too, quite willing to shoot any officer or soldier who failed to do his duty.[166]

Chuikov felt that street fighting assisted the Red Army. As he later commented:

> City fighting is a special kind of fighting. Things are settled here not by strength, but by skill, resourcefulness and swiftness. The buildings in a city are like breakwaters. They broke up the advancing enemy formations and made their forces go along the streets... The troops defending the city learned to allow German tanks to come right on top of them – under the guns of the anti-tank artillery and anti-tank riflemen; in this way they invariably cut off the infantry from the tanks and destroyed the enemy's organized battle formation.[167]

German infantrymen disliked street fighting, because it lost them the advantages of the *Blitzkrieg* strategy. In Stalingrad, every house, factory, railway station, hill and building had to be fought over bitterly.

Streets were littered with burned-out tanks, piles of rubble, twisted metal, crashed planes, empty shell cases and corpses. Fighting in Stalingrad even went on underground in the subterranean world of sewers, cellars, road tunnels and bunkers. German soldiers called the Battle of Stalingrad the 'Rat War' (*Rattenkrieg*). As one German general observed: 'The enemy is invisible. Ambushes out of basements, wall remnants, hidden bunkers, produce heavy casualties among our troops.'[168]

In Soviet histories, the official start date of the Battle of Stalingrad is 17 July 1942. On that day the German 6th Army clashed with the 62nd and 64th Soviet armies near the River Chur. The major German assault on the city, however, did not begin until just over a month later. This was on 21 August when the 6th Army under Paulus launched a tank attack along the River Don, then pushed along the bank of the Volga, blasting through Soviet defences with ease. In just two days the German forces were in the small town of Spartanovka, the most northerly suburb of Stalingrad. The tractor plant soon came under heavy fire and the two railway lines linking Stalingrad to the north and north-west of Russia were cut.[169]

The German attempt to capture Stalingrad was stepped up on 23 August, when the *Luftwaffe* launched one of the most deadly German air attacks of the entire war. Using 600 bombers and 1,000 tonnes of incendiary bombs, the German air force mercilessly carpet-bombed the city, setting fire to oil storage tanks, destroying factories, buildings, schools and residential properties, and cutting gas, water and electric power supplies. The sewage system no longer worked effectively. Stalingrad was bombed relentlessly for a further five days, leaving the cityscape filled with black smoke. According to Soviet sources, 40,000 people were killed, but the actual figure was about 25,000.[170]

Stalin summoned Georgy Zhukov, who had saved Moscow in 1941, to take charge of the defence of Stalingrad on 27 August 1942. On that day Stalin ordered Zhukov to go to the city and report back to him on how to turn around the dire situation there. At the same time, Stalin promoted Zhukov to the post of Deputy Supreme Commander of the Soviet Armed Forces, with Aleksandr Vasilevsky taking on Zhukov's former role as the Chief of the General Staff. Zhukov felt that if Stalingrad fell to the Germans, 'the south of the country would be cut off from the centre and will probably not be able to defend it'.[171] On 29 August he arrived in Stalingrad and immediately assembled three reserve units to launch an attack on the 6th Army. It began on 5 September, but was unsuccessful.

On 12 September Friedrich Paulus, the commander of the German 6th Army, visited Hitler at his headquarters in Vinnytsia. Also present were Franz Halder (not yet sacked) and General Maximilian von Weichs, the commander-in-chief of Army Group B. In his testimony at the Nuremberg Trial, Paulus claimed to have warned Hitler of his concerns about the weak Romanian, Italian and Hungarian troops protecting the exposed German flanks, but his warning apparently fell on deaf ears. There is no corroboration of this testimony, however. Paulus also stressed that the German plan to capture Stalingrad was based on Hitler's assumption that the Red Army was incapable of mounting a counteroffensive. When Hitler asked him how long it would take to capture the city, Paulus replied: 'About twelve days.'[172]

In Germany, by now, serious concerns were being expressed about the war dragging on through yet another winter. An SD report on public opinion in September 1942 commented:

> After the end of three years of war, the position of a large
> majority can be characterized by a certain resignation, partly
> reflected in an even stronger degree of war-weariness and
> frequently also expressed in remarks of the following nature:
> 'Who would have thought, after the great victories at the
> beginning of the war, that the war would take this course and
> drag on so long?' Or: 'How much longer will the war last?'[173]

According to Zhukov's memoirs, on 13 September 1942 he presented to Stalin, in the company of Aleksandr Vasilevsky, a plan for a bold Soviet counteroffensive designed to trap the 6th Army. It focused on the exposed flanks of Army Group B, which were defended by weaker and less well-equipped Romanian, Hungarian and Italian armies. Once these secondary forces were destroyed, the 6th Army would then be encircled inside Stalingrad and cut off from all sources of supply. German troops would then be slowly forced into surrender or death. Zhukov estimated that the preparations for this bold Soviet offensive (codenamed Operation Uranus) would take forty-five days. He would draw on reserves which had been set aside for the defence of Moscow, which it was now clear would not be needed.[174]

Zhukov's own version of the genesis of Operation Uranus has subsequently been called into question. There is no record in Stalin's appointment diary of any meeting on 13 September 1942 at all. Indeed, in 1946 Zhukov was demoted on a charge of taking all the credit for Operation Uranus. This charge of self-promotion was raised again in

[overleaf]
Fighting inside the factory district in
Stalingrad.

1957 when Zhukov was dismissed as the Soviet Defence Minister.

In reality the detailed plan for Operation Uranus – which was presented to Red Army Front Commanders on 4 October – was undoubtedly written by Aleksandr Vasilevsky. It did not singularly focus on the counteroffensive to encircle the 6th Army at Stalingrad, but it was framed as being one part of a much broader 'Winter Offensive' directed not just against Army Group B in Stalingrad, but against the position of Army Group Centre, too.[175]

The Battle of Stalingrad revolved around a series of German offensives to capture the city. The first began at dawn on 13 September 1942 in the south-central sector. This attack achieved some initial gains for the Germans with the major part of the old town captured and some penetration into the dockland area.[176] On 14 September German troops tried to capture Mamayev Kurgan, but the Soviet 13th Guards Rifle Division, commanded by the Spanish Civil War hero General Alexander Rodimtsev, was ferried across the Volga and counter-attacked, driving the Germans off the huge hill. Chuikov claimed this was a crucial intervention because it prevented the Germans from capturing the whole city.[177]

On the next day the Germans attempted to seize the 'Grain

Elevator', a huge concrete fortress on the west bank of the Volga. Around forty Red Army troops rebuffed ten German assaults to capture it on this one day alone. A soldier in the 6th Army, Wilhelm Hoffman, noted in his personal diary: 'Our battalion, plus tanks, is attacking the [grain] elevator, from which smoke is pouring. The elevator is occupied not by men, but by devils that no flames or bullets can destroy.'[178] The elevator was finally taken by German troops after a bitter four-day struggle.

On 27 September German forces attempted to take control of the whole heavily defended factory district. After a huge *Luftwaffe* raid, troops moved slowly forward through the falling rubble of the heavily bombed buildings. Somehow, the 62nd Army had survived this huge onslaught, but it was now confined to a narrowing strip of the riverbank in the factory district.

One of the most legendary acts of defence during the Battle of Stalingrad was the fifty-eight-day defence of a four-storey apartment building, located on 9th January Square, in the middle of the city, which took place between 27 September and 25 November 1942. It became known as 'Pavlov's House' in honour of the leader of its defence, Sergeant Yakov Pavlov. His men defended the building doggedly, fighting floor to floor and room to room until they finally held the building. Chuikov later claimed that more German soldiers lost their lives trying to capture 'Pavlov's House' than in the capture of Paris in 1940.[179] Pavlov became a national hero, but a Russian TV documentary in 2009 suggested that although he played a key role in the defence of the building, the real unsung hero of the battle was the much lesser-known Lieutenant Ivan Afanasiev.[180]

On 30 September 1942 Hitler returned to Berlin to deliver a speech at the opening of the Winter Relief Fund at the Sport Palace. He promised his audience that the occupation of Stalingrad would lead to a 'gigantic victory'. The worst days of the war in the Soviet Union had already passed during the winter of 1941–2, he said. Hitler once again repeated his warning to exterminate the Jews, who he claimed were the real influence behind President Roosevelt, who he described as 'this insane man in the White House'. He predicted that every state entering the war would emerge from it as an antisemitic state: 'The Jews once laughed about my prophecies in Germany. I do not know if they are laughing today or whether they no longer feel like laughing. Today, too, I can assure you of one thing: they will soon not feel like laughing any more. My prophecies will prove correct here, too.'[181]

Soviet troops in winter clothing fighting
for control of Stalingrad.

On 6 October Paulus suspended the first phase of the German offensive to capture Stalingrad. The German 6th Army now held most of the southern part of the city centre, including the huge Univermag department store on Heroes of the Soviet Union Square, which Paulus had turned into his own military headquarters. Even the central landing stage for shipping was under German control.

By now Stalingrad was a scene of unimaginable and indescribable desolation. Wilhelm Eising, a motorcycle dispatch rider with the German 16th Panzer Division, observed: 'The city centre with the main railway station and "Red Square" was a heap of rubble, the multi-storied buildings shell-damaged and gutted. Here and there half a chimney stack stood surrounded by the ashes of wooden buildings. The population had either fled or taken shelter in the suburbs, in ruins, cellars and caves.'[182]

As the fighting raged in Stalingrad, Himmler went to visit Mussolini in Rome on 11 October 1942. He found the Italian dictator in very good spirits, despite the continuing rumours in the Western press that his government was looking for a way to end the war. When the conversation turned to the so-called Jewish question, Himmler didn't mention the extent of the mass extermination of Jews. Instead, he claimed that a large number of Jews were dying because they were not used to hard physical labour. Himmler then openly admitted to Mussolini that Jews, including women and children, had been killed in mass shootings, but he indicated that this punishment was confined only to those engaged in partisan activity. Mussolini said that he completely agreed with Himmler's policy towards the Jews.[183]

At dawn on 14 October 1942 a second huge offensive was mounted by the German 6th Army in Stalingrad. Paulus deployed three infantry divisions, supported by 300 tanks, for this operation, with the aim once again of capturing the strategically important factory district. Chuikov later recalled there was 'fighting of unprecedented ferocity' during this phase of the struggle. The Tractor Factory was seized by the Germans on 16 October. On 23 October, the Red October Factory was occupied. On 27 October the Barrikady Factory fell to the Germans, too. By the end of October the whole of the factory district had been captured by the German army.[184]

This meant the survival of Stalingrad was now hanging by a thread. Yet the incredibly brave Soviet soldiers simply refused to give up. Massive Russian artillery bombardment from the left bank of the Volga helped the 62nd Army to survive the October onslaught. Red

Friedrich Paulus, Commander of the 6th Army, lifting his gloved hand.

Army reinforcements were ferried across the Volga, but on 18 October there was a lull in the fighting. 'From then on,' Chuikov recalled, 'the two armies were left gripping each other in a deadly clutch, the front became virtually stabilized.'[185]

In the first two weeks of November there was yet another suspension of the bitter battle for Stalingrad. The German soldiers of the 6th Army were now suffering from battle exhaustion. They were undoubtedly on top in the battle, but their morale was sinking. The house-to-house fighting had already inflicted enormous losses on the German infantry. This was especially true during the ferocious fighting for control of the factory district in late October. Between 21 August and 16 October 1942 the 6th Army suffered 40,000 men killed, wounded or missing.[186] A German corporal wrote in a despairing letter home: 'It's impossible to describe what is happening here. Everyone in Stalingrad who possesses a head and hands, women as well as men, carried on fighting.'[187] Wilhelm Hoffman, a German private, noted in his diary: 'Who would have thought, three months ago, that instead of the joy of victory we would have to endure such sacrifices and torture, the end of which is nowhere in sight? The soldiers are calling Stalingrad the mass grave of the *Wehrmacht*.'[188]

On 21 October Hitler sent a friendly letter to Mussolini on the twentieth anniversary of the Italian dictator's famous March on Rome in 1922. This event, Hitler insisted, had been a key inspiration to his own rise to power, and he once again stressed the deep connection between Italian Fascism and National Socialism. A key aim of this overly flattering letter was to raise Mussolini's flagging spirits. Hitler also mentioned his desire to soon meet Mussolini personally, but he felt that this was impossible at present due to the critical situation in the Soviet Union.[189]

In North Africa, meanwhile, the military initiative was passing decisively towards the Allies. On 23 October the British 8th Army launched an enormous tank-led offensive against German-Italian forces in Egypt to begin the Second Battle of El Alamein (Operation Lightfoot). The German tank commander Erwin Rommel – who had been on extended sick leave for several weeks – due to low blood pressure and intestinal problems – returned to North Africa on 25 October to take command of the flagging Axis defence operations. He immediately ordered a counter-attack, but this failed because of a severe shortage of fuel and ammunition.

On 2 November 1942 Montgomery launched another huge offensive

(Operation Supercharge). On the same day, Rommel informed Hitler that his army's strength was now 'exhausted after ten days of battle and not now capable of offering any effective opposition'.[190] The next day, Hitler advised Rommel to 'stand fast, yield not a yard of ground and throw every gun and every man into the battle'. Rommel had to fight on 'to victory or death'.[191]

On 4 November 1942 Rommel defied Hitler and issued an order to his troops to retreat. He then drove with his Panzer Corps all the way to Libya. Monty had reacted much too slowly to prevent this daring escape, but on 13 November Tobruk was recaptured by the Allied forces. It was a comprehensive rout of Rommel, who had been depicted as almost superhuman by the British press and in German propaganda. In fact, the Allied victory was due to an overwhelming equipment advantage, not tactical superiority. The Allies captured 30,724 Axis prisoners, most of whom were Italians, who had performed abysmally yet again. The Germans sustained 1,100 men killed, with 10,724 captured. Overall, the Axis nations had 25,000 men killed or wounded in the battle. It was the first major victory that the British and Commonwealth forces had achieved on land against the Germans since the war began in 1939.[192]

Hitler did not punish Rommel for disobeying his order. He decided to accept his excuse that a lack of fuel, rather than the superior military force of the British forces, was the key reason for the German defeat at El Alamein. Hitler realized that he had placed too much pressure on Rommel. At a conference at his headquarters in Rastenburg, Hitler commented:

> I really think one shouldn't leave a man in a position of such heavy responsibility too long. That gradually demoralizes his nerves. There is a difference if one is in the rear. There, of course, one keep's one's head. These people [generals] can't stand the strain on their nerves. One should really carry out the principle of not leaving a man in the theatre of war too long. That makes no sense. It is better to relieve him. Then someone comes in fresh.[193]

The Allies now spectacularly pressed home their military advantage in North Africa. On 7 November Hitler was travelling to Munich on his special train when it was suddenly halted in a forested area in Thuringia. There Hitler receive a telegraphed message from the Foreign Ministry warning him that an Allied invasion on the North African coast would occur within hours. When Ribbentrop boarded Hitler's

[overleaf]
British general Bernard Montgomery ('Monty'), the commander of the 8th Army.

train at Bamberg, he was so rattled by the news of the imminent Allied invasion that he urged Hitler to allow him to make overtures to Stalin for a separate peace, but Hitler angrily rejected this suggestion.[194]

As expected, on the following day British and American troops landed on the coasts of Morocco and Algeria and occupied French North Africa. The Allied landings were quite chaotic. If the invading forces had faced a heavily armed German defence force rather than poorly equipped French colonial troops, then the landings would probably have failed.[195]

Despite the dire news from North Africa, Hitler decided to go ahead with his traditional speech to the Nazi 'old fighters' in Munich's Löwenbräukeller on the anniversary of the 1923 Beer Hall Putsch. His speech was broadcast live on national radio and relayed to troops in Stalingrad. Hitler downplayed the Allied landings in North Africa and ruled out a negotiated peace with the Allies: 'From now on, there will be no peace offers.' Hitler then raised the prospect of victory in the Battle of Stalingrad, declaring:

> I wanted to reach the Volga, to be precise at a particular spot at a
> particular city. As it happens, it bore the name of Stalin himself.
> But don't think that I marched there for that reason, it was
> because it occupies a very important position. All the wheat from
> the vast Ukraine and the Kuban area converges there in order to
> be transported north... I wanted to capture it and, you should
> know, we are quite content, as we have as good as got it! There
> are a couple of bits left.[196]

After the Allied victories in North Africa, Hitler's patience with the Vichy government came to an abrupt end. His big worry was that if he did not act quickly the French colonies in North Africa would go over to the Allied side. The slippery pro-German French Prime Minister Pierre Laval, who had been restored to power on 18 April 1942, was summoned to Munich on 9 November. On the next day Hitler met him in Munich, in the company of Ciano, the Italian Foreign Minister. Ciano was standing in for Mussolini who claimed he was too ill to travel.

When Laval arrived, Hitler greeted him in a very distant manner. The French Prime Minister had no warning of what was about to unfold. Hitler explained that he wanted Laval to grant Axis troops access to all ports and airfields in French-controlled Tunisia. Laval indicated that if this were presented in the form of an ultimatum to Marshal Pétain then it was likely to be accepted.

What Hitler omitted to tell Laval during their conversation was that German troops had already been ordered to move into the Unoccupied Zone in France on the following day. At the same time, Italy seized Corsica and Savoy. There was no French resistance to either the German or the Italian military occupations even though they were clear breaches of the 1940 Armistice agreement. Hitler publicly announced that he would allow Pétain's government to remain in power in Vichy, but he left no doubt that all of France was now under full German occupation. Many French people thought that Pétain should have fled to North Africa at the end of this meeting and gone over to the Allied side.

Hitler wanted to seize the French naval fleet, too. It was anchored in Toulon, but as the German 7th Panzer Division entered the port on 27 November the French naval commander Jean de Laborde gave the order for his sailors to scuttle the entire fleet. The French destroyed seventy-seven vessels, including three battleships, fifteen destroyers, seven cruisers and twelve submarines. Some of the major ships were ablaze for several days. This destruction of the French naval fleet was incredibly helpful to the Allies and gave them a further advantage in the naval battle in the Mediterranean. For Hitler it was confirmation of his view that the French Vichy regime could not be trusted.[197]

On 8 November 1942 the French admiral François Darlan – a notorious collaborator with Hitler's government – was in Algeria visiting his son in hospital, during a pre-planned tour of the French colonies in Africa when he heard news of the Allied landings. Next a pro-Allied group seized control of Algiers and arrested Darlan.

Dwight D. Eisenhower, the Allied commander, realized that Darlan could greatly assist the Allies if he switched sides. On 10 November Darlan agreed to do so, arguing that Pétain was now a traitor and effectively a prisoner of Germany. Darlan ordered the ceasefire of all French forces in North and West Africa and urged them to join the Allied side. On 14 November Eisenhower appointed Darlan the High Commissioner of North and West Africa.

This prompted outrage from General de Gaulle, the leader of the Free French, but Roosevelt defended the move as a 'temporary expedient'. The American historian Arthur Funk later discovered that Darlan had been in talks with US diplomats for months before about switching sides.[198] Darlan's honeymoon with the Allies did not last long. On 24 December 1942, he was shot dead at his headquarters by twenty-year-old Fernand Bonnier de La Chapelle, a member of the

French Resistance opposed to the Vichy government's collaboration with Hitler. The assassin was summarily executed on the following day thereby avoiding interrogation of his motives.[199]

On 16 November 1942 German Field Marshal Friedrich Paulus launched his third and final major offensive to capture Stalingrad. Temperatures by now had plummeted to -20°C. Paulus used specially trained assault pioneer battalions to spearhead this assault. These units had special skills in operating in heavily fortified areas. The aim was to attack once more through the factory district and finally destroy Chuikov's extraordinarily brave 62nd Army. German troops managed to penetrate the grounds of the heavily defended Lazur chemical works, but the infantry could not capture it. The Germans had once again achieved very small gains in exchange for an enormous loss of life.

The great irony was that the 6th Army had already captured almost 90 per cent of the city, but no matter how hard they tried they could not dislodge the 62nd Army from a sixteen-mile strip along the west bank of the Volga. Until the Germans had captured this area, they could not claim total victory. The last attack on the factory district – aimed at the Red October Factory – finally petered out on 18 November 1942 due to troop exhaustion and lack of ammunition.

The whole world marvelled at the resilience of the Red Army in Stalingrad. It was portrayed by the Allied press as a classic David and Goliath struggle. How the 62nd Army survived the German onslaught in Stalingrad is difficult to explain without reference to the extraordinary courage, ingenuity, improvisation and 'never say die' attitude of the Red Army soldiers. Chuikov's own fearless bravery clearly inspired his soldiers. Under his command the greatly outnumbered 62nd Army became the masters of street fighting. They preferred to fight at night, using not just guns but knives and bayonets. By day, the Red Army troops made extensive use of snipers.

The most famous of these was Vasily Zaytsev, who was especially adept at knocking out German machine-gun nests. Because of Soviet snipers like Zaytsev, German soldiers feared moving about during daylight hours. Between 10 November and 17 December Zaytsev reportedly killed 225 enemy soldiers. He especially liked killing German officers: 'You watch a Nazi officer come out of a bunker, acting all high and mighty, ordering his soldiers every which way and putting on an air of authority. The officer hasn't got the slightest idea that he only has seconds to live.' On 22 February 1943 Zaytsev was awarded the title of 'Hero of the Soviet Union'. In 2001 he would be portrayed by Jude Law in the Hollywood film *Enemy at the Gates*.[200]

In the end the real knockout blow to the German 6th Army in Stalingrad was delivered many miles away. On 19 November 1942 one of the boldest and most spectacular military operations of the entire war began. Four Soviet army groups (Fronts) numbering 1 million men launched Operation Uranus at 5.20 a.m. with a huge artillery barrage, using 3,500 guns, mortars and rockets, accompanied by mechanized units. The two-pronged attack was first launched at the northern flank of the 6th Army, which was defended by the 3rd Romanian Army, commanded by General Petre Dumitrescu, and composed of ill-equipped infantrymen and cavalrymen. By 21 November these Romanian troops surrendered and 27,000 of them were captured.

From the southern flank, the Stalingrad Front struck against the 4th Romanian Army and sent the 4th German Panzer Army into a headlong retreat. The Romanian armies were now cut off from Army Group B. Within four days the Soviet pincers met up at Sovietsky village near Kalach-on-Don. The Soviet encirclement had been achieved by rapid cross-country tank movements.[201] A total of 240,000 German troops of the 6th Army were now trapped in Stalingrad.

Hitler was totally flabbergasted when first given the news of this Soviet masterstroke while he was staying at the Berghof. He immediately travelled by his special train to the Wolf's Lair in Rastenburg. There he met Chief of the Army High Command (OKW) Major-General Kurt Zeitzler on 23 November, who advised him to immediately order the 6th Army to withdraw. Hitler simply replied: 'We are not budging from the Volga.'[202]

The official OKW diary noted on 25 November 1942: 'The 6th Army, which is now surrounded, has held its fronts, though its supply situation is critical and, in view of the unfavourable winter weather and the enemy superiority in fighters, it is very doubtful whether the 700 tonnes of food, ammunition, fuel, etc., per day which the army has requested, can be transported to the pocket by air.'[203] On 26 November Adolf Hitler sent the following message to soldiers trapped in Stalingrad: 'My thoughts and those of the German people are with you in these grave hours! Whatever the circumstances, you must hold on to the Stalingrad position.'[204]

Göring foolishly promised Hitler that the *Luftwaffe* could supply the trapped German forces with 550 tonnes of supplies every day. However, his own *Luftwaffe* commanders told him only 350 tonnes was possible, even in good weather. Paulus reckoned that he needed 700 tonnes of daily supplies to survive. Speer thought that Göring himself did not believe his own claim that he could supply the trapped soldiers with supplies. 'People were afraid of telling the absolute truth,' Speer noted, 'and they wanted to please him [Hitler] with something that was cheering him up, and Göring saw Hitler in a desolate, depressive mood so he made his promise possibly without asking his generals beforehand.'[205]

The dug-in German soldiers of the 6th Army in Stalingrad were in a distressed state: suffering from cold, illness and lack of food. There was a spate of unexplained deaths, too, which had escalated rapidly in early December 1942. Soldiers were dying in large numbers of sudden heart failure, dubbed 'Stalingrad Heart'. Their rations had been steadily reduced, but initially doctors did not think it was 'starvation' alone that caused these mysterious deaths. Exposure to extreme cold seemed a much more likely cause. 'Stalingrad Heart' disproportionately affected young conscripts, with 55 per cent of the dead being soldiers aged between seventeen and twenty-one.

On 15 December Dr Girgensohn, the chief pathologist of the 6th Army, was sent to investigate the deaths in more detail. He conducted fifty autopsies on the victims of 'Stalingrad Heart', concluding that starvation was indeed the chief cause, inflaming the heart then affecting liver function and leading to multi-organ failure. He further noted that at the time of their deaths all of the affected soldiers were on severely reduced rations.[206]

Unsurprisingly, military historians have concentrated on the brilliantly executed Soviet counteroffensive outside Stalingrad in the latter months of 1942, but this has overshadowed the parallel but 'forgotten offensive' of the Red Army. Known as Operation Mars, it began six days after Operation Uranus and occured around the Rzhev–Vyazma salient, ninety-three miles west of Moscow. This Soviet offensive aimed to severely weaken the powerful German 9th Army, the key defence force of Army Group Centre. It was felt by Zhukov that if the Rzhev–Vyazma salient – which had been captured on 14 October 1942 – remained in German hands it posed a direct threat to Moscow. The Red Army had made several unsuccessful attempts to capture it during the spring and summer, but the Germans had held firm.

Zhukov claimed in his memoirs that Operation Mars was simply a diversionary attack to prevent German units moving south to deal with Operation Uranus, but it's unclear whether it was really part of a much more ambitious Soviet offensive to turn the tide in the entire German-Soviet War. Newly released Soviet archive materials now make it possible to appreciate the importance given to Operation Mars by the Red Army during the latter part of 1942 in spite of the life and death struggle going on in Stalingrad. Zhukov not only commanded Operation Mars but devoted more of his own time planning it than he did to Operation Uranus.

Unlike Operation Uranus, which was an attack on weaker and more disorganized Axis forces, Operation Mars took on the full might of the experienced soldiers of Army Group Centre. The German defenders of the 9th Army were well organized and skilled in defence. By 28 November 1942 the Soviet offensive against Army Group Centre had run into serious difficulties as the German forces launched well-aimed counter-attacks. The fierce fighting around the Rzhev–Vyazma salient raged on from 30 November to 15 December 1942. Once again, the *Wehrmacht* proved more than a match for the Red Army, and during an intensive battle for control of the city of Belyi, the Germans once again came out on top.

On 11 December Operation Mars reached its climax in the valley of the Vazuza River, with the Red Army launching a huge assault on German defenders, but losing 200 tanks in the process. Zhukov kept urging his forces forwards until 15 December, when he reluctantly ordered a retreat from Belyi and from the battle near the Vazuza River. Operation Mars was a total failure, but it is largely forgotten because of the extraordinary success of Operation Uranus and the encirclement of the 6th Army in Stalingrad. Zhukov had used massive mechanized forces during the attack, but the German army once again proved vastly superior. The Germans had defeated Zhukov's forces by skilfully employing small, well-directed mechanized units to meet the attack forces, and by deploying anti-tank weapons with deadly accuracy.

The Red Army's combat losses in Operation Mars were estimated by the 9th Army at 100,000 killed and 200,000 wounded or captured. Recently released official Soviet casualty figures indicate 70,373 were killed, captured or missing, with 145,301 severely wounded. The loss of Soviet equipment was equally devastating, with around 1,700 tanks and armoured vehicles lost – far exceeding the total number of tanks deployed in Operation Uranus. German losses were estimated as 40,000 killed, wounded or missing. These figures show that whatever occurred at Stalingrad, the German army was still far from defeated in the German-Soviet War.

Despite this, Operation Mars cannot be written off as a complete catastrophe for the Red Army. It kept the fearsome mechanized 9th Army tied down in the central sector of the whole front, while Operation Uranus was trapping the 6th Army in Stalingrad. It also proved a pyrrhic victory for the Germans. In the spring of 1943 Walter Model, the commander of the 9th Army, requested and received permission to finally abandon the bloody Rzhev–Vyazma salient.[207]

On 2 December 1942 Mussolini gave a speech to the Chamber of Fasci and Corporations. It was the first time he had addressed this parliamentary body for eighteen months. Il Duce spoke with surprising frankness of the difficult situation that Italy now faced in the war. He admitted that difficult times lay ahead for the Axis nations. It was clear, Mussolini predicted, that the Allies were likely to think of invading Italy in 1943 and he urged the Italian people to be ready to resist them. 'Now, comrades,' he said in conclusion, 'we must fight for the living ones, fight for the future, but also for the dead. We must fight so that the sacrifice of our dead be not in vain, so that the sacrifice of those who fell in the squadrons, of those who fell in the Ethiopian war, in the Spanish war, in the present war, be not in vain.'[208]

Meanwhile, the German situation in Stalingrad continued to worsen. On 7 December the 6th Army's chief quartermaster in Stalingrad noted: 'Rations cut to between a third and a half, so that the army can hold out until 18 December. Horses were starving to death and being eaten when they did so. Lice infestation of the clothes of soldiers was encouraging the rapid spread of disease.'[209] A German soldier called Heinz Pfennig later recalled:

> We were placed on short rations in December. Bread was doled
> out, there was rarely any extra food. Our potatoes were just dried
> potato flakes. At this point all our supplies were flown in. Then
> the first snow came and that was a big problem... We had no
> winter clothes and the only thing we could do was bundle up
> in the snow and wait for the enemy to come and get us. The
> Russians knew that time and the cold weather were on their
> side.[210]

Red Army soldiers started to taunt the Germans who were dug in trenches throughout the city. Loudspeaker messages constantly reminded them that they were now in a hopeless position and starving to death.

Hitler gave strict instructions that news of the Soviet encirclement of the 6th Army in Stalingrad should be kept from the German public.

The official German press release only mentioned that an attack by the Red Army in the northern sector of the front was being fiercely resisted. It was only on 8 December that the German public heard for the first time there had been an attack south of Stalingrad, but the huge Soviet encirclement was still not mentioned. However, letters home from soldiers to their loved ones in Germany soon helped to spread the news that the 6th Army was indeed surrounded inside Stalingrad.[211]

On 12 December Hitler briefly turned his attention to domestic matters by signing a decree concerning the legal status of the Nazi Party in Germany. A previous decree of 1 December 1933 declared that the Party was a key aspect of the unity of the state, but this clause was now removed. The Nazi Party was now demoted to a 'public corporation' under the total control of Hitler. Its rights and duties would be derived henceforth from tasks that Hitler decreed. Party law would determine its inner organization, but this would also be decided by Hitler alone. The movement towards a personal dictatorship in Germany was now complete.[212]

The brilliant tank commander Field Marshal Erich von Manstein – once described as the 'armoured-breakthrough magician' – was given the hopeless task of trying to rescue the 6th Army in Stalingrad under Operation Winter Storm (*Wintergewitter*). His plan was to cut a corridor in the Red Army encirclement of Stalingrad and open up a secure route for the 6th Army. The Red Army was expecting such an operation and had 60 divisions and 1,000 tanks ready and waiting to meet it.

There were some differences of opinion within the German High Command about the aims of Operation Winter Storm. Hitler viewed Manstein's plan as a means of reinforcing the 6th Army by opening a land supply line to it, rather than enabling it to break out and retreat. Many other German generals felt that it should be used to assist the 6th Army to break out.

On 12 December Manstein's newly formed Army Group Don – composed of the 4th Panzer Army, the 6th Panzer division (brought from France), and infantry units from the remnants of the 3rd Romanian Army – began Operation Winter Storm over snow-covered terrain. On 16 December, when Army Group Don had advanced to within forty miles of Stalingrad, Zhukov launched Operation Little Saturn: three Guards armies struck against the weak and poorly equipped Italian 8th Army, which retreated in long columns through the snow.

In London, meanwhile, the British government decided to make public details it had received of a murderous war against Jews being enacted by Hitler's government. On 17 December Anthony Eden, the British Foreign Secretary, made an astonishing statement in the House of Commons, objecting to 'the barbarous and inhuman treatment to which Jews are being subjected in German-occupied Europe'. Eden then read out an agreed statement from the British, United States and Soviet governments and their allies:

> The German authorities, not content with denying to persons of Jewish race in all the territories over which their barbarous rule has been extended the most elementary human rights, are now carrying into effect Hitler's oft repeated intention to exterminate the Jewish people in Europe. From all the occupied countries Jews are being transported, in conditions of appalling horror and brutality, to Eastern Europe. In Poland, which has been made the principal Nazi slaughterhouse, the ghettos established by the German invaders are being systematically emptied of all Jews except a few highly skilled workers required for war industries. None of those taken away are ever heard of again. The able-bodied are slowly worked to death in labour camps. The infirm are left to die of exposure and starvation or are deliberately massacred in mass executions. The number of victims of these bloody cruelties is reckoned in many hundreds of thousands of entirely innocent men, women and children.

The Allies, Eden added, condemned 'in the strongest possible terms this bestial policy of cold-blooded extermination'. They further declared that such atrocities 'can only strengthen the resolve of all the freedom-loving peoples to overthrow the barbarous Hitlerite tyranny. They reaffirm their solemn resolution to ensure that those responsible for these crimes shall not escape retribution.'[213]

Goebbels decided not to respond publicly to these accusations concerning the 'Final Solution' as he noted in his diary: 'We can't respond to these things. If the Jews say that we've shot 2.5 million Jews in Poland or deported them to the east, naturally we can't say actually it's 2.3 million. So we're not in a position to get into a dispute.'[214]

On 18 December 1942 Hitler asked Mussolini to urgently meet him at his military HQ in Rastenburg, but he once again claimed he was too ill to make the journey and sent Ciano to deputize for him. The atmosphere at the subsequent meeting was extremely tense. It was obvious that Italy's loyalty to Hitler was ebbing away. Ciano bluntly informed the Führer that Mussolini wanted Germany to end its war with the Soviet Union as soon as possible in order to free up troops for the Balkan and North African theatres. Hitler rejected this idea out of hand. There was, in any case, no chance whatsoever of Stalin considering a separate peace with Hitler or Mussolini.[215]

By now the critical situation at Stalingrad was common knowledge among the German public. On 18 December Martin Bormann sent a letter from the Reich Chancellery to all Nazi Gauleiters in the localities, reporting the increasingly hostile reaction of the public to the progress of the war as expressed in SD public opinion surveys. According to Bormann, those who were deeply negative were in the minority and their views were due to 'strained nerves'. As yet, there were no signs of a more general unrest among the public. Bormann urged the Nazi Party leaders to display unshakable optimism in public speeches about the war: 'Any doubts about a German victory and the justice of our cause must be silenced immediately by unassailable arguments and – if that does not help – by stronger methods using the example of our own struggle.'[216]

On 19 December Manstein, defying Hitler, gave the order for the 6th Army to break out from the south-west of Stalingrad, but Paulus informed him that 'it was too late and not possible'. Hitler did not want the 6th Army to break out at all, but to fight to the last man. On 21 December Manstein asked the Chief of the OKW Kurt Zeitzler for a final decision on whether the 6th Army could be allowed to escape. Zeitzler told him that Göring was still confident that he could continue sending them supplies by air.

On 24 December Manstein's army, having been halted near the Mishkova River, was in severe danger of encirclement itself. It was finally ordered to retreat on 28 December. The attempt to rescue the 6th Army had utterly failed. It had been encircled, starved and was now abandoned.[217] Paulus stood no chance of breaking out of the Soviet encirclement in Stalingrad. His troops were desperately short of vehicles, fuel and ammunition. Had the 6th Army moved into the open it would have been open to air attack.

Manstein's forces were now hastily diverted to assist the over-extended Army Group A in its retreat from the Caucasus mountain passes. Hitler had initially resisted this move, but Zeitzler finally persuaded him there was really no other option. In the end, Army Group A, which had been the spearhead of Operation Blue, was pushed 300 miles back to where it had originally started.

The 6th Army remained trapped in Stalingrad during Christmas

1942. German soldiers carved Christmas trees out of wood and created basic advent crowns. On Christmas Eve, German officers distributed their last meagre supplies of sparkling wine and spirits to the troops. After singing carols, soldiers crowded around a radio to hear a programme which began with the words 'This is Stalingrad', followed by German soldiers supposedly stationed in Stalingrad singing 'Silent Night' ('*Stille Nacht*'). It was, of course, a deception organized by Goebbels to delude the German public that all was well in Stalingrad.[218]

Count Friedrich von Solms, a German tank driver, later recalled what was really happening inside Stalingrad:

> Christmas was miserable. We ate cats and dogs; we only had
> a little bread. Even the horsemeat had run out. Our morale
> was bad. Russian broadcasts kept giving the numbers killed in
> Stalingrad. They talked about officers from our division who tried
> to escape in Russian uniforms. The soldiers didn't want to fight
> anymore, and the Russians weren't attacking. They let us wait and
> starve.[219]

Soviet soldiers were naturally much more optimistic. One wrote in a letter home: 'We are pushing the serpents back to where they came from.' Another observed: 'We have started pressing the enemy very strongly. Now we have encircled the Germans. Every week a few thousand are taken prisoner and several thousand are destroyed on the field of battle.'[220]

On 28 December Martin Bormann met Goebbels to discuss the planned celebrations in January 1943 for the tenth anniversary of Hitler's coming to power. Bormann stressed that the event should concentrate on the Führer's achievements since 1933 and avoid discussing the future. But Goebbels thought it was now more important than ever to stress the need for 'Total War', requiring greatly increased rearmament and the creation of a fully mobilized wartime economy.[221]

Bravely resisting the German summer offensive in 1942 came at a high cost to the Soviet Union. In 1941, the USSR had suffered 27.8 per cent of its total dead in the Second World War, but in 1942, the combined death toll from Operation Blue and the struggle in Stalingrad came to an enormous 28.9 per cent of all the Soviet fatalities in the entire German-Soviet War.[222]

Only a dictatorship as brutal as Stalin's, which placed a low price on individual human life, could have tolerated such enormous losses, but beneath this, we must not forget the exceptional personal bravery demonstrated by the ordinary soldiers of the Red Army. No one exemplified this do-or-die attitude better than Vasily Chuikov, the fearless commander of the 62nd Army inside Stalingrad, who later commented:

> The Germans underestimated our artillery. And they underestimated the effectiveness of our infantry against their tanks. This battle showed that tanks forced to operate in narrow quarters are of limited value; they're just guns without mobility. In such conditions nothing can take the place of small groups of infantry, properly armed, and fighting with utmost determination. I don't mean barricade street fighting – there was little of that – but groups converting every building into a fortress and fighting for it floor by floor and even room by room.[223]

1943

·

THE
WEHRMACHT
RETREATS

·

The looming military disaster at Stalingrad cast a huge shadow over the opening of 1943. German soldiers there were exhausted, demoralized and hungry. Hitler issued three New Year messages. In the first – directed to 'National Socialists and Party Comrades' – Hitler looked back over 1942, mentioned the success of the *Wehrmacht* in 'mighty battles' and predicted the winter 'cannot hit us any harder than last year. Afterwards, the hour will come when we will line up again and concentrate our forces to secure freedom, the future, and the life of the people. Someday, one power will be the first to fall in this struggle. We know it will not be Germany'.[1]

His second New Year message was addressed to the soldiers of the *Wehrmacht*. Hitler referred to the 'huge struggle on the Volga', which he admitted had led to a 'heavy toll in blood', but he refrained from mentioning the word 'Stalingrad'. He promised 'never to retreat from our enemies'. What he now desired was the defeat of the 'Jewish-capitalist vultures'. A German victory would be followed by a 'period of peacefulness'.[2]

Hitler's third message was sent privately to Friedrich Paulus, the commander of the 6th Army, to be read out to his beleaguered troops. Hitler wrote:

> In the name of the whole German people, I send you and your valiant army the heartiest good wishes for the New Year. The hardness of your perilous position is known to me. The heroic stand of your troops has my highest respect. You and your soldiers, however, should enter the New Year with the unshakable confidence that I and the whole German *Wehrmacht* will do everything in our power to relieve the defenders of Stalingrad and that with your staunchness will come the most glorious feat in the history of German arms.[3]

On 6 January 1943, the leading German army doctor in Stalingrad called the last month 'a large-scale experiment in hunger'.[4] On 8 January the Red Air Force dropped leaflets offering the trapped German soldiers rations, medical to the wounded and their repatriation to Germany if they agreed an 'honourable surrender'.[5] On that same day, three Soviet officers, holding up a white flag, entered the German lines on the northern perimeter of the city to present Paulus with a note from General Konstantin Rokossovsky, the commander of the Don Front. It read: 'The situation of your troops is hopeless. They are suffering from hunger, sickness and cold. The cruel Russian winter has scarcely begun. Hard frosts, cold winds and blizzards still lie ahead. Your soldiers are not provided with winter clothing and are living in appalling sanitary conditions.' Paulus was given twenty-four hours to reply. He telegraphed the Soviet surrender terms to Hitler, who emphatically rejected them.[6]

Once the Soviets had received this rebuff, the Red Army launched Operation Ring on 10 January, with a force of forty-seven divisions from the south and west of Stalingrad, numbering 280,000 men, 10,000 artillery guns and 250 tanks. Their aim was to break the final remnants of German resistance in the city.[7]

On 13 January the 6th Army quartermaster sent a radio message to *Wehrmacht* HQ, stating bluntly, 'We have no more bread, munitions and fuel.' In a letter home to his mother, an exhausted German soldier wrote desparingly: 'I can't move my legs any more, and it's the same with the others, because of hunger; one of our comrades died, he had nothing left in his body and went on a march and he collapsed from hunger on the way and died of cold, the cold was the last straw.'[8] Another German soldier informed his wife: 'Please don't be sad and weep for me when you receive this, my last letter. I'm standing here in an icy storm in a hopeless position in the city of fate, Stalingrad, encircled for months, we will tomorrow begin the last fight.'[9]

By now, there were even rumours circulating of cannibalism among German soldiers and many instances of suicide. The wounded were now left untreated. Few drugs, medicines or dressings were left. Frostbite was spreading. Many soldiers' fingers were so badly swollen they could no longer fit inside the trigger guards of their guns. Even if the Red Army had done nothing, the remaining German soldiers trapped inside Stalingrad would probably have starved to death by the middle of February.

The Allies, feeling supremely confident of the outcome in Stalingrad, decided to hold a conference between 14 to 24 January 1943 on future war strategy. It took place in the Anfa Hotel in Casablanca, French Morocco. Churchill and Roosevelt attended, along with their military Chiefs of Staff, but Stalin declined the invitation due to the critical

[overleaf]
Roosevelt and Churchill during a
photo-call at the January 1943 Casablanca
Conference.

stage of events in Stalingrad. At the heart of these Allied discussions were three issues: the expanding Mediterranean theatre of war, the opening of a Second Front in France, and future bombing strategy.

It was agreed to dramatically step up the area bombing of Germany during the course of 1943 to ease the pressure on the Red Army on the Eastern Front. There was intense debate over the benefits of daytime or night-time bombing. Churchill thought bombing by day was much too risky, but the Americans favoured it, because they believed it increased accuracy when hitting strategic targets. A deal was concluded in the end: the Americans would bomb by day and the British by night.

In a heavily attended press conference at the end of the proceedings in Casablanca and much to Churchill's surprise, Roosevelt announced that the Allies would now seek 'unconditional surrender' from their Axis enemies. There would be no negotiated peace settlement and no separate peace treaty by any of the Allied powers.[10] This would force Germany to fight on to the bitter end.

By 16 January the German pocket in Stalingrad had been reduced to an area measuring fifteen miles long and nine miles deep. A German major wrote: 'The implacable struggle continues. God helps the brave! Whatever Providence may ordain we ask for one thing, for strength to hold on! Let it be said of us one day that the German army fought at Stalingrad as soldiers never before in the world have fought. To pass this spirit on to our children is the task of mothers.'[11] On the next day the 6th Army was forced into the eastern half of the Stalingrad pocket. The chief German quartermaster noted ominously: 'The Army is no longer in any position to supply its troops.' Nearly all of the horses had now been eaten and there was no bread left to feed the troops.[12]

In Berlin on 22 January Albert Speer announced the Adolf Hitler Panzer Programme. The launch was intended to raise public morale at a time of deepening gloom. Tanks had a symbolic importance for the German army. Two new heavier model tanks – the Panther and the Tiger – were trumpeted by Speer at the launch as being part of a programme of 'miracle weapons' which would turn the tide in the war back in Germany's favour. Twice as many tanks were produced during 1943 as there had been in the previous year, but tanks accounted for only 7 per cent of total German armaments production.[13]

On the same day, the Red Army offered surrender terms to the 6th Army once more. Depressed, exhausted and suffering from dysentery, Paulus informed Hitler that his troops had run out of ammunition. He asked for permission to enter negotiations to surrender to the Red

Army. Hitler sent back a sternly worded telegram: 'Forbid surrender. The army will hold its position to the last soldier and last cartridge, and by its heroic contribution to the building of a defensive front and the salvation of Western civilization.'[14]

On 22 January the Soviets captured Gumrak, the last airfield serviced by the *Luftwaffe*. The German army was now driven into overcrowded underground cellars. There were by now 20,000 wounded soldiers with no medical supplies. On the streets, frozen corpses lay everywhere. The Red Army advance had split the Stalingrad pocket into three different small areas of the city.

On 25 January 1943 Hitler became worried about the impact in Germany of certain defeat in Stalingrad and what it might mean for his own political position. As a precaution, he decided to bring forward a law to weaken the power of the Reichstag. It had not met since 26 April 1942 and the current sitting was due to expire on 30 November 1943. If he did not act now then under the existing constitution elections for a new Reichstag would need to take place. To avoid this, Hitler signed a new decree ordering the extension of the current Reichstag until 30 January 1947. Henceforth, Hitler ceased using the title of Chancellor and signed all of his decrees simply as 'The Führer'.[15]

On 29 January Paulus sent a telegram to Hitler (in fact, it was most probably written by his adjutant, Colonel Wilhelm Adam), loyally stating: 'The 6th Army hails its Führer. The swastika flag is still flying over Stalingrad. May our struggle be an example for the present and coming generations, that we should never capitulate even in a hopeless position.'[16]

In Berlin, the commemorations of the tenth anniversary of Hitler's coming to power on 30 January 1933 were distinctly subdued. Hitler took no part in them at all, remaining ensconced in the Wolf's Lair. Göring was given the task of delivering the main radio address to the German people, highlighting the 'heroic struggle' of the soldiers ambushed in Stalingrad. Comparing their sacrifice to the selfless bravery of the Spartans at the Battle of Thermopylae in 480 BC, he predicted: 'A thousand years hence Germans will speak of this battle [for Stalingrad] with reverence and awe and will remember that in spite of everything Germany's ultimate victory was decided there.'[17] The broadcast finished with the playing of Bruckner's Fifth Symphony, a favourite of Hitler. The soldiers of the 6th Army listened with incredulity to Göring, taking no comfort in being cast in the role of sacrificial lambs to the slaughter. One soldier called it: 'Our own funeral speech.'[18]

In the evening – at the Berlin Sport Palace – Goebbels read out a prepared text of Hitler's anniversary speech to the packed crowd. The Führer stressed that there were only two possibilities left in the war: victory for the National Social revolution or a Bolshevik victory and enslavement. There was just one brief reference to Stalingrad: 'The heroic struggle of our soldiers on the Volga should serve as a reminder for everybody to do the utmost for the struggle for Germany's freedom and the future of our people.' Hitler predicted that Germany would gain ultimate victory in the war, and promised: 'A new life will begin to bloom on the sacrifices of the dead and the ruins of our cities and villages.'[19]

On that very same evening Hitler promoted Paulus to the rank of Field Marshal, fully realizing that no German soldier of such an illustrious rank had ever surrendered on the field of battle. Paulus knew full well it was an invitation to commit suicide, but he defiantly told one of his generals: 'I have no intention of shooting myself for this Bohemian corporal.'[20] By now Paulus was headquartered in the basement of the former Univermag department store building on Heroes of the Revolution Square in the city centre. A tattered swastika flag still fluttered forlornly on the balcony over the main entrance. The building was being constantly shelled. On the street outside, Red Army soldiers with flamethrowers were assiduously mopping up the final pockets of German resistance.

At 7.15 a.m. on 31 January 1943 a German officer came to the entrance of the store and signalled to the Red Army the willingness of German troops to surrender. Soviet troops then entered the building. In the basement they found hundreds of wounded German soldiers, as well as Paulus, who was lying on a camp bed, still in uniform but unshaven and looking miserable. He satisfied himself that he had not technically surrendered. After being captured, he was driven in his own staff car fifty miles to the Don Front Army headquarters outside Zavarykino. In a separate car, two of the other leading German officers – General Schmidt and Colonel Adam – followed.

After arriving, the Soviet officer Marshal Nikolay Voronov told Paulus, who was now wearing a warm Russian fur hat, 'Herr Colonel-General, it is rather late, and you must be tired. We have also been working a lot during the last few days. Therefore, we shall now discuss one problem which is urgent.' In reply, Paulus told Voronov that he was not a Colonel-General, but a Field Marshal. The Soviet officers present were surprised to have captured an officer of such a high rank and asked to see his identification papers.

Voronov then asked Paulus to issue surrender orders to the remaining German divisions still trapped in the northern part of Stalingrad so as to prevent any further loss of life. Paulus flatly refused to do so, saying that such an order would be 'unworthy of a soldier'. Voronov sneeringly replied that it was unworthy of someone who had already surrendered to force his soldiers to endure yet more unnecessary misery. In response, Paulus said that even if he signed a surrender order, the troops would probably disobey it. As it happened, after further artillery bombardment, the remaining German troops, commanded by General Karl Strecker, surrendered just before noon on 2 February 1943, two full days after the capitulation of Paulus. Before doing so, their commander telegraphed the following message to Hitler: 'Have fought to the last man to vastly superior forces. Long live Germany!'[21]

Hitler was totally disgusted by the surrender of Paulus. To his generals at the midday military conference at the Wolf's Lair on 1 February 1943 Hitler delivered a bitter tirade against Paulus and his fellow officers: 'They have surrendered there formally and absolutely. Otherwise they would have closed ranks, formed a hedgehog and shot themselves with their last bullet.' As he ranted on, the Führer became more emotional about what he saw as Paulus's betrayal: 'It hurts me so much because the heroism of so many soldiers is destroyed by a single spineless weakling – and the main thing is what he is going to do now. You have to imagine it: he [Paulus] comes to Moscow and sees the "rat cage" [in the notorious Lubyanka Prison]. He'll sign everything there. He will make confessions and appeal.' What most wounded Hitler was the fact that he had promoted Paulus to Field Marshal to give him a final consolation before killing himself: 'That's the last field marshal I shall appoint in this war.'[22]

The German defeat at Stalingrad was of such a magnitude that it could not be glossed over even by Goebbels's slick propaganda machine. The elite 6th Army, the fearsome 4th Panzer Army and the Romanian, Hungarian and Italian satellite armies had all been totally decimated. Hitler decided not to reveal to the German public the circumstances of the capture of Paulus and the other generals, but to instead stress the heroism of the German soldiers. His downbeat communiqué of 3 February was read out at 4 p.m. by a sombre radio news announcer:

> Fighting in Stalingrad has ended. True to its oath of allegiance
> to fight to the last breath, the 6th Army under the exemplary
> command of Field Marshal Paulus has succumbed to the
> superiority of the enemy and unfavourable circumstances... It

is not yet the time to describe the course of the operations that have led to this development. One thing can already be said today, however: the sacrifice of the 6th Army was not in vain. As the bulwark of the historic European mission, it defied for many weeks the assault of six Soviet armies... Generals, officers, non-commissioned officers and men fought shoulder to shoulder down to the last man. They died so that Germany might live.[23]

Straight after Hitler's message, Beethoven's Fifth Symphony was played in full, followed by 'Siegfried's Funeral March' from Wagner's *Götterdämmerung*. Hitler decreed three full days of national mourning. All places of entertainment and bars and restaurants were closed during this period.

Stalingrad was a mass grave in the middle of a dystopian landscape. There are no wholly reliable figures on the exact numbers killed there. Soviet records claimed 147,000 German dead and 91,000 captured: making a total of 238,000, with only 5,000 ever returning to Germany alive. In addition, there were 109,000 Romanian, 114,000 Italians and 105,000 Hungarian troops killed, wounded or captured between August 1942 and February 1943. The Soviet citizens recruited by the Nazis – the *Hiwis* – had losses of around 20,000. Soviet losses were astonishing, with 478,741 killed or missing and 650,000 wounded.[24]

The German people were deeply traumatized by the defeat at Stalingrad. An SD report, monitoring public feeling, noted: 'Above all, people are asking why Stalingrad was not evacuated or relieved and how it was possible, only a few months ago, to describe the military situation as secure and as not unfavourable. In particular, people discuss with a marked undertone of criticism, the underestimation of the Russian combat forces through which now a second time a severe crisis has been triggered.'[25]

Hitler's public reputation was undoubtedly damaged by the catastrophic defeat at Stalingrad. A report from the Nazi Gau for the East-Hanover area noted that Hitler was being blamed for having promised too much about the outcome of the war. Another Gau report from South Westphalia commented: 'On trains the Führer was being called the mass murderer of Stalingrad without the perpetrator being arrested and soundly beaten.'[26]

Within the Nazi elite there was now open talk of a 'leader crisis'. Goebbels, Speer and Göring believed that the home front needed to be mobilized much more vigorously to support 'Total War' and the three men agreed that a small war cabinet should be created. Hitler rejected this idea, but did agree to the creation of a 'Committee of Three' to centralize control over the war effort. Its members were Wilhelm Keitel, the Chief of the Armed Forces High Command; Martin Bormann, the head of the Nazi Party Chancellery; and Hans Lammers, the Chief of the Reich Chancellery. All of them were Hitler's dependable 'yes-men'. This Committee was supposed to make decisions independently of the various Reich ministries, with Hitler endorsing their initiatives, yet it was given no real powers. It met eleven times from January to August 1943, but it ran into opposition from the start and quickly declined into irrelevance. In its place Goebbels wanted to revive the Ministerial Committee for the Defence of the War to direct the war effort on the home front, but he lost his nerve when it came to submitting this idea to Hitler. In the end, nothing was achieved to make Hitler's government more efficient.[27]

Defeat at Stalingrad prompted Hitler to retreat even further from the public eye and he now rarely gave public speeches. He spent most of his time in the Wolf's Lair during 1943, the exception being a three-month stay at the Berghof in the spring, prompted by complete nervous exhaustion. Hitler was hardly ever in Berlin, the supposed centre of the German government. His aides noticed that he had stopped listening to music or watching films for relaxation.

Hitler's health was gradually worsening. He went to bed very late and got up late. Medical check-ups revealed high blood pressure and habitual stomach and bowel problems. Cardiograms showed the early signs of angina. He took all manner of pills for pain and to help his growing depression. For energy boosts he took amphetamine and vitamin injections, and sedatives to help him sleep. There were signs that he was developing Parkinson's disease, most notably a noticeable spasmodic trembling in his left arm and a stooped posture. He seemed much older than a man nearing his fifty-fourth birthday. Goebbels noticed Hitler's physical and mental deterioration around this time: 'The Führer has aged fifteen years during the three and a half years of war. It is tragic that the Führer has become such a recluse and leads such an unhealthy life. He never gets out into the fresh air. He does not relax. He sits in his bunker, worries and broods.'[28]

During February 1943 Stalin ordered the Red Army to build on its victory at Stalingrad by launching a series of simultaneous offensives on the Eastern Front. Once more Stalin over-optimistically assumed the German army was about to disintegrate. German army Group A had withdrawn from the Caucasus to set up a new defensive line on the so-called Kuban bridgehead. Many German soldiers, as they retreated, sang the lines of a famous marching song: 'Everything comes to an end / Everything passes away / We're moving back in winter / But we'll come back strong in May.'[29]

Between 2 and 5 February 1943 Soviet armies advanced on the lower River Don, capturing Rostov. On 14 February, Kharkov was also recaptured. This opened a dangerous 200-mile gap in the front line of German Army Groups South and Centre. These further military setbacks on the Eastern Front rattled Hitler. Between 17 and 19 February he met Manstein and his other leading commanders at Zaporizhia, the headquarters of Army Group South, telling them, pessimistically: 'We cannot mount any offensive this year. We must avoid risks. I think we should just take minor evasive actions.'[30] Manstein suggested a more limited counterstrike to halt the Soviet advance in the south, which Hitler sanctioned. Manstein came up with a bold plan to combine forces from Army Groups South and Centre to recapture Kharkov and thereby stem the tide of the Soviet advance on the Eastern Front.

This surprise German attack began on 7 March. Kharkov was surrounded in three days and then recaptured by the German army on 14 March. On 23 March Belgorod fell into German hands again. This ended the recent wave of German defeats and put the Red Army firmly back on the defensive along the southern front. Once again, Stalin had underestimated the power of the German army to quickly recover and stabilize the Eastern Front.

On 7 February Hitler delivered a two-hour speech at the Wolf's Lair to his Nazi Reichsleiters and Gauleiters. He still firmly believed in a German victory in the war, he said. The blame for the defeat at Stalingrad was not his or the *Wehrmacht*'s. He highlighted several factors which he thought had contributed to the catastrophe: Germany's weak allies, the Romanians, Italians and Hungarians; the dreadful winter weather conditions; and the failure of the *Luftwaffe* to supply the trapped troops inside Stalingrad. According to Hitler, the current crisis in the war was a psychological one and the role of the Party was now to stiffen up morale of the troops and the people on the home front.

Hitler also became convinced that Jews were acting as a driving anti-German propaganda force in the enemy states and 'we have nothing compatible with which to counter it'. As a result, even more radical measures were now required to counter the Jewish threat. Jews had to be completely eliminated from the Reich and all of Europe. If the German people turned out to be weak, then Hitler predicted, 'they would deserve nothing else than to be extinguished by a stronger people'.[31]

In Italy Mussolini replaced his military commander Ugo Cavallero – who was viewed as too servile towards the German High Command – with Vittorio Ambrosio, who was privately in favour of Italy ending its alliance with Germany and brokering a peace deal with the Allies. At the same time, Mussolini dismissed his untrustworthy son-in-law Galeazzo Ciano as Foreign Minister and took over the role himself. Ciano, who Hitler intensely disliked, was given the post of ambassador to the Vatican. Outside observers thought that this role would allow him to engage in secret discussions for a peace settlement with the Allies using the cloak of Vatican neutrality. German intelligence had cracked Italian cypher codes and they were fully aware of Ciano's double-dealing with the Allies.[32]

As his Undersecretary on Foreign Affairs Mussolini appointed Giuseppe Bastianini, another well-known critic of the Axis and previously an ambassador to Britain.[33] Mussolini tried to present his cabinet reshuffle as indicating his determination to uphold the Italian-German alliance, but it looked like an invitation to the Allies to open up talks for an armistice.

On 16 February Hitler sent a letter to Mussolini, expressing sympathy with Il Duce's continuing health problems. Hitler promised that he would now mobilize the German people for total war and he urged Mussolini to make a similar appeal to the Italian public. He ended by suggesting that they meet for talks soon at Schloss Klessheim. In reply, Mussolini reassured Hitler that Italy was prepared to fight to the bitter end.[34]

After the defeat at Stalingrad, Goebbels was acutely aware of the need to rouse the flagging German people to continue with the war. He began with a major speech at Berlin's Sport Palace on 18 February 1943. The audience was composed of 14,000 hand-picked Nazi fanatics, though Goebbels preferred to call it 'a cross section of the whole German nation'. His speech was broadcast live on German radio and granted blanket coverage in the newspapers on the following day not only in Germany but around the world.

Goebbels had shrewdly prepared the ground for his speech in the preceding weeks. On 17 January he published an article in *Das Reich* entitled 'Total War'. 'The more radical and the more totally we fight the war,' he had argued, 'the quicker shall come the victorious conclusion.' He promised the working population, 'especially mobilized women, that sponging loafers who don't want to relinquish any of their peacetime comforts despite the war will be pressed hard.'[35]

In his speech in the Sport Palace Goebbels emphasized repeatedly the determination of the German government to fight on until victory was secured. To achieve this required the population to accept radical new measures. Total war, argued Goebbels, was now the order of the day: 'We must put an end to the bourgeois scruples who even in this fight for existence want to operate on the principle of "make me an omelette, but don't break any eggs".' There was also a strong antisemitic flavour to Goebbels's argument:

> Behind the onrushing Soviet divisions we can see the Jewish liquidation squads – behind which loom terror, the spectre of mass starvation and unbridled anarchy in Europe. Here once more international Jewry has been the diabolical ferment of decomposition, cynically gratified at the idea of throwing the world into the deepest disorder and thus engineering the ruin of cultures thousands of years old, cultures which it never felt in common... We have never been afraid of the Jews and today we are less afraid of them than ever.

The speech gradually built up to a climactic ending, when Goebbels asked ten questions of the audience, including: 'Are you determined to follow the Führer through thick and thin in the struggle for victory and to put up with the heaviest burdens?' 'Is your trust in the Führer greater, more faithful and more unshakable than ever?' 'Do you swear a solemn oath to the fighting front that the country is behind it with its morale high and that it will give everything necessary to achieve victory?' Every question was answered with a resounding: *Ja!* ('Yes') by the packed crowd. Goebbels fired off more rhetorical questions, asking the crowd to endorse the mobilization of women for war work as well as the execution of opponents and war profiteers.

His final question – 'Do you want total war?' – was followed by another rousing 'Yes!' from the crowd, while his final words paraphrased the poet Theodor Körner in 1814 during the national uprising against Napoleon: 'And now people, stand up and storm, break loose!'[36] Wild cheering followed. It was a tour de force by Goebbels and a rousing declaration of the German government's determination to continue the war to the bitter end. Hitler, who had not been given a copy of the speech beforehand, described it as 'a psychological and propaganda masterpiece of the first order'. Other members of the Nazi elite suspected Goebbels of taking advantage of Hitler's absence to assume the role of unofficial Führer of the home front.[37]

Public reaction to the speech was generally favourable. Audiences cheered and applauded a newsreel of the speech, according to the SD observers present in the audience. On 26 February Goebbels told a Ministerial Conference that over 90 per cent of the letters he had received about the speech were favourable. An SD report on 22 February summed up public reaction to the speech thus:

> Its effect – and the [public opinion] reports were unanimous on this – was unusually great and on the whole very favourable. The morale of the population had reached a low point on account of the most recent developments on the Eastern Front, particularly the evacuation of Kharkov and were longing for an explanation of the situation. Dr Goebbels' speech, despite its frank description of the seriousness of the situation, had the effect of easing tensions and strengthening confidence and trust in the leadership.[38]

Yet the defeat at Stalingrad gave renewed hope to German opponents of Hitler's regime. These included the White Rose resistance group, which consisted of five close friends based at Munich University: the siblings Hans and Sophie Scholl, Alexander Schmorell, Christoph Probst and Willi Graf. The four men in the group were all medical students who had acted as medics in France, Poland and the Soviet Union outside university semesters. A popular lecturer, Professor Kurt Huber, also became involved in their resistance activities.

The White Rose produced six leaflets from June 1942 to February 1943. They were distributed either through the German postal system or delivered in the dead of night by members of the group. Names and addresses were chosen at random from professionals listed in local telephone directories. Recipients were encouraged to make copies of the leaflets and to pass them on.

Inge Scholl, Hans and Sophie's sister, later explained why they had chosen to distribute leaflets: 'They could have chosen to throw bombs, but that would have been at the cost of lives.'[39] Distributing leaflets might seem like a mild form of protest today, but in Hitler's Germany it amounted to high treason and carried the risk of execution.

The White Rose wanted to rouse educated sections of public opinion to oppose Hitler's regime in a non-violent way. The Nazi regime's encroachment upon organized religion was undoubtedly a key motivation in the group's formation. They all viewed Christianity as the basis for a moral regeneration in a post-Hitler Germany, although religious devotion does not fully explain their overall motivation. They

[left to right, top row]
Hans and Sophie Scholl, Christoph Probst,
Alexander Schmorell.

[bottom row]
Willi Graf , Kurt Huber, Roland Freisler,
known as 'Hitler's hanging judge'.

also promoted the idea of a federal and united Europe, and they wanted the restoration of democratic government. They thought that a community of nations would reduce the risk of a world war ever happening again.[40]

The first White Rose leaflet appeared at the end of June 1942. It began with the words 'Nothing is so unworthy of a civilized nation than to allow itself to be governed without opposition by an irresponsible clique that has yielded to base instinct.' The second leaflet – distributed early in July 1942 – castigated the German people for showing allegiance to a criminal regime. It also revealed the fact that 300,000 Jews had already been murdered in Poland in the 'most bestial way', and it called these killings 'the most frightful crimes against human dignity in the whole of history'.

The leaflet then asked directly: 'Why do German people behave so apathetically in the face of these abominable crimes so unworthy of the human race?' Realizing that readers of the leaflet might not be too concerned about Jews being killed, the Munich students added the following qualification: 'Perhaps someone might say the Jews deserved such a fate; this would be an incredible assumption. But assuming someone said this, how would he deal with the fact that the whole younger generation of Polish nobility was being annihilated?'

The third White Rose leaflet that followed a few days later was the most provocative to date. It advocated 'Sabotage in armaments plants and war industries. Sabotage in all gatherings, rallies, public ceremonies and organizations in the National Socialist Party.' It also mentioned influencing 'the lower social orders', emphasizing once again that the group saw its target audience as the educated members of the German middle class, ironically the backbone of Hitler's most loyal supporters and the least likely to support opposing him.

The fourth White Rose leaflet, which appeared in late July 1942, was an outright attack on Hitler's leadership. It claimed at one point: 'Every word that comes from Hitler's mouth is a lie. When he says peace, he means war, and when he blasphemously uses the name of the Almighty, he means the power of evil, the fallen angel, Satan.'

The first four White Rose leaflets were produced in small print runs of a few hundred. The majority of those who received the leaflets were 'loyal national comrades' and they handed them over to the Gestapo. The first leaflets made little impact at all.[41] It was recognized that a change of tactics was required if the White Rose was to make any real impact on German public opinion. To add some gravitas, the group recruited their own university lecturer, Professor Kurt Huber. They thought that his witty, anti-Nazi comments that punctuated his lectures meant he was a firm opponent of Hitler's regime, but in fact Huber was very much an old-fashioned conservative who thought Hitler had now gone too far and was leading Germany to military disaster. In a conversation with Hans Scholl and Alexander Schmorell, Huber told them that active resistance to Hitler's regime was impossible, but gradually he was drawn into the discussion surrounding the subject matter of further leaflets and offered advice.

The group tried to raise money to fund a more extensive leafleting campaign. Hans and Alex went to Stuttgart and met Eugen Grimminger, an accountant and a trusted opponent of Nazism. Grimminger sent them a cheque for 500 Reichsmarks to aid their resistance activities.

In late January 1943 10,000 copies of a fifth White Rose leaflet were printed. The aim was to reach a much wider audience. The leaflet was not released under the name of White Rose this time, but under the much more ambitious-sounding but misleading 'Resistance Movement in Germany'. No such organization existed. The leaflet was entitled 'A Call to Arms' and predicted: 'Hitler is leading the German people into an abyss. Hitler cannot win this war: he can only prolong it. The guilt of Hitler and his minions goes beyond all measure. Retribution comes closer and closer.' The leaflet then asked readers to 'Dissociate yourself from National Socialist gangsterism.' For the first time, a brief political programme was outlined, promising a post-war federal Europe based on freedom of speech, religion and the protection of citizens' rights.

By now the Gestapo was making a determined effort to track down the White Rose group. There was a fear that it was being sponsored by the Allies to undermine German morale. A special Gestapo task force was established, headed by the experienced officer Robert Mohr. He discovered the paper being used to print the leaflets; the envelopes and the stamps had all been purchased in Munich. Local post office clerks were now asked to look out for individuals purchasing large amounts of paper and stamps.

A linguistic expert produced a detailed psychological profile of the supposed sole author of the leaflets. He concluded that the leaflets were most probably written by someone with an academic or a theological background. Mohr was not yet fully convinced that the White Rose group was definitely based in Munich, because their leaflets had been distributed in several cities in southern Germany.[42] The members of the group could not be identified and placed under surveillance.

In the first week of February 1943, shortly after Germany's defeat at Stalingrad, Hans Scholl and Alexander Schmorell made a major error. Without consulting the other members of the group, they painted anti-Nazi graffiti – slogans such as 'Down with Hitler', 'Freedom' and 'Hitler the Mass Murderer' – in bold letters using large stencils on several city centre public buildings in Munich. The words were three feet high. At last, Mohr knew that the group was definitely based in Munich.

Kurt Huber's anger towards Hitler's government had intensified greatly after the defeat at Stalingrad. He decided to write the sixth leaflet of the White Rose himself. Entitled 'Fellow Students', it began by firmly placing the blame for the debacle at Stalingrad on Hitler, gloomily predicting the 'day of reckoning has come – the reckoning of German Youth with the most abominable tyrant our people have ever seen'. Huber further accused Hitler of destroying the 'moral fibre of the German people' and of plunging Germany into war. The leaflet ended by claiming that Germany would be dishonoured for all time if 'youth does not finally rise, take revenge and atone, smash up its tormenters and set up a new Europe of the spirit'.

Sophie and Hans Scholl decided to distribute the sixth leaflet on the university campus in Munich, even though the other White Rose group members had warned them a few days before that this would be much too risky. Ignoring them, Hans and Sophie decided to go ahead with their plan anyway. At around 10.50 a.m. on 18 February they skipped up a single flight of stairs into the imposing entrance hall of the university, known as the Lichthof, which derived its name from the huge glass-domed ceiling that casts daylight through the vast open space. The hallway was quiet and empty.

Sophie and Hans scurried around, placing small bundles of leaflets outside each lecture hall. When they reached the second floor, Hans placed a stack of leaflets on a marble balustrade. As the bell rang out to mark the end of the lecture period, Sophie impulsively and recklessly ran forward and pushed the leaflets over so that they fluttered down like confetti as the students left the lecture theatres.

Jakob Schmid, a 46-year-old university porter, saw the leaflets cascading down. He shouted 'Stop!' and ran upstairs to apprehend the culprits. When he confronted Hans and Sophie they made no attempt to escape. 'I went straight up to them,' Schmid told the Gestapo in a later statement. 'I told them they had to come with me' as 'they were under arrest'.[43] Sophie admitted that she had thrown the leaflets into the Lichthof, but denied that she or Hans had brought them into the university. Schmid, a loyal Nazi Party member, took Hans and Sophie to the office of Walter Wüst, the pro-Nazi university rector. The incident was immediately reported to the local Gestapo office based in the Wittelsbacher Palais.

Robert Mohr arrived in Wüst's office at 11.30 a.m. He asked to see the identification papers of the two students under suspicion, immediately noticing they were brother and sister. Mohr's first impression was that Schmid had made a mistake. Surely these two nice, well-mannered, middle-class students could not be the leaders of a group grandly calling itself the 'National Resistance Movement of Germany'.

Meanwhile, two Gestapo officers had meticulously collected up the leaflets the Scholls had scattered or placed around the Lichthof. When two piles of them were placed side by side they fitted perfectly into Sophie's briefcase. At that point Mohr decided to arrest them for further questioning. Sitting in a chair in the rector's office, Hans suddenly realized that he had in his jacket the hand-written draft of a seventh White Rose leaflet, written by Christoph Probst. He started to panic. He took it out of his pocket and tried to surreptitiously rip it up under his chair, while the backs of the Gestapo officers were turned. The eagle-eyed Schmid spotted him doing this and quickly retrieved not only the major portion of the leaflet, but the ripped-up pieces under the chair where Hans was sitting as well. Suspects about to be arrested often behave in irrational ways, so Mohr did not interpret this behaviour as a definite sign of the guilt of Hans Scholl.[44]

During their lengthy Gestapo interrogations Sophie and Hans initially stonewalled questions and denied involvement. The siblings were not, as was often thought, subjected to brutality and torture. They were progressively presented with incriminating material seized by the Gestapo from the apartment they shared near the campus. After a large quantity of stamps was placed in front of Hans, he finally broke down and confessed. When Sophie was told of her brother's confession, she accepted responsibility, too. Christoph Probst was also arrested and offered a frank confession, but asked for mercy due to the fact he was the father of three young infants and claimed he had already left the group before the Scholls were arrested.

Events now moved at a rapid pace. Paul Giesler, the local Nazi Gauleiter, wanted to make an example of the group. He felt a swift and brutal punishment would send a suitably discouraging message to anyone contemplating following their example. He telegraphed Berlin and requested a quick trial in the People's Court. The date was set for 22 February 1943.[45]

The three judges in the trial were sent from Berlin to conduct the proceedings. The lead adjudicator was Roland Freisler, known as 'Hitler's hanging judge' and one of the most brutal judges in the German criminal justice system. He was well known for his bullying of defendants, showering them with rapid-fire insults delivered at breakneck speed. His conduct was highly theatrical, but coldly calculated.[46]

Unsurprisingly, the trial of the Scholls and Christoph Probst was extraordinarily brief and it was over by lunch time. Despite Freisler's rage and invective, Hans and Sophie defended their actions with great bravery. Nevertheless, Freisler sentenced all three to death on charges of high treason, as well as creating an organization to carry out treason, aiding and abetting the enemy in time of war and encouraging the demoralization of troops. They had forfeited 'their honour as German citizens for ever', he concluded. The costs of the trial were to be charged to the estates and the families of the defendants.[47] The condemned prisoners were taken from the court in handcuffs and driven in separate police vans to Stadelheim Prison in Munich. The Scholls were allowed to see their parents before their executions.

At 5.01 p.m. Sophie Scholl, aged twenty-one, was executed by guillotine. Her brother Hans was next into the execution chamber. He was twenty-four. Christoph Probst was the third to be executed. He was twenty-three. But the cold and detached execution record noted one extraordinary detail. Before the blade fell on his neck, Hans Scholl had shouted: 'Long Live Freedom!'[48] The execution of the White Rose members sent a grim warning to anyone contemplating resistance in Hitler's Germany that they would pay for it with their lives.

The annual commemoration of the foundation of the Nazi Party took place in Munich on 24 February 1943, but Hitler did not attend. Instead, a text of his speech was read out by Hermann Esser, the editor of the *Völkischer Beobachter*. The war, Hitler wrote, had been instigated by the 'banking houses of New York and London, together with the Bolshevik Jews in Moscow'. He promised to 'break and crush the power of the Jewish international coalition. Mankind in its struggle for its freedom and daily bread, will gain final victory in this struggle.' He concluded with his familiar antisemitic prophecy, which was, of course, already coming true:

This fight will not end with the planned annihilation of the
Aryan but with the extermination of the Jew in Europe. Beyond
this, thanks to this fight, our movement's worldview will become
the common heritage of all peoples, even of our enemies. State
after state will be forced, in the course of its fight against us, to
apply National Socialist theories in waging this war that was
provoked by them. And in so doing, it will become aware of the
curse that the criminal work of Jewry has laid over all peoples,
especially through this war.[49]

Ribbentrop went on a four-day visit to Italy from 24 to 28 February
1943. The ostensible aim was to 'discuss the military situation', but the
visit was really designed to patch up Germany's faltering relationship
with Mussolini. Ribbentrop met Mussolini a day after arriving in Rome.
He told the Italian dictator the exact opposite of what he wanted
to hear: the war with the Soviet Union would carry on; a new Axis
offensive would be mounted in the summer, and a peace settlement
with Stalin was ruled out. Mussolini was extremely disheartened by
these comments, especially with Ribbentrop's declaration that the bulk
of German forces would still be concentrated on the Eastern Front,
rather than deployed to protect Italy from the growing Allied danger
in North Africa.

All that emerged from these talks was a joint statement issued
on 1 March 1943, which highlighted the determination of Germany
and Italy to continue the war with all the means necessary until the
complete destruction of enemy forces was achieved. After the Axis
victory, European people would be guaranteed productive work and
social justice in what was called 'the great European area'.[50]

In North Africa, Hitler's daring decision to prevent the Allies from
capturing Tunisia had stabilized the position. By 9 December 1942, the
newly established 5th Panzer Army – with 78,000 troops, supported
by 27,000 Italians – had occupied the former French colony. In early
March 1943, however, Anglo-American forces began to advance from
east and west on German positions in northern Tunisia. Allied naval
supremacy was also already severely disrupting supplies of oil to the
Axis forces stationed there.

A deeply pessimistic Rommel visited the Wolf's Lair and asked the
Führer to sanction the withdrawal of Axis forces from North Africa.
Hitler decided that the famed 'Desert Fox' was losing his nerve and he
recalled him to Germany, stating that he needed a prolonged leave of

absence. Rommel left Africa for the last time on 6 March 1943, but this fact was kept from the German public.

Hitler then ordered a German-Italian attack on Allied forces in front of the strongly defended Mareth Line, a system of pre-war fortifications built by France in southern Tunisia. Monty's 8th Army repulsed this poorly planned Axis attack. It now seemed clear – even to Hitler – that the numerically stronger, better-equipped and better-supplied Allies were bound to triumph sooner rather than later in North Africa, but he wanted to tie them down there for as long as possible.[51]

A new aspect of the war in Germany during 1943 was an intensified Allied bombing campaign. Bombing now became a key feature of everyday life for the German population. It began with the Battle of the Ruhr, from March to July 1943, which concentrated on Germany's industrial heartland of the Rhineland and Westphalia, home to more than 5 million inhabitants. It was one of the most economically important parts of the German war economy.

The Ruhr bombing campaign of the RAF began on the night of 5–6 March 1943 with a huge raid on the city of Essen, aimed at the headquarters of the key Krupp armaments business. British bombers were helped to track down targets using a new radio guidance system called 'Oboe'. A force of 442 British aircraft destroyed much of the city centre using incendiary bombs, leaving 479 people dead, 30,000 homeless and thousands more severely injured.[52] Goebbels visited Essen a few weeks later and, walking through the bomb-damaged streets, he thought the damage was 'colossal and indeed ghastly. The city must, for the most part, be written-off completely. The city's building experts estimate that it will take twelve years to repair the damage.'[53]

Between March and July 1943 there were twenty-six similar Allied air raids against cities in the Ruhr–Rhineland area, including Mülheim (10–11 March and 22–23 June), Duisburg (26–27 March), Dortmund (23–24 May), Düsseldorf (25–26 May and 11–12 June), Cologne (16–17 June), Krefeld (21–22 June), Wuppertal (24–25 June) and Remscheid (30–31 July). A foreman in the local municipal services witnessed the devastating Allied raid on Wuppertal:

> Hundreds of flak guns are roaring away. So far as we can see from this height, there are shells exploding in the sky. The air is humming with many aircraft engines. There are innumerable

searchlights wandering the sky. It's raining shrapnel... Later we
see an aircraft go down in flames. The whole thing [raid] goes on
for an hour and a half and then we can go home.[54]

These Allied air raids were hugely disruptive. Albert Speer, the
Armaments Minister, feared that Allied air raids in the Ruhr area
might cripple German arms production completely at first, but it
remained five times higher in 1943 than it was in 1942. The overall cost
in output of the raids in 1943 turned out to be the equivalent of just six
weeks' loss of industrial output. The cost for RAF Bomber Command
was enormous, however, with 872 aircraft destroyed.[55]

In some German areas that suffered major bomb attacks the usual
'Heil Hitler' greeting was met with a more defiant 'Good morning'
(*Guten Morgen*). A joke began circulating in Essen that reflected this
changing mood: 'A Berliner and an Essener were discussing the extent
of their damages. The Berliner exclaimed that the bombardment had
been so bad in Berlin that windowpanes were still shattering five hours
after the attack. The Essener replied, that's nothing; in Essen Führer-
pictures were still flying out of windows fourteen days after the last
attack.'[56]

In some areas Goebbels's 'Total War' speech was blamed for these
devastating Allied raids. Resentment of the government in Berlin was
at an all-time high, which led to a popular poem heard in the Ruhr
area:

> Dearest Tommies, do fly on.
> We're all miners put upon.
> To Berlin would be our guess,
> They're the ones who shouted 'yes'.[57]

The burial of air-raid victims was the responsibility of the already
overstretched German local authorities. A wide range of people was
involved, including the police and municipal workers, but all the heavy
digging and handling of the corpses was assigned to concentration-
camp inmates, forced labourers and prisoners of war. The dead needed
to be buried quickly to prevent the spread of disease. Hundreds of
corpses were put in hastily dug mass graves in local cemeteries. Foreign
workers killed in the raids were not generally placed in these mass
graves alongside 'national comrades', but were disposed of in local
crematoria.

Local Nazi organizations planned memorial ceremonies before the mass burials of members of the National Community. Nazi Party officials openly encouraged a 'cult of the dead', which included eulogies that elevated the bomb victims to the level of war heroes. The aim was to suggest that the sacrifice of civilians on the home front was the equivalent of the valiant death of a soldier on the battlefield. These ceremonies and rituals were an attempt to stiffen the public's resolve to fight on.[58]

There was a strong desire among the German people for revenge against the Anglo-American Allies but by the spring of 1943 the *Luftwaffe* was so overstretched it was unable to mount a sustained air war over Britain. In place of this, Goebbels promised the Germans that 'miracle weapons' were now being developed – most notably, the long-range V-1 and V-2 rockets – but these were not immediately available. An SD report on the public mood after a bomb attack on Dortmund noted: 'The mood and attitude among the population of ruined cities in the Ruhr has not altered greatly. The question of when the counter-blow is finally going to be made is asked more insistently every day.'[59]

German propaganda placed the blame for the air war squarely on the Allies. American airmen were especially singled out for criticism. It was suggested that they were gangsters, criminals and often 'racially inferior' black people (including a liberal use of the 'n-word'). A typical example appeared in the daily newspaper *Der Berliner Lokal-Anzeiger*:

> How can respect for other countries' cultural monuments be expected of people who have no culture of their own and whose heroes are gang bosses and cheating black boxers? [a reference to Joe Louis, the black World Heavyweight Champion] Is it the same breed of man that has come across the oceans from the USA, to bring culture to the countries of central Europe with their terror raids? The rabble, white or black, sits in Roosevelt's aircraft. The bomb is devoid of culture and will always be so.[60]

In these troubled times for Germany, Goebbels visited Hitler at the Wolf's Lair in March 1943. Hitler berated him for his poor response to the renewed Allied bombing raids. He also expressed his annoyance with his generals, who, he said, insulted his intelligence and 'cheated him whenever they could'. He thought that they had no respect for him whatsoever and regarded him as an unqualified upstart.[61]

Germany's strategic position in the spring of 1943 was undoubtedly very serious. Resources were overstretched on the Eastern Front and North Africa, and Hitler now needed to keep in mind the looming possibility of an Allied invasion in Western Europe. In early March detailed discussions took place on German military priorities for the spring and summer of 1943. Hitler gave his generals the freedom to decide strategy in a way that had not been seen since before the Battle of France in 1940.

Military planners in the German Army High Command (OKH), who were responsible for the management of the German-Soviet War, favoured moving on to the defensive after stabilizing the front during the summer, with just one quick offensive in a strategically important area. The High Command of the *Wehrmacht* (OKW), on the other hand, wanted to move to a wholly defensive strategy on the Eastern Front during the summer and gradually divert forces there to Western Europe.

In the end Hitler supported – albeit without any great enthusiasm – the OKH proposal for a quick, powerful and concentrated attack to weaken the offensive capacity of the Red Army. The plan presented to Hitler on 11 March 1943 at Army Group South headquarters suggested that Kursk should be prioritized for recapture using combined forces from Army Groups Centre and South.

Kursk was primarily an agricultural area around 315 miles south-west of Moscow and 150 miles north of Kharkov. It was demarcated by the towns of Orel in the south and Belgorod in the north, a distance 120 miles long and 60 miles wide. It was a key stopping point on the vital Moscow–Rostov railway line. What became known as the 'Kursk Salient' was really a gap that had opened in the operational areas of German Army Groups Centre and South. No one doubted that it made sense to close it.

Kursk had been originally captured by the German army on 2 November 1941, but recaptured by the Red Army on 8 February 1943. By regaining Kursk and the bulge surrounding it, the German army hoped to consolidate its position all along on the Eastern Front, thereby opening the way to possible future offensive action and freeing up troops for the looming war in Western Europe.

According to Heinz Guderian, it was General Kurt Zeitzler, the Chief of the Army General Staff, who wanted to make Kursk the top priority for a German summer offensive in 1943.[62] However, a close examination of German sources suggests that the key instigators of the Kursk plan were Rudolf Schmidt, the commander of the 2nd Panzer Army, and Günther von Kluge, the commander of the 4th Army. Both officers were attached to Army Group Centre.[63] They argued the huge

gap that existed in Kursk needed closing, and Zeitzler was persuaded this was a necessary priority.[64] This view was also supported by the influential Erich von Manstein, the commander of Army Group South, who thought that it would be better to eliminate the Kursk salient quickly before the spring rainy season (known in Russian as *Rasputitsa*) set in.[65]

On 13 March 1943, during a briefing to army commanders at the headquarters of Army Group Centre in Smolensk, Hitler issued 'Operational Order No. 5' for the 'Conduct of War during the Next Few Months on the Eastern Front'. It stated that after the build-up of strong tank forces, a pincer attack on the Kursk salient would be mounted, codenamed Operation Citadel (*Zitadelle*).

What Hitler did not realize as he left this important meeting to board a flight back to the Wolf's Lair: a group of dissident German military officers were plotting to kill him. The assassination plan was devised by Henning von Tresckow, the first general officer at Army Group Centre, under the code name Operation Flash. Tresckow was the nephew of the deposed commander of Army Group Centre, Field Marshal Fedor von Bock, who sympathized with the conspirators, but was not prepared to risk his life by joining them.[66]

Tresckow felt Hitler was 'the source of all misery' and thought the Führer's role in the *Wehrmacht*'s early victories in the Second World War had been greatly exaggerated. In Tresckow's view, the folly of what could be called 'Hitler's amateur strategy' was only revealed in the months after the German attack on the Soviet Union. Tresckow also felt that Germany's genocidal actions in the Soviet Union and in the extermination camps in German-occupied Poland would destroy the nation's honour once they were fully revealed. As he told a fellow officer, bluntly: 'This will still have an effect in hundreds of years, and it will not only be Hitler who is blamed, but rather you and me, your wife and my wife, your children and my children, that woman crossing the street and that lad kicking a ball.'[67]

Tresckow gathered relatively young, like-minded officers around him, such as Eberhard von Breitenbuch and Georg von Boeselager. All of them were determined to assassinate Hitler as soon as possible and negotiate a peace settlement with the Allies to end the war. Tresckow asked Colonel Heinz Brandt – who was travelling with Hitler, but was not part of the conspiracy – if he would deliver a present of two bottles of brandy to Colonel Hellmuth Stieff. This was not unusual. Personal packages of this type were often transported by officers on

German officer Henning von Tresckow.

planes, even those with the Führer on board. This package, however, contained a bomb. It was constructed with a light plastic explosive and a thirty-minute fuse was activated before it was handed to Brandt and the plane took off.

Tresckow now waited nervously for news of a plane crash, but Hitler's plane landed safely. The bomb had failed to detonate, most probably due to the cold temperature in the luggage hold. Once again Hitler had escaped death by a stroke of luck. Lieutenant Fabian von Schlabrendorff – who acted as a liaison officer between the resistance group in Army Group Centre and key figures in the broader conservative-military resistance – managed to retrieve the package containing the bomb from Brandt the following day and successfully defused it.[68]

On 21 March 1943 Hitler gave a speech in Berlin on Heroes' Memorial Day. It was his first public address since the German defeat at Stalingrad. He apologized for his lack of visibility in the preceding months, attributing it to having to deal with the military crisis on the Eastern Front, which he suggested had now been stabilized. It was the brave soldiers who had turned things around, he added. Hitler then reassured his listeners that the Reich remained strong and that the production of armaments was increasing. Once victory had been achieved the German National Socialist state would strive to eliminate all class differences and to create a true National Community.[69]

After the speech, Hitler visited an exhibition in the Old Armoury building (or *Zeughaus*) of captured Soviet military equipment, which had been collected by Army Group Centre. Waiting inside the entrance was a young member of the military resistance Colonel Rudolf-Christoph von Gersdorff, an intelligence officer who was attached to Army Group Centre. Gersdorff had agreed to act as a guide while Hitler toured the exhibition but he had also bravely volunteered to be a suicide bomber.

As Hitler entered the building, Gersdorff ignited a ten-minute delayed fuse on two small explosive devices hidden in his overcoat pockets. He expected Hitler to tour the exhibition for about half an hour, more than enough time for his bomb to go off, but Hitler passed by a few exhibits, then left in less than five minutes. Gersdorff had to rush to the nearest toilet in the building to defuse the bombs and, luckily, he succeeded.[70]

German military staff such as Gersdorff were best placed to strike a decisive blow against Hitler's regime. There were elements in the German army who still believed they had the right to remove a government which they deemed illegitimate in a *coup d'état* supported by military force. This element of resistance in the German army had originally emerged in 1938, when a group of conservative senior army officers – spearheaded by Lieutenant Hans Oster and Ludwig Beck, the Chief of the Army General Staff – had planned to overthrow Hitler during the Czech crisis. Their coup failed because it received no support from the leading figures in the General Staff, who remained loyal to Hitler – nor did it receive any encouragement from the British government under the champion of appeasement, Neville Chamberlain.[71]

The sequence of German military successes of 1939–40 meant that there was little prospect of overthrowing Hitler while his popularity was running at an all-time high. In this period, military resistance not surprisingly lay dormant. The German defeat at Stalingrad offered a fresh hope, however. This has led to the charge that the German military only resolved to overthrow Hitler's regime when he started to lose the war, so as to salvage the military power of the German army and not for genuine moral reasons.

At the heart of this conservative and military resistance to Hitler was the Beck–Goerdeler group, a complex network of dissidents which had built up gradually since 1938. The group grew primarily within the ranks of the traditional, upper-class, conservative elite in the civil service, the aristocracy and the military. They had gradually lost faith in Hitler's regime when it became clear that he no longer regarded them as equal partners.

Ludwig Beck was the leading military figure in the group.[72] The top civilian figure involved was the deeply religious

Ludwig Beck, the former chief of staff of the German army.

conservative Carl Goerdeler, the former German Minister of Prices, who had resigned in 1936 and who was also the mayor of Leipzig before he resigned that office in 1937. Goerdeler originally thought of Hitler as 'an enlightened dictator', but he became progressively estranged from the Führer's leadership, because of Hitler's religious intolerance, his desire for war and his persecution of the Jews.[73]

The Beck–Goerdeler group built up a secret network of military and political figures and established useful diplomatic contacts abroad. If the military coup succeeded then Beck would become the head of state in a provisional government; Goerdeler would take on the role of the Chancellor, with Social Democrat Wilhelm Leuschner becoming the vice chancellor, and Ulrich von Hassell, the former ambassador to Italy, the new German Foreign Minister.

The Beck–Goerdeler group wanted to create a German government that upheld the rule of law, free speech, religious freedom and social justice, within a system that allowed local government the freedom for ordinary people to make decisions. They wanted to broker a peace settlement with the Western Allies, but not with the Soviet Union, because the group took an anti-communist position and wanted Germany to remain a major military power. However, when this resistance group made informal approaches towards the West the response was extremely negative. The Allies were not prepared to negotiate a separate peace settlement that excluded the Soviet Union.

It's interesting to note that few communists or industrial workers were involved in the Beck–Goerdeler group. Left-wing Germans viewed cooperation with the military as unthinkable and still hoped that Stalin might come to

Carl Goerdeler, a key figure in the German resistance.

their rescue. Interestingly, no major socialist or liberal politician from the Weimar Republic was involved in the plot to overthrow Hitler either. Another group conspicuously absent from the resistance were businessmen, who remained wedded to the alliance of big business with Nazism.

The Beck–Goerdeler group could not decide whether to arrest or to assassinate Hitler. Goerdeler rejected assassination on religious grounds, arguing that a moral regeneration of Germany could hardly begin by defying the biblical commandment 'Thou shalt not kill.' Instead, he favoured gaining support from the Allies and then arresting Hitler and putting him on trial for his war crimes.

Hassell hoped to broker a peace settlement with the Allies once Hitler had been removed from power. However, he was worried that the Beck–Goerdeler group lacked a genuine popular leader who was not tainted by its association with the German army. Hassell wrote in his diary about the flaws of Goerdeler: 'He is too sanguine, always sees things as he wishes to see them, and in many ways is a real reactionary.'[74] As for Beck he was old, tired and in poor health.[75]

The Beck–Goerdeler group attracted some prominent military figures, most notably, Field Marshal Erwin von Witzleben, now retired, but previously the holder of several high-ranking positions in the German High Command. Witzleben would assume the role of commander-in-chief of the Armed Forces after the coup. Also involved were General Friedrich Olbricht, the head of the General Army Office based at the Bendlerblock in Berlin, and the deputy to Friedrich Fromm, the commander-in-chief of the Reserve Army (*Ersatzheer*); Major-General Karl Heinrich von Stülpnagel, the military-governor of occupied France; and Lieutenant-General Hans Speidel, the chief of staff of Army Group B in Western Europe. It's important to stress that this military conspiracy did not attract the most senior generals close to Hitler, who were naturally the best placed to kill him.

A number of diplomatic and intelligence personnel were also secretly involved, such as the Foreign Ministry official Ernst von Weizsäcker and a group clustered around the ardent monarchist Admiral Wilhelm Canaris, head of the *Abwehr* (the military intelligence service), as well as his chief of staff Colonel Hans Oster and the prominent Lutheran theologian Dietrich Bonhoeffer, who was also attached to the *Abwehr*. However, the resistance network within the *Abwehr* was broken by the Gestapo in April 1943 when Oster and Bonhoeffer were arrested, initially on foreign currency violations, but their resistance activities were subsequently discovered. In February 1944, Canaris was dismissed and the *Abwehr* was formally abolished.[76]

A diverse set loosely attached to the Beck–Goerdeler group was the Kreisau Circle. Formed in 1940, the group took their name from the castle of Count Helmuth von Moltke in Lower Silesia, where they held secret meetings and conferences. Moltke, who came from one of Prussia's best-known military families, felt that the resistance would only succeed if it came up with an optimistic vision of a post-Hitler Germany: 'A picture which will make it worthwhile for the disillusioned people to strive for, to work for, to start again and believe.'[77]

The Gestapo derisively called this small group the 'Counts Circle' due to the large number of aristocrats who were attached to it. Among its members – estimated at around twenty-four individuals – were Count Peter von Wartenburg, from a well-known family of Prussian nobles; Count Friedrich-Werner Graf von der Schulenburg, the Deputy Police President of Berlin; the diplomats Adam von Trott zu Solz and Hans Bernd von Haeften; the Social Democrats Carlo Mierendorff and Julius Leber and the Jesuit priest Alfred Delp.

The Kreisau Circle often discussed the shape of a new Germany after Hitler had been defeated by the Allies. On 24 April 1941, they produced a memorandum entitled 'Starting Point, Objectives and Tasks', expressing the belief that a post-Hitler German government must replace the cult of the leader and party with a democratic system in which self-governing, devolved regions would take charge for the benefit of local communities. This idea was modelled, to a certain degree, on the US federal system.

The Kreisau Circle also advocated an international tribunal to deal with Nazi war criminals and proposed the creation of an international body designed to end the conflict between European nations, much like the United Nations. They developed some tentative contacts with the Beck–Goerdeler group, although Moltke regarded Goerdeler as a conservative reactionary and ill-suited to move Germany away from militarism and extreme nationalism. The members of the Kreisau Circle opposed Hitler's assassination, preferring instead to wait for him to dig his own grave through military defeat. Moltke was arrested by the Gestapo on 19 January 1944, but his links with the military-conservative group were not initially uncovered.[78]

Within the military group a definite plan to assassinate Hitler emerged. In the spring of 1943, a new person entered the military conspiracy. This was Claus Schenk, Count von Stauffenberg who came from a Swabian aristocratic family. A devout Catholic, he was initially attracted to Hitler's anti-Versailles foreign policy. In 1939, he was enthusiastic about Germany's victory over Poland and as a member of Army General Staff he welcomed the Fall of France in 1940. His disillusionment with Hitler's leadership began when he heard about the atrocities of the SS on the Eastern Front after the invasion of the Soviet Union in 1941. Stauffenberg also deplored the persecution of Jews and the routine maltreatment of Russian POWs. In August 1942, Stauffenberg told a friend: 'They are shooting Jews in masses. These crimes must not be allowed to continue.' He informed a fellow officer around the same time: 'There is no point in telling Hitler the truth. No fundamental change is possible until he is removed. I am ready to do it.'[79] At this stage Stauffenberg was simply a disaffected lone wolf who knew nothing about the elaborate network of the military-conservative resistance.

General Kurt Zeitzler, who knew of Stauffenberg's dissident views, decided it might be a good idea to post him away from the central theatre of war on the Eastern Front. So in February 1943 Stauffenberg – now promoted to the rank of lieutenant colonel – was assigned to the 10th Panzer Division operating in Tunisia as a divisional chief in the North African campaign. On 7 April Stauffenberg's Horch jeep was hit by heavy machine-gun fire from an American Kittyhawk fighter bomber near Mezzouna. He suffered severe injuries: losing his left eye, most of his right hand and two fingers of his left hand. His back and legs were also riddled with shrapnel wounds. Given such serious injuries, Stauffenberg could easily have opted for medical retirement, but he chose not to for one single purpose: to kill Hitler. He was risking a great deal personally, as he had a devoted wife and five children.

After returning to Germany, Stauffenberg spent three months recuperating in a Munich hospital and underwent several follow-up operations. In September 1943 he gained a new post in the Reserve Army Office, based in the Bendlerblock in Berlin. He impressed his superior, the fervent anti-Nazi General Friedrich Olbricht, who soon introduced Stauffenberg to Henning von Tresckow and other leading figures in the military-conservative conspiracy.

It soon became obvious that Stauffenberg was a man of action and a skilled organizer. He injected energy into the idea of killing Hitler, but really had little in common with the conservative ideals of the Beck–Goerdeler group and was more in tune with the liberal outlook of the Kreisau Circle. Stauffenberg favoured the idea of creating a broad anti-Hitler coalition to include not just conservatives but also liberals, Social Democrats and trade unionists. By the late autumn of 1943 Stauffenberg had emerged as the leading army conspirator. There were six planned attempts on Hitler's life in the last months of 1943, but for one reason or another they all came to nothing.

Nevertheless, a detailed plan to overthrow Hitler's government was formulated. Code-named 'Valkyrie' it subverted an existing plan from 1942, which Hitler had already agreed and signed which was designed to save the Nazi regime if a coup was enacted. In Teutonic mythology, the Valkyries were warrior maidens who rode on horseback over battlefields to carry away the fallen to Valhalla, the seat of the gods. Valkyrie was intended to be launched in the event of serious internal unrest. In such an eventuality, the Reserve Army would take over the state to save Hitler's regime. For this reason, the Valkyrie plan was not communicated to the leading Nazi ministers, the SS, the SD or the Gestapo.

The military conspirators cleverly decided first of all to kill Hitler, then use the Valkyrie orders as a smokescreen to help the German army conspirators to institute martial law that would destroy Hitler's regime by arresting the key Nazi ministers and loyal generals, as well as the SS and party leaders. There was one serious flaw in this treasonous plan: the Valkyrie order had to be sanctioned by General Friedrich Fromm, the head of the Reserve Army. Fromm had so far expressed only lukewarm sympathy to the conspiracy, but no one really knew what he would do when asked to sanction an order that was, in effect, a plan for a military coup.[80]

The growth of the military-conservative resistance in the latter part of the war was part of a more general political battle between revolutionary National Socialism and Germany's traditional conservative elites, a struggle which had begun the moment Hitler came to power in 1933. In terms of social background, it's noticeable that many of the military conspirators belonged to the old Prussian nobility, which had always had little real enthusiasm for Nazi ideals. These old-school conservatives felt the previously high educational and elite recruitment standards of the *Wehrmacht* were being sacrificed to the National Socialist principle of selection based on performance. This meant younger people from outside the nation's traditional conservative-aristocratic elite were being promoted to officer class. The military conspirators believed they were helping to save the traditional German army from being completely Nazified.

Claus von Stauffenberg.

The worsening military position of Germany after Stalingrad had an unsettling impact on the nation's allies. There were plenty of rumours that many of them were looking to cut a deal with the Allies. In April 1943, Hitler – who had returned to the Berghof on 20 March and stayed there for the next three months – conducted a series of diplomatic meetings designed to stiffen the resolve of his allies and to bind them closer, encouraging them especially to step up their persecution of Jews.

On 3 April 1943 Hitler asked King Boris III of Bulgaria to increase anti-Jewish measures.[81] Italian dictator Mussolini visited between 7 to 10 April. The French Prime Minister Pierre Laval arrived on 9 April, but his request to regain French independence in the Vichy area was firmly rebuffed. On 12 and 13 April Hitler held talks with Ion Antonescu, the Prime Minister of Romania. On 16 and 17 April Hitler had meetings with Miklós Horthy of Hungary. On 18 April, there were talks with Hiroshi Ōshima, the Japanese ambassador to Germany; and on the following day the supine Norwegian Minister-President Vidkun Quisling arrived and was given a vague promise, according to his own account, of a restoration of Norwegian independence after the war. On 22 and 23 April diplomatic meetings were held with the Slovakian State President Josef Tiso and on 27 April he entertained Ante Pavelić, the Croatian military dictator.

Of all these diplomatic meetings in April 1943, the three most significant were with Mussolini, Antonescu and Horthy. The four-day talks with Mussolini were held at Schloss Klessheim near Salzburg. It had been thoroughly redecorated with new tapestries, marble floors and expensive carpets. The two men had not met since the April of 1942. At Salzburg station, Hitler greeted Mussolini – who was by this time thoroughly depressed and in poor health – with what an Italian diplomat described as 'emotional warmth'. Hitler thought his old friend looked like 'a broken man' and he wanted him to be examined by Dr Morell, but Mussolini declined this offer.

From the Italian point of view, Mussolini's first conversation with Hitler was a fiasco. Beforehand, Mussolini promised his chief of staff Vittorio Ambrosio to press Hitler to seek peace with the Soviet Union, so that Italian forces could be transferred home to defend Italy from an anticipated Allied assault. Face to face with Hitler, however, Mussolini completely lost his nerve and never once mentioned the subject of brokering a peace deal with the Soviet Union. Hitler monopolized the conversation and Mussolini remained mostly silent. In the bland joint statement that was released at the end of their talks, it was emphasized that Hitler and Mussolini were in total agreement on the conduct of the war.[82]

In a frank meeting with Antonescu, the Romanian Prime Minister, Hitler revealed that German intelligence knew full well that his government had already made diplomatic contact, concerning a peace settlement with the Allies. He warned him that the Allies would only allow Romania to exit the war on humiliating terms. In reply, Antonescu assured Hitler that he continued to give him his full support. Hitler was unconvinced and went on to criticize Antonescu for not dealing with the Jews harshly enough.[83]

The most tempestuous meeting of all, however, was with Admiral Miklós Horthy. Hitler told the Regent of Hungary that German intelligence knew that he was already considering making peace with the Allies. If Hungary jumped ship now, Hitler warned, it would drown. Goebbels, who was present, noted: 'The Führer minced no words and especially pointed out to Horthy how wrong his policies were in general, and especially with reference to the conduct of the war and the question of the Jews.'[84]

Hitler then told Horthy bluntly that his government needed to adopt much harsher measures against the 800,000 Jews still living in Hungary. He couldn't go on handling the Jews 'with kid gloves' and needed to treat them like 'the tuberculosis bacillus that can affect a healthy body'. It was not cruel to kill them, Hitler added, as 'the rabbit and the deer are shot so they cannot do harm'.[85] Replying, Horthy said that he had already taken away the livelihood of Jews, 'he surely couldn't beat them to death'.[86] Goebbels observed this exchange and noted in his diary:

> The Führer failed in convincing him [Horthy] of the necessity of stronger [anti-Jewish] measures. Horthy himself and his family are very much tangled up with the Jews and he will continue to put up a fierce resistance against actively attacking the Jewish problem in the future. He [Horthy] lists quite valid humanitarian arguments that do not, however, apply in this context. There can be no talk of humanitarianism regarding the Jews. Jewry must be thrown to the ground. The Führer made an all-out effort to convince Horthy of his views; however, he was only partially successful in this.[87]

On 13 April 1943 Radio Berlin announced the discovery of a mass grave of Poles in the Katyn Forest, west of Smolensk, and claimed they

had been murdered by Soviet 'Jewish NKVD commissars' in 1940.[88] Goebbels immediately realized the propaganda value of the discovery of a massacre associated with one of the Allies:

> We are now using the discovery of 12,000 Polish officers, murdered by the GPU [Russian State Political Directorate], for anti-Bolshevik propaganda on a grand style. We sent neutral journalists and Polish intellectuals to the spot where they were found. Their reports now reaching us from ahead are gruesome. The Führer has also given permission for us to hand out a drastic news item to the German press.[89]

On 16 April a detailed report on the massacre under the headline 'Jewish Mass Murder' appeared in the newspaper *Der Angriff*.[90]

The Soviet government denied any involvement in the Katyn massacre and tried to shift the blame onto the Germans. When the Polish government-in-exile called for an independent investigation by the International Committee of the Red Cross, Stalin severed diplomatic relations with them. Only in the early 1990s did the government of the Soviet Union finally admit responsibility for the mass executions in Katyn. In November 2010, the Russian State Duma finally approved a declaration blaming Stalin and other Soviet officials for ordering the killings.[91]

On 15 April 1943 the modified 'Operational Order No. 5' – drafted by Kurt Zeitzler, but signed by Hitler – stated: 'I have decided to launch Operation Citadel as the first of this year's attacks, as soon as the weather permits.' The order also stressed that the German assault must succeed rapidly and totally: 'It must give us the initiative for this spring and summer. For this reason, all preparations must be carried out with utmost care and energy.'[92]

The commanders of the German army groups involved welcomed Hitler's decision to finally order the offensive operation against Soviet forces in the Kursk salient. The first date set for the start of the assault was the beginning of May. On 3 and 4 May, Hitler held strategy meetings at the Berghof with his leading army group commanders to discuss the upcoming operation. Rather than the usual lengthy Führer military monologue, there was a genuinely open discussion on the plans. After a series of military setbacks, Hitler was no longer supremely confident about the best way forward on the Eastern Front. Hitler outlined what he described as 'Zeitzler's plan' for Operation Citadel, without either endorsing or rejecting it. Then he asked for the opinion of his leading generals on the plan.

The uncovered mass grave of the Soviet Katyn Forest Massacre.

Walter Model felt it needed some modification, particularly the allocation of more tanks. Manstein was more sceptical, saying an offensive in April would have had more chance of success. Günther von Kluge, the commander of Army Group Centre, was firmly in favour of Citadel, calculating that a military success there would restore his own army group to its previous pivotal role on the Eastern Front. Heinz Guderian – the newly appointed Inspector General of the Armoured Troops – felt the offensive was pointless and warned Hitler not to expect miracles from the recently introduced Panther and Tiger tanks, because both were currently having 'teething troubles' during military exercises. Speer, the Reich Minister of Armaments, also expressed serious doubts about the wisdom and purpose of the Kursk operation. Given the level of disagreement expressed at the meeting, Hitler decided to postpone the German attack until 12 June at the very earliest.[93]

When Guderian met with Hitler on 10 May 1943 to discuss how to further increase tank production, Guderian once again expressed serious misgivings about Operation Citadel: 'Do you believe, my Führer, that anyone knows where Kursk is? The world is indifferent whether we have Kursk or not. I repeat my question: "Why do you want to attack in the east, particularly this year?" In reply, Hitler said: 'You are quite right. The thought of this attack makes my stomach queasy.'[94]

On the morning of 19 April 1943, the day before the Jewish Passover, a heavily armed German assault group, directed by SS General Jürgen Stroop, arrived at the entrance of the Warsaw Ghetto. The purpose of this raid was to deport all the remaining ghetto inhabitants to the extermination camps. Stroop's force was composed of 9 officers and 821 other ranks of the Waffen-SS; 6 officers and 228 men of a German order police battalion, supported by 330 Ukrainian auxiliaries. The task force had three armoured vehicles, several tanks, some light cannon, machine guns and motorcycle outriders. From the outset, the Jews inside the ghetto refused to surrender, beginning the largest single revolt by Jews against Hitler's regime during the entire Second World War.[95]

Set up in October 1940, the Warsaw Ghetto stood on a site normally housing 160,000 people. It was a mile wide and two and a half miles long. Into this area 400,000 Jews were squeezed into overcrowded buildings, with inadequate food, water, sanitation and medical supplies. Jews were forbidden to leave the enclosed area except with permission to work in local factories.

In the summer of 1942 Himmler decided that Jews were not dying quickly enough in the Warsaw Ghetto. On 22 July 1942 he ordered the 'resettlement' of all 'unproductive Jews' there, meaning those incapable of work, to the extermination camps. By 3 October 1942, 310,322 Jews had been transported, mainly to the Treblinka extermination camp, where they were summarily gassed to death.

In January 1943 Himmler visited the Warsaw Ghetto and learned that the surviving Jewish population had been reduced to 40,000, all of whom possessed valid work certificates. A further 20,000 Jews were uncertified to work and were hiding in the many deserted houses in the ghetto. Himmler decided that all of the remaining Jews would be 'resettled'.[96] On 18 January 1943 a small contingent of SS troops arrived to deport them but met with armed resistance so determined and fierce that they decided to abandon the operation. Not until April did Himmler assemble sufficient forces to complete the planned deportations.

The incredibly brave resistance of Jews during the Warsaw Ghetto Uprising was led by two groups: (a) the Jewish Fighting Organization (ŻOB), founded in July 1942 by young Jewish men, but inspired by socialist and Zionist ideas and led by Mordechai Anielewicz. An estimated 500 armed fighters were attached to this group. (b) The Jewish Military Union (ŻZW), founded in 1939, which was a politically right-of-centre group composed mainly of committed Zionists and former officers of the Polish Army. This group, led by Dr Paweł Frenkel, mustered about 400 fighters, but they were much better armed than the ŻOB.[97]

The Jewish Warsaw Uprising was, of course, an uneven struggle from the start. Stroop's forces were more heavily armed. On the third day of the fighting, Stroop's forces began setting fire to ghetto buildings in order to flush out the rebels. On 8 May Stroop's forces killed the ŻOB leader Anielewicz and captured his command bunker.

In the latter stages of the rebellion small groups of defenders inside the ghetto adopted guerrilla tactics and went underground into cellars and sewers. Stroop's forces next tried to drown them by getting firemen to pump in gallons of water. As one surviving ŻOB member later recalled: 'We didn't have a rescue plan, because we didn't figure that any of us would survive.'[98]

On 16 May 1943, the last day of the Warsaw Uprising, Stroop noted in his detailed report: 'One hundred and eighty Jews, bandits and sub-humans were destroyed. The former Jewish quarter of Warsaw is no longer in existence. The large-scale action terminated on 20.15 hours by blowing up the Warsaw synagogue.'

[overleaf]
SS Major Jürgen Stroop (centre, wearing peaked cap), with his troops outside the Warsaw Ghetto.

Stroop took grisly pleasure in watching the Great Synagogue of Warsaw on Tłomackie Street, which had been built in 1877, burn to the ground, later commenting:

> What a marvellous sight it was; a fantastic piece of theatre. My staff and I stood at a distance. I held the electrical device which would detonate all the charges simultaneously. [Max] Jesuiter [a sapper SS officer] called for silence. I glanced over at my brave officers and men, tired and dirty, silhouetted against the glow of the burning buildings. After prolonging the suspense for a moment, I shouted: 'Heil Hitler' and pressed the button. With a thunderous, deafening bang and a rainbow burst of colours, the fiery explosion soared towards the clouds, an unforgettable tribute to our triumph over the Jews. The Warsaw Ghetto was no more. The will of Adolf Hitler and Heinrich Himmler had been done.[99]

Afterwards Stroop celebrated with a fine dinner, accompanied by wine and coffee. He then sent a brief self-congratulatory telegram to General Krüger in Cracow: 'The former Jewish quarter of Warsaw no longer exists.' According to Stroop's report on the Warsaw Ghetto, 57,065 Jews were killed or captured during the ghetto uprising; 631 underground bunkers were destroyed, and 36,000 Jews were deported, mainly to Majdanek concentration camp, where the majority were gassed. German forces suffered only sixteen dead and ninety wounded. The real number of German casualties was probably somewhat higher, however, and is estimated by the Jewish historian Marek Edelman at about 300 killed and wounded.[100] Once again, brave resistance had been brutally suppressed.

In a secret speech to Reichsleiters and Gauleiters on 7 May 1943, following the memorial ceremony in Berlin for the SA leader Viktor Lutze (who had been killed in a car crash), Hitler described the war as a battle between bourgeois and revolutionary states. He felt that 'bourgeois Britain' had been no match for Germany in the early stage of the war, but admitted the Soviet Union, underpinned by a fanatical revolutionary ideology, was now Germany's most formidable enemy. Hitler praised Stalin for ruthlessly removing all opposition in the Red Army and bringing an end to defeatism. The introduction of political commissars had further enhanced Red Army discipline. Hitler felt that Stalin had a further advantage because he was not being opposed by a conservative 'high society' group, as was the case in Germany.

Regardless of the strength of the Soviet forces, Hitler remained doggedly optimistic about a German victory: 'We still have to fight a great many battles, but they will undoubtedly lead to a spectacular success from whence the path to world domination is all but predetermined. Whoever controls Europe controls the world.' After the war, Hitler promised, Germany would create a united Europe and he concluded by predicting: 'There will never be any rebellion within the Reich against our leadership. The people will never think of such a thing. There is no Jewish leadership here for it. The criminals in such a serious crisis would be stood up against a wall.'[101]

On 10 May 1943 the Enabling Act, which allowed Hitler to rule without any legal restraint since 1933, was extended indefinitely. Instead of making a formal announcement of this to the Reichstag, Hitler chose to publish the news in a short message in the *Reich Law Gazette*, which read as follows: 'The Reich government will continue to exercise the powers bestowed upon it by virtue of the law of 24 March 1933. I reserve for myself the confirmation of these powers of the Reich government by the Greater German Reichstag.'[102]

In May 1943 the military situation of the Axis forces in North Africa deteriorated sharply after the crucial ports of Tunis and Bizerte were liberated by Allied troops. On 7 May the Americans captured Bizerte at 4.15 p.m. and, five minutes later, Tunis. On 13 May German army Group Afrika surrendered to the Allied forces. The British official history of the destruction of the Axis forces in North Africa claimed that 238,243 Axis prisoners were captured during this engagement; of those, 101,784 were Germans and 89,442 were Italians, with the rest being other Axis-allied soldiers. There were 8,500 Germans and 3,700 Italians killed in the conflict, with the British and Commonwealth dead numbered at 6,233. The American death toll was 2,715.[103] It was yet another catastrophic defeat for the German army. In terms of prisoners captured it was even worse than the final surrender in Stalingrad. To deflect any criticism from Rommel, the German press finally revealed that the popular field marshal had been recalled from Africa two months before the defeat.

Now that the core of Italian and German forces in North Africa had been destroyed or captured, an invasion of Sicily by the Allies seemed certain in the near future, then an assault on the Italian mainland was sure to follow. In a bitter letter to Mussolini, Hitler blamed Italian military commanders and even the Italian monarchy for the military catastrophe in North Africa.[104]

The air Battle of the Ruhr escalated on 16 and 17 May 1943 when the RAF launched Operation Chastise – more commonly known as the 'Dambusters' raid – on the Ruhr valley, using a new ingenious cylindrical bouncing bomb. It was developed by the talented engineer Barnes Wallis, who had forecast that a bomb released at a low height could skim over water and bounce on to its target, potentially inflicting greater damage than a traditional dropping bomb.[105] When Air Marshal Arthur 'Bomber' Harris was given a preliminary report on the likely effectiveness of these bouncing bombs, he wrote: 'This is tripe of the wildest description... not the smallest chance of it working.'[106]

The Dambusters raids – carried out by twelve heavy Lancaster bombers attached to the famous 717 squadron, led by Wing Commander Guy Gibson – were among the most audacious of all the Allied raids on Germany during the Second World War. The key strategic aim was to disrupt water supplies on mainland Germany for many months. The first target was the Möhne dam, which held 140 cubic tonnes of water. It took five assaults before the dam was finally breached. Karl Koldow, the chief minister of Westphalia, noted: 'The destruction of the Möhne dam is beyond imagination.'[107] The second target hit was the much larger Eder dam, with a water capacity of 214 cubic tonnes. These two dams provided the Ruhr with 70 per cent of the water used for industrial and drinking purposes for the 4.5 million inhabitants of the region. The bouncing bombs also struck the smaller Sorpe dam, containing 74 million cubic tonnes of water, but that dam proved much harder to breach. A fourth dam, the Ennepe, was hit by a single bomb, which also failed to penetrate it. As water surged into the valleys below there was heavy flooding. Wild rumours spread of 30,000 people being killed. To counteract this, the German local authorities decided to release an official figure of 1,579 killed, of whom 1,026 were foreign workers.[108]

A total of 133 crewmen from Britain, Canada, Australia, New Zealand and America took part in the Dambusters raids, of whom fifty-three were killed, three were captured but only eight aircraft returned safely. Due to the very high loss rate, future raids on dams were ruled out. Even so, the raids were highly publicized in the Allied media and the surviving airmen became national heroes.[109] The economic impact of the Dambusters raid was also greatly exaggerated by Allied propaganda. The predicted stoppage of water supplies to industry in the Ruhr proved over-optimistic. All the bombed dams were fully repaired within five months using a combination of soldiers, foreign forced labourers and prisoners of war.

The Dambusters raids were portrayed in the German press as 'the work of Jews', a typical headline being 'Jews Behind the bombing of the Dams'. Hitler approved of links being made in the press between Jews and the bombings.[110] Some Germans even thought that the bombing might be retribution for what the German government had done to the Jews already.[111]

At the end of May 1943 a report on public opinion from the various Nazi Gau districts was presented to the Party Chancellery. It made for gloomy reading. It was noted that German morale was plummeting with each successive military defeat and the intensification of the Allied bombing campaign. In Mainfranken people were now openly predicting that Germany would lose the war. In Upper Silesia, it was noted that some people were now blaming Hitler for the recent military reverses. The phrase 'I never voted for Hitler' was mentioned by locals several times. Soldiers on leave were becoming more critical, with one soldier commenting, 'We're only good for cannon-fodder.'[112]

A frequent suggestion by the public was for Hitler to take a prominent leading role once again. It was noted that ever since the attack on the Soviet Union he had completely retreated from public view. One SD report on the subject commented:

> Judicious and positive-minded citizens have remarked that it
> is not a good idea for the Führer to remain out of sight for too
> long. The nation wants to have its close relationship with the
> Führer confirmed by frequently receiving news of him. But in the
> course of the war it has become rare for a picture of the Führer to
> appear in the newspapers or in the newsreels; the same is true of
> speeches by the Führer.[113]

Even young people – previously some of Hitler's most passionate followers – were now exhibiting dissident behaviour. Disruptive youth groups in the major cities were at the heart of this teenage rebellion. One group, known as the Edelweiss Pirates, was composed of teenage boys aged between fourteen and eighteen. They were linked to other youth groups, including the Kittelbach Pirates, and the Roving Dudes.

The Edelweiss Pirates, who were predominantly working class, formed small gangs in major cities, including in Düsseldorf, Cologne, Duisburg, Essen and Wuppertal. A report by the Reich Ministry of Justice noted: 'In addition to the harmless ringing of doorbells, they have beaten up pedestrians. In some cases, they have smeared human excrement in the faces of national comrades.'[114] They wore distinctive checked shirts emblazoned with an Edelweiss flower, a white pullover, a windcheater, short trousers and white socks. They daubed graffiti on subways and public buildings, such as 'Down with Hitler – We want freedom' and 'Down with Nazi brutality'. They also went camping and invited girls, which was strictly prohibited on the Nazi-organized Hitler Youth camp trips. The Edelweiss Pirates often attacked members of the Hitler Youth in the newly built road subways.

The Düsseldorf Gestapo compiled detailed files on the Edelweiss Pirates. It was noted that most of the youths belonging to the group were working class, aged between sixteen and nineteen. Many had already lost fathers in the war. Most had full-time jobs and were not 'juvenile delinquents'. They were simply unwilling to conform to the rigid demands of the Hitler Youth.

In December 1942 the Gestapo mounted a series of raids throughout the Rhineland region, aiming to put an end to this teenage rampage. In Düsseldorf, ten different groups composed of 283 youths were arrested; in Duisburg 260 were taken into custody, and 196 were captured in Essen and Wuppertal. The Gestapo acted more ruthlessly towards them in the latter years of the war, and to deter others public hangings of the leaders often occurred in city centres.[115]

A quite different type of youth rebellion also emerged in Germany during war-time. Known by the Gestapo as the Swing Youth, its followers were middle class, educated and affluent, living in big cities such as Hamburg, Frankfurt, Berlin, Stuttgart and Dresden. They admired the American swing and jazz music popularized by big bands such as the Glenn Miller Orchestra and the black jazz trumpeter Louis Armstrong, whose records were banned from sale in Germany. As Frederich Ritzel, a former Swing Youth, put it: 'Everything for us was a world of great longing, Western life, democracy – everything was connected through jazz.'[116] Swing Youth set up illegal clubs and organized dance nights by hiring traditional ballrooms under the pretence that it was for traditional ballroom dancing. Some Swing Youth members even established their own swing and jazz bands. Gestapo reports on the Swing Youth emphasized the hedonistic pleasure these teenagers took in heavy drinking, high-energy dancing and an open attitude to sexuality.[117]

The followers of Swing Youth were mostly apolitical hedonists who wanted to establish a counter-identity from that of the Hitler Youth, but they were also symptomatic, in a limited way, of a strand of disillusionment in Germany with the rigid conformity demanded by Hitler's government. Totalitarianism in Germany was always much more propaganda myth than reality.

During June of 1943 a deeply hesitant Hitler postponed Operation

Citadel three times.[118] On 25 June he finally set the attack date as 5 July. Reinhard Gehlen, the head of the *Wehrmacht* Foreign Armies East military intelligence unit (FHO), thought Citadel was a 'decisive mistake'. In mid-June he warned: 'The Russians have anticipated our attack. The enemy has built many positions and has done everything to absorb our blow early on. It is therefore hardly likely that the German attack will break through.'[119]

There is little doubt that the Soviet military knew all about the German plans for Operation Citadel weeks before the attack began. Soviet intelligence had obtained details from several intelligence sources, notably the Swiss-based Red Trio Network, whose key agents were codenamed 'Werther' and 'Lucy'. This information was supplemented by Ultra, the British signals' intelligence unit. The British government sent a summary of all the decoded German messages to Moscow in the period 18–26 March 1943, providing 'irrefutable proof' of Germany's intention to attack the Kursk salient.[120] Yet the importance of this Ultra information in relation to the Battle of Kursk has been exaggerated. Ultra merely reinforced what the Soviets knew already. John Cairncross, a member of the famous Cambridge Five spy ring and based at Bletchley Park, related much more detailed information directly to Moscow than Ultra ever did.

In fact, the Soviets had much better information themselves, using their own intercepts of German army radio messages on the Eastern Front. Soviet air reconnaissance planes were monitoring the German troop build-up and several Soviet agents were deployed behind enemy lines, and deserting or captured German soldiers added even more information. Putting everything together, the Soviets knew that the planned German offensive was centred on the Kursk salient and would take place in early July.[121]

The Red Army High Command decided Soviet forces would deliberately soak up the German assault in the first phase of the attack using a system of three heavily reinforced defence belts, before mounting a devastating counteroffensive. By 1 July 1943 the Soviets had planted 600,000 anti-personnel mines, dug 3,000 miles of trenches in a criss-cross pattern, and created 310 miles of formidable anti-tank obstacles. The deepest minefields were placed at the points in front where the main thrust of the German attack was expected. These Soviet defensive strong points stretched as far back as thirty-five miles from the front line.[122]

On 1 July Hitler gave a speech to his military commanders. He reiterated once again that the war in Eastern Europe remained a 'battle for *Lebensraum*', and finally confirmed to them that Operation Citadel would begin on 5 July. Hitler claimed the various delays were due to waiting for enough tank reinforcements to be in place. The aim of the new summer offensive, he explained, was to inflict huge material and manpower losses on the Red Army, to capture Soviet prisoners and to prevent a Soviet counteroffensive.[123]

The relative strengths of the German and Soviet forces deployed at the Battle of Kursk are difficult to calculate, due to the incompleteness of the surviving sources. Even so, with the release of new Soviet records, historians have now reached something of a consensus on the likely size of the military strength available to each side.[124]

The *Wehrmacht* assembled strong and well-equipped forces. Army Group Centre, commanded by Günther von Kluge, was spearheaded by the experienced and formidable 9th Army, led by Colonel-General Walter Model. It would attack from the area of Orel towards the north of Kursk. The key objective was to break through Soviet defences along the Orel–Kursk highway and railway line.

South of Kursk, the German offensive would be led by Army Group South, under the hugely experienced Erich von Manstein, deploying the formidable 4th Panzer Army, led by Colonel-General Hermann Hoth. It also included three elite and ideologically loyal SS tank divisions: the *Leibstandarte* SS Adolf Hitler, *Das Reich* and *Totenkopf*. These attack units would mount a huge *Blitzkrieg* assault, aiming to break through Soviet defences in the south of the Kursk salient.

If successful, the two German assault groups would meet up in the middle of the bulge, thereby encircling and trapping the defending Soviet armies. As Major-General Theodor Busse recalled: 'It was essential that the rapid advance would force the enemy to bring up its reserves hastily and defeat them in quick succession.[125]

Defending the exposed flank of Hoth's tank forces was Army Detachment *Kempf*, also attached to Army Group South and commanded by General Hubert Lanz. Although this force had impressively recaptured Kharkov in March 1943, doubts were expressed within the German High Command as to its ability to meet a major Soviet counteroffensive on its own.

The German forces totalled 518,217 troops, 1,980 tanks, 570 assault guns, 570 tank destroyers and 260 self-propelled guns.[126] These force levels had been achieved only by redeploying forces from other sectors across the Eastern Front as a whole.

The Red Army had amassed numerically larger forces in the Orel–Kursk area to meet the German asssault, deploying four army groups (or Fronts): (a) the Central, numbering 510,983 troops and 1,607 tanks and assault guns; (b) the Voronezh, with 466,236 soldiers and 1,699 tanks and artillery guns; and (c) the West, totalling 226,043 men and 1,737 tanks and self-propelled guns. Held in reserve was the Steppe Front, with 449,133 troops and 1,632 assault guns. In total, the Red Army had 1.65 million troops, 6,675 tanks and self-propelled guns.[127]

In the air the *Luftwaffe* could call on 600 bombers, fighters and ground-attack aircraft. The Soviets defended with 700 fighters and bombers. Between 5 and 11 July 1943 the Soviets lost 439 aircraft, with 323 shot down in aerial combat, 57 by anti-aircraft fire, 11 in accidents and a further 48 damaged beyond repair. In the same period, the *Luftwaffe* lost just 66 aircraft. One of the main reasons for the huge disparity in the air losses between the two sides was the superior quality of the German fighter pilots. The Soviets relied much too heavily on young and inexperienced pilots.[128]

German army commanders believed that a well-prepared *Blitzkrieg* could still penetrate Soviet defences and that this would compensate for the numerical superiority of the Soviets. They also doubted whether the Red Army was yet capable of mounting sustainable counteroffensives against a German army skilled in mobile defence. This overconfidence led them to believe that the German army still held the upper hand on the Eastern Front.[129]

The Battle of Kursk was divided into three phases. The first phase was the period of Soviet defence, lasting from 5–11 July in the north of Kursk, and from 5–23 July in the south of the salient. The second phase was the Soviet counter-attack at Orel between 12 and 18 August 1943. The third phase was the second Soviet counteroffensive aiming to recapture Kharkov from 3–23 August. It's often suggested there was a lull in the fighting between 23 July and 3 August, but the war diaries from both sides suggest the fighting was continuous.[130]

On the first day of Operation Citadel, Hitler's 'Order of the Day' was read out to the German troops: 'Today you will launch a great attack whose outcome will have a decisive significance for the war. Your victory must strengthen the conviction of the entire world that resisting the *Wehrmacht* is useless. The powerful strike, which you will direct at Soviet armies this morning must shake them to their roots. The German homeland has placed its deepest trust in you!'[131]

The third major German summer offensive of the German-Soviet

War began at 3.30 a.m. on 5 July 1943, with the deafening roar of an artillery barrage on the Kursk salient. On the ground, Model's 9th Army moved slowly at first, advancing by only five miles on a disappointing first day. As one Panzer commander recalled: 'What happened at Kursk was unbelievable. I've never experienced it in war either before or since. The Soviets had prepared a defensive system whose extension in depth was inconceivable to us. Every time we broke through one position in bitter fighting, we found ourselves confronted by another.'[132]

The devastating strength of the Tiger and Panther tanks, and the equally destructive firepower of the Ferdinand tank destroyers, soon tipped the odds in Germany's favour. The Soviet T-34 was once the most formidable tank in operation on the Eastern Front, but the German Tiger with 88-mm guns was able to penetrate the armour of a T-34 from a mile away. However, only 147 Tigers were ever available for Operation Citadel.

The German Mark V Panther was a brand-new armoured vehicle, forty-five tonnes in weight with a top speed of 30 mph and huge 76-mm guns. There were 500 Panthers produced from January to June 1943, but they developed serious mechanical difficulties in battle, such as faulty gearboxes and fuel pumps, the latter often unexpectedly bursting into flames. It was very risky deploying them. A total of 200 Mark V Panthers were involved in Operation Citadel.

These German tanks were supplemented by the new heavy tank destroyer: the Ferdinand, named after its designer Ferdinand Porsche. Its box shape was fitted with an 8.8-cm cannon, the most devastating gun then available. It could penetrate the armour of an enemy tank from just over a mile away. In the spring of 1943, a total of ninety-one of these mechanical monsters was produced and eighty-nine of them were assigned to Model's 9th Army.[133]

After five days the battle, the northern part of the Kursk salient settled into a bitter war of attrition between the two sides. Kluge's forces failed to achieve the swift success Operation Citadel had envisaged, though they won the tank engagements decisively. It was the repeated bombardment by Red Army anti-tank guns which then hampered Kluge's progress. Meanwhile, Model's 9th Army had managed to puncture the first line of Soviet defences, but then screeched to a halt.

South of the Kursk salient, Manstein's Army Group South, spearheaded by the 4th Panzer Army, mounted the deadliest *Blitzkrieg* yet seen on any battlefield. The newer German tanks wreaked havoc. On 8 July a single Tiger tank engaged fifty Russian T-34s and destroyed twenty-two of them. On 9 July, the 4th Panzer Army had reached the Psel River, the last natural obstacle before Kursk. On the same day, the 2nd SS Panzer Corps seized Hill 252.2, a key strategic point overlooking Kursk and adjacent to the main railway line and highway.

On 12 July the now legendary Battle of Prokhorovka occurred between the two sides in a confined area just under two miles wide between the River Psel and the Storozhevoye Woods. Soviet legend suggested that 1,500 tanks were engaged in this battle, but recently released Soviet records suggest that the total armour on both sides came to 872 tanks. The Soviets originally recorded a German loss of 400 tanks on this day, including 70 Tigers. It's now clear that figure grossly exaggerated the actual German tank losses during the Battle of Prokhorovka. Judged purely on the tank losses of each side, the Germans decisively won the tank engagement at Prokhorovka. The battlefield records of the SS Panzer Units involved – SS Death's Head, SS Adolf Hitler and SS *Das Reich* – show that between 235 and 249 Russian tanks were put out of action. In contrast, the 2nd SS Panzer Army lost just ten tanks and only one Tiger. By the end of the battle, German tank units controlled the south of the battlefield and had even broken through to the third and final echelon of the Soviet defensive system.[134]

While all this was going on, Italy's position worsened. On 9 July Hitler received news that Allied assault forces had landed in Sicily. This could not have come at a worse moment. German troops in Sicily numbered just two divisions at the time, so any chance of holding the island depended on substantial reinforcements being sent there. Deeply alarmed by these developments, Hitler summoned Manstein and Kluge to an urgent military conference. The meeting took place on 13 July at the Wolf's Lair. Hitler spelled out the serious implications of the Allied move into Sicily, predicting that the next step for the Allies would be a landing on mainland Italy and possibly in the Balkans, too. New armies were needed to assist the Italians in meeting this Allied threat.

Therefore, Hitler decided Operation Citadel had to be abandoned. It was time to move to a defensive posture on the Eastern Front he thought.[135] Kluge, who thought the attack of the 9th Army was not progressing at all well, readily agreed with this decision. Manstein, however, disagreed, believing that his forces were poised to break through the Soviet defences. He later complained bitterly: 'And so the last German offensive in the east ended in fiasco, even though the

[overleaf]
The tank battle at Prokhorovka on
12 July 1943.

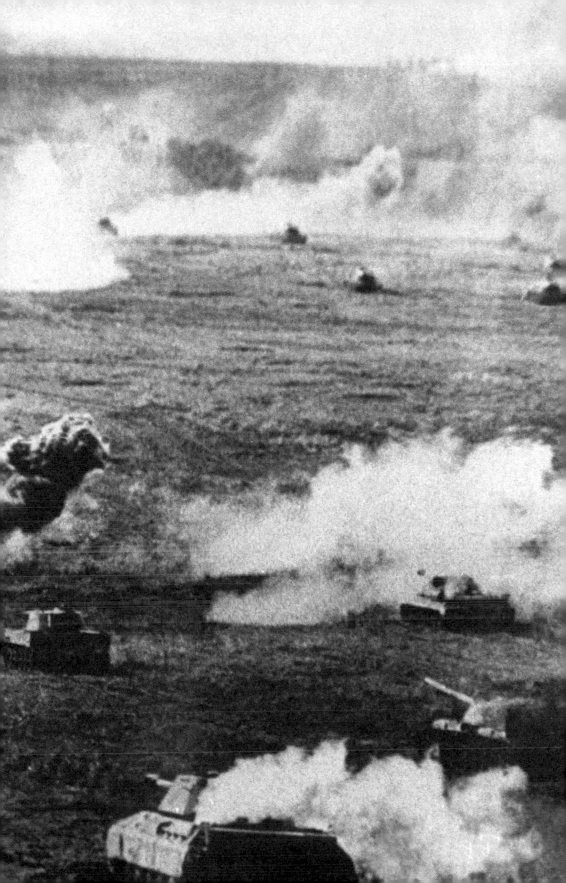

opposite two attacking [Red] armies... had suffered four times their losses in prisoners, dead and wounded.'[136]

Who was to blame for the failure to achieve overall victory at Kursk? Heinz Guderian didn't think it was Hitler alone as his other major generals thought. The plans for Operation Citadel were not Hitler's in the first place, he suggested, but the work of others, particularly Zeitzler, who had pressed Hitler to launch an offensive which the Führer had always doubted would be decisive from the beginning.[137] There is absolutely no reason to suppose, as Manstein later argued in his self-justifying memoirs, that if Operation Citadel had begun in May the Kursk salient would have been captured anyway.

Unlike his generals, when Hitler cancelled Operation Citadel he was looking far more broadly at the overall German strategic position in two theatres of war: in Eastern Europe and the Allied threat to Western Europe. Manstein was still focusing narrowly on gaining Kursk, a victory which stood little chance of being decisive anyway.[138] After 1945 it was commonplace for German army commanders to take all the credit for victories and to pin all the blame for military errors on Hitler, who became a convenient scapegoat for their own mistakes.[139]

Hitler left the Wolf's Lair on 18 July 1943, bound for Italy. His purpose was to try and raise the spirits of his demoralized ally Mussolini. On 19 July, the two dictators held their thirteenth meeting at the picturesque Villa Gaggia, near San Fermo in northern Italy. This secluded location required Hitler to land at Treviso Airport, then travel by train and limousine to his destination. The Italian entourage included Vittorio Ambrosio and Giuseppe Bastianini, plus a retinue of other diplomats and military officials. During the three-hour meeting Hitler delivered a monologue about the importance of the current struggle for the future of Europe. He urged Mussolini to crack down on his opponents at home, then blamed the poor leadership of the Italian generals for the military disasters in Tunisia and Sicily.

Before the meeting, Mussolini was urged by his military chiefs to tell Hitler that the Axis powers needed to broker a peace settlement with the Soviet Union. Once again, however, Mussolini remained silent, much to the disgust of his key foreign policy and military advisers. In the middle of Hitler's bitter harangue, a messenger arrived with news that the Allies were bombing Rome. Without even stopping to express sympathy, Hitler continued to insist on Germany's military superiority and ultimate victory.

After Hitler finally departed, Mussolini told Ambrosio that he wanted Italy to break from Germany and make a deal with the Allies. He said that he would write a letter to Hitler explaining this soon, but he never did. Mussolini's unwillingness to stand up to Hitler at this crucial meeting sealed his fate. Hitler was too fond of the sound of his own voice to realize this.[140]

By now Victor Emmanuel III of Italy (according to his own account) had already made up his mind to dismiss Mussolini. Support for Mussolini was draining away within the Fascist Party. For weeks its twenty-eight members had been calling for the Fascist Grand Council to be summoned for the first time since December 1939. Mussolini agreed to a meeting of this body on 24 July at 5 p.m. in the 'Parrot Room' in the Palazzo Venezia. Mussolini was blissfully unaware of what was about to happen. In his speech to the assembled members of the Grand Council, he admitted that the Italian people were now unanimously against the war, but he already knew the current conflict had always been unpopular. Mussolini concluded by proposing that Italy should fight to the finish alongside Germany.

This was not what his sceptical audience wanted to hear. A very acrimonious debate followed. Several speakers offered sharp and critical comments of Mussolini's conduct of the war. Count Ciano said that Italy had been betrayed by Germany. Dino Grandi, the President of the Italian parliament, then launched a blistering attack on Mussolini's policy of continued alliance with Germany, accusing him of betraying the Fascist Party and the Italian constitution.[141]

Grandi then introduced an ingenious but perfectly legal motion calling for the king to resume his full constitutional authority, including over parliament, foreign policy and the armed forces. This opened the door for Mussolini to be dismissed. This motion – the first in the twenty-year history of the Grand Council – was passed by nineteen votes to eight, with one abstention, at 2.40 a.m. on the morning of 25 July 1943. As the Italian Grand Council only possessed 'advisory powers' on paper, Mussolini didn't believe that he needed to do anything and could remain in power. Once home, he telephoned his mistress Clara Petacci, but during their conversation, which was bugged, he changed his mind, saying, 'It's all over now.'[142]

At 5 p.m. on 25 July Mussolini had a supposedly routine meeting with King Victor Emmanuel III at the Villa Savoia. The royal staff had telephoned Mussolini earlier in the day to tell him to wear a civilian suit for the meeting. After Mussolini sat down, the king told him that Italy was now broken militarily and that the situation required

Mussolini to resign with immediate effect.[143] Mussolini was replaced by a new broad-based national government, headed by the Italian general Pietro Badoglio, the conqueror of Abyssinia in 1935, but widely known to dislike Fascism and to be in favour of a peace settlement with the Allies.

At 11 p.m. Italian national radio broadcast the news of Mussolini's fall from grace. The Italian people flooded on to the streets, not to protest but to celebrate. Badoglio, fearing an immediate German occupation, insisted that Italy's alliance with Germany would continue, but privately negotiations had already begun for an armistice with the Allies.[144] The coup against Mussolini had been accomplished without bloodshed.

Meanwhile, Mussolini had been put under house arrest, then taken initially to the island of Ponza, before being shipped in secrecy to La Maddelana, an island on the northern tip of Sardinia. It was here that Mussolini began to write his garbled autobiography, which included ideas on the future of Fascism. On 28 August, Mussolini was moved again, this time to a hotel in the Campo Imperatore ski resort on the Gran Sasso mountains.

Mussolini's humiliating and ignominious fall from power was an unexpected bombshell for Hitler. Infuriated, he convened a meeting at the Wolf's Lair to discuss its implications with his leading generals. Ribbentrop, Göring, Himmler, Bormann and Goebbels were also present. Hitler told them he thought Mussolini had not resigned voluntarily. The coup against him had obviously been planned for some time. The Badoglio government's assertion that the alliance with Germany would continue meant absolutely nothing, he added. Hitler immediately ordered preparations for a German occupation of northern Italy, the arrest of anti-German political and military elite figures there, and the rescue of Mussolini, once his whereabouts became more clear.[145]

On 6 August 1943 members of the Badoglio government met with Ribbentrop and Keitel on a special Italian train. It was by now an open secret that the German army was poised to occupy Italy. Ambrosio asked why the German army was drafting reinforcements into Italy without asking for Italian permission. In reply, Ribbentrop said this was to meet the expected Allied invasion of the Italian mainland. Ribbentrop then asked Raffaele Guariglia, the new Italian Foreign Minister, if the Italian government had opened negotiations with the Western Allies. Italy remained a loyal ally, Guariglia replied, but he then pointedly advised Ribbentrop to 'make peace with the Russians as soon as you can'.

Ribbentrop offered an invitation for Victor Emmanuel III and Prime Minister Badoglio to visit Germany soon, in order to 'eliminate all possible misunderstandings'. The cool Guariglia smiled politely, saying he would pass on the invitation. After Ribbentrop boarded his special train to return to Germany, he sent a telegraph to Hitler, with a firm conclusion: 'The Italian government is preparing to do a deal with the Allies.' On the return train journey, Ribbentrop told August von Mackensen that he was dismissed as Italian ambassador with immediate effect. In his place Ribbentrop appointed Rudolf Rahn, one of the rising stars in the German Foreign Ministry.[146]

While the political drama in Italy continued, the Allied bombing campaign over Germany intensified. From 24 July to 3 August 1943, RAF Bomber Command – supported by the United States Army Air Force (USAAF) – carried out a series of destructive air raids on the port city of Hamburg, in an operation ominously code-named Gomorrah, after the biblical city destroyed by fire and brimstone.[147]

Hamburg, lying on the banks of the Elbe River in the north, was Germany's second-largest city. It was identified as a key urban target by Bomber Command in April 1943 even though it had the most extensive air defences of any German city. Not only did it possess a large number of searchlights and anti-aircraft guns, but it was also supported by fighter planes that could be launched from eight surrounding airfields.[148] The RAF planned to attack the most densely populated working-class districts during night-time, with the USAAF hitting strategic targets in daylight hours. Hamburg had already been subjected to many smaller-scale bombing raids – there had been 127 between 1940 and 1942, and 10 since the beginning of 1943 – but none were on the scale now planned.[149]

A new Allied technical innovation was introduced for the fresh Hamburg bombing missions: pilots dropped bundles of paper with metal foil on one side in order to blind German radar signals. These strips (codenamed 'Window') were the brainchild of Dr Robert Cockburn at the Telecommunications Research Establishment in Malvern. A German radar operator commented: 'None of the radar in Hamburg was functioning [during the RAF raids]: we did not yet know why. A paralysing terror began to creep over us. We felt like someone who has been given a rifle to defend himself, but is blindfolded.'[150]

The Hamburg raids occurred during a period of warm weather,

high humidity and good visibility. Perfect bombing conditions. Arthur 'Bomber' Harris told the RAF crews involved prior to departure: 'The Battle of Hamburg cannot be won in a single night. It is estimated 10,000 tonnes of bombs will have to be dropped to complete the process of elimination. To achieve the maximum effect of air bombardment, this city should be subjected to sustained attack.'[151]

The RAF air crews – including pilots from Britain, South Africa, New Zealand, Canada and Poland – left Britain at 9.45 p.m. on 24 July. The first bombs fell at 1 a.m. on 25 July, with 792 aircraft unloading 2,284 tonnes of bombs in just 58 minutes, primarily over the west of the city.[152] Roofs shattered, trees were flattened and windows were blown out. Fire spread like a hurricane, igniting whole neighbourhoods: schools, post offices, movie theatres, hospitals and railways stations were obliterated, as was the Tierpark Hagenbeck, a zoo founded in 1907. Many people suffocated in their cellars from the carbon monoxide gas generated by the firestorm. A member of the Hitler Youth called Otto Mahncke made his way through the bombed-out streets of Hamburg, trying to find his parents, in the aftermath of the first raid. On a street corner near his home he saw a woman pointing to her burning house, shouting: 'My baby! My baby!' Her infant had burned to death. Otto never found his parents.[153]

A young mother lay fast asleep on a small camp bed in the cellar of her apartment block when she was suddenly awoken by the deafening sound of bombs. Luckily, they missed her home. The next morning she walked through the eerily silent, deserted streets of Hamburg. She later described the scene in a letter:

> There was no gas, no electricity, not a drop of water, neither the elevator nor the telephone was working. It is hard to imagine the panic and chaos. There were no trams, no Underground, no rail-traffic to the suburbs. Most people loaded some belongings on to carts, bicycles, prams, or carried things on their backs, and started on foot, just to get away, to escape rather than stay in the devastating inferno of the city.[154]

The German Reich Statistical Office estimated that 10,289 people had been killed during the first raid. Only twelve RAF planes failed to return. A report by a local Hamburg police commissioner made grim reading:

The streets were covered with hundreds of bodies. Mothers
with children, men young and old, burned, charred or uninjured,
clothed or naked in waxen pallor like store window mannequins,
lay in every position, calm and peaceful or cramped, the agony
of their death on their faces. Shelters presented the same picture
even more gruesome in its effect, since it showed here and there
the last desperate struggle against a merciless fate.[155]

On 25 July 1943 the USAAF launched its first day-time raid,
concentrating on the dockland area, where most of the important
U-boat and aero-engine factories were located. The Americans
deployed the state-of-the-art Boeing B-17 heavy bombers (known as
the 'Flying Fortresses'), which flew at a high altitude up to 30,000 feet
and were equipped with bullet-proof windows and deadly machine
guns.

Around 1,200 USAAF crewmen were involved in its first raid on
Hamburg, but 150 never returned. The accuracy of American bombing
was patchy in spite of the daylight conditions: the Blohm und Voss
shipbuilding factory, the main railway line and two dry docks were all
damaged, but 60 per cent of the American bombs failed to hit their
targets.[156]

A second USAAF daylight raid took place on 26 July, but despite
briefly putting the Neuhof power plant out of action, it was equally
ineffective. During the two USAAF raids on Hamburg, 100 Flying
Fortresses were lost or severely damaged and 900 American airmen
were killed, wounded or missing. It once again illustrated the huge
dangers of daytime bombing.[157]

The second large British raid saw 787 RAF bombers arrive over
Hamburg on 28 July at 12.55 a.m. In the space of 50 deadly minutes
2,313 tonnes of bombs were unloaded on working-class areas to the
east of the city centre: Hammerbrook, Borgfelde, Hamm, Billwärder,
Hohenfelde and Rothenburgsort. These RAF incendiary bombs
created a huge and terrifying firestorm. With winds often reaching up
to 150 mph the streets became deadly fire tunnels. As Bill McCrea, an
RAF pilot involved in the raid, later recalled: 'It was an appalling sight.
Every so often it was burbling up, like a volcano.'[158] The human cost
was vast. An estimated 18,274 people died in this single raid, with the
loss of just 17 RAF planes. This extraordinary RAF raid shook the Nazi
hierarchy to its foundations. As Goebbels noted in his diary:

[overleaf]
The aftermath of the huge Allied bombing
raids on Hamburg in 1943.

A city of a million inhabitants has been destroyed in a manner unparalleled in history. We are faced with problems that are almost impossible of solution. Food must be found for this population of a million. Shelter must be secured. The people must be evacuated as fast as possible. They must be given clothing. In short, we are facing problems there of which we had no conception even a few weeks ago.[159]

On the following morning the streets of Hamburg were littered with naked corpses, their clothes burned off during the bombing. It was difficult to determine whether they were male or female. In one of the worst-affected areas, a German eye witness Hanse Jedlicka saw many people running over a bridge. 'One young woman sticks in my memory,' he later recalled. 'I still have a picture before my eyes. She came screaming out of the smoke over the bridge. She was completely naked and barefoot. As she came closer, I saw her feet were nothing but stumps. As soon as she found safety she fell down and died.'[160]

On 28 July the local Nazi Gauleiter Karl Kaufmann announced the evacuation of the whole city. In the following days around 900,000 people left. Every type of transport was commandeered for the exodus, including trains, lorries, buses, horse-drawn carriages and motor cars. At collection points bombed-out civilians demonstrated their anger. At a local railway station a distraught man was heard shouting, 'That Hitler! The pig should be hung!'[161]

Yet Hamburg's bloody ordeal was not over yet. Another large RAF raid began at 1 a.m. on 30 July, hitting the old town area, the docks, and some of the western suburbs of the city. An estimated 9,666 people were killed in this raid, but it was very costly to the RAF, with 28 planes shot down. The final RAF raid began at 1 a.m. on 3 August 1943. At the time Hamburg was experiencing a huge electrical storm, with thunder and lightning mixed with the deafening sound of exploding bombs. According to Bill McCrea, this raid was: 'An absolute shambles – entirely the fault of the Met men. We should never have gone, because this electrical storm came through Britain on the previous day. They [the weather forecasters] said it would be cleared.' It's been estimated that just eighty people were killed in this final raid but the RAF lost thirty aircraft.[162]

The Hamburg police authority meticulously catalogued the dead and missing. A card index was also compiled of every refugee who fled the city as a result of the raids. At the end of 1943, the Hamburg police recorded a total of 31,637 dead, but half of those were not identified by name. In May 1944, the official German cumulative death toll was placed at 38,975. By 1945 it was noted that 2,000 of those previously categorized as 'missing' had never been found and must have perished in the raids.[163] Most of the dead were buried in mass graves in Ohlsdorf Cemetery.

Despite the huge civilian death toll during the Hamburg raids, Arthur 'Bomber' Harris was extremely satisfied with the results: 'It was some time before the smoke of the burning city cleared away and air photographs of the damage could be taken. When this was done there was at last revealed a scene of unimaginable devastation. 6,200 acres in the most densely built-up district had been destroyed, 74 per cent of the most closely built-up parts of the city.'[164]

Amazingly, Hamburg was not as damaged economically as was first supposed. Foreign workers and forced labourers were soon sent back to work in the vital war industries, housed in makeshift barracks amidst the rubble-strewn streets. Furthermore, the vital port area was much less damaged than the city's residential areas. On 10 August some sections of the Hamburg road and tram system began operating again. Electricity and water supplies were then restored by the end of the month. By the end of November 1943, the telephone system was fully functioning, and 80 per cent of gas supplies restored. The recovery of industry in Hamburg was little short of miraculous. By the end of 1943, the aircraft industry in the city was operating at 91 per cent of its former capacity, with the chemical and shipbuilding factories running at 70 per cent of the pre-raid output figure. Overall, industrial output was back to 80 per cent of its pre-raid position in a few months. Far from achieving the knockout blow that Harris had predicted, the bombing of Hamburg had stiffened the resolve of the local population to fight on.[165]

In the Soviet Union during the summer of 1943 the Red Army mounted two major attacks as part of the Kursk Strategic Offensive. The first, codenamed Operation Kutuzov, began on 12 July and ended on 18 August. It was named in honour of the Russian general credited with saving Moscow during Napoleon's invasion of 1812.

It was really Operation Citadel in reverse, but much more successful. The initial attack aimed to split the German forces defending the Orel salient. It involved three Soviet army groups: the Bryansk Front – with 211,458 soldiers and 745 tanks and self-propelled guns – aimed to strike from the east. The Western Front – with 433,616 troops and 340 tanks and heavy guns – would move north.[166] These forces were supported

[overleaf]
Soviet troops advance during the Battle of Kursk.

by the Central Front, which also attacked from the south, with 675,000 soldiers and 1,500 tanks and self-propelled guns. These three huge Soviet armies numbering 1.3 million troops attacked the German 2nd Panzer Army and the 9th Army, which were both defending the Orel salient. In total the Germans had 300,700 men and 625 tanks and assault guns.[167]

The Germans were vastly outnumbered. The Soviet forces fought tank battles of extraordinary ferocity to break through the German defences at various points in the vicinity of Orel. Walter Model, the commander of the 9th Army, quickly decided to order a strategic withdrawal. Hitler surprisingly raised no objections to this, reluctantly accepting the Orel salient was not as important to hold as Kharkov and the economically useful Donets Basin. On 28 July Model withdrew his 9th Army to the so-called Hagen defensive position in front of the city of Bryansk. As they departed, German forces adopted a brutal 'scorched earth' policy in Orel, destroying large buildings in the city. On 5 August Soviet forces reoccupied Orel and by 18 August the Red Army had pushed the Germans back to their start position where they began the Battle of Kursk on 5 July 1943.[168]

Overall, Operation Kutuzov was a huge Soviet victory, but the costs were very high in men and equipment losses, with 112,529 Soviet dead or missing, 317,361 wounded, and 2,586 tanks and guns, plus 1,014 aircraft, destroyed.[169] Germany suffered a total of 25,515 dead or missing, 60,939 wounded, with 363 tanks and 218 planes destroyed.[170]

On 3 August 1943 the Red Army launched Operation Rumyantsev (also known as the Belgorod–Kharkov Offensive), which ran until 23 August 1943. Named after Russia's Foreign Minister in the run-up to Napoleon's unsuccessful invasion of Russia in 1812, it aimed to destroy the southern flank of Manstein's Army Group South, which was deployed to the south of the Kursk salient. Army Group South was defended by the fearsome 4th Panzer Army and Army Detachment *Kempf*, numbering a total of 213,000 troops in total, with 600 tanks and self-propelled guns. The Red Army, using nine Soviet armies from the Voronezh and Steppe Fronts, numbered 1.14 million troops, with 2,418 tanks and 13,633 assault guns available.[171]

On 5 August the Steppe Front began the offensive with an attack on Belgorod. Hopelessly outnumbered, the German soldiers quickly realized that defence was hopeless, so they evacuated the city on the evening of the first day. As the success at Orel occurred on the same day as the capture of Belgorod, Moscow radio was able to announce a double victory by the Red Army over the *Wehrmacht* during the summer months – this was the first time this had happened since the German-Soviet War began.

The Soviet military advance in the summer of 1943 continued relentlessly. On 10 August, Chuguev was recaptured. The next Soviet target was the fourth-largest city in the Soviet Union: Kharkov. Hitler issued an order on 13 August for the *Wehrmacht* to hold this strategically important city at all costs. He felt an evacuation of Kharkov would signal to Germany's remaining but wavering allies that the tide in the war was now turning decisively in favour of the Red Army on the Eastern Front.

The battle for Kharkov was therefore conducted in an extremely ferocious manner. On 20 August 1943 Hitler phoned Manstein to emphasize to him his steadfast determination to hold the city at all costs. In reply, Manstein told him that the situation in Kharkov was now completely hopeless: either the German forces abandoned the city forthwith or faced being trapped there, just as happened in Stalingrad in November 1942. Hitler, preparing himself mentally for the worst, ended their phone conversation by telling Manstein to hold the city 'if in any way possible'.

On 22 August German forces began abandoning Kharkov. On the next day the Red Army triumphantly marched in. Red flags were soon flying on buildings in the city. It was a deeply significant victory, as the Red Army had failed to retake Kharkov in 1942, had captured it in early 1943 and lost it again in March. This time it remained in Russian hands permanently.[172]

The decisive victory of the Red Army during Operation Rumyantsev was once again achieved at a very high cost in lives and equipment. The Soviets lost 71,611 men killed or missing, with 1,864 tanks, 423 artillery guns and 153 aircraft destroyed.[173] In comparison, the Germans suffered 8,933 dead or missing, with 240 tanks lost.[174] The huge disparity between Soviet and German losses was not, as is often supposed, wholly due to the superior tactics and weaponry of the German Panzer units, but by a better use of them, particularly the machine guns of the German infantry. Added to this was the devastating accuracy of German artillery and accurate bombing by the *Luftwaffe* against Soviet defensive positions.[175]

Yet the routine notion that Soviet quantity triumphed in the end over German quality requires qualification. The idea of 'Ivan the Primitive' versus 'Fritz the Efficient' on the Eastern Front was a German construct, reinforced by Nazi propaganda. It was then repeated in the memoirs and evidence of the German generals in war trials and was uncritically accepted in English-language histories during the Cold War era which had no access to Soviet records.

In reality, the Red Army slowly and painfully began to learn the operational art of war as the German-Soviet War progressed. By the summer of 1943 Soviet defensive fighting, combined with skilful counteroffensives, took the Germans completely out of their comfort zone. It was the Soviet counterpunch – as happened after the initial German attack at Kursk – that was now making a huge difference on the Eastern Front and driving the Germans into retreat.[176]

Nor can the high death rate of the Red Army be exclusively attributed to Stalin's undoubtedly oppressive and brutal Soviet system. It needs to be understood that historically Russian military strategy always had been wedded to an offensive strategy. Saving lives was never the Russian way of fighting wars, even during the Tsarist era. Russian leaders always felt wars of attrition were preferable because Russia had plenty of people and stood a better chance of winning a long war.

In the First World War, the armies of Tsar Nicholas II averaged 7,000 casualties per day between 1914 and 1917. Between 1941 and 1945 under Stalin the death toll was 7,950 per day. These two figures are similar enough to suggest that Stalin was following a long-standing Russian tradition in warfare, not one uniquely characteristic of his own regime.

The idea that Red Army officers regarded their soldiers as mere cannon fodder also requires some much-needed qualification. Soviet officers didn't let the foot soldiers take all the risks and do all the dying while they were sitting far away in the rear of battles. During the German-Soviet War (1941–45), a vast number of Soviet officers were killed in battle: 973,000, representing a death rate of 35 per cent. This shows that Soviet officers put their own lives on the line, which undoubtedly spurred on the ordinary soldiers under their command to follow suit. It's probably worth adding that Soviet losses began to diminish appreciably from the latter part of 1943 onwards until the end of the war. This was primarily due to the increased war supplies, higher-quality weapons, but also better leadership and improved organization within the Red Army.[177]

The breakneck advance of the Red Army on the Eastern Front in the summer of 1943 forced Hitler to issue 'Führer Order No. 10' on 12 August, ordering the creation of a defensive line of fortifications known as the East Wall (known as the Panther–Wotan line). On paper, this new boundary ran from Melitopol on the Sea of Azov, then along the lines of the Dnieper and Desna rivers, and north to Chernigov until it reached the Baltic. Hitler hoped this new 'East Wall' would allow the *Wehrmacht* to retreat no further. It was, of course, a pipe dream. German manpower and economic resources to build a huge defensive wall along the Eastern Front were now lacking. The Red Army was hardly going to sit back and allow it to be constructed.[178]

The huge defeat at Kharkov was really the beginning of a series of further retreats by the German army. By the start of September 1943, the Red Army had punched three huge holes in the section of the Eastern Front defended by Army Group Centre. The worsening predicament of German soldiers was summed up by a German commander on 2 September: 'Such a state of anxiety has arisen among the troops that draconian measures do not produce the desired results, but only the good example of officers and "kindly persuasion".' Discipline was now breaking down in a fashion unprecedented for the German army.[179]

During the summer campaign of 1943 the Red Army had pushed German Army Groups Centre and South back some 300 miles from Kursk to the River Dnieper. In the process, the Germans had lost the most economically valuable territory they had previously occupied. As the *Wehrmacht* retreated, its soldiers destroyed factories, bridges, government buildings, animals and anything else of economic value. There was a great deal of wanton violence and murder, too, as the Germans retreated over the Dnieper River. Many Soviet villages were razed to the ground. One German soldier, seemingly enjoying this orgy of destruction, wrote in a letter to his fiancée: 'The Russians will find only rubble from blown-up buildings and bridges.'[180]

Hitler continued to insist that German forces could not retreat beyond the Donets Basin, because of its economic and strategic importance. Hitler commented bitterly at this juncture: 'My generals think only of military matters and withdrawals. They never think of economic matters. They therefore have absolutely no understanding, if we give up the Donets area, then we lack coal. We need it for our armaments industry.'[181] On 3 September Manstein told Hitler bluntly at a military meeting there should be a German strategic withdrawal from the Donets Basin to a much more defensible position. Hitler at first refused to sanction it, but on 15 September, after a further meeting with Manstein, he finally accepted reality and approved the general retreat of Army Group South to a more defensive position behind the

River Dnieper, at roughly the same position reached by the *Wehrmacht* during July 1941. On 17 September, Bryansk was hastily evacuated by German troops. Smolensk was recaptured by the Red Army on 25 September, with little German resistance offered.[182]

The German war effort was undoubtedly in a state of deep crisis in the autumn of 1943. In September, Goebbels held two discussions with Hitler at the Wolf's Lair. The key topic of conversation was whether Germany should now open peace talks either with Churchill or Stalin. At the first meeting, Hitler said that it might be much easier to make a peace deal with the British government, because he thought Churchill was an anti-Bolshevist at heart and was pursuing purely British imperialist aims in the war. Hitler felt dangling the carrot of British domination in the Mediterranean might induce Churchill to conclude a peace deal with Germany. Goebbels disagreed, arguing that Stalin was a much more 'practical politician' and was more likely to be approachable for a peace deal than the 'romantic adventurer' Churchill.[183]

In his second discussion with Goebbels, Hitler completely changed his mind. It was personalities that counted in political talks not ideological principles, he stressed. Hitler now thought that negotiations with Churchill would lead nowhere, due to the British Prime Minister's personal hostility towards him. Hitler preferred to deal with Stalin, but he very much doubted whether Stalin would be willing to grant what Hitler wanted from a peace deal, because Stalin was now in a strong military position on the battlefield. In response, Goebbels made it clear to Hitler that 'we must come to some arrangement with one side or the other. The Reich has never yet won a two-front war. We must therefore see how we can somehow or other get out of a two-front war.'[184]

At a time when Goebbels was accepting the war was going very badly and might be lost, he commissioned his most ambitious wartime propaganda entertainment film: *Kolberg*. He wanted the film to encourage Germans to fight to the bitter end. The script was based on the autobiography of Joachim Nettelbeck, the mayor of Kolberg, who had led a stout defence of the besieged fortress town against Napoleon's invading army in 1807.

Directed by Viet Harlan and shot in vivid Agfa colour, with a budget of 7.6 million Reichsmarks (equal to 28 million euros today), *Kolberg* was the most lavishly produced entertainment film of the entire Nazi era. Many of the key Nazi propaganda themes came together in *Kolberg*: the growing mistrust of the army, the popular appeal to rally

Hitler greets Mussolini shortly after he was freed from Italian captivity by German paratroopers.

around the flag, the belief in a last-ditch defence of the Reich, the stoicism of the public in the face of destruction, and the hope of a last-minute miracle victory. Goebbels requisitioned 187,000 real soldiers and 4,000 sailors as extras during the filming. He even wrote many of the power-packed, patriotic speeches that appear in the film.

Kolberg portrays Nettelbeck as a true patriot determined to defend his town against Napoleon's superior forces or die heroically in the process. He recruits a local citizens' militia, but soon realizes he needs a charismatic Prussian leader to heroically defend the town. Nettelbeck sends the beautiful Maria (played by Kristina Söderbaum) on a dazzling white stallion to Königsberg, where the Court of Prussia has now retreated. Upon arrival, Maria persuades the aristocratic General Gneisenau to return with her to Kolberg to lead the citizens to defy Napoleon. In the end, the demoralized French decide to abandon the siege, whereas in reality the conflict ended with the Treaty of Tilsit. However, this hugely expensive attempt to boost German morale came far too late. *Kolberg* was not ready for release until 30 January 1945, by which time very few German movie theatres were still operational, due to Allied bombing raids. Few Germans ever saw what was probably the greatest work of Nazi film propaganda.[185]

Meanwhile, the crisis in Italy reached the critical level. On 3 September 1943 Allied forces landed on the Italian mainland at

Calabria. On the same day, a secret armistice agreement with the Allied armed forces was signed by General Giuseppe Castellano in Cassibile, Sicily. On 8 September, the new Italian government publicly announced Italy's unconditional surrender to the Allies. Italy was no longer capable of fighting, Prime Minister Badoglio told Hitler in a letter. On the next day, Victor Emmanuel III, Badoglio and his government abandoned Rome and journeyed by ship to Brindisi.

On 10 September Hitler, prompted by Goebbels, decided to speak to the German people about the rapidly deteriorating Italian situation in a recorded radio broadcast. Hitler claimed Italy's capitulation to the Allies had been expected for some time and he called the king, Badoglio and the army leadership 'traitors' who had betrayed Mussolini and the Italian people. Hitler absolved Mussolini of any blame for the military disaster, describing him as 'the greatest son of the Italian soil since the collapse of the ancient world'. The betrayal of the Italian army, he added, made very little difference to the overall military picture, because of the well-known military weaknesses of the Italians.[186]

The landing by the Allies on the Italian mainland did not lead to a swift victory. Instead between 1943 and 1945 Italy became a divided country. The *Wehrmacht* occupied the central and northern part of the Italian peninsula, including Rome, and mounted a well-organized and extremely effective defensive resistance. Of 3.48 million Italian soldiers, a million were disarmed and 600,000 were shipped off to Germany as military internees, then sent to labour camps and treated appallingly. A smaller kingdom in the south was established under Allied domination with the king and the Badoglio government as its figureheads. A strong German military fortification known as the Gustav Line ran south of Rome across the narrowest part of the Italian boot, with the natural mountain fortress of Monte Cassino as its strongpoint.[187]

Hitler was now determined to discover Mussolini's whereabouts and to rescue him. Thanks to tip-offs from Italian officials loyal to Il Duce, the Germans located Mussolini to a hotel at the ski resort of Campo Imperatore on top of the Gran Sasso, the highest range in the Abruzzo Apennine mountains. It's doubtful whether Mussolini wanted to be rescued. According to his own account, he was enjoying house arrest, even finding time to read Nietzsche's philosophy and poetry in depth.[188]

On 12 September 1942 the daring German rescue mission of Mussolini – Operation Oak – took place under the overall command of SS Lieutenant Colonel Otto Skorzeny. Ninety Waffen-SS commandos and paratroopers landed by glider planes near to Mussolini's hotel and quickly overwhelmed the 200 Carabinieri Troops standing guard outside it. In just ten minutes Mussolini was unceremoniously bundled into a tiny plane. After a perilous take-off, when the pilot nearly lost control of the aircraft, he was flown to Practica di Mare air base and then onward to Vienna, where he spent the night in the opulent Imperial Hotel.[189]

On 14 September Mussolini met Hitler at the Wolf's Lair and the two men embraced warmly outside the entrance to Hitler's bunker. Goebbels witnessed the meeting, noting: 'It was a deeply moving example of loyalty between men and comrades. I suppose there is nobody in the world who can fail to be impressed by so touching an occasion.'[190]

Mussolini's daring rescue was a welcome propaganda boost for Hitler, but was deeply embarrassing for the Allies. The German press portrayed it in heroic terms, suggesting that once again the Allies had been fooled by German ingenuity. On 18 September, Mussolini delivered a speech to the Italian people via Radio Munich, praising Hitler's unswerving loyalty and aiming criticism at the Italian Royal Family: 'It is not the regime that has betrayed the monarchy, it is the monarchy that has betrayed the regime.' He vowed all Italian traitors would be eliminated. The German public started to jokingly call Mussolini the 'Gauleiter of Italy' which was quite close to the truth. Hitler, who had once been so impressed by Mussolini, even regarding him as his mentor, was forced to admit to Goebbels that Il Duce was now a broken man. Mussolini always lacked the qualities of a world-wide revolutionary, he added. The friendship between Hitler and Mussolini was now pretty much over.[191]

On 23 September 1943, Mussolini became the leader of the newly created Nazi puppet Italian Social Republic (Repubblica Sociale Italiana or RSI). Hitler insisted that it should be a republic to emphasize a complete break with the Italian monarchy. Mussolini's title as 'Head of Government' reflected he was really a German appointee. Mussolini was used by Hitler to legitimize Germany's occupation of central and northern Italy. Mussolini later told a confidante that he had been given little choice in the matter, as Hitler had told him bluntly: 'Either you assume leadership of the Italian state or I will send in officials to govern Italy.'[192]

Rome remained the Italian capital, but Mussolini established his own headquarters in Salò, a small town near Lake Garda, midway between Rome and Venice. He now lived under German house arrest, guarded by the SS.[193] The Germans exploited the Italian economy for the war effort. Hitler appointed Rudolf Rahn, a career diplomat, as the new Plenipotentiary of the Greater German Reich at the National Fascist Government, but the real power in northern Italy rested with Field Marshal Albert Kesselring, designated as the supreme commander of German-occupied Italy.

Not surprisingly, Mussolini's rule – under direct German supervision – became more brutal and repressive. Mussolini took vengeance, at Hitler's insistence, against those who had betrayed him at the Grand Council meeting in July. Galeazzo Ciano, the former Italian Foreign Minister who was married to Mussolini's eldest daughter Edda, was put on trial in Verona. Found guilty, he was executed in Scalzi Prison on 11 January 1944, along with four other leading Fascists who had voted against Mussolini at the Grand Council meeting. Ciano was tied to a chair and shot in the back. His defiant last words were: 'Long live Italy!' His wife Edda managed to escape to Switzerland and took with her Ciano's diaries. They were published after the war and remain a key source for understanding the German-Italian diplomatic relationship.[194]

A notable feature of the Salò Republic was its persecution of Jews which again reflected Hitler's influence. On 16 October, 1,259 Jews were arrested in Rome by the SS and German police units, then transported to their deaths at Auschwitz-Birkenau. In November, the newly formed Republican Fascist Party defined all Jews and foreigners as 'enemies'. Of the 32,000 Jews who lived in the Salò Republic when Mussolini took over, only 837 survived the war.[195]

On the Eastern Front, the Red Army continued to advance relentlessly in the last months of 1943. At the centre of this phase of the struggle in the German-Soviet War was the important Battle of the Dnieper, which ran from 26 August to 23 December. This engagement involved 2.6 million Soviet troops, divided into five army groups. They faced 1.25 million Axis troops from Army Groups B, Centre and South. The Soviets changed their army group names from the Voronezh Front, Steppe Front, South-West Front and South Front to the 1st, 2nd, 3rd and 4th Ukrainian Fronts.

Pondering the successive run of German losses on the Eastern Front in late 1943, Captain Wilhelm Hosenfeld noted: 'The cause of our defeats is not the number of men and their equipment, but solely their morale, the lack of fighting spirit. Hitler has led the troops into the Russian wastelands and now they feel deserted, deceived and betrayed. That is the deepest cause of our reverses and it is what is going to lead to collapse.'[196]

By 30 September, the Red Army had established five bridgeheads on the west bank of the 400-mile-long River Dnieper, some of them seized in daring parachute raids. The German army was now outnumbered in manpower, tanks, artillery and aircraft. The Germans desperately tried to hold ground in front of the lower Dnieper on the west bank of the river, but German Army Groups North, Centre and South were all seriously undermanned, with many units now lacking significant tank or air support. It was only the German army's brilliantly improvised defensive manoeuvres that prevented a complete knockout blow being inflicted by the Red Army on the Eastern Front towards the end of 1943. [197]

These repeated setbacks in the Soviet Union prompted Hitler to lead a new drive to instil Nazi ideological zeal into Germany's High Command. On 16 October, he addressed a select group of *Wehrmacht* officers and key officials at the Wolf's Lair. He told them the traditional, detached German 'professional officer' was no longer enough. What the *Wehrmacht* now required was the 'political officer' who was 'a fanatical champion of our ideology'. Only officers of this type could save Germany from annihilation by 'Bolshevism and Americanism'.[198]

Soviet historians during the Cold War era tended to downplay the role of the United States in supplying the Soviet Union. Privately, however, Stalin was willing to admit that America's Lend-Lease supplies had been vitally important in the eventual Soviet victory in the German-Soviet War. The leading Soviet military commander Georgy Zhukov also agreed in his memoirs that American economic aid had been crucial to the Soviet war effort in the latter stage of the war. In 1943 the United States provided the Red Army with 77,000 jeeps, 151,000 light trucks and 200,000 large trucks. These were faster and more durable than the equivalent Soviet models. The list of other US supplies was equally impressive: 57.8 per cent of aviation fuel; 53 per cent of explosives; 50 per cent of copper, aluminium and rubber tyres; 56.6 per cent of railway rails and 11,075 railway carriages; 380,000 field telephones and 956,000 miles of telephone cable. Around 50 per cent of food supplies also came through Lend-Lease. Spam became a staple of Red Army soldier rations.[199]

SD reports on German public opinion during the autumn of 1943 now made extremely gloomy reading, with one commenting: 'It is striking that now a growing number of those [soldiers] on leave from the Eastern Front are coming home with pessimistic views, while a few months ago they still had an almost unshakable confidence and complete faith in the triumph of our arms.' Many soldiers were openly speaking of 'declining officer authority, inexperienced younger officers and rumours of carousing, sexual licence and black-racketeering giving the impression of a gradual demoralization across the Front'.[200]

In Germany, open displays of defeatism met with an increasingly harsh response by the People's Courts. In one case Theodor Korselt, a civil servant from Rostock, was sentenced to death for expressing the view while on a tram – after the announcement of Mussolini's resignation – that Hitler should do the same. Around this time, two senior branch managers of Deutsche Bank were executed for making similar 'defeatist' comments.[201]

The Gestapo's brutal crackdown on 'defeatists' helped to reduce public criticism. As the President of the Higher State Court in Bamberg observed on 27 November 1943:

> While a short time ago it was noticeable that there was a great
> lack of inhibition in the way rumours were passed on and
> political and military events were discussed in public, particularly
> in pubs, railway compartments, shops, etc., now, probably under
> the impression of the increasing number of death sentences
> against defeatists, this has been replaced by the greatest caution
> in all matters affecting the war and politics. So no one is prepared
> any longer to say what they think, on the contrary, everywhere
> there is a general unwillingness to engage in conversations about
> anything other than mundane matters.[202]

As Germany's military position progressively worsened, the Nazi leadership began to see the mass murder of the Jews as a sick consolation prize for military defeat. SS leader Heinrich Himmler – recently appointed to the additional government post of Minister of the Interior – played a leading role in this endeavour. Himmler was also keen to spread the blame for mass murder as the Allies promised Hitler and his leading cronies would face war crimes trials. With this fear in mind, Himmler summoned SS generals and the Nazi Gauleiters and Reichsleiters to Posen, the capital of the Warthegau. On 4 October 1943 Himmler delivered a three-hour speech to ninety-two SS officers in Posen town hall. A recording and a verbatim typescript of this speech has survived. It primarily offered an overview of the progress of the war. Himmler thought that the Soviet fightback on the Eastern Front was largely due to the ideological indoctrination of the Red Army by political commissars and he suggested that the *Wehrmacht* should now follow suit.

Himmler then declared, in a deeply significant moment in the speech: 'Today I am going to refer quite frankly to a very grave chapter. We can mention it now among ourselves quite openly and yet we shall never talk about it in public. I'm referring to the evacuation of the Jews, the extermination of the Jewish people.' He then praised the mindset of the SS men who had carried this out. As Himmler put it: 'To have endured this and at the same time to have remained a decent person – with exceptions due to human weaknesses – has made us tough.' The Final Solution was for Himmler 'an unwritten – never to be written – and yet glorious page in our history'. He then directly related this genocide of the Jews to the need to prevent a repeat of the undermining of the home front that had occurred in the latter stages of the First World War: 'We had the moral right, the duty to our people, to destroy this people which wanted to destroy us.'[203]

Himmler's second speech – very similar in content to the first – was delivered on 6 October 1943 at a conference of Reichsleiters and Gauleiters also in Posen town hall. The speech only came to light in 1970, when the Harvard historian Erich Goldhagen was inspecting Himmler's files, which had just been released to the German Federal Archives or Bundesarchiv. The Reich ministers Alfred Rosenberg, Joseph Goebbels and Albert Speer were also present, although Speer later tried to deny that he was ever there.

Himmler explained that certain defeatist attitudes had developed among the German population, but they had been dealt with ruthlessly by the courts. Himmler then said: 'I ask of you that which I say to you in this circle be really only heard and not ever discussed.' He then described the extermination of the Jews as 'the most difficult task of my life'. He justified the killing not only of Jewish men, but also of women and children:

> I decided to find a clear solution to this problem too. I did not consider myself justified to exterminate the men – that is to kill them or have them killed – and to let their children grow up to become the avengers against our own sons and grandsons. The difficult decision had to be taken to have this people disappear from the face of the earth.

Himmler's Posen speeches offer unequivocal evidence of the Final

Solution and his central role in carrying it out on Hitler's orders. The aim of his first speech was to praise SS men who had participated in the killings, while the second aimed to ensure key Nazi officials became knowing accomplices in the genocide to spread the guilt beyond the SS.[204] Goebbels, who attended Himmler's 6 October speech, noted in his diary:

> As far as the Jewish question is concerned, he [Himmler] gives a very unvarnished and frank presentation. He is convinced that we can solve the Jewish question throughout Europe by the end of this year. He proposes the harshest and most radical solution: to exterminate the Jews root and branch. It is certainly a logical solution, even if it is a brutal one. We have to take the responsibility for solving this issue in our time. Later generations will certainly not handle this problem with the courage and ardour that are ours.[205]

Ever since June 1941 the Eastern Front had been the centre of German strategy, but the military dangers to Germany's ultimate survival as a nation were no longer confined there. The Western Allies had now comprehensively defeated the Axis nations in North Africa, won the Battle of the Atlantic, invaded Sicily, occupied southern Italy, and were now mounting daily and devastating bombing raids on German cities. Realizing the growing threat in the west, Hitler issued 'Führer Directive No. 51' on 3 November 1943. It made clear that the decisive struggle against Bolshevism had previously justified placing the bulk of Germany's military strength on the Eastern Front: 'In the east, the vast extent of territory makes it possible for us to lose ground, even on a large scale, without a fatal blow being dealt to the nervous system of Germany.'

However, Hitler argued, it was 'very different in the West!' If the Allies breached German defences there, then 'the immediate consequences are unpredictable'. 'The danger in the East remains,' Hitler added, 'but a greater danger now appears in the West: an Anglo-Saxon landing!' He felt 'everything indicates that the enemy will launch an offensive against the Western front of Europe, at the latest in the spring, perhaps much earlier'. As a result, Hitler now claimed that defending the West from Allied invasion was the chief war priority, and predicted that Germany's struggle against Britain and the United States would be the 'decisive battle' that would determine the outcome of the war.[206]

On 8 November 1943, Hitler delivered a speech to the party faithful in Munich's Löwenbräukeller on the twentieth anniversary of the 1923 Beer Hall Putsch which still publicly emphasized the importance of the German-Soviet War. A recording was later broadcast on German national radio, although Goebbels admitted that he had to edit out 'a few clumsy turns of phrase'.[207] Hitler told his audience that only Germany could overcome the 'Bolshevik-Asian Colossus', which he predicted 'would assail all Europe until it was defeated'. Western Allied politicians were deluded in thinking that they could control what he called the Jewish-Bolshevik Soviet regime: 'The same men who believe they have found in Stalin the genius who will pull their chestnuts out of the fire for them, will live to see, perhaps sooner than they anticipate, how the spirits summoned from the underworld will strangle them.'

The swift collapse of Italy – which Churchill and Roosevelt predicted – had not occurred, Hitler added. The Allies were moving forward at a snail's pace in southern Italy and the German position had been stabilized. A landing on the Channel coast or in Norway would be much more difficult for them. The struggle in the east, he admitted, was the most difficult the German armed forces had to fight. The nation that would triumph there, he predicted, would seize the initiative in the war: 'our future depends on forcing the decision [on the Eastern Front] in our favour by a supreme effort. Every sacrifice which we make today stands in no relation to the sacrifices that will be demanded of us if we do not win this war.'

Hitler expressed deep sympathy to those suffering due to the air raids and he once again criticized the Allies for bombing defenceless women and children. Finally, he dealt with recent Allied press rumours which claimed he was suffering a nervous breakdown or that he had dismissed Göring, or that Göring had dismissed him, or that the *Wehrmacht* had dismissed the Nazi Party or vice versa, or that the generals had revolted against him, or that he had had all his generals arrested: 'You can rest assured: everything is possible,' he concluded, 'but that I lose my nerve is completely out of the question.'[208]

The Allied bombing campaign on Berlin was also stepped up markedly during the latter months of 1943. The renewed air battle over Berlin ran from 23 August 1943 to 24 March 1944, but the key period occurred from the end of November 1943 to the end of March 1944. It involved sixteen major attacks and seventeen smaller ones. After the devastation in Hamburg in July, there was a huge evacuation programme in Berlin to remove women and children to the remote countryside.[209]

[overleaf]
Berlin residents walking through the bomb-damaged streets of the city.

Arthur 'Bomber' Harris had always viewed Berlin as a key target. He thought his bombers could do to the German capital what they had done to Hamburg, but this never happened for a number of reasons. To begin with, Allied bombers were flying at the very end of their optimum range. The Allied 'Oboe' radar guidance system could not operate effectively at such a long distance. As a result, many Allied planes did not merely miss their targets but often missed Berlin altogether. Because it is a sprawling city, covering twenty-eight square miles, with wide boulevards and concrete buildings, the Allied bombing campaign on Berlin didn't produce the firestorms that ravaged more compact cities with narrow streets and half-timbered houses.[210]

The most intense period of sustained Allied bombing on Berlin began on the night of 18–19 November 1943 when 400 Lancaster bombers flew over the city, aiming to destroy key government buildings. However, due to poor visibility the damage inflicted was not severe. Two further raids followed on 22–23 and 23–24 November using 750 aircraft and were much more effective. These attacks were concentrated on the western districts of the city from the Tiergarten and Charlottenburg out to Spandau. Overall, the November attacks on Berlin killed 3,758 people, with 68,262 buildings destroyed and 500,000 people left homeless. It was during these raids that the famous Kaiser Wilhelm Memorial Church was damaged. Eyewitnesses were shocked by the scale of the destruction. One Berlin resident noted in a letter to her brother on 24 November:

> You can't imagine what a heap of ruins Berlin is! Between Zoo, Wittenbergplatz, Lützowufer and Einemstrasse there's hardly a habitable house standing. The embassy quarter is burnt out, the Hansa district and Moabit lie in ruins, at the Alexanderplatz, from Oranienburger Tor past the Stettin station to Reinickendorf it must be the same. All the main railway stations have been badly hit.[211]

Two further large Allied raids followed shortly afterwards. On 16 December the areas of Charlottenburg, Wilmersdorf and Kreuzberg were all hit heavily, resulting in 600 deaths. On 29 December, the Tempelhof and Neukölln areas suffered severe damage. The German journalist Ruth Andreas-Friedrich noted in her diary: 'We move rubble. We nail up corrugated board. Here we are without water, transportation or [electric] current. The telephone is dead too, and we learn only by roundabout ways whether our friends… are alive.'[212] For some Berliners the raids ignited a desire to live for the day. Another German journalist, Ursula von Kardorff, noted in her diary on 17 December: 'After every air raid I get the same feeling of an irresponsible vitality. One could embrace the world that has been given back to me. Presumably that's the reason why we so greedily grab every opportunity to have a party.'[213]

The Allied bombing of Berlin continued to the end of the war, but never again on the scale of the raids in late 1943. Harris later conceded: 'Judged by the standards of our attacks upon Hamburg, the Battle of Berlin did not appear to be an overwhelming success.'[214] Bomber Command lost 537 bombers, 2,690 airmen died and 1,000 were taken prisoner. The number of German civilians killed is a matter of dispute, with the lowest figure estimated at 4,000 and the highest at 9,390.[215]

At the end of 1943 the Allies were now supremely confident of defeating Germany. The 'Big Three' Allied leaders – Stalin, Roosevelt and Churchill – met to discuss war strategy in the Iranian capital of Tehran between 28 November and 1 December 1943. Despite his failing health, Roosevelt travelled 7,000 miles to meet Stalin for the first time.

The Tehran Conference marked a turning point in the dynamics of the relationship between the three Allied leaders. Churchill, the leader of a declining British Empire, now found himself relegated to a subsidiary role to the leaders of the two new military world superpowers: the United States and the Soviet Union. Stalin – worried the Germans might attempt to assassinate him – insisted the conference sessions were held in the heavily guarded Soviet embassy. Roosevelt and Stalin held talks privately together on the first day and the two men established an immediate friendly rapport. Roosevelt made it clear that he fully supported the opening of a Second Front in Western Europe. For his part, Stalin promised to join the war against Japan as soon as Germany was defeated.

The main disagreements in Tehran were between Stalin and Churchill. Over dinner, Stalin proposed the Allies took a very harsh line with the Germans after victory by executing 50,000 German officers. Roosevelt, wrongly thinking this was a cheeky joke, replied: 'Maybe 49,000 might be enough.'[216] Churchill was not amused at all, saying he would not sanction the cold-blooded murder of soldiers. Churchill said that only major war criminals should be put on trial. He then theatrically left the room, but was persuaded to return when Stalin told him that he was only joking. Churchill later recalled:

[overleaf]
The 'Big Three' Allied war leaders meet at the 1943 Tehran Conference (left to right: Stalin, Roosevelt, Churchill).

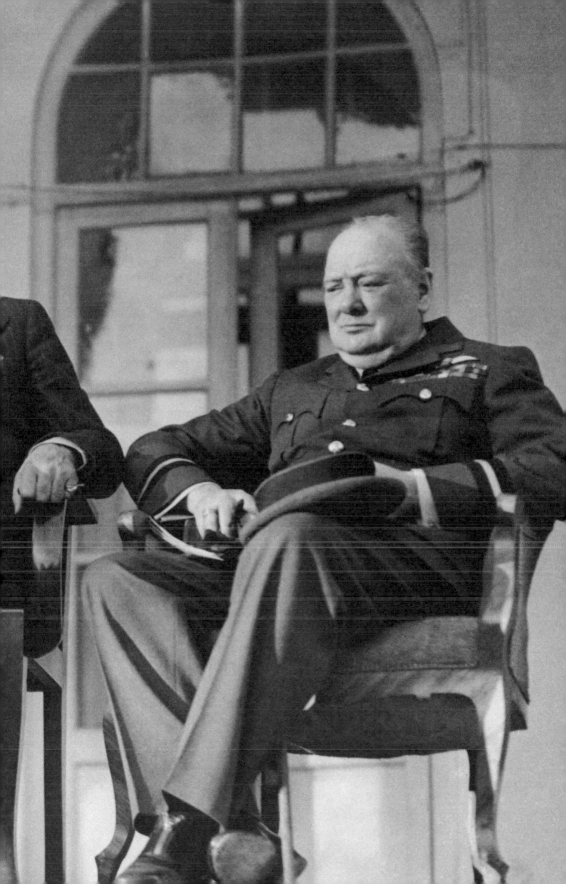

> Stalin has a very captivating manner when he chooses to use it,
> and I never saw him do so to such an extent as at this moment.
> Although I was not then, and am not now, fully convinced that
> all was chaff and there was no serious intent lurking behind,
> I consented to return, and the rest of the evening passed
> pleasantly.[217]

The conference dinner was interrupted by a short ceremony during which Churchill presented Stalin with a ceremonial sword made in Sheffield called the 'Sword of Stalingrad'. It was a present from George VI to the brave Soviet defenders of the city. Stalin raised the sword above his head, then kissed it. It was carried from the room by a Russian guard of honour, but the leading Red Army officer Clement Voroshilov managed to drop it as he left the dining room.[218]

The major topic of discussion at the Tehran Conference was Operation Overlord – the planned Allied landing in Western Europe. Roosevelt confirmed that the launch date had now been provisionally set for 1 May 1944. Churchill expressed some reservations about the whole operation, even casting doubt on whether the necessary shipping would be available in such a short space of time. Stalin promised to make his own contribution to the success of Overlord by launching a concurrent counteroffensive on Germany's Eastern Front to divert Hitler's forces from northern France. This placated Churchill somewhat, who, realizing he was outvoted anyway, finally accepted that the invasion of Western Europe would go ahead in May 1944.[219]

In Germany, the Tehran meeting was rightly interpreted as being part of an Allied plan to invade Western Europe in 1944. On 20 December, at a military conference, Hitler told his leading generals: 'There is no doubt that the attack in the West will come in the spring: it is beyond doubt.' He then predicted that the first landing point might be in Norway, which he felt would be 'disastrous for our entire northern army'. Hitler thought the landing in the west was being pushed by Roosevelt and he suspected that the British did not have their 'heart in this attack'. He felt the British government might be willing to consider a peace settlement to avoid it, even suggesting that Churchill was playing a crafty game by giving the supreme command of the operation to the Americans. This would allow Churchill to blame the Americans if it went wrong. The impending invasion prompted him to consider much more drastic defence measures, including the deployment of flamethrowers. He felt that once the Allies had invaded in Western Europe 'it will be relief', because he was confident that the German army could repel them in a head-to-head struggle.[220]

At a meeting with his leading naval commander Karl Dönitz on the same day, the likelihood of an Anglo-Saxon invasion of Western Europe in 1944 also came up. Hitler reiterated his view that he thought Churchill was getting cold feet about the whole idea. Hitler was not certain where and when the invasion would take place, but he expected landings in the Netherlands and in northern France, and probably early in 1944.[221]

On 22 December 1943 Hitler issued an order for the establishment of a leadership staff for the National Socialist Guidance of the *Wehrmacht*. He wanted officers to take a much stronger ideological line in future. The aim was to restore the spirits of the soldiers as they now fought in 'reverse gear'. The weapon of Nazi ideology, argued Hitler, was crucial in the long war of attrition that Germany now faced. To carry out this fresh ideological mission in the army, Hitler appointed General Hermann Reinecke, the chief of the *Wehrmacht* Office, to the post of Head of the National Socialist Leadership Staff. The aim was for all German servicemen to imbue themselves with National Socialist ideals. The order was an admission that Hitler's previous order to fully indoctrinate the *Wehrmacht* with Nazi ideals had not been implemented with sufficient vigour.[222]

During 1943 more than half of all the Soviet territory lost to the *Wehrmacht* since June 1941 had been recaptured. The Western Allies had cleared Africa of Axis troops, won the Battle of the Atlantic, captured Sicily, invaded the Italian mainland and were bombing German cities every day. Despite all of this, the Allies had not yet achieved a knockout blow, but Hitler's Germany was living on borrowed time.

1944
·
LOSING
BATTLES
·

•

In his traditional New Year message Hitler offered an overly optimistic review of the gloomy events of 1943, not even mentioning the catastrophe at Stalingrad. Similarly, the military disasters in North Africa and the Mediterranean – which he blamed on the 'shameful betrayal' of Mussolini by Victor Emmanuel III of Italy – were glossed over. Hitler then predicted the Western Allies would attempt a landing in Western Europe or in the Balkans during 1944, but claimed to be 'completely confident that wherever the Allies carry out their landing, they will be given an appropriate welcome'.

In a rare moment of candour, Hitler admitted the current struggle had led to psychological stress, which 'reaches the limit of what is bearable, even surpassing it at times'. This was particularly true not just for him personally but also for the *Wehrmacht* and German civilians who had to cope with the devastating effects of Allied air raids and the 'loss of so many personal belongings and small remembrances'.

Hitler forecast the Allied coalition, which he said was composed of 'Bolshevik-plutocratic conspirators and their Jewish wire-pullers', would soon collapse. He concluded optimistically: 'The year 1944 will make heavy and difficult demands on all Germans. The tremendous developments in the war will reach a crisis point in this year. We are completely confident that we will successfully ride it out.'[1]

At that time a fresh Soviet offensive – stretching across a 550-mile front line along the River Dnieper – was already moving forward. It was led by the four Soviet Ukrainian army groups (Fronts), numbering 2.23 million men and 2,600 aircraft. They faced the overstretched Army Group South, commanded by Field Marshal Erich von Manstein, now reduced to 328,000 men, supported by 109,000 Hungarian and Romanian troops, with just 199 tanks and 625 planes between them.

Under constant Soviet bombardment Army Group South had little choice but to retreat to a new defensive position running along the River Dnieper called the Panther–Wotan Line. Meanwhile, the 4th Panzer Army fell back from its besieged Kiev bridgehead towards Vinnytsia, forcing Manstein to move his military headquarters to

Ternopil, which was forty miles further west. The 1st Panzer Army also came under sustained attack near the western side of the bend of the River Dnieper.[2]

On 4 January 1944 Manstein, recognizing the danger his army group now faced, flew urgently to the Wolf's Lair to meet the Führer. He asked him to sanction several tactical withdrawals in the southern sector of the front, where the bend of the River Dnieper made a westward turn towards the Black Sea. Manstein also alerted Hitler to the possibility of a yawning gap opening up between Army Groups South and Centre. To avoid such a catastrophe, Manstein wanted the 1st Panzer Army to withdraw from the Dnieper Bend to assist the 4th Panzer Army. In his memoirs, Manstein noted that as he finished reading his gloomy report, Hitler fixed him with a steely gaze, then rejected all of his proposals, one by one, saying that they amounted to 'running away'.

At the end of the meeting, Manstein made a request to see Hitler privately, with only Kurt Zeitzler, the Chief of the Army General Staff, present. Hitler was extremely irritated that Manstein wanted to continue a conversation which he considered to be over. Speaking even more bluntly than he had at the earlier meeting, Manstein told Hitler that the successive defeats of the German army in the east were due not only to the numerical advantage of the enemy, but to 'the way we are being led'. He then suggested Hitler should appoint a new commander-in-chief for the Eastern Front, much like the role given to Field Marshal Albert Kesselring in northern Italy, and Field Marshal Gerd von Rundstedt in Western Europe.

Manstein later recalled that after listening to these comments, Hitler glared at him with 'a look which made me feel he wished to crush my will to continue. I cannot remember a human gaze ever conveying such willpower.'[3] Hitler rejected the implication that he was unfit to be the military commander and then questioned Manstein's own suitability as his replacement: 'Even I am not obeyed by my field marshals! Do you think that they would, for instance, obey you any better?' Manstein replied that his own orders were never disobeyed. Hitler then ended the discussion abruptly by informing him there would be no retreat for Army Group South. In effect, Manstein had been arguing for a restoration of the independence of the German commander in the field, but the days of a uniformed officer telling a political leader what to do were over – not just in Germany, but among all the Allied leaders, too.[4]

In fact, Army Group South did manage to halt the Soviet advance by staging a counter-attack against the 1st Ukrainian Front, which was heading in the direction of Uman and Vinnytsia on 24 January. Two Soviet armies were encircled, and 268 Soviet tanks were wrecked. The German army in the south had seemingly risen from the dead, thereby relieving the pressure on the 4th Panzer Army and halting the advance of the 1st Ukrainian Front. All of this was due to Manstein's brilliance on the battlefield, but one tactical victory was no longer enough to stem the tide of the Soviet advance.[5]

A new Soviet threat to Army Group South soon came further along the front line at a point where the German 8th Army, commanded by Otto Wöhler, was doggedly defending a thirty-mile bulge on the west bank of the River Dnieper, west of Cherkassy. On 5 January 1944, the 2nd Ukrainian Front launched a blistering attack on the 8th Army, which was desperately defending the industrial city of Kirovograd. The Soviet plan was to encircle the German defenders, and this was soon achieved, with the city being captured on 8 January.

Another huge Soviet assault followed on 24 January. The 1st and 2nd Ukrainian Fronts – numbering 336,700 men, 500 tanks, 5,300 artillery guns and 1,000 aircraft – launched another attack on the 8th Army and the 1st Panzer Army – this time from two directions. On 28 January the two Soviet army groups linked up, near the town of Zvenigorodka, encircling the Germans in a 45-mile-wide pocket, centred on the town of Korsun, which became known as the Korsun–Cherkassy Pocket.

Once again, as at Stalingrad in November 1942, a whole German army and a Panzer army were trapped. The number of German troops surrounded was estimated at 58,000. The Red Army brought up several infantry divisions to tighten the ring around Korsun. Hitler called the pocket a 'fortress on the Dnieper' and demanded that it should be held whatever the cost.

On 4 February Manstein put together a hastily assembled relief tank force, which managed to penetrate the outer Soviet ring surrounding Korsun, but it was soon pushed back by the sheer weight of Soviet numerical superiority. Another German relief attempt was made on 11 February, this time aiming to drive tanks into the centre of Korsun and capture the strategically important Hill 239, which overlooked the town. But this operation had to be abandoned due to a lack of fuel.

The Soviets offered the trapped German soldiers surrender terms, but these were rejected. On 15 February, Manstein defied Hitler's 'hold at all costs' order for Korsun and sent a radio message to the trapped soldiers there, ordering them to break out on the night of the 16–17

February. By now, the Korsun Pocket had shrunk to a rectangular area five miles long and three miles wide, containing just 45,000 German troops.

The Germans did break out in a daring move that surprised the Red Army, but they had to leave behind 1,450 badly wounded men. As they escaped, desperate German soldiers ran forward with only handheld weapons. Many were slaughtered in front of Hill 239. The survivors had to cross the fifteen-mile-wide and freezing-cold Gniloy Tikich River, before reaching the safety of German-held Lysjanka. German official documents listed the total escapees from the Korsun Pocket at 40,423, including the wounded who had been flown out at an earlier stage.[6] Soviet sources listed 24,286 Germans killed or missing, and a further 55,902 wounded between 24 January and 17 February.[7]

The Soviet press called the Korsun battle 'Stalingrad on the Dnieper'. This was something of an exaggeration, but it was undoubtedly another comprehensive Soviet victory. German propaganda preferred to present it as a heroic defensive operation, followed by a miraculous escape. The episode was further evidence that Army Group South was now crumbling in Ukraine.[8]

The next mortal threat to the German army came in the northern sector of the Eastern Front, threatening the position of Army Group North, which had 741,000 troops left. On 12 January, the Red Army began yet another bold offensive, codenamed Operation Iskra, which aimed to finally end the siege of Leningrad. It was spearheaded by two Soviet army groups – the Leningrad and Volkhof Fronts – who mounted a three-pronged attack from the east, south and west. The Soviets deployed 1.24 million troops, 1,475 tanks and 1,500 aircraft. A German officer offered his observations on the struggle for Leningrad in a letter to his wife: 'Here a battle is boiling which outdoes everything we've seen up to now. The Russians are advancing on three sides, we're living through hell. I can't describe it. If I survive, I'll tell you about it when we see each other. At the moment all I can say is one thing – wish me luck.'[9]

On 18 January two Soviet army groups linked up. On 27 January, the siege of Leningrad which began on 8 September 1941 – and lasted for 872 days – finally ended in a Soviet victory. Army Group North was now pushed back all the way to the Estonian border. On 22 January, Hitler replaced Field Marshal Georg von Küchler, the commander of Army Group North, with General Walter Model, a trusted practitioner of defensive warfare.

There has been a great deal of research on the Soviet death toll during the whole siege of Leningrad. A 'Commission to Investigate Atrocities Committed by the Fascist Occupiers' concluded there were 649,000 civilian deaths, with 632,253 due to starvation and 16,747 resulting from bombing and shelling. These figures were presented as accurate at the Nuremberg war crimes trials. The generally agreed figure put together from subsequent examinations of all the registered deaths now ranges from 650,000 to 690,000. It seems this too was an underestimate, because many deaths were never registered. A recent detailed demographic study now puts the death toll at 800,000.[10]

On 27 January Hitler addressed a group of field marshals and commanding generals at the Wolf's Lair. His speech concentrated on the necessity of ideological indoctrination for soldiers. From now on, he said, all officers must support the principles of National Socialism. At one point he turned to the question of the loyalty of officers in the *Wehrmacht*, declaring:

My generals and admirals. If Providence should actually deny us victory in this battle of life and death, and if it is the will of the Almighty that this war should end with a catastrophe for the German people, then it should really be so that you, my generals and admirals, would gather around me with upraised swords to fight to the last drop of blood for the honour of Germany – I say, gentlemen, that is the way it should really be.[11]

Suddenly and unexpectedly he was interrupted. Manstein, sitting in the front row, called out, seemingly ironically: 'And so it shall be Mein Führer.'[12] There followed an awkward silence. It was well known that Hitler disliked unsolicited interventions during his speeches or at military meetings. Staring the errant Field Marshal straight in the face, Hitler replied: 'If that is the case, we can never lose this war, never, come what may.' Hitler then ended his speech and left the room, his body language displaying deep irritation.[13]

Manstein later claimed his impudent interjection had been mischievous, implying that Hitler's desire for a fight to the death was not shared by his top generals. After he left the room, Hitler sent an aide to summon Manstein to his private study for a chat. Hitler warned Manstein never to interrupt him ever again during a speech, adding: 'How would you like it if someone broke in while you were addressing your own subordinates?'[14]

In late January 1944, Hitler discussed the worsening situation in Italy with Goebbels. The propaganda minister criticized what he termed the 'lazy' and 'cowardly' Italians at length. He then claimed that just before his execution Count Ciano had confessed that Mussolini had given Germany's plans to attack Belgium to a Belgian diplomat in 1940. Hitler replied that this only showed the underlying duplicity of Mussolini.[15]

By now, the war in Italy remained a stalemate along the Gustav Line of heavily defended German fortifications. This ran eighty-six miles from north of where the Garigliano River flows into the Tyrrhenian Sea towards the east: the narrowest part of the Italian boot on a map. It barred the Allied route to Rome. German defence of the north of Italy was further assisted by the natural defence offered by the Apennine mountains. The Allies had advanced just seventy miles in the previous six months, constantly hampered by rain, mud and a very stubborn and effective German defence. The only way the Allies could hope to outflank the Gustav Line was by launching amphibious landings further north.

With the upcoming D-Day landings being prepared, the Allies could not apply the force of numbers required to break this deadlock. The pattern of the war in Italy between the Allies and the Germans now consisted of the Allies attempting to move forward laboriously, then facing well-timed German withdrawals further north to establish another defensive position.

In the west of Italy, just above the Gustav Line, the Allies decided the two best areas to establish a foothold further north – opening the way to capture Rome – were Anzio, thirty miles from Rome, and the famous Benedictine abbey (founded in 529) at Monte Cassino, which dominated the nearby town of Cassino. This was a pivotal German defensive position along the Gustav Line.[16]

General Mark W. Clark, the overall commander of the 5th American Army, supported by the British and Commonwealth 8th Army, decided to attack Monte Cassino, which was defended by the elite German 1st Parachute Division. Allied troops assaulted the German defenders at Monte Cassino four different times between 17 January and 18 May 1944. Such was the difficulty in capturing this German stronghold that the Allies nicknamed it 'Murder Mountain'.

The Allies faced several difficulties in capturing Monte Cassino. To begin with, they were not skilled in difficult mountain warfare, which favoured defence. It was also almost impossible to apply air, artillery and tank power in such treacherous mountainous terrain.

Added to this, the German troops, with experience of the bitter German-Soviet War, were much better suited to fighting a dogged war of attrition.

On 22 January 1944 American forces led by General John Lucas mounted a surprise landing by sea at Anzio and managed to establish a tiny and precarious bridgehead, but when the Americans tried to move inland, they encountered strong German defensive positions and had to pause.

Hitler was concerned the Anzio landing was the prelude to a major Allied assault on Rome. On 28 April, Albert Kesselring, the overall commander of German forces in Italy, received an urgent telegram from the Führer asking him to issue orders to his troops of the need for a 'fanatical will' to hold ground during the fighting. 'The battle must be fought,' Hitler added, 'in the spirit of holy hatred for the enemy who is conducting a pitiless war of annihilation against the German people.'[17]

In the second Allied assault on Monte Cassino – launched on 24 January – American and French troops landed north of the Gustav Line, then quickly moved inland across the flooded Rapido Valley, north of Monte Cassino. There followed extremely fierce fighting between the Allies and the German 5th Mountain Division. By 31 January, the second Allied assault had come to a shuddering halt, with French forces suffering most with 2,500 casualties.[18]

These two costly military failures to put boots on the ground in Italy north of the Gustav Line led the Allies to switch to their formidable air and artillery power. In the third assault on Monte Cassino – between 15–23 March 1943 – Allied air crews unleashed 992 tonnes of bombs and 195,000 artillery rounds, repeatedly bombing the historic monastery. The Allied claim that German troops were occupying the monastery was firmly refuted by the Abbot of the monastery in a filmed interview for Italian and German newsreels.

The rubble left behind by the devastating Allied bombing of the abbey had the unintended consequence of making German positions even more impregnable than before. German paratroopers managed to defend the town with tactical flair for eight more days. On 23 March the Allies suspended the offensive at Monte Cassino, prompting an Allied debate about military strategy. Churchill was scathing about the lack of movement north. Clark felt substantial reinforcements were required before another assault could be attempted on Monte Cassino. Consequently, the war in Italy remained at a stalemate for the time being.

On 30 January 1944 a recording of Hitler's traditional speech to mark the anniversary of his coming to power was broadcast on national radio. The Führer's voice sounded noticeably weak and often faltering. Hitler concentrated on his two familiar hatreds, international Jewry and Soviet Bolshevism, offering the following prediction of the outcome of the war: 'One thing is certain: there can only be one victor, and this will either be Germany or the Soviet Union. A victory by Germany means the preservation of Europe, the victory of Soviet Russia means its destruction.' In the event of a German defeat the 'extermination' of the German people would follow, he warned, a goal which was 'the openly admitted intention of international Jewry'. Germany was therefore fighting not just for its own survival, but for the preservation of European culture and the entire continent.

Hitler then ran through a series of his achievements over the previous eleven years of National Socialist rule, claiming he had established a classless National Community (*Volksgemeinschaft*), which was now 'immune to all attempts at Bolshevik infection'. As a good example of equality of opportunity under National Socialism since he came to power, he cited the fact that in the *Wehrmacht* '60 per cent of the young officer corps comes from enlisted men', most of whom originated from the lower middle class.

Looking forward to the rest of 1944, Hitler predicted that it would make the harshest demands on the home front: 'No matter how much the storm rages outside the walls of our fortress, it will one day subside like every tempest. From behind the dark clouds, the sun will come out again and shine on those who remained steadfast and unshakable.'[19]

On 7 February 1944 Roosevelt asked Stalin not to allow the Polish border issue to undermine future international cooperation between the Allies. He also promised American neutrality between the Polish government-in-exile and the Soviet Union in their discussions to resolve the unresolved issues between them. Replying, Stalin informed Roosevelt that the Polish government-in-exile was extremely hostile to the Soviet Union and incapable of friendly relations.[20]

On 22 February Churchill delivered a statement on the international situation in the House of Commons. To dispel Soviet mistrust of British policy towards Poland, Churchill said the British government had never guaranteed any Polish frontier. He then made it clear that the exact territorial settlement in Poland would be determined once the Allies came to a final agreement on all European territorial arrangements at the end of the war. Churchill then said he

[overleaf]
Hitler with the Hungarian regent Admiral Miklós Horthy.

fully sympathized with the Soviets' desire for security, as it was now certain that the Soviet Union would liberate Poland:

> Twice in our lifetime Russia has been violently assaulted by Germany. Many millions of Russians have been slain and vast tracts of Russian soil have been devastated as a result of repeated German aggression. Russia has the right of reassurance against future attacks from the West, and we are going all the way with her to see that she gets it, not only by the might of her arms but by the approval and assent of the United Nations.[21]

On 26 February the Polish government-in-exile refused to recognize the Curzon Line, as suggested by the British government, as Poland's new eastern frontier after the war. On 3 March, Stalin rejected new British proposals to negotiate with the Polish government-in-exile over the disputed Polish-Soviet border question.

On 9 February Otto Bene, a German intelligence agent in the Netherlands, sent a report to the German Foreign Ministry noting that 108,000 Jews had already left the country on transports to Auschwitz-Birkenau, and that the round-ups of Jews in the Netherlands were continuing. In Amsterdam a young, intelligent, German-born Jewish teenager called Anne Frank was hiding with her family in the secret annex of a building, where her father Otto worked, along the canal at Prinsengracht 263. In her diary, she discussed the dreadful fate of the Jewish people under Hitler's rule. On 11 April 1944 she asked:

> Who inflicted this on us? Who has set us apart from all the rest? Who has put us through such suffering? It is God who has made us the way we are, but it is also God who will lift us up again. In the eyes of the world, we are doomed, but if, after all this suffering, there are still Jews left, the Jewish people will be held up as an example. Who knows, maybe our religion will teach the world and all the people in it about goodness, and that is the reason, the only reason, we have to suffer.

In another entry, Anne noted bitterly: 'We've been told that anti-semitism has cropped up in circles where once it would have been unthinkable. This fact has affected us all very, very deeply.'

On 4 August 1944 the local police, with the assistance of the Gestapo, arrested Anne Frank and the seven others hiding in the annex. Anne was transferred to a prison and subsequently transported by train to Auschwitz-Birkenau with her sister Margot. In January 1945, they were both deported from there to the Bergen-Belsen concentration camp in Germany. Anne and Margot died of typhus a few weeks later. Except for their father Otto, none of the other residents who hid in the Amsterdam annex survived the war.[22]

The Allied bombing campaign over Germany intensified in the early months of 1944. Between 20 and 25 February, the US Army Air Force, supported by the RAF, launched what became known as 'Big Week' (codenamed Operation Argument). It was a joint daylight strategic bombing campaign dubbed 'the biggest Allied air battle of the entire war'.[23] More bombs were dropped during 'Big Week' (amounting to 22,000 tonnes) than the *Luftwaffe* dropped on London during the entire Blitz of late 1940.

During 'Big Week' the *Luftwaffe* had been lured into a full-scale air battle with the Allies. Because the *Luftwaffe* lost 262 fighter planes, including 100 pilots, it had to abandon its tactic of maximum defence of the German mainland. The Americans lost 226 bombers and 28 fighters, amounting to 2,600 aircrew overall. The RAF lost 131 bombers, but whereas Allied losses represented just 6.3 per cent of overall air strength, *Luftwaffe* losses were much more damaging to German air power overall.[24]

By early 1944, the *Luftwaffe* was in a state of existential crisis. Göring decided to enlist the help of the Armaments Ministry to boost aircraft production. The result was the creation by Albert Speer in March 1944 of the Fighter Staff (*Jägerstab*), a newly created Nazi air task force. Speer, however, was in the midst of a physical and nervous collapse and effectively on sickness leave during which time he fell out of favour with the Führer.

In Speer's enforced absence, Karl Saur and officials from the Armaments Ministry took new measures designed to raise German aircraft production to meet the Allied threat. Between February to September 1944 monthly aircraft production rose from 1,323 to 3,538 planes. This was achieved in three ways. First, by raising the hours worked per week in aircraft factories to a back-breaking seventy-two. Second, by offering extra rations of food, sweets, cigarettes, alcohol, even underwear and socks as incentives to German workers to work much harder. Third, by using concentration-camp inmates, including Hungarian Jews drafted in from Auschwitz-Birkenau, who were forced to work even longer hours, but for meagre rations.[25]

After a meeting of Reichleiters and Gauleiters in the Wolf's Lair on 24 February Hitler departed for the Berghof, while the bunkers in Rastenburg were further reinforced by concrete now that Soviet aircraft were within striking distance. Life at the Berghof did little to raise Hitler's flagging spirits. As one of his secretaries Traudl Junge later recalled: 'The forced gaiety, the light conversations from guests could not hide the disquiet which we felt in our hearts.' Eva Braun, who was also in residence at the Berghof, had not seen her partner for months. She was shocked by the deterioration in his health and appearance. 'He has become old and sombre,' she told Junge. When she playfully joked to Hitler about his now stooping posture, he replied: 'That's because I have heavy keys in my pocket. Besides I carry along a pack of troubles.'[26]

Others in Hitler's inner circle also expressed concern about the state of Hitler's health. His knees often trembled involuntarily if he stood on his feet too long. If he placed a cup on a saucer it was often heard repeatedly rattlling before it was out of his hand. Hitler was once again plagued by the painful stomach cramps and digestive problems that had dogged him before the war. Dr Morell urged him to go to bed much earlier, but as a life-long sufferer from insomnia this advice was ignored. The late to bed late to rise sleep pattern continued.

On 24 February Hitler gave his only public speech of 1944 to the party faithful at Munich's Hofbräuhaus on the anniversary of the proclamation of the foundation of the Nazi Party in 1920. Hitler refused to allow it to be recorded or broadcast on national radio. In a brief speech, he told his most loyal supporters that he believed more firmly than ever in ultimate German victory. He also promised major retaliation against London for the bombing raids on Germany.[27]

Between 26 and 28 February 1944 Hitler held diplomatic talks with the now wavering Romanian leader Marshal Antonescu at Schloss Klessheim. Antonescu suggested putting out peace feelers to the Western Allies, but Hitler dismissed this idea. Hitler then demanded Romania become involved in an occupation of Hungary, but Antonescu refused unless he was promised the return of territory which had been transferred to Hungary in 1940.

Hitler gave Antonescu an up-beat assessment of the current strength of the West Wall. The Anglo-American Allies, he felt, would face enormous difficulties if they attempted a continental invasion. Should it fail, Hitler felt it was doubtful they would try again:

> The shock effect on public opinion in England and America of
> such a failure, and the enormous losses which it would inevitably
> incur, could not be overemphasized and would in all probability
> represent a turning-point in the war. With one blow large forces

would become available which could be deployed in the East, not only for a stabilization of the Eastern Front, but for an offensive against the Russians.[28]

On 3 March 1944 Hitler held a meeting at the Berghof with the ever-loyal Goebbels. He found Hitler was irate with the Hungarian government after reading a letter sent by Admiral Horthy on 12 February which demanded the withdrawal of nine Hungarian army divisions from the Eastern Front. Hitler then told Goebbels about German intelligence reports indicating secret talks were going on between the Allies and various Hungarian diplomats. Hitler promised to bring Hungary under German 'protection' soon and install a pro-Nazi puppet government there.[29]

On 8 March Hitler issued 'Führer Order No. 11', which called for the creation of fortified defence areas on the Eastern Front. These strongholds would deliberately allow troops to be encircled, to tie up as much enemy strength for as long as possible. It signalled Hitler's acceptance of a defensive war on the Eastern Front, but also revealed a willingness to sacrifice huge numbers of German soldiers.[30]

On 16 and 17 March 1944 Hitler met a select group of members of the Bulgarian Regency Council at Schloss Klessheim. He criticized them for what he viewed as the slow pace of the persecution of Jews in Bulgaria. He then admitted his own 'ruthless handling of the Jews' had turned them into 'inexorable enemies' of Germany, but he argued Jews would have been his bitter enemies in any case, and, by totally excluding them, he had 'completely eliminated the danger to [German] morale they represented'.[31]

On 18 March 1944 Hitler gave what turned out to be his last newspaper interview. He spoke by telephone to the Berlin correspondent of the Swedish newspaper *Stockholms Tidningen*. The purpose of the interview was to deny a recent report in the Swedish press suggesting Hitler had approached King Gustav V of Sweden to act as an intermediary in peace negotiations with the Allies. Hitler then discussed King Gustav's involvement in the negotiations for an armistice between Finland and the Soviet Union. The aim of Molotov, the Soviet Foreign Minister, in these negotiations, Hitler said, was to place 'a noose around the victim's neck in order to be able to tighten it at the right time'. The final goal of Bolshevism, he added, was 'the extermination of the Finns'.

When asked what he thought of the offer by Britain and the United

[overleaf]
The deportation of Hungarian Jews in 1944.

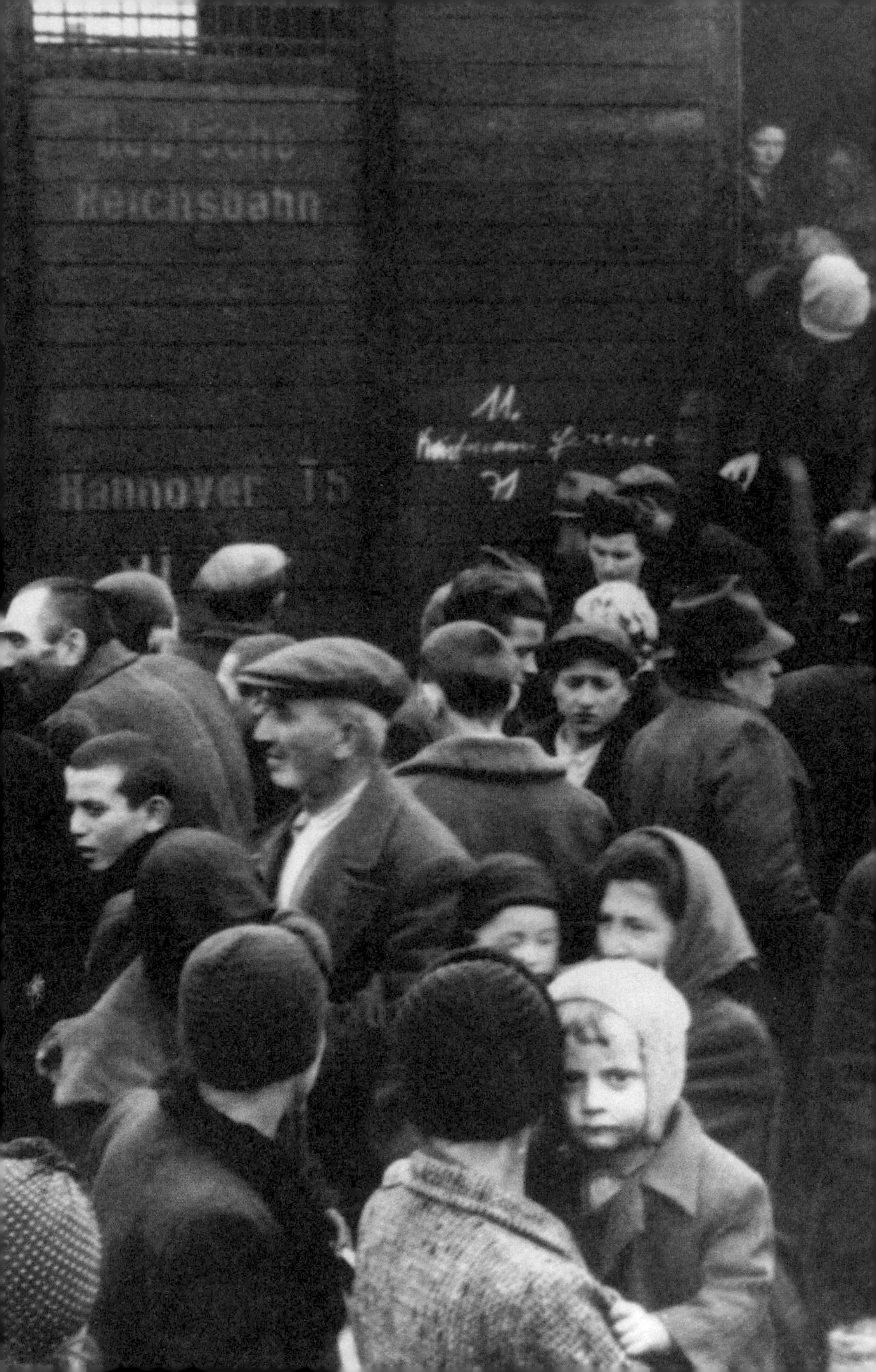
Reichsbahn
Hannover 15

States to act as a guarantor of a Soviet-Finnish armistice, Hitler dismissed it as a mere game-plan to make such an agreement more palatable to the Finns. The Anglo-Americans would not be able to restrain a victorious Soviet Union at the end of the war, he added. As for American guarantees in general, Hitler pointed out that Woodrow Wilson's famous 'Fourteen Points' were not respected during the Paris Peace settlement of 1919, and that the British guarantee to Poland in 1939 had ultimately proved utterly worthless.[32]

On the same day Miklós Horthy, the Hungarian regent – accompanied by his foreign and war ministers, plus his military Chief of Staff – arrived for talks with Hitler at Schloss Klessheim. Hitler greeted Horthy distantly, before asking to speak with him alone in his office with no advisers or interpreters present. Hitler then subjected the Hungarian regent to a daunting and bullying verbal attack, accusing him of double-dealing with the Allies, and of continuing to do nothing about the large numbers of Jews remaining in Hungary.

Because of all these alleged failings, Hitler told Horthy, he had already decided on a military occupation of Hungary. Hitler then demanded that Horthy needed to sign an agreement sanctioning this action straightaway. If Horthy refused, he said, German troops would invade. Horthy was further ordered to dismiss the 'unreliable' Prime Minister Miklós Kállay and replace him with the pro-German Döme Sztójay.

After listening to Hitler's bullying demands, Horthy angrily stood up from his chair, saying: 'If everything has been decided, there's no point staying any longer. I'm leaving.' He then walked briskly out of the room and demanded to be driven to his special train immediately. German Foreign Minister Ribbentrop, who was standing in the hall, said there had been an air-raid warning and Horthy couldn't leave. This was, of course, a delaying tactic. Ribbentrop then warned Horthy that if he didn't agree to the entry of German troops into his country, then he would be returning to Hungary as a German prisoner. Under this intimidation, Horthy finally agreed to install a pro-German puppet government, which became known as the Government of National Unity.[33]

On 19 March 1944, two divisions of the German army occupied Hungary. Their key aims were to forcibly keep Hungary in the Axis coalition and to eradicate Hungary's Jews. On 22 March Döme Sztójay, the right-wing former ambassador in Berlin, who was acceptable to Hitler, replaced Miklós Kállay as the Hungarian Prime Minister. He appointed two well-known antisemitic secretaries of state, László Endre and László Baky, to the Ministry of the Interior to assist in the proposed anti-Jewish measures. The German government appointed Edmund Veesenmayer as the new plenipotentiary in Hungary to supervise the anti-Jewish legislation. It gives us an insight into Hitler's all-consuming antisemitism that he decided to murder Hungary's 750,000 Jews while he was still embroiled in fighting a bitter defensive war against the Allies.

Since 1940 the Hungarian government had introduced a number of anti-Jewish measures, including the prohibition of marriages between Jews and Christians, the confiscation of Jewish-owned estates, and several orders for Jews to undertake forced labour. On 4 April 1944 all Jews in Hungary were required to wear the yellow star. SS and SD personnel were formed into the 600-strong Special Intervention Unit Hungary (*Sondereinsatzkommando Ungarn*).

The key figure behind the murder of the Hungarian Jews was Adolf Eichmann, who arrived in Budapest on 21 March 1944. He first of all set up his headquarters in the opulent Hotel Majestic, before acquiring a villa that was confiscated from a local Jew. Plans were soon drawn up to deprive Hungarian Jews of their remaining civil rights, and to confiscate their property and wealth. Jews were forbidden to own cars or even use public transport, their radios were removed and their phone lines cut off. Jews were also removed from all businesses, professions and government posts.

The mass murder of Hungarian Jews followed a four-stage process consisting of: concentration, ghettoization, deportation and murder. All these stages occurred with the full assistance and collaboration of the Hungarian police and local civil servants. Eichmann wanted to act quickly in order to avoid the sort of Jewish resistance that had occurred during the Warsaw Ghetto Uprising of 1943.

As part of the killing process, Hungary was divided into six numbered zones, matching the existing police districts. In each area, Jews were registered and concentrated. With a characteristic Nazi hatred of Jewish religious practices, Eichmann decided the round-ups of Hungarian Jews would begin on 16 April 1944, the day of the Jewish Passover. From that date until 3 July 1944 a total of 438,000 Hungarian Jews were summarily rounded-up, before being placed in sealed ghettos and other designated buildings dubbed 'yellow-star houses'.[34]

Eichmann planned to transfer every Hungarian Jew to the Auschwitz-Birkenau camp. Four train transports per day were scheduled, each carrying 12,000 Jews. This harrowing journey often took a week to complete. Hédi Fried, who travelled on one of those transports, later recalled: 'A hundred of us were pushed into each wagon, which normally held eight horses. We were tired, hungry, thirsty and rather apathetic. We allowed ourselves to be shoved in.'[35]

On 8 July 1944 the German Foreign Ministry was informed that 437,402 Hungarian Jews had been transported to Auschwitz-Birkenau. Of these 25 to 30 per cent were selected for forced labour and the rest were gassed immediately. On 9 July, the deportation trains were suddenly stopped on the orders of Horthy. By this time, however, only 150,000 to 200,000 Jews were still left alive in Budapest. The scale of the Hungarian genocide operation in 1944 exceeded even the brutal clearance of the Warsaw Ghetto between July and September 1942.[36]

On 21 March 1944 Manstein visited the Berghof to see Hitler. He asked Hitler to permit his battle-weary Army Group South to retreat over the River Dniester to form a new defensive line in Galicia. Hitler rejected this demand, then told Manstein that he held him personally responsible for the current difficulties of Army Group South. During a brief adjournment of the meeting, Hitler's adjutant Rudolf Schmundt told Hitler of Manstein's firm intention to resign if he was not permitted to retreat. When the talks resumed, Hitler offered Manstein some reinforcements drawn from the Western Front.

It was now clear that Hitler's relationship with Manstein had reached breaking point. On 30 March Hitler summoned Manstein to the Berghof and told him: 'I cannot use you in the South [as the commander of Army Group South].' Manstein replied: 'My Führer, please believe me when I say I will use all strategic means at my disposal to defend the soil on which my son lies buried.'[37] This made no difference. Manstein's glittering military career in the German army was over. On 2 April the loyal Nazi General Walter Model replaced Manstein and was also promoted to the rank of Field Marshal. At the same time, Army Groups South and A were renamed Army Groups North and South Ukraine to signal the symbolic but completely unrealistic aim of retaking Ukraine.

On 17 April Hitler made a rare public appearance in Germany when he attended the funeral in Munich of his loyal Gauleiter Adolf Wagner, who had suffered a stroke two years earlier which had incapacitated him. At the Nuremberg rallies of the 1930s it was Wagner who read out Hitler's opening proclamations. Hitler posthumously awarded him the German Order (*Deutscher Orden*), the highest decoration of the

Nazi Party, which had previously been awarded to the Reich Minister of Armaments Fritz Todt and to the leading SS figure Reinhard Heydrich.

Hitler celebrated his fifty-fifth birthday at the Berghof on 20 April 1944. In Berlin, Goebbels, as usual, organized several ceremonial events, including a special celebration in the State Opera House. This was attended by important figures in the army, state and party, and the Berlin Philharmonic Orchestra performed Beethoven's Eroica Symphony.[38]

On the German home front, the SD wrote a report in April entitled: 'Immoral Behaviour of German Women'. This noted that due to the extended length of the war, German women were now becoming more inclined to 'live it up sexually'. Wives of soldiers were singled out for special criticism for frequenting well-known bars where they reportedly met men and fraternized with foreign workers. One soldier received a letter from his wife in which she did not hold back her frustrated sexual feelings: 'I don't need to wait for you. I could have four men, if I wanted at any time. I've had enough [of a lack of sex]. I want it now too! I want to have a couple of strapping boys now.'[39]

On 22 and 23 April 1944 Mussolini met Hitler at Schloss Klessheim. The intention was to demonstrate to the world that Hitler and Mussolini's relationship was as strong as ever. It was Mussolini, very much the junior partner in status, who had surprisingly requested this meeting. For the first time, Hitler allowed Mussolini to speak at length. It proved a very awkward encounter. Mussolini expressed his dissatisfaction over the German seizure of the South Tyrol and Trieste, then he went further and complained about the flagging morale of Italian internees forced to work in Germany. He also pointed out the fact that recruitment to the new National Republican Army was difficult as potential soldiers feared they would be immediately shipped to Germany.

In reply, Hitler stressed Italian military recruits were required to train in Germany to toughen them up. He described Italian workers in Germany as 'lazy and communist' and mentioned that Italian troops fighting on the Eastern Front had been heard singing the left-wing anthem 'The Internationale'. Hitler made it clear to Mussolini that Italy had to continue to fight the Allies or Mussolini's regime would be crushed.[40] He then admitted he didn't know when an Allied invasion would occur, but British military activity indicated it would most likely come in the next six to eight weeks. Hitler felt the fate of Germany would be decided by the outcome of the invasion in the west: 'It is clear that a successful enemy offensive which succeeded in pushing through to Germany's industrial areas would bring about a decision.'[41]

On 26 April 1944 Hitler held a meeting with Goebbels, who noted in his diary afterwards:

> The Führer's hatred against the Jews has intensified even further. The Jews must be punished for their crimes against the European nations and in general against the entire cultured world. Wherever we can get hold of them, they should not escape retribution. The advantages of antisemitism do offset its disadvantages, as I've always said. All in all, a long-term policy in this war is only possible if one considers it from the point of view of the Jewish question.[42]

Meanwhile, the situation was worsening in the south of the Eastern Front. On 9 May 1944, the Red Army recaptured Sevastopol as part of the Crimean offensive. Humiliatingly, the German army was forced to flee the city by sea, under heavy air attack. Hitler's futile attempt to hold on to the Crimea had cost more than 57,500 German and Romanian lives, many of whom drowned during the hasty evacuation.[43] Hitler was nevertheless furious about the loss of the Crimea. General Erwin Jaenecke, the commander of the 7th Army, was blamed for the debacle and immediately dismissed. When the Soviet spring offensive paused, the German army had been pushed back in some sectors by as much as 600 miles.[44]

The Axis position in Italy was also coming under severe pressure. On 11 May 1944 the Fourth Battle of Monte Cassino began with 500,000 Allied troops drawn from ten different nations. Codenamed Operation Diadem, its aim was not only to break the stout German defence of the abbey, but to open the Liri Valley, the main route to Rome. The American 5th and the British 8th armies were supported by the Polish II Corps and the French Expeditionary Corps. The Allies faced the German 10th Army, supported by the poorly equipped Italian troops of the Salò Republic.

With these superior numbers, supported by devastating air and artillery power, the Allies finally broke the deadlock. On 18 May brave Polish troops – eager for revenge against Germans who had inflicted such terrible suffering on the Polish people – finally took Monte Cassino, forcing the German defenders to abandon it after fierce close fighting. It was the white and red Polish flag that flew above the ruins of the ancient abbey.

On 23 May, the Americans finally broke out of their Anzio bridge-head and forced the Germans into a headlong retreat. On 26 May, American General Mark Clark decided not to continue his drive northwards to encircle the bedraggled and retreating German 10th Army. That would have been the more sensible strategic option, but instead he moved his forces north-west to advance on Rome.

In a lengthy speech on 26 May Hitler spoke to officers involved in the newly instituted ideological training scheme for the *Wehrmacht* at the Platterhof Hotel, which was adjacent to the Berghof. Hitler praised the virtue of intolerance as a driving force in his ideology, before going on to emphasize how his leadership had helped to create a classless society in Germany.

In a remarkably revealing passage, Hitler spoke openly about the 'Final Solution'. The Jews were 'a foreign body' in the midst of the German people, he said, which had to be 'brutally and ruthlessly' extracted to ensure Germany's future survival as a nation: 'In removing the Jews, I eliminated in Germany the possibility of creating some sort of revolutionary core or nucleus bent on revenge.'

Hitler rejected the notion of dealing with the Jewish problem 'more humanly'. It was, he argued, a life-and-death struggle: 'If our opponents are victorious in this struggle, the German people will be eradicated. Bolshevism would slaughter millions and millions and millions of our intellectuals. Anyone not shot in the head would be deported. The children of the upper classes would be taken away and eliminated. This entire bestiality has been organized by the [Bolshevik] Jews.' Finally, he returned to his prophecy from 1939, which stated that in the event of a global war the Jews would be 'eradicated'. The audience reportedly applauded this. His sole aim, he concluded, in dealing with the so-called Jewish problem had been 'the maintenance of our race'.[45]

On 2 June Hitler ordered Field Marshal Albert Kesselring to abandon the Italian capital, because he felt that a bigger battle was looming in northern Europe. The Germans declared Rome an 'open city'. On 4 June American troops entered a largely empty Rome. Their commander Mark Clark had been determined to conquer it, mainly for reasons of personal vanity.[46] Rome's capture was poor compensation for the lost opportunity of encircling and capturing seven divisions of the German 10th Army, all of which had escaped north to take up new defensive positions. First, they moved to the Pisa–Rimini Line 150 miles north and then to the new Gothic Line north of the Arno River, thus ensuring the stalemate in Italy continued.

President Roosevelt in his radio 'fireside chat' said of the fall of Rome: 'The first of the Axis capitals is now in our hands. One up and two to go! It is perhaps significant that the first of these capitals to fall should have the longest history of all of them.' The victory had come 'at an excellent time, while our Allied forces are poised for another strike at Western Europe.'[47]

The four battles of Monte Cassino, plus the Anzio campaign and the capture of Rome, cost the Allies 105,000 dead, missing, wounded or captured.[48] German losses were estimated at 20,000 in total.[49] German dogged defence in Italy, coordinated by Albert Kesselring (dubbed 'Smiling Albert' by the Allies), exceeded even Hitler's expectations. Kesselring had bought the Germans time by fighting long, defensive battles and then ordering strategic withdrawals before his troops were encircled and captured.

D-Day occurred just two days after Rome fell. For Western historians D-Day (Operation Overlord) is the most famous military event in the entire Second World War. This is perfectly understandable, but something of a distortion to the overall picture. Despite enjoying overwhelming air superiority and a huge advantage in manpower and modern equipment, the Allied advance in the west was a slow, cautious and dogged struggle from D-Day to the end of the war.

The war in Western Europe was different in another important way from the German-Soviet War, because both sides fought in the west under the terms of the Geneva Convention. The horrific massacres inflicted by the German army and the SS *Einsatzgruppen* on the Eastern Front were – with a few exceptions – absent in the western theatre of war. German soldiers and airmen thought of their Western enemies as their racial equals, while they regarded their enemies in the east as heroic, but essentially subhuman. Similarly, the Allied soldier's contempt for Nazism was not based on a dislike of the German people or soldiers. As one typical American soldier put it: 'I didn't work up a great hate of the Germans. They were pretty good soldiers.'[50]

The lengthy planning for Operation Overlord began with the presentation of a report by a group using the acronym COSSAC (Chief of Staff to the Supreme Allied Commander), headed by Lieutenant-General Sir Frederick Morgan. The first draft of the invasion plan was presented at the secret Quebec Conference between 17 and 24 August 1943 and attended by Roosevelt and Churchill. Mackenzie King, the Canadian Prime Minister, hosted the event, but he was excluded from the secret military discussions. Various landing sites in northern France were outlined, with Normandy preferred, but at this early planning stage there was little detail on the size of the invading force required.[51]

Overlord took a more concrete shape from December 1943 after American Dwight D. Eisenhower was appointed as the Supreme Allied Commander. The D-Day amphibious landing (codenamed Operation Neptune) involved the Allied army, navy and air force. The aim was to establish a foothold in France first, then build up enough force to drive the Germans out of the country, thereby paving the way to Germany's defeat in Western Europe in the shortest possible time.

Four landing sites along the French coastline were seriously considered. Pas-de-Calais, the closest and narrowest point between Britain and France, was the obvious choice. It offered a quick route to the Netherlands and the German border. But it was rejected, because it was felt this was where the Germans would locate their best troops and it had the strongest defensive fortifications. Brittany and the Cotentin Peninsula were also considered, but they too were disregarded. The terrain there might allow the Germans a good chance to cut off the Allied advance. Normandy was then investigated. Not only was it the area least likely to be heavily defended by the Germans, but it was also within range of Allied airpower. It had no port facilities, but its long stretches of beach were considered ideal to facilitate a multi-pronged landing. It was Normandy that was finally selected for the D-Day landings.

The Allies planned to land on five beaches along a fifty-mile stretch of the Normandy coast. They named the beaches Utah, Omaha, Gold, Juno and Sword. The Americans would land at Utah and Omaha, the British at Gold and Sword, and the Canadians at Juno. The area of the proposed Allied landing was defended by the German 7th Army, commanded by General Friedrich Dollmann. Its soldiers were either very young or relatively old and many were on leave, mostly recovering from wounds or illnesses contracted on the Eastern Front. The 7th Army had been responsible for the coastal defence of Normandy and Brittany since 1941. These troops were not exactly the weakest link of the German army, but they were certainly vulnerable to a well-equipped army, with massive air support.

The lack of port facilities in Normandy was a real impediment to the successful execution of the Allied invasion plan. In northern France the nearest ports to the landing sites were Cherbourg and Le Havre, but both of these were in German hands and heavily defended.

[overleaf]
Dwight D. Eisenhower, Supreme
Commander of the Allied Expeditionary
Force in Europe.

There was little chance of capturing either of them intact. In the short term this lack of a serviceable shipping port would be overcome by the ingenious creation of two huge, floating, portable 'Mulberry Harbours'. These were floated across the English Channel and their creation was a remarkable feat of British engineering. They were to be used temporarily until a suitable port was captured, with Cherbourg – the nearest to the invasion area – highlighted as the first key target. Unfortunately, one of the Mulberry Harbours, constructed near Omaha Beach, was destroyed during a huge storm on 19 June.[52]

In the weeks leading up to the D-Day landings the Allies tried to trick the Germans into believing the intention was to land at Pas-de-Calais. This diversion plan was called Operation Fortitude. It involved creating in Kent and Sussex a fictional US 1st Army Group, located directly opposite Pas-de-Calais, complete with dummy tanks and vehicles. The supposed commander of this fictitious army group was General George Patton. False radio messages were even sent out in his name, giving details of the supposed invasion location. Secret service agents added to the subterfuge. It's clear German intelligence was successfully duped as Germany's military commanders put their strongest defence forces in Pas-de-Calais.[53]

Field Marshal Bernard Montgomery ('Monty') was the commander-in-chief of the Allied ground forces (called the 21st Army Group). Two other British officers – Air Chief Marshal Trafford Leigh-Mallory and Admiral Bertram Ramsay – commanded the air and naval operations, respectively. The armed forces involved in the Normandy landings were the American 1st Army, commanded by General Omar Bradley; the British 2nd Army, led by General Miles Dempsey; and the 3rd Canadian Infantry Division, with Major General Rod Keller in command. The initial D-Day landings involved 156,715 Allied troops. Of these 24,000 were airborne troops and 132,715 landed on the beaches: 75,215 British and Canadians, and 57,500 Americans. In addition, 195,700 naval crew were also assigned to give support to the landings.[54]

Hitler gave the task of repelling this invasion to two of his most experienced military commanders: Field Marshal Gerd von Rundstedt, the Supreme Commander West (*Oberbefehlshaber West* or *OB West*), had overall command of three army groups: Army Group B (7th and 15th armies, plus the 6th Panzer Army); Army Group G (1st and 19th armies), based in the south under the command of General Johannes Blaskowitz; and Army Group H (1st Parachute Army and 25th Army); as well as Panzer Group West, which had no control over the actions of Navy Group West or the *Luftwaffe* which was required for a coordinated defence of the coastal areas.

The second key German commander was the famous Field Marshal Erwin Rommel ('The Desert Fox'), who was relocated from northern Italy in December 1943 to take command of Army Group B, based in northern France. Hitler selected him initially to improve the western coastal defences (known as the West Wall). When Rommel arrived only 1.7 million mines had been laid there, but by May 1944 there were 4 million of them and a further half a million beach obstacles. Rommel was given a great deal of freedom of action, reporting directly to Hitler, even though Rundstedt was supposedly in overall command of Army Group B.[55] Rundstedt suspected that Hitler had sent Rommel to France to deliberately create a rivalry between the two German commanders and that he was overall commander in name only.

Rommel and Rundstedt held different views on how best to deal with the predicted Allied invasion. Both thought the main attack area would be in Pas-de-Calais and located the bulk of their defences there. Rommel, however, was convinced that the Allied attack must be stopped at the beaches or else the Allies would establish a firm bridgehead then break out of it and triumph. Rundstedt disagreed, arguing the decisive battle would not be fought on the beaches at all, but far behind the French coast. To this end, he decided the bulk of German tanks should be held in a strong central reserve ready to counter-attack the Allies as they moved inland from the coast.[56]

The exact number of German troops in the western theatre at the time of the D-Day landings is notoriously difficult to establish. The most reliable estimate now is that there were 865,000 troops overall, numbering 60 divisions based in France and the Netherlands, with a further 18 divisions stationed in Denmark and Norway. In addition, the *Luftwaffe* had 326,000 personnel, with a further 102,000 attached to the navy, plus 100,000 Waffen-SS and police personnel. In total, almost 1.4 million men, but these forces were defending the 2,000 miles of coastline stretching from the Netherlands to the Mediterranean.

At sea, the German navy (*Kriegsmarine*) was no match for the Allied navies at all. German Navy Group West (*Marinegruppenkommando West*), under the command of Admiral Walter Hennecke, did not have a single battleship or heavy cruiser available. There were thirty-one S-boats or Swift Boats, which were basically light torpedo craft. Between them they had just 124 torpedoes. The Germans had only fourteen U-boats in the range of the Normandy beaches on D-Day.

In comparison, on the morning of the D-Day landings, the Allied invasion armada numbered a staggering 6,939 vessels from eight different navies, including 1,213 warships, 4,127 landing craft and 277 minesweepers. In sum, the Allies enjoyed complete naval superiority.

The situation in the air was even more favourable for the Allies. The 3rd *Luftwaffe* Air Force was commanded by Field Marshal Hugo Sperrie, although overall command resided nominally with Hermann Göring but he remained in his Carinhall estate outside Berlin. The *Luftwaffe* had suffered heavy losses of fighter planes during the early months of 1944 during engagements over Germany and on the Eastern Front. On the day of the D-Day landings, the *Luftwaffe* had 90 bombers and 70 fighters in the air, facing 3,134 Allied aircraft, with 2,434 fighters and 700 bombers. As backup, the Allies had a further 9,000 planes, making an overall total of 12,000 aircraft. This amounted to complete air superiority at a massive ratio of almost 20 to 1.[57]

In Britain, weather forecasting played a crucial role in finalizing the date of the D-Day landings. On 4 June, Scottish-born Group Captain James Stagg, an RAF meteorologist and chief weather forecaster to General Dwight D. Eisenhower, recommended that Operation Overlord be postponed from 5 to 6 June, because he predicted the weather would be far more favourable then. Eisenhower decided to trust the accuracy of Stagg's weather forecast. As his Chief of Staff Walter Bedell Smith put it: 'It's a gamble, but it's a gamble worth taking.'[58]

On 4 June 1944 German weather forecasters informed Rommel of rising winds, choppy water and high tides in the English Channel until later in the month, which led them to believe the Allied landings would not occur until 19 June at the earliest. It was for this reason that Rommel decided to leave his command headquarters in La Roche-Guyon to travel by car to his detached house in Herrlingen, near Ulm, in the state of Württemberg-Baden. The purpose was to spend time with his wife Lucia on her fiftieth birthday. He had bought her a pair of stylish Parisian shoes as a present. After his wife's birthday lunch, Rommel then intended to visit Hitler at the Berghof to try and persuade him to increase the number of tanks and mortars in Normandy. 'The most urgent problem,' he noted in his diary, 'is to win the Führer over by personal conversation.'[59]

On the overcast morning of 6 June 1944 Allied troops landed on the five beaches in Normandy. It was a remarkable spectacle. The horizon was filled with ships and landing craft as far as the eye could see. The naval artillery bombardment was utterly deafening. The time designated for 'H-hour' was between 6 a.m. and 7.30 a.m. The Allies had estimated that casualties were likely to be very high on the first day.

The British met very little resistance as they landed 28,845 men on Sword Beach. As the easternmost landing area, it was strategically important due to its proximity to the ancient city of Caen, a key road hub to the rest of France. On one of the landing craft a company commander read out some stirring passages from Shakespeare's *Henry V* through a megaphone.[60] The British soon brought twenty-one amphibious tanks ashore and were then able to fight a combined arms battle to get off the beach. The 8,000 German defenders were composed of poorly equipped infantry with no artillery or tanks.[61]

The Canadians landed 21,400 troops on Juno Beach after a bumpy landing in rough seas. They met some stiff German resistance with bullets zipping all around them from the heavily fortified defensive positions. It was only after tanks and heavy artillery guns came ashore that the situation gradually improved. The Canadian advance was greatly assisted by skilled marksmen who made up 30 per cent of the Canadian landing force. Under heavy artillery and sniper fire, German resistance melted away. The Canadians swiftly linked up with British troops on Gold Beach to their right to form the central basis of the Allied bridgehead.[62]

On Gold Beach, the British landed 24,970 troops, also in very rough waters. There was some heavy tracer and machine-gun fire as the troops came ashore but their own deadly accurate naval and artillery weapons soon nullified the German defenders. The high-quality British commandos, using tanks and heavy armour, quickly moved off the beach and pushed inland, capturing Bayeux on the following morning.[63]

The landing by 34,250 mostly inexperienced American troops on Omaha Beach was not only the toughest of all the five Allied landings, but by far the most dramatic. This was the most heavily defended beach of all. Its primary strategic importance was that it lay between Gold and Utah beaches. Linking up with troops from those landing sites was critical in the formation of an impregnable Allied bridgehead.

The Omaha Beach landing has since featured in such Hollywood films as *The Longest Day* and *Saving Private Ryan*. Images of zipping gun fire, blood-filled water, immobile corpses and brave soldiers have elevated this landing to an almost legendary status. They gave the impression that every beach landing on D-Day was like that, but in fact

[overleaf]
US Soldiers preparing to land on Omaha Beach on D-Day 6 June 1944.

WORLD'S LARGEST EVENING NET SALE

The Eve

NO. 19,455   LONDON, TU

Monty is Leading the Gre

ALLIES INVAD

4,000 Ships and Thousand
Our Army Across Channel

WE DRIVE 10 MILES INLAND: HITLER THERE

A**N ARMADA OF 4,000 SHIPS, WITH SEVERAL THOUSAND SMALLER CRAFT, ALL BACKED BY 11,000 FRONT-LINE AIRCRAFT, TO-DAY CROSSED THE CHANNEL TO INVADE FRANCE.**

Mr. Churchill gave this news in the Commons to-day, three hours after an Allied communique —at 9.01 a.m.—had given the official news for which the world had been anxiously waiting— the invasion of Western Europe.

This is what the Allied communique said:

"**Under the command of General Eisenhower, Allied naval forces, supported by strong air forces, began landing Allied armies this morning on the northern coast of France.**"

As a supplement to this communique it was announced that General Montgomery is in command of the Army group carrying out the assault. This Army group includes British, Canadian and U.S. forces.

Later, it was officially revealed that the landings took place in Normandy between 6 a.m. and 8.15 a.m.

Shore Batteries Largely Quelled

Mr. Churchill, besides giving the invasion armada figures, told the Commons :

"**Massed airborne landings have been successfully effected behind enemy's lines. Landings on beaches are proceeding at various points at the present time. The fire of shore batteries**

A BIRD'S-E
INVASION VIE

I SAW THE ARM
FROM THE AI

From TOM DOWNF " Evening News " Reporter with the R

A**T** dawn to-day grim-fa fantrymen who for had lain hidden in woo villages of England, storm beaches in Northern Fran

From the radio operato of I plane I had seen man of the invasion fleet prepa sail. They were in a round which we circled times.

There were rows and ships, stretching away un faded into the haze which m and air merge into a back of blue

FULL VICTORY
—NOTHING LESS

EISENHOWER'S CALL
TO "CRUSADERS"

ing News

JUNE 6, 1944   ONE PENNY

BLACKOUT 10.57 p.m. to 5.0 a.m.
Moon rises 9.10 p.m.
Moon sets 6.31 a.m.

Assault on Europe
E FRANCE
of Other Craft Take
1,000 Planes

ST MALO

JERSEY

LA VIRE

BARFLEUR

CHERBOURG

ATTLE WILL GROW IN SCALE AND INTENSITY

remier's Glowing Confidence In Commons Statement To-day

R. CHURCHILL began his Commons statement to-day on the invasion by apologising for his absence earlier. Questions, he said, nt more rapidly than expected. He went on :

The House should, I think, take formal cognisance of the liberation of Rome by the Allied armies under the mmand of General Alexander, with General Clark, of United States Services, and General Oliver Leese, in mmand of the Fifth and Eighth Armies respectively.

his is a memorable and glorievent which rewards the nce fighting of the last five

---

SKY FILLED WITH PLANES FOR HOURS

"NOTHING LIKE IT BEFORE"

THE fiercest blitz of all time on the Continent was launched from Britain hour after hour throughout the night and to-day, smashing targets before the actual landings began, then giving all-out support to our landings.

From the South-East Coast came the report : "Nothing like it has been seen before. Aircraft seemed to be pouring out in enormous strength."

The attacks have been going on almost without stopping. Since last night our planes were still going out at noon to-day.

Across the East Coast, too, strong forces of Allied bombers went out, and there was great fighter activity.

Transport channels over Northern France were pounded throughout the night by Dutch Mitchells and R.A.F., Polish and Australian Mosquitoes of the R.A.F. 2nd Tactical Air Force.

Smoke Screens Laid

Attacks were concentrated on roads, railways, bridges, embankments, cuttings and junctions, and on other points in the transport network over a huge area where traffic blocks would be a nuisance to the enemy.

There was a large amount of cloud over France, and a number of the Mitchells did not bomb.

Mosquitoes nearly all found their targets. Pilots reported successful attacks on a convoy, rail and road junctions, and parked vehicles.

"There was very little movement on the roads," said one pilot. "Only the odd small convoy—probably the rations coming up."

R.A.F. Bostons were engaged in smoke-laying operations over the English Channel.

WE SECURE 2 BEACHHEADS

British and Canadians have secured beachheads at two points at least, and dug in.— Official.

MONTY : "WE ARE A TERRIFIC TEAM"

General Montgomery, on his eve of battle speech to war correspondents said : "I personally have absolute and complete confidence in the outcome.

"The party is in first-class shape to win the match."

He believed Rommel would aim at defeating operations on the beaches.

"We are a great allied team —a terrific allied team. The integration of the British Empire and America going out to battle together. I don't think any other two nations could have done it."

"I don't know when the war is going to end, but I don't believe the Germans can go on much longer with this business.

"The German soldier is terribly good, but I don't think the German general is as good as he used to be. He has been on the defensive a very long time, and I believe it must affect his mentality."

LANDINGS ON 80-MILE FRONT
—Berlin

German radio reported furious land and sea battles on an eighty mile front from Trouville to Barfleur on the tip of the Cherbourg Peninsula. Great masses of Allied airborne troops dropped deep behind German lines.

"WE LAND ON ISLANDS OFF FRANCE"

Allies gained foothold on several islands off coast of France.—German radio.

TIVOLI TAKEN, SAYS ALGIERS

Algiers radio reported French

Omaha was the exception. The German defenders were in concrete protected positions in a natural circular area of steep hills overlooking the beach, which explains why this was the most difficult landing area.

The inexperienced American troops landed in choppy seas, and twenty-eight of their thirty-one state-of-the-art Sherman tanks were launched too far from shore and promptly sank. This left those struggling ashore to face fierce German artillery bombardment and rapid machine-gun fire. Within minutes Omaha Beach was littered with American corpses and the sea was bright red. As one soldier later recalled, soldiers were screaming and crying out: 'If you stopped to help a guy, then there were two casualties not one. Because the moment you stopped you got shot.'[64]

At one point, Omar Bradley, the US commander, seriously considered evacuating his troops. It was the timely intervention of American and British naval destroyers – sailing dangerously close to the beach and firing huge naval guns with deadly accuracy – that saved the troops from obliteration and undoubtedly turned the tide. American troops were soon able to fight their way off the beach and the Omaha bridgehead was solidified over the next three days.[65]

The 23,250 American troops who landed on Utah Beach on the eastern foot of the Cotentin Peninsula were the luckiest of all Allied landing forces. Not only was the weather tranquil there, but the German army surprisingly had not deployed enough troops to defend it even though it was near the vital port of Cherbourg. The Allies were greatly assisted by troops of the 101st Airborne Division who were able to secure the flank of the advance up the beach. The defending forces, hopelessly outnumbered, were soon in disarray.[66]

By the end of D-Day, all five landing areas in Normandy were in Allied hands. Airborne troops had also secured the flanks of the invading force. By 12 June the soldiers who had landed on the five beaches linked up to form a solid bridgehead. The Second Front in Western Europe which Stalin had been calling for since 1941 had now finally been established. The two leading German army commanders Wilhelm Keitel and Alfred Jodl both agreed the situation in Normandy was extremely serious. They both felt that if the Allies succeeded in fighting their way out of their bridgehead, then France would be lost.[67]

Overall, D-Day went far more smoothly than the Allied planners had anticipated. A total of 75,215 British and Canadians, 57,500 Americans and 23,000 airborne troops had all made it ashore. By 15 June, five new airfields had been built within the Allied beachhead.

[previous pages]
The (London) *Evening News* reports the
D-Day landings.

A further seven would follow. The much-vaunted German beach obstacles were not in sufficient numbers to prevent the landings. Although often underappreciated, the Allied naval forces played a pivotal role, not only in the landings, but in clearing up the minefields on the beaches, supporting troops with devastating naval gunfire, which often destroyed enemy artillery, and supplying the landed troops with supplies of food, ammunition and equipment.

Allied casualty figures on D-Day were originally estimated at 10,000, with 2,500 killed. This figure is now regarded as an underestimate. The US National D-Day Memorial in Bedford, Virginia, has undertaken detailed research into D-Day casualties. Its lead researcher Carol Tuckwiller has confirmed that 4,414 Allied personnel were killed, with 2,499 of those American and 1,915 from the other nations involved. All these servicemen are given a bronze plaque within the memorial. These figures are now regarded as the most accurate estimate of the Allied fatalities on D-Day. One of the difficulties in establishing a definitive Allied death toll is that most of those listed as 'missing' were swept out to sea and their bodies were never found.[68] The vast majority of those who were killed perished as they landed on the beaches. There were nineteen Americans from the city of Bedford, Virginia, killed on Omaha Beach alone. They became known as the 'Bedford Boys'. It was the highest loss in any one American community, and it explains why the US Congress decided to locate its D-Day memorial there. Due to a lack of reliable records, the German casualties have been estimated between 4,000 and 9,000 killed, wounded or missing, although it now seems that the actual German death toll on D-Day could have been as low as 1,000.[69]

The Allied landings amounted to a disastrous failure of German military leadership and intelligence. First news of the airborne landings in Normandy was reported by Rundstedt to the German High Command at 3 a.m. Three hours later another German report highlighted Normandy as the key landing area. Hitler had not gone to bed until 3 a.m. He was asleep when the invasion was happening and apparently did not wake up until 10 a.m. He reacted remarkably calmly to the news, initially dismissing the landings in Normandy as a diversion from what he thought would be a second and larger invasion at Pas-de-Calais.

In the afternoon Hitler met the new Hungarian Prime Minister Döme Sztójay at Schloss Klessheim. General Walter Warlimont, who was present, noticed that Hitler 'put on an act' by behaving as if nothing

[overleaf]
The town of Oradour-sur-Glane, the scene of a brutal German massacre on 10 June 1944.

significant was happening. In a broad Austrian accent, he said to his Hungarian guests, 'So, we're off.' He told Sztójay that he had supreme confidence in Germany's 'ultimate victory'.[70]

In Britain, Winston Churchill gave a brief statement to the House of Commons on 6 June, saying: 'I can state to this House that this operation is proceeding in a thoroughly satisfactory manner. Many dangers and difficulties which appeared at this time last night to be extremely formidable are behind us. The passage of the sea has been made with far less loss than we apprehended.'[71]

On 10 June, with the attention of the world still focused on the battle raging in Normandy, yet another appalling German war crime was committed. The small French village of Oradour-sur-Glane, near Limoges, north of Toulouse, was completely destroyed by German soldiers, commanded by Adolf Diekmann, from a battalion of the 2nd Waffen-SS Panzer Division, *Das Reich*. This horrific massacre was a reprisal for the capture of a Waffen-SS officer Helmut Kämpfe on the previous day by some French resistance fighters. Members of the SS detachment were composed of Germans and collaborationists from Alsace, aged between seventeen and twenty-five.

German soldiers first sealed off the entire village, then ordered its inhabitants to assemble in the main square, ostensibly to have their identity papers inspected. The villagers duly gathered. Then the men were led inside six barns, which were set on fire. Anyone who came out

alive was killed by machine-gun fire. Only five men from the village survived. About 245 females were marched to the local church and locked inside it. Of these, 207 were children. A series of incendiary grenades were set off inside the church. Again, those who attempted to escape were mown down by machine guns. Only one woman, Marguerite Rouffanche, somehow survived, even though she was shot nine times.

The transformation of this peaceful little French village into a smoking ruin was truly shocking. In total, 642 men, women and children were killed in the Oradour-sur-Glane massacre. Almost a third of these innocent victims were children. The official report by the ruthless SS-*Das Reich* division claimed that the slaughter was a justified response to French Resistance activity in the area. After the war, the French leader Charles de Gaulle decided that the village should never be rebuilt and that it would serve as a permanent reminder of the brutality of the German occupation of France from 1940 to 1945.[72]

On 15 June 1944 the German government responded to the D-Day landings by dropping on London the new V-1 flying bombs ('V' for *Vergeltungswaffe* or 'vengeance weapon'). There was no clear understanding of what damage these V-1s might inflict on the British civilian population. Hitler viewed them as 'miracle weapons' that could turn the tide of the air war back in Germany's favour. The fuel in each flying bomb was calculated to run out when it reached its target area, at which point it fell to the ground and exploded. Due to the noise it made in the air, the V-1s were nicknamed by the British press as 'Doodlebugs'.

A total of 6,384 V-1s were fired from launch ramps and 16,000 from aircraft between June 1944 and March 1945, but only a third ever reached their targets. Many were brought down by fighter planes, barrage balloons and anti-aircraft fire. The top speed of the V-1 was 375 mph and a fighter plane could travel much faster.[73]

Churchill gave a report in the Commons on the impact of the V-1 Campaign on 6 July 1944. He explained that the British government was initially reluctant to give details on the German flying bomb attacks until 'we knew more about them and were able to measure their effect'. Churchill revealed that about 2,750 of these bombs had been released from France, but a great number never made it across the Channel or were shot down. So far, 2,752 British people had been killed and 8,000 injured in the attacks.[74]

It soon became obvious that the V-1 had done very little to dent

The German V-2 rocket.

British morale. They were certainly not the 'miracle weapons' German propaganda claimed. More hope was placed in a second associated weapon: the V-2 (technical name *Aggregat* 4). Powered by a liquid propellent rocket engine, this was really the world's first long-range ballistic missile. Each V-2 was launched fifty miles into the air on a planned trajectory, with four rudders on its tail fins, to reach its assigned target. It was brought into service in September 1944 and developed by Wernher von Braun, who would later become a key figure in the Apollo moon-landing programme.

The first two V-2 rockets aimed at Britain exploded on 8 September 1944, killing two people, although the German government did not tell the German public about the V-2s until 8 November 1944. An estimated 2,754 civilians were killed and 6,523 were injured in London from the V-2 attacks.

The German V-weapons project was hugely expensive, costing the equivalent of $40 billion in today's money. The treatment of slave labour during their production was so severe that more workers died of over-work producing these rockets than were killed by their use. These weapons made no difference whatsoever to Germany's fortunes in the war. The V-1s and the V-2s were an expensive irrelevance.[75]

On 26 June 1944, in the large coffee room of the Hotel Plattenhof, Hitler gave a speech to about a hundred leading figures in the war industries. Industrialists had recently been complaining to Albert Speer about the increasing interference of Nazi Party functionaries in war production. German industry had not been nationalized under Hitler's rule, but there were now fears that this might happen in the future.

Hitler's speech to the assembled businessmen on this day was largely based on notes provided by Albert Speer, who wanted Hitler to reassure industrialists that private capitalist enterprise would continue to flourish in post-war Germany. 'I do not care about peace today,' Hitler told the industrialists. 'I only care about victory! If we win this war, the German economy will receive such gigantic orders that it will be able to continue mass production in any event.'

Hitler then stressed his business policies had always been directed towards helping industry to thrive: 'The basis for all real higher development, indeed for the future development of all mankind will therefore be found in the encouragement of private initiative.' After victory, he promised, the 'greatest geniuses' of German businesses would thrive and enjoy a huge economic boom.

Speer noticed these seemingly reassuring statements received hardly any applause from the assembled group of industrialists. This led Hitler to adopt a much more strident and provocative approach in the latter part of his speech. He warned that in the event of a German defeat, the Soviet Union would wipe out capitalist business and businessmen, and that under Stalin's rule industrialists would face the stark choice of killing themselves, being shot in the head or being sent to Siberia.

Hitler next promised Germany's current difficulties on the battlefield would be overcome with one last superhuman effort: 'Whoever does not have a hard time in life cannot really rejoice in what he has accomplished. The birth certificate of a new empire is always written in blood, in blood and misery.' Victory would come, he said, because the 'German soldier is the best!' The Allies would be forced back: 'Let us wait and see whether they will conquer France.' Hitler ended his speech on a surprisingly religious note:

> Perhaps I am not what they call a sanctimonious hypocrite or
> pious. I am not that. But deep in my heart, I am a religious man;
> that is, I believe that the man who, in accordance with the natural

Two of the leading Soviet military commanders, Konstantin Rokossovsky (left) with Georgy Zhukov.

laws created by God, bravely fights and never capitulates in this world – that this man will not be abandoned by the Lawgiver. Instead, he will in the end receive the blessings of Providence.[76]

On 23 June a massive Soviet offensive on the Eastern Front began. It was planned to run in conjunction with the Battle of Normandy. It was codenamed Operation Bagration, after General Pyotr Bagration, the Russian prince who was mortally wounded at Borodino in 1812, one of the bloodiest battles of the Napoleonic Wars.

During the spring of 1944 the German High Command (OKH) had been expecting a Soviet summer offensive on the Eastern Front, but they predicted that it was most likely to come from north-western Ukraine, opposite Army Group North Ukraine, with the aim of capturing Poland, Romania and the Balkans, before moving to recapture the Baltic Coast. This seemed logical to the Germans, as the terrain in Ukraine was largely free of natural obstacles and favourable for tank advances.

German intelligence confirmed this assessment by observing a large proportion of Soviet tanks and bombers were located in this area. However, this was part of an elaborate Red Army deception which included fictional radio messages and the movement of troops, tanks and aircraft. To meet this perceived threat, the German High Command transferred most of the tanks attached to Army Group Centre to Army Group North Ukraine.[77]

The *Stavka* (Soviet High Command) concluded that Army Group North Ukraine, with its strong Panzer divisions, was now the strongest German force left on the Eastern Front. Soviet commanders had been impressed by its vigorous defence of the River Dnieper earlier in 1944. It was thought that the terrain in the Baltic, occupied by Army Group North, strongly favoured defence, too. This meant the best place for the Soviets to attack was the front occupied by Army Group Centre, known as the Byelorussian Balcony: a bulge in the front line, containing the vital communication line of Vitebsk–Mogilev–Bobruisk, plus the important railway hub of Orsha and the capital city Minsk.

The Byelorussian countryside with its forests, rivers and marshes was not really ideal for large mechanized operations, but it was decided by Soviet military planners that it was equally tough for attackers and defenders. A big advantage for the Soviets was the well-established partisan movement operating there, numbering 270,000 men. They were constantly disrupting German supply lines by blowing up trains, trucks and armoured vehicles, blocking roads with felled trees, and assassinating German troops and collaborators. Army Group Centre relied heavily for their supply chain on 110,000 Soviet rail workers, many of whom were secretly collaborating with the Soviet partisans.

On 20 May 1944, *Stavka* agreed on a sequenced cascade of Soviet summer offensives. First, an attack on Finland to knock it out of the war (launched on 9 June, which was initially unsuccessful). Second, a major assault on Army Group Centre, located in the Byelorussian Balcony. Third, an offensive in northern Ukraine in the direction of Army Group North Ukraine in front of Lvov. Fourth, an assault against Army Group South Ukraine, with the intention of knocking Romania out of the war, then threatening Army Groups E and F, currently occupying Greece and Yugoslavia, respectively.[78]

This was not a typical Soviet sweeping offensive across the whole front. Instead it concentrated on achieving a breakthrough in one sector, before moving on to the next. The first phase involved simultaneous thrusts at the flanks of Army Group Centre's defence of the Byelorussian Front, in the areas of Vitebsk, Bobruisk and Mogilev, before moving on to capture Minsk.

Army Group Centre, now commanded by the zealous Hitler loyalist Field Marshal Ernst Busch, was not prepared for such a gigantic Soviet offensive. Busch was generally regarded as an unimaginative plodder better at defence than attack. Once the most fearsome front-runner during the early *Blitzkrieg* victories of the German army in the Soviet Union in 1941, by the summer of 1944 Army Group Centre was in steep decline, full of immobile foot soldiers: with forty-six primarily infantry divisions, just one Panzer army and no independent larger Panzer division. In total, it contained 486,000 combat troops, plus 400,000 support staff.[79]

Army Group Centre had just 118 tanks and 377 assault guns. The low proportion of tanks to assault guns was a recognition that it was now primarily a static defensive force. For air cover, it relied on sixty-one fighters.[80] The key armies attached to Army Group Centre were: the 3rd Panzer Army (its title somewhat misleading, because it now contained no tanks at all), commanded by Georg-Hans Reinhardt and supported by the 2nd Army, led by Walter Weiss; the 4th Army under Kurt von Tippelskirch; and the 9th Army, with Hans Jordan in command. In support, and in case of emergency, was the Army Group Reserve, including the 20th Panzer Division, the only tank unit attached to Army Group Centre.

The Soviets had assembled a huge concentration of military power for Operation Bagration. There were four army groups (or Fronts) involved: the 1st Baltic, commanded by Ivan Bagramyan; and the 1st, 2nd and 3rd Byelorussian, led respectively by Konstantin Rokossovsky, Georgy Zakharov and Ivan Chernyakhovsky. The two coordinators of these huge army groups were Georgy Zhukov and Aleksandr Vasilevsky.

Rokossovsky's backstory was amazing. A veteran of the First World War, he was a victim of Stalin's army purges of the 1930s, ending up in a brutal Gulag prison camp from 1937 to 1940, where he endured torture and several beatings. In one incident several of his ribs were broken, nine of his teeth knocked out and his foot was bludgeoned with a hammer. He was once sentenced to death, but was reprieved at the last minute. In March 1940, with the Red Army short of experienced officers, he was suddenly released and rehabilitated. Stalin recognized that as Rokossovsky had already lived through hell he could cope with whatever happened on the battlefield. By June 1944, he was one of the most tactically gifted and energetic commanders in the Red Army.[81]

Overall, the Soviet attack forces contained 118 rifle divisions, eight tank and mechanized corps, thirteen artillery divisions, fourteen air defence divisions and six cavalry divisions. A total of 1.77 million personnel in all, including support staff. Of those, 1.25 million were battle-hardened combat troops. The Soviet advantage over the Germans in armoured equipment was even more advantageous, with 2,715 tanks and 1,355 assault guns.[82] In artillery, the four Soviet Fronts had 10,563 artillery pieces, 2,306 rocket launchers and 11,514 mortars between them. The other area of Soviet superiority was in the air. The Red Air Force had 7,000 aircraft available, including 2,318 fighters and 655 bombers.[83]

It's often stated that Operation Bagration began on 22 June 1944, the third anniversary of Operation Barbarossa, but it is now agreed by historians, using newly opened Soviet archives, that the actual start date was 23 June at 5 a.m. with a heavy double barrage of artillery fire.

The first Soviet military target was to capture the city of Vitebsk in the northern sector of the bulge in the Byelorussian Front. Soviet tanks moved forward rapidly, supported by fighter-bombers. A day later, 28,000 German troops from two weak *Luftwaffe* divisions and the larger 3rd Panzer Army were being pressed from three directions around the city. It was soon obvious the German forces were about to be swiftly encircled. Ernst Busch phoned Hitler to desperately ask for permission to withdraw, but Hitler flatly refused. So Busch followed Hitler's 'stand fast' order, which left his troops in a hopeless position. Inside Vitebsk, General Friedrich Gollwitzer decided to disobey Hitler's order and sanctioned a German breakout on 25 June. Those who escaped, leaving their equipment behind, soon found themselves in open countryside surrounded by Soviet tanks, troops and local vengeful partisans. One German soldier noted: 'Like hares before the hunt we raced through open fields, bullets chirping all around us.'[84] On 27 June, the remaining troops inside Vitebsk surrendered. The Soviets claimed that 20,000 Germans were killed and 10,000 captured in this battle, while the Germans claimed 5,000 were killed and 22,000 captured. Either way, it was a comprehensive German defeat.[85]

With the northern sector of the Byelorussian Balcony successfully breached, the next target for the Red Army was Orsha, a key rail and road hub containing the Moscow–Minsk highway which linked Smolensk with Orsha. Defending this area was the war-weary German 9th Army. The Soviets launched a powerful armoured drive against it, leading to panic among the German defenders, who soon became trapped in Orsha. Kurt von Tippelskirch, the commander of the 9th Army, realized the situation was irretrievable. He defied Hitler's orders and allowed his troops to break out. They hurriedly retreated over the River Berezina. On the evening of 26 June Soviet troops captured Orsha. A total of 28,000 Germans was killed or captured in this engagement.[86]

The next Soviet target was Mogilev, which lay on the River Dnieper. It was defended by Panzer Corps attached to the 4th Army. The city was an important rail junction and contained the key road link to Minsk. The 4th Army came under a devastating two-day artillery attack, beginning on 23 June 1944. Tippelskirch asked for permission to retreat over the River Dnieper, but Busch, acting on Hitler's orders, refused to allow it. Predictably, the troops of the 4th Army were soon completely overwhelmed by the advancing armoured units of the Red Army. Of the 8,000 Germans defending Mogilev, only 3,000 survived and were taken prisoner.[87]

The remainder of the hastily retreating 4th Army now moved to the town of Berezino. It stood on the site of Napoleon's famous crossing of the Berezina River during his ill-fated 1812 invasion of Russia. In a strange act of *déjà vu*, the 4th Army was now trying to cross that self-same river, but now under blistering modern artillery and air attack. Many of the German troops made it over the river before the bridge was blown up. They then began a lonely and pitiless slog on foot to

Minsk, which was still under German control. They never made it, with 50,000 of them becoming encircled and taken prisoner by the Red Army on the way to Molodechno, north of Minsk. From 23 June to 8 July 1944, the German 4th Army, which had begun as a force of 100,000 men, had been almost completely destroyed, its soldiers dead, missing or in captivity.[88]

In the meantime, Rokossovsky's formidable 1st Byelorussian Front, with twenty-seven infantry divisions, was advancing rapidly south towards Bobruisk and soon encircled 70,000 troops of the German 9th Army. Soviet troops soon broke through German defences, engaging in bitter, close-quarters combat at which they were now thoroughly skilled. Hitler, refusing to accept the facts, declared Bobruisk to be another fortified place. He dispatched the 20th Panzer Division to try and rescue the 9th Army.

On 26 June, Busch, the commander of Army Group Centre, flew to the Berghof in the hope of persuading Hitler to modify his 'hold fast' order for Bobruisk. The commander of the beleaguered 9th Army, Hans Jordan, went with him. Instead of acceding to their demands, Hitler summarily sacked the both of them on 28 June. Busch was replaced by the loyal Walter Model as the commander of Army Group Centre. Model retained his control of Army Group North Ukraine. Model was nicknamed the 'Führer's fireman', because of his record of retrieving hopeless battlefield situations. Jordon was succeeded by Nikolaus von Vormann. Tippelskirch, the commander of the decimated 4th Army, was replaced by Vincenz Müller.[89]

This fresh bout of military musical chairs conducted by Hitler did nothing at all to help the 9th Army, which was not only completely trapped in Bobruisk but cut off from its supply lines. A series of desperate breakout attempts was made, with about 15,000 troops managing to swim across the Berezina River but 5,000 badly wounded German soldiers were left behind. On 29 June, Bobruisk finally fell to the Red Army. The German 9th Army had been utterly decimated. The Soviets claimed 73,000 Germans were killed, wounded or captured in Bobruisk.[90]

Vasily Grossman, the Russian journalist, acting as a war correspondent for the Soviet *Red Star* (*Krasnaya Zvezda*) newspaper, witnessed the carnage in the city at the end of the battle in Bobruisk:

> When we entered Bobruisk some buildings in it were ablaze and others lay in ruins. To Bobruisk led the road of revenge! With difficulty, our car finds its way between scorched and distorted

German tanks and self-propelled guns. Men are walking over German corpses. Corpses, hundreds and hundreds of them, pave the road, lie in the ditches, under the pines, in the green barley. In some places, vehicles have to drive over the corpses, so densely they lie upon the ground. People are busy all the time, burying them, but there are so many that this work cannot be done in a day.[91]

On 30 June a completely stressed-out Kurt Zeitzler, the Chief of the Army General Staff, informed Hitler that he could no longer see the logic of holding fortified areas to the bitter end in the Soviet Union. He offered his resignation, but went instead on extended sick leave, apparently suffering from a complete nervous breakdown from which he never fully recovered. Hitler never spoke to him again and formally dismissed him from the German army in January 1945, taking away his pension rights and even refusing to allow him to wear a German army uniform ever again. Zeitzler was replaced on 21 July 1944 by Heinz Guderian.[92]

Meanwhile, the Red Army juggernaut on the Eastern Front rolled on. Soviet tanks now headed towards Borisov, which was held by the remnants of three bedraggled infantry divisions of the German 4th Army, plus a hugely depleted Panzer Corps. The city was surrounded by Soviet troops on 30 June. There followed some bitter street fighting, as many desperate German soldiers tried to flee the city and swim across the Berezina River. Most did manage to escape this time, but on 1 July Borisov was liberated by the Red Army after yet another stunning military victory.

The swift defeats at Vitebsk, Orsha, Mogilev, Bobruisk and Borisov were all disasters of the highest magnitude for Army Group Centre. In less than a week, the Red Army had smashed the German 4th and 9th armies, and decimated most of the 3rd Panzer Army, in the process destroying or capturing 366 armoured vehicles and 2,664 artillery pieces. The Red Army had in the process shattered a 250-mile-wide German-held front and advanced westwards by a whopping 100 miles.

The next Soviet target was Minsk, the capital of Byelorussia and the military headquarters of Army Group Centre. It was obvious that Minsk was about to fall, but once again Hitler refused to prevent this disaster by permitting an orderly and timely withdrawal. All the approaches to the city were doggedly defended by the 5th German Panzer Division, but this made no difference. By the end of June 1944 the Red Army was converging on Minsk from three different directions. There was heavy tank fighting between the Red Army and the German army to the north-west of Minsk on 1–2 August. The 5th Panzer Army was desperately trying to keep the Moscow–Minsk railway line functioning. German tanks took out 167 Soviet armoured vehicles, but their own tanks were progressively reduced during the bitter struggle from 120 to just 18.

Inside Minsk there was a strong sense of hopelessness among the 1,800 armed and 15,000 unarmed troops, plus their 12,000 support staff and 8,000 wounded. On 2 July, Hitler finally ordered an evacuation of Minsk. As German troops retreated they systematically demolished all the major factory buildings and cut off Minsk's electricity and water supplies, before escaping in a convoy of trucks and by rail.

In the end, Minsk had been secured without a fight, but as Zhukov later recalled: 'The capital of Byelorussia was barely recognizable. I had commanded a regiment there for seven years and knew well every street, and all the main buildings, bridges, parks, stadiums and theatres. Now everything was in ruins; where whole apartment buildings had stood, there was nothing but heaps of rubble.'[93] A German *Luftwaffe* infantryman wrote in a letter to his wife in East Prussia: 'If the Russians keep up the direction of their attack it will not be long before they are standing at your door.'[94]

In the period 23 June to 10 July 1944 the Red Army had completely decimated Army Group Centre with a huge demonstration of military power during Operation Bagration. The German army on the Eastern Front had now completely lost the strategic initiative. The destruction of Army Group Centre was the single greatest defeat any German army group ever suffered during the entire Second World War. The sudden breach in the central part of the Eastern Front placed huge pressure on Army Group North and Army Group North Ukraine, as a huge 43-mile gap had now opened between them.

The total number of German losses during Operation Bagration will probably never be known. It's estimated the Germans lost twenty-eight to thirty divisions, with seventeen of them destroyed. German losses were estimated at 399,102 men overall, with 26,397 killed, 262,929 captured or missing and 109,776 wounded.[95] On 17 July about 57,000 German troops were transported by train to Moscow, where they were paraded through the streets. Alexander Werth, the BBC's Russian correspondent, witnessed this ritual humiliation:

Particularly striking was the attitude of the Russian crowds lining the streets. Youngsters booed and whistled, and even threw things at the Germans, only to be immediately restrained by adults; men looked on grimly and in silence; but many women, especially elderly women, were full of commiseration (some even had tears in their eyes) as they looked at these bedraggled "fritzes". I remember one old woman murmuring, "just like our poor boys... *tozhe pognali na voinu* (also driven into war)."[96]

Soviet losses during Operation Bagration were 60,000 men killed, 8,000 missing and 110,000 wounded, with a loss of 2,957 tanks, 2,477 artillery pieces and 822 aircraft.[97]

There were many instances of revenge being taken against the brutal German occupiers. In Minsk, a Soviet partisan killed two German soldiers using a stake. He was convinced that they had killed his daughter Olya and his two sons. As he smashed in their skulls he repeatedly shouted, 'Here you are – for Olya! Here you are – for Kolya!' When they were dead, he placed their corpses up against a tree stump and continued to beat them.[98]

The local Soviet population were deeply relieved to be liberated. The German occupation of Byelorussia between 1941 and 1944 had been extraordinarily brutal. It was here that Hitler's racial war in the Soviet Union was at its most horrific. The local population were treated like animals by their German rulers. In mid-1941 the population of the area had been 10.5 million, but by the time it was liberated in 1944 only 6.2 million people remained there. Starvation and genocide accounted for up to 3 million of those deaths. Jews were the chief victims. There were 270 ghettos in the four German zones of occupation in Byelorussia and it is thought that up to one million Byelorussian Jews perished during the Holocaust there. In Vitebsk the Soviets discovered that all of the city's 37,000 Jews had been killed. Many other Byelorussians were deported to Germany to be used as forced labour and large numbers of them died of starvation in the concentration camps.[99]

It was now obvious that Hitler was leading Germany to a catastrophic military defeat. This gave a fresh boost to the military-conservative resistance. The leading figure in the project to depose Hitler was now undoubtedly Claus von Stauffenberg. For several months he had been coordinating discussions between the leading military conspirators. He now volunteered to assassinate Hitler.

On 7 June 1944 General Friedrich Fromm, the commander-in-chief of the Reserve Army, took Stauffenberg with him to a briefing with Hitler at the Berghof, introducing him to the Führer as a rising young star. Hitler, noticing Stauffenberg's eye patch, maimed left hand and lack of a right one, greeted him very warmly. Nothing impressed Hitler more than the scars of battle. Stauffenberg presented a brief outline of rapid mobilization measures by the Reserve Army.[100]

Fromm was a key figure as he alone was authorized to sign the Valkyrie orders, which would trigger the conspiracy, but he had not yet committed to the project and no one was sure whether he would sanction the Valkyrie order. Nevertheless, and for reasons that remain unclear, he moved Stauffenberg into a position that enabled him to kill Hitler. First he promoted him to the rank of colonel and then, crucially, he appointed him to serve as his Chief of Staff in the Reserve Army on 1 July 1944. Stauffenberg was now based in the War Office in the huge complex of offices inside the Bendlerblock building in Berlin. This high-profile post allowed him access to all of Hitler's military briefings and conferences.

Henning von Tresckow, who was serving in the German 2nd Army of the now devastated Army Group Centre, and another key supporter of the conspiracy, was heartened by Stauffenberg's appointment, commenting: 'The assassination must be attempted at any cost. Even if it should fail, the attempt to seize power in the capital must be undertaken. We must prove to the world and to future generations that the men of the German Resistance Movement dared to take the decisive step and to hazard their lives upon it. Compared to this subject nothing else matters.'[101]

The German military conspirators knew they could not expect support from the Allies. Churchill and Roosevelt regarded them as a bunch of disaffected 'militarists' and 'Prussian Junkers'. The Allies remained determined to impose 'unconditional surrender' on Germany, then to disarm the German army, occupy the country, and put the leading Nazis and generals on trial for war crimes.[102]

The military plotters feared being discovered by the Gestapo. In February 1944, Count Helmuth von Moltke was arrested and his Kreisau Circle uncovered. Then Admiral Wilhelm Canaris – leader of the *Abwehr*, the German intelligence service, and closely associated with leading figures in the conspiracy – was summarily dismissed by Hitler, who thought him at best disloyal and at worst playing a double game with the Allies. The *Abwehr* was now subsumed into Himmler's Reich Security Main Office. It could no longer act as an intelligence hub to the conspirators. Early in July 1944 the Gestapo arrested two prominent socialist members of the German resistance: Julius Leber and Adolf Reichwein. On 15 July, orders were issued for the arrest of Carl Goerdeler, the leading civilian political figure attached to the plotters. At Stauffenberg's insistence, Goerdeler went into hiding. It seemed the Gestapo was closing in on the leaders of the military-conservative conspiracy.

Stauffenberg believed it was only a matter of time before the Gestapo came knocking on his door. On 6 July he attended a two-hour military conference in the presence of Hitler at the Berghof, once again in the company of Fromm. This time Stauffenberg was carrying in his briefcase an explosive device, which the *Abwehr* had captured from a British SOE agent. Fromm had no idea what Stauffenberg was planning to do. The timer was activated by cracking a glass capsule containing acid, which then burned a wire that detonated the bomb. After being primed, the bomb would explode between ten and thirty minutes afterwards.

At this meeting Stauffenberg presented the official version of Operation Valkyrie, which allowed the army to seize control of the state in the event of a civil uprising or an invasion. It was designed to save Hitler's regime – not destroy it. Without asking any questions, Hitler approved the plan, which the plotters intended to subvert to assist their own *coup d'état*. Significantly, neither the SS nor the Gestapo were given copies of the top-secret Valkyrie plans. In effect, the Valkyrie orders offered the Reserve Army unlimited powers in an emergency that threatened the state.

Speer, who was present at the 6 July meeting, joked to Stauffenberg that his briefcase looked 'remarkably plump'. Unflustered, Stauffenberg smiled and said that as a young staff officer he had far too much paperwork. Stauffenberg never got the time alone to prime the bomb before leaving the meeting.[103]

On 11 July Stauffenberg was present at another military conference with Hitler at the Berghof. He had another unprimed bomb in his briefcase. This seemed to be a more determined attempt to kill Hitler, because Stauffenberg had ordered a plane at Salzburg Airport to fly him back to Berlin. Before the meeting Stauffenberg phoned two of the other leading military conspirators, Ludwig Beck and Field Marshal Erwin von Witzleben, and asked whether he should go ahead with the assassination attempt. They told him that Himmler needed to be present for the mission to be approved. Himmler wasn't there, so a very annoyed Stauffenberg had to abort his killing mission.

On 14 July Hitler left the Berghof for the very last time, journeying to the Wolf's Lair due to the deteriorating military situation on the Eastern Front which was getting progressively worse. On 15 July Stauffenberg was invited to attend yet another military briefing in Hitler's presence. By now, Stauffenberg's nerves were at breaking point. This attempt was also aborted, because he did not have time to activate the fuse of his bomb prior to the meeting.

Afterwards Stauffenberg phoned General Friedrich Olbricht in the Bendlerblock to tell him this news. Olbricht was very angry, because he assumed Hitler was already dead and had issued the first Valkyrie order at 11 a.m. on the same day, although luckily not the treasonable secret orders. Troops had even moved towards the Wilhelmstraße ready to occupy government buildings. The original Valkyrie order had to be hastily and embarrassingly withdrawn. Olbricht told Fromm that it was only a dummy exercise, but he was sceptical as to whether he was telling the truth. Olbricht made it clear to Stauffenberg that he would only activate the Valkyrie orders again after a definite confirmation of Hitler's death. After returning to Berlin, Alfred Kranzfelder, a friend of Stauffenberg's, told him a rumour was circulating among naval figures in Berlin that the Führer's headquarters would be blown up in a few days. Stauffenberg suspected that someone in the conspiracy was leaking information.[104]

Stauffenberg was next summoned to a meeting at the Wolf's Lair set for 1 p.m. on 20 July to discuss the plan for new recruits from the Reserve Army to be sent to the Soviet Union. The conspirators agreed that Stauffenberg had to attempt to kill Hitler at this meeting. However, no firm plans were agreed as to how best to carry out the assassination.

On the morning of 20 July Stauffenberg rose at 6 a.m. after a sleepless night at his opulent home in the affluent Berlin lakeside suburb of Wannsee. He fully realized that he had to make the attempt on Hitler's life on this day or abandon the project. Stauffenberg washed, shaved, dressed, wrapped up two bombs in a shirt and put them into his briefcase. He said goodbye to his wife and children. Outside his front gate a staff car with his personal driver was waiting. Inside was his loyal adjutant, Lieutenant Werner von Haeften, one of the conspirators from the Ministry of Foreign Affairs, who had agreed to accompany him and to assist him in priming the two bombs.

Stauffenberg and Haeften were driven to Berlin's Rangsdorf Airfield, where a plane was waiting to take off. Upon arrival at Rastenburg, at

Claus von Stauffenberg (left) stands near
to Hitler at the Wolf's Lair just days
before his assassination attempt on
20 July 1944.

around 10.30 a.m., the pilot was given instructions to have the plane ready any time after noon for the return journey. An army staff car was waiting to take both men on the short journey to the nearby Wolf's Lair.

It was a blisteringly hot summer's day. Security was tight at Hitler's military headquarters. The grounds were surrounded by electrified barbed wire and minefields. Signs warned trespassers of the deadly consequences of entering the compound without permission. It was guarded by elite SS men with trained and fearsome barking guard dogs. Stauffenberg and Haeften managed to get through three security checkpoints without their briefcases being examined.

Once inside, they were warmly greeted by the camp commander, who invited them to join him for breakfast, which they all ate under a large oak tree in the sunshine. After this, Stauffenberg visited the office of General Fritz Fellgiebel, the Chief Signal Officer. He was a key figure in the bomb plot. Fellgiebel's task was to pass on news of Hitler's death to the conspirators in Berlin after the bomb had exploded, then cut off the telephone and telegraphic communications at the Wolf's Lair for as long as possible.

Stauffenberg next went to see Field Marshal Wilhelm Keitel, the Chief of the Armed Forces High Command (OKW), in his office, at noon. Keitel, who knew nothing about the conspiracy, told Stauffenberg that as Mussolini was arriving by his special train at 2.30 p.m. to meet the Führer, the military conference had been brought forward from 1 p.m. to 12.30 p.m. Keitel asked Stauffenberg to keep his report very brief, because discussions on the deteriorating situation on the Eastern Front would now take priority. Due to the extreme heat the meeting was moved from the Führer's underground bunker to the barracks building above ground. It's sometimes wrongly described as a flimsy wooden hut, but the walls were reinforced with eighteen inches of concrete. Due to the heat, the windows were left open, which Stauffenberg realized would lessen the impact of the explosion. The room was rectangular in shape: thirty feet long and twelve feet wide. In the middle, dominating the room, was a sturdy oak table, resting on two heavy wooden supports.

A few minutes before 12.30 p.m., Keitel told Stauffenberg they both needed to hurry to the meeting. As they walked to the conference room, Stauffenberg, who had not yet primed the bomb, suddenly told Keitel he had left his belt and cap in Keitel's anteroom and needed to collect them and change into a fresh shirt. As Stauffenberg was disabled, this did not seem an unusual request to Keitel and the fact Haeften accompanied him likewise aroused no suspicion.

Major Ernst von Freyend offered his room for Stauffenberg to change his shirt. Once inside, Stauffenberg opened his briefcase and, using a pair of specially adapted pliers, with his three fingers, crushed the end of the acid primer of one bomb. Before the second bomb could be activated by Haeften, Sergeant-Major Werner Vogel knocked loudly on the door, informing them Keitel wanted Stauffenberg to rush to the meeting. Vogel later remembered that as he had half-opened the door, he could see Stauffenberg push 'an object' into his briefcase, but Vogel had no reason to be suspicious about what it was. The interruption was, however, crucial as it meant there was no time left to prime the second bomb. Haeften placed it in his own briefcase, unprimed.[105]

Stauffenberg next walked briskly to the meeting. He apologized to Keitel, who thought the delay was due to the obvious difficulty Stauffenberg would have putting on his belt and changing his shirt. When Stauffenberg entered the entrance to the conference barracks, he told the sergeant-major in charge of the telephone board to expect an urgent call for him from Berlin. Stauffenberg and Keitel walked into the conference room together at about 12.37 p.m.

The military conference was already under way. There were twenty-four people in the room. Hitler was standing, facing the open windows, inspecting a map of a battle area on the Eastern Front, with a magnifying glass. General Adolf Heusinger was simultaneously delivering a gloomy report on the dire military situation. Hitler recognized Stauffenberg and nodded in his direction.

Stauffenberg sat six feet away from Hitler, towards the end of the table, near to the entrance door. He put his briefcase under the table, inside one of the thick oak supports. Keitel then announced what Stauffenberg had come to talk about. Within a few minutes of sitting down, Stauffenberg got up and unobtrusively left the room. No one noticed. On his way out, Stauffenberg answered a pre-planned call from Fellgiebel, then put down the receiver and hurried out.

Meanwhile, inside the meeting, General Heinz Brandt leaned over the large table to look more closely at Heusinger's situation map, but he suddenly found Stauffenberg's briefcase was blocking his way. He moved it to the outside of the strong wooden table support. The previous year Brandt had innocently carried an explosive device on to Hitler's plane, although it had failed to detonate.

As Heusinger finally wound up his military report at precisely

[overleaf]
Hitler shows Mussolini the bomb-
damaged conference room at the
Wolf's Lair.

12.42 p.m. the bomb went off, destroying one of the walls and blowing out all of the windows. The huge oak table shattered. Wooden beams were on fire and some were dropping from the ceiling. Four people were killed as a result of injuries sustained in the bomb explosion: Heinz Brandt; Heinrich Berger, the stenographer; Rudolf Schmundt, Hitler's adjutant; and General Günther Korten. One eyewitness in the room recalled: 'There was nothing but wounded men groaning, the acrid smell of burning and charred remnants of maps and papers fluttering in the wind.'[106]

Stauffenberg was standing about one hundred yards away from the barracks room, chatting with Fellgiebel, when the bomb suddenly exploded. He was convinced everyone in the room must have been killed, but he needed to get out of the compound as quickly as possible, while confusion still reigned. A staff car was waiting to take him and Haeften to the nearby airstrip.[107]

The guards at the first checkpoint had heard the explosion and stopped the car. Stauffenberg jumped out, demanding to use the phone. He probably spoke to no one, but said into the receiver: 'I am allowed to pass.' The guard believed him and let the car go through the barrier. The second checkpoint proved much trickier. Alarm sirens were by now howling all around the compound. Stauffenberg's car was stopped again. His reassurance that he had permission to leave was not enough by itself to persuade the guard to let him pass. Stauffenberg asked him to call the commandant of the camp. The guard got through to Leonhard von Möllendorf, the adjutant to the camp commandant, and handed the phone to Stauffenberg who said he needed to get back to Berlin urgently. Möllendorf accepted his explanation.

At the final barrier Stauffenberg's car was stopped once more. He asked to use the phone yet again. The guard refused this request, but instead contacted Möllendorf himself to confirm Stauffenberg did indeed have permission to leave the compound. The guard then nodded him through the final barrier. Stauffenberg's unflustered composure during his exit from the Wolf's Lair was truly extraordinary.

His car now raced to the nearby airfield. Haeften, with the second bomb in his briefcase, threw it out of the car window. It was later retrieved by the Gestapo. At 1.15 p.m., the plane took off. With no radio communication on board, Stauffenberg and Haeften had no way of knowing whether the orders for Valkyrie had been issued in Berlin while they were in the air.

Meanwhile, back in the camp, a horrified Fellgiebel saw Hitler emerge from the smoke of the barrack building. He was clearly alive and not seriously injured. Fellgiebel appears to have contacted Fritz Thiele, the communications chief at the Bendlerblock in Berlin, around 1 p.m., to tell him Hitler was still alive. Thiele decided to keep this information to himself, until he gave details of what had happened at the Wolf's Lair to Fromm inside the Bendlerblock around 3 p.m.[108]

It's unclear whether Fellgiebel ever cut off communications from the Wolf's Lair to the outside world. At any rate, the telephone blackout did not last very long. There's no evidence Fellgiebel ever phoned Friedrich Olbricht, the key conspirator inside the Bendlerblock, to inform him the bomb had exploded, but Hitler was alive. It seems more likely only Thiele was told by Fellgiebel that Hitler was alive.[109]

The Führer had a miraculous escape. Hitler was covered in dust, his jacket damaged, his trousers and long johns torn to shreds, but his injuries amounted to a pierced eardrum, singed hair, several cuts and bruises to his legs (one hundred wooden splinters were later removed with tweezers), plus a cut arm and a bruised left hand. Hitler saw his survival as a gift from Providence. It was a sign, he thought, that his mission in the war would ultimately end in victory.[110]

One of his secretaries, Traudl Junge, saw Hitler enter the bunker, shortly after the explosion:

> I almost laughed at the sight of Hitler. He was standing in
> the little anteroom surrounded by several of his adjutants and
> servants. His hair was never particularly well cut, but now it was
> standing on end so that he looked like a hedgehog. His black
> trousers were hanging in strips from his belt, almost like a raffia
> skirt. He had thrust his right hand between the buttons of his
> uniform tunic; his arm was bruised. Smiling, he greeted us with
> his left arm. 'Well, ladies, everything turned out all right again.
> Yet more proof that Fate has chosen me for my mission, or I
> wouldn't be alive now.'[111]

In all the confusion, it was initially thought the bomb had been planted by forced labourers doing construction work in the camp. It was even thought Stauffenberg might be one of the fatalities. Then Sergeant-Major Arthur Adam, the telephone operator in the barrack building, recalled the 'one-eyed colonel' had left the building in a hurry just before the bomb exploded. Adam was rewarded generously by Hitler with a promotion, a new house and 20,000 Reichsmarks.[112] Others in the room then remembered Stauffenberg left his briefcase behind before leaving. The guards at the three checkpoints all

[overleaf]
Hitler bids goodbye to Mussolini for the
last time at the train platform at the Wolf's
Lair on 20 July 1944.

confirmed Stauffenberg left the compound shortly after the explosion. A call to Rastenburg Airfield revealed Stauffenberg's plane had taken off in haste, bound for Berlin. The bomb-damaged remnants of Stauffenberg's briefcase were soon found in the bomb wreckage. It was clear Hitler's would-be assassin was Stauffenberg.

Benito Mussolini arrived at the Wolf's Lair at about 3 p.m. for what proved to be his last ever face-to-face encounter with Hitler. The Führer took Mussolini with him to inspect the bomb damage, before commenting: 'What happened here today is the climax! Having now escaped death… I am more than ever convinced that the great cause which I serve will be brought through its present perils and that everything can be brought to a good end.' In reply, Mussolini commented, 'After [this] miracle it is inconceivable that our cause should meet with misfortune.'[113]

At about 5 p.m., Mussolini was having tea and cake inside the Führer's bunker. Also present were Göring, Ribbentrop, Dönitz and Keitel. They were already debating who was responsible for the bomb attack and the tensions between them were laid bare. Dönitz lashed out at the obvious disloyalty of the army. Göring supported him, then turned on Ribbentrop, claiming the assassination attempt was yet another failure of German intelligence. The discussion became ever more vicious, with Göring at one point calling Ribbentrop a 'dirty little champagne salesman'. In reply, Ribbentrop yelled: 'I am still the Foreign Minister, and my name is von Ribbentrop!'[114]

Then the brutality of the Night of the Long Knives in 1934 was brought up as an example of how to deal effectively with traitors. At this point, Hitler jumped to his feet, saying the Röhm Purge was nothing compared to the revenge he would now inflict on those involved in this betrayal. He would shoot them all: 'I'll put their wives and children into concentration camps and show them no mercy.'[115]

When this bizarre tea party was finally over, Hitler walked with Mussolini to his special train at about 7 p.m. Hitler stopped near the train to speak to a group of railway workers, commenting to them: 'I knew from the first that men of your sort were not involved. It's my deep conviction that my enemies are the "Vons" who call themselves aristocrats.'[116]

What happened next in Berlin on 20 July 1944 is far from easy to reconstruct from the surviving sources, because most of the key members of the conspiracy did not survive and the evidence of the leading Nazis involved must be treated with some caution. Many books on the Stauffenberg bomb plot also offer a confusing timeline of the events on the day. It's agreed Stauffenberg and Haeften's plane landed at Rangsdorf Airport in Berlin at 3.45 p.m. Haeften raced to a nearby phone box to call Olbricht to find out what was going on. Olbricht told him the Valkyrie orders had not yet been issued as it was unclear whether Hitler had been killed. Haeften said Hitler was most certainly dead.[117]

After this brief telephone conversation, Colonel Mertz von Quirnheim, another member of the conspiracy, issued the first Valkyrie order from the Bendlerblock at 4 p.m., without first seeking permission from either Fromm or Olbricht. This order was sent to General Paul von Hase, the Berlin Army Commander – also part of the plot. He summoned Major Otto Remer, commander of elite Guards Battalion *Großdeutschland*, to his office on the *Unter den Linden* at 4.10 p.m. Remer, a loyal Nazi, was not involved in the conspiracy. Hase fed to Remer the pre-prepared Valkyrie line: Hitler was dead and the SS had launched a coup to overthrow the state. To prevent this, the army was assuming power under martial law. Hase then ordered Remer's troops to cordon off the government area, place roadblocks outside key buildings and protect the Bendlerblock.[118]

Remer wrote a hand-written report on his key role in Berlin on 20 July two days later.[119] In the report, which has survived, Remer made clear Hase told him that Hitler had been killed and an uprising was under way. Even then, Remer felt Hase had 'not given me a clear picture', but he did believe a power struggle within the Nazi state was under way. Remer then made several telephone calls to find out whether the Führer was dead or alive, but he could get no firm confirmation either way.

Stauffenberg finally arrived in the Bendlerblock in Berlin around 4.30 p.m. He immediately injected some much-needed energy into what looked like a half-hearted military conspiracy. Stauffenberg, phone in hand, was soon issuing a flurry of instructions to district military commanders. Stauffenberg spurred Olbricht into action: he issued the remaining secret and treasonous Valkyrie orders to every military district and to all the German-occupied areas. Olbricht retrieved these orders from a safe in his office, then took them to Fromm, but he refused to sign them.

Fromm, who showed no desire to join the conspiracy, told Olbricht he had already spoken by phone to Keitel at the Wolf's Lair, who confirmed the Führer was alive with only minor injuries. The report was

accurate, but when Stauffenberg heard this he denounced it as a lie. Fromm then banged his fist theatrically on his desk, shouting, 'This is rank insubordination!' Fromm summoned Quirnheim who was told he was under arrest. Fromm then rushed at Stauffenberg, landing a single punch on him before being pulled off. Haeften pulled out his gun and pointed it straight at Fromm's face. Fromm was finally subdued, then locked in an adjacent office, which belonged to Major Ludwig von Leonrod, his own adjutant, who was assigned to guard him. The two men were provided with a bottle of wine and some sandwiches and told to stay there for the time being. The telephone line in the room was disconnected. What Fromm didn't know at this stage was that Hitler had already dismissed him as the Commander of the Reserve Army and replaced him with Himmler, who, though not in Berlin at this point, was given full powers to suppress the military coup.[120]

At 4.45 p.m. the Valkyrie coup escalated further when a teleprinter message was sent from the Bendlerblock to every military district commander in the *Wehrmacht*. It was prepared in advance and signed by the former Field Marshal Erwin von Witzleben, who was now supposedly the Supreme Commander of the Armed Forces. It read, in dramatic fashion:

> The Führer Adolf Hitler is dead. An unscrupulous clique of party leaders without front-line experience have exploited the situation to stab the fighting front in the back and to seize power for their own selfish ends. In order to maintain law and order in this situation of acute danger the Reich Government has declared a state of martial law and has transferred the executive power to me together with the supreme command of the *Wehrmacht*.[121]

By now Ludwig Beck, wearing a civilian suit, arrived at the Bendlerblock. He told staff there he was assuming the leadership of the state, and stressed the coup should continue, even if Hitler was still alive. Former Colonel-General Erich Hoepner who had been dismissed from the army by Hitler on 8 January 1942 and prohibited from wearing an army uniform – was next to arrive holding a suitcase containing his old uniform, which he promptly changed into. Beck had appointed him to replace Fromm as the Commander of the Reserve Army. At this point, that position was occupied by three different people: Fromm, Himmler and Hoepner.

The most important Nazi minister in Berlin on 20 July was the Propaganda Minister Joseph Goebbels, who began a decisive and

[clockwise from top left]
Friedrich Fromm, Werner von Haeften,
Otto Remer and Erich Fellgiebel, the
communications officer at the Wolf's Lair.

spirited counter-attack against the military rebellion. Goebbels, after several attempts, finally got through to Hitler by phone at 5 p.m. The national radio stations were all still under Goebbels's control, so he promptly ordered the *Deutschlandsender* radio station – which had a powerful transmitter able to broadcast throughout Europe – announce that Hitler had survived a treasonous bomb attack.

At 6.28 p.m., while the conspirators in the Bendlerblock dithered, a German radio announcer said: 'An attempt was made to assassinate the Führer using explosives… The Führer has not been injured, apart from slight burns and bruises. He has immediately resumed his work.'[122]

By now, Remer's troops arrived at the official residence of Goebbels. Albert Speer, who was inside with Goebbels, after being summoned by him, rang the Bendlerblock and asked to speak with Fromm, but was told he was 'not available'. Speer demanded to speak instead to Olbricht and told him the home of Joseph Goebbels was surrounded by troops. Olbricht said this must be a terrible mistake and he promised Speer he would put it right, before hastily hanging up.[123]

In Remer's own report he claimed he was ordered by Hase to place the Goebbels residence in lockdown, but in a later, post-war recollection Remer changed his story, claiming that it was Goebbels who had summoned him to give him a report about what was happening. Remer knocked on the door of the Propaganda Minister's home at 7 p.m. An assistant showed him in, then escorted him to the drawing room. Goebbels later claimed that before the meeting with Remer he went to his own bedroom, retrieved a box containing cyanide capsules and placed one in his pocket. This seems strange if Remer's post-war account is nearer the truth.

Remer told Goebbels that he would loyally obey his orders, even though the Führer was dead. Goebbels replied: 'What? The Führer still lives! I just talked to him on the telephone, the bomb plot failed.' In his most persuasive tone Goebbels asked Remer if he was faithful to the oath he had given the Führer. Remer said that he was.[124]

Goebbels then picked up the phone to ring Hitler. After explaining the purpose of his call, he handed the receiver to Remer. Hitler's unmistakable voice came on the line:

> Do you hear me? So I'm alive! The attempt has failed. A tiny clique of ambitious officers wanted to do away with me. But now we have the saboteurs of the front. We'll make short shrift of this plague. You are commissioned by me with the task of immediately restoring calm and security in the Reich capital, if

necessary by force. You are under my personal command for this purpose until the Reichsführer-SS [Himmler] arrives in the Reich capital![125]

Remer put down the phone, immediately realizing he was the unwitting dupe of the military conspirators. Goebbels then went out into his front garden and gave an impromptu and spirited speech to the waiting troops. He gave them the patriotic task of hunting down the 'traitors' inside the Bendlerblock and blocking all the surrounding roads.[126] Remer's troops, supported by SS *Panzergrenadiers*, soon secured the entrance to the Bendlerblock, but did not enter. As far as Remer was concerned, Fromm, the Commander of the Reserve Army, was handling the situation. In fact, inside the Bendlerblock an almost comical tragedy unfolded as this bizarre evening wore on.

By now, Witzleben had turned up from Zossen wearing his full army uniform to take up his role as the supposed new commander-in-chief of the German army. He walked into the office of General Eduard Wagner, who told him Hitler had survived the bomb attack. Witzleben then angrily confronted first Beck and then Stauffenberg, blaming each of them for what he called 'this bloody mess'. In less than an hour, Witzleben had left the building to return to his country estate and await the inevitable dire consequences of his decision to join the military conspiracy.[127]

A teleprinter message was issued from the Bendlerblock at 7.47 p.m. to all district German army commanders. It claimed the earlier national radio broadcast, sanctioned by Goebbels, was untrue: Hitler was dead. It further stressed that the Valkyrie orders should be carried out. At 8.08 p.m. the conspirators in the Bendlerblock announced by teleprinter the appointment of General Hoepner as the new Commander of the Reserve Army and the Supreme Commander of the Home Territory.[128]

To counteract this, two official responses were sent from Hitler's military headquarters in Rastenburg. At 8.30 p.m. Martin Bormann, Chief of the Nazi Party Chancellery, sent a circular telegram to every Nazi Gauleiter in Germany, which read: 'Simultaneously with the attempt to murder the Führer, army generals have attempted a putsch which must be and will be suppressed by all means... Only orders from the Führer and his men are valid and not the orders of disloyal reactionary generals.'[129] The response of the various military districts to the messages coming from Rastenburg and the Bendlerblock was

contradictory. In Paris and Vienna the occupying military authorities unwisely began to implement the Valkyrie orders, soon arresting SS and Gestapo officials, but in Germany itself the district military commanders did nothing, clearly accepting that Hitler was very much alive.

Otto John, a lawyer involved in the conspiracy, observed events inside the Bendlerblock on that fateful evening. He later recalled:

> In spite of the apparent turmoil, all I heard and saw, particularly
> snatches of Stauffenberg's telephone calls, gave me the
> impression that the whole army was up in arms against the Nazis.
> It never occurred to me at that moment that they could reverse
> the process and stop everything... I was sure Hitler was dead.
> I left at about 8.45 p.m. I went home to tell my brother what was
> happening at Rastenburg. We opened a bottle of champagne to
> drink to a glorious future.[130]

At 10.15 p.m. German radio made another announcement:

> For the second time in this war started by Jewry, a foul and
> murderous attempt has been made on our Führer's life, and again,
> as on 9 November 1939, Providence protected the man who holds
> in his hands the destiny of the German people... The German
> people will answer the cowardly attack on the Führer's life with
> a renewed profession of allegiance to its National Socialist ideals,
> virtues and duties and with the solemn promise to fight even
> more fanatically and to work even harder.[131]

The revolt was finally suppressed, not by Remer's troops, but by a group of younger Reserve Army officers inside the Bendlerblock. They were previously loyal to Olbricht, but after realizing that Hitler was alive, they decided to mount a counter-attack on the rebels. At 10.45 p.m. a group of them, led by Lieutenant Colonel Franz Herber, confronted Olbricht. During a brief exchange of fire, Stauffenberg was shot in his only functioning arm. Stauffenberg, Beck, Olbricht, Haeften and Quirnheim were soon disarmed and herded at gunpoint into Fromm's office.

Fromm, who had been released from his confinement by a loyal young officer, walked into his office, holding a revolver in his hand. 'You are my prisoners,' he told the captors. 'I have caught you in the act, committing treason and, according to existing legislation, you will all face a firing squad.'[132] He then announced his intention to hold an impromptu court martial. He wanted to eliminate those who might later incriminate him. Beck asked if he could use his own revolver to kill himself. Fromm granted him this request, but told him to do it

The Bendlerblock in Berlin, a key scene
of drama during 20 July 1944.

quickly. Beck tried and failed twice to put a bullet in his head. He was eventually finished off by an unnamed army sergeant. The fact Beck could not even kill himself summed up the ineptitude of the whole conspiracy.[133]

Fromm told the other conspirators to write letters of farewell to loved ones. Remer later recalled a message from Fromm for permission to hold the court martial was personally delivered to Goebbels and Speer by Colonel Ernst Bolbrinker. According to his own account, Speer drove to the Bendlerblock himself to try and stop the court martial. Speer arrived at midnight, but he was told by Ernst Kaltenbrunner, guarding the entrance, that no one – not even a minister of the state – could enter as the army was in the process of suppressing the armed rebellion.[134]

Inside the building, Fromm pronounced death sentences on the four leading conspirators, but he refused to even read out Stauffenberg's name. Such was his deep level of animosity towards him. Stauffenberg, Olbricht, Quirnheim and Haeften were then escorted downstairs at 12.30 a.m. to the courtyard of the Bendlerblock, which was illuminated by the dazzling headlights of parked armoured cars. A ten-man firing squad was swiftly formed by Fromm, using members of the Infantry Regiment *Großdeutschland*.[135]

Several witnesses present recalled the four men all met their deaths with calm dignity. Olbricht and Quirnheim were shot first. In a desperate act of bravery, the loyal Haeften jumped in front of Stauffenberg, as the shots aimed at him rang out. He was killed instantly. Finally, Stauffenberg, the driving force of the plot to kill Hitler, stood alone in front of the firing squad. Before the bullets hit him, he shouted defiantly, 'Long live holy Germany!'[136]

Fromm climbed on to the top of a military vehicle and delivered a rousing patriotic speech in support of the Führer. Remer claimed that he only entered the courtyard with his troops after the executions were all over. He delivered a verbal report of the day's dramatic events to Himmler shortly afterwards.[137] Fromm sent a telegram to Hitler, announcing: 'Attempted coup by irresponsible generals put down by force. All leaders executed.'[138] The corpses of Beck, Olbricht, Stauffenberg, Quirnheim and Haeften were taken away by truck and buried, without ceremony, at Berlin's Matthäikirche cemetery in the Schöneberg district. On the next day, Himmler ordered their bodies to be dug up, stripped of medals, then cremated and their ashes scattered.

Operation Valkyrie, the only methodically planned attempt to overthrow Hitler's government, had failed abysmally. The end was extremely amateurish. The biggest failure of the plotters was to stick too rigidly to their original plan once it became clear that Hitler was still alive. It was asking too much of Stauffenberg to think he could kill the Führer, fly back to Berlin and then lead the rebellion. Stauffenberg's chief accomplices at the Bendlerblock dithered, losing vital time, but with Hitler alive the coup was doomed anyway.

Once again, Hitler's amazing luck held out. A radio broadcast van was dispatched to the Wolf's Lair for the Führer to record a historic radio message in front of a small circle of trusted advisers. A few minutes after 12.30 a.m. on 21 July 1944 Hitler finally spoke to the German people of the dramatic day at Rastenburg:

> My fellow German men and women! I don't know how many attempts to assassinate me have been planned and carried out. But I am speaking to you today for two reasons, in particular: first, so that you can hear my voice and know that I am unhurt and in good health; second, so that you can hear the details of a crime for which there can be few comparisons in German history. A tiny clique of ambitious, unscrupulous and at the same time criminally stupid officers hatched a plot to remove me, and together with me virtually to exterminate the staff of the German High Command. The bomb, which was placed by Colonel Count von Stauffenberg, exploded two metres from the right of me. It very seriously injured a number of loyal colleagues of whom one has died. I myself am completely unhurt, apart from a few minor grazes, bruises and burns. I consider that to be a confirmation of the task given me by Providence to continue in the pursuit of my life's goal as I have done before... I am convinced that by crushing this tiny clique of traitors and conspirators we shall at last create the atmosphere in the rear at home which the fighting front needs. For it is an impossible situation if hundreds of thousands and millions of brave men are doing their best, while at home a tiny clique of ambitious and miserable types are continually trying to sabotage this. This time we shall settle accounts in the accustomed manner as National Socialists... I would like to give you, my old comrades in arms, a special greeting, glad that I have once more been spared a fate which had no terrors for me personally, but which would have brought terror to the German people. But I read into that the finger of fate pointing me towards the continuation of my work, so I shall carry on with it.[139]

In the early hours of 21 July Henning von Tresckow was asleep in his bedroom in the barracks of the German 2nd Army in Ostrov, about

213 miles from Munich, when he was suddenly awoken by Fabian Schlabrendorff and told the military coup had failed. Tresckow's response was quick: 'In the interrogation they will squeeze names out of me, and therefore I intend to shoot myself.' He added: 'I have done the right thing. I believe Hitler to be the arch-enemy not only of Germany but of the whole world.'

A few hours later, Tresckow stepped into the back seat of his staff car and ordered his driver Eberhard von Breitenbach to take him to a no man's land near the divisional headquarters of the 2nd Army, close to Białystok. After asking Breitenbach to stop, he then invited him to witness his suicide, but Breitenbach declined the offer. Tresckow walked along a tree-lined forest path, held a hand grenade below his chin and detonated it, dying instantly.

The official *Wehrmacht* report of his death stated that Tresckow had died 'a hero's death fighting in the front line'. He was buried with full military honours in his family's home town of Wartenburg, but when his involvement in the conspiracy came to light, his wife was arrested, his body exhumed and cremated without ceremony in Sachsenhausen concentration camp.[140]

General Carl-Heinrich von Stülpnagel, the military governor of German-occupied France, had made the mistake of implementing the Valkyrie orders on the night of the bomb plot far too early. Hitler ordered him to return to Berlin on 21 July to explain his behaviour. On his way, he stopped at Verdun – where he had fought in the First World War – and shot himself in the head. He did not die, but only succeeded in blinding himself. In his hospital bed, delirious on morphine, he kept muttering the name 'Rommel' repeatedly. He was brought before the People's Court in Berlin on 30 August, found guilty and slowly hanged on the same day.

In Berlin on 22 July Robert Ley, the fanatical leader of the German Labour Front, delivered a rousing pro-Hitler speech to a group of workers in a Berlin factory. It was broadcast live on national radio. Ley managed to pin the blame for the bomb plot simultaneously on Bolshevism and the Jewish international conspiracy:

> A worker said to me yesterday: 'Thank God it was not a
> worker.' Yes, all Germans in every walk of life are ashamed to be
> connected with such a murderer [Stauffenberg]. Bolshevism and
> reaction, arm in arm, paid by the Jews, traitors and cowardly dogs.
> And international ties. His wife was born in Poland, his sister-in-
> law is a Russian Bolshevist. There is the international plot. There

are the 'liberators' of Germany. No, we demand today that the [National Socialist] revolution should now make up for what if failed to do before. These creatures must be destroyed.[141]

In the days that followed, Goebbels organized a series of public demonstrations of loyalty to the Führer, which were attended by large crowds of loyal Germans. On 23 July newspaper editors were advised by Goebbels to give maximum publicity to such events. Editors were also told to say that only a few 'reactionary traitors' had been behind the plot – a small, 'snobbish', upper-class group that had delayed the conversion of the German army towards National Socialist ideals.[142]

SD reports on public opinion soon showed most Germans pinned the blame on a small group of traitors, mostly aristocratic officers. There is little doubt the public strongly opposed the assassination of Hitler in the midst of the war. All SD reports refer to the shock, dismay, indignation and deep anger about the coup attempt by the German people. Women were reported to have wept in the streets at the thought their Führer had been killed. A typical comment was 'Thank God the Führer is still alive.' Most Germans agreed with Hitler's view that he had been spared by Providence. It was also widely felt that Hitler's death would have made the situation worse. There was not a single instance of any person approving of the attempt on Hitler's life in the SD reports. Letters home from German soldiers indicate that the vast majority were equally horrified by the bomb attempt. Rather than weakening Hitler's popularity, the assassination attempt had the opposite effect.[143]

For Hitler, the military conspiracy was proof positive the German High Command had been sabotaging the German war effort all along. Hitler felt that his own accommodation with the conservative and aristocratic elites had led to military disaster. Hitler commented: 'We wiped out the class struggle on the Left, but unfortunately forgot to finish off the class struggle on the [conservative] Right.'[144]

One of the unintended consequences of the bomb plot was to destroy the independence of the German army. A firm and open commitment to Nazi ideals now became a prerequisite for all officers. The days of the detached, apolitical officer were finally over. On 29 July Heinz Guderian, with Hitler's blessing, issued an order stipulating that every Army General Staff Officer should now qualify as a National Socialist Leadership Officer (*Nationalsozialistischer Führungsoffizier* or NSFO) in an expansion of a scheme originally established in December 1943, but which had been implemented only half-heartedly since.

[overleaf]
Erwin von Witzleben struggles to keep up his beltless trousers during Freisler's questioning at the first bomb plot trial in August 1944.

The work of the NSFOs was now controlled by the Nazi Party. Officers had to demonstrate not only a command of military strategy, but also an exemplary understanding of Nazi ideological and political questions. As Hermann Reinecke from the NSFO put it: 'With the elimination of the traitors the last opponents of the decisive politicization of the *Wehrmacht* have been removed. The National Socialist Guidance work should now be able to proceed without any impediments.'[145] By the end of 1944, there were 1,000 NSFOs and 47,000 part-time members of the organization, and every one of them was a Nazi Party member. New guidelines were also issued to German officers which stressed that any sign of disloyalty or insubordination would be punishable by death.[146]

Hitler appointed Ernst Kaltenbrunner, the chief of the Reich Security Main Office, to head a commission called '*Sonderkommission 20 Juli 1944*' to investigate the Valkyrie bomb plot. This brought together 400 Gestapo and SS officers with updated reports sent frequently to Martin Bormann.[147] The Gestapo net was cast far and wide. Even families of conspirators were detained under the 'kin-detention' law (*Sippenhaft*). Before the bomb plot, the German army was allowed to investigate its own breaches of internal discipline, which helps to explain why the Gestapo had no real knowledge of how wide the conspiracy was. The Gestapo estimated that 7,000 people were arrested during its investigations into the bomb plot and 4,980 were executed, many of whom had no connection with the plot whatsoever. Among those executed were three field marshals, nineteen generals, twenty-six colonels and two former ambassadors.[148]

Himmler promised the entire Stauffenberg family would be 'exterminated'. Stauffenberg's wife and children were arrested, along with other members of his extended family, soon after the bomb plot. The youngest children were sent to orphanages, but neither Stauffenberg's wife nor his children were killed. It seems Himmler kept them alive as potential bargaining chips in any peace negotiations with the Allies.[149]

It was decided that the army conspirators should be dealt with by the civilian People's Court, rather than a military court martial. For this to happen, they were all dismissed from the army by the *Wehrmacht* Court of Honour. The first show trial of the 20 July bomb plotters occurred in Berlin's People's Court on 7–8 August 1944. It was chaired by the brutal, screeching Nazi Roland Freisler, wearing his blood-red robes. Hitler told him beforehand: 'I want them to be hanged, strung up like butchered cattle.'

The eight accused were Field Marshal Erwin von Witzleben, Generals Erich Hoepner, Paul von Hase, Friedrich Karl Klausing and Helmuth Stieff and the junior officers Albrecht von Hagen and Robert Bernardis, along with Count Peter Yorck, a cousin and close confidant of Stauffenberg. They all suffered extremely brutal interrogations at the hands of the Gestapo prior to appearing in court. The trial was filmed, directed by Hans Hinkel. It was given the title *Action X – Traitors Before the People's Court* and lasted for three and a half hours. Only short excerpts from the trial were ever shown in newsreels.

In his customary style, Freisler treated all the accused with utter contempt, repeatedly intimidating and humiliating them before the cameras and members of the public. Witzleben's ordeal was particularly harrowing. He looked like a broken man: unshaven and struggling to keep his trousers up as his belt had been confiscated along with his false teeth before he entered the court. 'You dirty old man,' Freisler bellowed at him, 'why do you keep fiddling with your trousers?' Nevertheless, all the defendants behaved with remarkable bravery. Count Peter Yorck was the most defiant under Freisler's venomous verbal onslaughts. Yorck told the judge that he had never been a Nazi, because he refused to 'renounce his moral and religious obligations to God'.[150]

All the accused were sentenced to death on 8 August 1944. They were sent for immediate execution at Berlin's notorious Plötzensee Prison. Hitler ordered the executions to be as slow and painful as possible. For this purpose eight meat hooks were attached to a steel rail, suspended from the ceiling. A thin hemp rope – not piano wire as was often reported – was placed around the neck of each of the condemned men, then attached to the meat hooks to deliberately prolong the agony. This macabre scene was reportedly filmed on the orders of Goebbels, but no copy of it has ever been discovered. It was similarly alleged Hitler had watched this film but again there is no conclusive evidence of this.[151]

The SD produced a detailed report on the public reaction to the first trial of the bomb plotters. Many Germans were surprised a public trial of such high-ranking figures occurred, but it was thought correct they be tried not by the *Wehrmacht*, but in a civilian People's Court as common criminals. There's no doubt in the minds of the whole population that the accused should have been sentenced to death. The ranting judge Roland Freisler made a strong and favourable impression. Many people in working-class areas said they enjoyed his ironic and often quick-witted put-downs of all of the accused. The vast majority felt the trial provided conclusive proof that 'those involved were

[overleaf]
The gruesome execution chamber in Plötzensee Prison in Berlin.

incapable of governing and that had the coup been successful it would have been incredibly disastrous for Germany'.[152]

In the months that followed, the Gestapo systematically hunted down most of the other key conspirators, many of whom were members of the aristocracy. Trials related to the bomb plot continued until the final weeks of the war. Erich Fellgiebel, who had seemingly cut the communications at Rastenburg, was arrested and brutally tortured. He insisted he acted alone and bravely refused to implicate others. He was sentenced to death by the People's Court on 10 August and executed on 4 September 1944.

Carl Goerdeler, who was to have been German Chancellor had the coup succeeded, went on the run. On 12 August, exhausted and hungry, he walked into a local beer hall in the village of Konradswalde in East Prussia and ordered some breakfast. A local woman immediately recognized him and she phoned the police. He was soon arrested. On 8 September 1944 Goerdeler was sentenced to death, but not executed until 2 February 1945. In his last letter he wrote: 'I ask the world to accept our martyrdom as penance for the German people.'[153]

Ulrich von Hassell, the one-time German ambassador to Italy, and Count Friedrich von der Schulenburg, the former German ambassador to Moscow, who had played a key role in the negotiations preceding the Nazi-Soviet Pact, were executed on 8 September and 10 November 1944, respectively.

General Erich Fromm – who vainly tried to cover up his own role – had been arrested on 21 July 1944, but his trial in the People's Court on a charge of 'cowardice' was delayed until February 1945. He was found guilty and allowed an execution by the traditional military method of firing squad on 19 March 1945.

Fabian von Schlabrendorff, a close confidant of Tresckow, endured several brutal Gestapo interrogations, but stubbornly and bravely denied any involvement in the military conspiracy. He was finally brought before the People's Court in Berlin, but on 3 February 1945, before his sentence was announced, a US Army Air Forces bomb hit the Justice Ministry and killed Roland Freisler, Hitler's fanatical judge, instantly. All the legal documents concerning Schlabrendorff's case were lost in the explosion and so Schlabrendorff was acquitted on a bizarre legal technicality.[154]

Helmuth von Moltke, the leading figure in the Kreisau Circle, had been arrested in January 1944, some months before the bomb plot. However, the Gestapo could find no evidence of his involvement in the conspiracy. Moltke eventually faced a trial in the People's Court after his case was reviewed by Freisler, who decided he deserved death, because he had discussed a new Germany based on democratic principles. Moltke's trial took place on 9 January 1945. He was found guilty and executed on the same day. In a letter to his wife, he noted that he was being hanged for his ideas and not his actions.[155]

Admiral Wilhelm Canaris, the former chief of the *Abwehr*, was arrested, but denied any involvement. Hans Oster, a key figure in the Valkyrie plot, also attached to the *Abwehr*, was taken into custody the day after the attempted assassination. The religious dissident Dietrich Bonhoeffer had been arrested on 5 April 1943, but remained in custody. On 4 April 1945 Canaris's secret diaries were discovered by the Gestapo. After reading some of their contents, Hitler immediately ordered the executions of Canaris, Oster and Bonhoeffer. They were all hanged on 9 April 1945 at Flossenbürg concentration camp.

In the weeks following the attempt on Hitler's life Germany's military situation deteriorated rapidly. In the Soviet Union, the Red Army continued to push westwards relentlessly. Soviet cities were recaptured in quick succession: Lida and Baranovichi on 8 July; Vilnius, the Lithuanian capital, on 13 July; Pinsk on 14 July; Grodno on 16 July; and Brest-Litovsk on 26 July.

Next the Red Army moved to crush Army Group North Ukraine, commanded by Colonel-General Josef Harpe, which had 900,000 troops, 900 tanks and assault guns and 700 aircraft. The Germans had established a defensive front concentrated on Brody and Lvov (now Lviv). On 15 July, Brody was encircled by the Red Army and captured seven days later. On 17 July, Soviet troops advanced on Lvov, capturing it on 27 July. On the same day, the heavily fortified city of Przemyśl fell into Soviet hands. On 18 July, the Red Army attacked Kovel and two days later broke through German defences there, too. By the end of July 1944 the Soviets were approaching the east bank of the Vistula, the largest river in Poland. On 31 July 1944 troops from the Red Army reached Praga, a suburb of Warsaw. By now, all the Soviet territory lost to the Germans since 22 June 1941 had been recaptured.

Despite the Soviet advance during the summer of 1944 the battle-weary Red armies had reached the limit of their supply lines. To capture Poland, the Soviets needed to cross the formidable geographical barriers of the Vistula and Oder rivers. In the southern sector of the Soviet advance, much of Lithuania was captured. The heavily defended eastern German border of East Prussia now came under direct threat.

On 17 August 1944, the Red Army entered the German Reich for the first time, near Schirwindt, but they were swiftly repulsed.

There was more agony for the Germans elsewhere. Army Group North Ukraine lost forty of its fifty-six divisions as the Red Army drove deep into Galicia in southern Poland, capturing Lemberg along the way. By the end of August 1944 most of Ukraine and eastern Poland was now in Soviet hands. In the Baltic region, Army Group North was fighting desperately to prevent being cut off from the main body of the German army. The relentless Soviet advance had opened a dangerous gap between Army Groups Centre and North. Hitler ordered the Baltic to be held at all costs, because Swedish steel, as well as nickel from Finland and oil shale – all vital to the German war economy – all flowed through it.

Army Group North, now numbering just 33 divisions, with a total of 200,000 men, was forced to retreat 130 miles north-west, evacuating most of Estonia, Latvia and Lithuania in the process, but it succeeded in preventing the Red Army from reaching the Baltic ports in bitter defensive engagements. It could not, however, prevent itself being cut off from East Prussia then surrounded on three sides by the Soviet forces. All German military efforts to re-establish contact on land with Army Group North failed. Supplies continued via the Baltic Sea, but these German troops would remain trapped until the very end of the war in Europe.[156]

On 16 October, the Red Army began its first major assault on East Prussia, advancing thirty-seven miles and capturing the border towns of Eydtkau, Ebenrode, and Goldap and Nemmersdorf. German soldiers were able to repel a Soviet assault on the East Prussian capital of Königsberg. On 23 October, German troops recaptured Nemmersdorf. What happened during the brutal Soviet assault on this small town remains a matter of controversy. There's little doubt Red Army troops were filled with feelings of revenge as they finally reached German soil. Soviet propaganda – distributed to the soldiers beforehand – was full of slogans such as: 'Take merciless revenge on the fascist child-murderers and executioners.'

A German soldier who assisted in the clearing-up operation in Nemmersdorf claimed he saw several crucified naked women nailed to barn doors, an old woman whose head had been split in two by an axe, and seventy-two women and children lying dead. All of the women, he noted, had been raped by Red Army soldiers.

A secret report by the German military police on the Nemmersdorf massacre, sent on 25 October 1944, offered a much less horrific account of what had happened. The corpses of twenty-six people, mainly elderly men and several women and children, were discovered. Most had been killed by a single bullet to the head. Only two of the women appeared to have been raped, as their underwear had been pulled down.

Goebbels was determined to use the 'atrocities' in Nemmersdorf for German propaganda purposes, cynically noting: 'I'll make use of it for a big press campaign' in order to show 'what the German people can expect if Bolshevism really gets hold of the Reich'. Sensational headlines soon followed, including: 'Bolshevik Bloodlust Rages in East Prussia Border Area' and 'The Raving of the Soviet Beasts'. These reports were full of graphic photos of the victims.[157]

Some Germans felt atrocity propaganda such as this was counterproductive. An SD public opinion report quoted one person as saying: 'They [the press] must surely realize that every intelligent person, when seeing these victims, will immediately think of the atrocities we [the Germans] have committed on the enemy soil – yes, even in Germany. Did we not slaughter the Jews by the thousands? Don't soldiers repeatedly tell of Jews who had to dig their own graves in Poland?'[158]

The Soviet advance on the Eastern Front had enormous political consequences. On 1 August 1944, the Polish underground resistance – led by the Polish Home Army (*Armia Krajowa*), commanded by General Tadeusz Bór-Komorowski – launched an uprising against German rule in Warsaw with the aim of liberating Poland's former capital city before the Soviets arrived.

The ill-fated Warsaw Uprising of 1944 went ahead without the agreement of the Polish government-in-exile in London, the Western Allies or the Soviet Union. Stalin, who disliked the 'London Poles', as he called them, told his Anglo-American allies that he thought the Warsaw Uprising was folly, throwing unarmed people against German tanks, artillery and aircraft in order to prevent a Soviet takeover of Poland. Stalin refused to send his exhausted troops to fight in another major city, especially in support of Poles for whom he had no sympathy. He had already created his own pro-Soviet puppet government-in-waiting in Lublin called the Polish Committee of National Liberation and preferred to use its members to form the nucleus of the post-war Polish government.

On 4 August 1944, Stalin – under pressure from Churchill and Roosevelt – met a delegation from the Polish government-in-exile,

[overleaf]
Warsaw in ruins after the failed uprising in 1944.

but insisted they agreed to somehow form a coalition with his own Polish Committee of National Liberation. The pro-Soviet 'Lublin Committee' had already agreed the new Polish border would be the one established at the end of the Polish War of 1939, known as the Molotov–Ribbentrop Line, and not the original 1919 border of Poland (the Curzon Line), which the 'London Poles' kept demanding.

Churchill described the Soviet inactivity during the Warsaw Uprising as 'strange and sinister'. He was sympathetic to the demands of the Polish government-in-exile and ordered a limited number of RAF supply drops which had fallen into German hands during the uprising. Roosevelt refused to exert any pressure on Stalin to intervene in Warsaw as he felt the defeat of Germany was a far more important priority. Roosevelt didn't want to become involved in the political future of the Eastern European countries being wrested from German control by the dominant Red Army.

It was against this broader strategic backdrop that the events of the Warsaw Uprising unfolded. Out of 25,000 members of the Polish Home Army in Warsaw, just 14 per cent were armed. They had just 108 machine guns, 844 sub-machine guns and 1,386 rifles, but precious little ammunition. On the first day 2,500 Poles were killed. In the first week 40,000 civilians were massacred in the Wola suburb alone.

Himmler was given the task by Hitler of brutally suppressing the Polish rebellion. To this end he deployed the notoriously brutal SS Kaminski and Dirlewanger Brigades, each composed of 6,000 men. During the sixty-three bloody days of the Warsaw Uprising some 10,000 Polish resistance figures were killed, but an additional 250,000 civilians – a quarter of Warsaw's population – were also brutally massacred, with German troops and paratroopers often using flamethrowers, gas-bombs and rapid-firing artillery, as well as flooding underground bunkers and hiding places. It's been estimated that 83 per cent of Warsaw's buildings were destroyed during the conflict. The surviving Polish inhabitants were brutally driven on long marches through the countryside to German concentration camps. Hans Frank, the governor of the General Government, reported: 'For the most part, Warsaw is in flames. Burning down the houses is the most reliable means of liquidating the insurgents' hideouts.'[159]

The Warsaw Uprising ended on 2 October 1944. During September, the Polish rebels opened up negotiations with the Germans for a ceasefire. The Germans, probably contemplating possible war crimes trials, decided to recognize the Polish rebels as 'combatants' and offered them protection as prisoners of war under the Geneva Convention.[160]

The rapid Soviet advance on the Eastern Front in late 1944 had other major political implications for Germany. Its Eastern European allies now began to fall like a pack of cards, with each defecting to the Allied side. It was the beginning of a new chapter in European history: the creation of a Soviet-dominated Eastern bloc of countries.

On 2 August Turkey broke off diplomatic relations with Germany and expelled Franz von Papen, the German ambassador. Papen met Hitler on 13 August and offered to broker a peace deal with the Allies, but Hitler rejected his offer which he thought would get nowhere.[161] On 23 August King Michael I of Romania, just twenty-two years old, led a successful coup to depose the pro-Nazi government of Ion Antonescu, then appointed Constantin Sănătescu as the new Prime Minister. This move was greeted enthusiastically by the Romanian people. The new government soon announced a ceasefire and switched sides by declaring war on Germany. It signed an armistice with the Soviet Union on 12 September, which accepted the Soviet occupation. The loss of Romania for Hitler was a total disaster. Germany had lost in the process vital oil supplies and the 30,000 German soldiers still stationed there who were captured by the Red Army.[162]

Two other German allies, Bulgaria and Finland, were the next countries to drop out of the Axis. Bulgaria was an ally of Germany, but it had never formally declared war on the Soviet Union. On 24 August, the Bulgarian government demanded the removal of German troops from its soil and declared its neutrality. This did not prevent the Red Army from invading Bulgaria on 8 September. On the following day, a coup in Bulgaria overthrew the government of Konstantin Muraviev. He was soon replaced by Kimon Georgiev of the Fatherland Front, who led a new coalition government composed of socialists and communists. Bulgaria then declared war on Germany, but it was still forced to accept a Soviet occupation.[163]

In August 1944, the Finnish government resumed peace talks with the Soviet Union. On 4 September, Finland suddenly broke off diplomatic relations with Germany. On 19 September, Finland and the USSR signed an armistice in Moscow, brokered by the State President and war hero Carl Gustaf Mannerheim. This finally ended the Finnish-Soviet 'Continuation War', which had begun in 1941. As part of the peace agreement, Finland had to transfer parts of Karelia and Salla and some islands in the Gulf of Finland to the Soviet Union. Reparations of 300 million US dollars were imposed and German troops expelled. A Soviet-led 'Allied Control Commission' was soon installed to enforce and monitor the armistice. Finland managed to survive the war with more independence than any other country in Eastern Europe and never became part of the post-war Soviet bloc.[164]

Churchill, fearing communism was about to spread to Greece, brokered a hard-headed agreement with Stalin for Greece to be placed in the British 'sphere of influence' in return for Britain agreeing the same for Romania. On 12 October German forces evacuated Athens, then the rest of Greece and Albania. The first British troops arrived in Athens on 14 October. Four days later the Greek government-in-exile returned to the capital in triumph. Conflict between the republican right and the communist left soon descended into a bitter civil war, however, which by 1945 left Greece in ruins and politically divided.[165]

Hungary was the next country to make a bid to free itself from German influence. At the end of August, the Regent of Hungary Miklós Horthy dismissed the Prime Minister Döme Sztójay, who had been installed after the German occupation in March 1944. Horthy then put a stop to the Jewish deportations, much to the annoyance of Hitler. On 7 September the Red Army crossed the Carpathian mountain region, meeting weak Hungarian resistance. The Hungarian cabinet then met to discuss an armistice with the Soviet Union.

Horthy opted to secretly negotiate with the Soviet government. On 11 October a draft armistice was signed in Moscow, but it was not due to be publicly announced until nine days later. In the meantime, however, news of secret Soviet-Hungarian negotiations leaked to the German Foreign Ministry. To put pressure on Horthy not to defect to the Soviet side, Ribbentrop hatched a plan more suited to a gangster film than the refined world of international diplomacy. Codenamed Operation Mickey Mouse, it involved German commandos kidnapping Horthy's son Miklós, then using him as a hostage to force his father to accede to German demands.

On 14 October Miklós junior was duly abducted in Budapest by Otto Skorzeny, who, it will be recalled, had rescued Mussolini from captivity the previous year. The young Miklós was reportedly unceremoniously put inside a rolled-up carpet, then bundled into the back of a lorry, bound for the Mauthausen concentration camp. In an act of patriotic defiance, Horthy, not giving in to Nazi blackmail at this stage, delivered a defiant speech on Hungarian national radio on 15 October 1944 which announced the armistice with the Soviet Union and he implored his people to revolt against the expected German response.

On the next day German tanks drove through the streets of Budapest, soon forcing Horthy to announce his abdication. A brutal German occupation of Hungary then followed, with Ferenc Szálasi, the leader of the Fascist Arrow Cross Party, installed as the Prime Minister of the new German puppet regime. This Government of National Unity was propped up by the German army and the SS. Horthy was taken to Germany and imprisoned. Hungary was besieged by the Red Army throughout the winter of 1944–45, but Budapest would not be captured by the Soviets until 13 February 1945.[166]

In Slovakia, during August 1944, pro-Soviet partisans led a popular uprising against the deeply unpopular government of Jozef Tiso. German troops were sent in to brutally suppress it. Tiso remained in office, but the country was occupied by German troops on 29 August 1944. Under a brutal German military occupation, Slovakia's remaining 8,000 Jews were rounded up, deported to Auschwitz-Birkenau, and most were gassed. The German occupation of Slovakia was only ended by Soviet invasion in April 1945.[167]

In Yugoslavia, Soviet troops captured Belgrade on 20 October. By this time most of the country was under the control of the popular communist partisans, led by Josip Tito. The Yugoslav National Liberation Army, which he commanded, numbered 800,000 men, organized into four well-organized armies. On 16 June 1944 the Tito–Šubašić Agreements had been signed in Vis, merging the Royal Yugoslav government-in-exile with Tito's communist partisans.

A new Yugoslavian provisional government took power on 1 November 1944 after German troops left. It was finally agreed the Yugoslav people would decide in a referendum what type of government they wanted at the end of the war. The independently minded Tito was worried Stalin just wanted him to act the role of Soviet cipher, which was something he was not prepared to do. In the end, Stalin decided to give Tito and Yugoslavia much more latitude than most of his other Eastern European satellite states after 1945.[168]

On the Western Front, the Battle of Normandy also raged on throughout that extraordinarily dramatic summer of 1944. On 17 June, Hitler had arrived by plane at his new Western European military headquarters: codenamed Wolf Canyon (*Wolfsschlucht II*), located in Margival near Soissons, close to the French border. It was constructed in 1942, but never used.

Upon arrival, Hitler chaired a conference in a bomb-proof concrete bunker complex called Command Centre W-II. He had summoned

Rommel and Rundstedt to discuss the progress of the Battle of Normandy. General Hans Speidel, Rommel's Chief of Staff, later noted:

> Hitler looked pale and sleepless. He played nervously with his glasses and with pencils of all colours, which he held in his hand. He was the only one seated, hunched on a stool, while the field marshals were kept standing. His earlier magnetic force seemed gone. After a brief, frosty greeting, Hitler bitterly expressed his displeasure at the successful landing of the Allies and accused the local commanders of mistakes and failures.[169]

When his turn to speak came, Rommel offered a frank assessment of the current military situation in the west and pointed out the Allied landing had succeeded due to enemy military superiority, particularly air and naval power. Rommel thought the Allies were deliberately picking small-scale engagements to grind down the less well-equipped German forces. He predicted the Allies would soon break out in force from their Normandy bridgehead, then punch a huge hole in the German lines and head straight for Paris. Under these circumstances, Rommel argued, the only sensible German strategy was to move back to a more defensible position, then to launch a counter-attack. Hitler rejected Rommel's gloomy prognosis and flatly refused to consider any retreats or withdrawals.

Rommel next urged Hitler to visit the German troops in Normandy to boost their morale – as Churchill had recently done with British forces. Hitler agreed to do so, but he never did. Rommel turned to 'political matters' and recommended Hitler should take steps to end the war by negotiation. This prompted Hitler to reply angrily: 'Don't worry about the continuance of the war, but about your invasion front.' Not long after this meeting, Hitler returned to the Berghof and never again set foot in France.[170]

The first significant advance by the Western Allies out of their Normandy bridgehead came on 18 June 1944, when American forces crossed the Cotentin Peninsula, cutting off the heavily fortified port of Cherbourg, which was being defended by 21,000 German troops. On 22 June, US bombers mounted a series of pounding raids on them, with 375 aircraft crippling German artillery positions. The US Navy then brought up three battleships, four cruisers and several destroyers to further assault the German defenders. Under such pressure, the Germans surrendered.

Cherbourg was the first French port captured by the Allies, but the Germans had wrecked it before they ever arrived. US Colonel Alvin G. Viney called it 'beyond a doubt the most complete, intensive and best-planned demolition in history'.[171] As a result, Cherbourg would not be available for use by the Allies – even in a very limited form – until the middle of August 1944.

Friedrich Dollmann, the German commander of the 7th Army, which had failed to hold Cherbourg, died on 28 June after Hitler had informed him that he would soon face a court martial. The official cause of death was a heart attack but Dollmann probably took cyanide.[172]

In the west of the Allied Normandy bridgehead, the Americans needed to move methodically and painstakingly through dense woodland and deep-rooted hedgerows (known as *bocage*) originally planted by Celtic farmers some 2,000 years before. These hedges were ten to twelve feet high and provided excellent natural cover and shelter. The Americans discovered charging through them could prove suicidal. They were largely impenetrable to tanks which placed a huge burden on the American infantry. Any significant break through German lines came only at the price of high casualties.

In the eastern part of the battlefield – where the British and Canadians were operating – the rolling open plains of the Calvados region offered a seemingly good opportunity for large-scale armoured assaults, except for the fact that the strongest German Panzer divisions were in this sector. On 26 June 1944 British forces began Operation Epsom, which aimed to capture Caen, the largest city in Normandy. The Germans contained this offensive, however, forcing the British to withdraw back to their original starting point. It was a setback for British forces, which suffered 588 men killed and 150 tanks damaged or knocked out. The Germans fared even worse, suffering 3,000 dead, missing or wounded, and the loss of 120 tanks.[173] In the first twenty-four days of fighting in Normandy the Germans lost 62,603 men, amounting to 2,608 per day.[174] By the end of June 1944, the Allies were already in a commanding position, even though they had not yet broken out of the Normandy bridgehead. The build-up of Allied troops was impressive. A total of 452,460 Americans, 397,818 British and Canadians, and 25,000 airborne troops had now landed in Normandy, some 875,278 troops in all and building up further all the time.[175]

On 29 June 1944 Hitler summoned Rommel and Rundstedt, his commanding generals on the Western Front, to a crisis meeting at the Berghof. The two generals wanted to tell Hitler the situation in the west was already hopeless, but Hitler warned Rundstedt at the start of the meeting to confine his report to his views on the situation in Normandy and make no comment whatsoever on the wider strategic dimensions of the conflict in the west. At this point, Rommel protested and was told by Hitler to leave the room.

On 1 July 1944, Hitler dismissed Rundstedt as the Commander of German Army Command in the West, replacing him with Günther von Kluge. He left Rommel in his post, though he now regarded him as a defeatist. Hitler felt dismissing Rommel, because of his fame, would attract adverse publicity, especially in Allied countries, and might damage German morale at home.[176]

On 8 July British and Canadian forces launched Operation Charnwood, another attempt to capture Caen. This time it was preceded by a huge Allied bomb attack on the old city, leaving it in ruins and killing an estimated 300–400 civilians. The British and Canadians managed to capture the northern half of the city before the Germans managed to retreat over to the northern bank of the River Odon.[177] It proved a hollow victory: reduced to rubble, Caen was strategically and economically useless. Allied bombing had killed French civilians for no real military advantage. German forces soon dug into new defensive positions on the opposite bank of the Orne River. This operation overlapped with Operation Windsor, led by the Canadian army, during which Carpiquet and its important airfield were captured. Field Marshal Montgomery decided not to advance over the Orne River due to the tenacity of the German forces stationed there. He thought that the capture of Caen had already been too costly as it was, with 3,817 men killed, missing or wounded, compared to a total of 2,000 German casualties.[178]

On 14 July 1944 the deeply frustrated Rommel sent a letter to Hitler outlining the critical situation now facing Army Group B in France. He raised again the devastating superiority of Allied artillery and air power, and predicted gloomily:

> In these circumstances we must assume the enemy will succeed in the foreseeable future – a fortnight to three weeks – in breaking through our own front line, above all that held by the 7th Army, and will go forward deep into France. The consequences will be incalculable. The troops are fighting with heroism, yet the unequal struggle is coming to an end. I must request you draw the necessary conclusions from the situation.[179]

Three days later Rommel was being driven around the Normandy battlefield in the front seat of his staff car, with three other officers as passengers. Hitler had forbidden Rommel to travel by plane out of fear that he might be killed, as had recently happened to several other high-profile German officers. At 6 p.m. Rommel's car was nearing the village of Vimoutiers when it came under intense Allied air fire. The driver, Sergeant Karl Daniel, was hit in the shoulder and lost control of the car. It left the road, struck a tree stump and rolled down a ditch, throwing Rommel violently out of it. Rommel had suffered life-threatening injuries, including a severe skull and cheekbone fracture, an eye socket injury and deafness in one ear. It's thought Charley Fox, a Canadian pilot, was responsible for the attack on Rommel's car.

After a period of intense hospital treatment in France, Rommel returned to his home in Herrlingen on 8 August to continue his recuperation. He continued to suffer from severe headaches, which made it difficult for him to sleep, and he was unable to open his left eye which remained heavily bruised and swollen. Rommel told his teenage son Manfred that his injuries were so serious his military career was over.[180] Günther von Kluge, already the Commander of German Army Command in the West, now took control of Army Group B.

On 18 July 1944 Operation Goodwood began with the British and Canadian 21st Army Group finally aiming to capture the rest of Caen. This was the first major effort to break out of the Allied bridgehead in Normandy and punch a significant hole in the German defensive line. Supported by heavy Allied bomb attacks, supported by large tank forces, a breakthrough seemed likely, but within two days, the German army, once more demonstrating extraordinary resilience in defence, held firm.[181]

Towards the end of July 1944, the deeply frustrated US Commander Omar Bradley felt the Allies really had to break out of their bridgehead if they were to triumph in Normandy. Bradley argued American forces should now apply their huge material advantage to launch a major

American military commander Omar Bradley.

attack at a designated weak point in the German defensive line.[182] The result was Operation Cobra, the first major offensive by American forces during the Battle of Normandy. The weak point selected to attack the Germans was a narrow five-mile-square area between the Normandy communes of Saint-Lô and Périers, where the 7th German Army and its associated Panzer units were located. The aim was to decimate the German soldiers there with mass carpet-bombing using 1,500 heavy bombers and 396 medium bombers, then to send in three American armoured divisions with 2,451 tanks, supported by a further eight infantry divisions, to create a corridor through which the American 1st Army could advance into Brittany and bypass the dreaded *bocage*.

This bold American offensive began on 25 July 1944 with a huge aerial attack in the selected killing zone. On the ground progress was at first slow, but two days later German resistance suddenly began to crumble. The bomb-saturated area looked like a landscape from the moon. Operation Cobra, largely an American operation, was the greatest demonstration of Allied brute force during the entire Normandy campaign.

Orders were issued from Hitler imploring the German troops to fight to the last bullet in the area of the American attack. It proved impossible, however, for even the most resilient German troops to stop this military juggernaut. US tanks decisively surged forwards through the gap the assault had created. By 28 July the German defences had completely collapsed. The Americans were now out in the open countryside in Normandy for the first time. Soon they had captured Avranches, then Coutances, a major road hub.[183]

The American breakthrough in Normandy rattled Hitler. At a military conference at the Wolf's Lair on 31 July Hitler seemed to accept fighting in the open field of battle in France was now becoming impossible: 'We can move some of our troops, but only in a limited manner. With the others, we cannot move, not because we don't possess air superiority, but because we can't move the troops themselves: the units are not suitable for mobile battle, neither in their weapons nor in their other equipment.'[184]

Despite this, Hitler ordered what he called a 'last throw of the dice' in Normandy: a risky counteroffensive (codenamed Operation *Lüttich*) in the hilltop town of Mortain, beginning on 7 August 1944. It aimed to push the Americans back from Avranches in order to buy time to prepare the old Siegfried Line or West Wall along the German border. By 13 August, the German counter-attack was contained by the Americans. The Germans were soon driven out of Mortain by a combination of devastating air and artillery fire.

American forces were now formed into the unified 12th Army Group, commanded by Omar Bradley, which incorporated the newly introduced 3rd American Army, led by the bold General George S. Patton. His fresh forces attacked west into Brittany, then pivoted eastwards, capturing Le Mans. Hitler described Patton as 'The most dangerous man they [the Allies] have.'[185] On 14 August 1944, further building on the American breakout from the Normandy bridgehead, Canadian, Polish and British troops drove south from Caen to begin Operation Tractable. The aim was to capture the strategically important town of Falaise and to trap the German forces congregated there.

On the following day, the Allies began Operation Dragoon, the code name for the Allied invasion of southern France. The goal was to secure the key ports on the French Mediterranean Riviera coast, thereby increasing the pressure on the already overstretched German forces. The US 7th Army landed in the south of France under Major-General Alexander Patch, swiftly defeating German forces located there in just four weeks, capturing the key ports of Marseilles and Toulon along the way. The poorly equipped German Army Group G, commanded by Johannes Blaskowitz, withdrew – with Hitler's agreement – to establish a new defensive line at the Vosges Mountains.

The Battle of the Falaise Pocket – the most decisive engagement during the Battle of Normandy – took place between 12 and 21 August 1944. It was the first battle of encirclement to be attempted by the Allies. The circular pocket around Falaise had been created by the advance of American, Canadian and Polish troops. The German 7th Army, the 5th Panzer Army and Panzergruppe Eberbach – the three main armies of German Army Group B – were now almost completely encircled, except for one route out: the Falaise–Argentan Gap, through which 40,000 to 50,000 Germans managed to escape.[186]

Nevertheless, the Battle of the Falaise Pocket was another comprehensive Allied victory. Most of German Army Group B, west of the River Seine, was destroyed. German forces in France were now retreating in complete disarray. As Eisenhower noted while visiting the battlefield afterwards: 'It was literally possible to walk for hundreds of yards at a time, stepping on nothing but dead and decaying flesh.'[187]

Hitler blamed Günther von Kluge, the commander of Army Group B, for the defeat at Falaise. Hitler even thought Kluge was

[overleaf]
General Charles de Gaulle enters Paris on
25 August 1944.

secretly negotiating a surrender with the Allies and dismissed him on 17 August. In fact, Kluge's telephone line had ceased to function for a day. Once communications were restored, Hitler summoned Kluge to Berlin. Kluge believed he had been implicated in the July bomb plot and committed suicide on 19 August without ever returning to Germany. A subsequent Gestapo investigation discovered Kluge had agreed to support the military conspiracy if Hitler was killed, but that he would withdraw this offer if the Führer survived.

It's been estimated 100,000 Germans were trapped in the Falaise Pocket, with 10,000 killed and 40,000 taken prisoner. Estimates as to how many escaped range between 20,000 and 50,000.[188] The Allied victory at Falaise is usually attributed to overwhelming air power, but Allied surveys of the battlefield show most of the Germans seem to have given up the fight early and left all their equipment behind. The RAF Operational Research Section counted 187 intact tanks and self-propelled guns, 157 armoured vehicles, 1,778 lorries, 669 motor cars and 252 artillery guns discarded by the Germans. A huge number of horses was also captured.[189]

In just ten weeks the Western Allies had liberated France from German occupation. The seeds of this overwhelming Allied victory were, of course, sown on the Normandy beaches on 6 June 1944. The Germans had failed to be in the right place at the right time then, and allowed the Allies to establish a solid bridgehead from which to make a decisive breakout, which was spearheaded by the Americans during the decisive Operation Cobra. During the entire Battle of France in 1944, the Germans suffered 240,000 killed, wounded or captured, with 41 divisions completely decimated. However, around 240,000 German soldiers crossed the River Seine and made it back home to fight another day.[190]

Paris was liberated on 25 August 1944. German forces abandoned the French capital without putting up a fight. The French Division *Blindée* (2nd Armoured Division) was given the honour of entering Paris first. A Provisional Government of the French Republic led by General de Gaulle, the leader of the Free French, was soon established. The French Resistance, a separate organization from the Free French, had engaged in brave partisan attacks, which assisted the Allied victory in France in 1944, but they were denied key positions in the new French government. This wound left deep scars on post-war French society.

On 31 August 1944 at a military conference Hitler expressed a firm commitment to continue the struggle against the triumphant Allies, commenting defiantly:

I live only for the purpose of leading this fight, because I know that if there is not an iron will behind it this battle cannot be won… If necessary we'll fight on the Rhine. It doesn't make any difference. Under all circumstances we will continue this battle until, as Frederick the Great said, one of our damned enemies gets too tired to fight anymore.[191]

In private, however, General Warlimont recalled Hitler being extremely depressed about Germans being forced to evacuate France. Warlimont also noticed: 'He [Hitler] made no reference to the opinion he had expressed only a few months earlier that this would be decisive in the outcome of the war. Nor did he refer to the fact that this meant the end of the vaguely expressed general strategy for 1944 to recover the initiative in the East once the invasion [in the West] had been defeated.'[192]

By 10 September 1944 Brussels, Sedan on the River Meuse, and the port of Antwerp had all been liberated, too. Allied soldiers now stood menacingly on the border of the heavily defended Netherlands and in the densely wooded Ardennes, the site of Hitler's greatest victory in 1940. The Germans had retreated in the west beyond the armistice line established in November 1918 of Ghent–Mons–Sedan.

The series of unmitigated military disasters during the summer of 1944 afflicting German positions in Eastern and Western Westphalia led to calls within the German elite to broker a peace settlement. Most of the leading figures in the Nazi elite – Goebbels, Göring, Speer and Himmler – all thought the only way out for Germany now was to try and seek a separate peace with either the Soviet Union or the Anglo-Americans, thereby dividing the Allied coalition. Goebbels claimed to have heard untrue intelligence rumours that the British government wanted to get out of its alliance with the Soviet Union and reach a compromise peace with Germany. Japanese diplomats were also urging the German government to make a separate peace deal with the Soviet Union.

On 20 September Goebbels prepared a lengthy memorandum on the idea of a separate peace with the Soviet Union, which he submitted to Hitler. Goebbels argued that Germany could not win a war on two fronts by military means. Ending the German-Soviet War first made sense as it would free up troops to repel the Western Allies. Goebbels also made clear that Ribbentrop was incapable of negotiating such an agreement. He suggested a new German Foreign Minister should be appointed – someone with the 'requisite clarity of vision and toughness, combined with a high degree of intelligence and flexibility'. He was effectively offering his own services for the job. Hitler never even replied to the memorandum.[193]

The German military collapse in France came as a huge shock to the German people. It meant the remainder of the war would now be fought on home soil. The German population, taken in by the propaganda of Joseph Goebbels for years, had not seen this defeat coming. SD opinion reports show that in September 1944 the mood of the people had reached its lowest point.[194]

The new buzz word in German propaganda became 'Total War'. On 25 July Hitler appointed Goebbels as the 'Reich Plenipotentiary for the Total War Effort'. It was a reward for the key role that Goebbels had played in crushing the 20 July bomb plot. Goebbels had been lobbying for this role ever since his famous speech on the subject on 18 February 1943 a few weeks after the defeat at Stalingrad. This new role gave Goebbels the power to issue decrees, although they had to be agreed with Himmler in his role as General Plenipotentiary of Reich Administration, as well as Martin Bormann, the Chief of the Party Chancellery and Private Secretary of the Führer, and finally Hans Lammers, the Chief of the Reich Chancellery.

The appointment of Goebbels to his new role reduced the standing of the technocratic Albert Speer, the Armaments Minister, especially as his much-touted 'miracle weapons' drive had made no significant impact in the war. It was obvious Speer was no longer Hitler's 'favourite', or as Goebbels accurately put it: 'I think we have somewhat let this young man become somewhat too big.'[195]

Goebbels did make an impact in helping to galvanize the German war effort. With the assistance of loyal Nazi Gauleiters he raised half a million new soldiers for the *Wehrmacht*, through several rationalization and austerity measures. Postal and rail services were drastically cut. The post office let go of 250,000 men and the railways 50,000, making these men available for army service. Theatres, cabaret clubs and other forms of entertainment were closed down, the number of orchestras greatly reduced; university study was limited, and companies producing goods deemed unnecessary for the war effort – such as toys, clothing and book publishing – were closed down.

Newspapers were reduced to a few pages. Film production was cut back drastically, although cinemas remained open. Domestic servants were restricted, freeing up 400,000 women for service in factories. Local government bureaucracy was reduced by simplifying government forms. The age limit for labour conscription for women was increased from forty-five to fifty, although a decree raising it to fifty-five was never implemented. Working hours per week for men were raised to sixty and to forty-eight for women. Goebbels even wanted to stop the production of beer and sweets, but Hitler vetoed this proposal. Speer agreed to the release of 100,000 unskilled workers from munitions factories for the *Wehrmacht*. By the end of October 1944, 451,800 men had been made available for the war effort and more than 400,000 women. In practice, however, many of the older men who became available proved unfit for military service.[196]

Hitler was always reluctant to impose the full cost of financing the war on the German public. He wanted especially to avoid the sort of collapse in German morale that had occurred in 1918, a fear that haunted him. For this reason, taxation in Germany remained low when compared to the Allies. On 4 September 1939, the War Economy Directive levied a 50 per cent surcharge on wages, but only for people who earned over 2,400 Reichsmarks a year, which affected just 30 per cent of all wage-earners. Only the top 4 per cent of earners ever paid the full surcharge. Hitler refused to increase income tax, even in the last phase of the war. German workers retained around 73 per cent of their pre-war income, compared to 38.1 per cent in Britain and 36.7 per cent in the United States.[197]

A major consequence of Hitler's decision not to raise tax revenue was to place the financial burden of the German war effort on increased government borrowing. This skyrocketed in 1944 to 60 per cent of German net national production. Most government spending went on the army. At the end of August 1944 the *Wehrmacht* was consuming more than the entire total national income of all German production during the boom years of the late 1930s. To prevent passing on inflation to the population, the government simply printed more money. From September 1944 to April 1945, the number of German banknotes in circulation increased by 80 per cent.[198]

In the autumn of 1944 Germany's dire military situation contributed to a sharp deterioration in Hitler's health. He had become prematurely old and seemed depressed and exhausted to those around him. He told his young secretary Traudl Junge around this time: 'I have so many anxieties. If you knew what decisions I have to take all by myself, no one shares responsibilities with me.'[199] Hitler's stomach cramps returned, his eyesight was now deteriorating, his left arm and hand often shook uncontrollably. The bomb blast on 20 July affected him much more seriously than he was willing to admit at the time. It led to deafness in one ear and new and frequent pains in his legs. He now walked much more slowly and his breathing was shallow. At a military conference on 31 July, he admitted to having severe dizzy spells: 'A moment like that can occur while walking and I have to pull myself together in order not to make a false step.' He also admitted his loss of balance now made speaking in public impossible.[200]

During September, Hitler felt so ill and run down that he took to his bed for a week. His personal physician, Dr Morell, whom Göring jokingly referred to as the 'Nazi Injection Minister', recorded that on 8 September Hitler was complaining of pressure around his right eye, and the Führer's blood pressure was very high. On 15 September Morell noted in his medical records that Hitler 'complains of dizziness, throbbing head and the return of involuntary trembling in his legs and particularly the left arm'.[201] On 16 September, it seems Hitler suffered a mild heart attack.[202] In mid-October Hitler confessed: 'The weeks since 20 July have been the hardest of my life. I have fought with a kind of heroism that no German could have dreamed of. In spite of serious pain, hours of dizziness and nausea, I have remained on my feet and fought against all this with iron energy.'[203]

The dental records of Hitler's personal dentist Dr Hugo Blaschke, Deputy Chief Dental Surgeon of the SS, noted that in 1944 Hitler regularly suffered from severe toothache and had ten new fillings fitted during the course of the year, even though Hitler had a phobia of the dentist's chair. Blaschke further noted that Hitler had bad breath, yellowing teeth, gum abscesses and severe gum disease.[204]

Morell's medical records show that Hitler's skin took on a yellowish appearance, indicating jaundice or hepatitis. Dr Erwin Giesing, a noted ear, nose and throat specialist, with a practice in Berlin, was brought to examine Hitler in the Wolf's Lair, and noted: 'The face was pale, slightly swollen, and there were large bags under bloodshot eyes.'[205] After Giesing listed an inventory of all the various medications Hitler was taking, he became immediately suspicious of two drugs in particular: an over-the-counter medicine called Dr Koester's Anti-Gas Pills, to combat flatulence, and Eukodal, a painkiller which was also available without a prescription. Giesing took them away for chemical analysis, without informing Hitler. He found they contained two poisons: strychnine, used in rat poison, and atropine, which paralyses the spinal column. Giesing was also concerned that Dr Morell was giving the Führer too many injections every day. Another doctor, Hanskarl von

Hasselbach, expressed similar concerns about Hitler's treatment.

Giesing told Hitler that in his opinion Morell's treatments were slowly poisoning him. Giesing prescribed eardrops for Hitler that contained cocaine to cope with his earache and severe headaches. According to Giesing's own report, Hitler thought these ear drops were 'wonderful' and made him feel 'lighter and carefree', and he took them whether he had earache or not.[206]

Morell angrily denied deliberately poisoning the Führer. He ordered his own chemical tests on the disputed drugs. These concluded the amounts of strychnine and atropine present were far too small to act as a poison. Morell claimed that Giesing was trying to replace him as Hitler's personal doctor. Hitler sided with Dr Morell in the dispute between his doctors. Giesing and Hasselbach were both reprimanded and prohibited from ever treating Hitler again in future. At the same time, Dr Karl Brandt, who had been Hitler's escort doctor since 1934, was also dismissed, because he had supported the attack on Morell. At the end of this dispute Hitler commented: 'I would like the matter involving anti-gas pills to be forgotten once and for all. You can say what you like against Morell – he is and remains my only personal physician, and I trust him completely.'[207]

In September 1944, the Allies believed the war would be over by Christmas. On 4 September, the British War Cabinet predicted that 31 December 1944 would be the likely end date of the Second World War. A British intelligence report suggested the Germans now had only nineteen divisions left with which to defend the West Wall. American commander Omar Bradley predicted that once the Allies crossed the Rhine the Germans would surrender.[208]

This proved wishful thinking. The spectacular advance of the Allies was undoubtedly a military triumph, but it created some severe logistical problems. Allied armies in the west, now numbering 2 million troops, had raced far ahead of their supply lines. The Allied war effort still relied to a great extent on the one remaining Mulberry Harbour in Normandy as the French rail system had been largely wrecked by Allied bombing. In its place, the Allies relied on truck convoys by the famous 'Red Ball Express', staffed mainly by black American soldiers, which at its peak operated 6,958 vehichles which carried about 12,500 tonnes of supplies each day. The capture of Antwerp in early September 1944 did not help to solve these supply problems, because the city was unusable for trade until 26 November 1944.

American commander Omar Bradley wanted to advance across

the Rhine on a broad front. In contrast, the British Field Marshal Bernard Montgomery, the leader of the 21st Army Group, wanted to punch a big hole in a weak point in the German front and then to cross the Rhine. Monty persuaded the overall Allied commander Dwight D. Eisenhower to sanction his own brainchild, for this purpose, codenamed Operation Market Garden. This huge airborne landing intended to move into the rear of the German defence of the Netherlands and capture five bridges, the most important being the great bridge over the Lower Rhine at Arnhem. If the plan worked, a route would then open up to the German industrial heartland of the Ruhr. General Patton doubted the wisdom of Monty's plan, however, noting critically in his diary: 'Monty does what he pleases and Ike [Eisenhower] says "yes sir".'[209]

On 17 September 1944, three airborne divisions landed in the Netherlands to begin Operation Market Garden. The Allies managed to reach four of the five designated river crossings, even though they were hampered by not having landed in exactly the right places. By 25 September, German heavy armour overseen by the resourceful Walter Model, Hitler's famed 'fireman', now entered the fray. The lone British battalion which attempted to capture the key bridge at Arnhem failed to achieve its objective.

Arnhem, the famous 'Bridge Too Far', was a very embarrassing Allied defeat. The Germans had decimated the Allied airborne division, killing 1,485 paratroopers and 499 airmen; a further 6,525 were taken prisoner and humiliatingly paraded for the German newsreels. German losses were 1,300 killed and 2,000 wounded.[210] Monty, the overconfident British commander, received most of the criticism at the time in the press and subsequent historians have accused him of overseeing a poorly planned operation which was driven by the personal glory of being the 'first to cross the Rhine'. Eisenhower has also been criticized by historians for letting Monty go ahead with such a risky adventure in the first place.

The Allied defeat at Arnhem ensured the Western Front became a stalemate during the last months of 1944, with the Germans defending the border areas tenaciously. The German army had shown it would not be easy to break down, defending on its soil. The only German city to fall into Allied hands in later 1944 was Aachen, which was captured by the Americans on 21 October.

With the Germans now determined to fight on, the Allies stepped up their bombing campaign. In the last two months of 1944, Allied bomber fleets launched a major air offensive against railway traffic and inland shipping across the whole of Germany. The air war now came to all the regions of Germany. Industrial cities were ablaze every night and reduced to rubble on the following mornings.

The impact on German society of these devastating Allied air raids was enormous. In many industrial areas, rail, tram, bus and river transport broke down completely. There were frequent power and gas supply cuts. On 11 November Albert Speer noted in his famous 'Ruhr Memorandum': 'If the industrial areas of the Rhineland and Westphalia were destroyed during these raids it would be decisive for the fate of the Reich.'

The anger of German civilians against Allied pilots was intense. Many were lynched if found alive after bailing out of their planes due to mechanical failure or before crashing. On 26 August 1944, six American airmen were summarily shot in Rüsselsheim. In Essen on 13 December three members of an RAF bomber crew were murdered by an angry local mob. The killing of Allied airmen by members of the public was not prosecuted by the German police or the courts. Exactly how many lynchings and murders of Allied airmen took place in the latter stages of the war is not known, but British and American military tribunals between 1945 and 1949 estimated that at least 350 such arbitrary killings occurred.[211]

Now that Germany faced an invasion, the position of the Nazi Party on the home front underwent a surprising revival. The role of the forty-two Nazi Gauleiters and seventeen Kreisleiters was significantly enhanced, not only to assist in the Total War drive, but also in the recruitment, organization and command of a new citizens' militia called the People's Storm (*Volkssturm*). The new force was announced in a decree signed by Hitler on 25 September 1944. Himmler officially launched the *Volkssturm* in a ceremony in East Prussia on 18 October, the anniversary of the 1813 Battle of the Nations, near Leipzig, during which the legendary *Landsturm* (a similar reserve force militia) had played an important role in liberating German territory from Napoleon's invading forces.

The *Volkssturm* conscripted all males aged sixteen to sixty who were not already serving in the armed forces. It was primarily composed of older men and younger members of the Hitler Youth. Most of the recruits served in their own urban district, constructing tank traps, planting mines and undertaking guard duty. The uniform amounted to a black armband with *Deutscher Volkssturm Wehrmacht* printed on it.

Conscripts were expected to provide all of their military kit, including a rucksack, a blanket and camp-style cooking equipment. It was not a serious military force that was going to make any difference against highly trained Allied soldiers. These older men and young boys were lambs to the slaughter. As an older recruit later recalled: 'After three hours' instruction from a holder of the Knight's Cross we were ready for action to use a bazooka. Our platoon had twenty-three members and for these twenty-three we got given twelve weapons. I didn't get one and didn't make an effort to. I didn't understand how they worked in any case.'[212]

During the on-going Gestapo investigation into the 20 July bomb plot Field Marshal Erwin Rommel, Germany's most famous officer, came under growing suspicion of being involved. Mystery still surrounds his precise role. The conspirators certainly put out feelers to him, but it's unclear whether Rommel knew anything about the actual plan to kill Hitler and he had no contact whatsoever with Stauffenberg.

There's little doubt Rommel favoured opening peace negotiations with the Western Allies, because, after the D-Day landings, he thought Germany was going to lose the war. There is, however, no evidence that he ever opened any peace negotiations with the Allies, whether formal or informal. General Heinrich Eberbach – who served in the spring of 1944 alongside with Rommel – said in a later conversation that was secretly recorded while he was in British captivity: 'Rommel said to me Germany's only possible hope of getting off reasonably well lies in our doing away with Hitler and his closest associates as soon as possible.'[213]

During the Gestapo's exhaustive investigation into the Valkyrie conspiracy, Rommel's name cropped up several times. The German *Luftwaffe* Lieutenant Colonel Cäsar von Hofacker, who was involved in the conspiracy, implicated Rommel, but only after being horribly tortured. He mentioned meeting Rommel on 9 July 1944 to try to win him over to the resistance. Hofacker recalled telling Rommel the full details of the bomb plot and quoted him as replying: 'Tell the people in Berlin they can count on me.' Hitler received a report on these revelations from Ernst Kaltenbrunner and decided Rommel must be questioned about them once he had recovered from his injuries.[214]

The Gestapo then discovered a list written by Carl Goerdeler of potential members of his post-coup government: Rommel's name appeared on it as a possible German president. At the Nuremberg Trials, Wilhelm Keitel, who knew him very well, said Rommel had supported the assassination attempt. Rommel's wife Lucia admitted her husband had a growing disdain for Hitler, but she thought he would not have agreed to support a plot to kill him and he certainly never discussed it with her.[215] Rommel's Chief of Staff, General Hans Speidel, who was closely connected to Goerdeler, was arrested on 7 September 1944. He told his Gestapo interrogators that Rommel favoured putting Hitler on trial for war crimes, but did not support killing him.[216]

On 19 September 1944, Martin Bormann received a detailed report from the Gestapo, compiled by Karl Kronmüller, which outlined in detail all of Rommel's alleged links to the military conspiracy.[217] On 27 September, Bormann presented a lengthy memorandum to Hitler, summarizing all the various accusations against Rommel, obviously culled from Kronmüller's earlier report. Bormann concluded that Rommel knew about the assassination attempt and he had made various promises of involvement in Goerdeler's post-coup government.[218]

It was decided that the Gestapo case against Rommel was strong enough to have him removed from the army and sent for trial at the People's Court, which would certainly result in his execution. Hitler, fully aware of Rommel's fame and popularity among the German people, thought publicly branding him a traitor would cause a media sensation, not just in Germany but in the Allied nations, too.

On 1 October 1944, Rommel, now realizing the evidence against him was building, wrote to Hitler, expressing his loyalty: 'You, my Führer, know how I have given all my strength and ability. Whether it be during the western offensive in 1940 or in Africa in 1941–43 or in Italy in 1943 or again in the West in 1944, I am completely consumed by the thought of fighting and achieving victory for your new Germany.'[219]

A few days later Hitler asked Rommel to come and meet him in Berlin. Rommel claimed he was still too ill to travel. Hitler regarded this as an admission of guilt. Accordingly, Hitler decided to offer Rommel two options: he could choose to defend himself personally with the Führer in Berlin or he could opt for a quiet 'honourable suicide'. If he chose the latter course, the German government would claim he had died of the injuries sustained in his car accident, grant him a state funeral with full military honours, and allow his widow to receive his full pension payments.

On 14 October 1944, two generals from Hitler's headquarters turned up at Rommel's home in Herrlingen at noon to make him an offer he couldn't refuse. They were Wilhelm Burgdorf, Rudolf Schmundt's successor as Hitler's chief adjutant, and Ernst Maisel, who was in charge of matters of 'military honour' in the army's personnel office. Once inside, they explained to Rommel that he was suspected of having been involved in the 20 July bomb plot and they outlined all the incriminating material that had been uncovered during the Gestapo investigation.

Rommel left the room in order to speak to his wife, saying to her: 'The Führer has given me the choice of taking poison or being dragged before the People's Court. They have brought the poison. They say it will take only three seconds to act.' Because Hitler had promised that if he chose suicide then nothing would happen to his family, Rommel told his wife he was going to accept.[220] His distraught wife pleaded with him to argue for his innocence in a public trial in Berlin. 'No,' Rommel replied. 'I would not be afraid to be tried in public, for I can defend everything I have done. But I know that I should never reach Berlin alive.'[221]

Rommel then went to his bedroom to put on his famous old Afrika Korps leather jacket and cap and held his field marshal's baton in his hand as he was led to the waiting Opel limousine. Burgdorf sat next to him on the back seat and Maisel got in the front seat alongside the driver, SS Master Sergeant Heinrich Doose.

They drove out of the village to a quiet, open forested area. Burgdorf and Rommel stayed in the car, while Doose and Maisel went for a brief walk. Bergdorf handed Rommel a single cyanide capsule, which he swallowed. Rommel died almost instantaneously. When Doose and Maisel returned in ten minutes, they saw Rommel, obviously dead, slumped forward on the back seat. His military cap had fallen off. Rommel's corpse was then driven to the Wagner School field hospital in Ulm. Burgdorf told the doctor not to examine the corpse because, 'Everything has already been arranged in Berlin.' Dr Meyer later recalled that it was obvious Rommel had not died from natural causes.[222]

The official German story – released to the public and the press – was that Rommel had died of a heart attack or a cerebral embolism, the result of a medical complication of the injuries he had sustained in his car accident in Normandy earlier in the summer. Hitler ordered an official day of mourning to commemorate a man he described as a 'war hero'.

Rommel was given a full state funeral, held – at his request – in Ulm not Berlin. His coffin was draped in swastika flags. As the 'Führer's Representative', Gerd von Rundstedt delivered a moving eulogy, saying of Rommel 'His heart belonged to the Führer.' At that time, Rundstedt had no idea that Rommel had been forced to commit suicide, on Hitler's explicit order. Rommel was cremated to avoid any future investigation into his death. No one outside Germany ever believed the official version of events.

Hitler didn't attend the annual commemoration of the 1923 Munich Beer Hall Putsch, which had been delayed until 12 November 1944. In his place, Himmler read out his speech. It focused on Hitler's familiar enemies: the Bolsheviks and the Jews. The Anglo-American democracies were depicted as the pawns of Jews, who had also helped create the 'Bolshevik beast of the world', which was now intent on exterminating the German people. The democracies could not see that victory for Soviet Bolshevism would lead to the smashing of their own bourgeois states. This was a fate Hitler promised would not happen to the Fatherland: 'As long as I live, Germany will not submit to the fate of European states swept away by Bolshevism.'

Hitler then mentioned the July bomb plot, promising: 'Whoever raises the sword or bomb against Germany will be ruthlessly and mercilessly annihilated. A few hours sufficed in order to suffocate the putsch of 20 July. It took only a few months to round-up and completely eliminate this coterie of dishonourable conspiratorial characters.'

Hitler next explained all of his time and energy was now devoted to bringing about a change of German fortune in the war: 'If at this time I speak little and not very often to you, my party comrades and German *Volk*, then I do this because of work; I work to fulfil the tasks with which time has burdened me and which must be fulfilled in order to bring about a turn of events.'[223]

On 20 November at 3.15 p.m. Hitler left the Wolf's Lair in Rastenburg for the last time. He travelled with his personal entourage on his special train to Berlin, with the blinds down on his carriage during the journey. 'I never saw Hitler so depressed and distracted as he was that day,' Traudl Junge later recalled. 'His voice hardly rose above a loud whisper; his eyes were lowered to his plate or stared absently at some point on the tablecloth. An oppressive atmosphere weighed down on the cramped, rocking cage in which we gathered together.'[224]

On 22 November 1944 Hitler underwent a minor operation in Berlin to remove a benign throat polyp. It left him unable to speak for a week. Beforehand, he was worried that he might lose his voice completely.[225] His long-term partner Eva Braun had come from Munich to stay with him in his private quarters on the second floor of

[overleaf]
Rommel's flag-draped coffin on top of his funeral gun carriage.

the Old Reich Chancellery while he recovered. After his operation, he communicated with her on little slips of paper.[226]

Hitler issued a special order to the *Wehrmacht* on 25 November, explaining what German army commanders should do in the event of encirclement by the enemy. In his view seemingly hopeless military positions could be overcome only by soldiers who were 'contemptuous of death'. If a German commander now wanted to give up a military struggle, he should first consult his other officers, then the non-commissioned officers, and finally the ordinary troops. If even one of them wanted to continue the fight, then the military command should be handed to that man, regardless of his rank.[227]

With winter approaching, Hitler knew a major Soviet offensive was a certain eventuality. He finally accepted no further offensive operations could be undertaken against the now formidable Red Army on the Eastern Front. As the Western Allies had not made a decisive breakthrough on the Rhine, Hitler decided to mount a surprise major offensive in the west, where the Allies least expected it: the densely forested Ardennes, the scene of Hitler's spectacular thrust through France in the summer of 1940.

The Ardennes offensive of 1944 started to germinate in Hitler's mind towards the end of the Battle of Normandy. The first steps towards its planning came at a meeting with his generals on 16 September, when Hitler suddenly announced: 'I have made a momentous decision.' He then explained an offensive in the west stood the best chance of success in the late autumn in bad weather, with muddy ground and foggy weather, all of which would weaken the impact of Allied air superiority.[228]

The mission was originally codenamed Watch on the Rhine (*Wacht am Rhein*), but was later renamed Operation Autumn Mist (*Herbstnebel*) in early December 1944. The Allies would call it the Battle of the Bulge. All previous German offensive operations had been planned by the High Command of the German Army (OKH), but this was the first one planned by the High Command of the German Armed Forces (OKW), commanded by the two Hitler loyalists – Wilhelm Keitel and Alfred Jodl.[229]

Hitler's ambitious goal for the Ardennes offensive of 1944 was for Army Group B – commanded by Walter Model, and composed of the 5th and 6th Panzer armies, supported by the 7th Army – to punch a deep hole in the Allies' defence front. In particular, the thinly defended line of the 1st US Army, numbering 83,000 troops, who were operating in the weakest sector of the Front in the Ardennes Forest, from Monschau to Echternach, a gap of almost a hundred miles. The aim was for the Germans to cross the River Meuse, then motor 125 miles to Antwerp, thereby cutting in two the Allied 21st and 12th Army Groups.

When the reinstated commander of the German Army Command in the West (OB-West) Gerd von Rundstedt first saw this plan, he called it a 'big solution' and felt it was unrealistic to think that a far distant Antwerp could be recaptured. He also felt that crossing the River Meuse was fraught with danger from deadly Allied bombers. Model also believed Hitler's aim of recapturing Antwerp was unattainable. Model came up with an alternative 'small solution' offensive that met with Rundstedt's approval. This involved a much more limited German attack on a 35-mile front south-west of Hürtgenwald, targeting the Allied forces in eastern Belgium and Luxembourg and wheeling north to retake Aachen from US forces. This plan had the virtue of bypassing the River Meuse.

When this 'Autumn Mist' plan was presented to Hitler, he saw it as a 'half-solution'. Hitler was determined to mount a much more dramatic offensive to send a message to the German people that he was determined to turn the tide in the war. He told Speer that if the offensive failed, 'I see no other possibility of bringing the war to a favourable conclusion.'[230]

Preparations for the German offensive in the Ardennes went on under strict secrecy. On 10 November 1944, Hitler signed the order for the final agreed offensive plan. It was entirely based on Hitler's original ideas but was drawn up by the OKW. The attack date was set for 27 November 1944, then moved to 10 December and finally to 16 December. Due to a successful German intelligence deception operation, including false radio messages, the Allies had no idea about the location or date of the attack.

The German armed forces assembled an impressive attack force, composed of three complete armies: the 5th and 6th Panzer armies and the 7th Army, totalling 406,342 men, 557 tanks, 667 tank destroyers and assault guns, and 4,224 artillery pieces. In support, the *Luftwaffe* provided 1,700 fighter aircraft, but not all of these planes could fly due to a serious shortage of fuel.[231]

On 11 December 1944 Hitler arrived at his new headquarters, codenamed the Eagle's Nest (*Adlerhorst*), a bunker complex that had been designed by Albert Speer. It was built in 1939–40 and located in the rural area of Langenhain-Ziegenberg in the Taunus Mountains in the state of Hesse. It was going to be the Führer's headquarters during the 1940 invasion of France, but it was never used back then. The bunker had three-foot thick concrete ceilings and walls and was poison gas-proof. Hitler would remain there until 15 January 1945.[232]

On 11 and 12 December Hitler addressed his generals in groups of twenty to thirty to discuss the upcoming 1944 Ardennes offensive. Most of those present were shocked by his appearance. He looked exhausted, mentally and physically. A shorthand record of his speech on 12 December has survived.

Hitler gave a lengthy historical overview of how he had reached this stage in his struggle for 'the life and death of Germany'. The themes were all too familiar. The European powers had always wanted to stop Germany gaining a dominant position on the continent, he said. They had always preferred a weak and divided Germany. The beneficiary of Germany's failure to ever gain a dominant position in Europe was the British Empire, which joined with France and Russia to encircle Germany in 1914. The war Germany had launched in 1939 was 'preventative', with the aim of setting Germany free of another 'encirclement'. Hitler admitted that rearmament had given Germany a potentially decisive advantage, but this had proved to be temporary.

It was always his intention, Hitler added, to wage war offensively to avoid the static war of defence that characterized the First World War and led to Germany's defeat. Hitler made no mention of his decision to invade the Soviet Union in June 1941, which had, of course, proved catastrophic. Instead, he emphasized the fact that the war must now be fought to the bitter end.

Hitler remained optimistic that Germany could turn the tide in the war because of the contradictory nature of the Allied coalition, which included the ultra-capitalist rising power of the United States, the declining British Empire, but also the ultra-Marxist state of the Soviet Union. All of these states, Hitler claimed, were under Jewish control. The differing aims of the Allied powers were now clashing and with a few military reverses this fragile alliance might well fall apart. The best place to attack this unstable coalition was in the west, he concluded, because he believed that the British and Americans could not cope if the German army inflicted 'gigantic' casualties on them.[233]

The Ardennes offensive was launched on 16 December 1944 under heavy cloud cover and in knee-deep snow which grounded Allied planes. The main thrust of the attack was carried out in the north by the 6th Panzer Army, supported by the 5th Panzer Army in the centre, with the 7th Army protecting the southern flank. In the first few days German troops made rapid progress. The German press were already calling the battle in the Ardennes a 'great victory'. The 5th Panzer Army penetrated up to sixty miles into the centre of Allied lines, capturing 23,554 Allied soldiers, but the Germans were never able to cross the River Meuse.[234]

Caught by surprise, the Allies recovered quickly, mounting a stubborn defence at Bastogne and St Vith, thereby delaying the German advance and allowing reinforcements from north and south to defend the bulge created by the German advance. When the cloudy weather finally cleared on 23 December, the Allies were able to exploit their devastating air superiority for the first time, with 5,000 aircraft constantly bombarding German tanks, and especially their long supply columns of fuel and ammunition. German fighters suffered heavy losses in fierce dog fights in the air. As General George Patton noted in his diary: 'The Krauts stuck his head in a meat-grinder. And this time I've got hold of the handle.'[235]

By Christmas Eve 1944 even the ever loyal and optimistic Walter Model thought this was one fire even he could not put out. He concluded the German offensive in the Ardennes had failed. On 27 December, Rundstedt confirmed that no reinforcements could be moved up the line. Meanwhile, Heinz Guderian on the Eastern Front requested a transfer of all available German forces to ward off an ominous military build-up by the Red Army on the River Vistula. Hitler dismissed this warning as 'rubbish'.[236]

On New Year's Eve 1944 at a dinner party in his Berlin home Joseph Goebbels told his invited guests that his new title of 'Reich Plenipotentiary for Total War' was quite hollow, because Allied bombs had already destroyed most of the country. His wife Magda, who had enjoyed perhaps more than a few glasses of wine during the evening, turned to her husband and said loudly: 'Why don't you tell these old soldiers that for the past three and a half years you have seldom managed to see the Führer? These people have the right to know this.'[237]

In Dresden, that same evening Victor Klemperer, the Jewish former university professor, wrote in his diary:

> The year draws to an end very disappointingly. Until well into the autumn I, and probably the whole world, thought it certain that the war would be over before the end of the year. Now the general feeling and mine also: Perhaps in a couple of months, perhaps in a couple of years.[238]

1945

·

FUNERAL
IN BERLIN

·

•

At five minutes past midnight on New Year's Day 1945 Adolf Hitler's instantly recognizable voice came on the German radio station *Großdeutscher Rundfunk*, to deliver a 26-minute recorded message. During the whole of 1944 Hitler had spoken only once to the German people on the radio after the failed assassination attempt of 20 July.

Hitler began by apologizing for not speaking regularly to the German people, but explained that this was due to his concentration on the all-consuming task of securing victory in the war. He admitted that in August 1944 Germany had been perilously close to defeat as 'one catastrophe followed another'. Since then there had been a stabilization of the military situation, although he made no mention of the faltering Ardennes offensive.

Hitler then warned the German people that the Allies, supported by the 'Jewish international conspiracy', wanted to tear the German people to pieces and to transport up to 20 million of them to foreign countries, leaving the rest of the population to starve. He promised to fight on with the 'greatest fanaticism' and would never capitulate, as happened in 1918. The choice for the German people was now 'living in freedom or dying in slavery'. He then referred to Frederick the Great, who through willpower and endurance had turned certain defeat into victory. Hitler concluded his speech with an unexpectedly Christian statement:

> I cannot close this appeal without thanking the Lord for the
> help that He always allowed the leadership and the *Volk* to find,
> as well as for the power He gave us to be stronger than misery
> and danger. If I also thank Him for my rescue [on 20 July 1944],
> then I do so only because through it I am happy to be able to
> continue dedicating my life to the service of the *Volk*. In this hour,
> as the spokesman of Greater Germany, I therefore wish to make
> the solemn avowal before the Almighty that we will loyally and
> unshakably fulfil our duty also in the new year, in the firm belief
> that the hour will come when the victory will favour for good the
> one who is most worthy of it, the Greater German Reich![1]

As Hitler's words were broadcast, the final German military offensive of the war was already under way. Codenamed Operation North Wind (*Unternehmen Nordwind*), it was a final desperate move to ease the pressure on the faltering Ardennes offensive. German troops thrust north-east of Alsace and Lorraine, with the aim of breaking through the lines of the under-strength American 7th Army and the French 1st Army in order to seize Strasbourg. The German attack force was led by Army Group G, commanded by Johannes Blaskowitz, and Army Group Upper Rhine (*Oberrhein*), commanded by Heinrich Himmler, who was taking part in a major army operation for the first time.[2]

Before the assault began, Hitler had delivered a lengthy briefing to his division commanders at Adlerhorst on 28 December 1944. He told them the survival of the German nation was now at stake. A victory for the Allies would mean the annihilation of Germany which would then be 'Bolshevized'. Above all, Hitler ruled out surrender: 'In my life I have never learned to know the word capitulation.'[3]

Operation North Wind initially took the Allies by surprise. On 7 January the German 19th Army was heading towards Strasbourg, before determined French defence forces halted them. Between 10 and 20 January 1945 German and American forces engaged in a series of tank battles. Gradually, however, the German momentum faltered, as the snow fell and turned to ice. On 25 January the German offensive was decisively halted near the French town of Haguenau. This was a costly engagement for both sides, with 14,000 American and 23,000 German casualties. The Germans, as usual, showed boldness in attack and doggedness in defence, gaining a tactical victory, but it was a strategic defeat for Germany because the operation neither lessened Allied pressure in the Ardennes nor captured Strasbourg.[4]

By now Hitler accepted the Ardennes offensive – his last military gamble of the war – had failed. On 16 January 1945 German troops were back in the same position they had occupied before the offensive began. On 26 January the Allies declared total victory in the Battle of the Bulge. It began with a surprise setback, followed by a swift rally, then an overwhelming victory. On 14 January at a military conference, Hitler, in a rare moment of candour, commented:

> I know the war is lost. The superior power is too great. I've been betrayed. Since 20 July everything has come out [regarding the treachery of the army] that I didn't think possible. Precisely those were against me who have profited most from National Socialism. I spoilt them all and decorated them. That's the thanks. I'd like most of all to put a bullet through my head.[5]

American casualty figures for the Battle of the Bulge, as recorded in the official report by the US Department of the Army, listed 105,102 casualties, with 19,246 killed, 26,246 captured or missing, and 62,489 wounded.[6] It was the largest American loss of life of any single battle of the entire Second World War. The German High Command estimated its own casualties at 81,834 of which 12,652 were killed, 30,582 were missing and 38,600 were wounded. Some historians have suggested that German casualties were as high as 125,000.[7]

On 15 January Hitler left his military headquarters in the Eagle's Nest to travel by his special train on a nineteen-hour journey to Berlin, arriving on the following day. Hitler realized the Eastern Front would now take centre stage. At first, he alternated between living in his apartment on the second floor of the old Reich Chancellery and underground in the Führerbunker.

This bunker complex, which lay beneath the old Reich Chancellery at 77 Wilhelmstraße, consisted of two separate shelters. The first was the Ante-Bunker (*Vorbunker*). Constructed in 1939, it was five feet beneath the cellar of a large reception hall in the old Reich Chancellery and it contained sixteen rooms and a staff canteen. This was connected via a long corridor to the main Führerbunker, which was accessed by a circular staircase. Built in 1944, the Führerbunker was twenty-eight feet below, at floor level, the surface of the old Reich Chancellery garden, with a roof made of ten-foot thick reinforced concrete. It had twenty sparsely furnished rooms, which branched off on each side of a long inner corridor. Hitler's private apartment was furnished with an upholstered bench, a desk and three armchairs. The main bedroom had an en suite bathroom and a dressing room, which was soon converted into Eva Braun's bedroom. Looming over the living room was a portrait of Hitler's military hero Frederick the Great by Anton Graff.

Next door to Hitler's apartment was a cramped conference room dominated by a large rectangular table. Usually two military briefings a day were held there: one in the afternoon, the other around midnight, which could go on until 6 a.m. Hitler would then go to bed and often not rise until noon.[8]

Also in the Führerbunker was a small dining room where Hitler took his meals with his four personal secretaries: Traudl Junge, Christa Schroeder, Gerda Christian and Johanna Wolf. The food was prepared by his personal cook and dietician Constanze Manziarly. Eva Braun often joined them when she took up permanent residence in Berlin from 7 March. She would sometimes escape the depressing atmosphere of the subterranean bunker and go upstairs to Hitler's apartment in the old Reich Chancellery, sometimes hosting small parties there for the secretaries and young officers at which records were played and they danced, drank champagne and smoked cigarettes.[9]

Also present in the Führerbunker was Hitler's Alsatian bitch Blondi and her four recently born puppies, including one (which became a favourite of Hitler's) called Wulf. Hitler's secretaries had their own office, with individual desks and typewriters. He would often pop in to their office to dictate letters, military orders and telegrams. His personal doctor Theodor Morell had his own surgery in the bunker with ample supplies of Hitler's favourite 'prescription drugs'.

The Führerbunker complex was completely self-sufficient. There was plentiful food and drink kept in large storerooms, while a noisy diesel generator provided electricity and powered the air-ventilation system. Well water was pumped in. Communications to the outside world included a telex machine, a telephone switchboard and a secure army radio system. Oxygen tanks were also available in case the diesel generator and the air conditioner failed.

Hitler found some consolation inspecting an illuminated scale model of his former hometown of Linz. Created by the architect Hermann Giesler, it was brought to the cellar of the old Reich Chancellery on 9 February 1945. Hitler liked to fantasize that Germany would miraculously win the war and he and Eva would retire to Linz. So beguiling was this idea that Hitler would often slip away during the day to gaze at the model, viewing it from different angles and checking the proportions of the buildings.[10]

Heinz Guderian, the Chief of the Army Supreme Command (OKH), had repeatedly warned Hitler defeat in the Ardennes would severely weaken the Eastern Front. On 9 January Guderian demanded that reinforcements be sent east because German intelligence reports were indicating a huge build-up of Soviet forces on the River Vistula. Hitler dismissed these reports as 'completely idiotic'. In response, Guderian described the Eastern Front as a house of cards. 'If the front is penetrated at any point,' he said, 'the whole thing would fall apart.' Hitler then told him bluntly: 'The East must rely on itself and survive on what it has.' This exchange reveals how out of touch with military reality Hitler now was. He seemed to have no realization of the numerical strength of the forces now facing Germany on the Eastern Front.[11]

Guderian's dire warnings proved correct. The Red Army, with 6.7

million troops available, had consolidated two huge bridgeheads on the west bank of the River Vistula, opposite Warsaw, during the latter part of 1944. Soviet forces were preparing for two simultaneous offensives across the Vistula–Oder and East Prussia, designed to pave the way to a comprehensive Soviet victory.

The Red Army was by now a fearsome fighting machine with professional officers, modern tanks, deadly artillery, huge air support and American-built trucks and jeeps. Soviet soldiers no longer feared the Germans. On the contrary, they were now ultra-confident after an unbroken series of victories.[12]

There was undoubtedly a strong desire for revenge among Red Army soldiers as they prepared for an assault on German soil. Soviet tank crews painted slogans on their vehicles such as 'Forward into the Fascist lair' and 'Revenge and death to the German occupiers'.[13] Many soldiers had lost close relatives in the war. One Soviet soldier recalled there being 'blind feelings of revenge' among the troops, while another admitted, 'We are taking revenge on the Germans for all the disgraceful things they did to us.'[14]

Stalin's chief anti-Nazi war propagandist was Ilya Ehrenburg, who wrote for the Red Army newspaper *Red Star* and became something of a hero with the troops. Goebbels claimed that Ehrenburg had written articles inciting Red Army soldiers to rape German women, but Ehrenburg later denied this, although he did admit to encouraging the Red Army troops to take revenge against German soldiers.[15]

The colossal Soviet Vistula–Oder Offensive involved two Soviet army groups (or Fronts as the Soviets called them). The 1st Ukrainian Front, led by Ivan Konev, would attack over the River Vistula on 12 January 1945, with Breslau as its ultimate target.

Heinz Guderian.

The 1st Byelorussian Front, commanded by Marshal Georgy Zhukov, would start its offensive on 14 January, its first objective was to capture Warsaw and then advance towards Berlin. Between them, the Soviets had 2.2 million men, 4,529 tanks, 2,513 assault guns, 13,763 artillery pieces, 4,913 anti-tank guns, 2,198 Katyusha multiple rocket launchers and 5,000 aircraft.[16]

Facing these numerically formidable Soviet forces was the under-strength German Army Group A, formerly Army Group North Ukraine, but adopting the title Army Group Centre on 26 January. By then its original commander Colonel-General Josef Harpe had been replaced by the fanatical Nazi Colonel-General Ferdinand Schörner. There were three armies attached to the reformed Army Group Centre: the 9th, 17th and the 4th Panzer. They were supported by the 1st Panzer and 1st Hungarian armies. In total, the Germans could muster 400,000 soldiers, 300 tanks and 600 artillery guns, supported by 300 fighter planes. The Germans were outnumbered by 5:1 in manpower in this sector of the Soviet assault.[17]

Simultaneously, the Red Army launched the East Prussian Offensive on 13 January 1945. This involved three more Soviet army groups: the 1st Baltic Front commanded by Ivan Bagramyan, the 2nd Byelorussian Front led by Marshal Konstantin Rokossovsky, and the 3rd Byelorussian Front, commanded by General Ivan Chernyakhovsky. These forces totalled 1.67 million men, 3,500 tanks, 25,000 artillery guns and 1,500 aircraft.[18]

Rokossovsky felt the East Prussian Offensive was of secondary importance to Stalin. He even suspected Zhukov had devolved to him command of the East Prussian Offensive to deny him the plum prize of leading the final Soviet assault on Berlin. There was some truth in this accusation as it was well known that Stalin did not want a Pole (Rokossovsky) to take the glory of capturing Berlin.[19]

Defending East Prussia was the reformed Army Group North commanded by Colonel-General Georg-Hans Reinhardt, who was replaced on 26 January by Lothar Rendulic and from 12 March by Walter Weiss. This German army group contained three armies: the 2nd and 4th, plus the 3rd Panzer. In total, 580,000 men, plus 200,000 poorly equipped *Volkssturm*. This group had 700 tanks and 700 aircraft.

The German forces aimed to create successive defence lines to a depth of 150 miles. A series of heavily fortified positions was built, using a combination of civilians, foreign labourers and prisoners of war. The German aim was to soak up the initial Soviet attack, then launch counter-attacks to push back the advancing Soviet forces. German commanders were pessimistic about their chances. A German military planning report gloomily predicted the Soviets would reach the border of Silesia in just six days after the opening of the offensive.[20]

The assault by Konev's 1st Ukrainian Front began with a huge artillery bombardment at 4.45 a.m. on 12 January 1945. It was freezing cold, but with little snow on the ground, which proved ideal conditions for the advancing T-34 Soviet tanks. The German officers ordered their troops to fight 'to their last breath' to defend German territory.[21]

The frozen battlefield soon became a smoke-filled wasteland. The headquarters of the 4th Panzer Army was obliterated and one German officer described the Soviet artillery bombardment as 'like the heavens falling on earth'.[22] In a matter of hours Soviet forces had penetrated twelve miles. On the second day of the offensive the Soviets held territory thirty-six miles wide and twenty-five miles deep. They had already captured the cities of Radom and Czętochowa. On 22 January, Soviet troops crossed the River Oder at Steinau. The German 4th Panzer Army was utterly decimated in this early engagement. In just ten days Konev's spearheads had driven deep into the vital German industrial area of Silesia. At the end of February, Silesia was safely in Soviet hands, representing an enormous blow to the German war economy. According to Albert Speer, the loss of Silesia led to a reduction of Germany's war production by a quarter, and it 'could not be compensated for by the bravery of our soldiers'. Speer thought Hitler should have brought the war to an end at this juncture.[23]

On 13 January, the Soviet assault on East Prussia began, striking first against the German 3rd Panzer Army, with the aim of quickly advancing to the state capital of Königsberg. Fighting in East Prussia was particularly brutal. The Germans mounted a dogged defence, but Soviet numerical strength gradually forced the Germans into retreat. Soviet tanks, attached to Rokossovsky's 2nd Byelorussian Front, decimated the defending German tank units.

On 18 January the 3rd Byelorussian Front achieved a decisive breakthrough between Schillen and Breitenstein. Within days, several East Prussian towns fell in succession, including Tilsit, Allenstein and Insterburg. The Red Army then reached Tannenberg, the site of a major German victory over Russia in August 1914. German defenders blew up the Tannenberg Memorial after hastily removing the coffin of former German President Paul von Hindenburg.[24]

By now, the 3rd Panzer Army near Königsberg was in danger of encirclement. The same fate soon faced the German 4th Army, as the Soviets cut off Königsberg from the rest of Germany. On 26 January General Friedrich Hossbach, its commander, bravely defying Hitler, ordered his troops to break out to the west. Hossbach was relieved of his command, but escaped execution. On the same day, Hitler's old military headquarters at Rastenburg, which the Germans had already blown up and abandoned two days earlier, was captured by the Red Army. By the middle of February 1945 almost the whole of East Prussia was now in Soviet hands.[25]

Heinz Guderian noticed that as the situation of the German army deteriorated, Hitler's rages at military meetings became much more uncontrollable. At the end of January 1945, when the Red Army had reached the River Oder and Guderian called for reinforcements, Hitler got so angry that he seized Guderian by his jacket lapels. On 13 February, after another blazing row between the two over the deteriorating situation on the Eastern Front, Guderian recalled Hitler 'stood there in front of me, beside himself with fury, having lost all self-control. After each outburst Hitler would stride up and down the carpet edge, then suddenly stop immediately before me and hurl his next accusation in my face.'[26]

It was obvious the relationship between the two men had now broken down irreparably. On 28 March, after Guderian's forces failed to recapture Küstrin, Hitler told him to take six weeks' 'sickness leave' due to heart trouble. Guderian was replaced by General Hans Krebs and never returned to active duty.

On 14 January Zhukov's 1st Byelorussian Front began its own assault over the River Vistula, attacking the defending 9th German Army. On the second day, Warsaw was completely surrounded. German troops evacuated the city on 17 January. Stalin granted the 1st Polish Army the honour of parading through the ruined city of Warsaw. Prior to this, Hitler had ordered that 'Fortress Warsaw' had to be held to the last man.[27] Other Polish cities, previously occupied by the Germans, now fell in quick succession. Kraków, Konev, Łódź and Posen were among them. On 23 January Soviet troops reached the River Oder between Oppeln and Ohlau. Five days later they crossed it, establishing a firm bridgehead on the western side of the river at Steinau.

Within the space of three weeks the Red Army had achieved yet another monumental military victory, effectively decimating the *Wehrmacht* as a fighting force on the Eastern Front. The Germans could no longer hold the Soviet juggernaut or mount any concerted counter-attacks. The end of the German-Soviet War now seemed in sight. The Soviets claimed 295,000 Germans were killed and 147,000 captured during the entire massive Vistula–Oder Offensive.[28] In fact, this is probably an underestimate. It now seems likely that 450,000 German soldiers lost their lives during the Soviet January–February offensives.[29] Soviet casualties were estimated at 43,000 men killed or missing, thus stressing how much the Red Army now dominated the battlefield.[30]

To try and cope with the unfolding catastrophe on the Eastern Front, Hitler created Army Group Vistula, under the command of Heinrich Himmler. It was given the hopeless task of maintaining a line of defence on the Oder and putting up a dogged defence of western Pomerania, plus the port city of Stettin. Himmler, the classic bureaucratic 'desk killer', proved totally unsuited to the role of an army commander.

On 11 March, Goebbels was told by Hitler that Himmler had failed to position the necessary anti-tank guns in Pomerania, as Hitler had ordered him to do, and promised to give 'a piece of his mind on the next available occasion to make clear that in the event of a repetition of such an instance, an irreparable breach would occur'.[31] There was no improvement in the military situation. By the end of March 1945, the whole of Pomerania, which Himmler's army group was supposed to defend, was now occupied by Soviets. Himmler was replaced on 20 March 1945 by General Gotthard Heinrici.

By now Himmler had suffered a complete nervous collapse and was confined to the health sanatorium of Hohenlychen, to be cared for by his own personal physician. Himmler's influence over Hitler was diminishing rapidly and he knew it. Hitler's growing displeasure with him was no doubt a factor in Himmler's decision to secretly try and broker a separate peace settlement with the Western Allies via the Swedish diplomat Count Folke Bernadotte. In this endeavour, Himmler, the key architect of 'The Final Solution', shamelessly pretended to be willing to repatriate Jews to neutral countries.[32]

By mid-February 1945 the devastating Soviet offensive on the Eastern Front paused, due to heavy fighting in East Prussia. Zhukov decided any drive on Berlin would require the consolidation of strong bridgeheads across the Oder, the replenishment of supplies, but also the mopping-up of any danger to the flanks of Konev and Zhukov's two key army groups and the detailed refinement of plans to capture Berlin.

The Soviet advance into Germany in early 1945 led to a mass exodus of Germans in East and West Prussia, Pomerania and Silesia, numbering over 2 million refugees. These long columns of desperate refugees walked westwards on ice-bound roads, with all of their possessions loaded on carts and every other available form of transport. A young woman who was part of this long retreat later recalled:

> We walked on in the direction of Danzig. On the way we saw gruesome scenes. Mothers in a fit of madness threw their children in the sea. People hanged themselves; others fell upon dead horses cutting out bits of flesh and roasting them on open fires. Women gave birth in the wagons. Everyone thought only of themselves – no one could help the sick and the weak.[33]

Many women fled in panic due to the high incidence of rape carried out by the advancing Soviet troops. It's been estimated that as many as 1.4 million German women were raped by Red Army soldiers in the eastern German territories, representing around 18 per cent of the total female population in these areas.[34] Many women were raped repeatedly by different bands of Soviet soldiers. Some German women asked Soviet troops to kill them afterwards. Many Soviet soldiers appear to have considered rape to be a much lower-grade war atrocity than the mass shootings of women and children carried out by the *Einsatzgruppen* in the Soviet Union. When Hitler was told of the rapes in East Prussia, he commented, angrily: 'They're not human beings anymore, they're animals from the steppes of Asia and the war I am waging against them is a war for the dignity of mankind.'[35]

The Soviet government knew what was going on. In one report from East Prussia, sent to the NKVD in Moscow, it was noted: 'Many Germans declare that all German women who stayed behind were raped by Red Army soldiers.' Numerous examples of 'gang rape' were cited involving 'girls under eighteen and old women'. Some victims were as young as eight.[36] Emma Korn told Soviet interrogators: 'Frontline troops entered the town. They came into the cellar where we were hiding and pointed their weapons at me and the other two women and ordered us into the yard. In the yard twelve soldiers in turn raped me.'[37] There were many instances of German women being gang-raped in front of their husbands. Soviet officers did little to stop the spread of the rape epidemic. They were more worried about clamping down on looting, drunken antics and the destruction of industrial machinery being carried out by the invading troops.

[overleaf]
A long trail of German refugees move westward as the Red Army advances into Germany.

The topic of rape by Soviet soldiers was a taboo subject among war veterans. Many Soviet soldiers claimed the sex with German women was consensual. Others tried to shift the blame to alcohol. Accusation of mass rape by Red Army troops is often viewed in Russia as a Western attempt to taint their victory in the 'Great Patriotic War'. Anthony Beevor's *Berlin* (2002), for example, was banned in the Soviet Union because it highlighted the rapes committed by the Red Army.[38]

As Soviet troops advanced into German territory for the first time, many were surprised by the high standard of living enjoyed by Germans. Some soldiers could not understand why the Germans had invaded the Soviet Union in the first place, because they seemed so well off. Others felt the Germans lived so well by pillaging the goods of the countries they occupied.[39]

When they liberated the German-run concentration camps, Soviet troops could see the very different treatment that was meted out to Soviet prisoners of war compared to American, British and French inmates. A report by the 1st Byelorussian Front noted Western Allied prisoners were always found healthy and well fed: 'They looked more like people on holiday than prisoners of war.' The Western POWs were not required to work and received Red Cross parcels. In contrast, Soviet prisoners were emaciated, suffered from severe starvation, were forced to undertake back-breaking hard labour and were denied Red Cross food parcels.[40]

Nazi propagandists tried to blame 'International Jewry' for the unfolding German military catastrophe. Typical was an article written by Joseph Goebbels called 'The Creators of the World's Misfortunes', which appeared in *Das Reich* on 21 January 1944. Goebbels claimed that 'Capitalism and Bolshevism have the same Jewish roots, two branches of the same tree that in the end bear the same fruit. International Jewry uses both in its own way to suppress nations and keep them in its service.' Stalin, Roosevelt and Churchill were, according to Goebbels, 'made by Jewry'. The Anglo-Americans presented themselves as 'upright men of civic courage, yet one never hears even a word against the Jews'. Even though the German government had broken the power of Jews in the Reich 'they have not given up. They did not rest until they mobilized the whole world against us.' Every Russian, British and American soldier was 'a mercenary of this world conspiracy of a parasitic race'.[41]

On 30 January 1945 a recording of Adolf Hitler's speech on the twelfth anniversary of coming to power in 1933 was broadcast on

German national radio. It would be the last time the German people ever heard his voice. He made no mention of the German defeat in the Ardennes offensive or the failure to halt the irresistible Soviet advance on the Eastern Front.

Instead, Hitler presented the peacetime period of 1933 to 1939 as one of great domestic achievements, only halted by a world war forced upon Germany by the 'Jewish international world plot', combining 'Jewish-Asiatic Bolshevism' and 'Anglo-American plutocracy'. Hitler warned his listeners that Britain and America would not be able to control the forces of Bolshevism they had unwittingly unleashed and would now themselves become the next 'victims of this destructive disease'. He then warned the German people of the dire consequences of Allied victory in the war: 'Whatever our enemies may plot, whatever sufferings they may inflict on our German cities, our German landscapes and above all on our people, all that cannot bear any comparison with the irreparable misery, the tragedy that would befall us if the Plutocratic-Bolshevistic conspiracy was victorious.'

Finally, Hitler implored the German people to 'gird themselves with a yet greater spirit of resistance until we can again – as we did before – put on the graves of the dead of this enormous struggle a wreath inscribed with the words: "And yet you were victorious." Therefore, I expect every German to do his duty to the last and to continue supporting this struggle with the utmost fanaticism.'[42]

To the Allies, Hitler's speech was tired and empty rhetoric. The German defeat was clearly only a matter of weeks away. The three major Allied leaders – Stalin, Roosevelt and Churchill – decided to meet to map out the future of Germany. This meeting – codenamed The Argonaut Conference – took place at Yalta in the Crimea between 4 and 11 February 1945. The location was a recognition of Stalin's strong diplomatic bargaining position. The last time the 'Big Three' had gathered was at the Tehran Conference in 1943. General Charles de Gaulle of France was not invited, which resulted in long-lasting resentment.[43]

The initiative for the Yalta Conference came from Roosevelt, who wanted Stalin to enter the war against Japan, once Germany had been defeated, but also to ask him to join a proposed 'World Organization', which would soon become the United Nations. This meant US policy makers made efforts not to provoke Stalin during the proceedings at Yalta. On the contrary, Roosevelt wanted to appease Stalin. It seemed to have worked, because on 5 April 1945 the Soviet government served

[overleaf]
The Allied leaders pose for the media at the Yalta Conference (left to right, Churchill, Roosevelt, Stalin).

notice of its intention to revoke the Non-Aggression Pact it had signed with Japan in 1941, thereby paving the way to join the war against Japan in the Pacific.

Churchill wanted to impress on Roosevelt how vital it was for post-war European stability for the Americans not to retreat into isolation from European affairs after the war, thereby leaving a political vacuum to be exploited by the now all-powerful Soviet Union. Churchill was also keen to emphasize the importance of democratic elected governments in Central and Eastern Europe, particularly in Poland.

Stalin pointed out the Western Allies had yet to cross the Rhine and remained bogged down in northern Italy, while the Red Army had the German army at its mercy on the Eastern Front and would capture Berlin in a matter of weeks. Stalin also reminded Churchill and Roosevelt how much the Soviet Union had suffered in the bloody struggle against German aggression and for this reason he wanted to prevent another invasion of his country at all costs. This meant the Western Allies needed to accept Central and Eastern Europe as a Soviet 'sphere of influence'. The American government was amenable to Stalin's demands. As James F. Byrnes, a member of the US diplomatic delegation, put it: 'It was not a question of what we would let the Russians do, but what we could get the Russians to do.'[44]

The treatment of a post-Hitler Germany occupied much of the Allied discussions at Yalta. Allied leaders confirmed that Germany must surrender unconditionally. There would be no separate peace agreements. Stalin favoured the total dismemberment of Germany for good, implying that no self-government would ever be offered in each of the three agreed zones of occupation. Roosevelt was inclined to agree with Stalin, but Churchill argued this demand required some further discussion. A committee of three representatives of the Allies was suggested, but this never met.

Further agreed proposals on the future of Germany included: (1) the complete demilitarization of Germany. (2) The creation of a Committee on the Dismemberment of Germany. (3) A programme of denazification implanted throughout the occupied zones. (4) Nazi war criminals would be hunted in Germany and in the other territories where their crimes had been committed. (5) Nazi leaders would be put on trial and executed.

Churchill gained Stalin and Roosevelt's mutual consent to allow France to be given one of the proposed zones of occupation in a post-war Germany, and also to be allowed to join the Allied Control Council for Germany. Churchill argued that the British needed France to share the burden of occupying post-war Germany for what was envisaged to be a lengthy period. Stalin insisted the French zone must be carved out of the existing British and US zones of occupation and this proposal was accepted.

Discussion then turned to the scale of reparations to be imposed on Germany at the end of the war. The Allies agreed to the establishment of a Reparations Committee, located in Moscow. Stalin suggested a figure of 20 billion US dollars ($280 billion in today's value), of which half would go to the Soviet Union. Churchill felt it would be better to initially seek reparations in the form of raw materials and forced labour, because he doubted Germany's capacity to pay for large financial reparations, at least in the immediate post-war period. In the end, the Reparations Committee accepted the Soviet figure, but only as a 'basis for discussion'.

The issue of Poland was also discussed extensively at Yalta. It was accepted by the Allies that Poland would be within the Soviet post-war 'sphere of influence' and the old Curzon Line would become the agreed eastern frontier of Poland. The real issue in dispute was how independent Poland would be in the post-war world. Churchill reminded Stalin and Roosevelt that Britain had gone to war in September 1939 to save Poland. As such, Churchill wanted a genuinely democratic and independent Poland to arise out of the ashes of war. Stalin, however, emphasized that for the Soviet Union the Polish issue was a matter of honour and security. He wanted to make sure that Poland could never again be used as an invasion corridor by Germany to attack the USSR. Stalin therefore favoured a Polish government of pro Soviet communists, although he paid lip service to Roosevelt and Churchill's demands for a democratically elected government.

It took three days of wrangling on the issue of post-war Poland before agreement was reached by the Allied leaders. Stalin agreed to democratic elections taking place in Poland and to the creation of a coalition 'provisional government' to include democratic leaders from inside Poland and some of those in exile. It was left to the Soviet Foreign Minister Molotov to thrash out more detailed proposals on the reorganization of Poland. At the end of the war, a communist pro-Soviet government was established in Poland, but no truly democratic elections ever took place, leaving many Poles feeling betrayed by the British and Americans at Yalta.[45]

The Yalta Conference ended with the release of an agreed communiqué by the Allies, which once again emphasized the only peace offer available to the German government was 'unconditional surrender' and it strongly implied that Germany's defeat would be followed by its occupation and dismemberment. Also issued by the Allies was a 'Declaration of a Liberated Europe', promising the people of Europe they would 'create democratic governments of their own choice'. This was quite similar to what was promised in the Atlantic Charter. It was, of course, not something that Stalin was ever likely to accept or implement.[46]

Two days after the Yalta Conference ended, Allied bombs rained down upon the historic city of Dresden, the capital of the German state of Saxony, which had a population of 750,000. This devastating attack was part of the final destructive stage of the Allied bombing campaign over Germany. Many German cities were severely damaged in this last destructive phase of the war, most notably Heilbronn, Stuttgart, Würzburg, Nuremberg and Munich. Pforzheim, known as the 'Gateway to the Black Forest', was also completely obliterated in a raid which killed 17,600 people, a quarter of the entire civilian population who lived there. Berlin was also targeted. On 3 February 1945, the German capital suffered the most damaging of all the 363 raids on the city during the war. It caused massive destruction, killing an estimated 3,000 people. The centre of Berlin was utterly devastated, with familiar streets, churches and government buildings destroyed. Even the old royal Hohenzollern Castle was burned to a shell.

The worst bomb attack was in Dresden, dubbed 'Florence on the Elbe'. It was full of beautiful baroque buildings and thousands of combustible timber and plaster-built houses. It was not a major industrial area, but it was not free of industry: there were 110 factories, employing 50,000 workers there, with most located in the suburbs – not in the target area of the Allied bombs. Dresden was not – as German propaganda later claimed – of no military significance at all. On 1 January 1945 Guderian had classified the city as a 'military strongpoint, a defensive area'.[47]

The terrifying bomb attacks on Dresden began on the evening of 13 February 1945: Shrove Tuesday. Two huge waves of RAF Avro Lancaster heavy bombers dropped destructive incendiary bombs all over the closely packed city centre. This was followed by further raids undertaken by US B-17 Flying Fortress bombers on the next day. In total, the Anglo-American air forces deployed 1,296 bombers. Allied losses amounted to just seven bombers, demonstrating the total air superiority the Western Allies now enjoyed over German air space.[48]

As the bombs exploded, trees crashed down, buildings were set aflame and collapsed into rubble. Soon a red-hot rash of small fires converged into a hellish firestorm, turning the narrow avenues and alleyways of the cramped cobbled streets into a fiery wind tunnel. Berthold Meyer, an engineering student, walked through the east of the city centre as the fires raged:

> Only someone who has been in such a sea of flame can judge what it means to breathe such an oxygen-deficient atmosphere... while battling against terribly hot, constantly changing currents of fire and air. My lungs were heaving. My knees began to turn weak. It was horrifying. Some individuals, especially older people, started to hang back. They would sit down apathetically on the street, or on piles of rubble, and just perish from asphyxiation.[49]

Ambulances and fire engines could not get through the blocked streets. Public transport halted. Water, gas and electricity supplies were cut off. The streets were littered with debris, ash, falling masonry and horrifically charred corpses. Margaret Freyer, who survived the raid, later recalled a vivid memory of the bombing: 'To my left I suddenly see a woman. I can see her to this day and shall never forget it. She carries a bundle in her arms. It is a baby. She runs, she falls, and the child flies in an arc into the fire.'[50]

Victor Klemperer met a young mother who told him what the city looked like a week later: 'There was a dreadful smell of corpses. The authorities estimated 200,000 dead (this was a huge exaggeration). There was a weak supply of water, no gas. There were no newspapers, except a leaflet from the Nazi authorities which threatens shooting for anyone who attempts to profit from the bombing.'[51]

The material damage in Dresden was equally enormous. The final report of the Higher Police and SS-Führer for the Elbe noted all of the following were destroyed: 24 banks, 26 insurance buildings, 31 department stores, 640 shops, 64 warehouses, 2 market halls, 31 large hotels, 26 beer halls, 63 administrative buildings, 3 theatres, 18 cinemas, 11 churches, 6 chapels, 19 hospitals, 39 schools, 5 consulates, a zoo, the railway system, the waterworks, 19 postal offices, 19 ships and barges, with 136 factories seriously damaged and 78,000 private dwellings completely destroyed and a further 64,500 seriously damaged.[52]

German news reports on the Dresden raid were initially guarded. Goebbels feared admitting the high number of casualties risked

[overleaf]
A forlorn statue overlooks the devastated German city of Dresden.

damaging the public's faltering morale. He was so outraged at the bombing in Dresden he told Hitler that he now favoured Germany abandoning the Geneva Convention and executing tens of thousands of Allied POWs as a reprisal. Even Hitler refused to sanction this.[53]

It was not until 16 February 1945 that the German News Bureau (DNB) finally issued its first press release on the Allied raids on Dresden. No casualty figures were given, but Dresden was portrayed as a city of culture without any war industries. On 4 March, an article in *Das Reich* claimed the aim of Allied bombing was 'to force us by mass-murder into surrender, so that they can carry out a death sentence on – as the other side expresses it – the surviving remnants.'[54]

On 25 February the Swedish newspaper *Svenska Dagbladet* claimed 200,000 people had been killed in Dresden. This figure, deliberately leaked by the German Propaganda Ministry, was a wild exaggeration, but it began something of a numbers game over the exact death toll in Dresden.[55] In early March 1945, the official Dresden police death toll – which was not released to the public – was 20,204. This figure had been reached after detailed research. Based on all the available evidence, a 2010 government report entitled the 'Dresden Commission of Historians for the Ascertainment of the Number of Victims of the Air Raids on the City of Dresden on 13–14 February 1945' used records from city archives, cemeteries and other official registers to come up with a maximum figure of 'up to 25,000'.[56]

The morality of the Dresden raid was questioned at the time and has been ever since. During a House of Commons debate on 6 March 1945 the Labour MP Richard Stokes echoed public concern about the raid when he objected to a policy of 'terror bombing' being used as a means of trying to 'shorten the war'. He also questioned why the Western Allies engaged in the blanket bombing of civilians while the Soviets – who did not – were enjoying much greater military success.[57] On 28 March 1945, Churchill responded to the growing public disquiet over the Dresden raids by ordering a halt to the carpet-bombing of German cities.

The historian Donald Bloxham has argued Dresden was a 'dispro-portionate act', but 'not comparable' to Auschwitz-Birkenau as a war crime. Similarly, Frederick Taylor agreed that the Dresden attack was 'immoral' and 'excessive', but that it fell some way short of being called a 'war crime'.[58] The German historian Jörg Friedrich has argued the Allied bombing campaign in the last months of the war served no real military purpose, because the German defeat was already inevitable and the attack on Dresden was of dubious validity.[59]

On 24 February 1945, Hitler delivered a speech to his Gauleiters in an undamaged part of the old Reich Chancellery. It was the twenty-fifth anniversary of the first proclamation of the Nazi Party programme in 1920, known as 'Foundation Day'. Most of those present hadn't seen Hitler since a previous meeting in August 1944. They were shocked by his physical appearance. He seemed old, his left arm trembled and he dragged his left leg as he walked.

Hitler spoke while seated in front of a table. He outlined how the previous struggles of National Socialism during the Weimar era had been overcome. Then he spoke of the current 'decisive hour' of the war, which would shape the coming century. He wanted to stiffen the resolve of those present to fight to the bitter end and never surrender.[60]

On the same day, the formal commemoration of the founding of the Nazi Party took place, as usual, in the Hofbräuhaus in Munich. It was impossible for Hitler to attend. The text of his speech was read out by Hitler loyalist Hermann Esser, the editor of the *Völkischer Beobachter*, and was broadcast live on German national radio. Hitler described the 'unnatural' alliance between 'exploiting capitalism and destructive bolshevism'. Providence, he continued, showed no mercy to weak nations, but it recognized the right to existence of sound and strong nations. The only way to stop the 'Jewish-bolshevist annihilation of nations and its Western European and American procurers' was 'extreme fanaticism' and 'stubborn steadfastness'. The Western Allies had made a pact with the 'Bolshevist devil' and 'will sooner or later become its victim'. If the Soviet Union won the war, he said, 'Germans would be dragged off to Siberia'.

Hitler promised to hand over power to a young generation if Germany won the war. His only remaining task as Führer was to strengthen the spirit of German resistance. He could accept any personal loss but not 'the weakness of my nation'. It was in times of the greatest distress that the German people showed its 'hardest character', he added. The struggle had to go on in order to avenge the wrongs committed by 'the international Jewish criminals'. In conclusion, Hitler stated defiantly: 'Twenty-five years ago I predicted victory for our movement. Today, filled as always with belief in our nation, I predict the final victory of the German Race.'[61]

On 4 March, Goebbels met Hitler in the old Reich Chancellery to discuss the possibility of opening peace talks with the Allies. Hitler told him he was concerned about the situation in the west and pessimistic about holding the Rhine. Nevertheless, he maintained a hope that the Allies would soon fall out with each other. Any initiative to open peace talks would most probably come from the Soviet Union, Hitler added, because Stalin was getting 'sick of quarrelling eternally with the Anglo-Americans'. Goebbels agreed that because Stalin – a dictator – had no need to worry about public opinion, he might undertake a U-turn in his war policy. After this frank conversation, Goebbels noted in his diary: 'The objective which the Führer has in mind is to discover some possibility for an accommodation with the Soviet Union and then to pursue the struggle against England [Britain] with brutal violence.' This conversation was, of course, pure fantasy. Germany was now heading towards certain defeat.[62]

In Western Europe, the supreme Allied military commander General Dwight D. Eisenhower had assembled 3.5 million men in three army groups, ready and waiting to finally cross the Rhine. The Allied forces consisted of the 21st Army Group in the north, commanded by Field Marshal Bernard Montgomery; the American 12th Army Group, led by Omar Bradley; and the 6th Army Group under the command of General Jacob L. Devers. Facing this huge force were 462,000 German troops, with a high proportion of them the raw and poorly equipped recruits of the *Volkssturm*.

As it turned out, the key Allied breakthrough in the west came by pure accident. On the afternoon of 7 March 1945, armoured forces

attached to the 1st US Army, commanded by General Courtney Hodges, reached a hill above the town of Remagen and saw that the Ludendorff Railway Bridge across the Rhine remained surprisingly intact. Not believing their luck, the Americans raced to the slopes of the river. Engineers cut the demolition wires left by the Germans. Some of the explosive charges did go off, shaking the bridge in several places, but it held firm. American tanks were then able to cross the Rhine for the very first time, quickly establishing a formidable bridgehead on the eastern bank. Crossing the bridge at Remagen was a pivotal moment in the battle on the Western Front.[63]

Hitler felt the Remagen incident was a consequence of the 'criminal neglect of duty' and 'cowardice' by those who were in charge of defending the bridge. Field Marshal Gerd von Rundstedt, the overall commander in the west, was summarily dismissed on 11 March 1945. It was the third time he had been dismissed by Hitler during the war. He was replaced by Field Marshal Albert Kesselring, who had so successfully contained the Anglo-American advance up the Italian peninsula.

Four German officers were primarily blamed for the disaster at Remagen: Majors Hans Scheller, Herbert Strobel and August Kraft and Lieutenant Karl-Heinz Peters. A 'flying tribunal' was quickly dispatched to administer fast-track justice. This 'mobile court martial' procedure was sanctioned in a decree issued by Hitler on 9 March 1945 for acts of cowardice and defeatism. These instant trials were presided over by three army officers, with two clerks recording the proceedings. In all cases the sentence was execution. The commander of Army Group B, Walter Model, chaired the Remagen 'Drum Head' Court Martial, which began on 13 March. A day later, Scheller, Strobel, Kraft and Peters were found guilty and executed by firing squad.[64]

Hitler's rage against the Army High Command increased as the military position of Germany deteriorated in the final months of the war. Over lunch one day in March, he told Christa Schroeder, one of his secretaries, of the difficulties he now faced:

> I am lied to on all sides, I can rely on no one, the whole business makes me sick. If I had not got my faithful Morell I should be absolutely knocked out... If anything happens to me, Germany will be left without a leader. I have no successor. The first, Hess, is mad; the second, Göring, has lost the sympathy of the people; and the third, Himmler, would be rejected by the Party – and anyway, is useless since he is so completely unartistic.[65]

The American 1st Army captured the
Ludendorff bridge at Remagen on
25 March 1945.

On 11 March Goebbels chatted with Hitler in the old Reich Chancellery. The key topic was once again the possibility of a peace settlement with the Allies. Hitler felt there was no chance of brokering a peace deal with the 'gangster' Churchill, who wanted to destroy Germany. As for the United States, its key war aim was to eliminate Europe as an economic competitor, but it needed the Soviet Union to join the Pacific War and for that reason alone Hitler felt that Roosevelt would not discuss a separate peace with Germany.

The only way to a peace settlement, in Hitler's view, was to drive the Soviet Union back in the east, because then he thought 'the Kremlin might show itself more accommodating towards us'. A separate peace in the east with Stalin would include an agreed partition of Poland, Germany retaining Hungary and Croatia, and freedom of movement to continue the war in the west. Goebbels noted afterwards that although he found Hitler's peace programme persuasive, 'there was no means of achieving it', given the dire German military position on the Eastern Front.[66] At no point did Hitler even mention accepting the non-negotiable Allied demand of unconditional surrender.

The crossing of the River Oder by the Red Army, then the Rhine by the Western Allies, prompted Albert Speer to write a lengthy memorandum to Hitler on 15 March 1945. In 'Drastic Measures to Defend the Reich at the Oder and the Rhine' Speer suggested the German economy would collapse in four weeks and went on to further warn Hitler that industrial installations, transport networks and public utilities should not be destroyed in a 'scorched earth' policy but preserved to ensure the future existence of the German people. The obligation of Germany's rulers – without regard to their own fate, Speer added – was to ensure that the German people were left with the possibility of reconstructing their lives in the future.[67] On 18 March Speer presented his memorandum in person to Hitler in Berlin, who responded to its contents bluntly:

> If the war should be lost, then the nation, too, will be lost. That
> would be the nation's unalterable fate. There is no need to
> consider the basic requirements that a people needs in order
> to continue to live a primitive life. On the contrary, it is better
> ourselves to destroy such things, for this nation will have proved
> itself the weaker and the future will belong exclusively to the
> stronger Eastern nation [the Soviet Union]. Those who remain
> alive after the battles are over are in any case only inferior persons,
> since the best have fallen.[68]

Hitler later commented on this meeting with Speer: 'Always when any man asks to see me alone, it is because he has something unpleasant to say to me. I cannot stand anymore of these Job's comforters.'[69]

On 19 March Hitler, completely ignoring Speer's advice, issued the 'Destructive Measures on Reich Territory Decree', subsequently called the 'Nero Order' (after the Roman emperor who supposedly engineered the Great Fire of Rome in 64 AD). In his edict, Hitler ordered the destruction of all military and industrial transportation and communications, plus electrical facilities, waterworks, bridges, railways, ships and warehouse stores in order to prevent them from falling into enemy hands. These measures were to be carried out by the military, working in conjunction with Gauleiters and Commissars for defence.

Hitler gratefully acknowledged Speer's 'great organizational talent', but then derided him as 'an artist by nature' and unsuited to a life-and-death crisis. He told Goebbels of his deep anger about Speer's memorandum, which he felt was influenced by capitalist industrialists. Hitler promised Goebbels that he would tell Speer to follow his orders or be summarily dismissed.[70] Goebbels felt Hitler now regarded Speer as a weak character and no longer trusted him.[71]

On 30 March 1945 Hitler and Speer had a face-to-face showdown in the old Reich Chancellery. Hitler criticized Speer for not being fully imbued with National Socialist fighting spirit. Speer bravely stood his ground, cleverly arguing that destroying factories was defeatist, as he thought they would be recaptured during a German counter-attack. This was enough to persuade Hitler to water down his original 'Nero Decree' by allowing arms production factories to continue to function.

Hitler then asked Speer whether he thought the war could still be won. In response, Speer said no. Hitler then told Speer he would give him twenty-four hours to see if he would change his mind on this point. On the following day Speer, blatantly lying, told Hitler: 'I stand unconditionally behind you.' Hitler seemed deeply moved by this expression of loyalty and shook Speer's hand warmly. As a further concession, Hitler agreed to Speer signing all of the demolition orders, under the terms of the 'Nero Decree'. In effect, Hitler was sanctioning Speer to defy his order.[72]

By now, the Allied advance in Western Europe was becoming overwhelming. The German cities of Cologne, Dortmund, Bonn and Bad Godesberg had all been captured. On 22 March, General George Patton's US 3rd Army, supported by the US 7th Army and the 1st Army, made the second successful Allied crossing of the Rhine at Nierstein

[overleaf]
The American 7th Army marches into
Nuremberg in April 1945.

535

and Oppenheim, south of Mainz. In a few days General Patton's forces had established a bridgehead seven miles wide and six miles deep.

On 23 March 1945 the Allied 21st Army Group – consisting of the British 2nd, the Canadian 1st and the American 9th armies – numbering 1.28 million men, launched Operation Plunder, the biggest Allied operation to cross the Rhine in force. The 21st Army Group took on the weakened German army Group H, commanded by General Alfred Schlemm, with just 69,000 troops defending, with the 1st German Parachute Army as its main source of strength. Schlemm was wounded in the initial stage of the battle and replaced by General Johannes Blaskowitz, who was given orders by Hitler to hold fast and fight to the last man.

The Allied operation went smoothly. Monty's forces, supported by 14,000 Anglo-American paratroopers, took part. They crossed the Rhine at Rees and Wesel in North-Rhine Westphalia, easily overpowering the worn-out and demoralized German soldiers, before pushing forward towards Bremen, Hamburg and Lübeck. Within a week the Allies had taken 30,000 Germans prisoner.

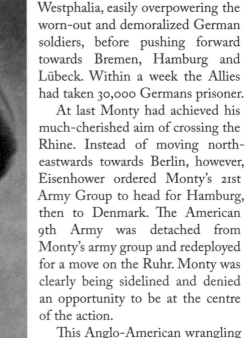

At last Monty had achieved his much-cherished aim of crossing the Rhine. Instead of moving north-eastwards towards Berlin, however, Eisenhower ordered Monty's 21st Army Group to head for Hamburg, then to Denmark. The American 9th Army was detached from Monty's army group and redeployed for a move on the Ruhr. Monty was clearly being sidelined and denied an opportunity to be at the centre of the action.

This Anglo-American wrangling did nothing to dent the relentless Allied advance in the west. One German city after another fell into Allied hands, including Mainz, Essen, Solingen, Darmstadt,

Walter Model, who killed himself after the German defeat in the Battle of the Ruhr.

Bochum, Mannheim, Wiesbaden and Frankfurt. In all these instances there was little German resistance. Local people were putting up white flags outside their homes.

The overall Allied operation – as conceived by Eisenhower – aimed for Omar Bradley's American 12th Army Group to encircle the Germans in the vital industrial area of the Ruhr. To this end, Eisenhower meticulously planned a classic pincer movement, involving the 1st US Army driving east from Remagen and the 9th US Army moving out of its bridgehead over the Rhine, then also heading east, spearheaded by the formidable 2nd US Armoured Division, nicknamed 'Hell on Wheels'. Both American armies would then link up to the rear of German army Group B and encircle it.

The plan worked perfectly. Army Group B was duly encircled on 1 April 1945, Easter Sunday, in one of the most expertly executed encirclements by the Western Allies of the entire war. German Army Group B, led by Walter Model, was trapped in an egg-shaped pocket, 30 x 75 miles, and subjected to relentless American air attacks. The position of the Germans was dire, but Hitler, predictably, refused to sanction a breakout. Instead, he promised to send a relief force under General Walther Wenck to assist Model. By 14 April, the trapped German forces were running out of fuel, ammunition and ideas.

US loudspeaker vans drove unimpeded through the streets, imploring the Germans to surrender. This time they did. The German 15th Army capitulated first. The next day, the Ruhr pocket was split in two. Model dissolved Army Group B, thereby allowing all of his men to surrender. On 18 April all the remaining German units gave up.[73] The number of German prisoners captured was a whopping 317,000.[74] There was one German soldier who didn't surrender: the fanatical Nazi Walter Model. He went on the run in a state of despair. On 21 April, Model shot himself in the head in a rural clearing surrounded by oak trees near Duisburg.[75]

The victorious Battle for the Ruhr Pocket caused the German administration in the area to collapse. Industrial production ceased. Electricity, gas, water and sewage services were severely disrupted. Bands of foreign forced labourers and released prisoners of war roamed the countryside, pillaging what goods they could find.[76]

The German front in the west was now wide open. This enabled US forces to drive rapidly and unhindered into the heart of Germany. More German cities fell, notably Düsseldorf, Cologne, Münster, Essen and Hanover. The Western Allied advance resembled a victory

[overleaf]
American troops captured huge numbers of German POWs after victory in the Battle of the Ruhr in April 1945.

parade. On 11 April 1945 the US 9th Army reached the River Elbe near Magdeburg and established a bridgehead there. The Americans were now just sixty miles from Berlin, pressing eastwards relentlessly into Thuringia and southwards into Saxony and Bavaria.

On 16 April American troops reached Nuremberg, the former citadel of National Socialism. The cities of Weimar, Leipzig, Halle, Jena, Chemnitz and Coburg all fell into Allied hands. The Western Allies advanced with light opposition, except in a few areas where they met more dogged, if brief, resistance. German people did not fear the Western Allies who were more likely to hand out chocolate rather than beatings.

The increasingly desperate military situation facing Germany led to a severe weakening of German public morale. At the end of February 1945 a report summarizing the public mood was compiled by the Propaganda Ministry. It noted a 'profound lethargy' among the middle classes, a typical comment being: 'In three months the war will be over.' Among the working classes in factories there was 'no grumbling', with the majority remaining 'faithful to the Führer'. There was, however, a group the report classified as 'the defeatists' who wanted the war to be over quickly and wished to surrender to the Anglo-Americans, who they saw as 'more civilized' and 'more humane' than the Soviets.[77] In his diary entry for 11 March Goebbels, who had seen the report, noted:

> The morale of the German people, both at home and at the front, is sinking ever lower. The Reich propaganda agencies are complaining very noticeably about this. The people thinks that it is facing a perfectly hopeless situation in this war. Criticism of our war strategy does not now stop short even of the Führer himself. He is reproached primarily for failure to take decisions on vital war problems, particularly those concerning personnel. The case of Göring is given special mention. The Führer should have changed the top-level personnel in the *Luftwaffe* long ago.[78]

Allied military advances in the east and west triggered hasty and poorly organized mass evacuations from German-controlled concentration camps. In January 1945, there were still 714,000 concentration camp inmates, most of them foreign slave labourers, although around 30 per cent of them were Jews. The SS didn't want slave labourers to fall into Allied hands, but Himmler issued no detailed plans as to where these evacuated prisoners should go and how they would be fed. The speed of the Allied advance often created panic among the guards of the concentration camps. The result was a series of poorly organized and merciless 'forced marches' or to describe them more accurately 'death marches'. Poorly clothed prisoners were forced to walk on icy roads and a great many perished along the way.[79]

The first major evacuation was from the notorious Auschwitz-Birkenau concentration camp, beginning on 18 January 1945. With the Red Army closing in on the camp, the killing installations had already been destroyed, but then a mass evacuation from the camp complex was arranged quickly and chaotically. Columns of prisoners were summarily marched out of the camp in freezing-cold conditions. However, around 7,000 prisoners – dubbed 'walking skeletons' by the Soviets – were too ill to move so they were left behind in the camp. They were discovered on 27 August 1945 when the Red Army entered the camp. The Soviets soon discovered piles of clothing, spectacles and luggage, revealing the huge extent of the genocide the Germans had carried out there.[80]

The SS guards who accompanied the prisoners on the 'death marches' were an assortment of experienced officers and elderly former soldiers or members of the *Volkssturm*. Many were ill-disciplined and exceptionally brutal. If news came of Red Army units advancing nearby, they tended to summarily kill any stragglers who could not keep up with the main body of the marchers.

This violence and abuse did not end when these bedraggled columns reached Germany. Many local communities, indoctrinated for years by Nazi racial propaganda, viewed the concentration camp prisoners as 'sub-human', and many spontaneous massacres occurred. No prisoner was safe, but Jews made up a large proportion of their victims. One of the most horrific Jewish massacres occurred in Pomerania at Palmnicken (or Yantarny in Russian). On 26 January 1945 about 3,000 concentration camp inmates were brutally murdered at the end of a thirty-mile trek from several concentration camps around Königsberg. They were taken to a nearby beach and driven into the ice-cold water where they were killed by machine-gun fire.[81]

The final wave of concentration camp evacuations occurred in Western Europe in April. On 6 April, 28,000 prisoners were evacuated from Buchenwald, but only 20,000 reached their destination of Flossenbürg a fortnight later. At Ohrdruf concentration camp around 1,500 political prisoners deemed to be 'dangerous' were summarily executed. The greatest death toll was at Bergen-Belsen. In March, 18,000 inmates died there and a further 9,000 perished in early April, before the camp was finally liberated by British troops. Allied soldiers

[overleaf]
A British soldier clearing up a huge pile of corpses that were found when Bergen-Belsen concentration camp was liberated on 15 April 1945.

543

brought local people into the camp to view the horrific crimes that had been committed in their name.[82]

It's been estimated that 250,000 inmates of the Nazi concentration camps died between the beginning of January and the end of April 1945, with half of that number being Jews. During April 1945, the last major concentration camps in Germany itself were finally liberated: Buchenwald and Dora (11 April), Bergen-Belsen (15 April), Sachsenhausen (22–23 April), Flossenbürg (23 April), Dachau (29 April), Ravensbrück (30 April), Neuengamme (2 May), Mauthausen-Gusen (5 May) and Stutthof (9 May).[83]

As Germany descended into chaos, state prisons were also hastily abandoned. It was decided prisoners would be categorized by the severity of their sentences and by Nazi racial criteria. The Ministry of Justice believed that the German public still had to be protected, so it rejected the mass release of prisoners regarded as harmless. This meant most state prisoners were also sent on fatal forced marches.[84]

On 5 April 1945, Eduard Weiter, the Commandant of the Dachau concentration camp, received a message from Gestapo headquarters in Berlin informing him that Hitler had ordered the execution of the 'special prisoner' Georg Elser, a former cabinet maker who attempted to kill him by planting a time bomb in the *Bürgerbräukeller* on 8 November 1939. On 9 April, Elser, now aged forty-two, was shot dead in his cell and his body burned in the camp crematorium. It was announced he had been killed in an Allied air raid. Despite the general agreement that Elser had acted alone in his 1939 assassination attempt, it seems fears remained he might have incriminating material to reveal to the Allies should he survive the war.[85]

On 7 April Goebbels noted in his diary that behind-the-scenes peace talks with the Western Allies – initiated by the German Foreign Ministry via Switzerland and Sweden – had got nowhere. The British were totally intransigent, the United States was not interested in a separate peace and the Soviet Union's demand for East Prussia was totally unacceptable to the Germans. Hitler, who thought these conversations were a waste of time, ordered them to cease immediately.[86]

At 1 p.m. on 12 April 1945 President Franklin D. Roosevelt was sitting at his desk in the living room of his 'Little White House' cottage in Warm Springs, Georgia. He had arrived there by train on 30 March, having to be carried into the cottage on a stretcher. The artist Elizabeth Shoumatoff was standing nearby, painting an official portrait of him. At 1.15 p.m. the President touched his head, complained of a sharp pain, then slumped back in his chair and lost consciousness. He was carried to his nearby bedroom by his doctors and died soon afterwards, having suffered a cerebral haemorrhage. His Vice-President Harry S. Truman became the new President of the United States and pledged to continue Roosevelt's policy in the war.

In Berlin on the following day Goebbels first heard the news of Roosevelt's death. He telephoned Hitler in a state of great excitement: 'My Führer, I congratulate you! Roosevelt is dead! It is written in the stars that the second half of April will be a turning point for us.'[87] Goebbels compared Roosevelt's death to that of the Tsarina Elizabeth of Russia, whose demise helped to split an enemy military coalition during the Seven Years' War, thereby turning the tide for Hitler's hero, Frederick the Great. The hand of Providence, thought Goebbels, had intervened once again to save the Führer from doom. It was, of course, all wishful thinking. Roosevelt's death made no difference to the hopeless military situation that Germany faced. It was no longer a matter of willpower, but firepower.[88]

On 13 April the Berlin Philharmonic Orchestra gave its final performance during the wartime period. Speer had organized the concert and Grand Admiral Karl Dönitz was the guest of honour. The concert included Beethoven's Violin Concerto, Bruckner's 8th Symphony and the dramatic finale from Richard Wagner's Twilight of the Gods (*Götterdämmerung*), one of Hitler's favourite operatic works. It ended with the Hall of the Gods being engulfed in flames. Afterwards, members of the Hitler Youth reportedly handed out free cyanide capsules to the departing audience.[89]

By now Berlin was a bomb-ruined city. Almost half of Berlin's dwellings were already destroyed. The city centre was a patchwork of ruined buildings, huge bomb craters and piles of rubble. About 52,000 inhabitants had already been killed in the air raids. A popular Berlin joke of the time was that optimists were learning English and pessimists Russian. Yet Berlin continued to function. Some cinemas, theatres, hotels, restaurants, shops and department stores remained open and 65 per cent of Berlin's factories were still functioning.

Commuters continued to travel daily on the underground U-Bahn and the overground S-Bahn railway systems. The Berlin Zoo full of animals was still functioning. Berliners seemed to disregard the obvious danger they were in. Léon Degrelle, a Waffen-SS officer, described the scene in the centre of the city, shortly before the Battle of Berlin began: 'The Hotel Adlon was still in operation, despite the bombs

[overleaf]
The shell-damaged Reichstag at the end of the Battle of Berlin.

and grenades that were already landing in the street. In the brightly lit dining hall waiters in tuxedos went on solemnly and unflappably serving people.'[90]

The population of Berlin, which in 1939 was 4.3 million, had fallen to 3.5 million by 1945. Of those, 60 per cent were women. The male population consisted of men mainly over fifty and younger men under thirty. In addition, there were about 500,000 refugees who had recently fled from Germany's eastern provinces, bringing with them horror stories of the mass rape, looting and drunken violence of the Red Army.[91]

No strategic or cohesive overall plan for the defence of Berlin was prepared in advance. Only when the Red Army reached the Oder River in January 1945 did defence preparations of the city really begin, with a few trenches being dug and anti-tank obstacles being erected on the eastern side of the city. Hitler said Berlin had to be defended to the bitter end. A series of defence lines was created by the Berlin Defence Area, commanded by General Hellmuth Reymann. They consisted of three concentric rings divided into eight defensive sectors, labelled A to H, starting in the east and moving clockwise.

The first, sixty miles in circumference, ran around the outskirts of the city, including the natural barrier of its rivers and lakes. Work gangs created barriers using masonry from bombed buildings, as well as obsolete railway carriages and tank barriers. The second ring of defence had a circumference of twenty-five miles. It followed the lines of the S-Bahn overground railway system, with fortified anti-tank ditches created and defence forces established in buildings overlooking all the key railway stations.

The third and most heavily defended section was in the heart of the city centre: the Wilhelmstraße district, known as the inner citadel or Sector Z (*Zentrum*). Here were located all the major government, diplomatic and civic buildings. These were surrounded by barricades, anti-tank traps and concrete blocks. Particularly strong defences were located around the Air Ministry, the huge Bendlerblock, the Reichstag, and the new and old Reich Chancelleries. Finally, there were three gigantic flak towers – anti-aircraft gun blockhouse towers – one in the Berlin Zoo and one in each of the parks of Humboldthain and Friedrichshain.

There was a distinct lack of manpower to defend all of these defensive strong points effectively. Only 60,000 poorly trained and ill-equipped forces were available to defend Berlin, consisting primarily of the poorly trained *Volkssturm*. Dorothea von Schwanenflügel was shocked when she encountered one young recruit: 'I went over to him and found a mere child in a uniform many sizes too large for him, with an anti-tank grenade beside him. Tears were running down his face and he was obviously very frightened.'[92] Clearly, the task of preventing Berlin from being overrun by the Red Army would fall on the trained German army troops outside the city.[93]

On 1 April 1945, Stalin chaired a planning meeting with his leading generals in the Kremlin to discuss the Battle of Berlin. The day before he had received a telegram from Eisenhower, indicating that Berlin was not a prime target of the Western Allies. This gave Stalin the green light to capture Berlin. Stalin saw how the fall of Berlin to the Red Army and perhaps even the capture of Hitler would be of enormous symbolic significance to the victory of the Soviet Union.[94]

For the Battle of Berlin – the last major battle of the German-Soviet War – the Red Army deployed three army groups. The 1st Byelorussian Front, the main assault force, commanded by Georgy Zhukov, would strike on a northerly route, thrusting centrally towards Berlin. The 2nd Byelorussian Front, led by Konstantin Rokossovsky, aimed to protect Zhukov's right flank by moving across the River Oder, outflanking Berlin from the south, taking Stettin and Rostock on the way. The 1st Ukrainian Front, under the direction of Ivan Konev, would attack across the Neisse and Spree rivers, then head for the southern outskirts of Berlin, thereby protecting Zhukov's southern flank. Flank protection of Zhukov's forces was a key part of the overall Soviet plan and was primarily designed to thwart a German counter-attack.

The overall aim for the Red Army was to comprehensively win the battle outside the city, then encircle Berlin and fight, street by street, inside the city against the weakest of the German forces. Zhukov estimated that the whole operation could be completed within twelve to fifteen days. The combined strength of the Soviet forces for the Battle of Berlin was 2.3 million troops, with 6,250 tanks and self-propelled guns and 7,500 artillery pieces.[95]

The German defenders deployed forces attached to the much-depleted Army Group Centre under the committed Nazi Ferdinand Schörner, with its main spearhead the 4th Panzer Army. It was supported by Army Group Vistula, now commanded by the defence specialist Gotthard Heinrici and consisting of the 9th Army and the 3rd Panzer Army.[96] All of these German forces would operate outside the city, with a total of 766,750 soldiers, 1,519 tanks and armoured vehicles and 2,224 aircraft.[97]

[overleaf]
Hitler inspects a group of Hitler Youth members on 20 April 1945, his 56th birthday.

On Hitler's orders, all the German troop commanders read out a proclamation to all soldiers on the Eastern Front. In this statement Hitler explained that he had been expecting this assault on Berlin by the 'Jewish-Bolshevik arch-enemy' since January: 'The Soviets intended to smash Germany and to eradicate our nation. You soldiers from the east today already know yourselves to a large extent what fate is threatening, above all, German women, girls and children. While old men and children are being murdered, women and girls are humiliated to the status of barracks prostitutes. Others are marched off to Siberia.'

Hitler further promised the Bolsheviks 'will bleed to death in front of the capital and the German Reich', and he had a warning for any waverers: 'Whoever does not do his duty at this moment is a traitor to our nation.' He asked German soldiers to 'look out for the treacherous few officers and soldiers who, to secure their own miserable lives will fight against us in Russian pay.'

Hitler concluded with a final rallying cry: 'In this hour the entire German nation looks to you, my soldiers in the East, and only hopes that by your fanaticism, by your arms and by your leadership, the Bolshevik onslaught is drowned in a bloodbath.'[98]

The Battle of Berlin began with a huge Soviet offensive along the Oder and Neisse rivers. At 3 a.m. on 16 April 1945 there was a deafening Soviet artillery bombardment, illuminated by 143 search-lights which shone for three miles across the battlefield. However, this first day was disappointing for Zhukov, because the German forces had retreated prior to the artillery assault. The first line of German defence, doggedly protected by the 9th Army, had not yet been breached. Rokossovsky's 2nd Byelorussian Front also struggled to force its way across the lower River Oder, south of Stettin. Once over the river, however, it pressed the German defenders relentlessly. Konev's 1st Ukrainian Front moved forward much more quickly, crossing the Neisse River at 130 different points and advancing nine miles across a seventeen-mile-wide front.

The most bitter fighting in the early stages of the Battle of Berlin occurred around two cities: Wriezen to the north and Seelow in the centre. The Germans put up a stout defence of the Seelow Heights. The breaking point in this battle came on 18 April when the sheer weight of Soviet numbers ground down the German defenders. By noon Seelow was finally captured. It proved a costly engagement with 30,000 Soviet dead and 12,000 German troops killed.[99]

On 18 April Mussolini, anticipating Hitler's birthday in two days' time, offered him best wishes for his 'historic mission' against 'Judaism and Bolshevism' in Berlin.[100] Hitler replied:

> The battle that we are waging for our very existence has reached its climax. With unlimited deployment of ammunition, Bolshevism and the troops of Jewry are doing all in their power to unite their destructive forces in Germany and throw our continent into chaos. In the spirit of dogged contempt for death, the German nation and all those who are similarly minded will halt this attack.[101]

On 19 April 1945, Goebbels delivered a national radio speech on the eve of Hitler's birthday, something he had done every year since 1933. 'Germany is still a land of loyalty,' he said. 'In the midst of danger that loyalty shall celebrate its greatest triumph.' Goebbels described Hitler as 'the core of resistance against the fall of the world. He is Germany's bravest heart and the people's most glowing will.' Goebbels ended by saying that every German was resolved to follow Hitler to the bitter end.[102]

Inside the old Reich Chancellery, on 20 April, the Nazi elite gathered to commemorate Hitler's fifty-sixth birthday. It was the last time all the key leaders of Hitler's government would ever meet as a group. Among those present were: Goebbels, Speer, Ribbentrop, Himmler, Göring and Bormann, plus the top defence commanders Dönitz, Keitel, Jodl, Burgdorf and Krebs. Most of them wanted to leave Berlin without further delay and head south to Bavaria. Hitler had already decided to split the command of the shrinking territory still under German control into a Northern Command Zone under Dönitz and a Southern Command Zone under Kesselring. If Berlin fell, these forces were expected to continue the struggle against the Allies.

Earlier in the day Hitler, dressed in a bulky grey overcoat, had emerged briefly from the Führerbunker to enter the Reich Chancellery garden. Here he inspected a group of sixteen-year-old members of the Hitler Youth from a 'Tank Destruction Unit', who were ordered to form a line to receive his personal congratulations for bravely defending Berlin. Hitler walked slowly along the line, shaking the hand of each of the youths who were all given a bravery award by Artur Axmann, the Hitler Youth leader. The Führer then gave a brief pep talk to the youths, telling them the Battle for Berlin must be won at all costs.[103]

In the early evening, Hitler announced to the Nazi elite that he wouldn't be leaving Berlin: 'I must bring things to a head here in Berlin or go under.'[104] Goebbels expressed a similar determination to stay in Berlin with his Führer to the very end. After receiving birthday greetings from all those present, Hitler left his guests to drink champagne and then retreated discreetly to his private apartment in the Führerbunker.

Eva Braun, who had arrived in Berlin from Munich on 15 April, continued the birthday party in the Reich Chancellery. She found a single gramophone record in the state room called 'Blood-Red Roses Speak of Happiness to You' and played it repeatedly. She danced, drank champagne and laughed and chatted with the guests.

On the same evening, two of the Führer's longest-serving ministers, Himmler and Göring, both declared their unswerving loyalty in the presence of Hitler. Nicolaus von Below, who witnessed this scene, noted: 'I had a sense that Hitler was paying Göring no attention now. It was not a nice moment.'[105] Himmler departed to Hohenlychen, north-west of Berlin, then secretly arranged a meeting with the Swedish diplomat Count Bernadotte with the aim of opening up peace talks with the Western Allies. Hitler's two long-standing secretaries Gerda Christian and Johanna Wolf also left for Bavaria that evening with his blessing.

On the following day, Konev's forces moved relentlessly towards Berlin from the south, capturing the hastily abandoned command centre of the *Wehrmacht* in Zossen on the way. To their astonishment, Soviet troops found the telephones were still ringing and teleprinters were still printing messages when they arrived. A Soviet soldier playfully picked up one of the receivers and said, 'Hello, Ivan here.'[106]

At the same time, Zhukov's forces began the first artillery barrage on Berlin. Hitler had already ordered a counter-attack by an SS force under the leadership of General Felix Steiner. Hitler called it Army Detachment Steiner and its aim was to attack the northern flank of the advancing 1st Byelorussian Front. But Steiner was in despair after receiving Hitler's order, because he did not have enough men or equipment to mount any sort of relief operation against the advancing Soviet forces.[107]

During his final days, Hitler exhibited unmistakable signs of a complete mental breakdown. On the evening of 21 April he retired to bed in a state of despair. His personal doctor Theodor Morell found him there in a very depressed mood. When Morell suggested he administer one of his 'energy-boosting' injections, Hitler exploded into a rage, accusing the doctor of wanting to drug him with morphine to put him on a plane to the south. He ordered Morell to leave the bunker for good, which he did on the following morning.[108]

On 22 April 1945 Hitler issued an order concerning 'Guerrilla Warfare' in the west, stating: 'We have to adopt the same method which was shown and taught us by the Russians in the years 1942–44. Our men have to infiltrate through the lines by ones or in small groups, supplied with sufficient ammunition, petrol and other materials, and must attack if they reach the rear areas where they can achieve complete surprise against the most sensitive points.'[109] However, there was never any possibility that any such organized partisan resistance by the Germans would have been able to resist the Allied onslaught in the west.

By now, due to the complete breakdown of telephone, radio and telegraphic communications, it was becoming impossible for Hitler to know exactly what was going on outside the Führerbunker. During the morning of 22 April, Hitler was continually on the phone, demanding news of the progress of 'Army Detachment Steiner'. Yet no one knew where Steiner was.

At the daily military conference, which began at 3 p.m., Hitler was informed that Soviet troops had now broken through the first defensive outer ring in Berlin and were flooding into the northern suburbs. Hitler asked once again for details about the progress of Steiner's combat group. There was a deafening silence which seemed to go on for ages. Then General Hans Krebs told Hitler that no counter-attack by Steiner had ever taken place, because his group had not yet been fully formed.

This discovery pushed Hitler to a mental breaking point. His deranged and furious rage is famously depicted in the film *Downfall*. Hitler ordered everyone to leave the conference room, except his leading army commanders Keitel, Jodl, Krebs and Burgdorf. To this small group Hitler vented his uninhibited anger and rage, accusing all of them of treachery, cowardice and betrayal. His loud shouting could be heard in the corridor outside the room. No one at the meeting had ever witnessed such a violent tirade from Hitler, and there had been many in his years as Führer.

Hitler even became so angry at one point that he threw across the table the coloured pencils he always carried with him to mark up battle maps. Hitler said that he could no longer go on and slumped back in his chair and said: 'Gentlemen, it's over. I shall stay here in Berlin and shoot myself when the moment comes. Anyone who wants can go now. Everyone is free to do so.' Hitler then said that he didn't want to fall into the hands of the Allies, dead or alive. He had no more military orders to give. If his military commanders looked for orders they should consult Göring: 'If it's a question of negotiating, Göring can do it better than I can.'[110] Keitel and Jodl left the bunker on the following day, taking up residence at temporary military headquarters at Krampnitz. Krebs and Burgdorf decided to stay in the Führerbunker.[111]

Hitler left the conference room, went to his private apartment, and shut the door to be alone with his thoughts. Bormann reassured those gathered outside Hitler's living quarters that he didn't think the Führer was serious about shooting himself. Jodl later summed up the day's events: 'Hitler has made the decision to stay in Berlin, lead the defence and shoot himself at the last moment. He said he could not fight for physical reasons and in any case would not personally fight as he could not risk being wounded and falling into the enemy's hands.'[112]

Hitler was seated in a chair, motionless, in his private apartment, when his secretary Traudl Junge opened the door and went in. Hitler looked up at her and commented, bitterly: 'All is lost, hopelessly lost.'[113] Eva Braun then came in, took hold of Hitler's hands and in a comforting tone of voice declared: 'But you know I will stay with you. I'm not letting you send me away.' Hitler then did something no one had ever seen before: he kissed Eva full on the lips.[114] His two younger secretaries, Traudl Junge and Gerda Christian, and his personal cook and dietician Constanze Manziarly all promised they would remain with him to the end. On 23 April Eva Braun wrote a letter to her sister Gretl, stating: 'There is still hope. But obviously we won't let ourselves be taken alive.'[115]

Hitler then summoned the ultra-loyal Joseph Goebbels to the Führerbunker at 5 p.m. He was the only person – apart from Bormann and Braun – Hitler still fully trusted. Goebbels, with his soothing voice and reassuring manner, tried to calm Hitler down. He promised Hitler that he intended to move to the bunker with his wife Magda and his six children. Traudl Junge recalled the moment when the Goebbels children arrived in the Führerbunker, later on the same day: 'The five little girls and the boy were happy and cheerful. They were pleased to be staying with "Uncle Führer" and soon filled the bunker with their games. They were charming, well brought-up, natural mannered children. They knew nothing of the fate awaiting them.'[116]

For the rest of the day, Hitler became surprisingly calm. He went to play on his own with the little puppy Wulf. Junge recalled: 'I suddenly felt very sorry for Hitler. A hopelessly disappointed man, toppled from the greatest heights, broken, lonely.'[117]

Hitler started preparing for his end. Julius Schaub, Hitler's personal adjutant, was summoned and given the task of disposing of Hitler's private papers and personal correspondence in the Reich Chancellery. Hitler's Naval Adjutant, Admiral Karl-Jesco von Puttkamer, was ordered to do the same with Hitler's papers held in the Berghof. Hitler's most criminal actions and orders would now be lost to history.[118]

News of Hitler's angry outburst was communicated to Himmler by his SS liaison officer in the Führerbunker Hermann Fegelein, the errant husband of Eva Braun's sister Gretl. This stiffened Himmler's resolve to seek a separate peace with the Western Allies. Göring was told about Hitler's meltdown by General Eckhard Christian, his own liaison officer in the Führerbunker. He received a report from General Karl Koller, the chief of staff of the *Luftwaffe*, informing him that Hitler had suggested Göring would be best suited to conduct peace negotiations during his outburst in the Führerbunker. Göring saw this as an invitation or an opportunity to immediately take over as Führer. He sought advice first on how to proceed from Hans Lammers, the State Secretary of the Reich Chancellery, who was also in Berchtesgaden at the time. Lammers brought Göring a copy of the Führer decree of 29 June 1941, which had stipulated that if Hitler died then Göring would be his successor.

Göring felt that Hitler, although not dead, was now totally incapable of governing Germany from the besieged Führerbunker and that soon he would probably take his own life.[119] Göring sent a carefully worded radio message to Hitler on 23 April. It read:

> My Führer!
>
> In view of your decision to remain in the fortress of Berlin, do you agree that I take over at once the total leadership of the Reich, with full freedom of action at home and abroad as your deputy, in accordance with your decree of 29 June 1941? If no reply is received by 10 o'clock tonight, I shall take it for granted that you have lost your freedom of action, and shall consider the conditions of your decree as fulfilled, and shall act for the best interests of our country and our people. You know what I feel for you in this gravest hour of my life. Words fail me to express myself. May God protect you, and speed you quickly here in spite of all.[120]
>
> Your loyal
> Hermann Göring

When Hitler read the message he was deeply outraged, describing Göring as a lazy, corrupt morphine addict. He then accused him of 'high treason' for which the penalty was death, but he promised to spare his life if Göring agreed to resign all of his government and military offices with immediate effect. Bormann interpreted Göring's actions as nothing less than an attempted *coup d'état*, which then persuaded the highly agitated Hitler to order Göring's immediate arrest. Bormann sent the following stiffly worded radio message to Göring: 'Your intention to take over the running of the state is high treason. Traitors are punished by death. Bearing in mind the merits that you have acquired over your work for the Party and state over the years, the Führer wants to refrain from resorting to the death penalty, but demands that you resign immediately on health grounds.'[121]

This incident showed Hitler's power as the Führer of Germany remained intact. On the following day, Göring and his entire staff were placed under house arrest by the SS in Obersalzberg. Goebbels bitterly commented on Göring's actions: 'That man was never a National Socialist. He just basked in the Führer's glory, he never lived by idealistic National Socialist principles. It's his fault that the German *Luftwaffe* failed, we have him to thank for it that we're sitting here now about to lose the war.'[122]

On the same evening, Albert Speer, with 'conflicting emotions', made one last visit to see Hitler in the Führerbunker. He met Hitler alone in his living room. 'In his welcome,' Speer later recalled, 'there was no sign of the warmth with which he had responded a few weeks before to my vow of loyalty.' Speer then admitted the 'Nero Decree' had never been carried out. After hearing this, Hitler displayed no anger at all. He then told Speer death would be easy now and a release, and emphasized once again that he didn't want to fall into the hands of the Soviets alive. As Speer prepared to leave, he felt Hitler had treated him during their encounter with calm indifference. It was proof positive the Hitler–Speer friendship was finally at an end, if it had ever been a friendship at all.[123]

At dinner Traudl Junge asked Hitler if he thought that National Socialism would ever be revived after his death, to which he replied: 'No, National Socialism is dead. Perhaps a similar idea will arise in a hundred years' time. But Germany is lost. It was probably not mature and strong enough for the task I intended it to perform.'[124]

By 25 April 1945, Berlin was now completely encircled by the Red Army after both the 1st Byelorussian and the 1st Ukrainian Fronts had linked up at Ketzin near Potsdam. A total of 464,000 Soviet troops were now deployed for the final operation to capture Berlin, with only 45,000 Germans left to defend the besieged city. Soviet troops soon moved to capture Tempelhof and Gatow, the two major Berlin airports. On the same day, American and Russian troops met up at Stehla and Torgau on the Elbe River, thereby cutting in two what remained of Hitler's German Reich.

The strongest German force still functioning near Berlin was the German 9th Army, but it was surrounded and isolated in a large pocket in the Spree Forest near the village of Halbe, south-east of Berlin. Hitler ordered its commander, General Theodor Busse, to hold his ground and mount a counter-attack. Busse knew this was impossible. All he could manage was to order a breakout from the pocket, which saved 30,000 soldiers out of the 60,000 who were either killed or captured by the Soviet forces.[125]

Hitler's last lingering hope of saving Berlin rested, in his own mind, on the German 12th Army, commanded by Walther Wenck. Hitler had redirected the 12th Army from defending the Elbe against the Americans to try to break the Soviet encirclement of Berlin. Wenck never seriously contemplated attempting to break through to Berlin, but he did provide an escape route for German soldiers who wanted to retreat westwards and surrender to the Western Allies.

General Helmut Weidling, attached to the trapped 9th Army, defied Hitler's 'stand fast' order and retreated to Berlin with a small corps of troops. Hitler ordered Weidling's immediate arrest and execution by firing squad for desertion and disobedience. On 23 April, the fearless and self-confident Weidling turned up at the Führerbunker to offer a spirited defence of his actions. Hitler was so impressed by him that he appointed him on the spot as the new 'Commandant of the Berlin Defence Area', replacing Lieutenant Helmuth Reymann.

What now went on inside Berlin was for the Red Army really a mopping-up operation against weak and poorly equipped German forces. As street fighting was important in the final phase of the battle, the commander of the Soviet 8th Guards, Army General Vasily Chuikov – the heroic defender of Stalingrad and dubbed 'The Man of Iron Will' – was assigned a key role in the final capture of the city.

Chuikov's attack groups were composed of infantry, tanks, assault guns and flamethrower units. During the night hours Soviet troops launched frequent smash-and-grab raids on German defensive positions. In daytime, the Soviets used smoke bombs to cover attack groups entering buildings. If the German defenders put up stiff resistance, Chuikov brought up heavy artillery guns and blasted the buildings and their occupants to pieces. The German defenders fought hard, but they crumbled quickly against such overwhelming force.[126]

Inside the Führerbunker, Hitler had recovered his composure from his meltdown three days earlier, but still clung to a fantasy that the 12th Army, stationed near Magdeburg, was heading towards Berlin in a rescue operation, linking up with the trapped 9th Army on the way. But the commander of the 12th Army, Walther Wenck, had neither the resources nor the military equipment to mount such an operation. The attack by the 12th Army was halted by the Red Army near Potsdam.[127]

At a military situation conference on 25 April a still deluded Hitler commented to Goebbels on the Battle of Berlin: 'This is now the decisive battle. If I win this battle, then I expect nothing in my personal name. But then I will be rehabilitated. Then I can eliminate a number of generals and lower officers, including in the SS, who have failed at decisive points.' Goebbels, who excelled in keeping up Hitler's sagging spirits, replied: 'If it doesn't go well and the Führer were to find an honourable death in Berlin, and Europe were to become Bolshevik, in five years, at the latest, the Führer would be a legendary personality and National Socialism a myth. He would be hallowed by his last great action.'[128]

On 26 April the *Luftwaffe* General Ritter von Greim, accompanied by the famous German pilot Hanna Reitsch, arrived in the Führerbunker. Greim was summoned from Munich by Hitler two days earlier. Reitsch had daringly landed their plane on the East–West Axis near the Brandenburg Gate, while under heavy Soviet anti-aircraft fire. One artillery shell ripped through the floor of the plane, hitting Greim's ankle, which was bleeding and fractured when he arrived. Greim's ankle was being placed in a plaster cast by Hitler's personal surgeon Dr Ludwig Stumpfegger when Hitler walked into the surgery in the Führerbunker. Hitler told Greim about Göring's 'traitorous ultimatum' and offered him the post of commander-in-chief of the *Luftwaffe*, while simultaneously promoting him to the rank of Field Marshal.

Reitsch, a devoted National Socialist, was quite willing to stay in the Führerbunker to the bitter end. When Hitler told her of his intention to commit suicide, she replied: 'The Führer must live so that Germany can live.' In response Hitler said: 'If I die it is for the honour of our country, it is because as a soldier I must obey my own command that I would defend Berlin to the last.'[129]

By 28 April 1945 the only part of Berlin the Red Army still didn't control was Sector Z: the citadel around the government sector. This area – running ten miles east to west and three miles deep – was now completely surrounded by Soviet troops. Retreat was no longer an option for its 10,000 remaining German defenders. A German soldier who witnessed the carnage in the city centre noted in his diary: 'There are seriously wounded, dying people, corpses everywhere and the nearly unbearable odour of putrefaction.'[130] On that same day Chuikov's 8th Guards Army crossed the Landwehr Canal, near the Tiergarten, and was now heading into the heart of the government district. The Red Army was now less than a mile away from the old Reich Chancellery and the Reichstag.

Berlin was slowly bleeding to death. In most areas electricity, gas and water services had now stopped. Newspapers were closed down. Even the Nazi newspaper *Völkischer Beobachter* ceased publication on 26 April. Rail, bus and tram services were no longer running. The distribution of goods and services had completely broken down. Postal and milk deliveries ceased. The official system of registering, collecting and burying dead bodies collapsed. Corpses were buried by grieving families themselves in gardens, cemeteries, parks and any open patches of land that could be found.

Looting became widespread. Shopkeepers were powerless to stop it. The huge Berlin department stores were systematically ransacked.[131] Hertha von Gebhardt, who lived in Wilmersdorf, witnessed the looting: 'The women hit each other, scratch each other, pour oil over each other, smear each other with jam, pour away good flour, good food, drag everything away by the hundredweight wherever they can. Revolting.'[132]

On the morning of 28 April 1945 radio and telephone contact between the German army and the Führerbunker was cut off. Ammunition was running out. In the early evening, Heinz Lorenz, a press officer at the Propaganda Ministry, was listening to a BBC radio broadcast when it reported that Himmler had made an offer of a German surrender to Eisenhower in exchange for a 'separate peace' with the Western Allies. This offer was rejected publicly by British Prime Minister Churchill and US President Truman, who both reported Himmler's request to Stalin. This showed the Allies remained united on the unconditional surrender of Germany.[133]

Lorenz rushed to the Führerbunker to tell Hitler his supposedly 'faithful Heinrich' Himmler had betrayed him. It was a horrible blow for Hitler. After a lengthy tirade against the 'worst act of treachery he had ever known', Hitler sat down and remained silent for several minutes, before saying, 'A traitor must never succeed me as Führer.' Hitler demanded immediate revenge. He ordered the injured pilot Greim to leave the bunker with Hanna Reitsch and make his way to Plön in Schleswig-Holstein to ask Dönitz to order Himmler's immediate arrest. They both left around 1 a.m. on 29 April.

A quicker route to revenge was much closer to hand in the shape of Himmler's Chief Liaison Officer in the Führerbunker, Hermann Fegelein, who had gone suspiciously absent without leave. Heinrich Müller, the chief of the Gestapo, was given the task of finding him. He appointed the SS Lieutenant Colonel Peter Högl for the task. Finding Fegelein proved relatively easy. He was in his apartment in Berlin, located at 4 Bleibtreustraße near Kurfürstendamm, in bed with a naked, unidentified woman, and hopelessly drunk.

Documents were then discovered in Fegelein's office in the basement of the old Reich Chancellery indicating he had full knowledge of Himmler's peace negotiations with Count Folke Bernadotte. Upon hearing this, Hitler ordered an immediate court martial. Shortly before midnight on 28 April Fegelein was escorted up to the Chancellery garden and summarily executed. The fact that he was married to Eva Braun's sister Gretl, who was pregnant, made no difference whatsover.[134]

Two other events occurred on the eventful day of 28 April: the first was the marriage of Adolf Hitler to Eva Braun and the second was the composition of Hitler's last will and testament. According to Traudl Junge, the dictation of the wills overlapped with the wedding celebrations.

The wedding of Hitler and Eva took place in the Military Conference Room in the Führerbunker shortly before midnight on 28 April. It seems only Eva, Traudl Junge and the diplomat Nicolaus von Below were given any prior notice of the marriage by Hitler. A local magistrate named Walter Wagner was hastily summoned to conduct the ceremony. Goebbels and Bormann acted as the legal witnesses. Wagner asked Hitler and Eva if they were both of 'Aryan descent' and free of hereditary diseases. Both replied 'yes'. As Eva began to write her surname with a 'B' on the marriage certificate, she immediately realised her nervous error and put a line through it, writing 'Eva Hitler, née Braun' instead.

Afterwards, a champagne wedding party took place in the cramped living room of Hitler's apartment. No one knew how to address Eva.

'You can safely call me Frau Hitler,' she announced to the guests. The idea of a wedding as a prelude to a double suicide is pretty bizarre, but it marked the exact moment when Hitler gave up and decided to recede into history.[135]

As the wedding celebrations continued, Hitler slipped away to the secretarial room to dictate his last will and testament to Traudl Junge. She took down every word in shorthand and typed it up in triplicate. Hitler began by reciting his 'Political Testament'. The first part was an overview of his explanation for why the war had started and the reasons for Germany's defeat. There was no hint of regret or remorse whatsoever. Hitler judged himself not guilty in the court of his own poisoned mind.

Hitler took absolutely no responsibility for any of the horrors that he had inflicted on the world. He denied he even wanted a war in 1939. It had been provoked 'exclusively by those international statesmen who either were of Jewish origin or worked for Jewish interests'. He had never wanted war with Britain or America at all. Three days before the attack on Poland in 1939, he continued, he proposed to the British government a reasonable solution to the Polish-German problem. This was flatly rejected, 'because the ruling clique in England wanted war for commercial reasons', and partly because it was influenced by 'propaganda put out by international Jewry'. It was 'the Jews' who were responsible for all of the deaths on the battlefield and in the bombed-out German cities.

Hitler then predicted Germany's role in the war would go down in history as 'the most glorious and heroic manifestation of the struggle for existence'. He promised that he would not allow himself to fall into the hands of the enemy, but he insisted:

> I have therefore decided to remain in Berlin and there to choose
> death voluntarily at that moment when I believe that the
> position of the Führer and the Chancellery itself can no longer
> be maintained. I die with a joyful heart in my knowledge of
> the immeasurable deeds and achievements of our peasants and
> workers and of a contribution unique in history of our youth
> which bears my name.

Oddly, there was no mention in his political testament of his bitterest enemy, the Bolsheviks, nor any explanation why he launched the unprovoked attack on the Soviet Union of 22 June 1941. Also missing was any reference to the National Socialist Party or the SS, the two organizations he created, except to state that he accepted that National Socialism was now a dead ideology. Hitler then insulted the German army, especially its highest-ranking officers, whom he chiefly blamed for the military disaster now facing Germany. He asked the commanders of the three armed services to prefer death to any cowardly resignation or capitulation. Nevertheless, he still claimed that the ultimate aim for the German people in the future was 'to win territory in the East'.

The second part of his 'Political Testament' dealt with his political succession and the members of the next government. He appointed naval commander Admiral Karl Dönitz to the posts of President of the Reich and Commander of the Armed Forces. This was a clear indication that Hitler believed that the army, the *Luftwaffe* and the SS had all betrayed him. He nominated Goebbels as the German Chancellor and Martin Bormann as the Party Minister. The ultra-loyal Ferdinand Schörner was made commander-in-chief of the army. Göring, Himmler and Speer were stripped of all their offices. Ribbentrop was replaced as Foreign Minister by Arthur Seyss-Inquart. Count Schwerin von Krosigk – Germany's Finance Minister since 1932 – kept his job, thereby surviving from 1933 to the bitter end.

Hitler's final piece of advice to the new German government and to the German people was to ask them 'to uphold the racial laws to the limit and to resist mercilessly the poisoner of all nations, international Jewry'. At 4 a.m. on 29 April 1945 Hitler finally signed his 'Political Testament', which was witnessed by the signatures of Goebbels, Bormann, Burgdorf and Krebs.[136]

Hitler then dictated his very brief 'Private Will and Personal Testament', nominating Bormann as his executor. He then explained why he had married Eva Braun and why they had now both decided to die together:

> Although during the years of struggle I believed that I could not undertake the responsibility of marriage, now, before the end of my life, I have decided to take as my wife the woman who, after many years of true friendship, came to this city, already almost besieged, of her own free will to share my fate. She will go to her death with me at her own wish as my wife.

Hitler left all of his remaining possessions to the Nazi Party, or, if it no longer existed, to the State. He donated his paintings to the founding of an art collection in 'my hometown of Linz'. Finally, he commented: 'My wife and I choose to die in order to escape the shame of overthrow or capitulation. It is our wish that our bodies be burned immediately in the place where I have performed the greater part of my daily work during the twelve years of service to the people.' The signing of this 'Personal Testament' was timed 4 a.m., and dated as 29 April 1945, but it was probably signed an hour later. The witnesses were Bormann, Goebbels and Nicolaus von Below. At no point did Hitler mention escaping from the bunker or going into exile.[137]

Goebbels, who was determined to share Hitler's suicidal fate, decided to dictate to Junge an 'Appendix to the Führer's Political Statement'. In it, Goebbels claimed he would defy Hitler's order to leave Berlin: 'In the nightmare of treason that surrounds the Führer in these most critical days of the war, there must be someone at least who will stay with him unconditionally until death.'[138]

On 29 April, news reached the Führerbunker of the deaths of the Italian dictator Benito Mussolini and his mistress Clara Petacci. On 18 April Mussolini left Lake Garda bound for Milan to try and negotiate an armistice with the Italian partisans and the Western Allies. However, on 27 April, he was captured by Italian partisans and taken to the small town of Dongo on the shore of Lake Como. The following day, in the small Italian town of Mezzegra, Mussolini and Petacci were summarily shot.

Their corpses were then transported to Milan, where they were suspended by their heels from the roof of a garage and petrol station on the Piazzale Loreto, surrounded by a cheering and baying mob. Their bodies were later cut down and thrown on the pavement where they were kicked and spat at by the crowd. There's no doubt Hitler learned of Mussolini's death, but it's not completely clear whether he knew all the full macabre details. If he did, then it must have stiffened his resolve to kill himself to avoid a similar humiliating end.[139]

Late in the afternoon of 29 April 1945, Hitler chaired his final military conference. General Helmuth Weidling presented a detailed report on the current military position outside the Führerbunker. It was a dire summary. Red Army troops were now in the nearby Tiergarten and Potsdamer Platz. Defending German forces had no tanks, no anti-tank weapons, little ammunition and no air-dropped supplies. Weidling predicted fighting in Berlin would come to an end within the next twenty-four hours. Hitler then asked SS Colonel Wilhelm Mohnke, the commander of the Citadel – the military fortress in the centre of Berlin – for his opinion. Mohnke agreed with Weidling's assessment. Hitler now seemed resigned to his fate. He now gave the order for German troops to break out from the Führerbunker 'in small groups'.[140]

At 7 a.m., on the morning of 30 April 1945, Major General Wilhelm Mohnke visited Hitler in his bedroom. Hitler was wearing his pyjamas and his dressing gown. Mohnke told him that the Red Army had now reached Wilhelmstraße and was now fighting a bitter battle on Potsdamer Platz, just 300 yards from the Führerbunker.[141]

Hitler decided to end his life on this day. Suicide was a self-destructive act of power for Hitler. It came as no surprise to those who knew him well. He frequently mentioned over the years that he would kill himself if Germany lost the war. His mortal downfall had to be total. He would take his chance that the judgement of history would be favourable towards him in Germany in the longer term. He had even given great thought to the method of taking his own life. He finally decided to take cyanide and shoot himself simultaneously. To test the cyanide capsules worked, he asked Dr Werner Haase to give one to his German Shepherd, Blondi. The dog died almost instantly.

At about 1.30 p.m. Hitler lunched for the last time with his two young secretaries, Traudl Junge and Gerda Christian, as well as his personal cook and dietician Constanze Manziarly. Eva did not join them. Before leaving the table, Hitler praised Constanze for her plain pasta and tomato sauce meal. It was the sort of bland meal he always enjoyed.

At 2.15 p.m. Hitler and Eva bade farewell to all the remaining high-ranking army officers still in the Führerbunker, as well as to Martin Bormann, Joseph and Magda Goebbels, his secretaries and other assistants. There were about twenty people in the corridor. Hitler went slowly along the line, shaking hands warmly with each of them.

At about 2.30 p.m. Hitler and Eva went into his personal apartment and locked the door. The only interruption came from Magda Goebbels, who knocked on the door, 'extremely upset'. When Hitler opened the door, Magda made an emotional appeal for Hitler not to kill himself. Hitler, visibly annoyed, did not say a word in response and promptly shut the door in her face.

It was at 3.30 p.m. when several witnesses in the Führerbunker reported hearing a single gunshot coming from inside Hitler's private apartment. Traudl Junge was sitting on a staircase with the six Goebbels children when she heard the shot. Young Helmut Goebbels, who was seated near her, shouted 'Bull's eye!'[142]

The Führerbunker.

Heinz Linge, Hitler's personal valet, was the first person to open the door to Hitler's living room. He was followed in by Bormann and Otto Günsche, Hitler's adjutant. Linge could smell the odour of burnt almonds, as he entered: a common scent of cyanide poisoning. Linge saw the corpses of Hitler and Eva on the sofa. 'There was a pool of blood on the carpet beside the sofa,' he later recalled. Artur Axmann, the Hitler Youth leader, also came into the room. He saw Hitler and Eva both clearly dead on the sofa and noticed a 'thin trail of blood' coming from Hitler's forehead.[143]

Linge later described the death scene in more detail. On the right side of the sofa was Eva, wearing a blue dress. Her legs were drawn up in front of her body, which probably happened as the cyanide took its deadly effect. She had no physical injuries at all and looked as if she was asleep. Her high-heeled shoes were on the floor. To her right was Adolf Hitler; his eyes were open, but he was obviously dead, too, with blood still dripping from a bullet hole in his right temple and still running down his face. His gun, a Walther PPK 7.65, lay on the floor. Linge felt Braun had taken cyanide and Hitler had shot himself.[144]

In accordance with Hitler's written and verbal instructions, the two

bodies were then wrapped in blankets and carried up the stairs. They were taken via the emergency exit to the garden behind the old Reich Chancellery. Linge and Dr Ludwig Stumpfegger jointly carried Hitler. Bormann bore Eva's corpse, but was soon relieved of this task by Erich Kempka, Hitler's chauffeur, who had brought some petrol to burn the corpses.

Hitler and his wife were then placed in a shallow pit and generously doused with petrol. After a few unsuccessful attempts, the bodies were eventually ignited by a thick roll of papers. As the two corpses were engulfed in flames a small group raised their arms in a final ghoulish Hitler salute. The group consisted of Martin Bormann, Heinz Linge, Joseph Goebbels, Otto Günsche and Erich Kempka, as well as the SS officers Peter Högl, Ewald Lindloff, Johann Rattenhuber and Hans Reisser. There were no words or eulogies at this impromptu Viking-style funeral.[145]

The Battle of Berlin was finally coming to an end. The Red Army was determined to take the Reichstag. A red Soviet flag was raised over the building at 10.40 p.m. on 30 April by 23-year-old soldier Rakhimzhan Qoshqarbaev. It was soon shot down by German snipers, who retook the building. It was on 2 May when the Red Army finally captured the Reichstag. A photograph of Qoshqarbaev raising the red flag over the building was re-staged by the Red Army naval officer and photographer Yevgeny Khaldei. It became one of the most iconic images of the Second World War.[146]

Countless legends and conspiracy theories have arisen around the circumstances of Hitler's death and the subsequent fate of his corpse. It's even been suggested that Hitler escaped from Berlin and went to live a quiet life abroad with Eva after the war. Argentina is the most often cited location, in this far-fetched scenario, but Hamburg, New York and Tokyo have all been mentioned. No convincing documentary evidence for any of these rumours has ever come to light. On the face of it, it's fairly certain Hitler and Eva died and that their corpses were disposed of just as the surviving eye witnesses describe and has been related here. This is the conclusion of a recent detailed and reliable evaluation of Hitler's death by the historian Luke Daly-Groves.[147] Even if Hitler had survived, his role in history ended with Germany's defeat in any case.

Albert Speer heard the news of Hitler's death on 1 May 1945. A few minutes later he was unpacking a case in a bedroom at the headquarters of Karl Dönitz. After putting a framed photo of Hitler on a bedside table, Speer began to weep uncontrollably. 'That was the end of my relationship to Hitler,' he said later. 'Only now was the spell broken, the magic extinguished. What remained were images of graveyards, of shattered cities, of millions of mourners, of concentration camps.'[148]

During talks concerning a ceasefire in Berlin on 1 May, General Hans Krebs informed the Soviets of Hitler's suicide. Georgy Zhukov phoned Stalin to tell him the news. Stalin replied with characteristic bluntness: 'So – that's the end of the bastard. Too bad that we did not manage to take him alive. Where is Hitler's body?'[149]

On 2 May a Red Army private Ivan Churakov spotted freshly turned soil in the old Reich Chancellery garden and began digging in the hope of finding buried Nazi gold. Instead he found the badly charred and unrecognizable remains of Hitler and his wife. Three days later these remains were dug up. Beneath them lay the corpses of two dogs, almost certainly Hitler's dog Blondi and her small puppy Wulf. On the following day, these four corpses, human and animal, were placed in wooden boxes and transported to the Soviet 3rd Shock Army headquarters in Buch, a northern suburb of Berlin.

On 8 May 1945 an autopsy was carried out on the remains by Lieutenant Colonel Faust Shkaravski, the Chief Expert on Forensic Science, in the mortuary of a military hospital in Berlin-Buch. One dog, undoubtedly Blondi, showed clear evidence of cyanide poisoning. Shkaravski noted the two human corpses were severely charred. Part of Hitler's skull was missing, clearly the area of the gunshot wound that killed him. The forensic scientist did not find a left testicle present in the male corpse. A fracture scar was noted on the right thigh. Hitler had sustained a similar injury from a gunshot as a soldier in the First World War.

Shkaravski managed to extract the upper and lower jawbones of both corpses for dental examination, noting Hitler's unusual and extensive bridge work. He found glass splinters from an ampoule of cyanide in the mouth of Hitler's corpse and the strong smell of bitter almonds in the mouth of the corpse of Eva. No toxicology tests were performed on either corpse.

There is no mention in Shkaravski's final report of a gunshot wound to Hitler, but he noted the whole of the skull was not present. The forensic expert offered the following conclusions on the two corpses: 'Death was caused by poisoning with cyanide compounds.' This discredited the theory that Hitler had shot himself. Instead the

Soviet autopsy opted for a more cowardly death, which, of course, suited Soviet propaganda.

On 11 May 1945 Hitler's dentist Hugo Blaschke and his dental technician compared the extracted lower jaws of both corpses with Hitler and Eva's dental records and concluded the two corpses were of Adolf Hitler and Eva Braun. This reliable dental evidence provides the most powerful corroboration of the numerous eyewitnesses who claimed that Hitler and Eva both died in the Führerbunker on 30 April 1945.[150] A further investigation into Hitler's death was undertaken by the Soviets between April and May 1946. It was headed by the expert forensic pathologist Pyotr Semenovsky. Ordering a fresh inspection of the furniture found inside the Führerbunker, he confirmed that blood was present on the sofa, indicating the death of Hitler was by a gunshot.

On 30 May 1946 a further excavation of the Reich Chancellery garden uncovered two fragments of what was thought to be Hitler's skull. One of them contained the exit wound of a bullet. Based on this evidence, Semenovsky concluded that Hitler had died of a self-inflicted gunshot wound. In 2009, however, DNA and forensic tests on the two skull fragments which were in a Soviet archive concluded they belonged to a woman under forty years of age but it was not determined whether this was Eva Braun.[151]

In 1947 Hugh Trevor-Roper had published his best-selling book *The Last Days of Hitler*. It was based on his own extensive investigation into circumstances surrounding Hitler's death, commissioned by the British government and undertaken in 1946.[152] Unaware of the Soviet investigation and its findings, Trevor-Roper based his own report primarily on the testimony of eyewitnesses who had been present in the bunker in the days leading up to Hitler's death. Trevor-Roper concluded that Hitler and Eva had both committed suicide in the Führerbunker on 30 April 1945 and that their bodies had been burned in the Reich Chancellery garden shortly afterwards. He could not ascertain what happened to their remains subsequently, however. This was not surprising as the Soviet Union never informed its wartime Allies how they had dealt with Hitler and Eva's remains. There are several discrepancies in the eyewitness accounts Trevor-Roper assembled, including a failure by some of those present to agree on the correct date of Hitler's death. These minor ambiguities in Trevor-Roper's account have nevertheless fanned the flames of doubt.[153]

There was, however, a much more conclusive West German investigation into Hitler's death. In 1952, the district court in Berchtesgaden near Munich began extensive legal proceedings to establish the precise date, time, location and circumstances of Hitler's death. During an extensive four-year investigation, a total of forty-two witnesses – most of whom had been in the Führerbunker at the time of Hitler's death – gave evidence under oath. They included Hitler's valet Heinz Linge and his personal adjutant Otto Günsche. Dr Hugo Blaschke, Hitler's personal dentist, and his assistant Käthe Heusermann, who worked in the dental clinic in the Reich Chancellery, both confirmed the teeth in the lower jaws of the corpses presented to them by Soviet investigators matched their own dental records for Hitler and Eva. These teeth were further matched to a skull X-ray of Adolf Hitler, which had been taken in July 1944 after the bomb plot.[154]

This final West German official government report concluded that Hitler and Eva had both died in the Führerbunker on 30 April 1945 just as every eyewitness present had suggested: Hitler by shooting himself and Eva by taking cyanide. It also suggested there was a 'distinct possibility' that Hitler had taken cyanide simultaneously, but this could not be fully confirmed from the surviving evidence. Hitler was declared officially dead by the West German government in 1956 and Eva in 1957.[155]

The Battle of Berlin did not last very long after Hitler's death. Martin Bormann sent Dönitz a radio message announcing that the naval chef had been appointed as the new German President in a 'caretaker government', although Bormann failed to mention Hitler was already dead. Dönitz's new government was initially based in Plön near Kiel in Schleswig-Holstein, but was soon forced to move to the northern port of Flensburg. The only purpose of this new government was to negotiate Germany's surrender, but the Allies refused to even recognize it as legitimate.

Also in accordance with Hitler's will, Joseph Goebbels became the new Reich Chancellor. Goebbels remained in the Führerbunker to make one last attempt to negotiate separate peace terms with the Soviet Union. General Hans Krebs was sent behind Soviet lines to discuss the matter with Chuikov, who told him that Germany's unconditional surrender was non-negotiable. Krebs could not accept this demand and returned to the Führerbunker.

Once Goebbels received this rebuff from the Soviets on the afternoon of 1 May 1945 he also decided to follow Hitler and commit suicide. A truly horrifying scene now played out in the eerie bunker.

Early in the evening Goebbels ordered the SS dentist Helmut Kunz to assist his wife in poisoning his six children. Kunz later claimed that he tried to persuade Goebbels and his wife Magda to spare their children. He even offered to place them under the protection of the Red Cross, but Goebbels snapped back, 'It's impossible. They are the children of Goebbels.'[156]

Shortly afterwards, Kunz entered the children's bedroom, accompanied by Magda. She told the children that the doctor was going to give them all a vaccination. Kunz said he then administered morphine injections to each child in turn. He noted the time in his medical notes: 8.40 p.m. Kunz, however, refused to poison the children with cyanide. This grim task was undertaken by Hitler's personal surgeon Dr Ludwig Stumpfegger, who entered the bedroom with Magda. She opened each child's mouth while Stumpfegger crushed a cyanide capsule into it. Soviet troops found bruising on Helga's face indicating she probably realized her fate and bravely struggled. These innocent children – Helga, Hildegard, Helmut, Holdine, Hedwig and Heidrun – were all victims of their parents' blind loyalty to Hitler and National Socialism.[157]

At 9 p.m. on 1 May 1945, with their children already dead, Joseph and Magda Goebbels said farewell to the few people still remaining in the bunker. They then walked upstairs to the old Reich Chancellery garden, accompanied by Günther Schwägermann, Goebbels's loyal adjutant. The couple each bit into a glass cyanide ampoule. This was noted in the Soviet autopsy report, although they may have shot themselves at the same time or perhaps it was Schwägermann who finished them off. Schwägermann set their bodies alight, but they were not badly charred when Soviet troops found them later and were easily identifiable.

On the same night, Martin Bormann, carrying a copy of Hitler's last will and testament, left the bunker. He was never seen again.[158] On the following day, Hans Krebs and Wilhelm Burgdorf, the last occupants of the Führerbunker, shot themselves with their own Luger pistols.

Hitler, Goebbels and other leading Nazis chose suicide, but they were not alone. A significant number of German people took their own lives, too. The most common reason for this was a desire to escape the consequences of Germany's defeat. Many were terrified of what a vengeful Red Army might do. Others simply could not live in a world without their Führer. From 30 April to 3 May 1945 a wave of suicides occurred in the small town of Demmin in the province of Pomerania. It's thought between 700 and 1,000 people took their own lives in this town in this brief period. The list of the dead included a wide spectrum of local townspeople: blue- and white-collar workers, doctors, tradesmen, shopkeepers, accountants, policemen, teachers, butchers and mechanics. Several methods of killing were used: drowning, gunshots, knives, razor blades, rope and cyanide.[159]

What occurred in Demmin was not an isolated case. Suicides occurred all over Germany and they were not confined to what would become East Germany either. In West Germany, many people saw no future for themselves. In Berlin there were 7,057 suicides in 1945, with 3,881 of those occurring in April. This was five times the usual suicide rate. In Neustadt, there was also a wave of suicides after the Americans occupied the town in March 1945. In Upper Bavaria local authorities registered ten times as many suicides between April and May 1945 than in the same months during previous years. Corpses hanging from trees became a familiar sight.[160]

At 9 p.m. on 1 May 1945 Radio Hamburg declared that the German government was about to make a 'grave and important announcement'. Solemn funeral music was played, including works by Wagner and Bruckner. At 10.20 p.m. the music suddenly stopped, followed by three drum rolls and a three-minute silence.

Then Karl Dönitz, the new German President, came to the microphone and said:

> German men and women, soldiers of the armed forces. Our Führer, Adolf Hitler, has fallen. In deepest grief and respect the German people bow. He early recognized the frightful danger of Bolshevism and dedicated his being to this struggle. At the end of this, his struggle, and his unswerving life's path, stands his hero's death in the capital of the German Reich. His life was a unique service for Germany. His mission in the battle against the Bolshevist storm-flood is valid for Europe and the entire civilized world.[161]

The first statement uttered by the new German President was a blatant lie. Hitler had committed suicide the previous day of course, but Dönitz preferred to depict him as a martyr dying a glorious death as a soldier in a scene that never occurred. In Dönitz's retelling of history, he then claimed Germany had not been fighting an Allied coalition, but was engaged in a singular ideological struggle against the Soviet Union.[162]

[overleaf]
Alfred Jodl, Chief of the Operations Staff for the German Armed Forces High Command, signing the 'First Instrument of Surrender' on 7 May 1945.

Dönitz had three aims before he sanctioned Germany's inevitable capitulation: first, to avoid unconditional surrender to the three major Allies; second, to preserve Germany as a sovereign state; and third, to preserve the *Wehrmacht* as a force in post-war Germany. More cynically, he hoped to negotiate a separate peace deal with the Western Allies and continue the war against the Soviet Union. This shows Dönitz shared many of Hitler's illusions, which ensured that the killing went on in Europe for another week, especially on the Eastern Front where fighting did not cease in some places until mid-May 1945.[163]

In the western theatre of war, there was a wave of surrenders, first in northern Italy and southern Austria on 2 May. On 4 May German forces in north-west Germany surrendered to Field Marshal Montgomery on Lüneberg Heath. On the following day, German forces surrendered in Denmark and the Netherlands. On 8 May the German army in Norway surrendered. On 9 May, the German forces on the Channel Islands gave up.

On 2 May 1945 General Helmut Weidling, the commander of the Berlin city garrison, surrendered to the Red Army. A Berlin housewife described the city as she emerged from her shelter: 'It was raining and felt very cold. Our legs were very shaky, walking in the street. Berlin as far as the eye could see was a smoking, smouldering ruin. Dead men lay on the ground and the living clambered over them carrying bedding and household articles.'[164]

Weidling, using a borrowed Soviet radio transmitter and loudspeaker vans, sent the following message to German soldiers: 'On 30 April 1945 the Führer committed suicide and in so doing deserted everybody who was loyal to him. You, German soldiers, were loyal to the Führer and were prepared to continue the battle for Berlin, although ammunition was in short supply and further resistance was pointless. I hereby declare an immediate ceasefire.'[165] During the sixteen-day Battle of Berlin, the Soviets sustained 81,000 men killed or missing.[166] The total German losses are notoriously difficult to calculate from the surviving sources, but the best estimate now suggests 100,000 military deaths outside the city, with a further 22,000 military dead inside the city and an additional 22,000 civilians killed during the final struggle.[167]

Alongside the tremendous and selfless bravery of the Red Army soldiers who captured Berlin came the shameful actions of many of those who engaged in the widespread rape of women. Records at Berlin hospitals recorded 130,000 rape cases and the true figure was probably much higher.[168] The Red Army's rape victims later recalled their harrowing ordeals. Ilse Antz was one. She lived in Wilmersdorf with her mother and her younger sister. One morning during the final days of the Battle of Berlin a Soviet officer entered her home, then took her to an upstairs room and stripped her naked. The officer had at first mistaken her for a man. 'I was not surprised,' Ilse later recalled. 'I was so thin from hunger I hardly looked like a woman.' The officer then raped her. As he left, he said, 'That's what the Germans did in Russia.' This was not the only instance of rape inflicted on Ilse's family. She was raped again by other Soviet soldiers and so were her mother and sister.[169]

A seventeen-year-old Berlin woman described what happened after a number of Red Army soldiers entered her home in Berlin:

> I counted them, there were eight Russians, yes... and I have to tell you, I did not cry, I didn't do anything, I whimpered, yes, because back then one heard, rape and then a shot in the head and I was incredibly afraid... They tore the clothes from my body, yes therefore I had nothing more on, nothing more at all... and the last one, he had me, and you know, I screamed... then I thought how many more still are coming, and then I constantly thought and when this is over then there will be a shot in the back of the head anyway.[170]

On 7 May 1945, the Dönitz government finally decided to un-conditionally surrender. A radio message – this time notably devoid of National Socialist rhetoric – was read to the German people by Schwerin von Krosigk, a leading minister in the new government, who admitted that 'Germany's strength has been overcome by the over-whelming power of our opponents. The continuation of this war would only have meant senseless bloodshed and pointless destruction.'[171]

At 2.41 a.m. on 7 May 1945 Alfred Jodl, representing the German High Command, signed the 'First Instrument of Surrender' at the headquarters of General Dwight D. Eisenhower in Rheims, France. It was to take effect at one minute after midnight on 8 May, although three German army groups – Army Group Courland, trapped in the Courland Peninsula, and Army Group Centre and Army Group Ostmark in Czechoslovakia, did not give up until 9 and 11 May 1945 respectively.[172]

When Stalin heard about the signing of the 'First Instrument of Surrender' in Rheims he was furious. He insisted it had to be signed again in Berlin to reflect the Soviet Union's enormous contribution to the overall defeat of Germany. The Western Allies agreed to this. Even

[overleaf]
The German armed forces sign the 'Final Instrument of Surrender' in Berlin on 9 May 1945.

so, the Western Allies celebrated 8 May 1945 as 'Victory in Europe Day'.

On that day a German surrender delegation was transported to Marshal Georgy Zhukov's headquarters in a technical school in Karlshorst in Berlin. The meeting began shortly before midnight. The German-signed acts of unconditional surrender already made to Montgomery in Lüneberg and in Rheims were officially ratified, and then the Germans signed the final document, called the 'German Instrument of Surrender' at 12.16 a.m. on 9 May 1945. Field Marshal Wilhelm Keitel represented the German army; Admiral Hans-Georg von Friedeburg the German navy; and General Hans-Jürgen Stumpff the German *Luftwaffe*. The Allied signatories to this historic document were Marshal Georgy Zhukov (Soviet Union), Air Chief Marshal Sir Arthur Tedder (United Kingdom) and General Carl Spaatz (United States), with General Jean de Lattre de Tassigny (France) acting as a legal witness. The document was backdated to 8 May 1945 to be consistent with the first signing in Rheims. In Russia, however, 9 May 1945 remains 'Victory Day'.[173]

In a victory speech, Stalin told the Soviet people:

> Comrades! Compatriots, men and women! The great day of victory over Germany has come. Fascist Germany, forced to her knees by the Red Army and the troops of our Allies, has acknowledged her defeat and declared unconditional surrender... Being aware of the wolfish habits of the German ringleaders, who regard treaties and agreements as an empty scrap of paper, we had no reason to believe their words. Since this morning, in pursuance of the act of surrender, German troops in mass have begun to lay down arms and surrender to our troops. This is no longer an empty scrap of paper. This is the real surrender of Germany's armed forces.[174]

Only hours after the 'German Instrument of Surrender' was signed in Berlin, the *Wehrmacht* broadcast its final radio message to the people of Germany:

> Since midnight the weapons on all fronts are now silent. On the orders of the Grand Admiral [Dönitz], the *Wehrmacht* has given up the fight which has become hopeless. Thus the heroic struggle which lasted nearly six years has come to an end. It brought us great victories but also heavy defeats. In the end the German *Wehrmacht* was honourably defeated by a huge superior force. The German soldier, true to his oath and with the greatest dedication,

has performed deeds which never will be forgotten. The home front supported him to the last with all its powers and suffering the greatest sacrifices. The unique achievement of the front and home front will find its ultimate appreciation in a future just verdict of history.[175]

With these unrepentant words, the Hitler years finally came to an end.

CONCLUSION
•
HITLER'S LONG SHADOW

G ermany's attempt to dominate the world by force threatened all of humanity. It took a hugely powerful coalition of the United States, the Soviet Union, and Britain and its allies to gain victory in a bitter struggle that lasted from 1 September 1939 to 9 May 1945 and claimed the lives of up to 60 million people. Hitler alone was primarily responsible for this catastrophe, but millions of German people, as well as generals, soldiers, sailors and airmen, supported his foreign policy, cheered his military triumphs and turned a blind eye to the persecution of the Jews. They all must share the collective guilt for Germany's war crimes and its catastrophic defeat.

Hitler was convinced Germany could only become a self-sufficient economic superpower by gaining living space (*Lebensraum*) and decided war was the best way to achieve his goal. Inextricably linked to Hitler's desire for living space was his fanatical belief that Germany was involved in a global, existential, racial struggle against international Jewry and Soviet Bolshevism. Hitler believed Jews controlled the political and economic power of his enemies. It was all distorted nonsense, of course, but Hitler acted upon this ingrained mindset.

In September 1939 there were 9 million Jews in Europe but by 1945 only 3 million were still alive. The German-led genocide against the Jews primarily took place in German-occupied Poland and the Soviet Union. Jews from all over Europe were transported to this killing zone and murdered there. Every single Jew was sentenced to death, for merely existing. As the German historian Eberhard Jackel put it: 'Never before had a state... decided to announce that a specific human group, including its aged, women, children and infants, would be killed as quickly as possible, and then carry through this resolution using every possible means of state power.'[1]

Hitler's obsessive hatred of Jews set the agenda for the Holocaust, but other dedicated National Socialists carried it out. The prime mover was undoubtedly the cold, detached bureaucrat Heinrich Himmler, who was in complete charge of the German terror system and the concentration camps. Hitler devolved great power and extraordinary freedom of decision-making to him. Himmler then devolved power to his own bureaucrats to carry out the mass murder. Himmler's *Einsatzgruppen* killing squads escalated the genocide against the Jews soon after Germany attacked the Soviet Union in June 1941, and then, in the spring of 1942, the Holocaust turned into a more systematic form of extermination during the horrific Operation Reinhard.

With the encouragement of Hitler and Himmler, antisemitism and fanciful ideas about racial purity spread like an epidemic throughout the Nazis' key terror organizations, such as the SS, the SD and the Gestapo, but also beyond these organizations to the vast number of bureaucrats who were willingly complicit in genocide. As Martin Bormann put it: 'National Socialist doctrine is entirely anti-Jewish, which means anti-communist and anti-Christian. Everything is linked within National Socialism and everything aims at the fight against Judaism.'[2]

Most of the middle-ranking bureaucrats within the SS and SD who carried out the 'Final Solution' were relatively young, educated to a high level and were committed National Socialists indoctrinated from an early age by Nazi racist and antisemitic ideology. These people were assisted by the existing 'conservative' bureaucracy in German society, men and women who were able to switch from one set of rules founded upon on the rule of law and democracy to a system based on extrajudicial murder and thuggish criminality, without ever seemingly engaging their consciences at any point.

Before opting for war in September 1939 Hitler – as was examined extensively in Volume 1 – had played a skilful and flexible diplomatic game. It had fooled his opponents and brought Germany an almost complete revision of the Treaty of Versailles without even firing a shot. Yet, even though he was very good at it, Hitler hated turning on the diplomatic charm. He was only prepared to compromise tactically in order to further his underlying and fixed ideological and military objectives.

The war Hitler had deliberately provoked in September 1939 was not the one he outlined in *Mein Kampf* (1925), in which he expressed a firm desire for an Anglo-German alliance that would give him a free hand to attack the Soviet Union. Britain was greatly admired by Hitler, who often said that he would like to emulate the British rule of India, which was administered by a small number of individuals. Hitler refused to accept his desire to create an empire on mainland Europe was any different from what the British had already achieved elsewhere. Yet the idea of an Anglo-German alliance – thereby giving Hitler a green light to dominate Europe – was something the British could never contemplate.

Instead, when the British government finally accepted Britain's position in the global order was threatened by Germany's unfolding war programme, it declared war on 3 September 1939. By then Hitler was entangled in a diplomatically astute non-aggression pact with his long-standing ideological enemy, the Soviet Union under Stalin. In 1939, therefore, Hitler was fighting the wrong war against what he saw as the wrong enemy. In 1941, when the United States also joined the conflict, after the Japanese air attack at Pearl Harbor, Hitler had yet another unexpected adversary.

In the early stages of the European war from 1939 to 1941 Germany gained a stunning series of military victories through a combination of military boldness and flexibility, including the defeat of Poland, France, Belgium, the Netherlands, Denmark, Norway, Yugoslavia and Greece. Yet these victories owed as much to the tactical errors of Germany's enemies and to sheer good luck than to any overwhelming German military power. Nevertheless, they made Hitler enormously popular in Germany.

Hitler's greatest error during this early period of impressive military victories was to allow the British Expeditionary Force (BEF) to escape from Dunkirk in May 1940. This was followed by the *Luftwaffe's* failure to achieve air superiority during the Battle of Britain in 1940. Hitler failed to see in both instances that Britain and its farflung empire had to be knocked out of the war completely or forced to accept an armistice if Germany stood any chance of winning the war. Hitler's half-hearted enthusiasm for Operation Sea Lion – the planned German invasion of Britain in 1940 – further confirmed his inability to realize that Britain, with its superior navy, its imperial allies and the material support it received from the money-rich United States, was very far from defeated.

Hitler tried to create an anti-British bloc in the autumn of 1940, but he failed to gain support for this from Spain, France and the Soviet Union. If in 1941 Hitler had devoted all of his considerable military forces to driving the British out of North Africa – instead of launching Operation Barbarossa – then Britain's ability to continue the war would have been seriously compromised and may even have forced the British government to capitulate.

Hitler probably started the war too early. Germany might have stood a better chance of winning the war in Europe if Hitler had waited until 1942 to launch it. Germany had only twenty-six operational U-boats in 1939 and yet it wreaked havoc on British merchant shipping. With a much larger force of U-boats a successful blockade of British ships might have been possible. If Hitler had also built up the strength of the *Luftwaffe*, then the Battle of Britain was potentially more winnable in 1942 than it was in 1940.

Another project that was in no way complete when Hitler embarked on war in 1939 was the so-called National Socialist Revolution. During the war, Hitler constantly went on about being surrounded by disloyal conservative aristocratic generals, judges and civil servants who did not believe in National Socialism. This was true and an admission of his own failure to Nazify Germany.

The much-trumpeted National Community (*Volksgemeinschaft*) – a consumer society free of class divisions, offering equality of opportunity, never happened. It was more propaganda myth than reality. Hitler did destroy communist and trade union organizations in Germany, but he never changed the country's underlying class structures through legislation or a redistribution of wealth and power.

The National Socialist government Hitler led from 1933 to 1945 was much too dependent on conservative nationalists. Little was done to Nazify the civil service, the judiciary and capitalist business enterprises. Hitler never brought industry under state control. Germans enjoyed low taxes and minimal state ownership, which are both traditional conservative policies aimed primarily at the middle classes. Hitler enriched capitalist businesses and made them his partner in all his schemes – even in mass murder. The German army retained a huge level of independence and at its highest levels was composed of upper-middle-class conservatives, few of whom were ever committed National Socialists.

As Hitler failed to change the existing class structure of German society he concentrated instead on eliminating his key political opponents, most notably, the communists and Jews, from German politics, the economy and society. He introduced policies designed to increase the 'racial purity' of the German population through the introduction of a wide-ranging programme of sterilization and then euthanasia. These policies were aimed against disabled people and a wide range of others, mostly lower down the social order, who were classed as 'anti-social', including Gypsies, homosexuals, alcoholics, vagrants, habitual criminals, prostitutes and even the long-term unemployed.

Hitler's government only really attempted to bring about a revolution in the heads of the German people, mainly through the skilful propaganda of Joseph Goebbels. The Nazis were most successful in mobilizing the population to support the idea of Germany once more becoming a great military power.

Hitler's image was also carefully stage-managed using propaganda. A Führer cult persuaded the German people to give Hitler their unconditional support and loyalty. Hitler became the embodiment of the patriotism of the German people. He persuaded them to trust him and to blindly follow him. This helps to explain why – even in the face of devastating Allied bombing campaigns from 1942 onwards, and then numerous military defeats – there was no collapse of German morale on the home front. The level of popular resistance to Hitler – according to Gestapo files – amounted to a miniscule 1 per cent of the German population.

On 22 June 1941, having abandoned the much more sensible course of trying to defeat Britain and its empire, Hitler ordered the hugely risky Operation Barbarossa. This brutal war of racial annihilation against the Soviet Union unleashed unprecedented levels of German violence and inhumanity. Hitler was the prime mover in the decision to attack the Soviet Union, and thereby opened up a new Eastern Front in the Second World War. For Hitler, this was the 'right war' – the one he had outlined in *Mein Kampf* – but it was also a war on two fronts that Germany stood much less chance of winning.

Hitler totally underestimated the military potential of the industrialized Soviet Union. He was tempted into his biggest gamble – and blunder – because he had won all of his previous battles so easily and at so little cost. He thought a swift victory could be achieved again. The German-Soviet War was a lesson in how wrong Hitler had been to dismiss Soviet power and organization.

The equally overconfident German Army High Command fell into the same arrogant mindset and failed to make adequate provision even for winter fighting during the period leading up to the failure to take Moscow in December 1940. Nor did the German generals take enough account of the vast logistical problems of fighting deep into the hinterland of the Soviet Union. German military planning was hampered by a failure to consider a plan B if their objectives were not achieved quickly.

In the Western popular imagination – particularly in Britain and America – the victory over the Nazis in the Second World War is rooted in the D-Day landings. Yet that narrative overlooks the enormous importance of the German-Soviet War in the defeat of Hitler's Germany. It must be understood that the war against the Soviet Union was Hitler's major preoccupation for most of the period from 1941 to 1945. Even in his final 'Political Testament', dictated shortly before his suicide, Hitler stressed that if Germany rose again from the ashes of defeat in a hundred years' time, its key objective should be to gain 'living space' once again in the east.

The Red Army was undoubtedly the main force behind the destruction of the German army on the battlefield. As was revealed in the preceding chapters, the monumental battles on the Eastern Front were on a completely different scale to the conflict on the Western Front. Out of every five German soldiers who died in the Second World War, four were killed by a soldier of the Red Army.[3] By 1941, 75 per cent of all Germany's fighting troops were fighting against the Soviet Union. Even in August 1944, towards the end of the Battle of Normandy, 66 per cent of all Germany's troops were still fighting bloody battles on the Eastern Front.[4]

The German government's official record, researched by the military historian Rüdiger Overmans, listed 4.3 million German military personnel dead or missing during the Second World War. A further 900,000 – conscripted from outside Germany's 1937 borders in Austria and East-Central Europe – were also killed fighting for the German cause.[5] One third of all German males born between 1915 and 1924 were dead or missing by the end of the war. In the summer of 1944, the German army had lost 589,425 dead on the Eastern Front, compared to 156,726 on all the other war fronts combined. The Western Allies killed a further 350,000 to 465,000 German civilians in bombing raids, most of these were civilians – not combat forces.[6]

The Soviet Union suffered a greater loss of life fighting the German army on the Eastern Front than any other power. The official Soviet record, compiled by the Russian Academy of Science, puts the Soviet military and civilian death toll in the German-Soviet War at 26.6 million, with 8.68 million of those being military deaths.[7] Other historians have suggested that the Soviet military death toll was in fact up to 11.5 million as the official Russian death total does not include the huge number of Soviet POWs who died, mostly from German maltreatment.[8] The Soviet civilian death toll was probably way above the official figure of 17.6 million and could even have been as high as 22.6 million, which, when the military deaths are added, brings a more accurate total of 34.1 million Soviets being killed due to German military aggression between 1941 and 1945.

In addition, the Soviet Union was left in utter ruins at the end of the war, its cities, villages and infrastructure totally destroyed. Economically, the Soviet Union never fully recovered from the ordeal it endured at the hands of Germany in the Second World War. Between 1940 and 1945, Soviet GDP fell by an enormous 18 per cent. By any measure, the suffering of the Soviet Union was truly appalling.

In comparison, the military losses of the Anglo-American Allies seem extraordinarily light. British military losses, including the navy and air force, totalled 383,700, with an additional 67,200 civilian deaths, mostly in German bombing raids. The United States suffered 407,300 dead, but only 12,100 civilian deaths. The Western Allies used tanks, artillery and devastating air power to defeat Germany in the western theatre of war, rather than putting at risk the lives of their foot soldiers. It was a strategy more suited to democratic countries who placed a greater value on human life than Stalin.

Yet the overall contribution of the Western Allies in the victory over the Axis powers was hugely significant. Without the substantial economic aid from the Western Allies – particularly the United States – the Soviet Union could not have mounted the huge offensives it did from 1943 to 1945. These US supplies were not merely food, but also equipment and transport vehicles. They helped to transform the Red Army into a fully mechanized and formidable fighting force, especially in the latter stages of the war.

The Allies' overwhelming victory at sea against German U-boats also ensured war and food supplies flowed freely. Large numbers of well-equipped American troops sailed across the Atlantic to fight in the final battles in North Africa, Italy and Western Europe. The sustained air bombardment of Germany also took its toll – and not only on civilians, but on Germany's wartime economy and infrastructure. Germany faced a draining Second Front in Western Europe from 1943 onwards that also assisted the Red Army grinding down the *Wehrmacht*.

The Anglo-American Allies also made a hugely important scientific and technological contribution to the victory of the Allies. They created radar technology and the bouncing bomb, as well as new fighter and number aircraft. They discovered that penicillin could be used to treat infected war wounds. They cracked the German Enigma codes at Bletchley Park and provided much better intelligence information than the Germans to the military commanders.

The Allies were lucky that Hitler did not devote enough time, energy and resources to building a German atomic bomb. A nuclear-armed Germany might have totally changed the course of the war. As it was, the US-led Manhattan Project led to the first functional nuclear bomb. On 6 August 1945, the United States dropped it on the Japanese city of Hiroshima, killing 80,000 people instantly, while tens of thousands more died later from radiation exposure in the years that followed. A second nuclear bomb fell on Nagasaki three days later, which led to the Japanese Emperor Hirohito announcing the Japanese intention to surrender on 15 August, known as V-J Day. The formal signing of the Japanese unconditional surrender came on 2 September 1945.

The question of whether it was primarily Hitler – with his fixed ideological ideas – that lost the war for Germany has long been discussed. He certainly judged himself one of the greatest historical figures who had ever lived, often comparing himself to Frederick the Great and Napoleon. Hitler expected everyone around him to recognize his greatness, but his personality was actually one of petty-minded egotism. This led, as we have seen, to frequent and often heated arguments with his generals.

Military decisions were debated between Hitler and his generals, with Hitler deciding on what he decided was the best course. Many times Hitler followed a course of action originally suggested by one of his generals. After the war was over, these aristocratic, nationalist and conservative generals pushed all of the blame on to Hitler, that 'mere corporal'. In their testimony at the Nuremberg war trials, and in their self-serving memoirs, these German generals agreed it was Hitler's poor military decision-making that led to Germany's defeat, the implication being if he had left the generals alone to make the decisions then Germany could have won the war.

Unfortunately, too many Western historians in the Cold War accepted this verdict uncritically. On closer inspection, it has been shown here that these self-same German generals raised no objections to the attacks on Poland and France, and eagerly supported Hitler's war of annihilation against the Soviet Union. They also knowingly supported and participated in the criminal orders and atrocities in the east, and never raised any objection to the mass murder of the Jews. They also took numerous bribes of land and money from Hitler. In truth, Germany's generals were willing collaborators in Hitler's plan to dominate Europe by force and they turned on him only when Germany began to lose the war.

Hitler had long been fascinated by the economic power of the United States, devoting many pages to this issue in his unpublished second book in 1928 – which was supposed to be the follow-up to *Mein Kampf*.[9]

To Hitler America was the economically self-sufficient, consumerist, capitalist superpower that he wanted Germany to emulate. Hitler loved American motor cars, gadgets and even Hollywood films. Hitler saw American power as being originally created by a strong Anglo-German 'Aryan' settler community which had been progressively compromised by mass immigration and Jewish influence. Hitler felt that the vast territory of the Soviet Union could be colonized in much the same way as German settlers had transformed America.

Hitler claimed he had not planned or wanted war with the United States. He frequently asked the Japanese government not to provoke war with America, but to attack the much weaker British forces in Southeast Asia. In fact, it was Hitler's ill-judged alliance with Japan that was the key factor in Germany declaring war on the United States in December 1941. This was an error, of course, but President Roosevelt had already decided America's global power and political interests were most threatened by Germany. It was inevitable, therefore, that whatever move Hitler made, Roosevelt would make defeating Germany his chief priority for the remainder of the war.

Hitler was also repeatedly hindered by his alliance with Italy. It's hard to think of a worse military ally than Benito Mussolini and Italy. Germany's military resources were constantly being diverted to assist Italy in Greece, the Soviet Union, North Africa, Sicily and finally on the Italian mainland itself. It would have been far better for Hitler if Italy had never entered the war at all. It would have been much better for Italy, too. Hitler and Mussolini were a marriage made in hell.

Another of Hitler's key strategic errors was his utter failure to coordinate the war efforts of his Axis allies or to even discuss with them an overall global strategy that might win the war. Hitler never even told his key allies about his own important military decisions beforehand, and, similarly, the Japanese government never gave Hitler prior knowledge of its attack on Pearl Harbor, and Mussolini often kept Hitler in the dark about his own military adventures, most notably, the Italian attack on Greece. The Axis powers also failed to exchange even basic intelligence information or details on new weaponry and naval strategy. The Japanese government refused to become involved in the war against the Soviet Union. In comparison, the Allies were much more coordinated, sharing information, strategy and the timing of supplies and offensives.

In the summer of 1942, Hitler's failure to capture Moscow the previous year led him to embark on a second huge offensive to defeat the Soviet Union in the hope of gaining the grain and oil resources that he required to sustain a long war. This resulted in the failed attempt to take Stalingrad, which resulted in a catastrophic defeat in February 1943. During 1943 Germany lost the Battle of the Atlantic, was on the retreat in the Soviet Union, had been driven out of North Africa, and was now bitterly defending the Italian mainland.

In the summer of 1944 Germany failed to prevent the D-Day landings and soon it had lost France and all the territory it had occupied in the Soviet Union since 1941. At this point in the conflict, any pragmatic German leader would have sought peace terms, but Hitler vowed to fight on to the bitter end against an overwhelming Allied coalition.

It was primarily Hitler who dragged Germany to disaster from 1943 onwards. By then he had abolished the independence of the judiciary, dispensed with the Reichstag and weakened the influence of the Nazi Party. Such was Hitler's dictatorial power by then that he was able to impose his own desires on his government, the military commanders and the entire German nation. Hitler, an instinctive gambler, believed in the power of his own will to change the course of events, but like every gambler he did not know when to stop.

The unconditional surrender of Germany in May 1945 spared the world any continuation of its criminal Nazi-dominated government, but it left Germany with its own sovereignty extinguished, its economy ruined, its armed forces abolished and with no functioning government. Furthermore, it was occupied by foreign armies.

Hitler, although dead, cast a long shadow over Germany. Between 1945 and 1949, Germany was divided into four occupied zones, each administered by the victorious Allies: the Soviet Union, the United States, Britain and France. On 23 May 1949 the democratic Federal German Republic (BRD) was created from the eleven states within the Allied administrative zones of Britain, France and the United States. The communist German Democratic Republic (DDR) began to function as a state in the Soviet occupation zone from 7 October 1949. With the onset of the Cold War, Berlin was bitterly divided between East and West, as symbolized by the erection of the Berlin Wall in 1961.

Germany was offered no peace settlement by the Allies. Instead, the major Nazi war criminals – excluding Hitler, Goebbels and Himmler, who had all committed suicide – faced a single trial at the International Military Tribunal at the Palace of Justice in Nuremberg. The defendants were all charged with crimes against peace, war crimes and crimes against humanity. The trial, which received huge international media

[overleaf]
Some of the defendants at the main
Nuremberg Trial of German war criminals.

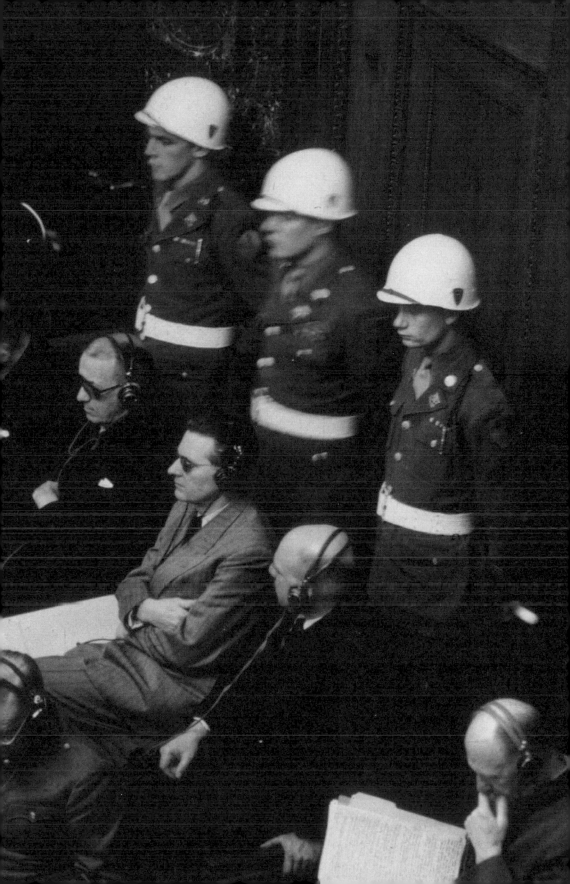

coverage, took place between 14 November 1945 and 1 October 1946. There were 403 court sessions during the proceedings.

There were originally twenty-four defendants at the main Nuremberg Trial, but Robert Ley, the leader of the German Labour Front, committed suicide only three weeks before the first trial began. Martin Bormann, though listed as 'missing', was tried in absentia. The twenty-two men who gave evidence at the Nuremberg Trial were: Hermann Göring, the former head of the *Luftwaffe* and the Gestapo; Karl Dönitz, who succeeded Hitler as German leader; the two former Foreign Ministers, Joachim von Ribbentrop and Konstantin von Neurath; Wilhelm Frick, former Minister of the Interior; Albert Speer, Munitions Minister; Rudolf Hess, Deputy Führer until May 1941; Franz von Papen, former Chancellor; Dr Hjalmar Schacht, former Economics Minister, and his successor Walther Funk; the industrialist Gustav Krupp von Bohlen und Halbach; Baldur von Schirach, former Hitler Youth leader; Arthur Seyss-Inquart, the Reich Commissioner of the Netherlands; Alfred Rosenberg, the Minister of the Occupied Eastern Territories; Julius Streicher, editor of the antisemitic newspaper *Der Stürmer*; Fritz Sauckel, Plenipotentiary in charge of forced labour; Hans Fritzsche, head of the news division of the Ministry of Propaganda; Hans Frank, Governor-General of the General Government; Ernst Kaltenbrunner, Chief of the Reich Security Main Office (RSHA); and the leading army officers Wilhelm Keitel and Alfred Jodl, plus Erich Raeder, the former chief of the German navy.

All defendants were subjected to intelligence tests prior to the start of court proceedings. The majority were classed as of 'above average' intelligence. At the top came Schacht (143), followed by Seyss-Inquart (141), Göring and Dönitz (138), Papen and Raeder (134). The rest recorded figures from 106 to 130. At the very bottom were the brutal Nazi Fritz Sauckel with a score of 118 and the crude antisemite Julius Streicher with a score of 106.[10]

All of the defendants tried to distance themselves from their war crimes by claiming that it was all Hitler's fault and they were only 'taking orders'. At the end of the trial, twelve of the defendants were given death sentences: Bormann (in absentia), Frank, Frick, Göring, Jodl, Kaltenbrunner, Keitel, Ribbentrop, Rosenberg, Sauckel, Seyss-Inquart and Streicher. Papen and Schacht were acquitted. No sentence was issued to Krupp – he would be dealt with at a later trial of businessmen. Prison sentences varying from ten years to life were imposed on the rest. Hermann Göring, the most famous Nazi at the trial, killed himself with a cyanide capsule on the night before he was due to be hanged.

There were twelve subsequent trials of high-ranking SS, military and government figures from December 1946 to April 1949, most notably of concentration camp officials, military officers, doctors, businessmen, judges, government officials and leaders of the *Einsatzgruppen*. The leaders of the *Einsatzgruppen* claimed at their notorious trial they were not cold-blooded murderers, but had been carrying out the orders of the Führer. Most of the defendants at the war crimes trials resorted to the same lame excuse. The industrialists were let off the hook completely and returned to run all of the major German companies which still exist to this day. The courts in the West German zones of occupation convicted only 5,228 defendants between 1945 and 1950 of war crimes. From 1945 to 1997, just 1,878 people ever faced trial in West German courts for war crimes committed in the Nazi era.[11]

During the period of the Allied occupation, from 1945 to 1949, all Germans went through a 'denazification' process, which aimed to remove all those who had been key members of the SS and Nazi Party. It was carried out in the western zones of occupation. As there had been 8.5 million members of the Nazi Party it was a huge task. It was reckoned about 45 million Germans were connected in one way or another with Nazi organizations.

The denazification process aimed to confront Germans with what they had done during the Nazi era, but it also encouraged a collective and selective amnesia. All Germans were required to fill in a short questionnaire (*Fragebogen*) asking questions about their involvement in Nazi organizations. Five categories of potential offender were listed: (1) Major offenders – these would face arrest, trial and sentencing; (2) Offenders – these included Nazi Party activists; (3) Lesser offenders – these would be given probation; (4) Followers and Fellow Travellers – they would be subject to possible employment restrictions; and (5) Exonerated – no sanctions.

Every German who experienced the denazification process wanted the prized certificate of blamelessness. This became jokingly known as the 'Persil Certificate' (Persilschein), a reference to the popular soap powder, which in newspaper advertisements promised to wash clothes 'whiter than white'. It was suggested Nazi war criminals were trying to wash their brownshirts white. Around 3 million Germans went through a more detailed denazification process. In the end, however, overstretched Allied officials accepted what they were told on the forms, which meant most Germans ended up being 'exonerated'.

There was no real purge of former Nazis in West Germany after 1945. Astonishingly, seventy-two judges of the notorious Nazi 'People's Court' were re-employed in the courts of the West German Federal Republic. In total, around 80 per cent of all former legal employees in West Germany kept their jobs. The same was true in the medical profession, the universities, the schools, the police force and the civil service. Between 1956 and 1961, a total of 66 per cent of the employees of the West German Interior Ministry were former Nazi Party members. There's little doubt former Nazis at the heart of the West German state and judiciary influenced the policy of not pursuing Nazi war criminals.

As part of the denazification process, the US Opinion Survey section conducted twenty-two surveys into German attitudes towards Hitler and National Socialism. It found 77 per cent of Germans thought that the murder of the Jews was 'unjustified', with 64 per cent thinking the persecution of Jews was the key reason for Germany's defeat. However, when Germans were asked if Nazism had been a bad idea, only 53 per cent replied 'Yes'. Among those under thirty, 60 per cent thought Nazism was 'a good idea, but carried out badly in the end'. Only 21 per cent thought Nazism had been 'bad' before the Second World War began. A total of 41 per cent of Germans expressed complete ignorance about what had happened in the concentration camps. In a further poll in 1950, only 38 per cent thought the Nuremberg Trials of Nazi war criminals had been fair.[12] Despite this, National Socialism – or even a fervent form of nationalism – never returned in West Germany prior to unification.

There was a similar denazification process in communist East Germany, but it was much more comprehensive. Anyone tainted with Nazi associations was removed from employment. The DDR presented itself as the embodiment of communist resistance to Hitler's regime. The most high-profile trials of Nazi war criminals in the DDR were the famous 'Waldheim Trials', which took place from April to December 1950. Of the ninety-one defendants, twenty-four were sentenced to death and seventeen of those were executed, a further thirty-one were given life sentences and the rest much shorter terms in prison.

Contrary to popular belief, the notorious East German secret state police, the *Stasi*, was not staffed by former Gestapo officers. Former Nazi Party members did not occupy key positions in the post-war East German judiciary either. In 1950 of the 1,000 East German judges, only one was a former Nazi Party member.[13]

The East German government repeatedly published damaging allegations concerning the lack of denazification in West Germany. In

1965, the National Front of the DDR published the so-called 'Brown Book', titled *War and Nazi War Criminals in West Germany*. It named a staggering 1,800 former leading Nazis who still held key positions in West Germany. The list included 15 government ministers, 100 generals and admirals, 828 senior judges and public prosecutors, 245 members of the foreign and diplomatic service, and 297 senior police officials, including former SS, SD and Gestapo officers. The West German government called it 'pure falsification' and the book was banned from sale. However, it turns out that the 'Brown Book' seriously underestimated the number of former Nazis who had retained prominent positions at the top of West German society.[14]

The people of East Germany suffered much worse deprivation in the post-war era than those in the affluent West, who enjoyed unprecedented prosperity and a stable parliamentary democracy dubbed 'The German Miracle'. The East Germans never received the huge injection of American funding through the Marshall Plan which had helped to rebuild the West German economy. In the same period, the cash-starved Soviet occupiers stripped East Germany of much of its industry and supported the repressive East German communist regime. Not surprisingly, the citizens of East Germany felt themselves to be the double victims of the Hitler years.

During the Cold War era, the Western Allies wanted to rehabilitate West Germany as a politically and economically strong bulwark against Soviet communism. This undoubtedly led to a softening of attitudes in the West towards Nazi war criminals. The West Germans were given an alibi by the Western Allies: pin all the blame on Hitler and his criminal Nazi regime.

This helps to explain the deafening silence surrounding the Hitler years in West Germany. There was a widespread unwillingness to discuss what had happened. Instead, self-pity became the norm. The 'Don't Mention the War' episode (called 'The Germans') of the classic British comedy *Fawlty Towers* was very close to the truth. In 1955, when the first Chancellor of the Federal Republic of Germany, Konrad Adenauer, was asked if West Germany was commemorating the tenth anniversary of the liberation from Hitler, he replied: 'You don't celebrate your defeats.'[15]

West Germans did feel a strong sense of victimhood, even though Germany launched the war, conquered much of Europe, enslaved and murdered millions of innocent victims, caused the deaths of millions of soldiers, destroyed countless cities and towns all over Europe, and murdered civilians on an unimaginable scale. Instead of showing contrition, the West Germans became preoccupied with their new prosperous life.

The murder of the Jews was a taboo subject. There was no single 'Holocaust Trial' ever mounted by the West or East German government. The term 'Holocaust' was not even in common usage in the immediate post-war era in West or East Germany. The most well-known Jewish victim of the Holocaust was, of course, the teenager Anne Frank, whose diary became a worldwide bestseller. In the subsequent Hollywood film, however, her Jewishness was downplayed. There are no scenes of her being a prisoner in Auschwitz-Birkenau or Bergen-Belsen.

It was the newly created state of Israel that brought the Holocaust to worldwide attention when it dramatically captured the high-ranking Gestapo official Adolf Eichmann on 11 May 1960. He was living in a quiet middle-class suburb of Buenos Aires in Argentina at the time.

Eichmann's sensational trial, which began on 11 April 1961, was broadcast on TV and radio and reported in newspapers around the world. The testimony of Jewish Holocaust survivors was given graphic expression for the first time.

Eichmann gave his testimony in a routine manner, coming across not as a Nazi fanatic, but as a sort of middle-class bank manager of death. He claimed to have sorted out the paperwork that ensured millions of people died, but was just a seemingly powerless cog in the wheel and was only 'taking orders'. The philosopher Hannah Arendt memorably summed up Eichmann's matter-of-fact attitude as the 'banality of evil'.

The Eichmann trial gave fresh impetus to a group of more radical West German lawyers who now wanted to bring Nazi war criminals to justice. This led to the most famous West German trials related to the Holocaust in the post-war period: the Frankfurt Auschwitz Trials, which took place between 20 December 1963 and 19 August 1965. These trials were given extensive media coverage. Twenty-two defendants were charged with murder and other serious crimes

Adolf Eichmann at his war crimes trial in Israel in 1961.

committed while they were working at the Auschwitz-Birkenau concentration camp. A total of 248 Holocaust survivors delivered harrowing testimonies. At the end of the trial, all but five of the accused were convicted, with six receiving life sentences. However, an opinion poll conducted at the time revealed that 57 per cent of West Germans were not in favour of any more Nazi war crimes trials.[16]

It was not until the 1970s that the Nazi period and the Holocaust were even included in the German school curriculum. It was really the American TV series *The Holocaust* – broadcast on West German TV in 1979 to an audience of 14 million – that led to a change of attitude, as the West German public began to see the Holocaust as a distinct Jewish experience.

Since the reunification of Germany in 1990 there has been a very noticeable willingness of younger Germans – who had no personal involvement in what happened during the Nazi era – to confront many inconvenient truths about the Nazi era. Steven Spielberg's epic *Schindler's List* (1993) prompted most German history teachers to take their students to see the film. The crimes of the *Wehrmacht*, once denied, are now fully acknowledged. The former SS-run German concentration camps of Bergen-Belsen, Dachau, Sachsenhausen are now moving memorials to the victims of Hitler's terror. All German schoolchildren now visit them as part of the school curriculum. In Germany in recent years there has been a flood of new documentaries, films and novels, as well as university courses, dedicated to the Holocaust and Nazi war crimes.

There's now a Holocaust memorial in the centre of Berlin. In 2001, a Jewish Museum opened and is now one of the city's leading tourist attractions. The German democratic government now makes frequent payments to former slave labourers of the Nazi era and to victims of the Holocaust. The heroism of those who stood up to the Nazis is also celebrated in Berlin's German Resistance Memorial Centre. It's now generally accepted most German people during the Nazi era were not just taking orders, but were enthusiastic supporters of Hitler and fought to the bitter end to preserve his criminal regime.

It would be a mistake, however, to assume all Germans have finally come to terms with the enormity of what happened during the Hitler years. The victims of Hitler's genocide and their families continue to suffer the pain and grief and the haunting memories. Adolf Hitler's long shadow over Germany and over humanity itself has not yet disappeared and it probably never will.

[overleaf]
The Memorial to the Murdered Jews of Europe in Berlin.

·

ACKNOWLEDGEMENTS
NOTES
BIBLIOGRAPHY
INDEX

·

Every book is a collaborative process. This book could not have been written without the advice and support of so many people. Once again, I must thank my wonderful literary agent Georgina Capel for her advice and support throughout the whole project and the whole team at Georgina Capel and Associates, especially Irene Baldoni and Rachel Conway.

A sincere thanks is also due to Anthony Cheetham for having faith in me to carry out such a huge project. The editorial team at Head of Zeus have been quite superb. The picture research and map creation was overseen by Juliet Brightmore, Clémence Jacquinet and Clare Gordon. The design of *The Hitler Years* by Isambard Thomas at Corvo is original and eye-catching.

I have also benefitted from the support and advice of a number of friends, colleagues and family during the period of the completion these two volumes. They were all mentioned at the end of Volume 1.

My greatest thanks must go to my wonderful wife Ann, who has shown amazing patience during my long hours engaged with this horrific subject and provided many insights on key issues as I discussed chapters with her. Without her support, I doubt I could have got through this huge project as during the writing process I suffered the deaths of my brother Michael and my sister Carol and in the past few months had illness of my own to cope with, though thankfully not serious.

Finally, I would like to thank all those brave service personnel, including my dad, who fought so bravely to defeat Hitler and his horrific and brutal regime. If they had failed, I would never have been able to write these books.

NOTES

**SOURCE ABBREVIATIONS
USED IN NOTES**

BAB
Bundesarchiv Berlin-Lichterfelde

BAK
Bundesarchiv, Koblenz

DGFP
Documents on Germany Foreign
Policy 1918–1945 [files of the
German Foreign Ministry,
Auswärtiges Amt, Berlin]

GWPA
German War Propaganda
Archive

HSW
Hagen Stadt Archives

HCD
Hansard's Parliamentary Debates,
House of Commons, 5th series

IfZ
Institut für Zeitgeschichte,
Munich

IWM
Imperial War Museum, London

JVL
Jewish Virtual Library

MGR
Memorial of the German
Resistance, Berlin

NA
National Archives, London

All publications are London,
unless otherwise stated.

CHAPTER I

1 *Sydney Morning Herald*, 1
January 1940.

2 DGFP, Series D, Vol. 8: *The
War Years 4 September 1939–18
March 1940* (Washington, DC,
US Government Printing Office),
No. 504, pp.604–609, Mussolini
to Hitler, 3 January 1940.
(Hereafter DGFP)

3 Ibid., No. 518, pp.636–40,
Memorandum, 10 January 1940.

4 Ibid., No. 531, pp.659–660, The
Ambassador in Belgium [Bülow]
to Foreign Ministry, 13 January
1939.

5 Ibid., No. 544, pp.674–5, The
Ambassador in Belgium [Bülow]
to Foreign Ministry, 17 January
1939.

6 See H. Sebag-Montefiore, 'The
Mechelen Affair', *Military History
Quarterly*, Vol. 20 (Spring 2008),
pp.48–55.

7 Hitler speech, Berlin, 24
January 1940, quoted in M.
Domarus, *The Essential Hitler:
Speeches and Commentary*
(Wauconda, IL: Bolchazy-
Carducci, 2007), pp.187–91.
(Hereafter: *Hitler: Speeches and
Proclamations*)

8 For details, see W. Warlimont,
Inside Hitler's Headquarters
(Novato, CA: Presidio Press,
1964), pp.66–81.

9 Hitler speech, Berlin, 30
January 1940, text at http://www.
hitler.org/speeches/

10 DGFP, Series D, Vol. 8, No.
591, pp.732–6, Conversation
between Hitler and Count
Massimo Magistrati on the
Occasion of his Farewell Visit,
2 February 1940.

11 For details see M. Doherty,
'The Attack on the Altmark
– a case study in Wartime
Propaganda', *Journal of
Contemporary History*, Vol. 38
(2003), pp.187–200.

12 DGFP, Series D, Vol. 8, No.
618, pp.779–83, Memorandum
by German Naval Attaché
in Norway, 17 February 1940.
For details see M. Doherty,
'The Attack on the Altmark',
pp.187–200.

13 The most detailed examination
of Case Yellow from the German
perspective is H. Jacobson, *Fall
Gelb: Der Kampf um den Deutschen
Operationsplan zur Westoffensive
1940* (Wiesbaden: Franz Steiner
Verlag, 1957).

14 The full text of the Manstein
memoranda can be found in MA-
BA, RH 19 1/26. The text of six
of the memoranda are reprinted
in E. Manstein, *Lost Victories:
The War Memoirs of Hitler's Most
Brilliant General* (London: TBS
The Book Service, 2004).

15 Hitler said after his first meeting with Manstein: 'Certainly a bright fellow with great operational talent, but I don't trust him.' See K-H. Frieser, *The Blitzkrieg Legend: The 1940 Campaign in the West* (Annapolis, MD: Naval Institute Press, 2005), p.376.

16 In his memoirs Halder tried to suggest that the 'Sickle Cut' plan was mainly his idea. See F. Halder, *Hitler as War Lord* (London: Putnam, 1949).

17 For details of the debate over Manstein's plan, see K. H. Frieser, *The Blitzkrieg Legend*, pp.60–99.

18 Hitler speech, Munich, 24 February 1940, *Hitler: Speeches and Proclamations*, pp.140–2.

19 For details see S. Hilton, 'The Welles Mission to Europe, February–March 1940: Illusion or Realism?', *The Journal of American History*, Vol. 58 (1971), pp.93–120.

20 *Hitler: Speeches and Proclamations*, pp.710–13.

21 For details see R. Petrow, *The Bitter Years: The Invasion and Occupation of Denmark and Norway, April 1940–May 1945* (London: William Morrow & Co., 1974).

22 DGFP, Series D, Vol. 8, No. 644, pp.831–33, Führer Directive for Fall Weserübung, 1 March 1940.

23 Ibid., No. 640, pp.821–9, Conversation between Ribbentrop and Mr Sumner Welles, Berlin, 1 March 1940.

24 Ibid., No. 640, pp.829–39, Memorandum by Weizsäcker, 1 March 1940.

25 Ibid., No. 649, pp.838–45, Conversation between Hitler and Mr Sumner Welles, Berlin, 2 March 1940. See also, *Hitler: Speeches and Proclamations*, pp.713–15.

26 Ibid., No. 663, pp.871–80, Hitler to Mussolini, 8 March 1940.

27 Ibid., No. 665, pp.882–93, Conversation between

Ribbentrop and Mussolini, Rome, 10 March 1940.

28 Ibid., No. 669, pp.898–909, Conversation between Ribbentrop and Mussolini, Rome, 11 March 1940.

29 See K. Fischer, *Hitler and America* (Philadelphia, PA: University of Pennsylvania Press, 2011), pp.27–8.

30 DGFP, Series D, Vol. 8, No. 671, pp.910–13, Conversation between Hitler and Colin Ross, Berlin, 12 March 1940.

31 Documents on German Foreign Policy, Series D, Vol. 9: *The War Years: March 18–June 22 1940* (Her Majesty's Stationery Office, 1956). Document 1, pp.1–16, Conversation between Hitler and Mussolini, 18 March 1940. (Hereafter DGFP)

32 John Toland, *Adolf Hitler: The Definitive Biography* (Ware, Hertfordshire: Wordsworth, 1997), p.601.

33 G. Ciano, *The War Diaries of Count Galeazzo Ciano, 1939–43* (Fonthill, 2015), p.168.

34 J. Holland, *The War in the West: A New History* (Corgi, 2015), Vol. 1: *Germany Ascendant, 1939–1941*, pp.231–2.

35 DGFP, Series D, Vol. 9, No. 39, Führer Directive, 2 April 1940.

36 Ibid., No. 41, Directive of the Chief of the High Command [Keitel] on Occupation of Denmark and Norway, 2 April 1940.

37 Ibid., No. 53, pp.84–5, Ribbentrop to Minister in Norway [Bräuer], 7 April 1940.

38 *The Times*, 5 April 1940.

39 For details, see D. Dildy, *Denmark and Norway 1940: Hitler's Boldest Operation* (Oxford: Osprey, 2007). See also, Holland, *War in the West*, Vol. 1, p.241.

40 DGFP, Series D, Vol. 9, No. 60, The Minister in Norway [Bräuer] to the Foreign Ministry, 8 April 1940.

41 See H. Dethlefsen, 'Denmark and German Occupation:

Cooperation, Negotiation or Collaboration?', *Scandinavian Journal of History*, Vol. 15 (1990), pp.193–206; J. Lund, 'Denmark and the New European Order, 1940–1942', *Contemporary European History*, Vol. 13 (2004), pp.235–56.

42 M. Mazower, *Hitler's Empire: Nazi Rule in Occupied Europe* (Allen Lane, 2008), pp.103–4.

43 For details, see H. Lunde, *Hitler's Pre-Emptive War: The Battle for Norway, 1940* (Newbury: Casemate, 2010).

44 For Quisling's role, see H. F. Dahl, *Quisling: A Study in Treachery* (Cambridge: Cambridge University Press, 2008).

45 DGFP, Series D, Vol. 9, No. 68, pp.104–105, Hitler to Mussolini, 8 April 1940.

46 Ibid., No. 69, pp.105–6, The Ambassador in Italy [Mackensen] to Foreign Ministry, 9 April 1940.

47 Ibid., No. 73, p.108, Schulenburg to Foreign Secretary, 9 April 1940.

48 Ibid., No. 83, pp.123–5, The Minister in Norway [Bräuer] to the Foreign Ministry, 10 April 1940.

49 Ibid., No. 95, pp.136–9, The Minister in Norway [Bräuer] to the Foreign Ministry, 11 April 1940.

50 Ibid., No. 99, pp.144–7, Conversation between Hitler and Hagelin, Berlin, 13 April 1940.

51 Ibid., No. 113, pp.161–2, The Minister in Norway [Bräuer] to the Foreign Ministry, 14 April 1940.

52 Ibid., No. 115, pp.162–4, Telephone Conversation between Ribbentrop and Bräuer, 14 April 1940.

53 Ibid., No. 118, pp.168–72, Note on Negotiations leading to the Resignation of Minister-President Quisling, 15 April 1940.

54 Ibid., No. 162, pp.230–1, Decree of the Führer Concerning

the Exercise of Government Power in Norway, 24 April 1940.

55 See Mazower, *Hitler's Empire*, pp.104–105; M. Burleigh, *Moral Combat: A History of World War II* (Harper Press, 2010), pp.194–6.

56 M. Hastings, *All Hell Let Loose: The World at War, 1939–1945* (Harper Press, 2015), p.48.

57 DGFP, Series D, Vol. 9, No. 168, pp.237–9, Hitler to Mussolini, 26 April 1940.

58 Ibid., No. 192, pp.275–7, Mussolini to Hitler, 3 May 1940.

59 Hitler speech, Berlin, 3 May 1940, *Hitler: Speeches and Proclamations*, pp.191–206.

60 HCD, Vol. 360, cols. 1073–1196, speech by Leo Amery, 7 May 1940.

61 For a detailed account of how the Norway campaign led to Churchill becoming Prime Minister, see N. Shakespeare, *Six Minutes in May: How Churchill Unexpectedly Became Prime Minister* (Harvill Secker, 2017).

62 DGFP, Series D, Vol. 9, No. 212, pp.299–301, Hitler to Mussolini, 9 May 1940.

63 Ibid., No. 232, p.321, Mussolini to Hitler, 10 May 1940.

64 Ibid., No. 231, pp.300–1, Führer Directive on Administration of the Occupied Territories of France, Luxembourg, Belgium and Holland, 9 May 1940.

65 J. Keegan, *The Second World War* (Pimlico, 1989), pp.53–4.

66 See Keegan, *The Second World War*, pp.45–72; H. Jacobson, *Fall Gelb*.

67 See D. Rottgart, '*Die deutsche Panzergruppe am 10/5/1940*', Part 1, *Zeitschrift für Heereskunde*, Vol. 49, No. 319 (May–June 1985), pp.61–7.

68 Frieser, *Blitzkrieg Legend*, pp.28–85.

69 D. Todman, *Britain's War: Into Battle, 1937–1941* (Allen Lane, 2016), Vol. 1, p.328.

70 R. Stolfi, 'Equipment for Victory in France in 1940',

History, Vol. 55, No. 183 (February 1970), pp.1–120. See also A. Horne, *To Lose a Battle: France 1940* (Penguin, 2007), pp.229–30.

71 Frieser, *Blitzkrieg Legend*, pp.44–54.

72 For details, see R. Kirkland, 'The French Air Force in 1940: Was It Defeated by the *Luftwaffe* or by Politics?', *Air University Review*, Vol. 36, No. 6 (1985), pp.101–18.

73 For a detailed analysis, see R. Jackson, *The Air War Over France, May–June 1940* (London: Ian Allan, 1974).

74 Keegan, *The Second World War*, p.53.

75 For a cogent overview of Gamelin as French military commander, see Horne, *To Lose a Battle*, pp.161–83.

76 Interview with André Beaufre in R. Holmes, *The World at War: The Landmark Oral History from the Classic TV Series* (Ebury, 2011), p.97.

77 See S. Dunstan, *Eban Emael: The Key to Hitler's Victory in the West*, Oxford: Osprey, 2005.

78 *Independent*, 14 September 2015.

79 Frieser, *Blitzkrieg Legend*, p.160.

80 J. Jackson, *The Fall of France: The Nazi Invasion of 1940* (Oxford: Oxford University Press, 2004), p.9.

81 A. Beevor, *The Second World War* (Phoenix, 2011), p.95.

82 Keegan, *The Second World War*, p.60.

83 Mazower, *Hitler's Empire*, pp.105–6.

84 DGFP, Series D, Vol. 9, No. 246, pp.343–4, Hitler Directive No. 11, 14 May 1940.

85 Frieser, *Blitzkrieg Legend*, pp.278–80.

86 Ibid., p.258.

87 DGFP, Series D, Vol. 9, No. 272, pp.374–5, Hitler to Mussolini, 18 May 1940.

88 Ibid., No. 276, p.379, Mussolini to Hitler, 19 May 1940.

89 Beevor, *The Second World War*, p.104.

90 DGFP, Series D, Vol. 9, No. 312, pp.427–9, Führer Directive, No. 13, 24 May 1940.

91 Frieser, *Blitzkrieg Legend*, pp.291–5.

92 Interview with Ferdinand Krones, in J. Steinhoff, P. Pechel, and D. Showalter (eds), *Voices from the Third Reich: An Oral History* (Washington, DC: Da Capo Press, 1994), p.77.

93 Interview with Walter Warlimont, in *World at War*, p.108.

94 Frieser, *Blitzkrieg Legend*, p.313.

95 R. J. Evans, *The Third Reich* (Allen Lane, 2003–2008), Vol. 3: *The Third Reich at War*, p.129.

96 For details, see W. Gardner, *The Evacuation from Dunkirk: Operation Dynamo, 26 May–4 June 1940* (Routledge, 2000).

97 Frieser, *Blitzkrieg Legend*, p.302.

98 DGFP, Series D, Vol. 9, No. 317, pp.436–9, Hitler to Mussolini, 25 May 1940.

99 Ibid., No. 356, p.483, Mussolini to Hitler, 30 May 1940.

100 Ibid., No. 357, pp.484–6, Hitler to Mussolini, 31 May 1940.

101 W. L. Shirer, *The Rise and Fall of the Third Reich: A History of Nazi Germany* (Folio, 2004), p.887.

102 See J. Lukacs, *Five Days in London, May 1940* (New Haven, CT: Yale University Press, 1999).

103 Todman, *Britain's War*, Vol. 1, pp.343–4.

104 The minutes of these meetings are within the National Archives, volumes CAB 65-7 and CAB 65-13, and are classified as War Cabinet Minutes WM 109 (40) to WM 188 (40).

105 Beevor, *The Second World War*, pp.109–11.

106 Interview with J. B. Priestley, *World at War*, p.111.

107 Shirer, *Rise and Fall*, pp.874–7.

108 Mazower, *Hitler's Empire*, pp.106–7.

109 *The Times*, 5 June 1940.

110 Evans, *The Third Reich at War*, p.230.

111 *Hitler: Speeches and Proclamations*, pp.737–8.

112 Ibid., pp.738–9.

113 See Shirer, *Rise and Fall*, pp.834–55.

114 Hastings, *All Hell Let Loose*, p.52.

115 DGFP, Series D, Vol. 9, No. 410, pp.542–3, Hitler to Mussolini, 10 June 1940.

116 Toland, *Adolf Hitler*, p.613.

117 Interview between Hitler and Karl von Wiegand, *Hitler: Speeches and Proclamations*, pp.715–19.

118 DGFP, Series D, Vol. 9, No. 433, pp.567–8, Führer Directive, No. 15, 14 June 1940.

119 Keegan, *The Second World War*, p.71.

120 A. Bullock, *Hitler and Stalin: Parallel Lives* (HarperCollins, 1991), p.751.

121 Keegan, *The Second World War*, p.70.

122 DGFP, Series D, Vol. 9, No. 479, pp.608–611, Record of Conversation between Hitler and Mussolini, 18 June 1940.

123 Ibid., No. 512, pp.643–52, Memorandum on Armistice Negotiations (First Meeting), Compiègne, 21 June 1940.

124 Ibid., No. 513, pp.652–4, Record of Telephone Conversation between General Weygand and General Hutzinger, 21 June 1940.

125 Ibid., No. 522, pp.664–71, Record of Second Day of Negotiations on the Armistice, Compiègne, 22 June 1940. For details of the full terms, see DGFP, Series D, Vol. 9, No. 523, German-French Armistice Treaty, 22 June 1940.

126 Frieser, *Blitzkrieg Legend*, p.318.

127 I. Kershaw, *Hitler, Vol. 2: Nemesis, 1936–1945* (Penguin, 2000), p.299.

128 Bullock, *Hitler and Stalin*, p.745.

129 See J. Harris, 'The Myth of the Blitzkrieg', *War in History*, Vol. 2 (1995), pp.335–52.

130 Burleigh, *Moral Combat*, pp.198–203.

131 Ibid., p.209.

132 See Mazower, *Hitler's Empire*, pp.107–10; Burleigh, *Moral Combat*, pp.202–17.

133 For a detailed analysis see A. Tooze, *The Wages of Destruction* (Allen Lane, 2007), pp.368–95.

134 Bullock, *Hitler and Stalin*, pp.749–51.

135 Documents on German Foreign Policy, Series D, Vol. 10: *The War Years: June 23–August 31 1940* (Her Majesty's Stationery Office, 1957), Document No. 26, p.27, Mussolini to Hitler, 26 June 1940. (Hereafter DGFP)

136 DGFP, Series D, Vol. 10, No. 166, pp.209–211, Hitler to Mussolini, 13 July 1940.

137 For a detailed examination, see M. Bunting, *The Model Occupation: The Channel Islands Under German Rule, 1940–1945* (Glasgow: BCA, 1995).

138 Beevor, *The Second World War*, pp.123–6.

139 DGFP, Series D, Vol. 10, No. 101, pp.111–13, The Jewish Question in the Peace Treaty by Franz Rademacher, 3 July 1940.

140 Bullock, *Hitler and Stalin*, pp.751.

141 Interview with Christabel Bielenberg, *World at War*, p.111.

142 DGFP, Series D, Vol. 10, No. 137, Conversation between Ribbentrop and Satō, Japanese Ambassador, 9 July 1940.

143 Ibid., No. 177, pp.226–9, Führer Directive No. 16: On Preparation of a Landing Operation against England, 16 July 1940.

144 Evans, *The Third Reich at War*, p.138.

145 Shirer, *Rise and Fall*, p.912.

146 Mazower, *Hitler's Empire*, pp.112–13.

147 Kershaw, *Hitler*, Vol. 2, pp.303–4.

148 See R. Müller, *The Enemy in the East: Hitler's Secret Plans to Invade the Soviet Union* (I.B. Tauris, 2015), pp.219–24.

149 DGFP, Series D, Vol. 10, Halder Diary Notes, 31 July 1940, pp.370–4. See also *Hitler: Speeches and Proclamations*, pp.370–4.

150 For detail on the course of the Battle of Britain, see R. Overy, *The Battle of Britain* (Penguin), pp.27–60; J. Holland, *The Battle of Britain: Five Months That Changed History* (Corgi, 2010).

151 Interview with Johannes Steinhoff, *Voices from the Third Reich*, p.81.

152 DGFP, Series D, Vol. 10, No. 270, pp.390–1, Führer Directive No. 17: For the Conduct of Air and Naval Warfare Against England, 1 August 1940. See also *Hitler: Speeches and Proclamations*, pp.743–4.

153 A. Cumming, 'Did Radar Win the Battle of Britain?', *The Historian*, Vol. 69 (2007), pp.688–705. See also L. McKinstry, *Operation Sea Lion: How Britain Crushed the German War Machine's Dreams of Invasion in 1940* (John Murray, 2014).

154 *The Times*, 21 August 1940.

155 For detail, see P. Bishop, *Battle of Britain: A Day-to-Day Chronicle 10 July–31 October 1940* (Quercus, 2010).

156 Interview with Johannes Steinhoff, *Voices from the Third Reich*, p.82.

157 Evans, *The Third Reich at War*, p.144.

158 Documents on German Foreign Policy, Series D, Vol. 11: *The War Years: September 1*

1940–January 1941 (United States Printing Office, Washington DC, 1960), Document No. 68, pp.102–5, Hitler to Mussolini, 17 September 1940. (Hereafter DGFP)

159 *Die Rothschilds* (1940). See I. Garden, *The Third Reich's Celluloid War: Propaganda in Nazi Feature Films, Documentaries and Television* (Stroud: The History Press, 2012), pp.78–84.

160 *The Jew Süss* (1940). For details, see S. Tegel, 'Viet Harlan and the Origins of the Jude Süss 1938–9: Opportunism in the Creation of Nazi-Anti-Semitic Propaganda', *Historical Journal of Film, Radio and Television*, Vol. 16 (1996), pp.515–31; D. Welch, *Propaganda and the German Cinema 1933–45* (I.B. Tauris, 2007); S. Hull, *Film in the Third Reich: Art and Propaganda in the Third Reich* (Simon & Schuster, 2011).

161 *Der ewige Jude* (1940). For details see Garden, *Third Reich's Celluloid War*, pp.238–46.

162 DGFP, Series D, Vol. 10, No. 413, pp.581–7, Documents on Second Vienna Award, 30 August 1940.

163 For details of the relationship between Franco and Hitler, see S. Payne, *Franco and Hitler* (New Haven, CT: Yale University Press, 2008).

164 DGFP, Series D, Vol. 11, No. 66, pp.93–8, Conversation between Hitler and Serrano Suñer, 17 September 1940.

165 Ibid., No. 70, pp.106–8, Hitler to Franco, 18 September 1940.

166 Ibid., No. 88, pp.153–5, Franco to Hitler, 22 September 1940.

167 Ibid., No. 73, pp.113–23, Record of Conversation between Ribbentrop and Mussolini, Rome, 19 September 1940.

168 Ibid., No. 79, pp.134–6, Record of Conversation between Ribbentrop and Mussolini, Rome, 20 September 1940.

169 Ibid., No. 118, pp.204–5, Three Power Pact between Germany,

Italy and Japan, 27 September 1940.

170 Ibid., No. 149, pp.245–59, Conversation between Hitler and Mussolini, Brenner Pass, 4 October 1940.

171 Ibid., No. 176, pp.291–7, Ribbentrop to Stalin, 13 October 1940.

172 Ibid., No. 199, pp.331–4, Mussolini to Hitler, 19 October 1940.

173 Ibid., No. 211, pp.353–4, Schulenburg to the Foreign Ministry, 22 October 1940.

174 Ibid., No. 212, pp.354–61, Conversation between Hitler and Pierre Laval at Montoire-sur-le-Loir Railway Station, 22 October 1940.

175 For an interesting interpretation of the Franco–Hitler meeting, see P. Preston, 'Franco and Hitler: The Myth of Hendaye 1940', *Contemporary European History*, Vol. 1 (1992), pp.1–16.

176 DGFP, Series D, Vol. 11, No. 220, pp.371–6, Conversation between Hitler and Franco, Hendaye Railway Station, 23 October 1940.

177 Bullock, *Hitler and Stalin*, pp.756.

178 Kershaw, *Hitler*, Vol. 2, p.330.

179 DGFP, Series D, Vol. 11, No. 227, pp.385–92, Conversation between Hitler and Marshal Pétain at Montoire-sur-le-Loir Railway Station, 24 October 1940.

180 For details of the significance of the Laval and Pétain meetings with Hitler, see M. Crevald, '25 October 1940: A Historical Puzzle', *Journal of Contemporary History*, Vol. 6 (1971), pp.87–96.

181 See J. Carr, *The Defence and Fall of Greece 1940–1941* (Barnsley: Pen & Sword, 2013).

182 Beevor, *The Second World War*, pp.147–50.

183 DGFP, Series D, Vol. 11, No. 245, pp.411–22, Conversation between Hitler and Mussolini, Florence, 28 October 1940.

184 Ibid., No. 323, pp.527–31, Führer Directive No. 18, 12 November 1940.

185 M. Bloch, *Ribbentrop* (Abacus, 2003), p.340.

186 Kershaw, *Hitler*, Vol. 2, p.334.

187 DGFP, Series D, Vol. 11, No. 325, pp.533–41, Record of Conversation between Ribbentrop and Molotov, Berlin, 12 November 1940.

188 Ibid., No. 236, pp.541–49, Record of Conversation between Hitler and Molotov, Berlin, 12 November 1940.

189 Bloch, *Ribbentrop*, p.342.

190 DGFP, Series D, Vol. 11, No. 328, pp.550–62, Record of Conversation between Hitler and Molotov, Berlin, 13 November 1940.

191 Ibid., No. 329, pp.562–70, Record of Conversation between Ribbentrop and Molotov, Berlin, 13 November 1940.

192 Bloch, *Ribbentrop*, p.343.

193 Bullock, *Hitler and Stalin*, p.764.

194 DGFP, Series D, Vol. 11, No. 352, pp.598–606, Record of Conversation between Hitler and Serrano Suñer, Berghof, 18 November 1940.

195 Ibid., No. 369, pp.639–43, Hitler to Mussolini, 20 November 1940.

196 Ibid., No. 383, pp.671–2, Mussolini to Hitler, 22 November 1940.

197 Ibid., No. 380, pp.654–62, Record of Conversation between Hitler and Antonescu, Berlin, 22 November 1940.

198 Ibid., No. 384, pp.672–8, Record of Conversation between Hitler and Draganov, the Bulgarian Minister, Berlin, 23 November 1940.

199 Ibid., No. 426, pp.748–51, Minister Neubacher to Minister Clodius, 29 November 1940.

200 Ibid., No. 417, pp.728–35, Record of Conversation between

Hitler and Cincar-Marković, Berghof, 28 November 1940.

201 Ibid., No. 452, pp.789–91, Hitler to Mussolini, 5 December 1940.

202 Ibid., No. 500, pp.582–3, Memorandum of Conversation between Admiral Canaris and Franco, Madrid, 7 December 1940.

203 Ibid., No. 488, pp.836–8, Führer Directive No. 18: Operation Attila, 10 December 1940.

204 Ibid., No. 551, pp.867–9, Führer Directive No. 20: Operation Marita, 13 December 1940.

205 Ibid., No. 510, pp.866–7, Pétain to Hitler, 13 December 1940.

206 Ibid., No. 532, pp.899–902, Führer Directive No. 21, Operation Barbarossa, 18 December 1940.

207 Hitler speech, Berlin, 18 December 1940, *Hitler: Speeches and Proclamations*, pp.745–7.

208 DGFP, Series D, Vol. 11, No. 564, pp.950–55, Conversation between Hitler and Darlan, Beauvais, 24 December 1940.

209 Ibid., No. 586, pp.990–4, Hitler to Mussolini, 31 December 1940.

CHAPTER 2

1 Hitler's New Year Message, 1 January 1941. Quoted in ww2today.com.

2 DGFP, Series D, Vol. 11, No. 597, pp.1005–10, German General [Rintelen] at the Headquarters of the Italian Armed Forces to the High Command of the *Wehrmacht*, 2 January 1941.

3 Adolf Hitler, *Hitler's Table Talk 1941–44* (Oxford: Oxford University Press, 1953), pp.9–10.

4 DGFP, Series D, Vol. 11, No. 606, pp.1018–1027, Record of Conversation between Hitler and Bulgarian Prime Minister,

Bogdan Filov, Berghof, 4 January 1941.

5 C. Browning, *Origins of the Final Solution: The Evolution of Jewish Policy 1939–1942* (Arrow, 2005), p.215.

6 Bullock, *Hitler and Stalin*, p.781.

7 Tooze, *Wages of Destruction*, pp.457–8.

8 Toland, *Adolf Hitler*, p.650.

9 DGFP, Series D, Vol. 11, No. 642, pp.1073–3, Führer Directive No. 22: Cooperation of German Forces with Italy in the Fighting in the Mediterranean Area, 11 January 1941.

10 Bullock, *Hitler and Stalin*, p.783.

11 DGFP, Series D, Vol. 11, No. 652, pp.1087–95, Record of Conversation between Hitler and Romanian Prime Minister Antonescu, Berghof, 16 January 1941.

12 Kershaw, *Hitler*, Vol. 2, p.347.

13 DGFP, Series D, Vol. 11, No. 672, pp.1127–1133, Record of Conversation between Hitler and Mussolini, Berghof, 19 January 1941.

14 Ibid., No. 670, pp.1145–51, Record of Conversation between Hitler and Mussolini in the presence of Ribbentrop, Keitel, Jodl, Rintelen, Ciano, Guzzoni, Marras, Berghof, 20 January 1941.

15 Kershaw, *Hitler*, Vol. 2, p.347.

16 Bloch, *Ribbentrop*, pp.348–9.

17 DGFP, Series D, Vol. 11, No. 677, pp.1140–3, The Ambassador in Spain [Stohrer] to Foreign Ministry, 20 January 1941.

18 Ibid., No. 682, pp.1157–8, Ribbentrop to Spanish Ambassador, 21 January 1941.

19 Ibid., No. 695, pp.1173–5, The Ambassador in Spain [Stohrer] to Ribbentrop, 23 January 1941.

20 Ibid.,No. 718, pp.1208–10, the Ambassador in Spain to Foreign Ministry, 27 January 1941.

21 Ibid., No. 725, pp.1217–18, Ribbentrop to Stohrer, 28 January 1941.

22 Ibid., No. 728, pp.1222–3, Stohrer to Foreign Ministry, 20 January 1941.

23 Ibid., No. 680, pp.1151–5, The Grand Mufti of Jerusalem to Hitler, 20 January 1941.

24 Ibid., No. 239, pp.488–9, Weizsäcker to Grand Mufti of Jerusalem, 8 April 1941.

25 Ibid., No. 514, pp.876–81, Record of Conversation between Ribbentrop and the Grand Mufti of Jerusalem, Berlin, 28 November 1941.

26 Ibid., No. 515, pp.881–5, Record of Conversation between Hitler and the Grand Mufti of Jerusalem, 30 November 1941.

27 Kershaw, *Hitler*, Vol. 2, pp.348–9.

28 Documents on German Foreign Policy, Series D, Vol. 12: *The War Years: February 23–June 22, 1941* (Her Majesty's Stationery Office, 1957), Document No. 17, pp.26–30, Hitler to Mussolini, 5 February 1941. (Hereafter DGFP)

29 Ibid., No. 76, pp.135–8, Mussolini to Hitler, 22 February 1941.

30 Fest, *Hitler*, p.645.

31 DGFP, Series D, Vol.12, No. 23, pp.42–4, Führer Directive No. 23: Guiding Principles for the Conduct of the War against the English War Economy, 6 February 1941.

32 Garden, *Third Reich's Celluloid War*, pp.46–51.

33 Ibid., pp.52–61.

34 DGFP, Series D, Vol.12, No. 22, pp.37–42, Hitler to Franco, 6 February 1941.

35 Ibid., No. 49, pp.96–8, Memorandum by State Secretary [Weizsäcker], 14 February 1941.

36 Ibid., No. 48, pp.88–96, Record of Conversation between Hitler and Cvetković, Yugoslav Prime Minister, Berghof, 14 February 1941.

37 Ibid., No. 78, pp.139–51, Record of Conversation between Ribbentrop and Ambassador Ōshima, Fuschl, 23 February 1941.

38 Tooze, *Wages of Destruction*, pp.459–60.

39 DGFP, Series D, Vol.12, No. 110, pp.197–9, Hitler to Mussolini, 28 February 1941.

40 Ibid., No. 121, pp.213–16, Schulenburg to Foreign Ministry, 3 March 1941.

41 Ibid., No. 121, pp.201–3, Hitler to İsmet İnönü, the President of Turkey, 1 March 1941.

42 Ibid., No. 161, pp.286–7, İsmet İnönü to Hitler, 12 March 1941.

43 M. Hauner, *Hitler: A Chronology of His Life and Times* (Basingstoke: Palgrave Macmillan, 2008), p.161.

44 F. McDonough, *The Holocaust* (Basingstoke: Palgrave Macmillan, 2008), pp.48–9.

45 D. Cesarani (ed.), *The Final Solution: Origins and Implementation* (Routledge, 1994), p.358.

46 Kershaw, *Hitler*, Vol. 2, p.354.

47 DGFP, Series D, Vol.12, No. 125, pp.219–20, Führer Directive No. 24: Regarding Cooperation with Japan, 5 March 1941.

48 Ibid., No. 195, pp.338–42, Directive of High Command on Operation Marita, 22 March 1941.

49 Keegan, *The Second World War*, p.122.

50 DGFP, Series D, Vol. 12, No. 207, pp.354–7, Conversation between Hitler and Cvetković, Yugoslav Prime Minister, Vienna, 25 March 1941.

51 Ibid., No. 217, pp.372–5, Minutes of Conference Regarding the Situation in Yugoslavia, 27 March 1941.

52 Toland, *Adolf Hitler*, p.653.

53 DGFP, Series D, Vol. 12, No. 224, pp.395–6, Führer Directive No. 25: Regarding Yugoslavia, 27 March 1941.

54 Ibid., No. 207, pp.369–71, Conversation between Hitler and

Hungarian Ambassador, Döme Sztójay, 28 March 1941.

55 *Hitler: Speeches and Proclamations*, pp.750–2.

56 Keegan, *The Second World War*, p.152

57 Bullock, *Hitler and Stalin*, p.775.

58 Browning, *Origins of the Final Solution*, p.223.

59 DGFP, Series D, Vol. 12, No. 261, pp.447–8, The Regent of Hungary to Hitler, 3 April 1941.

60 Ibid., No. 267, pp.458–60, The Minister in Hungary to Foreign Ministry, 5 April 1941.

61 F. Taylor (ed.), *The Goebbels Diaries, 1939–1941* (Sphere, 1982), pp.282–3. (Hereafter *Goebbels Diaries*)

62 DGFP, Series D, Vol. 12, No. 218, pp.376–83, Record of Conversation between Ribbentrop and Matsuoka, 27 March 1941.

63 Ibid., No. 230, pp.405–9, Record of Conversation between Ribbentrop and Matsuoka, 28 March 1941.

64 Ibid., No. 233, pp.413–20, Record of Conversation between Ribbentrop and Matsuoka, 29 March 1941.

65 Ibid., No. 278, pp.469–74, Record of Conversation between Ribbentrop and Matsuoka, 5 April 1941.

66 Ibid., No. 222, pp.386–94, Record of Conversation between Hitler and Matsuoka, 27 March 1941.

67 Ibid., No. 226, pp.453–8, Record of Conversation between Hitler and Matsuoka, 4 April 1941.

68 Bullock, *Hitler and Stalin*, p.790.

69 DGFP, Series D, Vol. 12, No. 333, p.537, Schulenburg to Foreign Ministry, 13 April 1941.

70 Ibid., No. 281, pp.475–8, Hitler to Mussolini, 5 April 1941.

71 Ibid., No. 289, p.485, Mussolini to Hitler, 6 April 1941

72 Ibid., No. 335, pp.538–41, Führer Directive No. 25, 13 April 1941.

73 See Beevor, *The Second World War*, pp.154–73.

74 DGFP, Series D, Vol. 12, No. 403, pp.636–7, Führer Directive No. 28: Operation Mercury, 25 April 1941.

75 Ibid., No. 419, pp.661–2, Memorandum by Weizsäcker, 28 April 1941.

76 Tooze, *Wages of Destruction*, p.479.

77 Shirer, *Rise and Fall*, pp.990–1.

78 Bullock, *Hitler and Stalin*, p.791.

79 Shirer, *Rise and Fall*, pp.998–1003.

80 Toland, *Adolf Hitler*, p.659.

81 Ibid, p.661.

82 Shirer, *Rise and Fall*, p.998.

83 *Goebbels Diaries*, p.364.

84 *Maisky Diaries*, p.356.

85 P. Longerich, *Goebbels* (Vintage, 2015), p.475.

86 *Goebbels Diaries*, p.364.

87 DGFP, Series D, Vol.12, No. 511, pp.797–806, Record of Conversation between Ribbentrop and Mussolini, Rome, 13 May 1941.

88 Keegan, *The Second World War*, p.139.

89 Evans, *The Third Reich at War*, p.155.

90 *Hitler's Table Talk*, p.12.

91 Browning, *Origins of the Final Solution*, pp.226–7.

92 DGFP, Series D, Vol. 12, No. 584, pp.940–51, Record of Conversation between Hitler and Mussolini, Brenner Pass, 3 June 1941.

93 Ibid., No. 614, pp.996–1006, Record of Conversation between Hitler and Antonescu, Munich, 13 June 1941.

94 Ibid., No. 622, pp.1021–2, İsmet İnönü, President of Turkey, to Hitler, 12 June 1941.

95 Ibid., No. 648, p.1051, German-Turkish Treaty, 18 June 1941.

96 J. Erickson, *The Road to Stalingrad* (Cassell, 1975), pp.97–8.

97 DGFP, Series D, Vol. 12, No. 643, pp.1047–1049, Hitler to Antonescu, 18 June 1941.

98 Erickson, *Road to Stalingrad*, p.89; Beevor, *The Second World War*, pp.188–9.

99 DGFP, Series D, Vol. 12, No. 660, pp.1066–1069, Hitler to Mussolini, 21 June 1941.

100 Fest, *Hitler*, p.647.

101 Documents on German Foreign Policy, Series D, Vol. 13: *The War Years: June 23–December 11, 1941* (Her Majesty's Stationery Office, 1964), Document No. 7, pp.8–11, Mussolini to Hitler, 23 June 1941. (Hereafter DGFP)

102 R. Overy, *Russia's War* (Allen Lane, 1997), p.76.

103 T. Marshall, *Prisoners of Geography: Ten Maps That Tell You All You Need to Know about Global Politics* (Elliot and Thompson, 2015), pp.1–30.

104 Keegan, *The Second World War*, p.141.

105 Tooze, *Wages of Destruction*, pp.436–7

106 Bullock, *Hitler and Stalin*, p.802.

107 Evans, *The Third Reich at War*, p.178; Erickson, *Road to Stalingrad*, p.98.

108 Keegan, *The Second World War*, p.142.

109 A. Roberts, *The Storm of War: A New History of the Second World War* (Allen Lane, 2009), p.141.

110 Hastings, *All Hell Let Loose*, p.142.

111 Roberts, *Storm of War*, p.154.

112 Toland, *Adolf Hitler*, p.673.

113 Hitler's Proclamation to the German People, 22 June 1941, *Hitler: Speeches and Proclamations*, pp.755–765.

114 N. Stargardt, *The German War: A Nation Under Arms, 1939–1945*, pp.159–60.

115 M. G. Steinert, *Hitler's War and the Germans: Public Mood and Attitude during the Second World War* (Athens, OH: Ohio University Press, 1977), p.127.

116 Ibid., p.122.

117 Ibid., p.128.

118 Toland, *Adolf Hitler*, p.674.

119 Todman, *Britain's War*, Vol. 1, p.656.

120 Ibid., pp.700–02.

121 M. Burleigh, *The Third Reich: A New History* (Macmillan, 2000), p.488.

122 DGFP, Series D, Vol. 12, No. 664, pp.1074–5, Conversation between Ribbentrop and Soviet Ambassador Dekanozov, 22 June 1941.

123 Beevor, *The Second World War*, p.191.

124 Overy, *Russia's War*, p.74.

125 Beevor, *The Second World War*, p.194.

126 Hastings, *All Hell Let Loose*, p.150.

127 Overy, *Russia's War*, p.79.

128 Erickson, *Road to Stalingrad*, p.141.

129 DGFP, Series D, Vol. 13, No. 14, The Ambassador in Japan to the Foreign Ministry, 25 June 1941.

130 Ibid., No. 35, pp.40–41, Ribbentrop to embassy in Japan, 28 June 1941.

131 Kershaw, *Hitler*, Vol. 2, pp.420–21.

132 Bullock, *Hitler and Stalin*, p.799.

133 Kershaw, *Hitler*, Vol. 2, pp.395–7.

134 N. Ohler, *Blitzed: Drugs in Nazi Germany* (Allen Lane, 2016), p.132.

135 Ibid., pp.137–43.

136 Hastings, *All Hell Let Loose*, p.148.

137 Fest, *Hitler*, p.651.

138 Beevor, *The Second World War*, p.195.

139 Stargardt, *The German War*, p.167.

140 C. Ross, P. E. Swett, F. d'Almeida (eds), *Pleasure and Power in Nazi Germany* (Basingstoke: Palgrave Macmillan, 2011), p.236.

141 Interview with Hans von Bittenfeld, *Voices from the Third Reich*, p.130.

142 Interview with Helmut Schmidt, *Voices from the Third Reich*, p.141.

143 Longerich, *Goebbels*, p.485.

144 DGFP, Series D, Vol. 13, No. 50, pp.55–9, Hitler to Mussolini, 30 June 1941.

145 Beevor, *The Second World War*, p.199.

146 Keegan, *The Second World War*, p.153.

147 Erickson, *Road to Stalingrad*, p.174.

148 DGFP, Series D, Vol. 13, No. 114, pp.149–56, Memorandum on Administration of Captured Territory of the Soviet Union, 16 July 1941.

149 Ibid., No. 119, pp. 163–5, Führer Directive on Administration of the Newly Occupied Territories, 17 July 1941.

150 Ibid., No. 134, pp.190–5, Hitler to Mussolini, 20 July 1941.

151 Ibid., No. 156, pp.220–2, Ambassador in Italy [Mackensen] to Foreign Ministry, 26 July 1941.

152 Ibid., No. 159, pp.225–7, Hitler to Antonescu, 27 July 1941.

153 Ibid., No. 164, pp.235–7, Führer Directive No. 34, 30 July 1941.

154 See McDonough, *The Holocaust*, pp.51–5.

155 V. Klemperer, *I Shall Bear Witness: The Diaries of Victor Klemperer*, Vol. 1: *1933–41* (Phoenix, 1998), p.524. (Hereafter *Klemperer Diaries*)

156 Interview with Karl Scheurenberg, *Voices from the Third Reich*, p.292.

157 Steinert, *Hitler's War*, p.134.

158 *Hitler's Table Talk*, p.87.

159 Ibid., pp.117–18.

160 Steinert, *Hitler's War*, p.137.

161 Ibid., p.137.

162 Tooze, *Wages of Destruction*, p.488.

163 Burleigh, *Moral Combat*, p.231.

164 Keegan, *The Second World War*, pp.157–8.

165 Ibid.

166 Ibid., p.159.

167 Ibid.

168 DGFP, Series D, Vol. 13, No. 265, pp.422–33, Memorandum of the High Command of the *Wehrmacht*, 'The Strategic Situation in Late Summer 1941', 27 August 1941.

169 Todman, *Britain's War*, Vol. 1, pp.668–81.

170 DGFP, Series D, Vol. 13, No. 209, pp.321–4, Briefing Notes for Hitler on the Roosevelt–Churchill meeting, 17 August 1941.

171 Ibid., No. 242, pp.383–8, Record of Conversation between Hitler and Mussolini, Wolf's Lair, 25 August 1941.

172 *Hitler: Speeches and Proclamations*, pp.718–19.

173 Bullock, *Hitler and Stalin*, p.810.

174 Overy, *Russia's War*, pp.90–92.

175 Hastings, *All Hell Let Loose*, p.159.

176 Bullock, *Hitler and Stalin*, p.811.

177 Overy, *Russia's War*, p.94.

178 Ibid., p.95.

179 DGFP, Series D, Vol. 13, No. 395, pp.634–7, Führer Directive No. 35, 10 October 1941.

180 Ibid., No. 388, pp.623–5, Directive of German High Command, 7 October 1941.

181 Erickson, *Road to Stalingrad*, p.227.

182 Overy, *Russia's War*, p.97.

183 DGFP, Series D, Vol. 13, No. 413, pp.667–9, Ambassador in Japan to Ribbentrop, 21 October 1941.

184 Ibid., No. 424, pp.687–97, Record of Conversation between Hitler and Ciano, Wolf's Lair, 26 October 1941.

185 Ibid., No. 433, pp.709–716, Hitler to Mussolini, 29 October 1941.

186 Ibid., No. 454, pp.749–55, Mussolini to Hitler, 6 November 1941.

187 Overy, *Russia's War*, p.114.

188 Toland, *Adolf Hitler*, p.688.

189 Beevor, *The Second World War*, p.233.

190 *Hitler's Table Talk*, p.142.

191 Bullock, *Hitler and Stalin*, p.814.

192 Shirer, *Rise and Fall*, pp.1028–9.

193 Keegan, *The Second World War*, p.167.

194 Interview with Karl Rupp, *Voices from the Third Reich*, p.129.

195 DGFP, Series D, Vol. 13, No. 564, pp.984–7, Führer Directive No. 39, 8 December 1941.

196 S. Fritz, *Ostkrieg: Hitler's War of Extermination in the East* (Lexington, KY: University of Kentucky Press, 2015), p.204.

197 Burleigh, *Third Reich*, p.497.

198 Ibid., p.496.

199 Bloch, *Ribbentrop*, pp.377–8.

200 Fritz, *Ostkrieg*, p.193.

201 Warlimont, *Inside Hitler's Headquarters*, p.208.

202 Toland, *Adolf Hitler*, p.696.

203 Hastings, *All Hell Let Loose*, p.164.

204 For a comparison of the economic and military strengths of the major powers, see Keegan, *The Second World War*, pp.170–78.

205 Evans, *The Third Reich at War*, p.332.

206 Cesarani, *Final Solution*, p. 448.

207 Ibid., p.454.

208 Fest, *Hitler*, p.658.

209 Ibid.

210 Overy, *Russia's War*, p.117.

CHAPTER 3

1 M. Domarus, *Hitler: Speeches and Proclamations, 1932–1945* (Wauconda, IL: Bolchazy-Carducci, 1977), Vol. 4, p.1821. The message, dated 31 December 1941, was also published in the *Völkischer Beobachter* on 1 January 1942.

2 Hitler meeting with Ōshima, 3 January 1942, in J. Noakes and G. Pridham (eds), *Nazism 1919–1945: A Documentary Reader*, Vol. 3: *Foreign Policy, War and Racial Extermination* (Exeter: Exeter University Press, 1983–98), pp.228–322.

3 For details, see W. Gruhl, *Imperial Japan's World War II, 1931–1945* (New Brunswick, NJ: Transaction Publishers, 2010).

4 Erickson, *Road to Stalingrad*, p.297.

5 A. Seaton, *Russo-German War 1941–1945* (Novato, CA: Presidio Press, 1993), pp.230–80.

6 Keegan, *The Second World War*, p.179.

7 For details, see T. Leonard and J. Bratzel (eds), *Latin America during World War II* (Lanham, MD: Rowman & Littlefield, 2007).

8 The timing of the beginning of the Holocaust is the subject of debate among historians. It is agreed that the key period was the autumn of 1941, with a huge escalation of mass murder during the course of 1942. For a very good discussion on this debate, see O. Bartov, 'Who Was Responsible and When? Some Well-known Documents Revisited', *Holocaust and Genocide Studies*, Vol. 6 (1991), pp.129–49.

9 M. Roseman, *The Wannsee Conference and the Final Solution:*

A Reconsideration (New York: Picador, 2002), pp.79–156.

10 Chełmno is one of the least-researched of the extermination camps. For a detailed analysis, see P. Montague, *Chełmno and the Holocaust: The History of Hitler's First Death Camp* (Chapel Hill, NC: University of North Carolina Press, 2012).

11 For a discussion of the aims of the Wannsee meeting, see E. Jäckel, 'On the Purpose of the Wannsee Conference', in J. Pacy and A. Wertheimer (eds), *Perspectives on the Holocaust: Essays in Honor of Raul Hilberg* (Boulder, CO: Westview Press, 1995), pp.47–63. Jäckel suggests that the key purpose of the Wannsee meeting was to gain agreement from Reich government agencies to accept that the sole authority for the 'Final Solution' rested with Heydrich and Himmler.

12 Obituary of Robert Kempner, *New York Times*, 17 August 1993.

13 For the full text of the minutes, see Roseman, *The Wannsee Conference*, pp.157–72.

14 Christian Gerlach has argued that Hitler only endorsed genocide on a European scale when the United States entered the war in December 1941, and he suggests that the Wannsee meeting was connected to that decision. See C. Gerlach, 'The Wannsee Conference, the Fate of German Jews, and Hitler's Decision in Principle to Exterminate All European Jews', *Journal of Modern History*, Vol. 70 (1998), pp.759–812.

15 See 'Extracts from the testimony of Defendant Lammers' in *Trials of War Criminals Before the Nuremberg Military Tribunals Under Control Council Law No. 10* (Case 11: Ministries Case), Vol. 13 (Washington, DC: District of Columbia General Printing Office, 1952), pp.414–30. The other defendants in this trial also denied that Wannsee represented a clearly spelled-out plan for genocide.

16 Roseman, *The Wannsee Conference*, p.105.

17 Ibid., p.106.

18 Ibid., p.104.

19 S. Friedländer, *The Years of Extermination: Nazi Germany and the Jews 1939–1945* (Phoenix, 2008), p.344.

20 IfZ FA/183/BL/61, Himmler to Glücks, 26 January 1942.

21 Evans, *The Third Reich at War*, p.266.

22 N. Wachsmann, *KL: The History of the Nazi Concentration Camps* (Little, Brown, 2015), p.295.

23 Stargardt, *The German War*, p.227.

24 Friedländer, *Years of Extermination*, p.332.

25 C. Goeschel, *Mussolini and Hitler: The Forging of the Fascist Alliance* (New Haven, CT: Yale University Press, 2018), pp.227–8.

26 Hitler speech, Berlin Sport Palace, 30 January 1942, *Hitler: Speeches and Proclamations*, pp.400–01.

27 L. Lochner (ed.), *The Goebbels Diaries* (Hamish Hamilton, 1948), p.27. (Hereafter *Goebbels Diaries*)

28 Ibid., p.30.

29 For an examination of the roles of Todt and Speer, see B. Taylor, *Hitler's Engineers: Fritz Todt and Albert Speer: Master Builders of the Third Reich* (Casemate, 2010).

30 A. Speer, *Inside the Third Reich* (Weidenfeld & Nicolson, 1970), p.272.

31 Ibid., p.279.

32 *Goebbels Diaries*, p.38.

33 Speer, *Inside the Third Reich*, p.276.

34 Ibid., p.291.

35 In his self-serving memoirs Speer tended to present a favourable image of his actions during the Third Reich. He often portrays himself as a Cary Grant figure in a Hitchcock film, but without the redeeming qualities. See G. Sereny, *Albert Speer: His*

Battle with the Truth (New York: Knopf, 1995).

36 Speer, *Inside the Third Reich*, p.295.

37 Tooze, *Wages of Destruction*, pp.552–84. See also R. Overy, *War and Economy in the Third Reich* (Oxford: Clarendon Press, 1995).

38 *Goebbels Diaries*, p.41.

39 *Hitler: Speeches and Proclamations*, pp.401–402.

40 Kershaw, *Hitler*, Vol. 2, p.505.

41 Hitler speech, Munich, 24 February 1942, *Hitler: Speeches and Proclamations*, pp.317–19.

42 Longerich, *Goebbels*, pp.513–14. See also *Goebbels Diaries*, p.75.

43 Stargardt, *The German War*, pp.228–9.

44 *Goebbels Diaries*, p.84.

45 Stargardt, *The German War*, pp.228–9.

46 For a definitive examination of the Operation Reinhard camps, see Y. Arad, *Bełżec, Sobibor, Treblinka: The Operation Reinhard Camps* (Bloomington, IN: Indiana University Press, 1987). See also B. Musial, 'The Origins of Operation Reinhard: The Decision-Making Process for the Mass Murder of the Jews in the Generalgouvernement', *Yad Vashem Studies*, Vol. 28 (2000), pp.112–53.

47 For the sinister role of Globočnik, see J. Poprzeczny, *Odilo Globočnik: Hitler's Man in the East* (Jefferson, NC: McFarland & Company, 2003); B. Rieger, *Creator of Nazi Death Camps: The Life of Odilo Globočnik* (Portland, OR: Vallentine Mitchell, 2007).

48 Globočnik to Herff, 27 October 1943, in H. Friedlander and S. Milton (eds), *Archives of the Holocaust: An International Collection of Selected Documents*, 26 vols, 1990–1995 (New York: Garland), Vol. 11, pp.335–7.

49 Arad, *Operation Reinhard*, pp.182–3.

50 For the role of the guards and auxiliaries who collaborated in

the Operation Reinhard camps, see P. Black, 'Foot Soldiers of the Final Solution: The Trawniki Training Camp and Operation Reinhard', *Holocaust and Genocide Studies*, Vol. 25 (2011), pp.1–99.

51 For the construction, organization and killing process at the Bełżec camp, see Arad, *Operation Reinhard*, pp.22–9, 68–74.

52 Cesarani, *Final Solution*, pp. 473–4.

53 The death toll at Bełżec is still the subject of some controversy. See D. Pohl and P. Witte, 'The Number of Victims of Bełżec Extermination Camp: A Faulty Reassessment', *East European Jewish Affairs*, Vol. 31 (2001), pp.15–22.

54 For the construction, organization and killing process at Sobibor, see Arad, *Operation Reinhard*, pp.30–43, 75–88.

55 For a detailed examination of the role of Franz Stangl, see G. Sereny, *Into That Darkness: From Mercy Killing to Mass Murder* (Pimlico, 1995).

56 Arad, *Operation Reinhard*, p.77.

57 NA-HW 16/23. The Höfle Telegram [to Adolf Eichmann], transmitted 11 January 1943. See also P. Witte and S. Tyas, 'A New Document on the Deportation and Murder of Jews in "Einsatz Reinhardt" 1942', *Holocaust and Genocide Studies*, Vol. 15 (2001), pp.468–86.

58 For the construction, organization and killing process at Treblinka, see Arad, *Operation Reinhard*, pp.37–43, 81–99.

59 Ibid., p.83.

60 NA- HW 16/23. The Höfle Telegram [to Adolf Eichmann], transmitted 11 January 1943.

61 BAK-NS19/2234/2, Progress Reports on the 'Administrative Conclusion on "Operation Reinhard"', March and November 1943.

62 Arad, *Operation Reinhard*, pp.170–73.

63 Ibid., p.174.

64 Ibid., p.379.

65 Evans, *The Third Reich at War*, p.294.

66 For the role of IG Farben at Auschwitz-Birkenau, see P. Hayes, *Industry and Ideology in the Nazi Era* (Cambridge: Cambridge University Press, 2000).

67 See Y. Gutman and M. Berenbaum (eds), *Anatomy of the Auschwitz Death Camp* (Bloomington, IN: Indiana University Press, 1994); F. Piper, *Auschwitz: Nazi Death Camp* (Oświęcim: Auschwitz-Birkenau State Museum, 2002).

68 See M. Nahon, *Birkenau: Camp of Death* (Tuscaloosa, AL: University of Alabama Press, 1989).

69 Cesarani, *Final Solution*, pp.536–42.

70 For the explanation of Rudolf Höss, see his memoirs *Commandant of Auschwitz (Age of Dictators 1920–1945)* (Weidenfeld & Nicolson, 2000).

71 Ibid., p.173.

72 F. Piper, 'Gas Chambers and Crematoria' in Y. Gutman and M. Berenbaum, *Auschwitz Death Camp*, pp.157–82.

73 Friedländer, *Years of Extermination*, p.505. See also G. Posner, *Mengele: The Complete Story* (New York: Cooper Square Press, 2000).

74 This harrowing topic is examined in a number of eyewitness accounts, most notably, S. Venezia, *Inside the Gas Chambers: Eight Months in the Sonderkommando of Auschwitz* (Polity, 2011).

75 Friedländer, *Years of Extermination*, p.508.

76 Y. Gutman, 'Social Stratification in the Concentration Camps', in Y. Gutman and A. Saf (eds), *In the Nazi Concentration Camps: Structure and Aims, the Image of the Prisoner: The Jews in the Camps*

(Tel Aviv: Kernermann, 1997), p.172.

77 McDonough, *The Holocaust*, pp.66–7.

78 Evans, *The Third Reich at War*, p.304.

79 Wachsmann, *KL*, pp.319–22.

80 T. Kranz, 'Ewidencja zgonów i śmiertelność więźniów KL Lublin', *Zeszyty Majdanka*, Vol. 23 (2005), pp.7–53.

81 *Goebbels Diaries*, pp.87–95.

82 For a detailed overview of the plight of foreign forced labour inside Germany, see Tooze, *Wages of Destruction*, pp.513–51. See also U. Herbert, *Hitler's Foreign Workers: Enforced Foreign Labour in Germany under the Third Reich* (Cambridge: Cambridge University Press, 1997); E. Homze, *Foreign Labour in Nazi Germany* (Princeton NJ: Princeton University Press, 1997); T. Allen, *The Business of Genocide: The SS, Slave Labour and the Concentration Camps* (Chapel Hill, NC: University of North Carolina Press, 2002).

83 Kershaw, *Hitler*, Vol. 2, p.507.

84 *Hitler: Speeches and Proclamations*, pp.285–7.

85 Ibid., pp.282–4.

86 Longerich, *Goebbels*, p.514.

87 Warlimont, *Inside Hitler's Headquarters*, p.230.

88 A. C. Grayling, *Among the Dead Cities* (Bloomsbury, 2006), pp.50–51.

89 J. Friedrich, *The Fire: The Bombing of Germany, 1940–1945* (New York: Columbia University Press, 2006), pp.70–71.

90 Steinert, *Hitler's War*, p.157.

91 R. Overy, *The Bombing War: Europe 1939–1945* (Penguin, 2014), p.118.

92 Friedrich, *The Fire*, p.73.

93 Longerich, *Goebbels*, p.535.

94 Hastings, *All Hell Let Loose*, p.273.

95 W. Churchill, *The Second World War*, Vol. 4: *The Hinge of Fate*

(Cambridge: Houghton, Mifflin and Company, 1950), p.107.

96 Hastings, *All Hell Let Loose*, p.293.

97 For the role of Bletchley Park in the intelligence codebreaking during the naval war, see T. Perera, *The Story of the ENIGMA: History, Technology and Deciphering* (Artifax, 2004).

98 For a detailed overview of the naval war, see Roberts, *Storm of War*, pp.351–74. For the German conduct of the naval war, see J. Showell (ed.), *Führer Conferences on Naval Affairs,1939–1945* (Stroud: The History Press, 2015).

99 Hitler War Directive No. 41, 5 April 1942, in H. Trevor-Roper (ed.), *Hitler's War Directives* (Pan, 1954), pp. 177–83. (Hereafter *Hitler's War Directives*) See also J. Hayward, 'Hitler's Quest for Oil: The Impact of Economic Considerations on Military Strategy 1941–42', *Journal of Slavic Military Studies*, Vol. 10 (1997), pp.97–124.

100 For details, see M. Edele, *Stalin's Defectors: How Red Army Soldiers Became Hitler's Collaborators, 1941–1945* (Oxford: Oxford University Press, 2017).

101 Stargardt, *German War*, pp.310–11.

102 The recent opening of Soviet archives has revealed Stalin's efforts to recruit Muslims to fight against Hitler. See J. Brill, 'A Soviet Jihad against Hitler: Ishan Babakhan Calls Central Asian Muslims to War', *Journal of the Economic and Social History of the Orient*, Vol. 59 (2016), online publication, at https://doi.org/10.1163/15685209-12341398.

103 GWPA, 'Advice to Speakers' on Food Rationing, 16 March 1942.

104 Steinert, *Hitler's War*, p.157.

105 Kershaw, *Hitler*, Vol. 2, pp.509–11.

106 Longerich, *Goebbels*, p.517.

107 Goeschel, *Mussolini and Hitler*, pp.229–31.

108 Fritz, *Ostkrieg*, p.245. See also H. Orenstein and D. Glantz, 'The Kharkov Operation, May 1942', *Journal of Soviet Military Studies*, Vol. 5 (1992), pp.611–86.

109 G. Roberts, *Stalin's General: The Life of Georgy Zhukov* (Icon, 2013), pp.150–53.

110 For details, see W. Adam and O. Rühle, *With Paulus at Stalingrad* (Barnsley: Pen & Sword, 2015).

111 Friedländer, *Years of Extermination*, pp.348–9. See also E. Brothers, *Berlin Ghetto: Herbert Baum and the Anti-Fascist Resistance* (Stroud: The History Press, 2012).

112 Darré played a leading role in developing the 'Blood and soil' ideology of the Nazi Party during its rise to power. He was a firm supporter of the expansion into Eastern Europe to gain *Lebensraum*. For Darré's role, see J. Farquharson, *The Plough and the Swastika: The NSDAP and Agriculture in Germany, 1928–1945* (Sage, 1976).

113 Backe was arrested by the Allies in May 1945 and was in captivity in Nuremberg when he committed suicide by hanging himself on 6 April 1947. He feared being taken into captivity in the Soviet Union.

114 *Hitler: Speeches and Proclamations*, pp.366–76.

115 For a detailed analysis, see G. Gerhard, *Nazi Hunger Politics: A History of Food in the Third Reich* (Rowman & Littlefield, 2015). See also Tooze, *Wages of Destruction*, pp.538–551.

116 N. Barr, *The Pendulum of War: The Three Battles of El Alamein* (Jonathan Cape, 2004), p.1.

117 Warlimont, *Inside Hitler's Headquarters*, p.247.

118 Beevor, *The Second World War*, pp.312–26.

119 Burleigh, *Moral Combat*, pp.304–307. For more detailed studies, see I. Miroslav, *The Assassination of Heydrich, 27 May 1942*, (Hart-Davis & MacGibbon,

1973); C. MacDonald, *The Killing of Reinhard Heydrich: The SS 'Butcher of Prague'* (New York: Da Capo Press, 1998).

120 War Directive No. 42: 'Instructions for Operations against Unoccupied France and the Iberian Peninsula, 29 May 1942, *Hitler's War Directives*, pp.184–186.

121 Kershaw, *Hitler*, Vol. 2, pp.517–18.

122 Steinert, *Hitler's War*, p.153.

123 Kershaw, *Hitler*, Vol. 2, pp.524–35.

124 MacDonald, *The Killing of Reinhard Heydrich*, p.182.

125 For details, see E. Stehlik, *Lidice: The Story of a Czech Village* (Lidice: The Lidice Memorial, 2004).

126 Burleigh, *Moral Combat*, p.307.

127 Warlimont, *Inside Hitler's Headquarters*, pp.239–41.

128 K. Geber (ed.), *Generalfeldmarschall Fedor von Bock: The War Diary 1939–1945* (Atglen, PA: Schiffer, 1996), p.501. (Hereafter *Bock War Diary*)

129 W. Gorlitz (ed.), *The Memoirs of Field-Marshal Wilhelm Keitel, Chief of the German High Command, 1938–1945* (New York: Cooper Square Press, 2000), p.178. (Hereafter *Keitel Memoirs*)

130 For details see A. Nelson, *Red Orchestra: The Story of the Berlin Underground and the Circle of Friends Who Resisted Hitler* (New York: Random House, 2009); S. Roloff, *Die Rote Kapelle: die Widerstandsgruppe im Dritten Reich und die Geschichte Helmut Rollofs* (Munich: Ullstein, 2002); S. Brysac, *Resisting Hitler: Mildred Harnack and the Red Orchestra* (Oxford: Oxford University Press, 2002).

131 See M. Melvin, *Sevastopol's Wars: Crimea from Potemkin to Putin* (Oxford: Osprey, 2017).

132 F. Halder, *The Halder War Diary* (Novato, CA: Presidio,

1988), pp.629–35. (Hereafter *Halder War Diary*)

133 D. Glantz and J. House, *When Titans Clashed: How the Red Army Stopped Hitler* (Lawrence, KS: University of Kansas Press, 1995), pp.295–6.

134 Bock had been dismissed in December 1941 as the commander of Army Group Centre, but Hitler decided to give him another chance by appointing him to lead Army Group South in February 1942.

135 A. Beevor, *Stalingrad* (Penguin, 2007), p.63.

136 For details, see N. Short, *The Führer Headquarters: Hitler's Command Bunkers, 1939–1945* (Bloomsbury, 2013).

137 *Time* magazine, 18 December 1939.

138 H. Görtemaker, *Eva Braun: Life with Hitler* (Penguin, 2012), pp.189–214.

139 Warlimont, *Inside Hitler's Headquarters*, pp.245.

140 Beevor, *Stalingrad*, p.75.

141 *Halder War Diary*, p. 646.

142 War Directive No. 45: 'Continuation of Operation Brunswick [Braunschweig], *Hitler's War Directives*, pp.193–7.

143 Beevor, *Stalingrad*, p.81.

144 Martin Bormann to Alfred Rosenberg, 23 July 1942, *Third Reich Sourcebook*, p.823.

145 J. Barber and M. Harrison, *The Soviet Home Front, 1941–1945: A Social and Economic History of the USSR in World War Two* (Longman, 1991), p.72.

146 Hastings, *All Hell Let Loose*, p.308.

147 Overy, *Russia's War*, pp.163–4.

148 Roosevelt to Churchill, 29 July 1942, in W. Kimball (ed.), *Churchill and Roosevelt: The Complete Correspondence* (Princeton, NJ: Yale University Press, 1984), Vol. 1, p.544.

149 See R. Neillands, *The Dieppe Raid: The Story of the Disastrous 1942 Mission* (Aurum Press, 2006).

150 NA- PREM3/ 76A/11. Churchill to Attlee, 16 August 1942.

151 *Halder War Diary*, p.649.

152 Keegan, *The Second World War*, p.184.

153 Warlimont, *Inside Hitler's Headquarters*, p.256.

154 Ibid., p.251.

155 *Halder War Diary*, p.664.

156 Warlimont, *Inside Hitler's Headquarters*, p.258.

157 *Keitel Memoirs*, p.181.

158 Ibid., pp.182–4.

159 L. Goldensohn, *The Nuremberg Interviews: Conversations with Defendants and Witnesses* (Pimlico, 2007), p.294.

160 Beevor, *Stalingrad*, p.145.

161 Warlimont, *Inside Hitler's Headquarters*, p.260.

162 Speer, *Inside the Third Reich*, p.333.

163 Fritz, *Ostkrieg*, pp.290–91; Roberts, *Second World War*, p.320.

164 Beevor, *Stalingrad*, pp.97–8.

165 Ibid., p.127.

166 Beevor, *The Second World War*, p.360.

167 Erickson, *Road to Stalingrad*, p.409. For Chuikov's own gripping account of the battle for Stalingrad, see V. Chuikov, *Battle for Stalingrad* (Ballantine Books, 1968).

168 Beevor, *Stalingrad*, p.149.

169 Erickson, *Road to Stalingrad*, p.369.

170 For a detailed analysis, see J. Hayward, *Stopped at Stalingrad: The Luftwaffe and Hitler's Defeat in the East, 1942–1943* (Lawrence, KS: University of Kansas Press, 1998). See also C. Bergström, *Stalingrad: The Air Battle: 1942 through January 1943* (Harmondsworth: Chevron Publishing Company, 2007).

171 Beevor, *Stalingrad*, p.117.

172 Ibid., p.129.

173 Steinert, *Hitler's War*, p.167.

174 Erickson, *Road to Stalingrad*, pp.390–1.

175 Roberts, *Stalin's General*, pp.168–9.

176 For a detailed examination of the first phase of the battle of Stalingrad, see D. Glantz, 'The Struggle for Stalingrad: Opposing Orders of Battle, Combat Orders and Reports and Operational Maps: Part 1: The Fight for Stalingrad's Suburbs, City Centre and Factory Villages, 3 September–13 October 1942', *Journal of Slavic Military Studies*, Vol. 21 (2008), pp.146–238.

177 Fritz, *Ostkrieg*, p.294.

178 Interview with Wilhelm Hoffman, *World at War*, p.285.

179 Beevor, *Stalingrad*, p.198. See also R. Burgess, *Pavlov's House* (Kindle, Richard Burgess, 2013).

180 *Legendary Redoubt*, Russian State TV, 2009.

181 Hitler speech, Berlin Sport Palace, 30 September 1942, *Hitler: Speeches and Proclamations*, pp.405–6.

182 Interview with Wilhelm Eising in R. Busch (ed.), *Survivors of Stalingrad: Eyewitness Accounts from the Sixth Army, 1942–1943* (Frontline, 2012), p.22.

183 BAB-NS 19/2410, Himmler to Ribbentrop, 22 October 1942.

184 For details of the struggle in the factory district in Stalingrad, see D. Glantz, 'The Struggle for Stalingrad: Opposing Orders of Battle, Combat Orders and Reports and Tactical Maps: Part 2: The Fight for Stalingrad's Factory District, 14 October–18 November 1942', *Journal of Slavic Military Studies*, Vol. 21 (2008), pp.377–471.

185 Keegan, *The Second World War*, p.188.

186 *Nazism*, Vol. 3, p.233.

187 Beevor, *The Second World War*, p.367.

188 Interview with Wilhelm Hoffmann, *World at War*, p.285.

189 Goeschel, *Mussolini and Hitler*, pp.233–4.

190 B. Liddle Hart (ed.), *The Rommel Papers* (New York: Da Capo Press, 1982), p.319.

191 Ibid., p.321.

192 Beevor, *The Second World War*, pp.374–9.

193 H. Heiber and D. Glantz (eds), *Hitler and His Generals: Military Conferences 1942–1945: The First Complete Stenographic Record of the Military Situation Conferences from Stalingrad to Berlin* (New York: Enigma Books, 2003), pp.46–7. (Hereafter *Hitler's Military Conferences*)

194 Beevor, *The Second World War*, p.379.

195 Ibid., p.385.

196 Hitler speech, Munich, 8 November 1942, Kershaw, *Hitler*, Vol. 2, pp.539–40.

197 Beevor, *The Second World War*, pp.382–5.

198 A. Funk, 'Negotiating the Deal with Darlan', *Journal of Contemporary History*, Vol. 8 (1973), pp.81–117.

199 See A. Verrier, *Assassination in Algiers: Churchill, Roosevelt, De Gaulle and the Murder of Admiral Darlan* (Macmillan, 1991).

200 For Zaytsev's own account of his sniping activities in Stalingrad, see V. Zaytsev, *Notes of a Russian Sniper* (Barnsley: Frontline Books, 2016).

201 Fritz, *Ostkrieg*, pp.307–11. For more detail, see D. Glantz, 'Soviet Military Strategy During the Second Period of War (November 1942–December 1942): A Reappraisal', *Journal of Military History*, Vol. 60 (1996), pp.115–50.

202 Keegan, *The Second World War*, p.190.

203 *Nazism*, Vol. 3, p.236.

204 Roberts, *Second World War*, p.336.

205 Interview with Albert Speer, *World at War*, p.286.

206 Beevor, *Stalingrad*, pp.303–07.

207 For a detailed assessment of Operation Mars, see D. Glantz, *After Stalingrad: The Red Army's Winter Offensive, 1942–1943* (Solihull: Helion & Co., 2011), pp.24–9; D. Glantz, *Zhukov's Greatest Defeat: The Red Army's Epic Disaster in Operation Mars, 1942* (Lawrence, KS: The University Press of Kansas, 1999).

208 Mussolini speech, Rome, 2 December 1942, Foreign Broadcast Intelligence Service, Federal Communications Commission, 1942. See also Goeschel, *Mussolini and Hitler*, p.236.

209 Beevor, *Stalingrad*, p.280.

210 Interview with Heinz Pfenning, *Voices from the Third Reich*, p.154.

211 Beevor, *Stalingrad*, pp.274–5.

212 *Hitler: Speeches and Proclamations*, p.320.

213 HCD, Vol. 385, cols 2082–2087, Anthony Eden statement, 17 December 1942.

214 Longerich, *Goebbels*, p.548.

215 Goeschel, *Mussolini and Hitler*, p.237.

216 Steinert, *Hitler's War*, p.169.

217 Beevor, *Stalingrad*, pp. 291–310.

218 Ibid., pp.312–14.

219 Interview with Friedrich von Solms, *Voices from the Third Reich*, p.173.

220 Beevor, *Stalingrad*, pp.314.

221 Longerich, *Goebbels*, p.549.

222 Hastings, *All Hell Let Loose*, pp.304–5.

223 H. Commager, *The Story of the Second World War* (Boston, MA: Little, Brown, 1945), p.167.

CHAPTER 4

1 Adolf Hitler, New Year Proclamation to National Socialists and Party Comrades, 1 January 1943. Transcript on Wikisource.

2 Adolf Hitler, Address to the *Wehrmacht*, 1 January 1943. Transcript on Wikisource.

3 BA-MA. RH 20/6.234, Hitler to Paulus, 31 December 1942.

4 Fritz, *Ostkrieg*, p.319.

5 Roberts, *Storm of War*, p.341.

6 Shirer, *Rise and Fall*, p.929.

7 Fritz, *Ostkrieg*, p.319.

8 Evans, *The Third Reich at War*, p.417.

9 Kershaw, *Hitler*, Vol. 2, p.547.

10 A. Wilt, 'The Significance of the Casablanca Decisions, January 1943', *Journal of Military History*, Vol. 54 (1991), pp.517–29.

11 J. Etcherkamp (ed.), *Germany and the Second World War*, Vol. IX/I: *German Wartime Society 1939–45: Politicization, Disintegration and the Struggle for Survival* (Oxford: Clarendon Press, 2015), p.583.

12 Beevor, *Stalingrad*, p.365.

13 Tooze, *Wages of Destruction*, pp.595–6.

14 Fest, *Hitler*, p.665.

15 *Hitler: Speeches and Proclamations*, p.292.

16 W. Craig, *Enemy at the Gate: The Battle for Stalingrad* (Penguin, 2001), p.372.

17 Göring speech, Berlin, 30 January 1943, *Bulletin of International News*, Vol. 20, 6 February 1943 (Royal Institute of Foreign Affairs), pp.100–04.

18 Beevor, *Stalingrad*, p.380.

19 Hitler's speech, 30 January 1933. Transcript on Wikisource.

20 Beevor, *Stalingrad*, p.381.

21 Ibid., pp.388–94.

22 Hitler Military Conference, 1 February 1943, *Hitler's Military Conferences*, pp. 57–71.

23 *Hitler: Speeches and Proclamations*, pp.767–8.

24 For the most reliable casualty figures at Stalingrad, see K. Friesel (ed.), *Germany and the Second World War*, Vol. 8: *The Eastern Front, 1943–44: The War in the East and on the Neighbouring Front, 1943–44* (Oxford: Oxford University Press, 2017), pp.14–15.

See also Fritz, *Ostkrieg*, pp.321–2; Evans, *The Third Reich at War*, p.420; Beevor, *Stalingrad*, p.398.

25 J. Noakes and G. Pridham (eds), *Nazism 1919–1945: A Documentary Reader*, Vol. 4: *The German Home Front in World War II* (Exeter: Exeter University Press, 1983–98), p.543.

26 Steinert, *Hitler's War*, p.191.

27 Kershaw, *Hitler*, Vol. 2, pp.568–77.

28 *Goebbels Diary*, p.200.

29 R. Citino, *The Wehrmacht Retreats: Fighting a Losing War, 1943* (Lawrence, KS: University Press of Kansas, 2016), p.63.

30 R. Toeppel, *Kursk 1943: The Greatest Battle of the Second World War* (Warwick: Helion & Co., 2018), p.21.

31 Longerich, *Goebbels*, p.556.

32 Bloch, *Ribbentrop*, p.404.

33 E. Wiskemann, *The Rome-Berlin Axis* (London: Collins, 1966), p.340.

34 Hitler to Mussolini, 16 February 1943, quoted in Goeschel, *Mussolini and Hitler*, p.240.

35 *Das Reich*, 17 January 1943.

36 GWPA, Goebbels speech, Berlin, 18 February 1943.

37 Longerich, *Goebbels*, p.561.

38 *Nazism*, Vol. 4, p.545.

39 H. Vinke, *The Short Life of Sophie Scholl* (Cambridge, MA: Harper & Row, 1984), p.108.

40 For more on the White Rose resistance group, see R. Hanser, *A Noble Treason: The Story of Sophie Scholl and the White Rose Revolt Against Hitler* (San Francisco, CA: Ignatius Press, 2012); I. Jens (ed.), *At the Heart of the White Rose: Letters and Diaries of Hans and Sophie Scholl* (Walden, NY: Plough Publishing, 2017); C. Moll, 'Acts of Resistance: The White Rose in the Light of New Archival Evidence', in M. Geyer and J. Boyer (eds), *Resistance against the Third Reich, 1933–1990* (Chicago, IL: University of

Chicago Press, 1992), pp.172–200; J. Newborn and A. Dumbach, *Sophie Scholl and the White Rose* (Oxford: Oneworld, 2018).

41 For English translations of all six White Rose leaflets, see McDonough, *Sophie Scholl: The Real Story of the Woman Who Defied Hitler* (Stroud: The History Press, 2010), pp.187–98.

42 BAB/ZC13267, Second Report on the White Rose Leaflets, Professor Harder, 18 February 1943.

43 BAB/ZC13267, Jakob Schmid Interrogation, 18 February 1943.

44 BAB/ZC13267, Gestapo Arrest Report, 18 February 1943.

45 BAB/ZC13267, Paul Giesler to Martin Bormann, 19 February 1943; Martin Bormann to Paul Giesler, 19 February 1943.

46 See H. Ortner, *Hitler's Executioner: Roland Friesler, President of the Nazi People's Court* (Barnsley: Frontline Books, 2018).

47 BAB/ZC13267, The First White Rose Trial, Transcript of Proceedings, 22 February 1943.

48 BAB/ZC13267, Execution Record, Hans Scholl, 22 February 1943. For a detailed analysis of the role of Hans Scholl, see J. Knab, *Ich schweige nicht: Hans Scholl and the White Rose* (Darmstadt: WBG, 2018). At the subsequent White Rose trials, Alexander Schmorell, Kurt Huber and Willi Graf were all sentenced to death and executed.

49 Hitler speech, Munich, 24 February 1943, *Hitler: Speeches and Proclamations*, pp.406–412.

50 Wiskemann, *Rome-Berlin Axis*, pp.342–5; Bloch, *Ribbentrop*, pp.405–6.

51 Bullock, *Hitler and Stalin*, pp.878–81.

52 R. Overy, *The Bombing War: Europe, 1939–1945* (Penguin, 2013), p.322.

53 *Goebbels Diary*, p.248.

54 Hagen Stadt Archives (HSH), *Diary of Romer*, 25 June 1943.

55 R. Hansen, *Fire and Fury: The Allied Bombing of Germany, 1942–1945* (New York: NAL Caliber, 2009), p.94.

56 Steinert, *Hitler's War*, p.203.

57 Ibid., p.202.

58 Etcherkamp, *German Wartime Society*, pp.397–8.

59 Ibid., p.451.

60 *Berliner Lokal Anzeiger*, 1 August 1943.

61 *Goebbels Diary*, pp.211–22.

62 D. Glantz and J. House, *The Battle of Kursk* (Lawrence, KS: University of Kansas Press, 1999), p.256.

63 Schmidt was soon accused of treason after a cache of letters critical of Hitler was uncovered, following his brother's arrest by the Gestapo on an unrelated matter. Schmidt went on leave and on 30 September 1943 he was discharged from the army.

64 Toeppel, *Kursk 1943*, p.22.

65 Ibid., pp.23–5.

66 For a detailed examination of Tresckow's role in the military resistance, see B. Scheurig, *Henning von Tresckow: Ein Preusse gegen Hitler* (Berlin: Propyläen, 2004).

67 Moorehouse, *Killing Hitler: The Plots, the Assassins, and the Dictator Who Cheated Death* (Bantam Books, 2007), p.183.

68 See F. Schlabrendorff, *The Secret War Against Hitler* (Boulder, CO: Westview Press, 1994).

69 Hitler speech, Berlin, 21 March 1943. Transcript on Wikisource.

70 Memorial to German Resistance (MGR) Berlin. Short biography of Gersdorff.

71 For details, see T. Parssinen, *The Oster Conspiracy of 1938: The Unknown Story of the Military Plot to Kill Hitler and Avert World War II* (Harper Perennial, 2004).

72 For a recent assessment of Ludwig Beck's role, see G. Buchheit, *Generaloberst Ludwig*

Beck: Ein Patriot gegen Hitler (Berlin: Lindenbaum, 2006).

73 For a detailed analysis of the role of Goerdeler, see G. Ritter, *The German Resistance: Carl Goerdeler's Struggle against Tyranny* (Allen & Unwin, 1958). For a more critical assessment, see P. Hoffmann, *Carl Goerdeler and the Jewish Question, 1933–1942* (Cambridge: Cambridge University Press, 2011).

74 *Nazism*, Vol. 4, p.603.

75 D. Orbach, *The Plots against Hitler* (Head of Zeus, 2017), p.182.

76 J. Waller, 'The Double Life of Admiral Canaris', *International Journal of Intelligence and Counter Intelligence*, Vol. 9 (1996), pp.271–89. See also A. Brissaud, *Canaris: The Biography of Admiral Canaris, Chief of German Military Intelligence in the Second World War* (New York: Grosset & Dunlap, 1974).

77 *Nazism*, Vol. 4, p.613.

78 For a detailed account, see G. Roon, *German Resistance to Hitler: Count von Moltke and the Kreisau Circle* (New York: Van Nostrand Reinhold, 1971).

79 Orbach, *Plots against Hitler*, p.176.

80 See J. Fest, *Plotting Hitler's Death: The German Resistance to Hitler* (Weidenfeld & Nicolson, 1996).

81 When King Boris continued to refuse to hand over Jews to Germany, a furious Hitler called him to a further meeting on 14 August 1943 at the Wolf's Lair. The king once again refused to send Jews to the death camps and to declare war against the Soviet Union. On 28 August 1943 King Boris died suddenly of a heart attack, aged forty-nine. There has been speculation that Hitler had him poisoned while he was at Rastenburg using a slow-acting poison, but this has never been conclusively proven.

82 Wiskemann, *Rome-Berlin Axis*, pp.346–8; Goeschel, *Mussolini and Hitler*, pp.241–3.

83 B. Delentant, *British Clandestine Activities in Romania during the Second World War* (Basingstoke: Palgrave Macmillan, 2016), pp.13–14.

84 *Goebbels Diary*, p.260.

85 *Hitler: Speeches and Proclamations*, p.412.

86 A. Hillgruber (ed.), *Staatsmänner und Diplomaten bei Hitler, Zweiter Teil: 1942–1944* (Frankfurt a. M.: Bernard & Graefe, 1970), p.240.

87 *Hitler: Speeches and Proclamations*, pp.412–13.

88 The confirmed death toll of the Katyn Massacre is 21,857. It included Polish army officers, policemen and members of the Polish nobility and intelligentsia.

89 *Goebbels Diary*, p.253.

90 *Der Angriff*, 16 April 1943.

91 BBC News, 26 November 2010, 'Russian parliament condemns Stalin for Katyn massacre'.

92 Fritz, *Ostkrieg*, pp.339–41.

93 Citino, *The Wehrmacht Retreats*, pp. 126–7.

94 L. Clark, *Kursk: The Greatest Battle: Eastern Front 1943* (Headline, 2011), p.193.

95 News of the Warsaw Ghetto Uprising was extensively reported in the British press. See *Manchester Guardian*, 7 May 1943 and *The Times*, 25 May 1943.

96 Cesarani, *Final Solution*, pp.603–604.

97 For a detailed examination, see D. Kurzman, *The Bravest Battle: The 28 Days of the Warsaw Uprising* (New York: Da Capo Press, 1993).

98 Cesarani, *Final Solution*, p.615.

99 K. Moczarski, *Conversations with an Executioner* (Englewood Cliffs, NJ: Prentice Hall, 1984), p.164.

100 See M. Edelman, *The Ghetto Fights: Warsaw 1941–1943* (Bookmarks, 1990). For an English translation of the Stroop Report on the ghetto uprising, see J. Stroop, *The Stroop Report: The Jewish Quarter of Warsaw is No More* (New York: Pantheon, 1979).

101 Hitler speech, Berlin, 7 May 1943, *Nazism*, Vol. 4, pp.249–50. For another summary of the speech, see *Goebbels Diary*, pp.276–82.

102 *Hitler: Speeches and Proclamations*, pp.292–3.

103 For details, see I. Playfair, et al., *The Mediterranean and Middle East*, Vol. 4: *The Destruction of Axis Forces in Africa*, History of the Second World War, Official Campaign History (Naval & Military Press, 1954).

104 Hitler to Mussolini, 19 May 1943, quoted in Goeschel, *Mussolini and Hitler*, p.244.

105 For a detailed analysis, see J. Sweetman, *The Dambusters Raid* (Weidenfeld & Nicolson, 1999).

106 Overy, *Bombing War*, p.324.

107 Westfälisches Archives [LWL – Archivamt für Westfalen], Koldow, Collection, Koldow to Dr Runte, 19 May 1943.

108 Stargardt, *The German War*, p.361.

109 Hansen, *Fire and Fury*, pp. 96–103.

110 *Goebbels Diary*, p.287.

111 Etcherkamp, *German Wartime Society*, pp.453–4.

112 Steinert, *Hitler's War*, pp.213–214.

113 *Nazism*, Vol. 4, p.547.

114 Ibid., p.450.

115 For a detailed analysis, see D. Peukert, *Inside Nazi Germany: Conformity, Opposition and Racism in Everyday Life* (Batsford, 1987).

116 See R. Willet, 'Hot Swing and the Dissolute Life: Youth, Style and Popular Music in Europe, 1939–49', *Popular Music*, Vol. 8 (1989), pp.157–63.

117 See M. Kater, *Different Drummers: Jazz in the Culture of Nazi Germany* (Oxford: Oxford University Press, 2003).

118 Operation Citadel was postponed on 6, 18 and 25 June 1943.

119 Fritz, *Ostkrieg*, pp.341–2.

120 NA, War Office [WO] 208/3573, fol. 265, 'Weekly Summary of Chief of Imperial General Staff for week ending 22 March 1943'.

121 Toeppel, *Kursk 1943*, pp.67–74. See also D. Glantz, 'Soviet Operational Intelligence in the Kursk Operation, July 1943', *Intelligence and National Security*, Vol. 5 (1990), pp. 5–49.

122 For a detailed assessment, see R. Harrison (ed.), *The Battle of Kursk: The Red Army's Defensive Operations and Counter-Offensive, July–August 1943* (Solihull: Helion & Co., 2016).

123 Toeppel, *Kursk 1943*, p.19.

124 Ibid., p.77.

125 Clarke, *Kursk*, pp.195–8.

126 Toeppel, *Kursk 1943*, p.78.

127 For details, see B. Wheatley, 'A Visual Examination of the Battle of Prokhorovka', *Journal of Intelligence History*, Vol. 18 (2019), pp.115–63. See also Fritz, *Ostkrieg*, p.343; Citino, *The Wehrmacht Retreats*, p.134.

128 Toeppel, *Kursk 1943*, pp.89–95. See also C. Bergström, *Kursk: The Air Battle: July 1943* (Hersham: Classic, 2007).

129 Glantz and House, *Battle of Kursk*, p.255.

130 Toeppel, *Kursk 1943*, pp. xv–xxi.

131 Clarke, *Kursk*, p.225.

132 Evans, *The Third Reich at War*, pp.486–7.

133 For details, see D. Fletcher (ed.), *Tiger! The Tiger Tank: A British View* (Her Majesty's Stationery Office, 1986); R. Forczyk, *Panther vs T-34, Ukraine, 1943* (Oxford: Osprey 2007); T. Jentz, *Germany's Panther Tank: The Quest for Combat Supremacy* (Atglen, PA: Schiffer, 1995).

134 Toeppel, *Kursk 1943*, p.128.

135 Citino, *The Wehrmacht Retreats*, p.200.

136 This self-serving line was adopted by Manstein in his memoirs and repeated in his testimony at the Nuremberg Trials. See E. Manstein, *Lost Victories* (Chicago, IL: Henry Regnery, 1958).

137 Toeppel, *Kursk 1943*, p.169.

138 Ibid., p.173.

139 Glantz and House, *Battle of Kursk*, pp.256–60.

140 Wiskemann, *Rome–Berlin Axis*, pp.352–3; Bloch, *Ribbentrop*, p.404.

141 P. Monelli, *Rome 1943* (Rome: Migliaresi, 1946), p.123.

142 G. Bianchi, *25 Luglio: Crollo di un regime* (Milan: Mursia, 1989), p.616.

143 Ibid., p.668.

144 Goeschel, *Mussolini and Hitler*, pp.246–8.

145 *Goebbels Diary*, pp.322–30.

146 Bloch, *Ribbentrop*, pp.414–15.

147 For detailed accounts of the Hamburg air raids in 1943, see K. Lowe, *Inferno: The Devastation of Hamburg, 1943* (Penguin, 2012); M. Middlebrook, *The Battle of Hamburg: The Firestorm Raid* (Phoenix, 2000); H. Brunswig, *Feuersturm über Hamburg: Die Luftangriffe auf Hamburg im Zweiten Weltkrieg und ihre Folgen* (Stuttgart: Motorbuch, 1978).

148 NA, AIR 40/1271, 'Target Committee Report, 9 April 1943'.

149 Overy, *Bombing War*, p.331.

150 Lowe, *Inferno*, p.113.

151 Rumpf, *The Bombing of Germany*, p.78.

152 Lowe, *Inferno*, pp.101–106.

153 Hansen, *Fire and Fury*, p.102.

154 Staatsarchive, Hamburg [SAH] Letter by Matilde Wolff Monckenberg, in Report of Hamburg Police President, 27 July 1943.

155 Steinert, *Hitler's War*, p.218.

156 Lowe, *Inferno*, pp.128–36.

157 Ibid., pp.163–73.

158 Ibid., p.193.

159 *Goebbels Diary*, pp.333–4.

160 Lowe, *Inferno*, p.227.

161 Ibid., p.239.

162 Ibid., p.281.

163 NA, AIR 20/7287, 'Secret Report by the Police President of Hamburg on the Heavy Raids on Hamburg, 1 December 1943'.

164 A. Harris, *Bomber Offensive* (Collins, 1947), pp.175–6.

165 Stargardt, *The German War*, pp.368–70; Overy, *Bombing War*, pp.337–8.

166 Citino, *The Wehrmacht Retreats*, pp.212–13.

167 Frieser, *The Eastern Front 1943–1944*, p.177.

168 Toeppel, *Kursk 1943*, pp.136–42.

169 G. Krivosheev, *Soviet Casualties and Combat Losses in the Twentieth Century* (Greenhill Books, 1997), p.262.

170 K.-H. Frieser (ed.), *Germany and the Second World War*, Vol. 8: *The Eastern Front 1943–1944: The War in the East and on the Neighbouring Fronts* (Oxford: Clarendon Press, 2017), p.189. (Hereafter *The Eastern Front 1943–1944*)

171 Krivosheev, *Soviet Casualties*, pp.81, 134.

172 Toeppel, *Kursk 1943*, pp.143–50.

173 Glantz and House, *Battle of Kursk*, pp.297, 395.

174 Frieser, *The Eastern Front 1943–1944*, p.107.

175 Toeppel, *Kursk 1943*, p.156.

176 Citino, *The Wehrmacht Retreats*, pp.204–208.

177 Overy, *Russia's War*, pp.212–15.

178 A. Noble, 'The Phantom Barrier: Ostwallbau 1944–1945', *War in History*, Vol. 8 (2001), pp.442–67.

179 Hastings, *All Hell Let Lose*, p.391.

180 Fritz, *Ostkrieg*, p.372.

181 Ibid., p.366.

182 For details on Hitler's worsening relationship with Manstein, see K. Campbell, 'Can Traits of a Successful Military Commander Be Those of a Good Intelligence Director? A Look at Field Marshal Erich von Manstein: Extraordinary Military Leader', *American Intelligence Journal*, Vol. 33 (2016), pp.111–20.

183 *Goebbels Diary*, p.347.

184 Ibid., p.386.

185 Garden, *The Third Reich's Celluloid War*, pp.160–69. See also F. Noack, *Viet Harlan: The Life and Work of the Nazi Filmmaker* (Lexington, KY: University Press of Kentucky, 2016).

186 P. Longerich, *Hitler: A Life* (Oxford: Oxford University Press, 2019), p.876.

187 Beevor, *The Second World War*, p.530.

188 Wiskemann, *Rome–Berlin Axis*, p.363.

189 See G. Annussek, *Hitler's Raid to Save Mussolini: The Most Infamous Commando Operation of World War II* (Cambridge, MA: Da Capo Press, 2005).

190 *Goebbels Diary*, p.363.

191 Ibid., p.378.

192 Goeschel, *Mussolini and Hitler*, p.271.

193 Ibid., pp.264–8.

194 See R. Moseley, *Mussolini's Shadow: The Double Life of Count Galeazzo Ciano* (New Haven, CT: Yale University Press, 1999); M. Salter and L. Charlesworth, 'Ribbentrop and the Ciano Diaries at the Nuremburg Trial', *Journal of International Criminal Justice*, Vol. 4 (2006), pp.103–127.

195 Goeschel, *Mussolini and Hitler*, p.272.

196 Etcherkamp, *German Wartime Society*, p.604.

197 R. Citino, *The Wehrmacht's Last Stand: The German Campaign of 1944–1945* (Lawrence, KS: University of Kansas Press, 2017), pp.22–7.

198 BA-MA/RL/19/69, 'Zanetti Report of Hitler Meeting at Rastenburg, 16 October 1943'.

199 Overy, *Russia's War*, pp.193–97.

200 Steinert, *Hitler's War*, p.227.

201 Ibid., p.227.

202 *Nazism*, Vol. 4, p.552.

203 For the full text of the speeches on 4 and 6 October 1943, see B. Smith and A. Peterson (eds), *Heinrich Himmler: Geheimreden 1939–1945* (Frankfurt am Main: Propyläen, 1974; see index, pp.268–77). See also a full text online at The Holocaust History Project, www.phdn.org/archives/holocaust-history.org/

204 Ibid.

205 Friedlander, *The Years of Persecution*, p.543.

206 *Hitler's War Directives*, p.219.

207 *Goebbels Diary*, p.411.

208 Hitler speech, Munich, 8 November 1943, *Hitler: Speeches and Proclamations*, pp.413–16.

209 Hansen, *Fire and Fury*, p.149.

210 Stargardt, *The German War*, pp.391–92.

211 Etcherkamp, *German Wartime Society*, p.338.

212 Moorehouse, *Berlin at War*, p.324.

213 *Nazism*, Vol. 4, p.572.

214 Harris, *Bomber Offensive*, pp.186–7.

215 Etcherkamp, *German Wartime Society*, p.389.

216 R. Gellately, *Stalin's Curse. Battling for Communism in War and Cold War* (Oxford: Oxford University Press, 2013), pp.176–9.

217 Bullock, *Hitler and Stalin*, p.906.

218 Ibid., pp.905–906.

219 G. Roberts, 'Stalin at the Tehran, Yalta and Potsdam Conferences', *Journal of Cold War Studies*, Vol. 9 (2007), pp.6–40.

220 *Hitler's Military Conferences*, pp.307–322. See also *Hitler: Speeches and Proclamations*, pp.768–70.

221 J.Showell (ed.), *Führer Conferences on Naval Affairs,1939–1945* (Stroud: The History Press, 2015), p.374.

222 Etcherkamp, *German Wartime Society*, p.614–15.

CHAPTER 5

1 Adolf Hitler, New Year Proclamation to National Socialists and Party Comrades, *New York Times*, 1 January 1944.

2 Citino, *Wehrmacht's Last Stand*, pp. 27–33.

3 E. Manstein, *Verlorene Siege* (Bonn: Athenäum, 1955), p.573.

4 Kershaw, *Hitler*, Vol. 2, pp.616–17.

5 Citino, *Wehrmacht's Last Stand*, pp.36–40.

6 D. Nash, *Hell's Gate: The Battle of Cherkassy Pocket, January–February 1944* (Southbury, CT: RZM, 2002), p.398.

7 Krivosheev, *Soviet Casualties*, p.100.

8 For a concise overview of the Battle of the Korsun Pocket, see Citino, *Wehrmacht's Last Stand*, pp.18–58. See also N. Zetterling and A. Franson, *The Korsun Pocket: The Encirclement and Breakout of a German Army in the East, 1944* (Drexel Hill, PA: Casemate, 2008).

9 A. Reid, *Leningrad: The Tragedy of a City Under Siege, 1941–1944* (Bloomsbury, 2012), p.384.

10 Ibid., pp.417–18.

11 Kershaw, *Hitler*, Vol. 2, pp.618–19.

12 Toland, *Adolf Hitler*, p.779.

13 Kershaw, *Hitler*, Vol. 2, p.619.

14 Manstein, *Lost Victory*, pp.510–12.

15 Goeschell, *Mussolini and Hitler*, pp.275–276.

16 For detailed studies on the Battle of Monte Cassino in 1944, see J. Ellis, *Cassino: The Hollow Victory: The Battle for Rome January–June 1944* (Aurum, 2003); R. Bohmler, *Monte Cassino: A German View* (Cassell, 1964); G. Forty, *Battle for Monte Cassino* (Ian Allen, 2004).

17 *Hitler's War Directives*, pp.232–3.

18 F. Majdalany, *Cassino: Portrait of a Battle* (Longman, 1957), p.91.

19 Hitler speech, German national radio, 30 January 1944. Full text in German in *Völkischer Beobachter*, 31 January 1944. For full text in English, see *der-fuehrer.org*. On the same day as the speech, the Berlin Sport Palace, the scene of many of his most famous speeches, suffered a direct hit during an Allied bombing raid and was destroyed.

20 R. Dallek, *Franklin D. Roosevelt and American Foreign Policy, 1932–1945* (Oxford: Oxford University Press, 1995), p.452.

21 HCD, Vol. 397, cols. 663–795, Churchill Statement on War and the International Situation, 22 February 1944.

22 Friedlander, *Years of Extermination*, pp.608–10.

23 For a detailed account, see J. Holland, *Big Week: The Biggest Air Battle of World War Two* (Corgi, 2019).

24 For American losses in 'Big Week' see A. Harvey, 'The Battle of Britain and "Big Week" in 1944: A Comparative Study', *Air Power History*, Vol. 59 (2012), pp.34–45. For British losses, see D. Caldwell and R. Muller, *The Luftwaffe over Germany: Defence of the Reich* (Greenhill Books, 2007), p.162.

25 Tooze, *War of Destruction*, pp.627–36.

26 Toland, *Adolf Hitler*, pp.779–80.

27 Kershaw, *Hitler*, Vol. 2, pp.623–4.

28 *Nazism*, Vol. 3, p.259.

29 Kershaw, *Hitler*, Vol. 2, pp.624–6.

30 *Hitler's War Directives*, pp.234–6.

31 Friedländer, *Years of Extermination*, pp.605–606.

32 Hitler interview, *Stockholms Tidningen*, 19 March 1944.

33 For a detailed account, see G. Ránki, 'The German Occupation of Hungary', *Acta Historicae Academiae Scientiarum Hungaricae*, Vol. 11 (1965), pp.261–83.

34 For detailed accounts, see R. Braham, *The Politics of Genocide: Holocaust in Hungary*, 2 vols (Boulder, CO: Columbia University Press, 2001); R. Patai, *The Jews of Hungary: History, Culture, Psychology* (Detroit, MI: Wayne State University, 1996).

35 Cesarani, *The Final Solution*, p.711.

36 Ibid., pp.700–702. See also Kershaw, *Hitler*, Vol. 2, p.628.

37 *Hitler's Warriors*, TV documentary, ZDF Television, 1998.

38 Kershaw, *Hitler*, Vol. 2, p.632.

39 Stargardt, *The German War*, p.421.

40 For detailed accounts of the 22–23 February 1944 meetings, see Goeschel, *Hitler and Mussolini*, pp.276–8; Wiskemann, *Rome–Berlin Axis*, pp.386–7.

41 *Nazism*, Vol. 3, p.259.

42 Friedländer, *Years of Extermination*, p.604.

43 See R. Müller, *Der letzte deutsche Krieg 1933–1945* (Stuttgart: Klett-Cotta, 2005), p.200.

44 Kershaw, *Hitler*, Vol. 2, p.630.

45 Hitler speech, Platterhof, 26 May 1944. Full text at *der-fuehrer.org*. See also Kershaw, *Hitler*, Vol. 2, pp.636–7.

46 For a detailed study of Clark's role, see M. Blumenson, *Mark Clark: The Last of the Great World War II Commanders* (New York: Congdon & Weed, 1994). For Clark's own account, see M. Clark, *Calculated Risk: The War*

Memoirs of the Great American General* (Enigma, 2007).

47 Franklin D. Roosevelt, *Fireside Chat*, No. 29 'On the Fall of Rome', 5 June 1944. Full transcript at *millercenter.org*.

48 J. Ellis, *Cassino: The Hollow Victory: The Battle for Rome: January–June 1944* (Aurum, 2003), p.469.

49 A. Axelros, *Real History of the Second World War: A New Look at the Past* (New York: Sterling, 2008), p.208.

50 M. Hastings, *Armageddon: The Battle for Germany 1944–45* (Pan, 2004), p.2.

51 M. Gilbert, *The Second World War: A Complete History* (New York: Henry Holt, 1989), p.491.

52 For details, see G. Hartcup, *Code Name Mulberry: The Planning, Building and Operation of the Normandy Harbours* (Barnsley: Pen & Sword, 2011).

53 For a detailed study, see J. Levine, *Operation Fortitude: The Greatest Hoax of the Second World War* (Collins, 2012).

54 L. Ellis, G. Allen and A. Warhurst, *Victory in the West*, Volume 1: *The Battle of Normandy* (Naval & Military Press, 2004), pp.521–33.

55 For the German preparations in the west prior to D-Day, see A. Wilt, *The Atlantic Wall: Rommel's Plan to Stop the Allied Invasion* (New York: Enigma, 2004).

56 C. Messenger, *The Last Prussian: A Biography of Field Marshal Gerd von Rundstedt 1875–1953* (Brassy's, 1991), pp.158–9.

57 For a concise overview, comparing the military strength of the Allied and German forces in the build-up to D-Day, see Citino, *The Wehrmacht's Last Stand*, pp.109–156.

58 D. Crosswell, *Beetle: The Life of General Walter Bedell Smith* (Lexington, KY: University of Kentucky Press, 2010), p.622.

59 Toland, *Adolf Hitler*, p.784.

60 J. Holland, *Normandy '44: D-Day and the Battle for France: A New History* (Bantam Press, 2019), p.183.

61 For details, see K. Ford, *Battle Zone Normandy: Sword Beach* (Stroud: Sutton Publishing, 2004), pp. 86, 112.

62 See C. Stacey and C. Bond, *The Victory Campaign, 1944–1945*, Vol. 3: *The Official History of the Canadian Army* (Ottawa: The Queen's Printer, 1966), p.112.

63 S. Trew, *Battle Zone Normandy: Gold Beach* (Stroud: Sutton Publishing, 2004), pp.83–4.

64 Holland, *Normandy '44*, p.162.

65 See S. Badsey, *Omaha Beach* (Stroud: Sutton Publishing, 2004).

66 For details, see K. Ford and S. Zaloga, *Overlord: The D-Day Landings* (New York: Osprey, 2009), p.165.

67 Warlimont, *Inside Hitler's Headquarters*, pp.429–30.

68 A. Whitmarsh, *D-Day in Photographs* (Stroud: History Press, 2009), p.87. See also *Daily Telegraph*, 6 June 2016.

69 Ford and Zaloga, *Overlord*, p.335.

70 Warlimont, *Inside Hitler's Headquarters*, p.427.

71 HCD, Vol. 400, cols 1323–4, Churchill statement in House of Commons, 6 June 1944.

72 For a detailed examination, see P. Beck, *Oradour, The Massacre and Aftermath* (Barnsley: Pen & Sword, 2011).

73 See A. Young, *The Flying Bomb* (Shepperton: Ian Allen, 1978).

74 HCD, Vol. 401, cols 1322–39, Churchill statement in House of Commons, 6 July 1944.

75 For a detailed analysis, see T. Duggan, *V2: A Combat History of the First Ballistic Missile* (Yardley, PA: Westholme, 2005). See also Evans, *The Third Reich at War*, pp.660–66.

76 Hitler speech, Platterhof, 26 June 1944, Tooze, *Wages of*

Destruction, pp.634–6. See also Speer, *Inside the Third Reich*, pp.485–8.

77 For details of Soviet preparations for Operation Bagration, see R. Armstrong, *Soviet Operational Deception: Red Cloak* (Fort Leavenworth, KS: Combat Studies Institute, 1989).

78 Citino, *Wehrmacht's Last Stand*, pp.165–6.

79 Fritz, *Ostkrieg*, p.409.

80 A. Tucker-Jones, *Operation Bagration and the Annihilation of Army Group Centre* (Barnsley: Pen & Sword, 2009), p.27.

81 See B. Solotov, *Marshal K. K. Rokossovsky: Red Army's Gentleman Commander* (Warwick: Helion and Co., 2016).

82 Fritz, *Ostkrieg*, p.409.

83 Tucker-Jones, *Operation Bagration*, pp.7–8.

84 Citino, *Wehrmacht's Last Stand*, p.180.

85 Tucker-Jones, *Operation Bagration*, pp.59–60.

86 W. Dunn, *Soviet Blitzkrieg: The Battle for White Russia, 1944* (Boulder, CO: Lynne Reiner, 2000), pp.149–50.

87 Tucker-Jones, *Operation Bagration*, p.63.

88 Citino, *Wehrmacht's Last Stand*, pp.181–90.

89 Fritz, *Ostkrieg*, p.417.

90 Citino, *Wehrmacht's Last Stand*, p.197.

91 Tucker-Jones, *Operation Bagration*, pp.69–70.

92 Kershaw, *Hitler*, Vol. 2, p.650.

93 Tucker-Jones, *Operation Bagration*, p.77.

94 Beevor, *The Second World War*, p.592.

95 Frieser, *Ostfront*, pp. 593–4.

96 Tucker-Jones, *Operation Bagration*, p.86.

97 Ibid., p.85. In *When Titans Clashed* (p. 298) Glantz and House estimate that Soviet losses were much higher, with 180,000

dead or missing and 340,000 wounded or sick.

98 Beevor, *The Second World War*, p.592.

99 Tucker-Jones, *Operation Bagration*, p.126.

100 P. Hoffman, *Stauffenberg: A Family History, 1905–1944* (Montreal: McGill-Queen's University Press, 2003), p.239.

101 F. Schlabrendorff, *They Almost Killed Hitler* (New York: MacMillan, 1947), p.103.

102 Bullock, *Hitler and Stalin*, p.701.

103 Speer, *Inside the Third Reich*, p.509. See also Hoffman, *Stauffenberg*, p.200.

104 Shirer, *Rise and Fall*, p.108. For details on Olbricht's role, see H. Schrader, *Codename Valkyrie: Friedrich Olbricht and the Plot Against Hitler* (Yeovil: J. H. Haynes Publishing, 2009).

105 Hoffman, *Stauffenberg*, p.165.

106 Moorhouse, *Killing Hitler*, p.203.

107 For details on the timeline of events leading up to the bomb explosion on 20 July 1944, see G. Thomas and G. Lewis, *Defying Hitler: The Germans Who Resisted Hitler* (New York: Caliber, 2009), pp.414–26; Orbach, *The Plots against Hitler*, pp.210–240; Kershaw, *Hitler*, Vol. 2, pp.655–83; Shirer, *Rise and Fall*, pp.1104–1082.

108 Hoffman, *Stauffenberg*, p.268.

109 IfZ Report by Dr Helmut Arntz, adjutant to Erich Fellgiebell, ED/88/2.

110 For a vivid eyewitness account of the explosion and its aftermath, see Alfred Jodl's '*Der 20 Juli 1944 im Führerhauptquartier*', BA-MA. N/69/3.

111 T. Junge, *Hitler's Last Secretary: A Firsthand Account of Life with Hitler* (New York: Arcade Publishing, 2011), p.130.

112 Thomas and Lewis, *Defying Hitler*, p.426.

113 Shirer, *Rise and Fall*, p.1056.

114 Bloch, *Ribbentrop*, p.440.

115 Shirer, *Rise and Fall*, pp.1056–1057.

116 Fest, *Hitler*, p.714.

117 H. Gisevius, *Bis zum bitteren Ende* (Zurich: Fretz und Wasmuth, 1946), pp.517–18.

118 Etcherkamp, *German Wartime Society*, p.871.

119 Imperial War Museum, London, 'Statement by Major Otto Ernst Remer Concerning the Events of 20 July 1944', Berlin Documents, 2010. (Hereafter IWM) Remer's contemporary account must be treated with caution because he changed some of it during post-war interviews.

120 For a more sympathetic view on Fromm's role on 20 July, see B. Kroener, *General Friedrich Fromm: Der Starke Mann im Heimatkriegsgebiet: Eine Biographie* (Paderborn: Schöningh, 2005), pp.682–701.

121 *Nazism*, Vol. 4, p.621.

122 Ibid., p.622.

123 Speer, *Inside the Third Reich*, pp.517–18.

124 IWM, Remer Report on 20 July 1944.

125 Speer, *Inside the Third Reich*, pp.518–20.

126 In accounts of 20 July 1944 the exact time of Remer's meeting with Goebbels ranges from 5.30 p.m. in Shirer to 7 p.m. in Hoffman. Based on Remer's timeline it was probably nearer to 7 p.m.

127 Gisevius, *Bis zum bitteren Ende*, pp. 558–60.

128 *Nazism*, Vol. 4, p.622.

129 Ibid., p.623.

130 IfZ Zeller Papers, Otto John's account of the telephone conversations in Bendlerblock on 20 July 1944, ED 88/2. For a full account of John's role, see O. John, *Twice Through the Lines: The Autobiography of Otto John* (Macmillan, 1972). For the quote from John, see F. McDonough, *Opposition and Resistance in Nazi Germany* (Cambridge: Cambridge University Press, 2001), pp.56–7.

131 *Nazism*, Vol. 4, p.624.

132 Orbach, *The Plots against Hitler*, p.236.

133 E. Zeller, *Geist der Freiheit: Der Zwanzigste Juli* (Munich: Rhinn, 1952), p.338.

134 Speer, *Inside the Third Reich*, p.521.

135 IWM, Remer Report on 20 July 1944.

136 Zeller, *Geist der Freiheit*, pp.399–400.

137 IWM, Remer Report on 20 July 1944.

138 Ullrich, *Hitler*, Vol. 2, p.468.

139 For full transcripts see *The Times*, 21 July 1944. See also *Nazism*, Vol. 4, pp.626–7. For the German text, see H. Jacobsen and E. Zimmermann (eds), *20. Juli 1944* (Bonn: Berto-Verlag, 1961), pp.185–9.

140 See Orbach, *The Plots against Hitler*, pp.241–3; Thomas and G. Lewis, *Defying Hitler*, pp.439–41.

141 *Nazism*, Vol. 4, pp.626–7.

142 Ibid., pp.628–9.

143 Steinert, *Hitler's War*, pp.264–74.

144 Thomas and G. Lewis, *Defying Hitler*, p.442.

145 Etcherkamp, *German Wartime Society*, pp.915–17.

146 I. Kershaw, *The End: Germany 1944–45* (Penguin, 2012), pp.46–7.

147 Ullrich, *Hitler*, Vol. 2, p.477.

148 IfZ- ZS 249/III, Investigation Files of the Public Prosecutor, Land Court Munich on '*Sonderkommission 20 Juli 1944*' (photostat for IfZ on 24 March 1953). See also Thomas and G. Lewis, *Defying Hitler*, pp.442–3.

149 Hansen, *Disobeying Hitler*, p.64.

150 Shirer, *Rise and Fall*, pp.1070–1071.

151 BAK, N/1340/21, Speer to Erich Fromm, 1 July 1973. In this letter, Speer wrote: 'It can be safely assumed that Hitler watched the film.'

152 *Nazism*, Vol. 4, pp.630–31.

153 Thomas and G. Lewis, *Defying Hitler*, p.444.

154 Moorhouse, *Killing Hitler*, p.208.

155 See Moltke's letters to his wife in H. Moltke, *Letters to Freya, 1939–1945* (Vintage, 1995).

156 For detailed accounts of the Soviet advance during the summer of 1944, see S. Zaloga, *Bagration 1944: The Destruction of Army Group Centre* (Oxford: Osprey, 1996); P. Adair, *Hitler's Greatest Defeat: The Collapse of Army Group Centre, June 1944* (Leicester: Brockhampton Press, 1996); W. Dunn, *Battle for White Russia: The Destruction of Army Group Centre, 1944* (Harrisburg, PA: Stackpole Books, 2008).

157 Kershaw, *The End*, pp.111–17.

158 Steinert, *Hitler's War*, p.288.

159 M. Hastings, *Armageddon: The Battle for Germany 1944–45* (Pan, 2004), pp.114–23.

160 For brief accounts of the Warsaw Uprising of 1944, see Stargardt, *Germany's War*, pp.434–41; Beevor, *The Second World War*, pp.609–612; Roberts, *Storm of War*, pp.536–9; Bullock, *Hitler and Stalin*, pp.939–44; Evans, *The Third Reich at War*, pp.621–24. For more detailed studies, see J. Ciechanowski, *The Warsaw Uprising of 1944* (Cambridge: Cambridge University Press, 1974); N. Davis, *Rising '44: The Battle for Warsaw* (New York: Viking, 2004).

161 For Turkey's role during the Second World War, see S. Deringil, *Turkey's Foreign Policy During the Second World War: An 'Active' Neutrality* (Cambridge: Cambridge University Press, 2004).

162 For a detailed study on the role of Romania, see M. Axworthy, C. Scafes and C. Craciunoiu, *Third Axis, Fourth Ally: Romanian Armed Forces*

in the *European War 1941–1944* (Arms and Armour, 1995).

163 R. Bideleux and I. Jeffries, *The Balkans: A Post-Communist History* (Routledge, 2007), pp.84–5.

164 For details on Finland's role, see O. Vehviläinen, *Finland in the Second World War* (Basingstoke: Palgrave, 2002).

165 For details, see M. Mazower, *Inside Hitler's Greece: The Experience of Occupation, 1941–44* (Yale University Press, 2001).

166 Bloch, *Ribbentrop*, pp.450–1. See also M. Fenyo, 'Some Aspects of Hungary's Participation in World War II', *Eastern European Quarterly*, Vol. 3 (1969), pp.219–29.

167 Bullock, *Hitler and Stalin*, pp.944.

168 Ibid., pp.947–51. See also B. Mamula, 'The National Liberation War in Yugoslavia, 1941–1945', *The Journal of the United Services Institution*, Vol. 130 (1985), pp.52–6.

169 For Speidel's account of the meeting, see H. Speidel, *Invasion 1944: Ein Beitrag zu Rommels und des Reiches Schicksal* (Tübingen: Rainer Wunderlich, 1949), pp.112–24.

170 Citino, *Wehrmacht's Last Stand*, pp.246–9.

171 Ibid., p.242.

172 *Frankfurter Allgemeine Zeitung*, 19 August 2003.

173 L. Clark, *Battle Zone Normandy: Operation Epsom* (Stroud: History Press, 2004), p.109; J. Buckley (ed.), *The Normandy Campaign 1944: Sixty Years On* (Routledge, 2006), p.87.

174 Holland, *Normandy '44*, p.358.

175 Ibid., p.366.

176 Citino, *Wehrmacht's Last Stand*, pp.251–52.

177 Stacey and Bond, *The Victory Campaign*, p.160.

178 S. Trew, *Battle Zone Normandy: Battle for Caen* (Stroud: Sutton Publishing, 2004), p.46.

179 *Nazism*, Vol. 3, pp.262–3.

180 Hansen, *Disobeying Hitler*, pp.45–6.

181 For details, see C. Dunphie, *The Pendulum of Battle: Operation Goodwood, July 1944* (Barnsley: Leo Cooper, 2005).

182 O. Bradley, *A Soldier's Story* (New York: Holt, 1951), pp.326–46.

183 For details, see J. Carafano, *After D-Day: Operation Cobra and the Normandy Break Out* (Boulder, CO: Lynne Rienner, 2000); C. Pugsley, *Operation Cobra: Battle Zone Normandy* (Stroud: Sutton Publishing, 2005).

184 *Hitler's Military Conferences*, pp.445–6.

185 P. Caddick-Adams, *Snow and Steel: The Battle of the Bulge* (Arrow, 2014), p.19.

186 Stargardt, *Germany's War*, p.444.

187 Ibid.

188 See C. D'Este, *Decision in Normandy: The Real Story of Montgomery and the Allied Campaign* (Penguin, 2004), pp.430–31; C. Wilmot, *The Struggle for Europe* (Ware: Wordsworth, 1997), p.424.

189 Caddick-Adams, *Snow and Steel*, p.24.

190 Hastings, *All Hell Let Loose*, p.556.

191 Bullock, *Hitler and Stalin*, pp.954–5.

192 Warlimont, *Inside Hitler's Headquarters*, p.457.

193 H. Trevor-Roper (ed.), *The Goebbels Diaries: The Last Days* (Martin Secker & Warburg, 1978), pp.634–7. (Hereafter *Goebbels Diaries*)

194 Kershaw, *The End*, pp.60–61.

195 Longerich, *Goebbels*, pp.641–47.

196 Kershaw, *The End*, pp.75–7.

197 V. Ullrich, *Hitler: Downfall, 1939–1945* (The Bodley Head, 2020), p.365.

198 Tooze, *Wages of Destruction*, pp.642–44.

199 Junge, *Hitler's Last Secretary*, p.142.

200 *Hitler's Military Conferences*, p.462.

201 Kershaw, *Hitler*, Vol. 2, p.727.

202 Caddick-Adams, *Snow and Steel*, p.53.

203 Ohler, *Blitzed*, p.201.

204 Ibid., p.55.

205 Ibid., pp.195–96.

206 Ibid., pp.198–99.

207 Ibid., p.213.

208 Hastings, *Armageddon*, pp.17–20.

209 Beevor, *The Second World War*, p.634.

210 M. Middlebrook, *Arnhem 1944: The Airborne Battle* (Viking, 1994), pp.439–41.

211 Etcherkamp, *German Wartime Society*, pp.458–66.

212 *Nazism*, Vol. 4, pp.648.

213 S. Neitzel, *Tapping Hitler's Generals: Transcripts of Secret Conversations* (Frontline, 2007), p.103.

214 Ullrich, *Hitler*, Vol. 2, p.478.

215 Hansen, *Disobeying Hitler*, p.55.

216 Shirer, *Rise and Fall*, p.1077.

217 BA-MA, N/117/20, report by Karl Kronmüller to Martin Bormann concerning Field Marshal Rommel, 19 September 1944

218 P. Remy, *Mythos Rommel* (Munich: List Verlag, 2002), p.292.

219 Ullrich, *Hitler*, Vol. 2, 479.

220 J. Yaqoob, 'Death of the Desert Fox: Rommel son's account of his last moments after Hitler ordered him to take a cyanide pill or be arrested', *Daily Mail*, 30 December 2012.

221 Orbach, *The Plots Against Hitler*, p.259.

222 Shirer, *Rise and Fall*, p.1078.

223 For the full text of Hitler's speech, read by Himmler on 12

November 1944 in Munich, see *der-fuehrer.org*.

224 T. Junge, *Hitler's Last Secretary: A Firsthand Account of Life with Hitler* (Skyhorse, 2011), p.147.

225 Caddick-Adams, *Snow and Steel*, p.54.

226 H. B. Görtemaker, *Eva Braun: Life with Hitler* (Allen Lane, 2011), pp.224–5.

227 *Hitler's War Directives*, p.288.

228 Citino, *Wehrmacht's Last Stand*, p.369.

229 A vast amount has been written about the Battle of the Bulge. See, for example, C. MacDonald, *Time for Trumpets: The Untold Story of the Battle of the Bulge* (New York: Harper Collins, 1997); A. Beevor, *Ardennes 1944: Hitler's Last Gamble* (New York: Viking, 2015); J. Toland, *Battle: The Story of the Battle of the Bulge* (Lincoln, NE: Bison Books, 1999).

230 Stargardt, *Germany's War*, p.478.

231 T. Dupuy, *Hitler's Last Gamble* (New York: Harper Collins, 1994), p.18.

232 Caddick-Adams, *Snow and Steel*, p.4.

233 Hitler speech, Adlerhorst, 11 December 1944, *Hitler: Speeches and Proclamations*, pp.791-3. See also Citino, *Wehrmacht's Last Stand*, pp.366–8 for a succinct summary.

234 Kershaw, *Hitler*, Vol. 2, p.744.

235 Roberts, *Storm of War*, p.507.

236 Bullock, *Hitler and Stalin*, p.958.

237 Toland, *Adolf Hitler*, p.839.

238 V. Klemperer, *To the Bitter End: The Diaries of Victor Klemperer*, Vol. 2: *1942–1945* (Weidenfeld & Nicolson, 1999), p.370. (Hereafter *Klemperer Diaries*, Vol. 2)

CHAPTER 6

1 Hitler, New Year Proclamation, German Radio, 1 January 1945, *Hitler: Speeches and Proclamations*, pp.416–26.

2 For details, see C. Whiting, *The Other Battle of the Bulge: Operation Northwind* (New York: Avon Books, 1992).

3 Hitler speech, Adlerhorst, 28 December 1944. For full text, see *der-fuehrer.org*.

4 See Citino, *Wehrmacht's Last Stand*, pp.407–420.

5 Kershaw, *Hitler*, Vol. 2, p.747.

6 Army Battle Casualties and Non-Battle Deaths in World War II, Final Report, 7 December 1941–31 December 1946 (Washington, DC:, Department of the Army, 1953), pp.1–33.

7 C. Bergström, *The Ardennes: Hitler's Winter Offensive, 1944–1945* (Havertown, PA: Casemate, 2014), p.425.

8 J. Fest, *Inside Hitler's Bunker* (Pan, 2012), pp.16–24. See also S. Lehrer, *The Reich Chancellery and Führerbunker Complex: An Illustrated History of the Seat of the Nazi Regime* (Jefferson, NC: McFarland, 2006).

9 Görtemaker, *Eva Braun*, pp.229–30.

10 Bullock, *Hitler and Stalin*, p.970.

11 Citino, *Wehrmacht's Last Stand*, p.427. This exchange comes from Guderian's memoirs.

12 For details, see C. Duffy, *Red Storm on the Reich: The Soviet March on Germany, 1945* (Routledge, 1991).

13 Beevor, *Berlin*, p.17.

14 Fritz, *Ostkrieg*, p.450.

15 See J. Rubenstein, *Tangled Loyalties: The Life and Times of Ilya Ehrenburg* (Tuscaloosa, AL: University of Alabama Press, 1999).

16 These figures are cited in Duffy, *Red Storm on the Reich*, pp.24–5. Citino in *The Wehrmacht's Last Stand* (p.424) estimates

the Red Army's strength at 2.25 million men, 7,000 tanks and 4,700 aircraft.

17 Fritz, *Ostkrieg*, p.441.

18 Citino, *Wehrmacht's Last Stand*, p.430.

19 Beevor, *Berlin*, p.15.

20 Fritz, *Ostkrieg*, p.441.

21 R. Bessel, *Germany 1945: From War to Peace* (Simon & Schuster, 2009), p.26.

22 Beevor, *Berlin*, p.17.

23 In his testimony at the Nuremberg Trial on 20 June 1946, Albert Speer said that once Silesia had fallen he knew the German military economy would collapse in weeks.

24 Bessel, *Germany 1945*, p.28.

25 For a detailed examination of the Soviet assault on East Prussia, see P. Buttar, *Battleground Prussia: The Assault on Germany's Eastern Front, 1944–1945* (Oxford: Osprey, 2010).

26 Shirer, *Rise and Fall*, p.1103.

27 Beevor, *Berlin*, p.21.

28 For a good overview of the Vistula–Oder operation, see Glantz and House, *When Titans Clashed*, pp.238–48.

29 K. Bahm, *Berlin 1945* (Barnsley: Pen & Sword 2001), pp.51–2.

30 Glantz and House, *When Titans Clashed*, p.300.

31 H. Trevor-Roper, *The Goebbels Diaries: The Last Days* (Pan, 1979), p.103. (Hereafter *Goebbels Diaries*)

32 For details on Hummler's efforts to broker a peace settlement with the Western powers, see F. Bernadotte, *The Curtain Falls* (New York: Alfred A. Knopf, 1945).

33 *Nazism*, Vol. 4, p.665.

34 Kershaw, *Hitler*, Vol. 2, p.763.

35 Junge, *Hitler's Last Secretary*, p.145.

36 A. Beevor, 'They raped every German female from eight to 80', *Guardian*, 1 May 2002.

37 Beevor, *Berlin*, p.29.

38 Ibid., pp.30–32.

39 Fritz, *Ostkrieg*, p.451.

40 Beevor, *Berlin*, p.85.

41 GWPA, Joseph Goebbels, '*Die Urheber des Unglücks der Welt*', *Das Reich*, 21 January 1945.

42 GWPA, Hitler speech, German National Radio, 30 January 1945. Full text also available at *wikisource.org*.

43 For detailed discussions of the proceedings at Yalta, see D. Preston, *Eight Days at Yalta: How Churchill, Roosevelt and Stalin Shaped the Post-War World* (Pan Macmillan, 2019); S. Plokhy, *Yalta: The Price of Peace* (Penguin, 2011).

44 C. Black, R. English, J. Helmreich, C. Issawi and J. Adams, *Rebirth: A Political History of Europe since World War II* (Boulder, CO: Westview, 2018), p.61.

45 D. Loizos, 'The Polish Question at the Yalta Conference', PDF available, *researchgate.net*, January 2003.

46 See Bullock, *Hitler and Stalin*, pp.960–1967. For the full proceedings of the Yalta Conference, see I. Skelton, Combined Arms Research Library, Digital Library, *cgsc.contentdm.org* (PDF).

47 F. Taylor, *Dresden: Tuesday 13 February 1945* (Bloomsbury, 2005), p.238.

48 For a detailed analysis, see P. Addison and J. Crang (eds.), *Firestorm: The Bombing of Dresden* (Pimlico, 2006).

49 Taylor, *Dresden*, p.333.

50 J. Carey, *Eyewitness to History* (New York: Avon Books, 1987), pp.608–611.

51 *Klemperer Diaries*, Vol. 2, pp.398–405.

52 Taylor, *Dresden*, p.408.

53 Ibid., p.420.

54 *Das Reich*, 4 March 1945.

55 *Svenska Dagbladet*, 25 February 1945.

56 F. Taylor, 'How Many Died in the Bombing of Dresden?', *Der Spiegel* Online, 10 February 2008.

57 HCD, Vol. 408, cols 1847–1930, comment by Richard Stokes, MP, 6 March 1945.

58 Addison and Crang, *Firestorm*, p.180.

59 See Friedrich, *The Fire*, pp.310–315.

60 Kershaw, *Hitler*, Vol. 2, pp.779–80.

61 Text of Hitler's Proclamation, read out by Hermann Esser at Hofbräuhaus, Munich, 24 February 1945. Full text at TVR, *jewishvirtuallibrary.org*.

62 *Goebbels Diaries*, pp.40–44.

63 For details of Remagen, see K. Hechler, *The Bridge at Remagen* (New York: Ballantine, 1957). See also L. Izzo, 'An Analysis of German Mistakes Leading to the Capture of Ludendorff Bridge at Remagen', Military History Anthology (Fort Leavenworth, KS: Combat Studies Institute, 1984).

64 See L. Brune and J. Weiler (eds), *Remagen im März 1945: Eine Dokumentation der Schlussphase des Zweiten Weltkriegs* (Hrsg. vom Friedens-Museum, 1993).

65 Bullock, *Hitler and Stalin*, p.973.

66 *Goebbels Diaries*, pp.108–109.

67 H. Schwendemann, '"Drastic Measures to Defend the Reich at the Oder and the Rhine..."', A Forgotten Memorandum of Albert Speer of 18 March 1945', *Journal of Contemporary History*, Vol. 38 (2003), pp.597–614. See also A. Mierzejewski, 'When Did Albert Speer Give Up?', *Historical Journal*, Vol. 31 (1980), pp.391–97.

68 Stargardt, *The German War*, p.508.

69 Beevor, *Berlin*, p.151.

70 *Goebbels Diaries*, p.250.

71 Ibid., p.275.

72 Beevor, *Berlin*, pp.156–7.

73 For a succinct summary of the Battle of the Ruhr Pocket, see Citino, *Wehrmacht's Last Stand*, pp.435–45. See also the following detailed study: D. Zumbro, *Battle for the Ruhr: The German Army's Final Defeat in the West* (Lawrence, KS: University Press of Kansas, 2006).

74 S. Zaloga and P. Dennis, *Remagen 1945: Endgame against the Third Reich* (Oxford: Osprey, 2006), p.87.

75 For Model's role, see C. D'Este, 'Model', in C. Barnett (ed.), *Hitler's Generals* (Phoenix, 1989). See also M. Stein, *Generalfeldmarschall Walter Model: Legende und Wirklichkeit* (Bissendorf: Biblio-Verlag, 2001).

76 For a detailed examination of the collapse of administration in Germany, see H. Mommsen, 'The Dissolution of the Third Reich: Crisis Management and Collapse, 1943–1945', *Bulletin of German Historical Institute*, Vol. 27, (2000), pp.9–23.

77 Steinert, *Hitler's War*, p.302.

78 *Goebbels Diaries*, pp.112–13.

79 See D. Blatman, 'The Death Marches, January–May 1945: Who Was Responsible for What?', *Yad Vashem Studies*, Vol. 28 (2000), pp.155–202. Wachsmann argues that the high death toll on the 'Death Marches' was a by-product rather than a deliberate policy. See Wachsmann, *KL*, pp.585–6.

80 See D. Blatman, *The Death Marches* (Cambridge, MA: Harvard University Press, 2011).

81 A. Kossert, '"Endlösung on the Amber Shore": The Massacre in January 1945 on the Baltic Seashore – Repressed Chapter of East Prussian History', *Leo Back Institute Yearbook*, Vol. 49 (2004), pp.3–22.

82 See B. Shephard, *After Daybreak: The Liberation of Bergen-Belsen* (Pimlico, 2006).

83 Cesarani, *Final Solution*, pp.748–59; Wachsmann, *KL*, pp.585–6.

84 Kershaw, *The End*, p.231.

85 For a detailed assessment, see H. Ortner, *The Lone Assassin: The Incredible Story of The Man Who Tried to Kill Hitler* (New York: Skyhorse, 2012).

86 *Goebbels Diaries*, p.312.

87 Shirer, *Rise and Fall*, p.1110.

88 Kershaw, *Hitler*, Vol. 2, pp.791–2.

89 Beevor, *Berlin*, p.189. See also *Spectator*, 19 October 2013.

90 W. Kempowski, *Swan Song: A Collective Diary of the Last Days of the Third Reich, 1945* (New York: W. W. Norton & Company, 2015). (Hereafter *Collective Diary*)

91 C. Ryan, *The Last Battle* (Hodder & Stoughton, 1966), p.17.

92 Moorehouse, *Berlin at War*, p.363.

93 For the official report on the German preparations for the defence of Berlin, see B. Carruthers (ed.), *Götterdämmerung: The Last Days of the Wehrmacht in the East* (Barnsley: Pen & Sword, 2012).

94 For a detailed assessment of the Soviet documents related to the Battle of Berlin, see Erickson, *The Road to Berlin*, pp.531–640.

95 Citino, *Wehrmacht's Last Stand*, p.456.

96 For Heinrici's role as commander of Army Group Vistula, see BA-MA N/265/108, ff 2–9, Generaloberst Heinrici, 'Bericht Heeresgruppe Weichsel im April 1945'.

97 Glantz, *When Titans Clashed*, p.373.

98 Hitler proclamation: 'Soldiers on the German Eastern Front', 16 April 1945. Full text: Wikisource.

99 Hastings, *Armageddon*, p.540.

100 Goeschel, *Mussolini and Hitler*, p.288.

101 *Collective Diary*, p.2.

102 Fest, *Inside Hitler's Bunker*, pp.51–2.

103 Ibid., p.48.

104 Junge, *Hitler's Last Secretary*, p.159.

105 *Collective Diary*, p.83.

106 Erickson, *Road to Berlin*, p.581.

107 BA-MA N/265/108, ff 19–22, Heinrici report, 15 April 1945. For Steiner's own account, see F. Steiner, *Die Armee der Geächteten* (New York: Ishi Press, 2011).

108 Beevor, *Berlin*, p.275.

109 Hitler's Order to Western Armies Concerning Guerilla Warfare, 22 April 1945. Full text: Wikisource.

110 Bullock, *Hitler and Stalin*, pp.977–8.

111 IWM, FO 645/155 Interrogation of Wilhelm Keitel, 10 October 1945. See also Beevor, *Berlin*, pp.275–6.

112 Fest, *Hitler*, p.738.

113 Junge, *Hitler's Last Secretary*, p.162.

114 Ibid., pp.162–3.

115 Görtemaker, *Eva Braun*, p.235.

116 Junge, *Hitler's Last Secretary*, p.168.

117 Ibid., p.166.

118 Beevor, *Berlin*, p.277.

119 R. Manvell and H. Frankel, *Göring: The Rise and Fall of the Notorious Nazi Leader* (New York: Skyhorse, 2011), p.315.

120 For the full text, see Shirer, *Rise and Fall*, p.1116.

121 *Collective Diary*, p.133.

122 Junge, *Hitler's Last Secretary*, p.182.

123 Speer, *Inside the Third Reich*, pp.639–40.

124 Junge, *Hitler's Last Secretary*, p.175.

125 For details of the fate of the 9th Army, see T. Le Tissier, *Slaughter at Halbe* (Stroud: Sutton Publishing, 2005).

126 For Chuikov's own account, see V. Chuikov, *The End of the Third Reich* (Moscow: Progress Publishers, 1978), pp.198–211.

127 See D. Bradley, *Walther Wenck, General der Panzertruppe* (Osnabrück: Biblio Verlag, 1982).

128 *Hitler's Military Conferences*, pp.723–5.

129 Shirer, *Rise and Fall*, pp.1119–1120. For detail on Reitsch, see C. Mulley, *The Women Who Flew for Hitler: The True Story of Hitler's Valkyries* (Pan, 2018).

130 Fest, *Inside Hitler's Bunker*, p.89.

131 Ryan, *The Last Battle*, pp.348–9.

132 *Collective Diary*, p.287.

133 See M. Allen, *Himmler's Secret War: The Covert Peace Negotiations of Heinrich Himmler* (Robson, 2005).

134 J. O'Donnell and U. Bahnsen, *The Bunker: The History of the Reich Chancellery Group* (Boston, MA: Houghton Mifflin, 1978), pp.182–4.

135 Junge, *Hitler's Last Secretary*, p.186.

136 Hitler's Political Testament. 29 April 1945, *Hitler: Speeches and Proclamations*, pp.804–08.

137 Hitler's Personal Testament, 29 April 1945. Ibid., p.809.

138 Shirer, *Rise and Fall*, p.1128.

139 Fest, *Inside Hitler's Bunker*, p.107.

140 Erickson, *Road to Berlin*, p.604.

141 *Collective Diary*, p.213–14.

142 Fest, *Inside Hitler's Bunker*, p.115.

143 *Collective Diary*, p.296.

144 H. Linge, *With Hitler to the End* (New York: Frontline, 2013), p.199.

145 A. Joachimsthaler, *The Last Days of Hitler: The Legends, The Evidence, The Truth* (Brockhampton Press, 1999), pp.197–8. For Rattenhuber's account of the burning of the corpses, see V. Vinogradov, J. Pogonyi and N. Teptzov, *Hitler's Death: Russia's Great Secret from*

the Files of the KGB (Chaucer Press, 2005), pp.183–96.

146 See B. Brennan and H. Hardt (eds.), Picturing the Past: Media, History and Photojournalism (Urbana, IL: University of Illinois Press, 1999), pp.122–57.

147 See L. Daly-Groves, Hitler's Death: The Case Against Conspiracy (Oxford: Osprey, 2019).

148 Speer, Inside the Third Reich, p.653.

149 Erickson, Road to Berlin, p.609.

150 H. Eberle and M. Uhl (eds), The Hitler Book: The Secret Dossier Prepared for Stalin (John Murray, 2005). For the full Soviet autopsy report of 8 May 1945, which remains in the President of the Russian Federation Archive in Moscow, see U. Völklein (ed.), Hitlers Tod: Die Letzen Tage in Führerbunker (Göttingen: Stedl, 1998).

151 See D. Marchetti, I. Boschi and M. Bollaci, 'The Death of Hitler', Journal of Forensic Science, Vol. 50 (2005), available online at: www.astm.org. See also Guardian, 1 October 2013.

152 See H. Trevor-Roper, The Last Days of Hitler (Macmillan, 2002).

153 Perry-Groves, Hitler's Death, p.14.

154 IfZ, 'Report of Proceedings to Determine Hitler's Death', Munich, 25 October 1955. Gb 05/01/1.

155 IfZ, 'Expert Assessment on Hitler's Death', 1 August 1956, Gb 05/01/2.

156 Beevor, Berlin, p.380.

157 Ibid., pp.380–1.

158 It was suggested that Bormann had escaped to South America, but on 7 December 1972 his remains were recovered during an excavation by construction workers. Forensic examination indicated death by cyanide. Dental records and subsequent DNA tests confirmed that the corpse was Bormann.

159 F. Huber, Promise Me You'll Shoot Yourself: The Downfall of Ordinary Germans in 1945 (Penguin, 2019), pp.46–71.

160 See C. Goeschel, 'Suicide at the End of the Third Reich', Journal of Contemporary History, Vol. 41 (2006), pp.153–73.

161 Karl Dönitz speech, Hamburg Radio, 1 May 1945. Full text JVR, www.jewishvirtuallibrary.org

162 See IWM, FO 645/155, 'Karl Dönitz Interrogation, 12 September 1945', for his explanation of why he delayed ending the war.

163 Bessel, Germany 1945, pp.124–5.

164 Hastings, Armageddon, p.549.

165 Moorehouse, Germany at War, p.380.

166 Krivosheev, Soviet Casualties, p.157.

167 See E. Ziemke, 'Germany and World War II: The Official History', Central European History, Vol. 16 (1983), pp.398–407.

168 Ibid., p.376.

169 Ryan, The Last Battle, p.380.

170 Bessel, Germany 1945, p.118.

171 See R. Kaltenegger, Schörner: Fieldmarschall der Letzen Stunde (Munich: Herbig, 1994).

172 See R. Hanson, 'Germany's Unconditional Surrender', History Today, Vol. 45 (May 1995).

173 Collective Diary, p.300.

174 Bessel, Germany 1945, p.133.

CONCLUSION

1 Bullock, Stalin and Hitler, p.1074.

2 McDonough, Holocaust, p.133.

3 I. Tharoor, 'Don't forget how the Soviet Union saved the world from Hitler', The Washington Post, 8 May 2015.

4 Fritz, Ostkrieg, pp.369–470.

5 R. Overmans, Deutsche militärische Verluste im Zweiten Weltkrieg (Oldenburg: De Gruyter, 2000), pp.147–8.

6 Fritz, Ostkrieg, p.470.

7 Krivosheev, Soviet Combat Losses, p.79.

8 V. Zemskov, 'About the scale of casualties of the USSR in the Great Patriotic War', Demiscope, 11 October 1918. See also C. Hartman, Operation Barbarossa: Nazi Germany's War in the East, 1941–1945 (Oxford: Oxford University Press, 2015), p.157. Hartman suggests a Soviet military dead figure of 11.4 million.

9 Fritz, Ostkrieg, p.474.

10 G. Gilbert, Nuremberg Diary (Cambridge, MA: Da Capo Press, 1995), pp.30–1.

11 F. McDonough, The Gestapo: The Myth and Reality of Hitler's Secret Police (Coronet, 2015), pp.237–8.

12 S. Gordon, Hitler, Germans and the Jewish Question (Princeton, NJ: Princeton University Press, 1984), pp.371–7.

13 Ibid., p.241.

14 See Nationale Front des Demokratischen Deutschland, Germany Staatliche Archivverwaltung Dokumentationszentrum (Berlin: Zeit im Bild, 1965).

15 See M. Sontheimer, 'Why Germans Can Never Escape Hitler's Shadow', Der Spiegel online, 10 March 2005.

16 The Guardian, 31 August 2017.

BIBLIOGRAPHY

BOOKS AND ARTICLES

Place of publication is London, UK, unless otherwise stated.

Adair, P. *Hitler's Greatest Defeat: The Collapse of Army Group Centre, June 1944* (Leicester: Brockhampton Press, 1996)

Adam, W. and Ruhle, O. *With Paulus at Stalingrad* (London: Pen & Sword, 2015)

Addison, P. and Crang, J. (eds.) *Firestorm: The Bombing of Dresden* (London: Pimlico, 2006)

Allen, M. *Himmler's Secret War: The Covert Peace Negotiations of Heinrich Himmler* (London: Robson, 2005)

Allen, T. *The Business of Genocide: The SS, Slave Labor and the Concentration Camps* (Chapel Hill, NC: University of North Carolina Press, 2002)

Aly, G. *Aktion T4 1939–1945. Die 'Euthanasie'-Zentrale in der Tiergartenstraße 4* (Berlin: Rotbuch, 1989)

Aly, G., Chroust, P. and Pross, C. *Cleansing the Fatherland: Nazi Medicine and Racial Hygiene* (Baltimore, MD: Johns Hopkins University Press, 1994)

Annussek, G. *Hitler's Raid to Save Mussolini: The Most Infamous Commando Operation of World War II* (Cambridge, MA: Da Capo Press, 2005)

Arad, Y. *Belzec, Sobibor, Treblinka: The Operation Reinhard Camps* (Bloomington, IN: Indiana University Press, 1987)

Armstrong, R. *Soviet Operational Deception: Red Cloak* (Fort Leavenworth, KS: Combat Studies Institute, 1989)

Badsey, S. *Omaha Beach* (Stroud: Sutton Publishing, 2004)

Bajohr, F. *Aryanisation' in Hamburg: The Economic Exclusion of the Jews and the Confiscation of their Property in Nazi Germany* (New York: Berghahn, 2002)

Bankier, D. *The Germans and the Final Solution: Public Opinion under Nazism* (Oxford: Blackwell, 1996)

——— (ed.) *Probing the Depths of German Anti-Semitism: German Society and the Persecution of the Jews, 1933–1941* (New York: Berghahn, 2000)

Barber, J. and Harrison, M. *The Soviet Home Front, 1941–1945: A Social and Economic History of the USSR in World War II* (London: Longman 1991)

Barkai, A. *From Boycott to Annihilation: The Economic Struggle of German Jews, 1933–1943* (Harrisburg, PA: Brandeis University Press, 1990)

Barr, N. *The Pendulum of War: The Three Battles of El Alamein* (London: Jonathan Cape, 2004)

Bartov, O. 'Who Was Responsible and When? Some well-known documents revisited', *Holocaust and Genocide Studies*, Vol. 6 (1991), pp. 129–49

Bauer, Y. *The Holocaust in Historical Perspective* (Seattle, WA: University of Washington Press, 1978)

Baynes, N. (ed.) *The Speeches of Adolf Hitler*, 2 vols (Oxford: Oxford University Press, 1942)

Beck, P. *Oradour: The Massacre and Aftermath* (Barnsley: Sword & Pen, 2011)

Beevor, A. *The Second World War* (Phoenix, 2011)

Behnken, K. (ed.) *Deutschland-Berichte der Sozial democratischen Partei Deutschlands (SOPADE), 1934–1940*, 7 vols (Frankfurt am Main: P. Nettlebeck, 1980)

Bergström, C. *Kursk: The Air Battle: July 1943* (Hersham: Classic, 2007)

——— *Stalingrad: The Air*

Battle: 1942 through January 1943 (Harmondsworth: Chevron Publishing Company, 2007)

Bernadotte, F. *The Curtain Falls* (New York: Alfred A. Knopf, 1945)

Berschel, H. *Bürokratie und Terror: Das Judenreferat der Gestapo Düsseldorf, 1935–1945* (Essen: Klartext, 2001)

Bessel, R. *Germany 1945: From War to Peace* (London: Simon & Schuster, 2009)

Bielenberg, C. *Ride Out of the Dark: The Experience of an Englishwoman in Wartime Germany* (Boston, MA: G. K. Hall, 1968)

Bishop, P. *Battle of Britain: A Day to Day Chronicle 10 July–31 October 1940* (London: Quercus, 2010)

Black, P. 'Foot Soldiers of the Final Solution: The Trawniki Training Camp and Operation Reinhard', *Holocaust and Genocide Studies*, Vol. 25 (2011), pp. 1–99

Blatman, D. 'The Death Marches, January–May 1945: Who Was Responsible for What?', *Yad Vashem Studies*, Vol. 28 (2000), pp. 155–202

——— *The Death Marches* (Cambridge, MA: Harvard University Press, 2011)

Bloch, M. *Ribbentrop* (Abacus, 2003)

Blumenson, M. *Mark Clark: The Last of the Great World War II Commanders* (New York: Congdon & Weed, 1994)

Bohmler, R. *Monte Cassino: A German View* (London: Cassell, 1964)

Bradley, D. *Walther Wenck, General der Panzertruppe* (Osnabrück, Biblio Verlag, 1982)

Bradley, O. *A Soldier's Story* (New York: Holt, 1951)

Braham, R. *The Politics of Genocide: Holocaust in Hungary*, 2 vols (Boulder, CO: Columbia University Press, 2001)

Brill, J. 'A Soviet Jihad against Hitler: Ishan Babakhan Calls Central Asian Muslims to War',

Journal of the Economic and Social History of the Orient, Vol. 59 (2016), online publication, at https://doi.org/10.1163/15685209-12341398

Brissaud, A. *Canaris: The Biography of Admiral Canaris, Chief of German Military Intelligence in the Second World War* (New York: Grosset & Dunlap, 1974)

Broszat, M. *The Hitler State: The Foundation and Development of the Internal Structure of the Third Reich* (Longman, 1981)

———, et al. (eds) *Bayern in der NS-Zeit*, 6 vols. (Munich-Vienna: Oldenbourg, 1977–1983)

——— *Hitler and the Collapse of Weimar Germany* (Oxford: Berg, 1987)

Brothers, E. *Berlin Ghetto: Herbert Baum and the Anti-Fascist Resistance, Stroud* (The History Press, 2012)

Browning, C. *The Origins of the Final Solution. The Evolution of Jewish Policy 1939–1942* (Arrow, 2005)

Brunswig, H. *Feuersturm über Hamburg: Die Luftangriffe auf Hamburg im Zweiten Weltkrieg und ihre Folgen* (Stuttgart: Motorbuch, 1978)

Brustein, W. I. *Roots of Hate: Anti-Semitism in Europe before the Holocaust* (Cambridge: Cambridge University Press, 2003)

Brysac, S. *Resisting Hitler: Mildred Harnack and the Red Orchestra* (Oxford: Oxford University Press, 2002)

Buchheit, G. *Generaloberst Ludwig Beck. Ein Preußer gegen Hitler* (Berlin: Lindenbaum, 2006)

Bullock, A. *Hitler: A Study in Tyranny* (Penguin, revised edn, 1962)

——— *Hitler and Stalin: Parallel Lives* (HarperCollins, 1991)

Bunting, M. *The Model Occupation: The Channel Islands Under German Rule, 1940–1945* (Glasgow: BCA, 1995)

Burleigh, M. *Death and Deliverance: 'Euthanasia' in Germany 1900–1945* (Cambridge: Cambridge University Press, 1994)

——— *Ethics and Extermination: Reflections on Nazi Genocide* (Cambridge: Cambridge University Press, 1997)

——— *The Third Reich: A New History* (Macmillan, 2000)

Burleigh, M. and Wippermann, W. *The Racial State: Germany 1933–1945* (Cambridge: Cambridge University Press, 1991)

Burleigh, M. *Moral Combat: A History of World War II* (HarperPress, 2010)

Burrin, P. *Hitler and the Jews: The Genesis of the Holocaust* (Arnold, 1994)

Busch, R. (ed.) *Survivors of Stalingrad: Eyewitness Accounts from the Sixth Army, 1942–1943* (London: Frontline, 2012)

Buttar, P. *Battleground Prussia: The Assault on Germany's Eastern Front, 1944–1945* (London: Osprey, 2010)

Caddick-Adams, P. *Snow and Steel: The Battle of the Bulge* (London: Arrow, 2014)

Caldwell, D. and Muller, R. *The Luftwaffe over Germany: Defence of the Reich* (London: Greenhill Books, 2007)

Campbell, K. 'Can Traits of a Successful Military Commander Be Those of a Good Intelligence Director? A Look at Field Marshal Erich von Manstein. Extraordinary Military Leader', *American Intelligence Journal*, Vol. 33 (2016), pp. 111–20

Caratano, J. *After D-Day: Operation Cobra and the Normandy Break Out* (Boulder, CO: Lynne Rienner, 2000)

Carr, J. *The Defence and Fall of Greece 1940–1941* (Barnsley: Pen & Sword, 2013)

Carruthers, B. (ed.) *Götterdämmerung: The Last Days of the Wehrmacht in the East* (Barnsley: Pen & Sword, 2012)

Cesarani, D. (ed.) *The Final Solution: Origins and Implementation* (Routledge, 1994)
—— *Eichmann: His Life and Crimes* (Heinemann, 2004)
Cesarani, D. (ed.) *The Final Solution: The Fate of the Jews, 1933–1949* (Macmillan, 2016)

Childers, T. *The Third Reich: A History of Nazi Germany* (Simon & Schuster, 2017)

Chuikov, V. *Battle for Stalingrad* (London: Ballantine Books, 1968)

Ciano, G. *The War Diaries of Count Galeazzo Ciano, 1939–43* (Fonthill, 2015)

Ciechanowski, J. *The Warsaw Uprising of 1944* (Cambridge: Cambridge University Press, 1974)

Citino, R. *The German Way of War: From the Thirty Years' War to the Third Reich* (Lawrence, KS: University Press of Kansas, 2008)
—— *The Wehrmacht's Last Stand, The German Campaign of 1944–1945* (Lawrence, KS: University of Kansas Press, 2017)

Clark, L. *Battle Zone Normandy: Operation Epsom* (Stroud: History Press, 2004)
—— *Kursk: The Greatest Battle: Eastern Front 1943* (London: Headline, 2011)

Clark, M. *Calculated Risk: The War Memoirs of the Great American General* (London: Enigma, 2007)

Commager, H. *The Story of the Second World War* (Boston, MA: Little, Brown, 1945)

Conot, R. *Justice at Nuremberg* (New York, NY: Harper and Row, 1983)

Craig, W. *Enemy at the Gate: The Battle for Stalingrad* (London: Penguin, 2001)

Crevald, M. '25 October 1940: A Historical Puzzle', *Journal of Contemporary History*, Vol. 6 (1971), pp. 87–96

Crew, D. (ed.) *Nazism and German Society 1933–1945* (Routledge, 1994)

Crosswell, D. *Beetle: The Life of General Walter Bedell Smith* (Lexington, KY: University of Kentucky Press, 2010)

D'Este, C. *Decision in Normandy: The Real Story of Montgomery and the Allied Campaign* (London: Penguin, 2004), pp. 430–31

Dahl, F. *Quisling: A Study in Treachery* (Cambridge: Cambridge University Press, 2008)

Dallek, R. *Franklin D. Roosevelt and American Foreign Policy, 1932–1945* (Oxford: Oxford University Press, 1995)

Davis, N. *Rising '44: The Battle for Warsaw* (New York: Viking, 2004)

Dawidowicz, L. *The War against the Jews 1933–45* (Pelican, 1979)

Dedencks, M. *Heydrich: The Face of Evil* (Greenhill, 2006)

Degras, J. (ed.) *Soviet Documents on Soviet Foreign Policy* (Oxford: Oxford University Press, 1939)

Deringil, S. *Turkey's Foreign Policy During the Second World War: An 'Active' Neutrality* (Cambridge: Cambridge University Press, 2004)

Deschner, G. *Heydrich: The Pursuit of Total Power* (Orbis, 1981)

Dethlefsen, H. 'Denmark and German Occupation: Cooperation, Negotiation or Collaboration?', *Scandinavian Journal of History*, Vol. 15 (1990), pp. 193–206

DGFP *Documents on German Foreign Policy* (Series D), Vol. 11: *The War Years: September 1 1940– January 1941, 1940* (Washington, DC: United States Printing Office, 1960)
—— *Documents on German Foreign Policy* (Series D), Vol. 13: *The War Years: June 23–December 11, 1941* (London: H.M.S.O., 1964)
—— *Documents on German Foreign Policy* (Series D), Vol. 8: *The War Years: 4 September 1939–18 March 1940* (Washington, DC: US Government Printing Office),

No. 504, pp. 604–609; *Mussolini to Hitler, 3 January 1940*
—— *Documents on German Foreign Policy* (Series D), Vol. 10: *The War Years: June 23–August 31 1940* (London: H.M.S.O., 1957)
—— *Documents on German Foreign Policy* (Series D), Vol. 9: *The War Years: March 18–June 22 1940* (London: H.M.S.O., 1956). Document 1, pp. 1–16, *Conversation between Hitler and Mussolini, 18 March 1940*

Diest, W. *The Wehrmacht and German Rearmament* (Toronto: University of Toronto Press, 1981)

Dildy, D. *Denmark and Norway 1940: Hitler's Boldest Operation* (Oxford: Osprey, 2007)

DGFP, Series D, Vol. 13, No. 564, pp.984–7, Führer Directive No. 39, 8 December 1941

Doherty, M. 'The Attack on the Altmark: A Case Study in Wartime Propaganda', *Journal of Contemporary History*, Vol. 38 (2003), pp. 187–200

Domarus, M. *The Essential Hitler: Speeches and Commentary* (Wauconda, IL: Bolchazy-Carducci, 2007)

Duffy, C. *Red Storm on the Reich: The Soviet March on Germany, 1945* (London: Routledge, 1991)

Duggan, T. *V2: A Combat History of the First Ballistic Missile* (Yardley, PA: Westholme, 2005)

Dunn, W. *Battle for White Russia: The Destruction of Army Group Centre, 1944* (Harrisburg, PA: Stackpole Books, 2008)

Dunphie, C. *The Pendulum of Battle: Operation Goodwood, July 1944* (Barnsley: Leo Cooper, 2005)

Dunstan, S. *Eban Emael: The Key to Hitler's Victory in the West* (Oxford: Osprey, 2005)

Dupuy, T. *Hitler's Last Gamble* (New York: Harper Collins, 1994).

Eberle, H. and Uhl, M. (eds,) *The Hitler Book: The Secret Dossier Prepared for Stalin* (London: John Murray, 2005)

Edele, M. *Stalin's Defectors: How Red Army Soldiers Became Hitler's Collaborators, 1941–1945* (Oxford: Oxford University Press, 2017)

Edelman, M. *The Ghetto Fights: Warsaw 1941–1943* (London: Bookmarks, 1990)

Ellis, J. *Cassino: The Hollow Victory – The Battle for Rome January–June 1944* (London: Aurum, 2003)

Ellis, L., Allen, G. and Warhurst, A. *Victory in the West*, Volume 1: *The Battle of Normandy* (London: Naval & Military Press, 2004)

Erickson, J. *The Road to Stalingrad* (London: Cassel, 2003)

Etcherkamp, J. (ed.) *Germany and the Second World War*, Vol. IX/I: *German Wartime Society 1939–45: Politicization, Disintegration and the Struggle for Survival* (Oxford: Clarendon Press, 2015)

Evans, R. J. (ed.) *The Third Reich*, 3 vols, Vol. 1: *The Coming of the Third Reich*; Vol. 2: *The Third Reich in Power*; Vol. 3: *The Third Reich at War* (Allen Lane, 2003–2008)
—— *The Third Reich in History and Memory* (Little, Brown, 2015)

Farquharson, J. *The Plough and the Swastika: The NSDAP and Agriculture in Germany, 1928–1945* (London: Sage, 1976)

Fenyo, M. 'Some Aspects of Hungary's Participation in World War II', *Eastern European Quarterly*, Vol. 3 (1969), pp. 219–29

Fest, J. *Hitler* (Penguin, 1982)
—— *Plotting Hitler's Death: The German Resistance to Hitler* (London: Weidenfeld & Nicolson, 1996)
—— *Inside Hitler's Bunker* (London: Pan, 2012)

Fletcher, D. (ed.) *Tiger! The Tiger Tank: A British View* (London: H.M.S.O., 1986)

Forczyk, R. *Panther vs T-34, Ukraine, 1943* (Oxford: Osprey 2007)

Ford, K. *Battle Zone Normandy: Sword Beach* (Stroud: Sutton Publishing, 2004)

Forty, G. *Battle for Monte Cassino* (London: Ian Allen, 2004)

Frei, N. *National Socialist Rule in Germany: The Führer State, 1933–1945* (Oxford: Blackwell, 1993)

Freiser, K. (ed.) *Germany and the Second World War*, Vol. 8: *The Eastern Front, 1943–44: The War in the East and on the Neighbouring Front, 1943–44* (Oxford: Oxford University Press, 2017)

Friedlander, H. and Milton, S. (eds) *Archives of the Holocaust: An International Collection of Selected Documents*, 26 vols, 1990–1995 (New York: Garland)

Friedländer, S. *The Years of Extermination: Nazi Germany and the Jews 1939–1945* (London: Phoenix, 2008)

Friedrich, J. *The Fire: The Bombing of Germany, 1940–1945* (New York: Columbia University Press, 2006), pp. 70–71

Frieser, K.-H. *The Blitzkrieg Legend: The 1940 Campaign in the West* (Annapolis, MD: Naval Institute Press, 2012)

Fritz, S. *Ostkrieg: Hitler's War of Extermination in the East* (Lexington, KY: University of Kentucky Press, 2015)

Fröhlich, E. (ed.) *Die Tagebücher von Joseph Goebbels*, Vol. 1: *Aufzeichnungen 1923–1941*, 9 vols; Vol. 2: *Diktate 1941–1945*, 15 vols (Munich: K. G. Saur, 1993–2000)

Funk, A. 'Negotiating the Deal with Darlan', *Journal of Contemporary History*, Vol. 8 (1973), pp. 81–117

Gamelin, M. *Servir* (Paris: Plon, 1947), 3 vols

Garden, I. *The Third Reich's Celluloid War: Propaganda in Nazi Feature Films, Documentaries and Television* (Stroud: The History Press, 2012)

Gardner, W. *The Evacuation from Dunkirk: Operation Dynamo, 26 May–4 June 1940* (London: Routledge, 2000)

Geber, K. (ed.) *Generalfeldmarschall Fedor von Bock: The War Diary, 1939–1945* (Atglen, PA: Schiffer, 1996)

Gerhard, G. *Nazi Hunger Politics: A History of Food in the Third Reich* (London: Rowan and Littlefield, 2015)

Gerlach, C. 'The Wannsee Conference, the Fate of German Jews, and Hitler's Decision in Principle to Exterminate All European Jews', *Journal of Modern History*, Vol. 70 (1998), pp. 759–812

Gilbert, M. *The Second World War: A Complete History* (New York: Henry Holt, 1989)

Gisevius, H. *Bis zum bitteren Ende* (Zurich: Fretz and Wasmuth, 1946), pp. 517–18

Glantz, D. 'Soviet Operational Intelligence in the Kursk Operation, July 1943', *Intelligence and National Security*, Vol. 5 (1990), pp. 5–49
—— 'Soviet Military Strategy During the Second Period of War (November 1942–December 1942): A Reappraisal', *Journal of Military History*, Vol. 60 (1996), pp. 115–150
—— *Zhukov's Greatest Defeat: The Red Army's Epic Disaster in Operation Mars, 1942* (Lawrence, KS: The University Press of Kansas, 1999)
—— 'The Struggle for Stalingrad: Opposing Orders of Battle, Combat Orders and Reports and Operational Maps, Part 1: The Fight for Stalingrad's Suburbs, City Centre and Factory Villages, 3 September–13 October 1942', *Journal of Slavic Military Studies*, Vol. 21 (2008), pp. 146–238
—— 'The Struggle for Stalingrad: Opposing Orders of Battle, Combat Orders and Reports and Tactical Maps, Part 2: The Fight for Stalingrad's Factory District, 14 October–18 November 1942', *Journal of Slavic Military Studies*, Vol. 21 (2008), pp. 377–471
—— *After Stalingrad: The Red Army's Winter Offensive, 1942–1943* (Solihull: Helion and & Co., 2011)

Glantz, D. and House, J. *When Titans Clashed: How the Red Army Stopped Hitler* (Lawrence, KS: University of Kansas Press, 1995)
—— *The Battle of Kursk* (Lawrence, KS: University of Kansas Press, 2004)

Glass, J. *Life Unworthy of Life: Racial Phobia and Murder in Hitler's Germany* (Basic Books, 1997)

Goeschel, C. 'Suicide at the End of the Third Reich', *Journal of Contemporary History*, Vol. 41 (2006), pp. 153–73
—— *Mussolini and Hitler: The Forging of the Fascist Alliance* (London: Yale University Press, 2018)

Goldensohn, L. *The Nuremberg Interviews: Conversations with Defendants and Witnesses* (London: Pimlico, 2007)

Goldhagen, D. *Hitler's Willing Executioners: Ordinary Germans and the Holocaust* (Abacus, 1996)

Gorlitz, W. (ed.) *The Memoirs of Field Marshal Keitel* (New York: Stein and Day, 1966)
—— *The Memoirs of Field Marshal Wilhelm Keitel: Chief of the German High Command, 1938–1945* (New York: Cooper Square Press, 2000)

Gorodetsky, G. (ed.) *The Maisky Diaries: Red Ambassador to the Court of St James, 1932–1943* (New Haven, CT: Yale University Press, 2015)

Görtemaker, H. *Eva Braun: Life with Hitler* (Penguin, 2012)

Gruhl, W. *Imperial Japan's World War 2: 1931–1945* (London: Transaction Publishers, 2010)

Gutman, Y. and Berenbaum, M. (eds) *Anatomy of the Auschwitz Death Camp* (Bloomington, IN: Indiana University Press, 1994)

Halder, F. *Hitler as War Lord* (London: Putnam, 1949)
—— *The Halder War Diary* (Novato, CA: Presidio, 1988)

Hanser, R. *A Noble Treason: The Story of Sophie Scholl and the White Rose Revolt Against Hitler* (San Francisco, CA: Ignatius Press, 2012)

Hanson, R. 'Germany's Unconditional Surrender', *History Today*, Vol. 45 (May 1995)

Harris, A. *Bomber Offensive* (London: Collins, 1947)

Harris, J. 'The Myth of the Blitzkrieg', *War in History*, Vol. 2 (1995), pp. 335–52

Harrison, R. (ed.) *The Battle of Kursk: The Red Army's Defensive Operations and Counter-Offensive, July–August 1943* (Solihull: Helion & Co., 2016)

Hartcup, G. *Code Name Mulberry: The Planning, Building and Operation of the Normandy Harbours* (Barnsley: Pen & Sword, 2011)

Hartmanns-Gruber, F. (ed.) *Akten der Reichskanzlei: Regierung Hitler, 1934–1945*, 5 vols (Munich: Oldenbourg, 1999–2012)

Harvey, A. 'The Battle of Britain and "Big Week" in 1944: A Comparative Study', *Air Power History*, Vol. 59 (2012), pp. 34–45

Hassell, U. *The Ullrich von Hassell Diaries, 1938–1944: The Story of the Forces Against Hitler Inside Germany* (Barnsley: Frontline Books, 2011)

Hastings, M. *Armageddon: The Battle for Germany 1944–45* (London: Pan, 2004)
—— *All Hell Let Loose: The World at War, 1939–1945* (HarperPress, 2015)

Hauner, M. 'Did Hitler want World Domination?', *Journal of Contemporary History*, Vol. 13 (1978)
—— *Hitler: A Chronology of His Life and Times* (Basingstoke: Palgrave Macmillan, 2008)

Hayes, P. *Industry and Ideology: IG Farben in the Nazi Era* (Cambridge, MA: Harvard University Press, 1987)
—— *Industry and Ideology*

in the Nazi Era* (Cambridge: Cambridge University Press, 2000)

Hayward, J. 'Hitler's Quest for Oil: The Impact of Economic Considerations on Military Strategy 1941–42', *Journal of Slavic Military Studies*, Vol. 10 (1997), pp. 97–124
—— *Stopped at Stalingrad: The Luftwaffe and Hitler's Defeat in the East, 1942–1943* (Lawrence, KS: University of Kansas Press, 1998)

Heiber, H. and Glantz, D. (eds) *Hitler and His Generals: Military Conferences 1942–1945: The First Complete Stenographic Record of the Military Situation Conferences from Stalingrad to Berlin* (New York: Enigma Books, 2004)

Herbert, U. *Hitler's Foreign Workers: Enforced Foreign Labour in Germany under the Third Reich* (Cambridge: Cambridge University Press, 1997)

Heston, L. and Heston, R. *The Medical Casebook of Adolf Hitler: His Illnesses, Doctors and Drugs* (William Kimber, 1979)

Hiden, J. and Farquharson, J. *Explaining Hitler's Germany: Historians and the Third Reich* (Totowa, NJ: Barnes and Noble, 1983)

Hillgruber, A. (ed.), *Staatsmänner und Diplomaten bei Hitler, Zweiter Teil: 1942–1944* (Frankfurt a. M.: Bernard & Graefe, 1970)

Hilton, S. 'The Welles Mission to Europe, February–March 1940: Illusion or Realism?', *The Journal of American History*, Vol. 58 (1971), pp. 93–120

Hoffman, P. *Stauffenberg: A Family History, 1905–1944* (Montreal: McGill-Queen's University Press, 2003)
—— *Carl Goerdeler and the Jewish Question, 1933–1942* (Cambridge: Cambridge University Press, 2011)

Holland, J. *The Battle of Britain: Five Months That Changed History* (Corgi, London, 2010)

——— *The War in the West: A New History*, Vol. 1: *Germany Ascendant, 1939–1941* (Corgi, 2015)

——— *Big Week: The Biggest Air Battle of World War Two* (London: Corgi, 2019)

——— *Normandy '44: D-Day and the Battle for France: A New History* (London: Bantam Press, 2019)

Holmes, R. *The World at War: The Landmark Oral History from the Classic TV Series* (Ebury, 2011)

Homze, E. *Foreign Labour in Nazi Germany* (Princeton, NJ: Princeton University Press, 1997)

Höss, R. *Commandant of Auschwitz (Age of Dictators 1920–1945)* (London: Weidenfeld & Nicolson, 2000)

Huber, F. *Promise Me You'll Shoot Yourself: The Downfall of Ordinary Germans in 1945* (London: Penguin, 2019)

Hull, S. *Film in the Third Reich: Art and Propaganda in the Third Reich* (London: Simon & Schuster, 2011)

IMT *Trials of the Major War Criminals before the International Military Tribunal*, 42 vols (Nuremberg: International Military Tribunal, 1947–1949)

——— *Nazi Conspiracy and Aggression (Documents from the Nuremberg Trials of the Major War Criminals)*, 8 vols (Washington, DC: US Government Printing Office, 1946–1948)

Jäckel, E. 'On the Purpose of the Wannsee Conference,' in J. Pacy and A. Wertheimer (eds.), *Perspectives on the Holocaust: Essays in Honour of Raul Hilberg* (Boulder, CO: Westview Press, 1995), pp. 47–63

Jackson, J. *The Fall of France: The Nazi Invasion of 1940* (Oxford: Oxford University Press, 2004)

Jackson, R. *Air War Over France, May–June 1940* (London: Ian Allan, 1974)

Jacobsen, H. *Fall Gelb: Der Kampf um den deutschen Operationsplan zur Westoffensive*

1940 (Wiesbaden: Franz Steiner, 1957)

——— (ed.) *General Franz Halder: Kriegstagebuch, 1939–1943*, 3 vols (Stuttgart: W. Kohlhammer, 1962–1964)

Jens, I. (ed.) *At the Heart of the White Rose: Letters and Diaries of Hans and Sophie Scholl* (Walden, NY: Plough Publishing, 2017)

Jentz, T. *Germany's Panther Tank: The Quest for Combat Supremacy* (Atglen, PA: Schiffer, 1995)

Joachimsthaler, A. *The Last Days of Hitler: The Legends, The Evidence, The Truth* (London: Brockhampton Press, 1999)

——— *Hitlers Liste: Dokumente Privater Beziehungen* (Munich: Herbig, 2003)

John, O. *Twice Through the Lines: The Autobiography of Otto John* (London: Macmillan, 1972)

Junge, T. *Hitler's Last Secretary: A Firsthand Account of Life with Hitler* (New York: Arcade Publishing, 2011)

Kaltenegger, R. *Schörner: Feldmarschall der Letzten Stunde* (Munich: Herbig, 1994)

Kater, M. *Doctors under Hitler* (Chapel Hill, NC: University of North Carolina Press, 1989)

——— *The Twisted Muse: Musicians and Their Music in the Third Reich* (Oxford: Oxford University Press, 1997)

——— *Different Drummers: Jazz in the Culture of Nazi Germany* (Oxford: Oxford University Press, 2003)

Keegan, J. *The Second World War* (Pimlico, 1989)

Kempowski, W. *Swan Song: A Collective Diary of the Last Days of the Third Reich, 1945* (New York: W. W. Norton & Company, 2015)

Kershaw, I. *Hitler*, Vol. 2: *Nemesis, 1936–1945* (Penguin, 2000)

——— *The End: Germany 1944–45* (London: Penguin, 2012)

Kimball, W. (ed.) *Churchill and Roosevelt: The Complete Correspondence* (Princeton, NJ: Yale University Press, 1984)

Kirkland, R. 'The French Air Force in 1940: Was It Defeated by the Luftwaffe or by Politics?', *Air University Review*, Vol. 36, No. 6 (1985), pp. 101–118

Klemperer, V. *I Shall Bear Witness: The Diaries of Victor Klemperer*, Vol. 1: *1933–41* (Phoenix, 1998)

——— *To the Bitter End: The Diaries of Victor Klemperer*, Vol. 2: *1942–1945* (London: Weidenfeld & Nicolson, 1999)

Knab, J. *Ich schweige nicht: Hans Scholl and the White Rose* (Darmstadt: WBG, 2018)

Kossert, A. ' "Endlösung on the Amber Shore": The Massacre in January 1945 on the Baltic Seashore – Repressed Chapter of East Prussian History', *Leo Baeck Institute Yearbook*, Vol. 49 (2004), pp. 3–22

Kranz, T. 'Ewidencja zgonów i śmiertelność więzniów KL Lublin', *Zeszyty Majdanka*, Vol. 23 (2005), pp. 7–53

Krivosheev, G. *Soviet Casualties and Combat Losses in the Twentieth Century* (London: Greenhill Books, 2004)

Kroener, B. *General Friedrich Fromm: Der Starke Mann im Heimatkriegsgebiet: Eine Biographie* (Paderborn: Schöningh, 2005), pp. 682–701

Kurzman, D. *The Bravest Battle: The 28 Days of the Warsaw Uprising* (New York: Da Capo Press, 1993)

Le Tissier, T. *Slaughter at Halbe* (Stroud: Sutton Publishing, 2005).

Lehrer, S. *The Reich Chancellery and Führerbunker Complex: An Illustrated History of the Seat of the Nazi Regime* (Jefferson, NC: McFarland, 2006)

Leonard, T. and Bratzel, J. *Latin America during World War 2* (Lanham, MD: Rowman and Littlefield, 2007)

Levine, J. *Operation Fortitude: The Greatest Hoax of the Second World War* (London: Collins, 2012)

Liddle Hart, B. (ed.) *The Rommel Papers* (New York: Da Capo Press, 1982)

Lochner, L. (ed.) *The Goebbels Diaries* (London: Hamish Hamilton, 1948)

Lowe, K. *Inferno: The Devastation of Hamburg, 1943* (London: Penguin, 2012)

Lukacs, J. *Five Days in London, May 1940* (New Haven, CT: Yale University Press, 1999)

Lund, J. 'Denmark and the New European Order, 1940–1942', *Contemporary European History*, Vol. 13 (2004), pp. 235–56

Lunde, H. *Hitler's Pre-Emptive War: The Battle for Norway, 1940* (Newbury: Casemate, 2010)

MacDonald, C. *Time for Trumpets: The Untold Story of the Battle of the Bulge* (New York: Harper Collins, 1997)

MacDonald, C. *The Killing of Reinhard Heydrich: The SS 'Butcher of Prague'* (New York: Da Capo Press, 1998)

Majdalany, F. *Cassino: Portrait of a Battle* (London: Longman, 1957).

Mamula, B. 'The National Liberation War in Yugoslavia, 1941–1945', *The Journal of the United Services Institution*, Vol. 130 (1985), pp. 52–6.

Manvell, R. and Frankel, H. *Göring: The Rise and Fall of the Notorious Nazi Leader* (New York: Skyhorse, 2011)

Marchetti, D., Boschi, I. and Bollaci, M. 'The Death of Hitler', *Journal of Forensic Science*, Vol. 50 (2005), available online at: www.astm.org

Marshall, T. *Prisoners of Geography: Ten Maps That Tell You All You Need to Know about Global Politics* (London: Elliot and Thompson, 2015)

Mazower, M. *Inside Hitler's Greece: The Experience of Occupation, 1941–44* (London: Yale University Press, 2001)

—— *Hitler's Empire: Nazi Rule in Occupied Europe* (Allen Lane, 2008)

McDonough, F. *Opposition and Resistance in Nazi Germany* (Cambridge: Cambridge University Press, 2001)

—— with Cochrane, J. *The Holocaust* (Basingstoke: Palgrave Macmillan, 2008)

—— *Sophie Scholl: The Real Story of the Woman Who Defied Hitler* (Stroud: The History Press, 2010)

—— (ed.) *The Origins of the Second World War: An International Perspective* (Continuum, 2011)

—— *The Gestapo: The Myth and Reality of Hitler's Secret Police* (Coronet, 2015)

McKinstry, L. *Operation Sea Lion: How Britain Crushed the German War Machine's Dreams of Invasion in 1940* (London: John Murray, 2014)

Melvin, M. *Sevastopol's Wars: Crimea from Potemkin to Putin* (Oxford: Osprey, 2017)

Messenger, C. *The Last Prussian: A Biography of Field Marshal Gerd von Rundstedt 1875–1953* (London: Brassy's, 1991)

Middlebrook, M. *Arnhem 1944: The Airborne Battle* (London: Viking, 1994)

—— *The Battle of Hamburg: The Firestorm Raid* (London: Phoenix, 2000)

Mierzejewski, A. 'When Did Albert Speer Give Up?', *Historical Journal*, Vol. 31 (1980), pp. 391–97

Miroslav, I. *The Assassination of Heydrich, 27 May 1942* (London: Hart-Davies, MacGibbon, 1973)

Moczarski, K. *Conversations with an Executioner* (Englewood Cliffs, NJ: Prentice Hall, 1984)

Moll, C. 'Acts of Resistance: The White Rose in the Light of New Archival Evidence', in M. Geyer and J. Boyer (eds.), *Resistance against the Third Reich, 1933–1990* (Chicago, IL: University of Chicago Press, 1992), pp. 172–200

Moltke, H. *Letters to Freya, 1939–1945* (London: Vintage, 1995)

Mommsen, H. 'Hitler's Reichstag Speech, 30 January 1939', *History and Memory*, Vol. 9 (1977)

—— 'The Dissolution of the Third Reich: Crisis Management and Collapse, 1943–1943', *Bulletin of German Historical Institute*, Vol. 27, (2000), pp. 9–23

Montague, P. *Chełmno and the Holocaust: The History of Hitler's First Death Camp* (Chapel Hill, NC: The University of North Carolina Press, 2012)

Moorhouse, R. *Killing Hitler: The Third Reich and the Plots against the Führer* (Vintage, 2007)

—— *The Devil's Alliance: Hitler's Pact with Stalin, 1939–1941* (The Bodley Head, 2014)

—— *First to Fight: The Polish War 1939* (The Bodley Head, 2019)

Moseley, R. *Mussolini's Shadow: The Double Life of Count Galeazzo Ciano* (New Haven, CT: Yale University Press, 1999)

Mühlberger, D. *Hitler's Voice: The Völkischer Beobachter, 1920–1933*, 2 vols (Oxford: Peter Lang, 2004)

Müller, I. *Hitler's Justice: The Courts of the Third Reich* (Cambridge, MA: Harvard University Press, 1991)

Müller, R. *Der letzte deutsche Krieg 1933–1945* (Stuttgart, Klett-Cotta, 2005)

—— *The Enemy in the East: Hitler's Secret Plans to Invade the Soviet Union* (London: I. B. Taurus, 2015)

Mulley, C. *The Women Who Flew for Hitler: The True Story of Hitler's Valkyries* (London: Pan, 2018)

Musial, B. 'The Origins of Operation Reinhard: The Decision-Making Process for the Mass Murder of the Jews in the Generalgouvernement', *Yad Vashem Studies*, Vol. 28 (2000), pp. 112–53

Nahon, M. *Birkenau: Camp of Death* (Tuscaloosa, AL: University of Alabama Press, 1989)

Nash, D. *Hell's Gate: The Battle of Cherkassy Pocket, January–February 1944* (Southbury, CT: RZM, 2002)

Neillands, R. *The Dieppe Raid: The Story of the Disastrous 1942 Mission* (London: Aurum Press, 2006)

Neitzel, S. *Tapping Hitler's Generals: Transcripts of Secret Conversations* (London: Frontline, 2007)

Nelson, A. *Red Orchestra: The Story of the Berlin Underground and the Circle of Friends Who Resisted Hitler* (New York: Random House, 2009)

Newborn, J. and Dumbach, A. *Sophie Scholl and the White Rose* (Oxford: Oneworld, 2018)

Noakes J. and Pridham, G. (eds) *Nazism 1919–1945: A Documentary Reader*, 4 vols, Vol. 1: *The Rise to Power, 1919–1934*; Vol. 2: *State, Economy, Society, 1933–1938*; Vol. 3: *Foreign Policy, War and Racial Extermination*; Vol. 4: *The German Home Front in World War II* (Exeter: Exeter University Press, 1983–98)

Noble, A. 'The Phantom Barrier: Ostwallbau 1944–1945', *War in History*, Vol. 8 (2001), pp. 442–67

O'Donnell, J. and Bahnsen, U. *The Bunker: The History of the Reich Chancellery Group* (Boston, MA: Houghton Mifflin, 1978)

Ohler, N. *Blitzed: Drugs in Nazi Germany* (Allen Lane, 2016)

Orbach, D. *The Plots Against Hitler* (London: Head of Zeus, 2017)

Orenstein, H. and Glantz, D. 'The Kharkov Operation, May 1942', *Journal of Soviet Military Studies*, Vol. 5 (1992), pp. 611–86

Ortner, H. *The Lone Assassin: The Incredible Story of The Man Who Tried to Kill Hitler* (New York: Skyhorse, 2012)

—— *Hitler's Executioner: Roland Friesler, President of the Nazi People's Court* (London: Frontline Books, 2018)

Overy, R. *War and Economy in the Third Reich* (Oxford: Clarendon Press, 1995)

Parssinen, T. *The Oster Conspiracy of 1938: The Unknown Story of the Military Plot to Kill Hitler and Avert World War II* (London: Harper Perennial, 2004)

Patai, R. *The Jews of Hungary: History, Culture, Psychology* (Detroit, MI: Wayne State University, 1996)

Payne, S. *Franco and Hitler* (New Haven, CT: Yale University Press, 2008)

Perry-Groves, L. *Hitler's Death: The Case Against Conspiracy* (Oxford: Osprey, 2019)

Petrow, R. *The Bitter Years: The Invasion and Occupation of Denmark and Norway, April 1940–May 1945* (London: William Murrow & Co., 1974)

Peukert, D. *Inside Nazi Germany: Conformity, Opposition and Racism in Everyday Life* (London: Batsford, 1987)

Piper, F. *Auschwitz: Nazi Death Camp* (Oswiecim, Poland: Auschwitz-Birkenau State Museum, 2002)

Plokhy, S. *Yalta: The Price of Peace* (London: Penguin, 2011)

Pohl, D. and Witte, P. 'The Number of Victims of Belzec Extermination Camp: A Faulty Reassessment', *Eastern European Jewish Affairs*, Vol. 31 (2001), pp. 15–22

Poprzeczny, J. *Odilo Globocnik: Hitler's Man in the East* (London: McFarlane and Company, 2003)

Posner, G. *Mengele: The Complete Story* (London; Cooper Square, 2000)

Preston, D. *Eight Days at Yalta: How Churchill, Roosevelt and Stalin Shaped the Post-War World* (London: Pan MacMillan, 2019)

Pugsley, C. *Operation Cobra: Battle Zone Normandy* (Stroud: Sutton Publishing, 2005)

Ránki, G. 'The German Occupation of Hungary', *Acta Historicae Academiae Scientiarum Hungaricae*, Vol. 11 (1965), pp. 261–83

Rees, L. *The Holocaust: A New History* (Viking, 2017)

Reid, A. *Leningrad: The Tragedy of a City Under Siege, 1941–1944* (London: Bloomsbury, 2012)

Remy, P. *Mythos Rommel* (Munich: List Verlag, 2002)

Ribbentrop, J. *The Ribbentrop Memoirs* (Weidenfeld & Nicolson, 1954)

Rieger, B. *Creator of Nazi Death Camps: The Life of Odilo Globocnik* (London: Portland, 2007)

Ritter, G. *The German Resistance: Carl Goerdeler's Struggle against Tyranny* (Allen & Unwin, 1958)

Roberts, A. *The Storm of War: A New History of the Second World War* (Allen Lane, 2009)

Roberts, G. *Stalin's General: The Life of Georgy Zhukov* (London: Icon, 2013)

Roloff, S. *Die Rote Kapelle: Die Widerstandsgruppe im Dritten Reich und die Geschichte Helmut Rollofs* (Munich: Ullstein, 2000)

Roon, G. *German Resistance to Hitler: Count von Moltke and the Kreisau Circle* (New York: Van Nostrand Reinhold, 1971)

Roseman, M. *The Wannsee Conference and the Final Solution: A Reconsideration* (New York: Picador, 2002)

Ross, C., Swet, P. and Almeida, F. *Pleasure and Power in Nazi Germany* (Basingstoke: Palgrave Macmillan, 2011)

Rottgart, D. 'Die deutsche Panzergruppe am 10/5/1940', part 1, *Zeitschrift für Heereskunde*, Vol. 49. No. 319 (May–June 1985), pp. 61–7

Rubenstein, J. *Tangled Loyalties: The Life and Times of Ilya Ehrenburg* (Tuscaloosa, AL: University of Alabama Press, 1999)

Ryan, C. *The Last Battle* (London: Hodder & Stoughton, 1966)

Salter, M. and Charlesworth, L. 'Ribbentrop and the Ciano Diaries at the Nuremburg Trial', *Journal of International Criminal Justice*, Vol. 4 (2006), pp. 103–27

Schacht, H. *Account Settled* (Weidenfeld & Nicolson, 1949)

Scheurig, B. *Henning von Tresckow: Ein Preusse gegen Hitler* (Berlin: Propyläen, 2004)

Schirach, B. *Ich glaubte an Hitler* (Hamburg: Mosaik Verlag, 1967)

Schlabrendorff, F. *They Almost Killed Hitler* (New York: MacMillan, 1947).
——— *The Secret War Against Hitler* (Boulder, CO: Westview Press, 1994)

Schleunes, K. A. *The Twisted Road to Auschwitz* (Champaign, IL: University of Illinois, 1970)

Schmidt, P. *Hitler's Interpreter* (Stroud: History Press, 2016)

Schrader, H. *Codename Valkyrie: Friedrich Olbricht and the Plot Against Hitler* (Yeovil: J. H. Haynes Publishing, 2009)

Schwendemann, H. '"Drastic Measures to Defend the Reich at the Oder and the Rhine...", A Forgotten Memorandum of Albert Speer of 18 March 1945', *Journal of Contemporary History*, Vol. 38 (2003), pp. 597–614

Seaton, A. *Russo German War, 1941–1945* (London: Presidio Press, 1993)

Sebag-Montefiore, H. 'The Mechelin Affair', *Military History Quarterly*, Vol. 20 (Spring 2008), pp. 48–55

Sereny, G. *Albert Speer: His Battle with the Truth* (London: Knopf, 1995)
——— *Into That Darkness: From Mercy Killing to Mass Murder* (London: Pimlico, 1995)

Shakespeare, N. *Six Minutes in May: How Churchill Unexpectedly Became Prime Minister* (London: Harvill Secker, 2017)

Shephard, B. *After Daybreak: The Liberation of Bergen-Belsen* (London: Pimlico, 2006)

Shirer, W. L. *Berlin Diary: The Journal of a Foreign Correspondent, 1934–1941* (Sunburst Books, 1997)
——— *The Rise and Fall of the Third Reich: A History of Nazi Germany* (Folio, 2004 edn)

Short, N. *The Führer Headquarters: Hitler's Command Bunkers, 1939–1945* (London: Bloomsbury, 2013)

Showell, J. (ed.) *Führer Conferences on Naval Affairs, 1939–1945* (Stroud: The History Press, 2015)

Siemens, D. *Stormtroopers: A New History of Hitler's Brownshirts* (New Haven, CT: Yale University Press, 2017)

Solotov, B. *Marshal K. K. Rokossovsky: Red Army's Gentleman Commander* (Warwick: Helion & Co., 2016)

Sontag, R. and Beddie, J. (eds) *Nazi-Soviet Relations, 1939–1941: Documents from the Archives of the German Foreign Office* (Washington, DC: US Government Printing Office, 1948)

Speer, A. *Inside the Third Reich* (Weidenfeld & Nicolson, 1970)

Speidel, H. *Invasion 1944: Ein Beitrag zu Rommels und des Reiches Schicksal* (Tübingen: Rainer Wunderlich, 1949)

Stacey, C. and Bond, C. *The Victory Campaign, 1944–1945*, Vol. 3: *The Official History of the Canadian Army* (Ottawa: The Queen's Printer, 1966)

Stargardt, N. *The German War: A Nation Under Arms, 1939–1945* (Bodley Head, 2015)

Stein, M. *Generalfeldmarschall Walter Model, Legende und Wirklichkeit* (Bissendorf: Biblio-Verlag, 2001)

Steinhoff, J., Pechel, P. and Showalter, D. (eds) *Voices from the Third Reich: An Oral History* (Washington, DC: Da Capo Press, 1994)

Stolfi, R. 'Equipment for Victory in France in 1940', *History*, Vol. 55, No. 183, (February 1970), pp. 1–120

Stroop, J. *The Stroop Report: The Jewish Quarter of Warsaw is No More* (New York: Pantheon, 1979)

Sweetman, J. *The Dambusters Raid* (London: Weidenfeld & Nicolson, 1999)

Taylor, B. *Hitler's Engineers: Fritz Todt and Albert Speer: Master Builders of the Third Reich* (London: Casemate, 2010)

Taylor, F. (ed.) *The Goebbels Diaries, 1939–1941* (London: Sphere, 1982)

Tegel, S. 'Viet Harlan and the Origins of the Jude Süss 1938–9: Opportunism in the Creation of Nazi-Anti-Semitic Propaganda', *Historical Journal of Film, Radio and Television*, 16 (1996), pp. 515–31

The Trial of Adolf Eichmann: Record of Proceedings in the District Court of Jerusalem, 9 vols (Jerusalem: Israel Minister of Justice, 1992–95)

Thomas, G. and Lewis, G. *Defying Hitler: The Germans Who Resisted Hitler* (New York: Caliber, 2009)

Toland, J. *Adolf Hitler* (Ware, Hertfordshire: Wordsworth, 1997)
——— *Battle: The Story of the Battle of the Bulge* (Lincoln, NE: Bison Books, 1999)

Tooze, A. *The Wages of Destruction: The Making and Breaking of the Nazi Economy* (Allen Lane, 2007)

Toppel, R. *Kursk 1943: The Greatest Battle of the Second World War* (Warwick: Helion & Co., 2018)

Trevor-Roper, H. (ed.) *Hitler's War Directives* (London: Pan, 1954)
——— (ed.) *The Goebbels Diaries: The Last Days* (London: Martin Secker & Warburg, 1978)
——— (ed.) *Hitler's War Directives, 1939–1934* (London: Pan, 1983)

Trew, S. *Gold Beach: Battle Zone Normandy* (Stroud: Sutton Publishing, 2004)
────── *Battle Zone Normandy: Battle for Caen* (Stroud: Sutton Publishing, 2004)

Tucker-Jones, A. *Operation Bagration and the Annihilation of Army Group Centre* (Barnsley: Pen & Sword, 2009)

Ullrich, V. *Hitler, Vol. 1: Ascent: 1889–1939* (The Bodley Head, 2016)

Vehviläinen, O. *Finland in the Second World War* (Basingstoke: Palgrave, 2002)

Venezia, S. *Inside the Gas Chambers: Eight Months in the Sonderkommando of Auschwitz* (London: Polity Press, 2011)

Verrier, A. *Assassination in Algiers: Churchill, Roosevelt, De Gaulle and the Murder of Admiral Darlan* (London: MacMillan, 1991)

Vinke, H. *The Short Life of Sophie Scholl* (Cambridge, MA: Harper & Row, 1984)

Vinogradov, V., Pogonyi, J. and Teptzov, N. *Hitler's Death: Russia's Great Secret from the Files of the KGB* (London: Chaucer Press, 2005)

Wachsmann N. *KL: The History of the Nazi Concentration Camps* (Little, Brown, 2015)

Waller, J. 'The Double Life of Admiral Canaris', *International Journal of Intelligence and Counter Intelligence*, Vol. 9 (1996), pp. 271–89

Warlimont, W. *Inside Hitler's Headquarters, 1939–1945* (Novato, CA: Presidio, 1964)

Weinberg, G. *The Foreign Policy of Hitler's Germany: The Road to World War II* (New York: Enigma Books, 2005)

Weizsäcker, E. *Memoirs* (Gollancz, 1951)

Welch, D. *Third Reich: Politics and Propaganda* (Routledge, 2002)
────── *Propaganda and the German Cinema 1933–45* (London: I. B. Taurus, 2007)

Wheatley, B. 'A Visual Examination of the Battle of Prokhorovka', *Journal of Intelligence History*, Vol. 18 (2019), pp. 115–63

Whiting, C. *The Other Battle of the Bulge: Operation Northwind* (New York: Avon Books, 1992)

Whitmarsh, A. *D-Day in Photographs* (Stroud: History Press, 2009)

Willet, R. 'Hot Swing and the Dissolute Life: Youth, Style and Popular Music in Europe, 1939–49', *Popular Music*, Vol. 8 (1989), pp. 157–63

Wilmot, C. *The Struggle for Europe* (Ware: Wordsworth, 1997)

Wilt, A. 'The Significance of the Casablanca Decisions, January 1943,' *Journal of Military History*, Vol. 54 (1991), pp. 517–29
────── *The Atlantic Wall: Rommel's Plan to Stop the Allied Invasion* (New York: Enigma, 2004)

Wiskemann, E. *The Rome–Berlin Axis* (Fontana, 1966)

Witte, P. and Tyas, S. 'A New Document on the Deportation and Murder of Jews in "Einsatz Reinhardt" 1942', *Holocaust and Genocide Studies*, Vol. 15 (2001), pp. 468–86

Wittman R. and Kinney D. *The Devil's Diary: Alfred Rosenberg and the Stolen Secrets of the Third Reich* (William Collins, 2016)

Wragg, D. *Plan Z: The Nazi Bid for Naval Supremacy* (Pen & Sword, 2008)

Young, A. *The Flying Bomb* (Shepperton: Ian Allen, 1978)

Zaloga, S. *Bagration 1944: The Destruction of Army Group Centre* (Oxford: Osprey, 1996)

Zaloga, S. and Dennis, P. *Remagen 1945: Endgame against the Third Reich* (Oxford: Osprey, 2006)

Zaloga, S. and Ford, K. *Overlord: The D-Day Landings* (New York: Osprey, 2009)

Zaytsev, V. *Notes of a Russian Sniper* (London: Frontline Books, 2016)

Zeller, E. *Geist der Freiheit: Der Zwanzigste Juli* (Munich: Rhinn, 1952)

Zetterling, N. and Franson, A. *The Korsun Pocket: The Encirclement and Breakout of a German Army in the East, 1944* (Drexel Hill, PA: Casemate, 2008)

Ziemke, E. 'Germany and World War II: The Official History', *Central European History*, Vol. 16 (1983), pp. 398–407

Zumbro, D. *Battle for the Ruhr: The German Army's Final Defeat in the West* (Lawrence, KS: University Press of Kansas, 2006)

INDEX

R